# ETCHED IN MEMORY

# ETCHED IN MEMORY
## The Building and Survival of Artistic Reputation

Gladys Engel Lang and Kurt Lang

The University of North Carolina Press

Chapel Hill and London

Library of Congress Cataloging-in-Publication Data

Lang, Gladys Engel.
   Etched in memory : the building and survival of artistic
reputation / by Gladys Engel Lang and Kurt Lang.
      p.   cm.
   Includes bibliographical references.
   ISBN 0-8078-1908-5 (alk. paper)
   1. Etching, British.   2. Etching—19th century—Great Britain.
3. Etching—20th century—Great Britain.   4. Artists and patrons—
Great Britain.   5. Etching, American.   6. Etching—19th century—
United States.   7. Etching—20th century—United States.
8. Artists and patrons—United States.   9. Art and society—Great
Britain.   10. Women artists—Great Britain.   11. Art and society—
United States.   12. Women artists—United States.   I. Title.
NE2043.25.L36   1990
767'.2'094209034—dc20                                    89-70715
                                                            CIP

This book was published with the assistance of the H. Eugene and
Lillian Lehman Fund of the University of North Carolina Press.

The paper in this book meets the guidelines for permanence and
durability of the Committee on Production Guidelines for Book
Longevity of the Council on Library Resources.

Manufactured in the United States of America

94   93   92   91   90      5   4   3   2   1

*For Our Granddaughters*
*Esmé Lang von Hoffman*
*and*
*Ariella Kahn Lang*

# Contents

# Illustrations and Tables

## Illustrations

All illustrations are from prints in the possession of the authors. They appear in this book following page 226.

*Figure*

## Tables

# Preface

Beginning in the mid-nineteenth century, there took place a revival of etching as an original form of creative expression. It began in France, moved across the Channel to England and, after a premature stillborn delivery, established itself in the early years of the new century in the United States. Artists in each of these countries helped renew an interest in the potentialities of the acid-bitten copperplate for the production of original images. They adopted the label *peintres-graveurs*, or painter-etchers, to distinguish themselves from those who used the etching technique solely as an adjunct to reproductive engraving or for some less artistic, more narrowly commercial purpose. As etchers, these artists cultivated a certain delicacy of expression, emphasizing the cleanly etched line and relying for their aesthetic effects on the contrast between dark ink and light paper. In this way they were reviving the example of Rembrandt and other etchers of the seventeenth century.

All three countries passed through a similar but not identical cycle in the production and popularity of etchings. Each experienced a gradual buildup in the number of professional painter-etchers, in the number of etched plates produced, and of public interest in original etchings. This growth continued through the 1920s but then, with the economic crash, came to a grinding halt. Public enthusiasm for etching waned. By the early 1930s the etching market had completely collapsed; World War II put an end to what was left of it. Once-coveted prints, greatly diminished in value, were stored away in attics and basements to become victims of worms, mice, mildew, and general neglect. Some acquired solely for speculative purposes were destroyed along with other now-worthless stock certificates.

While most of the etchers once acclaimed were forgotten along with their prints, some were more forgotten than others. The names of some leading practitioners—such as Camille Pissarro or Dunoyer de Segonzac in France, Augustus John or Graham Sutherland in England, and Childe Hassam or John Sloan in America—are still widely recognized and their prints much sought after, but each of these had, in his lifetime, achieved some fame as a painter. The end of the boom had the most disastrous consequences for artists who had devoted most of their energy to etching. Today their names are known only to a handful of curators and experts, and even museum inventory lists often lack such elementary but vital information as birth and death dates. Among the most forgotten are the many British women whose special virtuosity in the medium had once been heralded.

It was these gaps in the collective memory—catching our attention as we were looking into the relationship between artistic productivity and changing popular taste—that stirred our interest in reputation as a central sociological problem. As sociologists we wanted to understand the dynamics of the process whereby some producers of culture but not others come to be considered worth remembering. Art historians are more likely to focus on the big names on the assumption, so it seems, that artists who are forgotten are not worth remembering. Such an assumption runs counter to our own approach. It may not even be consistent with reality, once one leaves the pantheon of the acknowledged "greats" to look at the minor figures.

From the perspective adopted throughout this book, a reputation evolves through a social and collective process; its survival is similarly mediated through interested individuals and by their proximity to archives. The specifics may vary with historical circumstance, but the basic ingredients are everywhere the same. A reputation is, above all, a social construction; it expresses a shared belief about the probity, generosity, ability, achievement, etc., of a known person. "Deserved" or not, nearly every reputation has some basis in fact. In the case of artists and other creators of culture, it inevitably rests in some way or manner on the products that they produce. But this linkage, as our case histories document, can be indirect and is certainly influenced by existing opportunities and prevailing taste, both of which are eminently social and have little to do with characteristics intrinsic to the art objects themselves.

This view may not sit well with those critics and other experts who earn their own reputations as arbiters of what is good and thus deserving of remembrance. We nevertheless believe that the materials we present (bolstered by the illustrations) lend support to our case. For some years, one of our empirically oriented colleagues had been challenging us to subject this mildly irreverent position to some experimental test. Partly at his urging, we prepared a dozen slides of artistic etchings, unlabeled as to title and name, gender, generation, or nationality of the artist. We grouped them into six pairs, each similar in technique and subject matter but by artists of quite different reputation. One image in each pair was by an artist still well remembered, the other by someone more or less forgotten. These pairs were shown to two groups—first to those attending a session on the sociology of culture at a national meeting and later to a class on the history of film-making. Those present were asked to do two things—to identify the image in each pair they found artistically more appealing, and then to indicate how "obvious" this difference was. Few of our respondents, though conversant with aesthetic criteria, knew much about the genre and were unlikely to have recognized by name any of the artists represented.

This little exercise hardly meets the standards of a scientific experiment. After all, our respondents were judging reproductions of etchings, not the originals. Also the sample of judges might more fittingly be described as "haphazard" than as "random." In spite of these deficiencies, the reactions, when tabulated, drove home a point. Preferences for images by the more renowned artists hardly exceeded those for the less well known or nearly forgotten ones. We assure the skeptical reader that we were careful *not* to select bad examples by the more famous etchers or otherwise deceive our respondents. In fact, we included, though not within the same pair, one of the best known prints by one of the most renowned etchers of the period and another we ourselves had purchased for £2, the price of its frame, in one of the junkier stalls in London's Portobello Road (see figure 46). Asked to single these two out among the twelve shown, correct identifications were within the range of what one would expect in a random distribution. Both groups gave the largest number of mentions to more than one "wrong" print.

We recognize that scholarly interest in this particular period and genre of printmaking remains modest. On the other hand, since the late 1970s there has been a revival of collectors' interest, stimulated at least in part by the publication of Guichard's handsome reference book, *British Etchers, 1850–1940.* The author, who is not an art historian but a collector, provided capsule biographies and illustrations of work by 373 etchers he judged to be "major." The names of more than one thousand other artists who produced etchings in these years were simply listed under the heading of "minor" etchers. Both the small type and the lack of other information suggests their presumed unimportance.

The book, which has become a standard reference for many curators, galleries, and collectors, now certifies the reputation of those singled out for special treatment. As a result, some almost-forgotten etchers have gained a new hold on memory, while the reputations of others, their names lost once more among the ranks of "minors," are, in fact, downgraded. That may not have been the author's intent, but as our study of painter-etchers shows, it is precisely this kind of publicity that influences what people take the time to look at, creates a demand, raises the price, and ultimately establishes a reputation that is likely to last.

In examining the relationship between popular taste and artistic careers as part of a more general sociology of reputation, we see ourselves as having broken some new ground. For one thing, in order to highlight the problematic, we have deliberately directed our attention to artists working in an art often denigrated as "minor." Yet one finds rich material here for studying the nonsurvival of reputation, a neglected subject. More than in "big" art, some of the most distinguished practitioners have, for all practical purposes, been so nearly erased from the collective memory that they are unlikely ever again to achieve visibility through posthumous rediscovery. The basis for such an assertion will become apparent in these pages.

Also, our research strategy is somewhat uncommon. It approximates a scavenger hunt conducted over some ten years for whatever scraps of data we could ferret out on some of the more forgotten artists. This is a reversal of the more usual and less risky procedure of working from an unmined or only partly mined cache of readily available data. Yet this approach, though costly in terms of time and travel, paid off in ways we could not have anticipated.

Perhaps even more important is the attention we have paid to the passage of time. The experiences of our subjects exemplify the interplay of history with their own personal biographies. What matters is the point in time when the two come together. Thus, in the building of a reputation such factors as gender, family background, "talent," and personal wealth are shown to exert an influence, but the amount of influence and the way it makes itself felt depend on various other contingencies that change with time. These include access to adequate training and the popularity of an art genre, as well as the social and political climate. For example, the young woman who aspired to an art career in the nineteenth century certainly encountered different problems in reputation building than those who followed next century, no matter how similar their talent or family background may have been, no matter that both entered school at the same age. So too, the timing of an artist's death affects the chance that the reputation achieved in a lifetime will endure into posterity.

Posthumous reputations, so runs our thesis, are sustained by the preservation of tangible things associated with the deceased artist. The principle applies equally, though with some variation, to other areas of culture production. With this in mind, we have in the concluding pages of this book developed some ideas about how the factors that govern the endurance of artistic reputations operate in other areas of creative activity. We could not pursue these comparisons to their end without unduly lengthening a manuscript that already had to be considerably cut in the interest of marketability. But we hope that sociologists of culture and knowledge production who have so far paid scant attention to the linkage between reputation and archiving will be sufficiently intrigued to give the subject the attention it deserves. The selections that result from reputation building become especially relevant with the new, almost unlimited, technological capacities for information storage.

When we began our work in the 1970s, there was precious little empirical research on either collective memory or on reputation, the two subjects central to our study. Among the handful of sociological sources on memory on which we could draw, of particular value were the seminal studies by Maurice Halbwachs, W. Lloyd Warner, and Fred Davis. We also read with considerable profit the observation by Charles H. Cooley on fame and the more detailed study by Edgar Zilsel on genius. Additional leads came from remarks by Ernst Kris on the biography of the artist, by Harold Rosenberg on the importance of widows in the management of their husbands' artistic reputations, by Harvey G. Lehman on literary reputations (which forms the basis for some of the speculations by Robert Escarpit), and by a line of inquiry on science pioneered by Robert K. Merton and several of his students.

The time must have been ripe for a sociology of reputation. Since we first circulated our thinking in the form of memoranda and proposals, there have appeared studies on commemoration by Barry Schwartz; on art worlds (with an extensive treatment of artistic reputations) by Howard Becker; on the French art market by Raymonde Moulin; on the revival of Renaissance plays by Wendy Griswold; on literary reputations by Karl-Erik Rosengren, by Gaye Tuchman and Nina Fortin, and by Hans-Matthias Kepplinger; and on reputations in sport by Allen Guttmann, Raymond Schmitt, and Wilbert M. Leonard. Several highly informative case studies of reputations have revealed patterns that show similarities with our etchers. Jane Tompkins has dealt with the reputation of Nathaniel Hawthorne, John Rodden with that of George Orwell, Michéle Lamont with that of Jacques Derrida, and Robert Kapsis with that of Alfred Hitchcock as an *auteur*. Not to be overlooked are Gary Taylor's work on the "reinvention" of Shakespeare and two other monumental studies: David Lowenthal, an art historian, is the author of *The Past Is a Foreign Country*; Leo Braudy's *The Frenzy of Renown* is a similarly extensive and discursive treatment of fame by a literary historian.

These titles are no more than the tip of an iceberg that is rapidly surfacing. Our own conceptualization was already in place by the time most of this recent literature on reputation was generally available. While we have made mention of it, where applicable, we have made no attempt to discuss in any detail how our own work complements or differs from that of others. We consider that an unnecessary, even pretentious, exercise that would border on the kind of pedantry we have worked hard to avoid in presenting our findings. Similar considerations have moved us to keep the technical vocabulary of the sociologist to a minimum. The sociologically oriented reader will recognize the theories—especially those related to the "creativeness" or social production theories of culture that inform our analysis. But for the larger audience—especially those drawn from the arts and humanities—whose attention we seek, an overspecialized vocabulary that critics would only describe as jargon would likely be off-putting, as well as more a barrier than an aid to understanding.

So many people and institutions have helped along the way that we include most in a separate acknowledgment section at the back of the book. Here we mention only a few to whom we owe a special debt. We are, above all, grateful to the National Humanities Center in North Carolina for the opportunity, as fellows, to devote an academic year in preparing an early draft of this manuscript. We should thank every member of its administrative, library, and secretarial staffs, as well as all members of our 1983–84 class for inspiration and help along the way. Here let us give special thanks to Charles Blitzer, Kent Mullikin, John O'Connor, Jean Leuchtenburg, Alan Tuttle and, among the fellows, those whose interests most often intertwined with ours, William Rorabaugh, Robert and Helen Lane, Anthony LaVopa, John Shelton Reed, William Newman, Vincent Carretta, Lance Bertelsen, Olaf Hansen, Martin Meisel, Michael Shapiro, and Herbert Bailey. Also, during our residence, Arthur Marks, Professor of Art at the University of North Carolina-Chapel Hill, provided a welcome opportunity to discuss our study with a group of graduate students in art history. At S.U.N.Y.-Stonybrook Dan Weldon helped by admitting Kurt Lang to his printmaking class, while Frank Beaver at the University of Michigan let us use his film seminar for the "experiment" mentioned in this preface.

St. Antony's College, in Oxford, where we were Senior Member Associates, helped us get started on this project in 1978. Then, during a sabbatical in 1981, we were housed at M.I.T., thanks to the good offices of Russ Neumann and the late Ithiel de Sola Pool. Among those whose hospitality later made it possible to pursue our searches in England were Ellen Mackintosh in Cambridge, Judy and Colin Seymour-Ure in Canterbury, Sylvia and Jeremy Tunstall in London, and Evangeline and John Dickson in Ipswich. Professors Kevin Lang and Shulamit Kahn, then resident in Irvine, made our extended search for data in Southern California possible. Ned Polsky, of Biography House, sheltered us in New York City, as did Philip Ennis, when our hunt took us to Middletown, Conn.

Along the way we have profited from critiques of papers we delivered in various forums in various parts of the world; we owe a lot to scholars who have worked actively to promote this kind of scholarly exchange by founding and building the Culture Section of the American Sociological Association into one of its major divisions. Among these scholars, we owe special debts to Richard A. Peterson, Vera Zolberg, Howard S. Becker, Ann Swidler, Michael Schudson, Judith Blau, Judith Balfe, Muriel Cantor, and her deeply missed partner, Joel Cantor. Schudson, along with Peter Clarke and Susan Evans, critiqued the paper we prepared for the Scholars Conference on Communication and Collective Memory at the University of Southern California in March 1986, in which we first extrapolated our findings on the survival of artistic reputation to other areas of culture production. This manuscript has been read in its entirety by three leading sociologists of culture: Gaye Tuchman, whose kudos heartened us; Vera Zolberg, whose perceptive reading of our work she will hopefully find reflected in the final product; and Richard A. Peterson, who suggested a scheme for shortening it. Diana Crane generously photocopied some hard-to-get material on American etchers from the Bibliothèque Nationale. Glenna Lang, a fine art illustrator, and Alexander von Hoffman, a historian at the Harvard School of Urban Design, read and helped with the first chapter, always a stumbling block, while a number of friends and colleagues, especially James Beniger and Kent Mullikin, have been supportive in the process of finding the right publisher. We are sure we have. In the course of our careers, we have worked with many editors, but we have encountered few so caring, erudite, and pleasant to work with as Paul Betz. Finally, we thank the Institut für Publizistik at the

Johannes-Gutenberg-Universität, Mainz, West Germany, where we spent the summer of 1989 as guest professors, for providing student assistance in checking some bibliographic references. At the Seattle end, where our home base is, at the University of Washington, communication researcher Peggy Bieber and historian Phil Roberts did yeomen service, in our absence, by searching our home library and files for footnote information.

# Note on the Illustrations

The prints reproduced in this volume were selected to give adequate representation of the range of subject matter and techniques used by artists associated with the painter-etcher movement, of men and women printmakers, and of the largely forgotten or relatively neglected among them. Each artist whose work is illustrated is mentioned in the text, but specific plates are noted there only when directly relevant to the discussion.

Figures 1 through 5 are included as historical background; Figures 7 through 17 are prints from the earlier revival period. The rest are grouped by subject matter rather than in chronological sequence. Figures 9, 11, 12, 13, 14, 15, 20, 22, 25, 26, 27, 34, 35, 40, 44, 45, 46, and 54 represent the work of largely forgotten artists, all of whom (except for Nora Lavrin) died before the revival of interest in the prints of the period.

# ETCHED IN MEMORY

I

# Introduction: Reputation and Fashion

In 1924 Billy Gabriel, a middle-aged manager of the Westminster branch of a London bank, nearly murdered his wife because she had "murdered" his etching. In a fit of rage, jealous of his devotion to his collection, of the love he lavished on his "beauties," she had torn into a hundred pieces his passionately cherished print of Whistler's *The Balcony*. Fingering the fragments, he faced her with hatred in his eyes: " 'You're mad,' he said, 'Mad! That's what you are. . . . You've killed that. It never did you any harm. . . . By God, I'll not be with you in the house another five minutes. You're a murderess.' " Billy Gabriel, the hero of Hugh Walpole's not-so-tall tale, did not murder his wife. Rather, he left her, "took a charming cottage in the country, made a beautiful collection of etchings," and presumably lived happily ever after.[1]

The story appeared in a popular magazine in the 1920s, when etchings in England as in the United States had become absolutely à la mode. The Gabriel described by Walpole, himself a collector, was a true *amateur d'estampes*, a print lover with a consuming passion for etchings. He had bought the Whistler print—a beautiful impression—from a Bond Street art shop for £160; only a few years before it had sold for just £120. Still, Gabriel had thought his a good buy; the asking price could easily have been £200—near equal to that of a new car. Indeed, the print would double in value by 1929. But after the market crash, the monetary value of his "beautiful collection of etchings" would have shrunk disastrously.[2] That exquisite *Sussex* by McBey (figure 18), which Gabriel might have acquired for £140 in 1925 was valued eight years later at a tenth of that—£15. In 1938 it could scarcely be given away; in one auction it sold for exactly five shillings. Had it lost its aesthetic appeal?

Gabriel had started collecting in response to an inner urge to acquire beautiful things. But how could a man have come to love an etching even more than his wife? Gabriel, we are told, had long dreamed of owning some pictures—"pictures in the vague, so vague and so impossible that he never breathed this particular ambition to anybody and for himself had scarcely formulated it. He only knew that they were to be real, original pictures. Pictures touched, themselves, by the hand of the original artist." One time, when on his lunch hour, he noticed a box labeled "No Print In This Box More Than Five Shillings" near the door of a shop by the British Museum. His eye was caught by "a little landscape, a thing simple enough—a hill, a clump of trees, a cow, and a horseman. But how beautiful! How quiet and simple and true! And the real thing. Not a copy, although it was not a drawing. In the left-hand corner there was scribbled a name, 'Everdingen.'" Having paid five shillings for this black-and-white treasure, he left the shop, not knowing why he had been so strangely stirred. He did not even know exactly what an etching was. "Driven still by a mysterious sense of drama, he stopped in a bookshop and bought a little book entitled, 'Prints and Etchings: All About Them.'"[3]

From this book he learned that his etching was an intaglio print, derived from a drawing lightly "scratched" with a needle on an acid-resisting wax previously applied to a smooth copperplate. This drawing had then been "bitten" into the metal by immersing it in an acid bath.[4] Only the exposed portions, where the needle had removed the wax coating, would be eaten away. The plate, once cleared of wax, had been inked and carefully wiped so as to leave ink only in grooves created by the action of the acid. In a last step the plate, between blankets, was passed through a press, which, by dint of great pressure, extracted the ink from the etched lines on to the paper, producing that "magic of a line"—black on white—cherished by so many art lovers. With such painstaking care had Gabriel's etching been produced.

The entire process of wiping and inking the plate and passing it through the press had to be repeated for each impression. An artist well-versed in the technique could pull an indefinite, though not an infinite, number of copies from a single etched plate, with each impression (or print or proof) being essentially a replica of the others but with no two copies ever exactly the same. Thus, Gabriel's Everdingen, though a kin to many others, was as original as a painting (figure 1). Not only had it been touched by the hand of a master, but it was his alone to possess and get to know.

Having acquired a taste for etching, Gabriel soon bought six more: a Samuel Palmer, a Daubigny, a Legros, a Hollar, an Appian, and a William Strang; the last, at £5, was the most expensive. He bought more books and took a subscription to the *Print Collector's Quarterly*. Before long he was spending an hour or two every Saturday afternoon in the British Museum print room, studying etchings he could never dream of possessing. Then, as he gained confidence in his own judgment, he most probably acquired, though Walpole does not say so, etchings by younger artists, including the French and Americans whose work was being featured in art magazines and shown in the windows of Bond Street dealers.

Print lovers with the same passion to possess as Gabriel helped fuel the etching mania of the 1920s. Indirectly they created another type of collector more wedded to money than art but attracted by the opportunities for investment or ready to speculate. Investors mostly set their sights on dead masters, whose oeuvre could no longer increase and was therefore bound to rise in price. Speculators were more likely to go for highly touted contemporaries. They were betting that once a newly issued edition, numbering perhaps seventy-five prints, by James McBey, the renowned Scottish etcher, had sold out, the price would skyrocket, and it usually did. They regarded their prints as if they were stock certificates and were only too ready to dump them when their value diminished after Black Tuesday of 1929. The reaction of the *amateurs d'estampes*, like Gabriel, to the market crash was more complicated. Economic adversity probably reduced their ability to collect what they truly loved, but some of the more fickle were already being seduced and weaned away, as the 1930s began, by new art styles just coming to the fore.

## The Etching Cycle

What ended with the crash was a vogue, the final phase of a longer change in artistic taste whose beginnings go back to the mid-nineteenth century. This taste cycle—the subject of our next chapters—exemplifies the extent to which artistic artifacts are commodities, their "utility" and consequently their value dependent on the vagaries of taste. One usually refers to such a rise and fall of interest as a fashion phenomenon. Things in fashion are coveted not so much for characteristics intrinsic to them but because they bestow a certain prestige on their owners, even make them objects of envy.[5] To this extent, then, taste is as much influenced by value as value is influenced by taste. Both together affect the production of art.

In characterizing the etching revival as a movement carried by fashion, we do not mean to trivialize it, only to recognize that, in the still prevailing hierarchical view of the arts, the position of etching remains that of a "minor" art. Much of what survives as original work was in fact derivative, inasmuch as the visual ideas were developed largely as an adjunct to painting and then incorporated into etching. Many etchers were primarily painters who used the etched plate to translate their already successful images into a form that would make them available to a larger audience. Since etchings, far more than paintings, are items of personal consumption, one can also argue that they are more subject to fashion trends.

This taste cycle in etching struck us as uniquely suited for an investigation into the effects of such changes on (1) artistic productivity, (2) the building of artistic reputation, and (3) the selective survival of reputation within the collective memory. How much were artists influenced by public demand in taking up etching? Did they cease to etch when the public stopped buying? How did they make names for themselves as etchers? To what extent were they starting from scratch or merely exploiting reputations they had already earned in another art medium? And last, why should the names and works of some once well reputed etchers have been all but forgotten while those of others survive?

Why should the rise and fall of etching be so suitable for such study? First, etchings, unlike paintings, exist in multiples, owing to the number of copies (impressions) that can be pulled from any single etched plate. Therefore, the sale of any one impression does not necessarily remove a print from the market; even after a published edition—usually somewhere between thirty and one hundred copies[6]—has been sold out and the plate canceled, some copies will sooner or later appear for resale. It is possible, as one print collector put it, to look at *all* surviving prints by an artist, decide which you would most like to have, and then "with good luck and time . . . have some chance that you would find it."[7] Therefore, the records of print sales allow a more continuous tracking of the popularity (or value) of a "single" work than is possible in the case of a painting, subject only to the proviso that the quality of an impression and its state of preservation also affect price.

Second, the continuing circulation of what is essentially, though not exactly, the same image makes the movement of the prices for etchings a more valid measure of the rise and fall of an artist's standing than the auction prices for quite different paintings with the same signature. The record prices commanded by "big" art at auctions that have attracted so much attention can result from no more than a single determined collector bidding against a museum curator for a unique work. The art market quickly responds by attracting wealthy buyers, some of whom are only looking for investment values.

Third, collectors of etchings operate in a larger market than the collectors of paintings: the total impressions of etchings pulled by professional artists between 1850 and 1940 number quite literally in the millions. Being so widely available, etchings by any artist cost less than his or her paintings, which puts them within the reach of people of moderate means. Billy Gabriel, for instance, could never have collected paintings by Old Masters or even by Impressionists, but all but the most coveted prints by stars such as Whistler and McBey would have been well within his reach. It follows that the market for etchings was less affected than the market for paintings by the purchases of museums or, even, by the foibles of a small number of major collectors intent on possessing an especially rare or fine impression of a print.

Fourth, etching (like printmaking generally) is a less solitary activity than painting, so that the social, economic, and cultural factors facilitating or impeding the building of an artistic reputation can be brought into sharper relief. Etchers often collaborate; they tend to share and join in experimenting with their latest techniques. They are also more dependent on help when it comes to printing the full edition of a successful plate. Some are simply not skilled in handling the heavy press, but even those who insist on mastering the whole process find this part of their work tedious. Most prefer, once a plate has been proofed, to have someone else do the printing. This division of labor mandates a close working relationship, with the artist monitoring the proofs until a satisfactory result is achieved. In addition, etchers, like painters, are dependent on dealers to reach their clientele. These same dealers may also function as "publishers": they commission a plate, arrange for its printing, and sometimes even obtain the copyright. The precise nature of the relationship between etchers and dealers varies. How painter-etchers during the revival banded together to advance their cause and, in the process, their own careers should become clear within these pages.

## Artistic Reputations

Reputations fluctuate with fashions. Indeed, John Locke linked the two in speaking of a law of fashion established by opinion and reputation as governing many areas of life.[8] Specifically, reputations persist insofar as people accept what is said about the character and abilities of others, including those with whom they are not personally acquainted. Whether or not the attributions and claims can be factually substantiated matters little. They still function as objective social facts with discernible consequences. Even persons who dissent from the prevalent view are forced to acknowledge the existence of a reputation. As regards one's own reputation, most people consider it among their most prized possessions, even though it cannot, like material goods, be inherited or directly passed on to someone else. Reputations have to be earned and validated, but once established, they are entitled to legal protection, much like other property, so that a person whose reputation is damaged through malice or negligence can seek redress through the courts.

An artistic reputation expresses the consensus about an artist's standing within some community. Understanding its dynamics requires that we distinguish between its two aspects: recognition and renown.

*Recognition* refers to the esteem in which "insiders" hold the artist. It depends primarily on evaluations of artistic output by persons significant in the artist's professional world, especially teachers, colleagues, and discerning connoisseurs. Recognition over a lifetime can be gauged by such measures as election to artistic societies, acceptance of the artist's work in juried exhibitions, and awards won. But such honors do not, in themselves, make an artist famous. The recognized artists still have to be discovered by the larger community.

*Renown* represents a more cosmopolitan form of recognition, measured by how well the artist is known beyond the network of professional peers. For this, artistic achievement does not suffice. Renown requires publicity, and its achievement turns more on what critics write about an artist, on dealer promotion, on sales, and on museum acquisitions than on the judgment of peers. Although only a small number of visual artists ever reach the pinnacle of celebrity status, they have arrived—or achieved renown—when their names have become established currency outside the more intimate world of fellow artists and admiring clients.

It is this renown, and not just the recognition from peers, that lifts an artist several rungs up the ladder to lasting stardom. Here the network of critics and dealers is crucial. In the heyday of the etching revival critics often functioned as go-betweens, first putting the artist in touch with a gallery (or publisher) then following with a laudatory review or vice versa. Early champions of etching, such as Philippe Burty in France, P. G. Hamerton in Britain, and Sylvester R. Koehler in the United States, set themselves the dual mission of promoting the medium among artists and educating the public to its charms. Yet none of them was at all loath to promote a particular artist he deemed worthy. The line between scholarly presentation and commercial promotion in etching was no more easily drawn than in the other visual arts.

Once an artist has become a valuable property, greatness begins to feed on itself. The high prices the work now commands bring further attention. Soon the publicity turns the artist into a persona until, in the extreme instance, anything touched by his or her hand comes to have value for that reason alone. The adulation that the few great artists have enjoyed in their lifetime is reinforced by legend, such as the myth that grew up around one of our etchers, Augustus John: during his adolescence, it was said, he had been miraculously transformed into a genius when, in a diving accident, he hit his head on a rock and emerged from the water a magnificent draftsman![9] While John never lived up to the exorbitant expectations of his Slade School peers, the art (including etchings) that he produced during his long career was good enough, in tandem with his highly unconventional behavior, to keep him in the limelight for the rest of his life.

In the artist's productive years, this kind of renown attracts those seeking art for investment and others hoping to make names for themselves as collectors. It leads to stories in popular magazines and newspapers and to reproductions of the artist's work in prestigeful art publications. Even before the artist's death archivists start the bidding for the memorabilia—the records, correspondence, photographs, but especially the pictures, prints, and sketches to be had for the asking. The remnants of a renowned artist's life stand a far better chance of being preserved than similar effects left by less publicized figures. These residues are the stuff of which scholarship is made; they facilitate the preparation of a catalogue raisonné, and they serve to keep the image of the artist alive.

Much of art historical writing focuses on the great names, so that a small number of major figures stand out as markers around which to locate those many other names that pad out the biographical dictionaries of artists. The art of these focal figures becomes invested with a certain mystique, and the attribution of greatness to its creators lends a special aura to whatever has been touched by their hand. This preoccupation with reputation spills over to the consumer of art. The public feels awe in their presence, so much that the mere hint of a connection to an esteemed artist suffices to produce "beauty" in an object that might otherwise be honored with only a passing glance. Thus Baudelaire, an influential tastemaker, wrote rather contemptuously of the "people who go to the Louvre, walk quickly past a large number of most interesting, though secondary, pictures without throwing them so much as a look, and plant themselves, as though in a trance, in front of a Titian or a Raphael, one of those which the engraver's art has particularly popularized. . . . Happily from time to time knight errants step into the lists—critics, art collectors, lovers of the arts, curious-minded idlers, who assert that neither Raphael nor Racine has every secret, that minor poets have something to be said for them, substantial and delightful things to their credit."[10] While it might not be too difficult to tell the "majors" from the "minors," as E. B. White points out in his semiserious essay on poets, this distinction begs the far more complicated and important question of "whether what they write is any good or not."[11]

The excessive, though not in any way unique, concern of the modern age with the identity of a work's creator is linked to three historical developments. It could not have happened without the prior elevation of the skills and artisanship associated with the creation of visual images to the status of a fine art. Painters, sculptors, and architects did not always nor everywhere have such standing. In antiquity, the social and intellectual prestige of what are now indisputably fine arts was far lower than the surviving residues would lead us to believe. Until the very end of the Renaissance, as Kristeller has reminded us, these visual arts were confined to the artisans' guilds so that painters were "sometimes associated with the druggists who prepared their paints, sculptors with goldsmiths, and architects with masons and carpenters."[12] Only gradually with the founding of academies and the development of an extensive theoretical and critical literature did painting gain recognition as a fine art. For a long while, etching continued to be considered a craft.

A growing interest in the persona of the artist, well documented by Zilsel, is indicated by the increasing number of artists who signed their works and by the appearance of compendiums of biographies of artists.[13] The most famous of these reference sources was, and remains, the *Lives of the Painters* by Vasari, himself a highly successful though hardly a major artist, who, having amassed a fortune from his painting, was moved to record the lives of the most renowned and esteemed artists out of a genuine indignation that so much talent should have remained concealed and buried for so long. Vasari's own place in historical memory rests less on his painting than on the popularity of this tome, which, though first published in the sixteenth century, continues in print right down to the present.[14]

Implicit in both the elevation in status of the visual arts and the focus on the persona of the creators is a third development: the idea of the artist as a superior individual. Noble art, said Ruskin, with whom this idea was hardly original, is "nothing less than the expression of a great soul" and should be understood as the "labour of a particular class of men."[15] He also proclaimed as "a rule in art-economy, that original work is, on the whole, cheapest and best worth having" because one got more satisfaction and tired less of good art by a master.[16] Such art, even if only a pen drawing or watercolor, was sure to last, whereas anyone who purchased a *copy* of a great painting could consider himself as "having purchased a certain quantity of mistakes." Even studies produced by great artists solely "for their own use should be sought after with the greatest eagerness; they are often to be bought cheap; and in connection with the mechanical copies, would become very precious."[17] What held for the studies and sketches from the hands of a master would, presumably, also hold for their etchings, an inference not lost on those pressing a claim for the superiority of painter-etching over reproductive engraving.

Ruskin's insistence on the value of originals by superior artists as expressive of true genius had an unmistakably elitist flavor; yet his meaning was readily misconstrued. Before long, the "originality" of an artist was reduced to an emblem of his or her personal identity, and nothing more. In this more democratic view, sincerity and spontaneity of personal expression sufficed as signs of another kind of genius, the genius that inheres in everyone by virtue of being human. No "divine" gift was required; what mattered was the nonreplicability and uniqueness of the work. According to the new "aesthetics of the sketch," the originality and sincerity of an initial spontaneous expression was assumed to suffer if reworked too meticulously in the studio.[18] Etching was uniquely compatible with this assumption. In substituting the etching needle and acid bath for cuts made with the engraver's burin, the artist gained a freedom that had been impossible when the hard steel plates were cut by muscular force. Impressions printed from etched plates, when skillfully handled, retained their spontaneous quality and resulted in the softness that had so seduced Billy Gabriel.[19] That they were originals was certified by the artist's signature, a distinctly modern practice.

## Studying Reputation

The new cult of individuality, no matter how democratic in principle, hardly obliterated all invidious distinctions. Although painter-etchers advanced their fortunes collectively, not everyone shared equally in the rewards from the newly won popularity of the medium. But works of art can not always speak for themselves. They have to be brought to people's attention as something worth looking at. From this perspective, we examine how social networks, publicity, and promotion function to build a reputation and use these same factors to explain why some artists, but not others, remain in high repute and/or command high prices after their death.

In emphasizing the influence of social factors, we do not mean to discount the importance of the aesthetic element as the basis for a reputation. Admittedly, it was the pleasure we ourselves found in looking at their prints that first led us to the etchers. But even had we turned to the experts, it would have been impossible to solicit agreement on the appropriate aesthetic criteria. All too frequently the arbiters of contemporary taste have offended the taste of posterity. Roger Fry stated the problem in one of his last lectures: "We all tend to believe that there is an orthodox standard of values—that Michelangelo *is* greater than Meissonier and Raphael than Raffaëlli in some objective sense." But the history of taste contains so many reversals of generally accepted judgments that "one must abandon all hope of making aesthetic judgments of universal validity."[20] As an example, Fry cited the Italian primitives, neglected from about 1500 to 1850, after which not to admire Botticelli was to render oneself an outcast in the art world. In like manner the artists of the seicento, such as Guido Reni, who had reigned supreme in the eighteenth century, later came close to being taboo. Another example, chronicled by Reitlinger in *The Economics of Taste*, is the precipitous drop by the 1920s in the prices of paintings by those early avant-gardists, the Pre-Raphaelites. Works that had been the rage a generation before, when back on the market, brought not one-tenth of their former peak value.[21]

Such extreme fluctuations in reputations make one skeptical about the existence of valid and objective, much less eternal, judgments on art. There are, to be sure, critics and aesthetes who write off these often cited reversals as evidence of previous "mistakes." They never cease educating the public to defer to the authoritative standards they proffer. But supposing, Fry asked, that one could actually

> demonstrate by reasoning as cogent as that which forbids us to believe that the earth is flat, that . . . Rembrandt was the greatest artist that ever lived and that, by the same method, [one] could establish an exact scale for valuing any particular work of art. . . . [This] knowledge that a work of art has a high aesthetic value is absolutely useless

to us. . . . No doubt after we had experienced intense aesthetic pleasure from a work it might be a satisfaction of our self-esteem to know
that its absolute aesthetic value was 75 out of a possible 100 marks.
We might enjoy *ourselves* more, but it would not increase by a tittle
our enjoyment of the work itself.[22]

No argument will prevent some from writing off the etching revival on similar grounds. It was, after all, only a minor chapter in the
history of art. What makes it worthy of our attention, despite its subsequent neglect, are the many strategically placed persons who once
took it very seriously. So did the artists whose careers and fates we will
be discussing. For us the issue is not whether or not they deserved their
reputations or have rightly been written off but rather *how* this selection has come about. To address this issue, we have to look beyond the
artists whose names appear in most of the art histories at those whom
just about everyone has ignored.

In selecting individuals into our study, we did not interpose our
own aesthetic judgments but deferred instead to that of their contemporaries, as gauged from records of exhibitions, reviews, awards, and
other indicators. These are less than perfect yardsticks. But all our
subjects, by these measures, were once recognized for accomplishments in printmaking; a few had even come close to achieving a degree
of renown sufficient to guarantee them lasting fame through the ages.

## Searching for Lives

In studying the dynamics of reputation we adhered to what historians call prosopography, or collective biography. We selected 126 British and 160 American artists, all of whom had achieved a minimum of
recognition as etchers (a few as printmakers in a closely allied medium)
sometime between 1880 and 1940. Our procedure was designed to
yield a sample that would enable us to compare etchers of different
gender and generation in two countries where opportunities for entry
into and advancement in art careers were clearly different.

The sample was selected in two steps. We began by developing a
list that included as nearly as possible *all* women etchers that met our
standard of lifetime achievement. This was easier in Britain, where we
could draw on the membership roster of the Royal Society of Painter-
Etchers (RSPE) for its first fifty years (1881–1930). Membership in
that organization was clearly based on merit and limited to a maximum of fifty fellows, elected upon approval of a diploma work by its
council. An additional number of associates, up to a combined total of

150, could also be admitted. While the RSPE had, from its founding, been more open to women than most other artistic societies, women still had to clear more hurdles than men, so that their election as fellows, or even as associates, can be read as compelling evidence of peer recognition. To compensate for the possible establishmentarian bias of this criterion, we added the names of women whose work had been positively mentioned in at least two of five major print reference sources from the period.[23] Nearly all of these women had been members of other prestigious graphic societies. The resultant list of sixty-three women is not altogether exhaustive. As our work progressed, we did come across a few others who might have been included had we not restricted the initial search to these specific sources.

As the second step, we compiled a similar but obviously much larger list of men, from which we selected an equal number, each matched with a women with the identical or near-identical year of birth. The two procedures yielded 126 etchers, evenly divided by gender and similarly distributed with regard to birth and time of entry into an art career.

Analogous procedures produced a sample of 160 American etchers. Here, the selection process was complicated by the lack of an official status comparable, in any strict sense, to that of fellow (or associate) in a Royal Society.[24] Nor was there any other list of nationally recognized etchers to form the basis for a sample that could, if needed, be expanded. We had to go to a variety of sources to compile our basic list of names. These include the catalogs of major print exhibitions, membership rosters of etching clubs, and surveys and histories of the graphic arts.[25]

The resultant lists include some of the most illustrious names in etching, such as Muirhead Bone and John Taylor Arms, along with a number of artists known mostly for their paintings but whom we selected because they also etched. Walter Sickert, Laura Knight, and Graham Sutherland, among the English, and J. Alden Weir, John Marin, and John Sloan, Americans, fall into this category. But most of the names will be unfamiliar to anyone without a thorough knowledge of etchings from the period.

Nor had most of the names been familiar to us when we first began searching for biographical data; moreover, we could not readily ascertain the birth or death dates of a considerable number. Print rooms and standard biographical dictionaries, which could supply these vital facts for all but a few of the men, had nothing or little to offer on the women; some were not even listed in the standard compendiums. Obtaining information on social origins, schooling, marital status, parenthood, and other influences that enter into both career choices and the prospects of future success was still more difficult. We wanted to know how these artists had supported themselves—their sources of income and its adequacy, how they had fared within the distributional networks of dealers and publishers. Other things to consider had to do with the size of their output, the subject matter of their prints, the range of their work in other media, their participation in art associations and exhibitions at home and abroad, their connections to dealers, publishers, critics, and museum curators and to members of the social, intellectual, and literary elites of their countries. And, where such data were available, we took note of sales and prices, of reproductions of their prints in magazines and art journals, of critical acclaim in reviews, and of the prizes and honors they had taken.

Let it be understood that for many of the artists selected for study, particularly the women, most of this information was—to understate the problem—difficult to come by. We picked up clues wherever we could find them, hardly knowing where they might lead us; one birth date we found on a tombstone in an old cemetery. A few we never found at all. Instead of starting with a cache of documents, which we could then analyze, we worked from our lists, pursuing whatever leads we had, looking at published and unpublished biographies, autobiographies, diaries, letters, and such other personal documents—wills, testaments, marriage and birth certificates—as could be located. In a few cases, we were able to track down and get information from relatives or friends of forgotten etchers and, to our delight, even interview a small number of the women and men who were still alive.

Because these sundry sources did not provide all the information we would have needed, our conclusions are not primarily based on a statistical argument. Where we have meaningful figures, we present them, but we do this cautiously. More often than not, we have relied on vignettes of lives and careers and the fate of artists' work since the end of the etching cycle, selecting from the biographies incidents and experiences that are in some significant way representative. Moreover, instead of simply dropping "missing cases," as is customary in quantitative analysis, we have tried to use what material we have to make inferences about the reason for the disappearance of the rest.

## Presenting Our Findings

We begin in Part I with the indispensable historical context, recounting how the etching revival flourished as it moved from France to Britain and America and then faltered. Making use of life histories, in

Part II we consider how, during this cycle, reputations were built. Finally, in Part III we consider how and why reputations were sustained or lost.

In Part I we show that the death of etching in the eighteenth century is a myth, much exaggerated by those who hailed its revival, and that the practitioners of what became known as painter-etching never meant their art to become wildly popular. In France the revival movement was production-driven: while professional artists revived the art, it came into fashion because others, with little encouragement from the artists themselves, developed a mechanism for rationalizing its production and distribution. The English revival was an expressive movement, practiced and promoted by the people, some of them amateur artists, who got it going. Whereas in France, publishers and publicists built a demand and then recruited artists, the British artists, mostly by themselves, built a public and the organization needed to establish the legitimacy of etching as a fine art. They became the beneficiaries, and later the victims, of a boom they could not have created on their own. The American revival was a grass-roots artists' movement, which through collaborative effort built an infrastructure for educating the public and creating a demand. Ultimately, the revival was not just another victim of bad times—as commonly believed—but its demise was hastened by stirrings wholly internal to the art world.

In Part II, on reputation building, we show that our artists were not born to be, but made a decision to be, artists (Chapter 5), and they learned to be artists mainly in school—there was, in the precise sense, no fully self-taught artist among them (Chapter 6). Nor was their initiation into etching a matter of pure chance but a function of gender, generation, and nationality (Chapter 7). In Chapter 8, we show that what greatly mattered for the aspiring artist was to be in the right place at the right time. Beyond this, we dispose of certain myths about the influence of money, or lack of it, on artistic output. Neither having or not having to take on a job—like teaching or portrait-painting or illustrating—was necessarily counterproductive; insofar as such jobs were means to an end, each had its advantages and disadvantages. Nor was the quality of their oeuvre negatively affected by the need to earn a living. Here, and later in Part III, we counter Germaine Greer's depiction of "Love" as necessarily an obstacle in women's race for recognition; especially mutuality—where two artists made the race together— could be a bonus. Finally in Chapter 9, we look at reputation building as a social (collective) process that has also to be understood in its historical context. Here we consider two sets of influences: first is the part played by "insider" networks in recognition as an artist and of "mediator" networks in the achievement of renown; second is the opportunity structure as changed by external events, like social catastrophes—including war and economic depression—over which the artist has little if any personal control.

While gender is a constant theme throughout Part II and is shown to mediate the effects of personal contingencies on productivity and visibility, the subject is not tackled directly until Chapter 10, where we inquire into the posthumous survival of reputation. Theoretically informed by the concept of collective memory, we try to account for the disappearance of the many once well recognized British lady-etchers. First disposing of some popular explanations—that they were not good enough, serious enough, or chose trivial (that is, feminine) subject matter—we find our answer in the relation of age and longevity to the fashion for their artistic medium, to "fate" in the sense of being born and/or dying at the wrong time, and in certain ingrained self-expectations of feminine behavior. Thereafter, in Chapter 11 we take a more general look at the selective survival of reputation within the collective memory, stressing the importance for visual artists of the preservation of the original oeuvre. Where such preservation is not assured, the posthumous durability of reputation depends, we find, on the artist's own lifetime initiatives to project his/her reputation, on the availability of survivors, on linkages to networks that facilitate entry into the cultural archives, and on symbolic associations with emerging cultural or political identities. Finally, we consider whether our conclusions about the process of reputation-survival are generalizable to other fields, such as music, literature, and science, involving creative activity.

# Part I

The Etching Revival: A Taste Cycle

# 2

# Etching Reborn

By the mid-nineteenth century the art of etching had become the stuff of poetic love songs. "Know ye what etching is?" asked a Dutch poet, "It is to ramble on copper."[1] And in a more satiric vein, in an ode to a noble lady, Thomas Hood marveled that "prepared by a hand that is skillful and nice, / the fine point glides along 'like a skate on the ice.' "[2] By the 1920s the phrase, "Come up and see my etchings!" was conjuring up visions of seduction. At least the line floated in and out of cartoons and jokes.[3] So evocative of danger to unwary innocence was an invitation to look at someone's etching collection that the phrase seems to have caught the attention of Hollywood censors. How else to explain a film roué inviting a blond stenographer to come up and see his Rembrandt *lithographs*?[4]

One linguistic authority suggests that the phrase, with its 1890-ish or Edwardian tone, likely existed in "sophisticated" urban society long before the age of the flapper when etching was all the rage.[5] Indeed, people had been looking at etchings for a long time, as the medium does have a long history. The process, it is generally agreed, was an outgrowth of the decorative work of armorers, of jewelers, of watch and clock workers. Exactly when engraving on steel and other metals was first used to produce prints is not firmly established. But there is a record that Tomasso Finiguerre "about the year 1450 took rubbings from his engraved work on pax, silver goblets, spoons, or what not. He found that by applying pressure on the back of some material he obtained an impression from the grease or dirt in his incised work," apparently with the help of some sort of printing press.[6] Most early prints from metal plates were engravings cut with a burin. The earliest known and dated etching "is a highly decorative representation of a woman standing while she dips one of her feet in a foot-bath bitten into iron by Urs Graf, a German or Swiss, in 1513."[7] There are five etchings, also on iron, by Albrecht Dürer, executed between 1515 and 1518.[8]

The development of etching qua etching came when an etching-ground made up of wax was first used as an acid-resister, probably in the early seventeenth century by a Swiss, Dietrich Meyer. Before this, most etchers were more truly engravers, depending on acid only to reinforce lines already cut into the hard metal with an échoppe, graver, or point. The possibility of drawing a needle through the wax coating with only the slightest resistance gave the artist a new degree of spontaneity almost equal to drawing with pen or pencil. The real genius of etching was "the very *antithesis* of the formality of line-engraving."[9] Engraving, with which many artists supported themselves, was viewed as the art of commerce; etching, however, could be practiced for pure pleasure.

Most early etchings, like the engravings of the time, were made after drawings and paintings of noted artists. This had completely changed by the middle of the seventeenth century, when there were etchers everywhere, and many of them, especially in Holland, were preoccupied with landscapes. Etching became for these artists a means of recording the familiar things around them: interiors, marketplaces, the streets and, notably, the countryside.[10]

## Rembrandt van Rijn

Rembrandt, better than anyone else, personifies etching as it evolved in the seventeenth century. Between 1628 and 1664, he etched hundreds of plates, often changing and reworking them after impressions had already been pulled. He was a virtuoso with the etching needle if ever there was one. Some critics, Hind among them, still believe that in the range of his genius he stands alone. Hamerton, the Anglo-Saxon guru of the etching revival, characterized the kind of homage given to Rembrandt as too uncritical and more in "the nature of worship or adoration."[11] And although he still remains by common consensus the greatest etcher of all time, he was by no means a lone laborer. Working in Holland at the same time were Anthony Van Dyck, the great portrait etcher, and such other recognized landscape etchers as Lucas van Uden, Jacob van Ruisdael, Antoni Waterloo, Jan Haeckert, and Allart van Everdingen, whose little etching had so seduced the hero of Walpole's story. Ruisdael's work was later to have a strong influence on John Crome, the landscape painter and etcher from Norwich. Other lauded names were Paul Potter, known for his etchings of cattle, and Reynier Nooms (remembered as Zeeman), to whom Charles Meryon, one of the later "etching gods," was to dedicate his set of Paris etchings.

It cannot be said, however, that Rembrandt was the inheritor of any "great legacy in the conventions of etching" when, while still resident in Leiden, his hometown, he started to etch the people around him—beggars, cripples, and relatives. Repeated efforts by scholars to trace the origin of his comprehension of the varied capabilities of the medium to predecessors have not yielded the sources of his technique.[12] Nor have we found any credible account of what motivated his earliest attempts, dating from around 1625, when he was still in his teens.[13] Some have reacted to the deification of Rembrandt as lone genius by questioning the attributions, especially of the early work in Leiden. Among these early detractors were two key figures in the nineteenth-century revival: Francis Seymour Haden, who set out to prove that many of the etchings Rembrandt was supposed to have made before 1640 were in fact the work of his pupils;[14] and Alphonse Legros, who made himself "leader of the extreme left in the destructive ranks" when, based on his personal feelings for technical excellence, he threw aside "the whole weight of history" in reducing the Rembrandt oeuvre to a paltry 71 plates compared with the 293 that Hind, in his 1912 catalog, was prepared to accept as authentic.[15]

That Rembrandt did indeed borrow ideas has been documented by R. H. Fuchs, who points out that he was not only an avid art collector but also a part-time dealer in art.[16] Rembrandt is known to have purchased prints and drawings at public sales as early as 1635. These acquisitions were not simply for display but to teach the pupils who came to him for etching lessons. *The Death of the Virgin*, executed a good year after Rembrandt had bought a series of Dürer woodcuts, was developed, though not in any way copied, from one of these compositions. *Abraham and the Angels*, first printed in 1656, can be traced to a copy Rembrandt had made of an Indian miniature of the Mogul period. And the details of Rembrandt's self-portrait of 1639 reveal the artist's familiarity with two Italian masterpieces—Titian's *Portrait of a Man* and Raphael's portrait *Baldassare Castiglione*, which had made their way to Amsterdam that very year.

None of this should persuade us to consider Rembrandt's achievements less awesome than they were. But it has been alleged that the once mightily acclaimed artist fell completely out of favor toward the end of his life and that, thereafter, he came close to being forgotten. According to Laver, "neither in painting nor etching was the old Rembrandt accepted as a model even by his own countrymen. His etching had little, if any, immediate influence."[17] Not until the middle of the nineteenth century were his superlative powers fully recognized by French landscape artists, who began to search his prints for clues to his technical and artistic mastery of the process.[18] To be sure, Rembrandt's fortunes took a bad turn in 1642, when he offended the community with his unconventional group portrait known as *The Night Watch*. Satisfied with this work, Rembrandt refused to make any changes, paint a new one, or refund the money to the civic guards, each of whom had paid 100 guilders to sit for him. That same year his wife had died. With both his own money and that which she had entrusted to him tied up in his house and in his valuable art collection, he was forced to borrow considerable sums. As long-continued wars and civil strife brought hard times for patrons, art dealers, and artists, Rembrandt fell into debt. And, as if this were not trouble enough, scandal followed when his servant, a peasant girl, bore him a child and he could not, under the terms of his wife's will, afford to marry her. By 1656 he was declared bankrupt. His property, including the larger part of his collection of etchings and drawings, was auctioned off at a fraction of its value.

In Rembrandt's lifetime, so Slive assures us, his etchings were in continuous demand by collectors and by graphic artists, who used them to study his techniques.[19] However, two tendencies had combined toward the end of his life to reduce somewhat the popularity of his prints. One was a change in taste that favored the new classicist art from Italy in the form of bright, clear painting. Even erstwhile Rembrandt patrons, it seems, could not resist the etched reproductions of such paintings and sculptures that were published in the year of his death and the year following.[20] A second tendency had to do with changes in Rembrandt's own style. Instead of closely hatched lines of shading, he now sought rich pictorial effects from variations in tone heavily dependent on the tint of the ink left on the surface of the plate in the printing. He even reworked plates that had already received public acclaim so as to produce a darker version, one in which his subtle lines became hard and heavy. In this he was obviously going counter to the movement in public taste.[21]

Critics who after his death came to judge Rembrandt's painting according to the canons of classicist art ridiculed his penchant for ugly women and for a despicable lack of taste in depicting such elements as two dogs copulating that figure in the canvas *St. John Preaching*.[22] Unable to reach the heights of a Raphael or Michelangelo, so charged

these critics, he preferred to be perverse.[23] Nevertheless, the attention
these detractors paid his paintings is testimony to Rembrandt's continued importance as an artist.[24] His etched work, on the other hand,
rarely came in for equally harsh criticism. Evidence of the esteem this
continued to enjoy exists in its cataloging. Before he died, Clement de
Jonghe, who had published some of Rembrandt's etchings, had listed
every one of the seventy-three sheets of Rembrandt prints individually
by title.[25] Accounts of the artist's life and other catalogs of his etched
oeuvre, beginning with the one published by Bartsch in Vienna in
1797, would follow.[26] By the middle of the eighteenth century, there
were reports that "all the wild scrabbles, scratches, etc., done by him
or thought to be done by him were being sought." A circle of English
collectors, centered around the artist and art dealer Arthur Pond, generated a "madness to have [Rembrandt's] prints,"[27] reversing the decline in prices expected after an artist's death. Thus, a first state of
*Christ Healing the Sick*, widely known as the "Hundred Guilder Print"
because Rembrandt sold an impression for that sum, brought 84 guilders (£7) in 1755. The same copy sold for just over £33 in 1798, then in
1809 for over £41. In 1847, with the revival in France just getting
under way, another impression was bought in at an Amsterdam sale
for near £140, to be sold again in the early 1860s to Samuel Palmer,
the painter-etcher, for £1,180.[28]

## Etching in Eclipse? The Eighteenth Century

Most histories of etching show a near void in the production of
etching from Rembrandt's death in 1669 until the "rediscovery" of his
work some 150 years later, but this is not to be taken literally. How
vast was the void? Surely, etchers of the first rank were not wanting. In
Spain there was Goya and in England there were the great satirists—
Hogarth, Rowlandson, and Gillray. Moreover, etching in Italy may
have reached its zenith in the hands of such practitioners as Canaletto,
Tiepolo, and Piranesi.[29] And while the etched work of Watteau in
France was too rare to have had much impact on his contemporaries,
one cannot overlook François Boucher, Jean-Jacques de Boussieu,
Norblin de la Gourdaine, and especially Gabriel de Saint-Aubin, who
is now recognized as an experimental etcher par excellence.[30] At a less
lofty level of achievement, the compiler of a dictionary of British etchers has noted that from 1610 on, there was "scarcely a year that failed
to produce its British Etcher, to say nothing of the numberless foreigners."[31] Nor should one ignore amateur artists like the *fermier général*

La Live de Jully; the manufacturer J. de Jullienne, the friend and pro-
tector of Watteau; and the Marquise de Pompadour, who liked to
dabble with the needle and actually became a pupil of Boucher.[32] And
in England, cultured ladies and gentlemen not yet old enough to assume full adult responsibilities took to etching as "a delightful hobby,
easily to be classed among the 'polite arts.'" A collection of such
amateur etchings done between 1713 and 1813 is housed in the Print
Room of the British Museum.[33] But to the sophisticated taste of the
eighteenth century, an etching had an "unfinished" and superficial
look. The demand was for the magnificently rich copies from line
engravings of portrait paintings by Reynolds, Van Dyck, and other
luminaries. Some etchers, when not apologizing for the apparent hasti-
ness of their prints, actually strove to make them appear like line
engravings.

Nor was the etched work of Rembrandt really lost in the eighteenth century. It had only been "misplaced" and was still there to be
found early in the nineteenth. Avid collectors and professional artists
had helped preserve the best of the past. One of the finest collections
of Rembrandt etchings was assembled by Heneage Finch, Fourth Earl
of Aylesford.[34] Among artists who copied or imitated Rembrandt, and
thereby assured his continuing influence, was a noted portrait painter
by the name of Benjamin Wilson; his works, when shown by a practical jokester to several important connoisseurs, were readily accepted as
originals.[35] There were others who etched in the style of Rembrandt,
including Thomas Worlidge, who did a number of heads, and Arthur
Pond, remembered for his portrait of Alexander Pope. Most notorious
among the copyists was Captain William Baillie, who managed to
deceive the experts with his copy of *The Three Trees* and achieved a
dubious sort of fame by restoring the plate of the great etcher's "Hundred Guilder Print," which had come into his possession, and dividing
it into four pieces. Impressions from these partial plates were still
circulating in the twentieth century.[36] It is estimated that within the
four decades after 1748 nearly a third of Rembrandt's etchings, including most of his landscapes, were copied by amateurs and professionals.[37] These copies came to pose problems for posterity confronted
with the riddle of what was authentic Rembrandt and what was "*after
him.*"

Thus, etching in the eighteenth century was not dead; it had simply gone out of fashion and, in a sense, underground. As a marketable
art form, especially in England and France, it served only as a hand-
maiden to more sought after printed work.

## The Art of Painter-Etching Reborn

J. R. W. Hitchcock noted in 1886 the "incongruity in alluding to an art which has existed, and at times flourished for three hundred years, as if it were born yesterday."[38] Yet, if etching was not born in the nineteenth century, it was certainly reborn in the spirit of Rembrandt and the landscape etchers of the seventeenth century.

The many clearly incestuous accounts of the etching revival, though pointing to France as the starting place, begin with different individuals and at different times.[39] We opt for 1841 as a starting date, when Charles Jacque, an engraver of maps in Paris, tried his hand at an etching after Rembrandt's *Head of an Old Woman*. After this first attempt, he turned to copying and analyzing other Dutch masters of etching, including Rembrandt's rendering, *A Pig*. Pigs came to figure prominently in many of Jacque's 470 plates, most of them landscapes, which also depict sheep, chickens, peasants, and children.[40] (See figure 2.) In fastening on Jacque for the date of this rebirth, we are aware that the etchings of the Barbizon painter, Charles Daubigny, actually pre-date those of Jacque and are better remembered. We similarly pass over others caught up in Jacque's enthusiasm, such as Jean-Baptiste-Camille Corot, who produced some fourteen etchings between 1845 and 1871 mainly for relaxation,[41] and Jean-François Millet, whose earliest plates were directly inspired by Jacque. Théodore Rousseau etched only four plates, although one of these (*Chênes de Roche*), published after his death, is considered a masterpiece.[42] Jules Dupré, a pioneer of the School of Barbizon, figures hardly at all in the history of French etching, except for his dictum that artists should "paint on their good days and their bad, but etch on their good ones only."[43]

Jacque was the first of the Barbizon painters to devote himself preeminently to etching. In his zeal to master the technique, he got the revival going by rediscovering many forgotten processes. Part of the small cadre of landscape painters working in Barbizon, he was, like so many of his contemporaries, completely out of sympathy with the then current academic style and sought inspiration from the work of his Dutch predecessors. Etching became for him a preferred means of translating his ideas directly from nature into prints.[44] He was certainly the most prolific of the Barbizon etchers and, in his own time, the most popular. Editors and publishers overwhelmed him with commissions that he did not refuse. As a result, his later etchings have none of the "charming poetry of his good period; they betray the boredom of a wearied spirit."[45] On the other hand, it was the etchings of

Jacque's colleague, Jean-François Millet, today considered the greatest of the Barbizon painter-etchers, that brought that struggling artist his first recognition. Dating chiefly from 1855 to 1863, Millet's prints were not mentioned by Hamerton in either the 1868 or the 1876 edition of *Etching and Etchers*.

A plate that Millet etched raised an issue much debated during the revival: who stands to profit from the deliberate limitation of the products of artistic creativity? When in 1869 Millet was commissioned to do an etching for *Sonnets et eaux-fortes*, with the stipulation that the plate be destroyed after publication, he objected but then agreed after hearing that Corot, Daubigny, and others had complied with a similar request.[46] He found the destruction of plates "a most brutal and barbaric thing," as he wrote his future biographer. "I am not good enough at commercial calculations to understand the idea behind it; but I know that if Rembrandt and Ostade had each made one of these plates they would not have been destroyed."[47] Upon his death, his etched plates were stored in a strong box, sealed by order of the court until one of his heirs should come of age. Frederick Keppel, the New York print seller, who was present when the box was opened, saw that the plates were not worn from use and quickly arranged for an edition by the finest copperplate printer in England. It was he who had the plates destroyed to prevent any further printing of presumably inferior editions, thereby protecting the artist's posthumous reputation as an etcher. Millet, had he been alive, might have preferred that his plates be steel-faced for a larger print run.[48]

The point is that when these artists began to etch, there was hardly a market for their prints. They etched because the process suited their individual temperaments. Jacque set the pace, and together they helped to dispose of the idea that etching was easy and best suited for dilettantes. Yet one does not yet find within this group of painters any missionary zeal to "spread the word" about the ecstasy of etching. It was left to others to convince the outside world of its charm.

## The Trendsetters

In the earlier half of the nineteenth century, French art students had certainly not been encouraged to try their hand at etching. Hence it is hardly surprising that Jacque, who had worked for an engraver, was the only one of the Barbizon painters with real training in etching techniques. The rest learned from each other and by studying old prints. As their work caught the attention of other artists, the ranks of etchers began to swell until, by the 1850s, etching could be said to be in vogue among artists—the fashionable thing at which to try one's hand, even if the public had not yet caught on.

A major trendsetter in addition to the Barbizons was Charles Meryon who, along with Rembrandt and Whistler, is universally judged one of the greats of etching. (See figure 4.) He was taught to etch by Eugène Bléry, who had him copy paintings. Then somewhere among the bookstalls bordering the Seine, Meryon came upon Zeeman's prints. These sketches of a long-gone Paris by the Dutch etcher, some of which Meryon copied, so inspired him that he later dedicated *Eaux-fortes sur Paris*, his first set of twenty-two etchings, to the long-dead artist. Meryon was, however, unlike the Barbizons, a loner, not part of any circle, a paranoiac who died young in an asylum. Gabrielle Niel is the only one among a host of French architectural etchers who apparently came under his direct tutelage, but only insofar as he showed her how to prepare a plate for printing.[49] As for Meryon's etchings, it was only during the last decade of his life, when he was already in an asylum, that they came to be appreciated. The poet-critic, Charles Baudelaire, among others, had done his best to make Meryon's work known, while several well-recognized artists, including Félix Bracquemond, sought to befriend him. But Meryon's paranoid delusions caused him to treat his would-be benefactors as if they were enemies. Only after his death in 1868, with the market for etchings booming, did a demand for his work develop.

Neither of two other artists who played a major role in the rebirth of etching in France was French. Both American-born James Abbott McNeill Whistler and his English brother-in-law, Francis Seymour Haden, came to etching by way of a "nonartistic" profession. Whistler had designed and etched, while still a young man, for the drawing division of the United States Coast Survey, where the making of topographical maps was the principal activity. Haden, in the course of his medical studies, had scratched anatomical subjects on metal plates. He already was an admirer and collector of Rembrandt prints. His own earliest plates, six scenes of Italy, were etched in 1844, just before he entered medical practice. It is also possible that he attended night classes at the Ecole des Beaux-Arts while pursuing his medical studies in Paris, but the "mystery of why Haden began to etch and how he learned to use the medium" with such assuredness remains basically unresolved.[50] Like Jacque, he adopted Rembrandt as mentor and was often in France, where he took a strong interest in the pioneer etchers. Once he called on Meryon in his lodgings, chose a few prints, and departed after paying the price demanded. But Meryon, believing that his treasures had been stolen, ran out to retrieve them and then wrote a letter to the *Gazette des beaux-arts* to warn its editor against Haden.[51] Haden was more successful with Whistler, who in the days before they became bitter enemies gladly accepted his financial help.

Whistler, the son of a military man, had been expelled from the United States Military Academy and then, after a brief period as a draftsman in Washington, D.C., persuaded his mother to let him study art in Paris. He arrived in November 1855, just after the publication of Meryon's *Eaux-fortes sur Paris* and Daubigny's *Cahier d'eaux-fortes*. Whistler made his own debut in 1856 with his *Douze eaux-fortes d'après nature*, a series known as his French set. One of these prints, *La Vieille aux loques* (figure 3), clearly shows Jacque's influence; another, *La Mère Gérard*, is Rembrandtesque. Most were drawn during a summer's ramble with a friend, during which Whistler carried in his knapsack small copperplates prepared (grounded) in advance for on-the-spot etching. Whether Whistler, before this, had been in personal contact with Jacque or any of the pioneer French etchers we do not know, but he had his plates printed in Auguste Delâtre's shop, which they all frequented, and so surely he knew their work. Their publication made Whistler, aged twenty-four, a major etcher overnight. The set sold for 2 guineas, bound as a drawing room album or separately framed, whichever the subscriber preferred. For the enterprise to succeed, he needed fifty subscribers; Haden in London and his mother back home each promised to find him twenty-five.[52]

It was shortly after completion of his French set that Whistler first met Alphonse Legros, who had learned to etch in the drawing school of Lecoq de Boisbaudran and who, though even younger than Whistler, had already had two works hung in the Salon. Despite incessant work—in painting, etching, drawing, lithography—and a circle of supportive friends, he had a hard time eking out an existence. It was therefore not too difficult for Whistler, after he moved to England, to persuade the young Frenchman to follow. Their presence there, as we shall see, was subsequently to influence the course of the British revival. Before he deserted France, Legros had been anointed by the critic, Philippe Burty, along with Bracquemond, as one of two *"pontifes de la nouvelle église"* (popes of the new church).[53] Bracquemond was a most important catalyst who assisted others to master etching techniques and to find outlets for their work. "The art," wrote Beraldi, "could not have found a stronger champion."[54] Apprenticed at fifteen to a lithographer, he was inducted into the art world by a neighbor of his family, the painter Joseph Guichard, who gave him drawing and painting lessons and encouraged the boy to etch. From odd prints bought on the quays of Paris, from study of the entry on *la gravure* in a borrowed volume of Diderot's *Encyclopédie*, and with some help from a printer, he made his first etching in 1849.[55] His first sale of a copperplate was *Birds Nailed on a Barn*, bought by Cadart, the Paris publisher, for 24 francs—a small sum, indeed! But it was a critical link in the promotional network that was soon to make etching à la mode.[56]

## Etching à la Mode

Before midcentury the production of original etchings in France was not highly organized, and there was only loose collaboration among those who worked in the medium. Schools offered little in the way of formal training. Painter-etchers responded to their own expressive needs rather than to any public demand—theirs was an elite art, reinvented by artists for themselves. The movement, if that is what it was, amounted to nothing more than a few artists banding together on the basis of some affinity they experienced. Baudelaire believed that etching could never become wildly popular; nor, in his view, should it. An etching was too personal and consequently too aristocratic.[57] Certainly as practiced by those who revived it, this art form was destined to have only limited appeal, to be forever the favored medium of the few rather than of the many.

Prior to 1860, there had been no real French market for etchings. Plates by Daubigny and some other etchers that appeared in *L'Artiste* from the 1840s stirred some interest but not much in the way of public demand. Meryon's critically acclaimed *eaux-fortes* sold hardly at all. Whistler's first plates, greatly admired by his circle of friends, had first to make their way in London. The basically individual mode of creation and casual marketing at the time contradicted the way they were produced. Inherent in the medium was the potential for mass distribution. The essential next step in the revival was the diffusion of this intrinsically elite art form to a larger public. In other words, etching could never become truly in fashion except by organizing the activities relevant to its processing. The revival eventually "took off" in France when it found a *publisher*, an *artist-printer*, and a *spokesman*. Together, but with little encouragement from the artists, these three created a mechanism for rationalizing the production of prints and for distributing and establishing a market for their output.[58]

The publisher was Alfred Cadart. A keen sympathizer since the first stirrings of the revival, he was to organize the Société des Aqua-fortistes, the first etching association in France. It was active from 1862 to 1867. From whom the first suggestion came is a matter for conjecture. Bracquemond, Legros, and the writer Hippolyte Babou have each been credited with persuading Cadart to take the initiative in its organization. In comparison with the many etching societies that were to form later, the aquafortistes were in their mode of operation quite frankly commercial.[59]

To attain its stated aim, "the extension and perfection of etching," it began to issue *Eaux-fortes modernes*, a monthly publication of five original etchings. The yearly subscription price for all sixty was 50 francs. A deluxe edition of twenty-five was priced at twice that amount, while proofs could be purchased individually for one and a half francs each.

To become a member an artist had to submit a "planche de reception," a presentation or acceptance plate. The initial membership included artists who had never etched, who had not etched for a long time, or who had spent no more than a day or so on Cadart's premises learning the basics. Women, too, were admitted on an equal basis. The statutes called for no office other than that of *éditeur*, a post assumed by Cadart. The choice of plates to be published was placed in the hands of a five-member jury that was rotated each month. The etcher received a flat price plus half of what was realized from any sale outside the regular subscription. While not required to hold more than one meeting a year, the members seem to have shared a certain amount of conviviality.[60]

The first issue of *Eaux-fortes modernes* contained a blistering manifesto that defended the domain of "artistic" reproduction against the inroads of photography, which was blamed for the "commercial death" of fine line engraving as a form of illustration.[61] But engraving may have died by its own hand because it was too slow. Publishers often had to wait years for a plate in which they had invested significant sums of money. In terms of speed, etching was more competitive.[62] Thus, *The Burial of the Burin*, an allegorical print by Buhot published as a frontispiece for an issue of *L'Illustration nouvelle*, shows the dead body of the engraving tool being carried away in a hearse as modern etching comes "thundering on in the form of an express train." But this was not until 1877. Thirteen years earlier, with *Eaux-fortes modernes* in successful operation, Théophile Gautier had already sounded the clarion call: "Etching, almost abandoned since the seventeenth century, has become one of the expressions of French art."[63] Cadart's shop was turned into a meeting point for a movement whose code was individualism. The "dainty little catalogues" of Maison Cadart contained the names of "all the greatest etchers of the day."[64]

In purely quantitative terms, the venture proved extraordinarily successful. The prints published by the society during its short life came to form one of the largest series of etchings in the world, amounting to 323 plates, which, if they had been printed in editions of only one hundred each, would have totaled well over 30,000.[65] It was succeeded by another monthly, *L'Illustration nouvelle*—already mentioned—and by *L'Album Cadart*, which was issued annually, starting in 1874.

And what about quality? Here the verdict is mixed. Hamerton judged that the Société had published "a good many plates that tried to be fine but were not . . . yet they rarely addressed . . . the taste of the vulgar."[66] Hind's judgment a half-century later was harsher: Cadart, he wrote, had done his "most to bring third-rate work to the fore."[67] In the opinion of Martin Hardie of the Victoria and Albert, Cadart's publications contained "an endless number of indifferent prints [but] . . . every now and then, in turning the volumes over, one comes upon a real gem, which more than atones for the inferiority of a score of other plates."[68] Certainly the selection of plates was not always artistically discriminating, and the printing, though closely supervised, did not always bring out the best in each. Allowance has to be made for the peculiar conditions under which these early publications were produced. For one thing, the public had not yet learned to distinguish between original etching and the line engraver's interpretation of a painter's work. Also, the popularity of mechanical processes was fast increasing; most people were of the opinion that photographic reproductions rendered reality better than any artistic copy. To meet this competition, publishers had to sell their etchings at prices hardly higher than those of photographs. In 1873 Cadart advertised Meryon's masterful *Ministère de la Marine* at 3 francs, most of Bracquemond's proofs at 2 or 3 francs, and Haden's *Bords de la Tamise* at 4 francs. It was this unavoidable "commercialism . . . [that] kept alive an art which would otherwise have been forced to give ground to productions of the mechanical press."[69]

The printer who helped transform the nineteenth-century etching world was Auguste Delâtre (1822–1907). Employed to print the landscape etchings of Charles Jacque and Louis Marvy, he was an artist in his own right.[70] He had learned to draw, gone on to study the etchings of the Old Masters, and discovered for himself how by skillful printing one could obtain varied effects from a single plate. With two presses bought from Jacque, he set up his own shop to become the "high-priest of printing." So great was his reputation that etchers came to insist on proofs printed by Delâtre himself, passing over the many other copperplate printers in Paris. Almost every plate etched in Paris by such as Meryon, Jacque, Bracquemond, Jacquemart, Corot, Millet, Daubigny, Delacroix, Haden, and Whistler passed between the rollers of Delâtre's press. He is credited with having personally printed some 90,000 proofs over a lifetime, in addition to which he several times left Paris for London, first to set up an etching class at the National Art Training School, where he gave daily lectures, and again in 1871, after a Prussian shell had shattered his presses, to set up shop across the Channel for a full year.

The revival of etching still required publicists and poets to sing its praises. The leading figure on this front was Burty. As art critic for the *Gazette des beaux-arts*, he could be counted on to review, with enthusiasm, the various print exhibitions and publications of the aquafortistes. He also made sure that each issue of the *Gazette* contained an adequate number of artistic etchings, including some by Corot, Millet, and other heralded Barbizon painter-etchers. His survey of etching in France, published in *Renaissance littéraire et artistique*, was the first history of the movement. In promoting the art, Burty was assisted by etchers who were themselves untiring publicists for their art. For one, Legros persuaded Manet to contribute his *Les Gitanos* to *Eaux-fortes modernes*. Bracquemond, with equally close connections to the Impressionists, proved a ceaseless advocate for the needled copperplate. And Maxime Lalanne, himself a well-reputed etcher, wrote the first *Treatise on Etching*. A highly popular manual for artists, it also had good sales among a public curious about the technique.

Among the poets who did their literary best to give etching a new lease on life, the most enthusiastic was clearly Baudelaire. For him the revival of the almost obsolete technique signified the personal force and distinction he so valued. Also, he sensed that poetry and etching supplemented one another quite naturally: "The sharpness of the etched line deepening the impressions of form and color conveyed more faintly by the words, and these, in turn amplifying the ideas and sentiments that the artists were able to indicate only indirectly and symbolically in the pictures."[71] Not only Baudelaire but also Victor Hugo found Meryon's etchings "splendid" and especially "dazzling," the novelist himself being inspired to take up etching. The closest union between poet and etcher came with the publication of *Sonnets et eaux-fortes* in 1869, printed in an edition of 350 with contributions from a large number of the major (and some minor) poets and etchers of the period. Hugo appeared not as a poet but as an etcher and, appropriately enough, the volume was dedicated to Burty.

## Fashion and Fad in France

"The glorious period that was opened after about 1860 ended in 1880 in a crisis," Léon Rosenthal wrote in 1909.[72] The very success of etching against which Baudelaire had earlier cautioned was also the cause of its downfall. A "little unpopularity," he had proposed, was a "sort of consecration," but, as he feared, a little popularity had inspired a multitude of mediocre imitators.[73] Nevertheless, France was never hit by the same mania or craze that later overwhelmed England and America. Even at the height of the vogue, the little shops along the quay in Paris had etchings by Jacque, Daubigny, and others, priced at a franc or so (then worth about nineteen cents), that went unsold. The American collector Samuel P. Avery snapped up some of these bargains, including an "exceptionally good proof" of a Daubigny, which he then induced the artist to sign.[74] The output of original etchings by an increasing number of artists was more than adequate to satisfy the demand. The progressive fatigue gradually bankrupted Cadart. Although his firm ceased publication in 1881, this insolvency affected mostly himself. The glut on the market halted the overproduction of etchings without choking off the revival itself. New societies formed, this time mostly with painter-etchers themselves taking the initiative in order to signal the vitality of their art. The Société Artistique des Aquafortistes, launched in 1885, leaned rather toward reproductive etching but also offered some original work. This was followed in 1889 by the Société des Peintres-Graveurs Français, which still exists today and, at one time or other, counted most of the distinguished names in French etching among its members.

Let us suggest some reasons why the revival in France never reached the peak of popularity that it later did in Britain and the United States nor, after the bubble burst, fell so far in public esteem. At no point in time did etching in black and white become the printmaking technique most favored by French artists and the art public. Because it had to compete not only with line engraving but equally and perhaps even more so with lithography, wood engraving, and all forms of color prints, there was no critical mass of practitioners whose reputations were built nearly completely on etching and who depended for their livelihood on collectors betting on continually escalating prices. This brake on the boom turned out to be a brake on a possible bust as well.

A second reason is that the revival in France was more closely tied to book and journal illustration than in the other countries. Though etching as a form of illustration could hold its own better than engraving in the competition with the as yet primitive photoreproductive processes, it faced a more serious challenge from color, particularly in a period dominated by the Impressionist painters. Several who excelled in etching—Johan Berthold Jongkind, Mary Cassatt, Camille Pissarro, Pierre Bonnard, for example—experimented with color techniques first developed in poster art. There was real continuity within the French print world. The leading color printer was none other than Eugène Delâtre, son of Auguste Delâtre who had introduced an earlier generation to the magic of a black line. The 1890s saw a number of color publications along the lines of Cadart's *Eaux-fortes nouvelles*, all of them short-lived, with contributions from painter-etchers. In 1898, some of these printmakers formed themselves into the Société de la Gravure Originale en Couleur, but it took them six years to mount their first exhibition.[75]

None of this is meant to denigrate the contribution of the painter-etcher movement as it developed in France. In the 1870s, no other country could rival it in the number of thoroughly accomplished etchers. "For every artist who practiced etching in Whistler's day," Malcolm Salaman estimated in 1913, there are now "perhaps fifty scratching their visions on the copper-plate."[76] Some of these, like Jean-Louis Forain, Auguste Brouet, Edgar Chahine and Auguste Lepère went on to produce little masterpieces. And it can safely be said that, by the time the Great Depression of the thirties hit, most modern French painters and sculptors had at some time in their careers executed etchings for sale, for book illustration, or simply for their own enjoyment. And, in the doing, they had proved themselves more experimental than their counterparts across the Channel.

French artists had taken the first steps to revive etching in the spirit of the Dutch landscape artists, but it was simply not taken as seriously there as it would be taken in England. Especially after about 1880, etching always had serious rivals in the other print media. In short, it was only one of many such techniques with which artists could experiment, and in France it never occupied quite the same status within the art world.

# 3

## Export to Britain

In John Crome, John Sell Cotman, George Vincent, Henry Ninham, and the rest of the Norwich School, England had, early in the nineteenth century, its own counterpart to Barbizon. Had these landscape painters etched "not merely 'for pleasure or for remembrance,' but with the London press and a London publisher at their back, we should have had a real English revival of etching which would have anticipated that of France," so wrote Martin Hardie, long-time curator of prints and drawings at the Victoria and Albert.[1] Yet, because they lacked a publicist, like Burty, and a master copperplate printer, like Delâtre, their early accomplishments had little resonance. Only after Whistler and Legros, fresh from the ferment in France, carried the revival across the Channel did English etching find an equivalent spokesman in Philip Gilbert Hamerton and a Delâtre in the person of Frederick Goulding. Nor did any of its several publishers measure up to Cadart. Instead, the role of key catalyst was assumed by a most unusual "amateur"—Sir Francis Seymour Haden, for whom etching was, to begin with, only a pleasant diversion from a highly successful career as a surgeon. His mission was to establish its legitimacy as a fine art.

### Professionals and Amateurs

British landscape etching, imported from Holland by immigrant artists in the seventeenth century, had just about managed to survive through the eighteenth. Many of these early etching efforts were more nearly "sketching" than etching. A true British gentleman had to know something about art, preferably making, collecting, or performing it. Drawing and etching landscapes fit this requirement admirably and, in keeping with it, Crome, a conscientious drawing master, was understandably reluctant to publish etchings made only as a means of instructing his pupils.[2] The difference between the professional and the amateur etcher was less a matter of commitment than of economic status. Both might have professional ties to London print sellers, but amateurs—many of them women—were sufficiently well off to confine their art to what pleased themselves and their circle. If they published at all, it was usually for a very limited clientele, who then assembled these prints into folios to be studied and enjoyed at leisure. There did come about, however, a significant change in the conventions of print consumption. Eighteenth-century *amateurs d'estampes*, though enjoying prints for their beauty, were prone to consider them expendable. They would paste, glue, or pin them in books or onto walls. One collector actually used landscape prints to wallpaper an entire room. It was not until the nineteenth century that prints in England were considered works of art worthy of preservation. A curator of prints and drawings at the British Museum invented the mat mounting, used to this day, to protect the etched surface from possible mishandling and damage. Also invented was the solander box, which sheltered stored prints against changes in temperature and humidity.[3]

Despite this change in attitude, the revival in England was never to lose entirely its amateur character. Walter Sickert, in his disdain for "The Old Ladies of Etching Needle Street," characterized the movement as nothing more than "an interesting and sincere amateur revival, closely based, to begin with, on the professional revival in France." Etching had become so popular, he complained, that too many of its carriers were amateurs who, having failed to master drawing, had been urged to try their hand at etching to see if they could get better effects.[4] The etching "hobby" did indeed have the seal of approval from Queen Victoria, herself an amateur, and Prince Consort Albert. In 1840, after receiving proper instruction from Edward Landseer, the royal rulers turned out a series of plates—sketches of children and dogs, portraits, and so forth.[5] These became the focus of a public scandal when proofs, stolen by the assistant to a printer at Windsor, found their way to a publisher named Strange, who then, quite unabashedly, announced "A Descriptive Catalogue of the Royal Victoria and Albert Gallery of Etchings." For six weeks, the suit to keep the catalog from being published received full coverage in *The Times*.[6]

The considerable publicity given the matter of the purloined prints reminds us that in this period of growing affluence, writers were urging people to cultivate a taste that could as readily as not extend to original etchings. Ordinary people had, however, not yet learned to enjoy art in their own homes. The whole episode also reminds us of the essentially aristocratic nature of etching production as a pastime. The leisure and money required for quality paper, copperplates, printing material, and services were obvious impediments to its complete democratization.

## The Etching Club and the Junior Etching Club

The origins of the Etching Club, formed in 1838 and later referred to as the "Old Club" to distinguish it from its younger offspring, were not so frankly commercial as those of the Société des Aquafortistes. But while the club rejected a suggestion, made at an early meeting, that the French marketing techniques be adopted, its artistic purity of purpose can easily be overstated.[7] In forming the club the members were less interested in encouraging each other or others to etch than in earning enough from the publication of sumptuously illustrated books of the kind then in fashion to compensate for the time their etching would take from their work as painters. All eight men present at the first organizational meeting were successful painters; several were to become Royal Academicians. Although for a few etching was as much a labor of love as of work, there was nothing dilettantish about the attitudes of any of them. Still, most lived in the same London borough of Kensington and found diversionary joys and social fellowship in their common enterprise.

The troubles of the club in the near half-century of its existence arose from a dilemma: how to make rules strict enough for efficiency and yet elastic enough for comfort. According to the initial rules, each member was to bring a plate "carefully wrought, bit in, and proved ready for printing" to each regular monthly meeting. But not everyone complied. After two founding members, remiss on more than two occasions, were made to resign, the club "as a temporary measure" began to meet not every month but only every six weeks. One member thought this a step in the wrong direction. His motions to impose fines or to turn over to others work not finished on time "were generally passed, but . . . always rescinded at the next meeting" when members balked at paying the half-guinea demanded of them.[8]

The first project completed by the club was an illustrated edition of Oliver Goldsmith's poem, *The Deserted Village*, with forty plates and seventy-nine little etchings. When the book earned money, it raised a new and thorny question: Should all contributors share equally in the proceeds? Or, should so much be allowed for each published plate and, if so, should more be allotted for large plates than for small ones? What troubles lay ahead becomes apparent in reading the convoluted scheme devised for profit sharing.

> Each member shall be provided with a numbered list of all the plates and shall write against each omitting his own how many shares (not less than one nor more than eight) he considers due to it—and these being added up and averaged with the number of members will determine how many shares each etching is entitled to—Then the whole number of shares being added together and the sum to be shared divided thereby will give the worth of each share, and this multiplied by the number of shares adjudged to each member will give his aggregate of the division of the profits.[9]

But members could not agree on what gave merit to an etching. The more old-fashioned among them, trained in engraving and aware of the time required for elaboration, thought in terms of pay per hour of work. To them the summary lines of the younger French-trained etchers hardly looked time-consuming. How, then, could these etchers' plates be worth as much as theirs?

Conflict over this issue ultimately led to the demise of the Old Club in the 1870s but not before interest in its activities had first been diminished by the prosperity its members were experiencing. Their success was not untypical. From the 1860s to the turn of the century, established artists and especially Royal Academicians could earn more from painting than from the elaborately detailed etchings still favored by collectors.[10] Even Samuel Palmer, the least financially solvent member, feared losing more remunerative work in watercolor. He was a slow worker, as he confided to Hamerton, "because I cannot otherwise get certain shimmerings of light, and mysteries of shadow; so that only a pretty good price would yield a journeyman's wages. . . . [And] I can get 100 guineas for quite a small drawing, which does not occupy nearly the time of some of my etchings."[11]

Another problem had arisen from the time-honored practice of having plates printed by a commercial firm. After Haden joined in 1858, he seized every opportunity to promote the idea that the finest proofs could only be pulled by the artists themselves or under their direct supervision.[12] It took over a decade of badgering for Haden to convince the club to entrust the printing of their second volume of etchings to Goulding, the esteemed master printer. That volume, with two Hadens, one Palmer, one Millais, and sixteen other prints, turned out to be a financial success. The club realized £525 in profits. Yet

Haden's triumph was but the prelude to disaster when members failed to agree about how to divide this amount among the contributors. Haden's proposal for a division into equal shares for each plate had some support. Arrayed against him were John Everett Millais and Charles West Cope, who knew that Palmer had spent much time and extreme care on his only plate and was really in dire financial straits. They requested that the profits be divided equally among all contributors regardless of the number of plates each had contributed. After four or more meetings and much dissension, Haden carried the day, but at considerable cost. The old cordiality was gone; Palmer was deeply offended, and the affair left a rift that kept the club from meeting for four years.[13] When it finally reconvened, Haden did not attend. Two years later, in April 1878, he resigned from a club effectively defunct save in name, bidding a fiery farewell, so he wrote, "in defense of the liberty of the Etcher." By this time he was ready, with "his genius and irascibility to promote the greatness and embitter the existence of other associations," especially one that he could effectively dominate.[14]

The Junior Etching Club, founded on 17 June 1857, became the pride and joy of its parent group. Its objective and its constitution were modeled on that of the Old Club and there were places for up to twenty-five men (*sic*). Two of the more forward-looking juniors had made the "radical" proposal that ladies be admitted as members but, when put to a vote, this "lost by a large majority." Otherwise, membership in the Junior rather than the Old Club was simply a function of age and no reflection on either talent or prior experience. Thus, Samuel Palmer was admitted to the Old Club in 1850, at age forty-five, after submitting a modest plate, his first ever, whereas Whistler, just turning twenty-three, was tapped for the Junior Club although he was already enjoying a certain notoriety from his French Set, then on view at the Royal Academy.

Neither of the two clubs had anywhere near the influence on etching in England that the Aquafortistes had in France. The Old Club survived for nearly a half-century, until 1885. All told, its members collaborated on nine major illustrated books—about one every fourth year of its existence. Several members also contributed to Hamerton's influential *Etching and Etchers* (1868) and to the magazines that he launched. "Their work was well drawn, pretty, sincere in its way, but (the work of Samuel Palmer excepted) shows little appreciation of the spirit of etching."[15] The most sought-after illustrated book to come out of the Junior Club was *Passages from Modern English Poets*. Its forty-seven plates include one of the thirty or so now acclaimed etchings by Charles S. Keene (*Scene of the Plague in London 1665*), another by Millais (*Summer Indolence*), and two by Whistler (*The Angler*, also known as *The Thames*, and *A River Scene*, also known as *The Punt*). Yet the book in its entirety comes no closer to being a collection of masterpieces than those of the Old Club. The problem was that "most of the members were more devoted to illustration than to etching, and indeed cared very little for the medium employed."[16]

Whistler, who attended just three meetings of the club, was completely out of sympathy with this use of etching as a method of illustration. He had initially refused to contribute a plate to *Modern English Poets* but finally changed his mind when prevailed upon by friends, who told him that otherwise its publication would be seriously delayed by the death of a member who had been scheduled to provide two etchings.[17] But the break with book illustration had to be made if etching were to take off. Millais's experience surely proved that a series of etchings on miscellaneous subjects could be more remunerative than this kind of collective enterprise. In 1859, his annual income had amounted to £3,000, of which £800 came from woodblocks for magazine illustration.[18] Yet the club never acted on Whistler's proposal, made in 1862, to establish a periodical that would publish plates by members. When it was dissolved in the seventh year of its existence, it was because its members saw little prospect of gain. Like its longer-lived predecessor, the Junior Club was at least partly the victim of market forces.

## England Finds Its Burty

At this point Hamerton stepped in. An unsuccessful etcher with such passionate love for the art that he could never put down the needle, Hamerton believed that the big mistake of the Old Club was to have catered to an uneducated public.[19] Hence he took it upon himself to cultivate the English taste by rejecting the etched reproductions of paintings, including artists' re-creations of their own work, with which the Printsellers Association, formed by thirty-one London dealers, was flooding the market. The first edition of Hamerton's *Etching and Etchers*, which appeared in 1868, made a strong case for painter-etchings, designed and etched by artists themselves, as deserving more admiration than the public was prepared to grant them. It was a handsome volume, issued with thirty-five original etchings, one printed from an old plate by Rembrandt.

No one could have been more surprised than Hamerton himself at how quickly this volume, published at a guinea and a half, sold out. Within ten years it became a collectible and quadrupled in value. Through much of the book Hamerton not only deplored the English taste but had little that was good to say about the artists in the two etching clubs—Whistler and Haden excepted: "Sustained energetic work . . . is not encouraged here, as it is in France . . . nor . . . is there much of that heroic temper amongst English artists which will persevere in an unremunerative pursuit, simply for the love of it, and from a feeling that a noble art ought to be kept alive for its own sake."[20] In reflecting on the differences between England and France, he was, however, inclined to exonerate the artists and find the greater fault with the public: "The ordinary Englishman measures the graphic arts exclusively by their powers of imitation; he has no conception of any higher faculty in the artist, or any wider liberty. . . . We know that the real labour of the artist (though the vulgar may not be aware of it) consists, not in giving a mirror-like image of things precisely as they are, but in a personal and original *interpretation* of their aspects, far, indeed, from the literal truth of a reflection on metal or on glass."[21]

A contrary view, impressed upon students by Ruskin in his Oxford lectures, underlay many of these critical reviews. One in the *Morning Post* asserted that "the needle, the burin, the pencil, the brush,—these are all machines or tools worked by the hand to copy what the eye beholds, and the faithfulness of the copy constitutes the merit of the work. No graphic delineation can portray the invisible, no artist can figure feeling; this must be extracted by spectators themselves out of the imitated forms, as the artist's was excited by the view of the originals."[22] The reviewer for *The Times* likewise quickly dismissed the idea that etching might be the one art with room for interpretation as too novel to be taken seriously. The opinions of such critics were reinforced by the Royal Academy, which at a time when the Paris Salons were giving an entire room over to etchings and lithographs, could spare such efforts no more than a corner of one remote room. The section had a placard labeled "Engravings" lest it be overlooked by visitors. Hamerton was touched to find the words "*and* Etchings" scribbled in pencil underneath the big black printed word of the sign, as if someone had wanted " 'to let the people know that the art was in existence.' " He suspected that the scribbler was Haden.[23]

In Hamerton the English etching renaissance had found its Burty. The apparent success of *Etching and Etchers* spurred him to find additional means for spreading the word. In 1879, he launched *The Portfo-*

*lio*, an art monthly similar in format to *L'Artiste* and *Gazette des beaux-arts* and addressed to a "cultivated class of readers."[24] Each of the early issues contained an illustration by an English etcher; yet the pool of possible contributors who met Hamerton's standards was so quickly exhausted that he came to rely mostly on continental artists. Nevertheless, determined to encourage his compatriots to etch, he next issued a practical manual for anyone who might want to learn; then, to expand the market for etchers, he founded two other art journals, *English Etchings* (1881–91) and *The Etcher* (1879–83), the second of which carried a column with "Practical Notes on Etching." Bound into each issue were usually three (steel-faced) etchings—all this at a cost of £0.3.6 and, for the truly discerning collector, there was the opportunity to purchase a limited edition proof of these same etchings, each printed on Japanese paper and signed by the artist.

Together these ventures resulted in a "remarkable development . . . of the [artist's] taste for etching." Where five years ago there might have been an educated public sufficient to support publication of *The Etcher*, its editor noted in 1880, one would have been at a loss to find "the etchers and variety of etchers to keep it alive." All this had changed with the translation of Lalanne's *Treatise on Etching* into English. Votaries of etching, formerly numbered by tens, could now be numbered "by hundreds."[25]

## Francis Seymour Haden

If Hamerton was the chief publicist for the British revival, Haden can be considered its pontiff. His main contribution was the promulgation of a doctrine and the creation of an organization to give the painter-etcher movement legitimacy. The task he took upon himself was two-purposed: to establish original etching as a fine art and to raise the professional status of its practitioners to equal that of other visual artists. He worked valiantly for both causes.

Here are the tenets of the Haden "gospel," distilled, as they must be, from his writings and "proclamations," since he himself never issued a set of formal rules in this or any form:

Etching is an art form superior to line-engraving ("the comparison of the etching-needle with the burin is the comparison of the pen with the plough").
The original etching, designed and executed by the artist, is superior to the reproductive etching, which is nothing but a copy.
The beauty of an etching lies in its use of line.

The highest attainment in etching depends on the economy of line, on the ability of the artist to suggest a great deal with a minimum number of lines. (This is the doctrine of linear economy or "the labor of omission.")

Etching is the least suited of all the arts to the half-educated artist: "The faculty of doing such work supposes a concentration and a reticence requisite in no other art."

Printing is an integral part of the etcher's art—it should be undertaken by the etcher himself or, if that is impossible, by some specialized and competent printer such as Delâtre or Goulding, working closely with the artist.

If etching is freer and more suggestive than other arts, it follows that it is also more intellectual.

The following comparison of etching with painting and sculpture is in Haden's own words:

Etching being an art which expresses itself by lines, and the line since there are none in nature, being the acme of conventionalism, how comes it that we attach either beauty or value to the etched line? It is precisely because the best art is conventional—that is to say suggestive rather than imitative—that one may properly do so. With the relatively coarse materials at his disposal, the painter does not seek to reproduce the morning mist and the noon-day haze—he seeks to suggest it. The sculptor does not make his statue of marble because marble is like human flesh but because, while it permits perfection of form, marble suggests for human flesh a purity which it is the peaceful province of art to claim for it. If he painted the eyes and eyebrows to make his statue "like nature" he would descend at once from the region of art into the abyss of realism, and instead of exalting humanity, degrade it.[26]

Haden's missionary zeal should not be taken as altogether disinterested. He must have had his eye on his own election to that body when he pressed the Royal Academy to admit etchers as artists in their own right rather than as Associate Engravers—an equivocal title at best. Lord Frederic Leighton, president of the Academy, is said to have told the surgeon-etcher, "Set your mind at rest, my dear fellow, you will never be an Academician." Haden allegedly replied, "Set your own mind at rest, my dear fellow, I am the President of my own Academy."[27] His "Academy" was the society he formed in 1880 that later, with the granting of a royal charter, became the Royal Society of Painter-Etchers (RSPE). Haden was its president. No longer did he have to fight the adherents of an older, more academic and illustrative tradition still dominant in the Old Club, which he despised.

By his deeds as by his preachments, Haden helped transfuse the French revival to Britain. After two of his prints, submitted to the Royal Academy under the nom de plume H. Dean, were accepted for hanging and after his *Etudes à l'eaux-fortes* were published, at Burty's urging, he quite unexpectedly found a ready clientele for them in London. It was the year of the great crash of the London Stock Exchange, yet his etchings, when exhibited at Colnaghi's on Bond Street, were not only praised by eleven newspapers but attracted ready buyers. Within weeks 120 copies were sold at what was then the high price of 15 guineas; in Paris he had sold only ten at the much lower price of 350 francs. With 180 sets printed from an intended edition of 250 (one plate broke when run through the press while others showed signs of premature wear), it has been estimated that his gross receipts may have been as high as £2,500. Be this as it may, fourteen years later, in 1880, a set went for 30 guineas at auction; sold individually, the copies would have yielded a dealer twice that amount.[28] While in the long run the dealers may have profited, Haden reportedly lost a considerable sum on the venture—each set had cost him 18 guineas, more than the original price at which they were sold.

Haden made his financial coup in 1870 with the *Breaking-up of the Agamemnon*. Too large for *The Portfolio*, for which it had originally been commissioned, the *Agamemnon* became, if not the first, then one of the first English prints to be offered for subscription as a single print, not as part of a series. It was enormously popular. Sales of impressions from the plate, published in two states, totaled £2,500, making it the most financially successful etching ever published.[29] The ever-cantankerous Joseph Pennell branded Haden as "the first, and still, I imagine, far the most successful business etcher of modern times." He was, so Pennell wrote, in the habit of steeling his plates before turning them over to Goulding to "print as much alike as he could."[30] But the chief motivation in Haden's career was certainly not commercial. He would have agreed with Baudelaire that a little bit of "unpopularity" was necessary if the public was to come to regard etching as more than another form of decoration or illustration.

Nevertheless, no one would dare argue that Haden was always consistent in what he advocated or that his behavior never contradicted the views he championed. For example, he had often railed against the preliminary sketch, holding that the etcher should work directly from nature, with a rapid execution, and not linger over details; a plate should be etched, bitten, and finished the same day. Yet, it appears that fewer than 10 percent of his own plates were completed at one sitting. Nor did he etch directly from nature as often as he claimed; like others, he frequently relied on sketches and even on photographs.[31] He also pressed vigorously the principle that the economy of line so important to the appeal of etching favored small plates. In this he was only following the footsteps of the Dutch etchers, of Legros and, above all, of Whistler, who had done more than anyone else to release etchers "from the necessity of filling every inch of their plates . . . and won [for etchers] the liberty to be slight, sketchy, and suggestive."[32] Haden would have agreed that small plates were ideal for "working from nature," yet, perversely, his very popular *Agamemnon* was an outsized 7¾ inches high and 16½ inches wide. Nor was his claim to have sketched it from nature credible. When he told some house guests that, while on his way to a formal dinner, he had seen the beleaguered ship in the Thames at Greenwich, sat down on a pier pile, pulled the plate out of his dress coat-tail pocket and began his etching, one skeptical listener inquired what size plates fitted in his ordinary coattail pockets. With that the subject abruptly changed.[33]

## The Master Printer

Before Haden could turn his attention to founding his "own Academy," etching had to develop a firmer infrastructure. The foundation stone was laid when etching was introduced into the curriculum of the National Art Training School in South Kensington. After Auguste Delâtre's visit to England, when he gave daily demonstrations of the preparation of plates, their biting, and printing, the class fell into the hands of two engravers. Then, in 1875 the Frenchman Legros took it over, and thereafter the class was always taught by an etcher.

So long was Legros's tenure at South Kensington—and later the Slade—that he is often said to have introduced the fervor for etching among British artists. But original etching could not have advanced so far and fast as it did without the master printer to whom Legros, Whistler, and Haden owed so much. Frederick Goulding's father and grandfather had both been copperplate printers. Apprenticed to Day and Company at fifteen, Goulding used his spare time to take classes at South Kensington and to attend lectures at the Royal Academy. Then, one day "a strange looking gentleman, with eye-glass, tall cane, and black slouch hat" had come to the office and insisted on "proving" his own plates. The man was Whistler who, working with Goulding, recognized for the first time that "something of the artist's mind could pass through the finger-tips of the printer to the inanimate copper."[34] After this auspicious start, Goulding often went to Whistler for a day's printing. Like Delâtre, the printer also became an avid etcher and connoisseur.

Goulding, as a young printer, had also met Haden during a demonstration of a press for Day and Son at the International Exhibition in London. Though he had gone to the surgeon's house several times after this meeting to look at Haden's etchings and Rembrandt collection, he did not print an edition for him until 1867. After that, and for the rest of Haden's life, the two were in constant touch. When Haden lectured about etching, Goulding would be at his side to demonstrate the art of printing, always bringing his own press and materials. Meanwhile—or, to be exact, in 1876—Goulding was made assistant to Legros in the etching class at South Kensington; he also began working with him one night a week at the Slade. Soon his services were in such high demand that he bought and set up his own printing business.[35] More and more, as Legros's responsibilities at the Slade increased, Goulding found himself taking charge of the South Kensington class until finally in 1882 he was formally appointed as instructor. His contribution to English etching received official recognition in 1890, with his election as the first Master Printer of the Royal Society of Painter-Etchers.

## The Royal Society of Painter-Etchers

The Royal Society of Painter-Etchers was Haden's brainchild.[36] Its origin can be traced to a meeting he called on or about 31 July 1880. The six men present constituted themselves as a provisional council consisting, in addition to Haden, of Legros, Heywood Hardy, Robert Macbeth, James Tissot, and Hubert Herkomer, all of them junior by far to the now sexagenarian Haden. The meeting was opened by Haden with a reading of a "sketch" of his scheme. Herkomer could "only recall the presence of Professor Legros (who did not understand English and was sketching all the time), and of M. Tissot (who confined himself to vowing vengeance against the dealers). I was too inexperienced then to see the drift of the scheme."[37]

In organizing the society, one of Haden's stated objectives was to get the Royal Academy to cease treating painter-etchers as though they were "pariahs." Line engravers, though long accepted into the fold, had only won permission in 1876 to use the letters A.R.A. and R.A. (Associate of the Royal Academy and Royal Academician) after their names. Might not painter-etchers at least be elected as Academy Engravers? Toward this end Haden proposed a campaign to persuade Academy painters to learn to etch their own pictures. When Academicians proved unreceptive to the idea, Haden abandoned it on the ground that they were too old: etching could successfully be taught only to the young.

The second of Haden's objectives was to upgrade the status of etching by emphasizing the difference between an original etcher and a mere copyist. To drive the distinction home, he adopted the term "painter-etcher," an obvious translation of the French *peintre-graveur*. Though accepted, the term was at first considered an affectation.

A third objective, to which Haden would devote most of his energies, was to get the work of the growing number of original etchers before the public. Though their etchings were beginning to be published by the print sellers and shown in some galleries, in the Black and White Exhibitions and even at the Academy, there they were easily overlooked: "Diminutive in size, through the teachings of their school, and delicate in treatment, they so shrink away amongst their more forcible comrades that they are never seen save at a disadvantage having to scramble for position with demonstrative efforts of every hue against the products of the crayon, the brush, the pencil, and the pen."[38] The solution: original etchers had to hold their own exhibitions.

In 1881 Haden, as president of the fledgling RSPE, issued an invitation to artists of all nationalities to send their original etchings for an "allcomers" exhibition that would demonstrate the "state of the art in [England] and ascertain whether the material existed for the formation of a Society having for its object its further promotion."[39] One hundred twenty-six artists submitted over 500 prints, of which 491 were hung. Haden and Legros exhibited twelve each. Most entries came from oil and watercolor painters rather than old-fashioned engravers. Most conspicuous by his absence was Whistler, whose etchings of Venice, when shown at the Fine Art Society, had caused a great stir, but out of pique against his brother-in-law, he not only sent no prints but did his best to spoil the opening.[40] Overall the response had been sufficiently favorable to encourage a repeat performance the following year. These exhibitions became an annual event and a central focus of RSPE activity through war and depression. They functioned as an effective marketing device for individual artists and helped the society raise money. The annual call for plates was an incentive to individual members to continue work in the medium.

To begin with, the RSPE had no formal membership beyond its

hastily formed provisional council, but Haden quickly moved to expand this. Invited to serve were Hamerton, a few interested curators and connoisseurs, as well as some prominent artists, including the president of the Royal Academy and several members of the Old Etching Club. The following year, with the election of sixty-seven fellows and honorary fellows, fifty of whom had exhibited at the Allcomers, the society had become a viable international body. Eight Americans were among the early members: James D. Smillie, Frank Duveneck, Otto Bacher, Frederick S. Church, Henry Farrer, Stephen Parrish, Thomas *and* Mary Nimmo Moran—for membership was open to women from the beginning.

Election to membership came to rest with the council, to whose artistic judgment applicants submitted an etching. Subsequent admissions increasingly reflected the new breed of British painter-etchers trained at the Slade or in the etching class at South Kensington. By 1887 it had become imperative to restrict the number of members if election was to continue to be a mark of distinction. However, a proposed limit posed a different danger: the society might turn into an exclusive club of elders, and the young talent that abounded would be discouraged. The solution was to establish two grades of membership: fellows, limited to fifty, and associates. Neophyte etchers would first have to pass muster as associates, after which, if found deserving, they could be advanced to fellow. The practice duplicated that of the Royal Academy.

In the year following, Haden's ambition to have his own Academy came still closer to fulfillment when the society, by a grant from the Crown, received the right to use the prefix "Royal." Having failed to obtain the representation in the Royal Academy he so longed for, Haden could take pride in the society he had created, which now took "its place definitely among those Societies [such as the Old Water Colour Society], which, like itself, were founded for the encouragement of special branches of the Fine Arts, and which, also, like itself, [had] long been subject to this form of ostracism."[41] Thereafter, each member of the RSPE would be granted a Diploma by the Royal Crown for the Art of Original or Painter-Engraving.

But the now-Royal society still had one more group to contend with: the Printsellers Association. Its power resided in rules that prohibited any of its twenty-one commercial member-firms from selling proofs above a certain value unless these had actually been printed by one of them. Oddly enough, artists, printers of steel and copperplates, and others connected with the printing trade held membership along with print sellers and publishers, thereby prohibiting a publisher member from employing a printer unless that printer was also a member. Such a rule was bound to irritate painter-etchers like Whistler and Haden, who were keen on keeping the production and distribution of proofs in their own hands. But the association remained a major gatekeeper so that less-established artists who refused to print, publish, and sell through its auspices were likely to render themselves and their work invisible.

Gradually, but only after some skirmishes, the RSPE won its battle with the print sellers. An initial victory ensued when a respected publisher about to issue a large etching by Robert Macbeth ran up against this rule. Both the publisher and the artist were eager to have the edition pulled by Goulding, but the master printer had declined to join the association on the simple ground that the publishers were clearly going "beyond what is equitable in compelling him to join: 'What would you say,' he had asked, 'if the printers were to form a society and make a rule that all publishers should be *compelled* to belong to it, or they would not work for any of them?' "[42] Understandably, in this instance, both publishers and print sellers managed, in their own best interest, to overlook their own rule. Finally, in 1892, with the connivance of some of the leading houses in the trade, the RSPE succeeded in gaining an exception so that its members, including Goulding, might print their own etchings.

The painter-etchers had also managed to develop their own marketing outlets. As early as 1881, Robert Dunthorne, under the sign of "The Rembrandt Head" in Vigo Street, had begun to deal *exclusively* in original etchings. His was the first firm to do so and through this activity did much to foster the revival of the art form. The RSPE formally recognized his contribution by appointing him as their official publisher in 1892. Meanwhile, invitations for the society to hold collective exhibitions outside London started to come in. Though reluctant to accept most of these, it did respond positively to one from Liverpool and another from Derby, Haden's ancestral home.

## Ne Desilies Imitator

By the end of the century Haden and his "academy" had raised the status of original etching to new heights. The letters A.R.E. or R.E. (Associate Royal Etcher, Royal Etcher), testimony to royal recognition, were valued prizes. Though no more than 50 could be R.E.s at any one time, by 1900 almost 200 artists had been elected to membership.

Production had grown correspondingly. Over 7,000 prints, nearly all of them original painter-etchings, had been shown in RSPE annuals over the past two decades. These would have added up to well over half a million impressions on the conservative assumption of an average edition of seventy-five.[43] The motto chosen by Haden for the royal diploma—*Ne desilies imitator* (Do not stoop to be a copyist)—was well on the way toward acceptance, and in 1894 Haden himself had been knighted for his contribution.

Now Sir Francis, at the peak of success, apparently set out to undo much of what he had done by reversing his earlier position. He took a stand against banning reproductive engravings from the annual exhibition, actually proposing that the name of the organization be changed to the Society of Painter-Etchers *and* Engravers. What he foresaw in his new vision was "not just the restoration of original etching but the re-infusion into all forms of the engraver's work of those personal qualities which make engraving in the hands of great painters a fine art."[44] A transformed RSPE would become the center of a worthier school of English engraving, whose works would displace the prints, mostly from big plates, that the Printsellers Association was pouring out at a rate of about 45,000 impressions a year.[45]

The only rational explanation for Haden's belated and unlikely championship of reproductive engraving was his admiration for Frank Short, his designated heir, himself a superb etcher as well as an authority on all engraving processes. Short had expended much effort on interpreting other masters, especially on completing Joseph Mallord William Turner's *Liber Studiorum*, an engraved record of landscape composition. Yet if Haden by his contentious championing of "original engraving" intended to defend Short, his tactics were unnecessarily circuitous and heavy-handed. There would have been few objections to the exhibiting of Short's mezzotints after Turner. There was much to be said for allowing an original painter-etcher already elected as such to include an occasional metal-plate reproduction, "so long as it was a good work of art approved by the Council, especially if it was a pioneer of an improved style or method."[46] It may have crossed Haden's mind that the new type of reproductive engraving by Short (and a few others) could too easily be exploited by the despised Printsellers Association. To forestall this, it was better to give it a home in his Royal Society.

Whatever his reasoning and motives, Haden by his autocratic and often erratic management was now hindering more than helping the spread of his gospel. In his insistence that members first exhibit all new work at the RSPE, he sought to override the artists' wishes. Haden simply would not yield and caused two of the most eminent etchers— William Strang and David Y. Cameron—to leave the society in protest. Still, Haden could not now disrupt his academy as he had once disrupted the Old Etching Club. A barrier had been crossed, and nothing could any longer stop the expanding demand for British etchings. Collectors on both sides of the Atlantic had grown in number, while reduction of estate duties and other advantages to be gained from the tax system contributed to a shift from public to private patronage of art. There had been world exhibitions in Chicago in 1893, in Paris in 1895, and in Brussels in 1897. London newspaper reviews of smaller shows also stimulated interest, as did the photomechanical reproduction of works of art in books and journals on the subject. The year 1893 had seen the first number of *The Studio*, devoted largely to the arts and crafts movement. Exhibition societies were mushrooming. Some of these provided alternative outlets to the RSPE, among them the International Society of Sculptors, Painters, and Gravers, with Whistler as its first president, and The Society of Twelve, a joint enterprise by such acclaimed painter-etchers as George Clausen, William Strang, William Rothenstein, David Y. Cameron, and Muirhead Bone, later joined by Francis Dodd and Walter Sickert.

Notwithstanding the growing public interest in the new style of modern etching favored by the RSPE, it had not yet cornered the entire print market. More accurately, the print public had become effectively divided into two segments: those who flocked to the exhibitions of the RSPE to enjoy the delicate and expressive (mainly) landscapes and those who still felt that there was nothing quite as artistic as a very large elaborate etching that represented a commonplace, rather than individual, vision of its theme. In reviewing the 1895 RSPE exhibition, it occurred to Wedmore that in no other art were the demands of connoisseurs and the public "divided by so sharp a gulf as the art of etching."[47] The loyal following the painter-etchers were enjoying was still more likely numbered in the hundreds than in thousands, hardly enough for artists to live off their original etched work, however well received by critics.

In the ten years before the Great War this situation was to change dramatically. The appearance of *The Print Collector's Quarterly* in 1911 was both a response to and a stimulant to growing demand. Certainly by 1912, prices for first-rate examples of etchings by Whistler, Haden, Cameron, and other eminent practitioners had attained levels beyond the reach of the ordinary print lover, who would "certainly have to make up his mind, once and for all, to abandon all idea of collecting nothing but early 'states.' "[48] The concern of collectors for states, signatures, numbering, and so forth was a new twist. Collectors of the old school, who bought what they liked and paid no attention to whether or not a print was signed, whether it was a first state, or whether it was pulled early in the edition, were coming to be displaced by a new breed more concerned with rarity and whatever else seemed to make certain prints a good investment.

The First World War put little more than a temporary brake on the development of a real craze. At the war's end there was a pent-up demand, and a whole host of new publications delayed by the war catered to the connoisseur: *The Bookman's Journal and Print Collector, Modern Etchings and Their Collectors* by Thomas Simpson, *Making and Collecting Etchings* by Hesketh Hubbard, and *Etchers and Etching* by Joseph Pennell. Artists, too, formed new organizations. The Society of Graphic Art, a rival to the RSPE, had the famous Frank Brangwyn as president but did not follow its example in forming a Print Collectors Club as a means of developing a public. By the time that Martin Hardie delivered his lecture inaugurating the club, 90 percent of the limited number of subscriptions had already been reserved. In the course of his talk, he described the collecting of etchings as a "loophole of retreat." He referred to two collectors he knew, "of whom one hid his Camerons and Bones lovingly in his office desk, while the other, when he bought something 'à un prix qu'on n'avoue pas à sa ménagerie,' ["at a price one does not admit to his household"] would invite a guest to Sunday lunch, and not till then, when Madame must perforce withhold her views, would he produce his new treasure." The moral, advised Hardie, was that all should enroll their wives as members of the Print Collectors Club.[49]

So here we are once more reminded of Billy Gabriel, the *amateur d'estampes*, whose wife murdered his etching. In England his ranks had begun to swell after the war, until soon etching was truly à la mode. The artists were the obvious beneficiaries of a boom they could never have created on their own. But analysis of this boom phase of the etching cycle, and its effects on artistic reputations, requires that we first catch up with the story of the Revival across the Atlantic.

# 4 🐉

## On to America: Boom and Bust

The craze for etching came to America in a series of minicycles. Interest was initially stirred in 1866 when the Frenchman, Alfred Cadart, came to New York prepared to proselytize for the art. But the steady production of etchings did not really begin until a decade later, when a group of artists organized themselves into the New York Etching Club. Then, once again, the intense activity that was generated, stimulated by demand, proved to be short-lived and, by the turn of the century, very little original etching was being published. The final boom-and-bust cycle that culminated in the crash of 1929 was set in motion by the etching collectives. They had reawakened interest in the medium and developed their own distribution channels. This chapter traces the origins of these taste cycles and their effect on artistic productivity, then looks at the forces that put a final end to the etching revival in America and Britain.

### Etching Comes to America

The beginnings of what is now known as the American etching revival were largely derivative. Although the arts in America had reached a take-off point and begun to develop a certain momentum after the Civil War, no artist's education was as yet considered complete without a sojourn abroad to study the masters. Collectors, too, including the connoisseurs of etchings, continued to favor imports over the art of their native land. While even in colonial times America had had its homegrown printmakers, the lack of schools of instruction and competent masters mean that they had had to learn the rudiments of their craft through improvisation and experimentation, often with very indifferent results. The outlook for printmaking improved with the influx of highly skilled engravers from abroad, some of whom had been trained in art and passed this interest, along with their craft, to

53

their sons—sometimes their daughters—and to friends. The more artistically inclined found an outlet in the developing market for reproductive engravings, but most were employed at embellishing silverware or designing banknotes and federal currency—jobs they could hardly consider artistic even in the broadest meaning of that term.[1] Many who drew upon the copperplate did so "with little idea of its unique requirements and with results of no artistic value."[2]

Nonetheless, a notable number of leading American artists who flourished during the first half of the nineteenth century began their artistic careers as engravers.[3] Some of these were producing etchings a full half-century before the revival really got under way. Robert W. Weir, drawing instructor at West Point, had "copied some of Rembrandt's etchings as to be with difficulty detected, and was on the eve of turning [his] attention seriously to the publication of etchings from various old pictures in the possession of different gentlemen in New York, but, like many other things of the kind, it fell through, after the first or second plate was finished."[4] Others, though not very many, had turned to the medium years before Cadart crossed the Atlantic to spread the word. Samuel F. B. Morse, better remembered as an inventor, had been copying Italian pictures. George Loring Brown, a Bostonian, had made etchings of Rome in 1853 and 1854, but these were published only after his return from abroad years later.[5] John G. Chapman, a highly skilled craftsman, had executed innumerable designs on copper for Harper Brothers and the American Tract Society.[6] His little landscape etchings—at least, the best of them—have been expertly judged "remarkably good for the time."[7] The first edition of his instructional *American Drawing Book* (1847) makes no mention of etching; the 1858 edition, however, published after the author had permanently settled in Rome, contains clear and sound instructions of a very modest sort.[8] It guided R. Swain Gifford in his experiments with etching while he was yet in his early teens and helped him, despite many failures and the acid-ruin of his clothes, ultimately to master some of the processes. Some of his etchings were published as early as 1865 or 1866.[9]

These early efforts were isolated and sporadic. Despite some public "how-to" demonstrations by English-born John Sartain, nothing resembling the tradition of the peintres-graveurs in France had had much chance to develop. The first serious attempt to transplant that tradition and to create an appropriate infrastructure came with Cadart's visit to New York. Besides some paintings he obviously wanted to sell, he brought with him a "rare collection of etchings" as well as sufficient etching supplies with which to demonstrate the process.[10]

How much interest the visit inspired among artists is difficult to ascertain. Immediate results were paltry, and Cadart was hardly the "Lafayette d'Art" conquering a whole new continent for the cause of etching that legend would have it.[11] The seeds of interest he planted could not flourish until the ground had been more fully prepared.

Looking back on the visit a quarter-century later, Henry Russell Wray contended it had been a stimulus to "wealthy men in Boston, New York, Philadelphia and western cities [to gather] into their portfolios valuable impressions, from the study of which many of our artists credit their first etching inspiration."[12] This initial influence was augmented in 1868 by two other events: the first New York showing of etchings by Whistler and the publication of Hamerton's *Etching and Etchers*, which was said to have been "read from the Atlantic to the Pacific" and stirred much interest among artists as well as a small circle of discerning collectors.[13] But this still left those inclined to venture into the medium very much to their own devices. They could not count on technical advice or assistance. Samuel Colman, who had been collecting etchings "for some years" before trying to make one, gave up "after several years of trials . . . on account of the difficulty in having plates printed in a satisfactory manner."[14] The dearth of adequately skilled copperplate printers, of presses, and even of ordinary etching tools was apt to discourage anyone lacking the ingenuity demonstrated by Henry Farrer six years after he came to America at age nineteen. In 1868 he made a first "serious attempt" at etching only after he had succeeded in fashioning a small press and all the paraphernalia of etching. Having tried "many of Mr. Hamerton's new-fangled notions," he found them "simply devices for wasting time, so that with the exception of bordering wax, I adhere to the methods of work that as Mr. Gifford says was found good enough for Rembrandt."[15] Whether or not Farrer had followed Hamerton's instruction for building a press or sought help from local craftsmen is uncertain.

Nor were there American art magazines comparable to *L'Artiste*, *Gazette des beaux-arts*, *Zeitschrift für bildende Kunst*, and Hamerton's *Portfolio*, all richly illustrated with modern original and reproductive etchings. Opportunities for artists to publish whatever etched work they were moved to create were limited. American firms favored lithography, a cheaper method of printing images in large numbers.[16] In these circumstances, it was a fondness for the medium rather than the prospect of financial gain that moved an artist to turn to the etching needle. Not surprisingly, of the 209 modern etchings hung at the 1876 Centennial Exhibition in Philadelphia, the largest number yet assembled in America, 130 were by foreigners, mostly French, while

77 of 79 American works were submitted by just two artists—Peter Moran and Edwin Forbes.

This was Moran's first venture into the medium, and it gained him both a medal and a special exhibition at the National Academy of Design the following year. Twelve of these works were then chosen for publication in a portfolio, reportedly "the first printed etchings of any pretension ever purchased outright by a noted publisher in this country."[17] This does not by itself signify that modern etching had gained public acceptance. In fact, the centennial catalog actually listed the exhibited etchings as "engravings." And when, on the strength of the recognition accorded Moran, the Fairmount Park Association commissioned the artist to execute an etched plate of *The Dying Lion*, a sculpture group it had just purchased, the venture soon turned sour. Many subscribers had expected to receive an engraving. Being unfamiliar with etchings, they considered themselves to have been swindled. Dealers refused to handle the print.[18]

## The New York Etching Club

Such was the milieu into which the New York Etching Club was born, largely through the exertions of two enthusiasts. Leroy Milton Yale was a physician and, like Haden, a dedicated amateur etcher. But the main impetus came from a small number of artists led by James David Smillie, who had been trained by his father as a banknote steel engraver, a métier he had abandoned to become a fine watercolorist. The idea for the club was the brainchild of A. W. Warren, a painter and Civil War illustrator. Before his death in 1873, Warren had written Smillie urging the forming of an etching club. The "poor fellow," thought Smillie, was "ahead of his time [but] I got into the habit of talking about it . . . to Yale [until] he proposed that we do something." The two then wrote a constitution, called a meeting at Smillie's studio, and organized a club that elected Yale as president and Smillie as secretary and treasurer.[19]

Fewer than half the twenty or so artists gathered by invitation for its first meeting on 2 May 1877 had any prior acquaintance with etching. Everyone watched Smillie "grounding" a plate to be drawn on by Gifford. They went through the entire process until at the end "an elegant brother [Yale], who had dined out early in the evening, laid aside his broadcloth, rolled up the spotless linen of his sleeves, and became for the time an enthusiastic printer." He passed the etched plate through the heavy steel rollers of the press and "in another moment, finding scant room in the pressing crowd, the first-born of the

New York Etching Club was being tenderly passed from hand to hand."[20] Thereafter the club would meet on the second Monday of every month.

By holding classes, by providing a press on which proofs could be printed, and through informal discussion, the club encouraged artists to work in the medium. Within three years, its members had etched over 120 plates, which were discussed at their regular meetings, some of these being exhibited in the shows of the American Society of Painters in Watercolor at the National Academy.[21] From 1882, by which time the club claimed twenty-eight resident and five nonresident members, it published its own annual catalogs, the first listing 282 etchings. The last was issued in 1893. And while the art historian, Sadakichi Hartmannn, may have been right in judging that there was "not one great etcher among them,"[22] these charter members of the club did help to launch a genuinely grass-roots movement.

Within five years similar groups, which sought to combine "the ideal interests to be subserved by the advantages of fellowship with the more practical aim of becoming publishers, either directly or indirectly, of the etched work of their members," had sprung up in Cincinnati, Philadelphia, Boston, Brooklyn, and Baltimore.[23] Not all of them were mere clones of the New York organization. The artists who in 1880 founded the Philadelphia Society of Etchers were certainly more at home with the medium, but their number was small and remained so; by the time they held their first exhibition in 1882, they could muster only eight active members. Their bylaws called for an exchange of prints among members every other month, a practice which one recruit considered an overly "severe tax."[24] The Brooklyn Etchers Club, founded by artists in 1881, also welcomed collectors, who were eligible to buy limited edition prints as a privilege of membership, but the Brooklyn Scratchers Club, which followed within a year, was limited to professional artists. The movement quickly spread to the West Coast, where some once well known artists belonging to the San Francisco Art Association pooled their resources to import an etching press from France.[25] Little of their etched work has survived and next to nothing is known about the membership of the club they formed. It could not have survived for very long.

## The Mediators

To describe the American revival as a grass-roots artists' movement for which the infrastructure had yet to be built is not to deny the important mediator role played by a handful of collectors and a network of art dealers whose interest in modern European etchings put them clearly ahead of their time. Men like S. P. Avery, the wealthy New York picture dealer, and James L. Claghorn, president of the Pennsylvania Academy of Fine Arts, had close connections with the artistic community and were prepared to open their private collections to artists for viewing and study.

Thus it was that the first catalog of Whistler etchings was published in 1874, mainly with the help of Avery, who paid half the cost of printing fifty copies and, in return, received half the edition.[26] Also, it is to the study of impressions in the folios of wealthy collectors that many artists credited their first etching inspiration.[27] Even before the Philadelphia Society of Etchers was born, Joseph Pennell had become acquainted with the English tradition by "going over the prints at Claghorn's . . . , where, in the corner of his upstairs print room, Sunday after Sunday afternoon was spent studying Whistler and Haden."[28] Moreover, Claghorn first called Pennell's street scenes of Philadelphia to the attention of Frederick Keppel, the New York dealer, who became the artist's agent for three decades. Alerted, Keppel had immediately written to say that on his next trip to Philadelphia he would call on Pennell "in reference to their sale."[29] Other firms that sold and published prints were Christian Klackner (the publisher for Winslow Homer), M. Knoedler and Company, and Hermann Wunderlich, whose director—E. G. Kennedy—had been buying Whistlers in the 1870s. This network of dealers developed only gradually. For a long while the selling of prints in America had been in the hands of book dealers, like F. B. Patterson, who had issued Henry Farrer's etched views of old New York. Keppel himself had got his start as a book dealer. It was the unexpected success that he had in selling a portfolio of prints purchased, out of kindness, from a down-and-out London print seller that persuaded him to shift. The New York print shop he opened in 1868 was to become a major distribution channel for both European and American prints.

Neither can one overlook the contribution of Sylvester R. Koehler to the American revival as both advocate and publisher. His knowledge of graphic processes was gained over the ten years he spent as technical manager with the leading American firm in color lithography, a position he left to devote himself more fully to the study of art. His first project was to translate into English Lalanne's well-known treatise on etching.[30] This effort was supplemented by visits to many places, where he would lecture and make contact with local artists. It was slow going; dedicated "converts" were hard to come by.

In 1880 as the local lyceum guest lecturer in Salem, Massachusetts, he spoke on the fine art of etching. To demonstrate the process, he called on Harriet Frances Osborne, a local drawing teacher then in her middle years, to draw a little landscape on the plate he had prepared for her. But technical support was insufficient to sustain whatever enthusiasm Koehler may have generated. Osborne did produce a half-dozen plates—"charming intimate glimpses of the venerable wharves and sea-worn houses of the coastal town of Salem," but these represent most, probably all, of her etching oeuvre.[31]

But it was above all through his *American Art Review*, a handsome publication that featured original etchings, that Koehler encouraged some soon-to-be-well-known etchers by introducing their work to a larger public than they had hitherto known. The *Review* was his most ambitious project. Koehler had planned a print run of 5,000 for the first issue, hoping that demand might soon warrant an increase, but that hope never materialized; no issue ever sold out.[32] There were only some 1,200 to 1,500 subscribers, many of whom failed to renew. Accomplished American etchers were in similarly short supply. As an incentive to artists, Koehler offered to advertise the fifteen artist's proofs each had the right to retain and to provide contributors with a supply of proofs on Japan paper that they could sell on their own.[33] Nothing seems to have come of this offer; nor did it save the *Review*. But he managed to put together and arrange for the publication of a number of portfolios of original etchings, some in collaboration with the New York Etching Club.

In November 1882, Haden himself came to America to spread the word. The event had been fully prepared. Present as special guests at New York City's Lotos Club, where he spoke, were such established artists as Eastman Johnson and Elihu Vedder and such mainstays of the revival as Smillie, Kruseman van Elten, and Mary Nimmo Moran. Haden's fame had preceded his visit, and there was much interest in his views. The halls where he appeared were often packed. When he talked to the New York Historical Society in a room able to seat 600, extra seats had to be added. The lecture itself was a "rather discursive" attack on engraving, which, though later qualified, stirred much opposition.[34] A Boston critic took Haden to task for casting aspersions on the burin as an instrument simply in order to raise the status of etching.[35] Even Smillie, trained engraver that he was, felt that Haden, with his intemperate attack, had weakened "the force of his argument" and so later declared himself *not* to be one of the Englishman's followers.[36]

Just the same, interest in original etching continued to grow. The same decade saw the appearance of a number of books illustrated with original etchings, some of them from plates published by Koehler that had remained in the hands of Estes and Lauriat, the printers. In 1882 the Art Interchange Publishing Company of New York initiated the publication of semimonthly portfolios like those published between 1883 and 1889 by Koehler, edited by the critic Ernest Knaufft with comment on the artist and/or the impression.[37] Ripley Hitchcock, in Philadelphia, put together similar publications. Meanwhile, etching was coming into use for the free rendering of popular paintings and for illustrating books. The first such volume was the rather costly *Poets and Etchers* (1882), containing poems by Longfellow, Whittier, and others, illustrated with etchings. Between 1883 and 1889, the indefatigable Koehler managed to edit at least six illustrated books. Located in Boston, he was appointed temporary curator of a collection of prints owned by Harvard University but on long-term loan to the Boston Museum of Fine Arts. When that museum set up its own print department, Koehler was the logical choice. As curator of prints, he was now in a strategic position to promote the cause of the original print then being popularized by his European counterparts. This he did until his death in 1900.[38]

## The Public

What John Sartain, the master engraver, had in mind when he noted in 1880 that a gradually growing "passion for etching . . . [has] quite lately . . . intensified into a perfect furor," was the young artists' preference for working with the needle, not the burin.[39] Koehler was moved to protest the notion, obviously mistaken, that the "lively interest [that has] . . . lately been taken in etching" was merely faddish and akin to the "keramic craze" or the "decorative craze," neither of which was equal in high-mindedness and seriousness to etching.[40] Etching, however, had become all too popular. Even department stores were beginning to serve as marketing channels. But what was attracting thousands to buy etchings? Their interest did not mean, so Hitchcock observed, that a new "army of buyers has suddenly been educated up to a point of discriminating appreciation . . . [only that it] has become fashionable to show an interest in and love for etchings."[41] Propelled in large part by merchandising, this "ripple, which increased in size and spread in a popular tidal wave over the country," could hardly last.[42] As early as the mid-eighties, acute observers sensed the unease of collectors, who were beginning to go back to the line engravings and etchings of early masters, whose artistic status was fixed and whose value could be measured by an assured standard. Sales of modern etchings were falling off. They had risen as a proportion of all sales of etchings from a mere 2 percent in 1875 to 73 percent in 1883. During the previous two seasons the upward trend had leveled off, falling to a 62 percent share in 1885.[43]

Commercial exploitation led to the treatment of any etching as a thing of indisputable beauty. Demand was met at the expense of quality. "To supply the art-craving of a people insatiable with the greed of a new appetite," lamented Smillie, "presses with relays of men, working night and day, are laboring to supply the demands of our great cities, and carloads—literally carloads—of signed artist proof etchings are being sent to plains and prairies, Rocky Mountain homes and far Pacific slopes."[44] The printing of large editions encouraged carelessness. "Unintelligent, or at least unsympathetic, workmen . . . enter a field wherein they deem that popularity may quickly and easily be won, putting the etcher's serious, beautiful and individual craft in danger of degenerating into mistaken rivalry with other forms of graphic expression." There were simply too many large, showy, "finished" etchings that "try to be as unlike etchings, as like steel engravings or elaborate drawings as possible."[45]

So great was the newly won glamour of etchings that publishers were prompted to commission etched rather than engraved renderings of popular paintings, regardless of whether the artists commissioned had the requisite combination of skills. In a countermove, the New York Etching Club took steps to bar such reproductive work from its exhibitions.[46] Several of its members joined the new Society of American Etchers, a group formed for the explicit purpose of limiting the size of editions in order to assure the status of their art. The stamp of the society, affixed to every proof issued, was to guarantee the print's quality and authenticity.[47] But the damage had already been done. There is little dispute that, in catering to demand, the publishers had managed to kill the goose that had laid the golden eggs. In an 1892 article, written for a Viennese publication, Koehler judged American etching to have peaked five or six years ago and to be on the "downgrade."[48]

Once the fad had become a bore, publishers withdrew from the overstocked market and etchers directed their activities into other channels. Asked to provide names whose work could be included, along with that of other Americans working in Europe, in a special number of *The Studio* being readied for the summer of 1902, Smillie cited difficulties: "At this time practically no etching is being done and from those who have etched it is difficult to get the desirable ones for your purposes."[49] Some of the champions of etching had passed away, while others were directing their energies toward more lucrative lines of work.[50] Smillie and Mielatz were among the few who continued to etch: Smillie taught at the National Academy, where none of his students were "finished" etchers,[51] and Mielatz was listed as the only officer of the now inactive New York Etching Club.[52]

## In Hibernation

Despite the decline of the market, etching in America, once revived, did not die again; it only went into hibernation. The New York Etching Club ceased to hold exhibitions after 1893, but a few painter-etchings could still be seen at the annual show of the American Watercolor Society. By the turn of the century, there were signs of a gradual recovery—new opportunities for studying prints, for studying printmaking, and for support through illustration. Print dealers, for their part, were cultivating a more educated public.

The U.S. National Museum had established a Graphic Arts Section; the Boston Museum of Fine Arts had set up a print department based on a minor collection. Still, neither of these collections, assembled since the 1880s, then contained more than a few, if any, modern etchings. The Boston Museum had repeatedly rejected the advice of Koehler, its own print curator, that it purchase the large collection it had on permanent loan from Harvard. But Koehler was working hard to change this situation. Using the proceeds from his careful deaccessioning of duplicates, he managed, from 1897 on, to acquire sufficient modern prints to lay the foundations for the first print department of its kind in the United States.[53] A real leap forward on the archival front came with the establishment of the first print room in New York City, when S. P. Avery donated his superb collection of etchings and lithographs by Whistler, Haden, and French artists—only after it had been refused by the Metropolitan Museum of Art—to the New York Public Library.[54] These holdings grew in number during the long curatorship of Frank Weitenkampf, who persuaded artists to donate prints to the library and mounted many an exhibition of their work.

New opportunities to study printmaking became available: in 1889 the National Academy of Design, having received as a gift a complete set of etching equipment, started an etching class taught first by Smillie and then, after his retirement, by Mielatz. A Saturday etching class met at the Art Students League from 1906 on. It was taught, at different times, by George C. Senseney, Charles Henry White, and others, but the etching studio, with its one press, remained "barren and bleak" until 1921, when Joseph Pennell began to teach there.[55] On the other coast, formal etching instruction was available as early as 1908 at the University of California in Berkeley.

And even while artistic etching was dormant, many American artists were able to make a comfortable living by illustrating for magazines. Among the numerous second generation etchers (born in the 1870s) supporting themselves as illustrators were Troy Kinney, Eugene Higgins, and Ernest Haskell. Also, American print galleries were happy to stock prints of Old World scenes by artists who were wholly or partly expatriate and to promote these along with the works of established European masters, for which the market had never quite disappeared. The "indispensable prerequisite for a successful career was to have etched, at least once, a 'series' of views of Italy, France, England, Germany, or of London, Paris, and Venice in the manner of the roaming [Otto] Bacher," who had been a follower of Duveneck and Whistler.[56]

This time it was the fine print dealers who took the initiative in keeping etching alive. Firms like Keppel in New York and Albert Roullier in Chicago did more than just sell prints; they issued a number of informative booklets that, though essentially sales catalogs, also contained, along with illustrations and biographical sketches, explanations of the art of etching. Keppel featured a number of still young Americans who had perfected their art in Europe, while Roullier's promoted "native" artists.[57] They had to overcome the prejudice that an etching that had "not made one trip across the Atlantic, even when done by an American, was . . . lacking in some tangible distinction; and at least another decade would have been required for Whistler prints to have gained their preeminent position if they had come out of Portland, Oregon, instead of London. . . . [It was even considered] a little uncouth of an etcher not merely to be born in Texas but to do his work there."[58]

In 1911, with one eye on their own fine print trade, Keppel and Fitzroy Carrington, an associate, launched *The Print Collector's Quarterly*. It was to focus chiefly on "recognized great masters of engraving and etching, both old and modern," with one number each year devoted to "such contemporary etchings as seem worthy of the serious consideration of collectors." The first number had practically no text but featured illustrations of etchings by Whistler, Haden, Meryon, and

Cameron from the Tracy Dows collection, "recently purchased by Messrs. Frederick Keppel & Company." Readers were also promised a special summer number, in addition to the four issues, "should the acquisition of any collection of prints of prime importance render such an extra issue desirable."[59] Later issues were, to be sure, more informative and, until it folded during World War II, it was a singularly strong influence on collectors, who looked to it for guidance.

Neither these and other efforts of dealers to cultivate an educated print public nor the demand for illustrations sufficed to send artists flocking to the medium. But they did provide a fertile ground and the artistic seed, once planted, was bound to germinate and develop a life of its own. The second decade of the new century witnessed the rise of etching collectives that seized the initiative to promote their own art, something the New York Etching Club had failed to do.

## Etching Collectives: A Reawakening

Among the artists newly attracted to what they saw as the charm of the etching craft was Bertha E. Jaques. She became the moving spirit behind the Chicago Society of Etchers (CSE) and, for many years, its effective, hardworking secretary-treasurer. As early as 1903 she had gathered around her a small group, which included Earl H. Reed, Otto J. Schneider, and Ralph M. Pearson, all of whom had turned to etching on their own initiative, mostly with improvised tools.[60] By the time the CSE came into being, the earlier societies, with the sole exception of the Society of American Etchers, were extinct. Years of quiescence had taken their toll. In 1911 when the new organization held its first open exhibition, it "dredged up," in the words of its vice-president, "the flotsam of twenty years. Forgotten portfolios were overhauled, and the collection, even with a jury devoted to new things, had a retrospective look. . . . The mass of this work was sufficient to show how long etching had been stifled."[61] It took two more annuals for this backlog to clear and for the CSE to transform itself into an effective vehicle for the encouragement and showing of new work. Especially, its organizers were not content to reach a local public. By the third year of its existence, traveling exhibitions sent out by the CSE were reaching twenty-seven American cities, and soon it was drawing members not just from around Chicago but from as far away as New York, San Francisco, and even abroad. Jaques made herself the hub of an international network, keeping up a voluminous correspondence and lending a hand wherever etchers and printmakers sought to associate with kindred spirits.

The CSE also pioneered new ways of promoting prints, first by using its rather considerable proceeds from exhibition sales to purchase etchings for donation to the Chicago Art Institute and, second, by establishing an associate membership category. With dues set at $5, nonartists were invited to lectures and entitled to one of the CSE's annual publications—either a privately printed book designed and illustrated with one or more original etchings by artist members or a signed etching by one of them. Artists and art lovers were both served by this practice, as evidenced by the spurt in membership. The CSE quickly grew from 22 active and "nearly 100" associate members at the end of its first year to 52 active and 197 associate members a year later. Even America's involvement in the war could not halt its growth; by 1918, members numbered 119 and associates 215.[62]

Meanwhile, similar groups were forming clear across the country. The California Society of Etchers was organized by West Coast artists, many of whom had had only the most rudimentary training in the craft.[63] Within two years, in 1915, it had about fifty members, whose work had been shown not just in California museums but at the Panama-Pacific International Exhibition. By 1916 membership stood at eighty, by 1917 at ninety, but then it seems to have peaked at ninety-five in 1918.[64] The ultimately more successful Print Makers of Los Angeles, later renamed the Print Makers Society of California, was launched when eight artists living near Los Angeles, joined by six other invitees, banded together to awaken interest in printmakers and their work. Unlike the CSE that inspired it, their association, though dominated by etchers, was hospitable to art in any of the print media. The driving force behind this collective came from two local artists: Benjamin C. Brown, an established Southern California artist, and his younger brother Howell, who did the day-to-day work that made the organization flourish. His vast correspondence, involving "thousands of letters each year," which left him neither "the time nor the freshness of enthusiasm to express himself in etching or water colors as he could," may account for his failure to make more of a name for himself.[65]

Growth was slow at first—only twenty-nine members by 1918—possibly because all work had to clear a "jury of admissions." But the organization prospered in the 1920s after it added to its one annual "club" exhibition a second international exhibition, open to printmakers all over the world, held at the Los Angeles Museum of Art.[66] Soon there were more submissions than could possibly fit on limited wall space, and membership was reaching an unwieldy level.[67] Faced with this prospect, the officers decided that thereafter membership would be granted by invitation only to artists whose works, when hung, were judged to be *"of such merit that we would like to have them as members."*[68] In other respects—reliance on associate members, offers of presentation prints, and traveling shows—the Printmakers followed the CSE model. In the small communities of the American Southwest, where art exhibitions were a rarity and galleries nonexistent, prints from its traveling shows were exhibited in private homes.[69]

The first etching collective in New York was the short-lived Association of American Etchers, known to have held its "second annual" exhibition of one hundred prints in 1914 with twenty-eight artists, some of them also members of the CSE.[70] Plans for this exhibition to travel to other cities and to Europe seem to have been disrupted by the outbreak of war. At about the same time came the New York Society of Etchers, with twenty-five charter members and associate memberships open to interested parties. The catalog of its first exhibition stated, correctly or incorrectly, that New York City offered etchers no facilities for public exhibition. This situation the society sought to rectify by dedicating itself to the "furtherance of the art of etching and the *allied graphic arts.*"[71] Even its first exhibition included lithographs and wood-block prints along with the etchings.

Other societies followed in quick succession. The Brooklyn Society of Etchers was organized in 1916.[72] The principle of jury selection for all entries to its exhibitions would be strictly enforced with one exception: the society invited fifteen artists of high standing to send one work each *hors concours*. Of the 400 submissions for the first exhibition, so many were of high quality that the 196 put on display was nearly double the number initially planned for.[73] The Painter-Gravers of America, founded in New York in 1917 with Albert Sterner as chairman, was primarily aimed at fostering the "work of younger men [*sic*]" and, like the Brooklyn Society, limited membership to American artists while insisting that there "shall be no jury either in spirit or form."[74] There was a good deal of contact among these collectives; in fact, some names showed up on nearly every roster. Arthur S. Covey, the first president of the New York Society, was also a founding member of the Brooklyn Society; so was Earl Horter, its secretary. Covey likewise had a hand in founding the Painter-Gravers, while Horter was represented among the twenty-eight exhibitors in the 1914 show of the Association of American Etchers. Anne Goldthwaite, Eugene Higgins, Ernest Roth, Albert Sterner, Mahonri Young, and others were actively involved in at least three of these collective ventures to promote artistic etching. Many of these New York artists also held nonresident membership in out-of-town organizations.

While little is known about the many ephemeral groups in other cities, the Print Club of Philadelphia represents a particularly interesting variant. The club, founded by a small group of well-to-do women, claims to be the "oldest organization of club nature devoted to the graphic arts in the United States."[75] Its first and private exhibition had been put together by W. H. Nelson of the magazine *International Studio*. This was in 1916. Bertha Jaques, herself a contributor to that exhibition, came to Philadelphia to lend a hand; artists from other cities also rallied to its cause. So successful was the club that it soon acquired its own clubhouse. Its facilities—including a library and an etching press—were open to use by any artist or student who desired to apply.

Managed by lay persons with the support of wealthy patrons, the Philadelphia club sold as well as showed prints, including those of the great masters. Likewise, the Print Club of Cleveland, formed and incorporated in 1919, owes its existence less to the needs of artists than to the interest of lay persons. Friends of the Cleveland Museum of Art united both to increase their own knowledge of prints and to aid the museum to "acquire a print collection of high excellence."[76] The moving spirit was a collector who over the years had donated a large number of prints to the museum and whose widow continued their generous annual gift. The Cleveland club also commissioned prints for distribution to its members with proceeds going to the museum.

Momentum

In the aftermath of the Great War there were unmistakable signs of an etching revival: "Museums and print rooms and print societies and teachers and professors and schools of the graphic arts spring up all over the place.—The only thing lacking," wrote Joseph Pennell to Hans W. Singer, his German curator friend, "is the great artist—no really good man has appeared—and most of those of promise have their heads turned at the faintest breath of success and vanish."[77] But Pennell was a conservative in art no less than in his politics. He clearly felt uncomfortable with the inevitable change brought on by four years of unprecedented slaughter, and he was totally out of sympathy with modernist currents. But the statement also expressed his distress at what he considered the lack of proper technical training in the art schools of America.[78] The United States, at the time, had nothing resembling the nationwide art-school system in Britain. For many artists, the informal tuition offered by the etching collectives was the only training available.

These collectives, whatever their deficiencies, were the main carriers of a significant movement in art. They offered encouragement and practical help, and they provided a showcase whereby artists, especially the younger ones, could get their work before the public. Visibility posed no less a problem for a new generation in Britain, where the *numerus clausus* of the Royal Society of Painter-Etchers (RSPE) could be a barrier. With turnover slow, there simply were more eligible applicants than vacancies. Moreover, the RSPE had for many years barred from its exhibitions anything other than "engravings" on metal or wood. Lithographs, modern woodcuts, and color prints of any kind were unacceptable. Such restrictions on numbers and on what was acceptable encouraged the formation of societies similar to the American collectives. The Senefelder Club was exclusively for lithographers, while wood engravers and the makers of color prints formed their own societies. The Society of Graphic Art, organized during the postwar boom and dedicated to "uphold and maintain the interests of all forms of art which do not use colour as a means of expression," accommodated artists unable to find a home in the more establishmentarian RSPE. There was also a Glasgow Society of Painter-Etchers for artists working in Scotland. The more successful artists moved on from these societies to become associates and, ultimately, fellows of the more prestigious RSPE.

The rise and fall of participation in etching can be traced through the membership figures in these collectives. In the early 1920s, just before etching really took off, the *unduplicated* membership in the three main British etching organizations was somewhat over 200. But some indisputably eligible artists—including some leading etchers—deliberately opted out. D. Y. Cameron, a Royal Academician, had long ago resigned from the RSPE; neither Muirhead Bone, long associated with the New English Art Club, nor James McBey had ever joined. All three met the consistently high demand for their output through their publishers. The directory of etchers, engravers, and lithographers in the first volume of *Fine Prints of the Year* shows dozens of others listing themselves as etchers but not affiliated with any collective. Although this directory is not necessarily complete, it can be accepted as fairly representing the population of etchers whose prints were being actively marketed nationally. Thus, based on membership in the collectives and selective use of the directory, we estimate that there were some 250 *recognized* painter-etchers active in Britain in the early 1920s. This, let it be added, is a highly conservative estimate.

The diversity of the art scene makes such a numerical estimate of

American painter-etchers even more problematical. For one thing, there was no single dominant etching society, such as the RSPE. The claim of the president of the CSE, near its beginnings, that his organization included "practically every American etcher of prominence" would become hard to sustain.[79] The CSE was also open to foreign artists, who were invited not only to exhibit regularly but also to contribute presentation plates for distribution to its lay members. Its active membership, including nonresidents, at the beginning of the 1920s stood at over one hundred. The directory in the first volume of *Fine Prints of the Year* contains names of 151 artists who were either associated with one or more of the etching societies or listed themselves as etchers. Complementing this with information on the membership of the etching societies suggests that, at that time, the United States had near 175 active and *recognized* professional painter-etchers or about 30 percent fewer than Britain. Again, this is a highly conservative estimate that omits many "occasional" etchers, those at the beginning of their careers, and those preeminently oriented toward a local market.

## The Etching Boom

During the Roaring Twenties etchings were being turned out by the tens of thousands each year. But to what extent does the increase in output reflect an increase in individual productivity, that is, in the average number of plates published by any individual artist? For an answer we turn to the one consistent data set available—to the annual directories in *Fine Prints of the Year*, where names of plates executed in the preceding twelve months, sometimes together with edition size, are listed, based on information submitted by the artists themselves and by leading publishers.[80] Again, the data are not without flaws: some artists (or publishers) undoubtedly failed to respond to directory inquiries. Nor can one assume a consistency in reporting habits among artists or for any one artist from one year to the next. Obviously, an etching issued by a publisher intent on sales was more likely to be listed than one that the artist sought to market on his or her own. And—especially important—the artist had, one way or another, to have come to the attention of Malcolm Salaman, the general editor of the series.

In fact, a comparison of directory data for some individual artists with that available from their catalogues raisonnés suggests that the listings account for between one-fourth and one-third of the plates they actually produced in these years. The slippage is probably greater in America because the print distribution network there was less developed than in Britain, and British prints were to dominate the American market well into the depression years. Nevertheless, *Fine Prints of the Year*, though a British publication, went to some length to appeal to Americans. Incomplete as it may be, this fifteen-year source of serial data, running from 1924 to 1938, provides a picture of aggregate trends consistent with that ascertained by looking at individual case historics.

The columns in table 4.1 labeled "artists" chart the number of painter-etchers reporting at least one etching having been produced in any given year. This is a stringent criterion. Thus, the 113 British etchers listed in the 1923–24 directory is smaller than the combined number of fellows and associates of the RSPE. And there are but 41 Americans listed at a time when the CSE alone had over 100 members. One can at least assume that the measure reflects trends in productivity within a group of etchers most active in the fine print market.

The productivity curves, measured by the total number of plates in the two countries (columns labeled "plates"), diverge somewhat. The British etchers got off to an earlier start, but their output fell off more precipitously as the depression hit, whereas the American output did not peak until the 1929–31 triennium and thereafter consistently outstripped that of the British.

The early build-up in Britain reflects mainly the influx of young artists. Their careers having been interrupted by war, they had completed their formal art training and were now ready to enter a promising and potentially lucrative field. Comments at the time of the 1927–28 dip attributed it to previous overproduction. But it was the complete collapse of the market, especially in America, on which British etchers had always counted, that led to the sharp decline during the thirties both in the number of actively productive etchers and in output. Many artists—especially the younger ones not yet fully established—abandoned etching for watercolor, for a more lucrative career in commercial art, or for the security of a teaching position.

During the year of the crash, American output caught up with that of the British. But the gap had begun to close before this. Following a big spurt in American activity during the 1927–28 season, growth in the number of etchers listing one or more prints exceeded that in Britain, and the fall-off following the crash was gentler. By 1932–33, there were actually fewer active painter-etchers in Britain than in the United States. The reversal in the last year for which we

Table 4.1
Etchers and Plates Produced, 1923–1938

| Year | British | | | American | | |
|---|---|---|---|---|---|---|
| | Artists | Plates | Average Plates per Artist | Artists | Plates | Average Plates per Artist |
| 1923–24 | 113 | 511 | 4.5 | 41 | 170 | 4.2 |
| 1924–25 | 130 | 567 | 4.4 | 44 | 249 | 5.6 |
| 1925–26 | 124 | 598 | 4.8 | 45 | 222 | 4.9 |
| 1926–27 | 120 | 671 | 5.6 | 78 | 447 | 5.7 |
| 1927–28 | 116 | 554 | 4.8 | 97 | 542 | 4.9 |
| 1928–29 | 162 | 592 | 3.6 | 139 | 543 | 3.9 |
| 1929–30 | 153 | 523 | 3.5 | 117 | 515 | 4.4 |
| 1930–31 | 143 | 439 | 3.1 | 139 | 604 | 4.3 |
| 1931–32 | 104 | 351 | 3.4 | 119 | 412 | 3.5 |
| 1932–33 | 92 | 280 | 3.0 | 116 | 402 | 3.5 |
| 1933–34 | 94 | 295 | 3.1 | 91 | 271 | 3.0 |
| 1934–35 | 62 | 140 | 2.7 | 72 | 196 | 2.7 |
| 1935–36 | 55 | 170 | 3.1 | 101 | 222 | 2.2 |
| 1936–37 | 60 | 193 | 3.2 | 91 | 206 | 2.3 |
| 1937–38 | 50 | 135 | 2.7 | 89 | 194 | 2.2 |

Source: *Fine Prints of the Year*, 1924–38, vols. 2–16; 1924 actually covers about six months of 1923 and six of 1924.

have listings is dramatic: during the preceding twelve months, there were twice as many active American as British painter-etchers and, collectively, they had executed roughly 50 percent more plates.

Whatever the differences between the two countries, the depression had the same adverse effect on productivity in Britain and America. The output of etched plates per individual (the columns labeled "average") in both countries was highest in 1926–27 and steadily declined from 1928–29 on, until in 1937–38 it was about half of what it had been ten years before. The average size of editions decreased simultaneously, causing an even sharper drop in the total number of new impressions entering the market.

Some of the momentum that carried American productivity past the crash resulted from the "competitions, the friendly rivalry of societies and exhibitions in many centres, widely distributed [and] the prizes offered to attract talent" on which Britons must have cast an envious eye.[81] These included the Northwest Printmakers Society, which was organized in 1928 and held its first exhibition the year following. Odd as it may seem, new collectives were constantly forming even as the economic depression deepened; there were the Prairie Printmakers in Wichita, Kansas (1931); the Society of Washington (D.C.) Etchers (1933), open—its name notwithstanding—to all printmakers; the Print Club of Albany (1933); the Honolulu Print Makers (1933); the Indiana Society of Print Makers (1934); the Southern Printmakers Society in Mount Airy, Georgia (1935); and the Lone Star Printmakers (1937). Print clubs patterned after the one in Philadelphia sprang up in Buffalo (1929), Syracuse (1932), Dallas (1935), and other cities, while a group of dentists and physicians, who etched as a hobby, got together in New York to launch a Haden Etching Club. One observer estimated that in 1938 there were "about 26" such groups in the country, most of them by this time open to all printmakers.[82]

There was no comparable grass-roots movement in England, causing a distinguished curator there to lament that "at the present moment in America [1936] . . . etching is more popular than in Great Britain."[83]

## The Buying Public

Just how popular had etching become before it once more fell out of favor? We must distinguish between its appeal to artists and its popularity in the more precise sense, but public enthusiasm is far more difficult to "measure" with any degree of confidence. We have described how quickly the Print Collectors Club in Britain became a great success; there must have been some pent-up demand waiting to be satisfied, for the ceiling set on subscribers was quickly reached. In America, too, quotas were readily filled and often exceeded. The number of *amateurs d'estampes*—with a passion to possess etchings—may have numbered no more than a few thousand, either in Britain or the United States, but the buying public—not to speak of the viewing public—was far larger. It would have included the many persons who did not subscribe to any club but might treat themselves to a print as the occasion arose.

How large was the market for etchings? The following calculations may suggest the magnitude of the etching craze. In 1926, a year near the height of the boom, etchers in the two countries recorded over 1,100 plates (table 4.1). If we assume an average edition size of fifty, this would have put some 55,000 new impressions on the market. The same tabulations suggest that in the decade from 1923 to 1932 near 8,700 plates were produced, which, if an average number of impressions were pulled, would have yielded about 435,000 etchings. If the "average" collector bought as many as four prints a year, the number of persons participating in the etching market over these years would have had to be at least 10,000. Furthermore, since the lists on which this estimate rests includes only between one-fourth to one-third of the etched output by recognized artists, the print-buying public was no doubt greater by far, probably no less than 30,000 to 40,000.

These estimates are highly conservative. They give us an inkling of how widely diffused the urge to possess etchings was before disaster struck. This popular demand was, assumedly, what drove up prices, in some instances to meteoric heights. But the question of what had created the demand has no simple answer.

Generally speaking, the speculation in modern etchings was to a large degree a side effect of a generally bullish market for art, traceable to the growth of wealth and of discretionary income. In Britain, the demand for paintings of all kinds had risen rather phenomenally in the latter part of the nineteenth century, when "artists were like colts turned loose in clover fields."[84] This upswing in the art market is easily documented with prices realized at auctions. In 1892, a year of intense international competition for art treasures, when foreign collectors and curators first entered the English art market in large numbers, more than fifty pictures sold for a price equal to or in excess of £1,400.[85] The next time this happened was in 1908, when the art auction market really took off. Several new records were established before the Great War caused a big drop. Only toward its end did prices once more pick up, until in 1919, the first year of peace, an unprecedented one hundred pictures were bought for above £1,400. Thereafter auction prices reached ever new heights, only to come crashing down at the end of the decade, along with everything else.

The pioneers of the etching revival reaped little benefit from this boom in "big art." The only prints that sold at auction for over £20 before the last decade of the nineteenth century were mainly old engravings, most notably "the beautiful old colour prints of the eighteenth and at the beginning of the nineteenth centuries," which were being rediscovered after a period of long neglect.[86] There was, of course, the occasional master print by Rembrandt or Hollar—Rembrandt's *Portrait of Jan Six* (second state) sold for £505 in 1883—but not much of this appreciation spilled over to contemporary etchings. Even Whistler had no great success with his second Venice set when it came on the market the same year as the Rembrandt print. The prints and engravings listed as "modern" at these auction sales were nearly all reproductions of paintings, their value influenced as much by the name of the painter who had created the image (*pinx*) as that of the engraver (*sculpt*) who had translated it.

By 1897, when collectors were just beginning to turn their attention to modern etching, the Venice set by Whistler, which had previously gone for a song brought £82 at a British auction; Axel Haig's *Interior at Burgos* realized £33, and Haden's *Shere Mill Pond*, £31, sums which in those days amounted to real money. A well-known collector recalled how, in 1908, when his interest lay in old mezzotints, he had been reluctantly persuaded by a friend to visit an exhibition at the Gutekunst Gallery. Two plates caused his "transfer of affection": *L'abside de Notre Dame* by Charles Meryon and *Mytton Hall* by Seymour Haden, both on view in their first states.[87] All the while original painter-etchings were becoming so visible at auction sales that some felt that the boom for them had already peaked—but, of course, it had not. Demand for the older type of engraving and for prints with "a marked degree of antiquity" remained very high until at least 1920.[88]

From America, things looked just a bit different. Almost overnight etchings had become a popular form of art, with Americans acquiring many of the best prints appearing for sale in Britain.[89] As early as 1919, the critic Charles DeKay observed that there were two collectors of etchings to every one who acquired a painting, watercolor, or drawing. "Etching ha[s] become a species of art which closely resemble[s] merchandise"; in no other branch of art had offerings been so completely catalogued and prices so specified that buyers could know exactly what they were buying.[90] Not that this attitude was peculiarly American. In Scotland the buying and selling of etchings by the Swede, Anders Zorn, and by their own D. Y. Cameron was described as "a sort of stock exchange transaction."[91] The speculative fever at the December 1920 sale of the Gutekunst collection caused recently published etchings to be sold for more than some fine Rembrandt etchings. Zorn's work, unlike that of Cameron, was published in large editions, yet nearly every one of his plates was oversubscribed before it even came on the market. One originally offered at 5 guineas by Colnaghi's rapidly advanced in price to 15 and 20 guineas.

What drove up the price of a print were the reputation of its creator, its rarity, and its subject matter. Any signature—whether in pencil or ink—added to the value of a print, all the more so if the artist was already a "name." Plates by such established painters as Frank Brangwyn in Britain or Childe Hassam in America were usually published at higher prices than equally worthy plates by less-known printmakers. For truly renowned etchers, buyers were always ready to pay premium prices. If enough people fancied a plate by Cameron, McBey, or Bone, the price quickly soared.

As to rarity, some restricted the size of their editions in order to create an imbalance between supply and demand, but output was also limited by the energy and time it took to print as many impressions as the market might absorb. James McBey, who did his own printing, would lose "printing interest" in a plate after pulling some twenty or thirty impressions: "If I print another forty or so, it is only because collectors may want to possess them, but after seventy-six in all, I do not intend to go on."[92] Most etchers would print, up to some limit, whatever number of good proofs a plate would yield. The plates of some drypoints might show wear after no more than twenty or thirty impressions.

Subject matter affected price, especially when combined with rarity, as exemplified by Cameron's *Five Sisters, York*. Published in an edition of thirty (plus an undisclosed number in three earlier but incomplete states) and heavily touched with drypoint, this etching, described by Rinder, as "perhaps the loveliest of great English windows . . . [in] a light-interpenetrated design" caught the public's fancy.[93] It seemed to have found something arty, even mysterious about church interiors, and the York stained glass window was, of course, almost as famous as those at Chartres or at Notre Dame de Paris.[94] As soon as the edition had sold out, collectors started to go after it, including some who had never seen an impression but learned that it was worth possessing. Within three years, two impressions at the same auction went for roughly five times what they had originally cost.[95] Only a year later, in 1911, another impression sold for 175 guineas (£183. 15.0) and, by 1912 at the Wedmore sale, the price reached a temporary peak of £250. At least six more impressions came up at auction in the next few years, all at prices under 200 guineas (£210), until a new record of $1,675 (about £350) was reached in 1922 at an auction in America. This was by no means the end. Further sales brought $3,200 (about £667) and, in England, £620 and £630, the highest price up to then ever paid for a print by a contemporary etcher.

Not that stained glass windows were the only key to popularity and high prices. Bone's scenes of urban demolition and of old buildings also commanded high prices at auction. A copy of his *Ayr Prison* (edition of forty-one), perhaps the earliest of his more famous prints, was first marketed in 1905 at £2.2.6. Four years later, a copy sold for £21; the auction price reached £100 by 1912. Then, in 1929, at the height of the boom, it sold for £365, which at the then current exchange rate would have been roughly $1,750. Having once made a name for himself, Bone was able to set a publication price of £12.12.0, £15.15.0, and even £26.5.0 for his later etchings.

Some prints were popular because they exuded an "atmosphere." Seymour Haden's admired *Sunset in Ireland*, executed in 1863, became so great a favorite that even inferior impressions might do well at auction. The popularity of Cameron's *Ben Ledi* (Gaelic for "The Hill of God") rests on its ability to evoke the rugged Scottish landscape. McBey's *Dawn; the Camel Patrol Setting Out*, based on a sketch that he made while serving as an official war artist to the Palestine Expeditionary Force, experienced the most meteoric rise of all. Published in 1919, the edition of seventy-six was immediately snapped up. The price steadily climbed on resale until it reached $2,500 (about £530) in 1929. Still other subject matter that could put the price of a print beyond the means of the ordinary collector included portraits, either of famous persons or of classically beautiful but distant women, such as those by Gerald Brockhurst. *Adolescence*, his rendering of a teenage girl contemplating her nude body in a mirror, was a tour de force. Published in 1932, the third year of the depression, it was priced at an extraordinarily high £31.10.0—or $150—and thereafter quickly escalated at auction. Certain subjects appealed especially to hunters, sailors, sportsmen, dog lovers, children, or whomever. Thus, the works of two renowned artists whose etchings consistently brought the highest publication prices fall in this category: Frank Benson, who depicted wild fowl and hunting scenes, and Arthur Briscoe, who showed sailors fighting rough waters.

Indirectly most etchers benefited from this upward movement in auction prices and from the publicity that surrounded sales. Caught up in the craze, some uninformed buyers could be enticed to pay top prices for prints with little or no artistic merit. Yet literally scores of fine etchings by less well known and younger artists, some on a par with work obtainable only at premium prices, could still be had directly from publishers for 3 to 6 guineas in Britain or for $15 to $25 in America, and some top quality impressions by seasoned artists were still to be had for no more than twice these amounts. So keen was the perception of some collectors that "it [was] no new thing for a young etcher to attain acknowledgment, and even notoriety, within a few months."[96]

## The Bubble Bursts

Everybody seemed to be benefiting from the boom. Artists—neophytes and veterans alike—could afford to work in a medium suited to their temperament. Print clubs were flourishing, print dealers prospering. With assistance from solicitous critics, there had been mobilized a public comprising two types of print buyers: the *amateur d'estampes*, who responded to the aesthetic appeal of the original print, and the speculator, driven by publicity surrounding the more spectacular sales. Things were obviously too good to last forever. The day of reckoning was bound to come.

It came on Black Tuesday, the day the stock market crashed and brought just about everything else down with it. Turnover on the New York Stock Exchange declined from a volume of 1,125 million shares in 1929 to 425 million in 1932. Within twenty-eight months, the Dow-Jones industrial average had shriveled to a little more than one-tenth of its high just before the crash.[97] Art, too, was down sharply but, judged against the collapse of the stock market, did not fare too badly. An art market price index of 165 at its peak still stood at 50 in 1933. Importation of art declined by 8 percent, and the production of artists' materials by almost one-half. Speaking of the New Deal period, Richard McKinzie goes so far as to suggest that the slump in art may actually have had a modestly positive side benefit. Insofar as it curtailed purchases by the wealthy, it would also have done "much to smash the snobbishness and artificiality which had characterized American art."[98]

One response to the sudden economic instability was to boost home products. As a result, the vogue for prints continued, even if at a greatly diminished level of strength. For the time being at least, etching societies continued to hold their customary annual exhibitions and, as we have seen, participation actually grew in the early phase of this winter of economic misery.

There is no question that for many artists, in America as in Britain, the downturn spelled economic disaster. But given their dependence on exports to America, the British were less able to bear the near total collapse of their own indigenous market. If at first the demand for prints there appeared less subject to fashion than the picture market, this was due to the time it took for the prices of quality prints (the Rembrandts, the Whistlers, the Hadens) to tumble.[99] For a while prices for a small number of prints by living artists also held steady. Thus, an impression of Cameron's *Five Sisters* still brought £300 at auction in 1931, as did two of his *Ben Ledi*. In fact, in a year when oils by only three living British painters cleared the 100 guinea mark, Bone's *Manhattan Excavation*, published at 25 guineas in 1928, could still bring in nearly 62 guineas as late as 1932. Measured against the fall in the cost of living, which in one year was down by nearly 40 percent, prints by this small elite of etchers continued to do well. But ultimately they, too, became victims of the slump, their prices falling in proportion with others. There was some feeling among the less fortunate against the luminaries. William P. Robins, a respected British etcher, felt that McBey, as much as any dealer, was responsible for "ruining the market" with the outrageously high prices he had charged for his prints.[100]

It was not just the speculators who suffered from the depreciation of inflated values. Among genuine collectors it had been common practice to finance new acquisitions by selling off those prints in their collections which no longer appealed to them. With their taste having changed, or been broadened by connoisseurship, they were able to use the profits from rising prices to finance purchases of as yet undiscovered talent. Falling prices caused this type of collector to drop out of the market.

Further adding to the sluggishness of the print market were the miscalculations of dealers responding to what appeared to be an insatiable demand. In exploiting the market for all it was worth, they had published more than could be absorbed. The practice of overselling the future prospects of young etchers whose first work they published can be likened to the method of the first edition book-ramp. Some reputations were greatly harmed, as artists of great promise moved from being overrated to being "degraded far below their undoubted merits, so that their prints [passed] through at Sotheby's in batches of three or four at a time for a pound or two," where in the late twenties they were fetching up to £30 apiece. In 1940, this London auction house held a one-day sale devoted entirely to modern etchings. Seventy prints of high quality by "one of the best of [the] younger etchers, whose work [had] frequently been hung at the Royal Academy and . . . received much praise from the critics" could be purchased for less than the original price of one.[101]

The depression fell most heavily on the younger artists used to selling enough prints to survive on the proceeds. Graham Sutherland, born in 1903, arrived on the scene when the boom was well under way and managed to earn around £700 from his etchings and drawings. He was producing a maximum of four plates a year, pulling seventy-five copies priced at 4 guineas apiece. With his best customers in the United

States, he "*had* to teach" when the American recession came along.[102] Two of his friends—E. Bouverie-Hoyton and Robin Tanner—made similar shifts, while others escaped into commercial art.

American etchers, though with some delay, were affected by a similar chain of events: "For the first time in several seasons," wrote Susan Hutchinson in reviewing prints made in 1934, "there has been a marked diminution in the number of producing etchers, although the quality of work submitted is well up to that of previous years. Some appear to have turned to more lucrative fields, some have been painting and some are unaccounted for."[103] One of those lost to the art was Anton Schutz, who had come to America in 1924 to escape the postwar inflation in Germany. A most successful etcher of urban scenes with a remarkable business sense, he found it advantageous to set up his own company for the sole purpose of publishing his own etchings and those of other artists. Newspapers dubbed him the "financial etcher," partly because of his business success, partly because his drypoints depicted "the New York Stock Exchange, Wall Street vistas and the towering skyscrapers of lower Manhattan."[104] For him, 1929 turned out to be a real boom year. After earning $30,000 in the three months ending 1 April 1930, things began to go steadily downhill. His company received fewer and fewer orders; clients even asked him to accept returns. By early 1932, his net income from etching for the entire year was less than $1,000. He abandoned etching and switched his enterprise to publishing fine art reproductions in collotype.[105] Martin Lewis, though hardly as prolific as Schutz and disinclined to work on commissions, had been highly regarded for the marvelous feel with which his etchings and drypoints depicted city life and its atmosphere. Two of them, when published by Kennedy and Company in 1929, carried premium prices: *Relics* sold for $150, and *Fifth Avenue Bridge* for $100. The following year the *Glow of the City*, his masterpiece, still carried a price tag of $48 (figure 50). But insufficient sales forced him to sell his house and, ultimately, to give up etching.

Gerald Geerlings, like Lewis a recorder of urban scenes published by Kennedy, recalled how from time to time he would stop in to find the absolute stillness in the gallery "unnerving" and would ask if there "was any justification for new plates." Because his income from prints had become "almost negligible," he illustrated architectural articles to fund his six-month trips to London, where he could concentrate on etching, but found this an unsatisfactory solution to his problems: "I found it impossible to have a dual personality: on the one hand, trying to etch on a copper plate a 'social document' or a distilled cityscape portrayal, entirely divorced from any thought of financial reimbursement; and, on the other hand, being a combination of craftsman, architect, and wordsmith, with financial involvement."[106]

The effects from the instability of economic conditions were deeply felt by artists in both countries.

## The Lure of Alternative Mediums

The etching revival was not, however, just another victim of bad times. Its demise was speeded by stirrings wholly internal to the artistic community. Long before the depression set in, other methods of printmaking had been attracting printmakers and print lovers. Most of these were not technologically innovative; what was new was a willingness on the part of artists to adopt, for their own purposes, techniques already in commercial use. As a result, etching was facing competition from lithography and from block prints on wood and even linoleum. These mediums had long been used extensively for illustration but there had been only occasional attempts to exploit their full artistic potential.

The French and, of course, Whistler had shown what could be done with lithography, and others had followed their lead. The Senefelder Club, as noted, had been formed for the express purpose of lending encouragement to lithography, with Pennell as its first president and John Copley its secretary. Both were also etchers. In the United States, where artist-lithographers did not formally organize themselves into a separate group, a similar movement toward lithography began when George C. Miller, a commercial lithographic printer, set up shop in 1915 to turn his talents exclusively toward artistic lithography. Bolton Brown moved into lithography and lithographic printing about the same time. Other lithographic workshops for artists followed. Together they provided a real incentive for artists to work on stones. Not only Pennell and Copley but many others of the older generation of etchers, such as Albert Sterner, "Pop" Hart, and Frank Armington, were as comfortable drawing on stone as needling their copper. Some, like the much younger Yasuo Kuniyoshi, experimented with etching only to embrace lithography as a more congenial alternative.

The woodblock was another competitor to the copperplate. Yielding a relief print, it could be printed from the same press as the type, which made it uniquely suitable for book illustration. The printing of original designs from blocks actually required no press at all nor even a very skilled printer. Artistic wood-block printers found homes in several of the existing printmaking societies. Even the exclusive RSPE was moved, after the Great War, to amend its bylaws and admit two wood engravers: Noel Rooke and Gwen Raverat. But this did not prevent the formation of a separate Society of Wood-Engravers. Americans pioneering the revival of the original woodcut had less need for an organization of their own, since several printmaking collectives had always welcomed them into their ranks. The close affinity among printmakers is underlined by the number who, like Norman Janes in England and Howard Cook in America, won recognition as etchers *and* wood engravers; the latter worked with equal dexterity in lithography.

The editors of *Fine Prints of the Year*, originally devoted only to etchings and engravings, were cognizant of the inroads being made by other print media. By 1934, in the depths of the depression, they were acknowledging that a truly "representative collection of the year's graphic art in America," where printmaking remained more alive than in Britain, "would have to include lithographs and block prints as well as etchings and engravings."[107] Two years later the magazine was giving equal attention to work on stone and wood.

The shift to these other print mediums was tied to broader stylistic changes, in particular the movement away from an academic and representational mode toward what is usually subsumed under the term "modernism." A cleavage between the traditional and the new existed everywhere; printmaking was no exception. The "modernists" within the art world looked on the etching societies and on most of the print galleries as bastions of conservatism. Colnaghi's in Britain and Keppel and Kennedy in America certainly favored etchers in the more traditional mold. Some "modernists" ceased taking their prints to these galleries because they never showed anything that they themselves liked.[108] But Deighton, in London, and Weyhe, in New York, felt less bound by accepted practice, and the American Institute of Graphic Arts, in its first traveling exhibition of *Fifty Prints*, decided to "deviate" from the practices of other annual print exhibitions by giving equal space to both camps. Ernest Roth was asked to select prints to represent the highest achievements in traditional printmaking; Ralph Pearson was asked to do the same for the modernists.[109]

About three-quarters of the twenty-five traditional prints were etchings, but among the moderns they were a minority. Yet the line between the two styles was still easily crossed. Not everyone who continued to draw very precisely from nature or from life was necessarily out of sympathy with others who took greater liberties. Artists whose prints had been selected for the conservative group included John Sloan, representative of the path-breaking "Ash Can School," and "Pop" Hart, a very experimental printmaker, while some of the so-called modernists, like Harry Wickey, J. J. Lankes, Peggy Bacon, and Ralph Pearson himself, continued to work in an essentially representational mode and could, on these grounds, have as logically been classified as conservative. Eugene Higgins could not be pigeonholed; in 1926 he was represented by one print in each category.

As bad times persisted, the involvement of American artists in the social scene found expression in their prints. This, too, hardly amounted to a radical break with the past. Printmakers were drawn to a critical realism in the tradition of Steinlen and Forain. Some of the younger etchers made effective use of their etching skill for sharp and biting satirical comment. William Auerbach-Levy had long doubled as a cartoonist for several publications. One of the noteworthy differences between the British and American etchers was the greater isolation of those in the Old World from the political crosscurrents of the thirties.

What finally put painter-etching hors de combat after the Second World War was the turn away from nature, life, and politics together with the ascendancy of the color print. The turn toward abstraction among American printmakers was already evident before the war but was greatly strengthened in 1940 when S. W. Hayter moved his Atelier 17 from Paris to New York. In this atmosphere, many older printmakers and their followers found themselves pushed aside by a newer breed of Hayter disciples. A few became converts but not John Taylor Arms, president of the American Society of Etchers, who had, unhappily, to acknowledge to a younger like-minded colleague that times had changed: "You and I and a few of our pals are getting our works tossed out of shows like the proverbial 'old shoes' these days. You were thrown out of the Academy and the Pennell Show. I was thrown out of the Brooklyn Museum Show. Stow Wengenroth and Roi Partridge are two others rejected by the Brooklyn Jury. Kennedy and Company, our dealers in New York, took it as quite an affront. I was rejected by the Los Angeles Drawing Show not so long ago. Seems as if, old hats that we are, the juries can look at us with a cold 'Gromyko.' "[110] The last remark was a reference to the icy stare of the diplomat representing the Soviet Union at the United Nations. Arms went on to explain that he no longer had an official place in the National Academy, having been removed "unceremoniously" as first vice-president and as a member of the council.

Even more revealing is a letter from Ralph Pearson, once in charge of selecting modernist prints for *Fifty Prints*, in which he dissociated himself from the excesses of the turn away from realism. Taking exception to the term "abstract expressionism," he complained that it "over-dignifies the revelers of chaos. . . . I hate to see [abstract art] stretched to cover smears and dribbles and doodling." His later comments were even more critical: " 'Personality expression' in the raw (via D'Amico at the Modern [Museum of Modern Art]) belongs in the department of psychology, not art."[111]Looking back at his own career, Pearson felt that, despite some marvelous testimonial letters from students and readers of his books, his relations with art museums had been checkered. They had exhibited his "etchings copiously many decades ago" but never since was there ever "a financial lift via purchases or in any other way. . . . Fashions certainly do change; my greatest disillusion has been that chaos could become the 'latest style.' "[112] Other print-makers from the 1920s and 1930s who refused to go along with the new art movement encountered equal neglect.

Still, it must be acknowledged that the painter-etchers as a group had been indifferent, if not downright hostile, to important developments in poster art, commercial printing, and chromolithography, which, together with the Japanese woodcut, had provided the inspiration for the truly remarkable color prints produced by French artists as early as the 1890s.[113] As always, there were exceptions. Theodore Roussel, an associate of the RSPE and long-serving president of the Society of Painter-Gravers in Colour, was much preoccupied with color experiments, as was the highly versatile Nelson Dawson, R.E. Robertine Heriot, a Roussel protégé, and Elyse Lord, the most popular of the newer British color printers, worked outside the RSPE and never exhibited there. Lord's drypoints, overprinted with color from woodblocks, and usually with an Oriental motif, were much in demand. It was a harbinger of the future that they continued to sell at 12 to 15 guineas in the depressed market of the thirties.

In America, etchers experimenting in color were apt to be less segregated. Among the older generation, George Elbert Burr, Charles Mielatz, Bertha Jaques, Zella de Milhau, "Pop" Hart, Bertha Lum and, especially, Helen Hyde, had enhanced their reputations with color renditions of their intaglio prints, mostly drypoints and etchings. Even Arms himself had printed in color but mostly as an experiment. Helen Hyde took off for Japan, where she was directly influenced by first-hand study, as was Bertha Lum, who, like Lord and Hyde, added color from woodblocks using a technique of her own invention. The Japanese print had a more indirect influence on the younger generation of color printers who came together in Provincetown around 1915.[114] For a while, until the group dispersed after the war, their work was prominent in many woodblock shows. B. J. O. Nordfeldt, Maud Squire, Margaret Patterson, and other participants in the group had all been active etchers.

Notwithstanding all this activity, the color print did not come into its own until the Graphic Arts Division of the Works Progress Administration Federal Arts Project brought together a large number of American printmakers, thereby facilitating an expansion of the technical possibilities in various printmaking techniques. It was here that Russell T. Limbach, an experienced lithographer, made his first color lithograph in 1935. As a supervisor he could instruct others in the process so that, by 1938, an exhibition with twenty-three color lithographs by sixteen artists could be held. Sales were sufficient to suggest that color lithography, a heretofore neglected medium, might achieve the kind of mass popularity it had never had, even in Europe. Explorations of the color woodcut under the guidance of Louis Schanker led to similar spurts of creative activity. The project also issued a mimeographed handbook on the serigraph as a vital expressive medium for artists.[115] In the words of one participant, these workshops "popularized lithography, the woodcut, serigraphy, and most of all color printing" as the first step in the extraordinary search for innovation in the postwar decade.[116]

Printmakers who refused to go along with any of these style changes soon found themselves bypassed, inasmuch as the public's long on-again off-again love affair with the black-and-white etching was, once more, off again.

# Part II

## The Building of Reputation

::ILL:: 19359   ::Borrower:: XIM   ::ReqDate:: 940315 ::Status:: RENEWAL OK
::OCLC:: 20825806   ::NeedBefore:: 940414 ::RecDate:: 940323 ::RenewalReq:: 940520
::Lender:: VYF,*XNC,XBM,XQM,YQM   ::DueDate:: 940420 ::NewDueDate:: 940520
::AUTHOR:: Lang, Gladys Engel.
::TITLE:: Etched in memory : the building and survival of artistic reputation

::IMPRINT:: Chapel Hill : University of North Carolina Press, c1990.
::VERIFIED:: OCLC/U OF NC 1990
::PATRON:: MCCUE,H/FAC
::SHIP TO:: UPS:Ithaca College Library/ILL Gannett Center/Danby Rd./Ithaca, N
14850.Library Rate::ILL/Ithaca College Library/Ithaca,NY 14850
::BILL TO:: Same
::SHIP VIA:: UPS/Library Rate   ::MAXCOST::   ::COPYRT COMPLIANCE:: CCL
::FAX:: (607) 274-1539
::E-MAIL:: BHOGREN@ITHACA.EDU
::BORROWING NOTES:: Please cond on negative response.
::LENDING CHARGES::   ::SHIPPED:: 940321 ::SHIP INSURANCE::
::RETURN TO:: Lorette Wilmot Library ILL/Nazareth College/4245 East Ave./Box
8950/Rochester, New York 14618-0950

Harry McCue
Fine Art (Carrache)

# 5   🌀

# Nature and Nurture: Decisions for Art

A British painter, looking back at a career that began in the late nineteenth century, conceded that his father had been absolutely right to oppose his desire for a life in art. "Today," he wrote in 1925, "I would rather be shot than encourage any boy or girl to be a painter, a writer, an actor or a musician."[1] His father's had been but a natural wish to spare a son or daughter the lifetime of insecurity that all but a few of the most fortunate art practitioners inevitably faced. Art as a profession was not quite respectable, less than economically viable, and fit for well-bred men and women only if they did not make it their main source of livelihood.

It is against such a background of discouragement that we want to consider how and when the painter-etchers whose lives we studied first came to think of themselves as artists. Were most of them "born to art," knowing almost from their first breath that there was no other life for them? To what extent was their profession inherited, passed on to them across generations? How important was childhood immersion in a cultural milieu supportive of artistic talents and aspirations? What obstacles had to be overcome? These are some of the questions we seek to answer while keeping in mind differences between generations, gender, class, and the institutional support available in Britain and America.

## Precocity and Temperament

We begin by considering the still popular notion that artists are "born to art," that art is more a calling than a profession. Those born to a life in art, argued John Ruskin, will never be good at anything else. Their artistic gift—except for the very greatest, like Leonardo da Vinci—is "not joined with others; [therefore] your born painter, if you don't make a painter of him, won't be a first-rate merchant, or lawyer."[2] Evidence for such inborn and irrepressible precocity can be found in the lives of great painters. Legend has it that Giotto, while yet a boy, had drawn pictures of the sheep hè tended. Others, like Raphael, Michelangelo, Titian, Rembrandt, and Salvatore Rosa seem to have imbibed their taste for drawing along with their maternal milk. Sir Thomas Lawrence had at the tender age of five, without the benefit of any art instruction, drawn portraits of visitors to his parents' home. Likewise, Benjamin West, later president of the Royal Academy, was alleged to have completed pen-and-ink drawings at age seven, before he had ever seen a picture. A more recent exemplar is Picasso, who could draw even before he could talk.

Accounts that speak in awed tones of the infant artist's uncanny imitative skill, bordering on the magical, contain mythical and projective elements, usually injected into these life histories after their subjects' death.[3] One cannot, however, deny the underlying reality, of which such stories are but an embellishment. Many future artists do indeed give early signs, if not of divine gifts, then of an eidetic rather than an auditory memory, of a preference for the visual mode of thought and communication, of reproductive dexterity, or at least of an urge to draw and produce images. Some such evidence is contained in one-third of our life histories; in many other cases we simply lack documentation. For the artists themselves, the origins of these early impulses may remain a lifelong puzzle. Thus, Anna Lea Merritt, the portrait painter and etcher, was still puzzled as a very old lady as to "why a small child [like herself], who heard no talk about art, should have a fixed determination to make pictures."[4]

There are, indeed, few artists who cannot, when asked, dredge up some family lore or memory about their artistic precocity. And this holds for our etchers: it was said of Loren Barton that while yet in the nursery she painted with the milk she was supposed to drink; of Diana Thorne, an etcher of animals, that she was already "fashioning" her four-legged creatures as a child; of Peggy Bacon that she began drawing at eighteen months, before she could yet talk; of Hester Frood that by age three she was always standing on a chair and drawing; of John Taylor Arms that as a child he always had a pencil in his hand; and of Raphael Soyer (as of his brothers) that he drew constantly.[5] As for artists' own recollections, Charles Tunnicliffe's earliest memory of a boyhood on a Cheshire farm was scribbling "shapes and marks which were supposed to be horses and cows . . . and, when I had exhausted all the available clean paper in the house, I had to content myself with pencil scribbles on the white-washed walls of the shippons and stables."[6] John Marin started drawing "virtually at the age of three or four . . . scrawls of rabbits and things"; he called this his most "industrial" period.[7] Less credible is the claim of Mortimer Menpes that his artistic career began in South Australia as a one-year-old, sketching on the floor as he lay on his stomach.[8]

To assess the true extent of such precocity among professional artists is almost impossible. The notion that artists are "born to art" has been perpetuated through their own memoirs and by their biographers who, along with publicists, journalists, and even sociologists, have a proclivity for asking artists when they first showed signs of being gifted. One painter-etcher best set the matter straight when queried about how early her talent had become manifest. She had had "pretty much of an impulse as a child," she replied, "*but then all children do.*"[9] Studies of childhood drawing would bear her out.[10] These early proclivities are too common to explain who becomes an artist.

Psychological testing of much older art students points to strong skills in visual perception, the form in which artists express themselves.[11] Awareness of such ability can become an important influence on career choice. Thus, the highly successful James McBey recalled that in his first years in school, "I could memorize anything visual and, having studied a map, I could from memory reproduce it accurately and in detail without effort. Great was my astonishment when I saw that none of my schoolmates, all cleverer than I, had the same faculty."[12] As a young boy, Walter Sickert was collared by a headmaster whose caricature he had been drawing in class but for which, unbelievably, he escaped punishment. Much later he found that the drawing, which was confiscated, had been saved and framed.[13] Also precociously adept was fifteen-year-old Eileen Soper, who had two etchings exhibited at the Royal Academy, an achievement "sensational enough to draw crowds of smilingly sceptical Private Viewers."[14] The Italian-American Pamela Bianco attracted attention with drawings exhibited in Turin when she was but eleven.[15] The most celebrated of our "young geniuses" were the English twins, Edward and Maurice Detmold, who first exhibited at the Royal Academy at age thirteen, then experimented, and by fifteen had become adept in mezzotint (the most demanding of the intaglio processes) and were making color prints.[16]

It does not follow that this kind of precocity is a prerequisite for ultimate recognition and success. D. Y. Cameron, according to his cataloguer, was definitely no prodigy but relied on prodigious effort and determination to bring out the "poet-seer" in him.[17] Sensitivity to visual beauty also counted. Instead of a special talent in drawing, Theodore Roussel confided to his critic-friend and biographer-to-be that as a child he had secretly taken pleasure in watching "the grey light in the early morning, the dew on the flowers, the gradual change of aspect of all things from those hours until the splendour of noon, the mysterious light playing in a forest of stems of a bank of scabiosa. . . . There were also the changes of colour in the sea, and later the aspect of the town [in Brittany] when we came back there in the Autumn. . . . That I should have felt these things at such an age may be strange, but it is most scrupulously true."[18] Roussel did not opt for art until he was nearly twenty.

Whatever the origin and nature of childhood sensitivities and impulses, they have somehow to be implemented. Gwen Raverat "always liked pictures, as long as I can remember anything." Then, from the time she was nine, when she began her drawing class, she "always kept a sketchbook going and drew everything [she] saw."[19] Even more intense were the spurts of activity that Wanda Gãg described as her "drawing fits," during which the teenage girl would shut herself off from the rest of the world for days on end in response to an inner compulsion.[20]

Another element in the decision for art is the perception of the artist, whether a painter or writer or musician, as someone who has managed to avoid being caught in a more prosaic career. Signs of such disaffinity were apt to appear in school. These etchers, like other artists, often described themselves as unpromising students. School was drudgery for someone who knew, as did Harry Wickey, that he wanted more than anything else to be an artist and "could see no reason for studying things bearing little relation to it."[21] Others admitted to having had "a slow ear and no head for arithmetic" or "little aptitude for scholarship."[22] Such disclaimers are often contradicted by later successes in the very areas of implied ineptness. Thus, an aversion to commerce among those of middle-class origin was not inconsistent with hard bargaining over the financial terms related to their dealings in art.[23]

Sickert exemplifies the multitalented person. He had been unhappy at his first school and managed to get himself expelled from a second, allegedly for selling doughnuts to schoolmates for a profit. This, if the charge was true, would have been the only time that Sickert exhibited any real head for business. He was as a rule most casual, if not indifferent, in disposing of his work. Nor could he be considered an academic failure. His sister recalled that as a teenager, he had "surrounded himself with friends . . . and somehow managed to make a fair acquaintance with the classics and mathematics while he seemed to be preoccupied with other matters."[24] He had a short career as an actor and throughout his life was a prolific writer of reviews and essays filled with foreign phrases that give testimony to his linguistic accomplishments.

The combination is by no means unique. Some highly celebrated writers took up the pen only after putting down the brush. William Thackeray had worked in a Paris atelier and published some satirical drawings before he wrote *Vanity Fair*, which he himself illustrated. And, had it not been for his wife's strong objections, Henrik Ibsen, who had painted a good many pictures by the time he was thirty-five, might have had a career in painting instead of drama. The two talents seem most completely fused in two artist-poets: William Blake, who had been trained as an engraver, and Dante Gabriel Rossetti, of the Pre-Raphaelite brotherhood. Ruskin himself not only wrote verse before he was seven but was displaying a decided ability for drawing by the time he was eleven.

Several painter-etchers likewise wrote poetry and had it published. A. Hugh Fisher, from England, earned a reputation (however "minor") as both etcher and poet. He also left a vivid account of his travels as a member of the British civil service.[25] A more common sequence was from illustrating the books of others to writing and illustrating one's own. In this way Clare Leighton, an Anglo-American wood engraver, came to write fourteen books, including the well-received *Four Hedges* and *Southern Harvest*. Peggy Bacon made herself known for the books she wrote and illustrated for children, as did Hilda Cowham, Thomas Handforth, Elizabeth Olds, Eileen Soper, and Wanda Gág. A talent for writing is also evident in the remarkable number of published and unpublished autobiographies, memoirs, and letters left behind by these etchers—by the better known, such as Mary Cassatt, Augustus John, C. R. W. Nevinson, Gwen Raverat, Clare Leighton, and Wanda Gág, as well as less conspicuous figures, including Jerome Myers, Harry Wickey, Ilse Bischoff, Zella de Milhau, and Charles Tunnicliffe. We counted a total of forty such books by our 286 British and American etchers, several published posthumously. And the number may still grow; there are an undetermined number of unpublished diaries (some still sealed) and memoirs left for others to edit and make public.[26]

While it may be natural for artists to write and talk about their art and in this way share their experiences, redundancy between the eye and the ear may be more problematic. Whoever speaks can learn to write, but musical expression demands a specially sensitive ear, says Cecil Gray, the musical historian. While graphic representation is readily put to the service of literary aims, only the abstract play of colors begins even to approximate the condition of music. Some composers, like Felix Mendelssohn, tried their hand at painting, but with no great success.[27] Yet there were at least two of our etchers who—like the artist Paul Klee—wavered between a musical and an artistic career before settling on the latter. Several others were accomplished performers: Irwin Hoffman in his later years abandoned graphics to make musical instruments, and Kathleen Jefferies was both a recognized painter-etcher and a fellow of the Royal Academy of Music.

We come back to Ruskin's doctrine: Are those born with the temperament and endowment to be artists unfit to do well at anything else? Avant-garde doctrine posits a fundamental incompatibility between the artist inspired to create and more ordinary people preoccupied with money-making. As Pelles points out, an artist's work has come to be associated with pleasures that the rest of us associate with leisure.[28] This is what makes the drudgery and tedium of working in the studio something more than just work. And yet the nature of the precise quality that we think of as artistic temperament or creative ability remains elusive even for psychologists. What can be said is that whatever potential resides in the genes stands little chance, unless nourished and reinforced, of ever being realized. The family milieu is of obvious importance as the first source of stimulation and encouragement. We now want to search the lives of our etchers to assess what influences, whether a parent's workshop or the family parlor, moved them in their early years toward art.

## Occupational Inheritance through the Workshop

Everyone knows that children frequently take up their fathers' careers: physicians follow their physician fathers into medicine, ministers are influenced by family tradition, and officers may come from a long line of military ancestors. Such occupational inheritance is no less common among artists. Both Giovanni Bellini and Jacob van Ruisdael overshadow their less-famous painter fathers.[29] Among early Americans, the painter Charles Willson Peale may have assured that his sons would follow in his footsteps by christening them Rembrandt and Raphael. The Wyeth family by now encompasses three generations of distinguished artist-illustrators.

Nineteen percent of the British and 14 percent of the American etchers about whom dependable information could be obtained had one or more parents and/or were in close contact with a relative (an uncle, an aunt, or a grandparent) who were themselves professional artists. These proportions are in line with those in other professions that tend toward an early choice.

Nor, on this score, was there much difference between the men and the women, even though before the nineteenth century "the proportion of male painters who were *not* related to other painters [was] nearly as high as the proportion of women who were."[30] A spot check of women listed as engravers in the *Inventaire de la Bibliothèque Nationale* in Paris (after 1800) reveals many, especially among the earlier practitioners of the craft, who were either daughters or wives of engravers, or both. That this should have been so is altogether natural. Wives and daughters were often commandeered to help with the preparation and printing of plates and readily picked up the elements of the craft. Yet, by the time most of our etchers were born, with formal educational opportunities for women expanding, women were less dependent on a father as role model and sponsor. This helps explain the near parity between genders in occupational inheritance.

Having a parent-artist was, however, a dominant factor in career choice. As the daughter of an artist, Wanda Gāg, the eldest of seven surviving children, felt she had not only a right but a "filial" obligation to live out her father's unfulfilled ambition. He was a Bohemian immigrant who had found his way to New Ulm, Minnesota, late in the nineteenth century, totally unaware that no artist could survive in a "mediocre Western village" with the "vitiating spirit of Main Street."[31] To support a large family, Wanda's father decorated houses and churches on weekdays but "on Sundays, for his inner satisfaction, he painted pictures in his attic studio," into which the children were sometimes admitted but only if they behaved. When he died, Wanda, though only fifteen, was consumed by a passion for art and a determination to be an artist. With her mother mortally ill, there was pressure from the community, which provided a small relief allowance, to "forget about school, stop drawing, and clerk in a local school to help support the family."[32] This could forever have put an end to her ambition. Yet Wanda kept alive her father's unfulfilled yearning for a formal art education under able teachers, perhaps even in Europe. Dying, he had called her to his bedside and, as he took her hand, said faintly (in German), "What papa couldn't do, Wanda will still have to finish." And this she did, while making it possible for her brothers and sisters to finish high school. Her quest for an art career reads like a soap opera, but then sometimes soap operas imitate life.

We found more daughters than sons inspired, against all obstacles, to live out a parent's dream. Denise Lebreton Brown, youngest of our British etchers, lost her father late in the Great War, when she was just seven.[33] Even sixty years later, she still spoke admiringly of his superb draftsmanship. But economic pressure had forced him into a commercial partnership with another man able to letter but not draw. She also remembered how shortly before his death she had received from him her first painting set. In the schools she attended, she took no more than the routine art classes and, upon finishing secondary school, her mother wanted her to train as a secretary—the "sensible thing" for a young woman going on the job market in the late 1920s. But she "hated" even the thought of it. The dead father's influence on the daughter persisted. She made her way to the Hornsey School of Art, which proved to be "sensible" preparation for a scholarship that enabled her to attend the Royal College of Art. It was there that she "got into etching."

It was the mother, and not the father, of Dame Laura Knight, who "willed" the daughter to do what had been denied to her for want of money. When carrying Laura, the last of her three children, she had prayed as she painted and drew that her own passion for art might be transmitted to the child in her womb. Her husband, whom she had married at seventeen, had by then deserted his family.[34] She turned to art for a living, holding classes for private students in a room in her house as well as teaching at a school, while she herself attended evening classes at the local art school. When baby Laura gave signs of unusual talent, a "born artist" with an uncanny facility for drawing, this was for the mother the God-sent gift she so desired. It made her feel that life was worthwhile. Dame Laura quotes her as saying when her daughter was only a few years old, "You will be elected to the Royal Academy one day."[35] One doubts that, in the England of the 1870s, a provincial in such meager circumstances could have uttered so improbable a prophecy for a little child. But chance or circumstance caused Laura to heed her mother's urging, as she lay dying of cancer in 1892, to wait and marry an artist who would share and encourage her ambitions for recognition and fame.

Only Gág and Knight, so far as we know, had their occupations so directly "willed" to them, but others were the objects of their parent-artists' hopes and dreams. One still discerns the quiet satisfaction of an aging father expressed in a letter written by the artist, Ernest Blumenschein, to his sister. Conscious that his productive years were passing, he was relieved to find that his daughter, Helen, had at last found herself in her work: "I feel I can rest easy as she is going to keep up the high standards for which her parents strove. She was a problem with her nice mamma slaving for her all the time, but at last she is digging in to the deep qualities of creative life and her last lithograph is a comfort to her dad."[36] Helen, who by then was just thirty, worked principally as a lithographer. Just how she came into her artistic inheritance is uncertain. She was a late child, born after her father had given up illustration and his teaching post at the Art Students League to move to Taos, where he turned his full attention to painting, specializing in Southwest Indian subjects. But her mother, also a professional artist, was a city person and not at all anxious to give up the creature comforts and cultural attractions of New York for the Wild West. She also wanted the best schools for her daughter. As a result, much of the first ten years of Helen's life were spent in that art mecca with her mother.

New York evidently agreed with Helen. In her letters to Ernest, Mary Blumenschein reported Helen to be doing very well at school, practicing her violin, growing at a rapid rate, and getting to be more darling every day.[37] At one point Helen was taking dancing lessons, but nothing in her parents' correspondence indicates that she showed talent for drawing or that they were at all concerned about this. Following long periods of separation, the family was at long last permanently reunited in Taos. Only then did the daughter, sharing so closely her parents' life in the studio, turn to art as a career. She did a stint at the Art Students League and was sent off to Paris. Upon her return, the trio, known as the "Blumeys," kept studios in the same adobe building on Ledoux Street in Taos.

Paul Cadmus exemplifies a direct and uncomplicated transmission of the artistic calling from two parents, both of them painters, to both their children. Cadmus is said to have announced with "forthright assurance" at the age of nine, after a carefree summer with the family at the seashore, "I am going to be a marine painter and sister is to be a portrait painter." Encouraged by his parents, he left high school at fourteen to enter formal art study at the National Academy of Design. The sister, too, was to train as a professional painter.[38]

This last vignette, even more than the others, suggests that children are enticed by the presence of a role model long before a conscious career choice has to be made. They can understand what it means to be an artist. A second advantage for children of artists is the availability of instruction, however informal. Visual expression in any form, as painting, drawing, or etching, demands a certain dexterity. Guidance on these matters is readily at hand before children ever leave the nursery. In this respect, J. Alden Weir, the painter and etcher who became president of the National Academy of Design, had an unusually favorable situation. Under the fatherly tutelage of Robert W. Weir, drawing instructor at the United States Military Academy, the boy began to study and make copies of Old Masters. He was also advised by a much older half-brother, a landscapist and later head of the Yale School of Art.[39] Young Weir's family "inheritance" may even have extended to etching. The father, working as a copyist while yet a young man in the 1820s, had produced rather close duplicates of some of Rembrandt's etchings. He had thought of turning his "attention seriously to the publication of etchings from various old pictures" but ceased after the first or second plate.[40]

Evidence of children learning to etch from their fathers was obtained for only four artists: James D. Smillie, Ian Strang, Orovida Pissarro, and Eileen Soper.

Smillie, born in 1833, was the son of an engraver-craftsman, adept in etching as in several other graphic processes. He remembered having etched his first plate in his father's shop when he was but seven years old—a "foolish little thing" that he had drawn upon a card plate of copper, with his father laying the ground and biting it in. His real introduction to professional life came six years later when he copied *Quails* from a book about dogs, for which he laid the ground and bit the plate himself. But he also confessed to having been "so ardent—so impatient—so blindly in a hurry to complete my work . . . that when everything was ready and father told me to pour on the acid I caught the turpentine bottle and deluged it with that causing, of course, instant destruction."[41] The only impressions of the subject to survive come from a second early plate. Smillie was the oldest of the male etchers in the sample. Growing up in an era when the adoption of the father's craft by a son was all but taken for granted, he was destined to remain in his father's shop for nearly two decades, during which they cooperated closely in reproductive engraving as their primary business activity. With the elevation of etching to an artistic medium and the aesthetic elitism that accompanied it, Smillie came to consider his inheritance an obstacle. Much as he admired his father, who had helped him develop into a technical virtuoso, he became preoccupied with how "to counteract the influence of years of service in the cause of line-engraving, with its formality, and of commissions to do reproductive work not worthy of his powers." He was to remain his own severest critic.[42] His correspondence is full of self-doubt, invoking his "engraver's education and . . . comparative unfamiliarity with what may be done by an etcher-painter" and his habituation to "the use of a steel rather than a copper plate" to account for any failings.[43]

Two women absorbed their skills from fathers who were themselves very much a part of the etching revival. One, Eileen Soper, who exhibited at so young an age, had been tutored by her father, George, who had studied etching under Frank Short and was a fellow of the Royal Society of Painter-Etchers (RSPE). When he sent his own work to the Print Makers Society of California, he also sent along some prints by Eileen. They were accepted and received favorable notices, which then encouraged her to submit work for the Royal Academy Exhibition. The father had set the course for his daughter's career.

The other, Orovida Camille Pissarro, was clearly "born to art." She inherited not only the name but also occupation of her illustrious grandfather, the French Impressionist, and of his son Lucien, who had settled in London and made a name for himself as a wood engraver. Orovida, as she signed herself, was an only child. During almost all of her working life, she lived with or near her parents, and her father served both as mentor and professional confidante. She also had four artist uncles, one of whom, before his premature death at the age of twenty-three, had been making "dry points of the most ingenious arrangement" by scratching with an old nail on zinc fallen from the roof. When Lucien sent Camille a drawing by five-year-old Orovida, the grandfather was impressed: "Diable, voilà encore un artiste en perspective. . . . Kiddy [as her family called her] se revèle dessinateur, c'était écrit. Ses dessins sont déjà pleins de sentiment, d'élégance et de laisser-aller."[44] Neither father nor grandfather ever doubted that she would one day join them in the studio. It was, as Lucien put it, "in her blood."[45]

British critics agreed that it was "only natural" for a Pissarro to be so talented.[46] But her mother, though herself trained as an artist, was dead set against her only child following family tradition. As Esther Pissarro never ceased to remind her daughter, there was no financial security in it. Believing it to be more remunerative, she had her unwilling "Kiddy" study music instead. However, the mother's opposition weakened somewhat when Orovida took up etching, since she could more readily visualize its commercial prospects in illustration.[47] But here Orovida was still following a well-beaten path, for grandfather Camille, after developing an eye ailment that prevented his painting outdoors, had more and more turned to prints, even buying a press from Delâtre and urging his son to share in work which, though done only by a few, he found "as interesting as painting."[48]

Orovida, in her later years, tended to downplay the debt to her father Lucien, who she claimed had given her "only occasional advice," and to insist that she had learned etching techniques, at which she excelled, from a book.[49] Yet, she must have watched Camille pulling prints and impressions, since her first seven plates were run off his press under the supervision of her uncle Paul. Other reinforcement came from family acquaintances. Among the callers on alternate Sundays when her mother was "at home" were men from the world of prints, who encouraged the girl to think of herself as an artist.[50]

Like Soper and Orovida, Ian Strang inherited his occupation from a father who was himself a pioneer in the etching revival. William Strang, having married young, found it hard to "feed [his five children] on copper plates."[51] Yet, whatever the father's misgivings, two of his sons followed him into the etching world. Of Ian Strang it is said that he was allowed to go his own way without encouragement or discouragement. He never worked directly under his father, and most of his student years were spent abroad. Yet there were disadvantages to having had so renowned a father. Critics have suggested that not only Ian's etching but also that of his younger brother David, who became a leading copperplate printer, was inhibited by working too closely under the tyrannical eye of the moody Scot. They speak of the father's influence on Ian's work, of its having "a granite dourness and a hardness"—as if this were as much a matter of heredity as of example.[52]

## The Cultural Inheritance

The cultural milieu of the family of origin affects the likelihood that talent will be recognized and encouraged. As a rule, it is at the higher socioeconomic levels of society that personal expression through music, writing, and drawing is most likely to be valued. Most of this interest is not in any sense vocational; creative activity is viewed primarily as a pleasant pastime, as an escape from more mundane obligations, and to some extent as an ostentatious display of superior status.

Some of the men and, even more so, the women in our sample— especially the British women born before 1880—grew up in homes where the company of artists was actively sought, where it was fashionable not only to arrange for a daughter's music lessons but also to provide instruction from a drawing master at school or sometimes privately. Teaching her to draw and sketch was, as one authority put it, intended chiefly "to occupy maidens' minds with a harmless pursuit. . . . Painting in water colours was considered a particularly safe occupation for a young lady," with the drawing master or mistress at private seminaries having also "to ensure that each of the fee-paying young ladies produced a presentable copy of an engraving to be viewed by their mammas on the annual open day."[53]

The childhood of Catherine Maude Nichols, the oldest of the British women (born in 1847) and the first "lady fellow" of the RSPE, was spent in just such a milieu. Her father, a much-respected surgeon, was a dedicated Liberal, and at one time mayor of Norwich, and her parental home a meeting place for the leading literary and political lights of the city. Several members of the family had an intimate acquaintance with painting. For some generations, they had rented a large farm near where the venerable Norwich artist, John Crome, used to paint. Two of "Kate's" aunts were reputed to have received lessons from him for some ten years. Dr. Nichols collected oil paintings. He hoped his daughter would be a painter of oils and willed her money for that explicit purpose.

Nichols dated the love of art she "inherited" from the time she was six years old and began by drawing from natural objects. As she grew older, she taught herself from a skeleton belonging to her father, followed this with the usual year or two of tuition under a clever drawing mistress and then with a couple of terms at the local art school. She later insisted—even boasted—that she was completely self-taught, that no professors had ever instructed her in the use of oils, watercolor, miniature work, or etching. Her real training, she said, came through painting from flowers and buds and from visits first to English and later to Continental galleries, as well as from many sketching tours. In this she may have made a virtue of necessity. For in these early Victorian times, women with serious intentions found professional art training hard to obtain, not only in Britain but even more so across the Atlantic.

Anna Lea Merritt, a Philadelphian born in 1844, grew up in a far less artistically supportive milieu. Her well-to-do Quaker parents were ready to send her to the best schools available to women, to educate her mind, but they had neither much regard nor sympathy for her obvious artistic talent. Black silhouettes were the only portraits permitted in a home altogether "without picture-papers or picture postcards or picture books or photographs or advertisements or posters or any pictorial display whatever."[54] Hence it was a wonderful day for her when she was taken by a kind grandmother to a small exhibition of English watercolors: "There were many beautiful pictures, but the enthralling one was *The Light of the World* by Holman Hunt. . . . With that picture, the influence of art on me immediately began. From that day I craved the power of expression. . . . It was only necessary to provide the pencils and paper."[55]

But art had as yet no firm foothold in the United States, and the idea of a woman becoming a professional artist, even though there were some, seemed quite far-fetched. Most people simply did not think of women as artists or of artists as women.[56] When another Philadelphian, also born in 1844, insisted at age sixteen that, contrary to the wishes of her affluent parents, she "must" study art, they sent Mary Cassatt off quietly to the Ladies' Classes at the Pennsylvania Academy of Art. The Civil War made it difficult to head for Europe, and besides, her father once declared that he would almost rather see her dead than become an artist.[57]

Nevertheless, it is most unlikely that Nichols or Merritt or Cassatt would ever have become artists, despite their resolute early desire, had they not been born into a milieu where someone recognized their talent and where the families had the means of nurturing it. The women etchers of a later generation had an easier time of it.

One of these was Sylvia Gosse, daughter of Sir Edmund Gosse, an eminent Victorian man of letters and a central figure in the artistic and literary world of London. Her mother, Ellen ("Nellie") Epps, from a wealthy mercantile family of cocoa importers and chemists, had aspired to be a painter and gave in to Edmund's persistent courtship only after he pledged to allow her to paint every day, which she did, even after her three children were born.[58] Still, Sylvia's artistic inheritance derived more from the drawing room than from the studio.

The Gosses knew almost everybody "worth knowing" in Victorian London. In their home there was the constant excitement of people coming and going. Aunt Laura Epps was a regular exhibitor at the Royal Academy and wife of the celebrated painter, Sir Lawrence Alma-Tadema. Among her mother's closest friends were two of her former classmates at Queen's College, Harley Street: Catherine Maddox Brown, daughter of the Pre-Raphaelite painter, and Theresa Thornycroft, both of whose parents (and brother) were well-known sculptors. Thornycroft's son was Siegfried Sassoon, the war poet and also a close friend of Gwen and Jacques Raverat. Regular callers included Thomas Hardy, Henry James, Robert Browning, Walter Crane, Rudyard Kipling, and Rider Haggard.

The rarefied atmosphere obviously rubbed off on young Sylvia. She was encouraged to paint and draw from an early age. As she happily wandered about the house, she would stop to sketch anything that pleased her, most usually birds and animals. Her father took pride in the promise she showed. He saw to it that she had training up to professional standards to supplement the art classes for children that she took from still another aunt who was a figure painter.[59] After her formal training at St. John's Wood School of Art and the Royal Academy Schools, she became a pupil of Walter Sickert, another visitor to the Gosse household.

Not only did the family circles of Gwen Raverat and Sylvia Gosse overlap, but the parents of both were well acquainted. Gwen's father, George Darwin, the son of the famous naturalist, was the Plumian professor of astronomy and experimental philosophy at Trinity College, Cambridge, at the same time that Edmund Gosse held the Clark lectureship in English literature there. Although Gwen's mother amused herself by painting, as befitted a lady in her position, she was not by temperament a dilettante. She was convinced that every girl should be brought up to have some occupation; having settled on Gwen's becoming a mathematician, she was disappointed at her daughter's "obvious mathematical idiocy."[60] The main artistic stimulus came from a drawing teacher with whom Gwen took lessons and who became the center of her existence.[61] The teacher took the children to sketch buildings, streets, trees, and animals. She taught them about architecture and perspective and anatomy. The opportunities were there for Gwen to seize. She was only thirteen when she saw one of the big Rembrandt exhibitions in Amsterdam, which sent her "absolutely mad." She came to treasure a little book of reproductions of Rembrandt drawings and etchings someone had given her, even slept with it by her bed for several years. It was this series of influences that gradually caused her career aspiration to crystallize.[62]

Some men, too, benefited from a stimulating and supportive milieu. For one, there was C. R. W. Nevinson, who owned up to being "unlike most artists born into the most exquisite intellectual ambiance." He was the son of a well-known writer; his mother was well educated, fluent in French, and hooked into artistic circles. Both parents were as much at home on the Continent as in London. As a young boy, Nevinson recalled, he was privy to all kinds of conversation and gossip—about the latest *bon mot* of Whistler or Oscar Wilde; about the bold bad doings at the Langham, the famous art club; or about Gordon Craig, later Isabella Duncan's lover, who lived nearby. He, too, began with private drawing lessons and was permitted to draw at the studio of his teacher, who sometimes took him along in his gig to sketch architecture. By age fifteen, Nevinson had devoured Camille Mauclair's books on Renoir, Manet, Degas, Sisley, and Pissarro, and he had heard of Gauguin and Cézanne and even of the " 'mad' paintings of van Gogh some five years before their 'discovery' by Roger Fry and the dealers." During discussions, which also touched on literature, politics, and music, some artist might take him aside to talk painting for hours. Nevinson, like most boys from such privileged families, was sent off to an elite boarding school (a "hell on earth"), but after a few unhappy years he went off to St. John's Wood, then more or less a preparatory school for the Royal Academy Schools.[63]

## Competing Social Values

Gosse, Raverat, and Nevinson were the beneficiaries of an unusually supportive milieu. Others were advantaged by social connections or family wealth. To estimate how many painter-etchers came from such privileged backgrounds, we broke down the sample as best we could by social origin. Information was often sketchy. Nevertheless, we conclude with some confidence that, judged by wealth and/or education of parents, at least one quarter were inheritors of cultural capital. Many more women than men—especially among the British—fall into this category. The majority of other men and women were not, however, impoverished. Nor did they come from what might today be considered a culturally deprived background. A more modest milieu could still function as a bridge, even if only to the extent that a child's developing interest was shared and stimulated by some other relative or family friend. To be sure, the bridge was just as much economic as cultural insofar as parents were able to provide a son or daughter with the extended moratorium on self-support they most needed before they could stand on their own feet as artists. Some parents in quite modest financial circumstances were willing to sacrifice to facilitate a talented child's success in his or her calling. Just slightly under 10 percent came from families so poor as to exclude any such possibility. Those who managed to overcome this obstacle were mostly men (table 5.1).

Nevertheless, even today, the bridge from the middle-class world into art can be a shaky one. Parental resistance is grounded in the ambitions they harbor for their offspring. When confronted by the announcement of a serious career intent, parents have to face up to the

Table 5.1
Etchers' Class Background, by Gender (in percent)

|  | British | | American | |
|  | Women | Men | Women | Men |
| --- | --- | --- | --- | --- |
| Social/economic elite | 21 | 14 | 21 | 4 |
| Highly educated | 40 | 27 | 25 | 8 |
| Other "middle class" | 33 | 27 | 49 | 62 |
| Modest/manual/poor | 6 | 32 | 5 | 25 |
|  | N = 48 | N = 44 | N = 61 | N = 71 |

obvious difference between school success in the form of teachers' approval, school prizes, and acknowledgments in graduation programs and, occasionally, in local papers and occupational success, defined in terms of financial rewards and social prestige.[64] Their fear for their children's future is twofold: that they will never attain the material symbols of success and may never even be able to support themselves and that they will fall victim to the reputedly bohemian life that artists lead. Aesthetic and expressive values conflict with the values of economic success and social respectability.

To overcome their parents' objections etchers could marshal the support of respected authorities or convince them by a succession of failures in more acceptable fields. William Rothenstein recognized that his father was "proud enough of my drawings, and of the praise they won from his friends, [but] hoped that I would nevertheless do as most solid merchants' sons then did, and follow in his footsteps." Faced by his son's stubborn persistence, he finally agreed to seek outside judgment on whether the boy's drawings showed talent sufficient to justify serious study and to abide by that judgment. The famous Hubert Herkomer, head of the Bushey School of Painting, from whom the verdict was sought, rendered a positive opinion and suggested that young Will, then only fifteen, study at a local art school and then come to Bushey. A bit later, upon the further advice of the son of a wealthy local merchant who was also a gifted artist, the boy was sent off—to his delight—to the Slade School in London.[65]

The widowed father of Augustus John was even more set against a career in art for his son, even though he himself was fully alive to the claims of culture, knew his Latin, could on occasion quote a few lines from Virgil, played the piano, had composed a few pieces of his own, and in later life gave regular Sunday performances on the organ in the little local church. His deceased wife had filled her leisure by drawing and painting. But he intended his son to follow him into law. As a temporary accommodation between the two, Augustus was to join the army. The father was moved finally to accept the inevitable by highly favorable reports from the headmaster of the local Tenby (South Wales) art school where his son had been taking classes.[66] Augustus, on the other hand, believed that his father looked upon him as "an unsatisfactory type of fellow, moody and unpredictable, with no sense of figures nor respect for the value of money; it was certain I would never be any good in business: perhaps Art might be just the thing for me, since it involved irregular hours, few social obligations and no arithmetic. . . . The suspicion, almost amounting to certainty, that I was determined to go my own way irrespective of [my father's] views, no doubt moved him as a man of peace to take the easier risk."[67] The father's account also took note of the son's persistence: "Obstacles put in his way would only have strengthened his determination to become an artist." The earnestness Augustus put into his request to attend the Slade first led him to think he might after all make an artist and ultimately moved him to give his consent.[68]

Whoever held the purse strings had the upper hand in these conflicts. John Marin had first to "prove" himself a failure to his widowed but "comfortably well off" father with no interest in art. Except, perhaps, for some reproductions of French pictures, the home of the two aunts responsible for his upbringing had little to inspire such visions.[69] Neither his aunts nor his father ever expected him to do other than earn a conventional living. So, after high school and a brief stint at Stevens Institute in New Jersey, he was sent off to work, first for a wholesale notion house, where he got into trouble by scrambling orders. Then, for nearly four years, he moved through a succession of architects' offices and finally set up for himself. Marin was twenty-eight before his aunts were ready to admit that, having failed at all else, he might do no worse in art. The father was persuaded to keep his son in funds for the two years he then spent at the Pennsylvania Academy of Arts.[70]

Illness intervened in several instances to spare a son the more demanding career, military or naval, that socially ambitious parents had planned for him. In one case, the father was a painter of humble origin, who had married "above himself" to a woman with all the cultural advantages of travel and education. She was interested in music and determined that her son should have a musical career. Should that prove impossible, she meant him to become an officer in the British Navy or, failing that, to study law. He passed the examination for the Royal Naval Training College, but a bout with acute appendicitis, followed by hospitalization for five months, put an end to these plans. The son, Phillip Evergood, completed an academic education and was admitted to law at Cambridge University, where he managed to spend progressively more time on art and finally, with parental approval, dropped out to enroll at the Slade.[71]

Not every artist-parent is a willing professional role model for his or her children. Oswald Sickert, a landscape painter who had achieved neither fame nor much in the way of financial rewards, eventually gave two sons to art despite his strong misgivings. He is described as someone who lived only for art and music. Mindful of his own struggles and disappointments, he wanted a career with a more promising future for his son, Walter, and, stern father that he was, positively forbade him to study art but compromised by letting him enter the theater. His opposition weakened only after Walter appeared to have secured his future by an engagement to a woman with money of her own. The marriage, however, ended in divorce and, despite Sickert's very considerable artistic success, he was never without financial woes. But he was more fortunate than his younger brother, Bernard, who had to wait until after his father died, when Walter managed to persuade their mother that Bernard was unsuited for other than an art career.[72]

Reginald Marsh, on the other hand, "was almost literally born an artist."[73] He owed this birthright to a grandfather, whose money had enabled his parents to follow their artistic calling. But this same grandfather now insisted on a conventional education for Reginald at Lawrenceville School and thereafter at Yale, where he was forbidden to enter the life class. What he learned about art, he picked up in the artistic home environment and by his own constant drawing. He became the star illustrator for the *Yale Record*. The grandfather's wealth had thus created a cultural capital that was then passed on as an occupational inheritance through an intervening generation.

The precarious balance between the two sets of values—aesthetic expression and material well-being—is illustrated in the case of Peggy Bacon's parents. Her mother was a painter of miniatures; her father of landscapes, figures, and murals. Peggy grew up as a much-cherished only child, sharing her parents' varied cultural and intellectual life. They took her to museums, to the theater, and furnished her with large quantities of the best art materials but never directly encouraged her to be an artist. Very early in her life, the sojourns with her parents in search of landscapes and other subjects to paint put her in easy contact with painters, illustrators, and writers. The fateful year for Peggy was her last year of high school. In February, she went to see the Armory Show with her father. That summer she turned down Smith College, a school for "brainy" girls, where she had already been accepted, in favor of studying art. "Her parents wept; as artists themselves they understood the hardships that she would face." In October, her father, depressed by "a lack of patrons and the dearth of critical attention to his paintings," became a suicide in his New York studio. Undeterred by this tragic demonstration of artistic misfortune, Peggy was back in art school by the end of November, with friends of her parents paying the expenses. It would have been easier for her to have turned to Greek and Latin studies, as her parents had wished and in which she had excelled.[74]

An altogether different kind of parental resistance resided in the high value some put on social respectability. Many persons with no acquaintance or understanding of artwork falsely associate it with a frivolous life-style built on an equally precarious economic existence. Such a life, judged unacceptable for a son, was considered even more inappropriate for a daughter.

Oliver Hall, who grew up in a "luxurious home" at Tulse Hill in London, had completely "inartistic" parents, who did everything to discourage their son's interest in art despite early evidence of a distinct talent.[75] A variant on this story is that of George Elbert Burr. In Missouri, where he grew up in circumstances far less opulent than those of Hall, his father rejected the son's interest in things artistic not only for their impracticality but also as a sign of "softness." It might be fit for a woman, such as his wife, who had daily instructed the small boy in drawing and painting, but was wholly unbecoming in a man. This macho attitude was common in many parts of America, where frontier mores still prevailed and the conditions of life left little room for aesthetics. Young Burr found himself forced to go to business school, after which he joined the family's small-town hardware business. He complied for a full five years while managing to squeeze in three months of tutelage in Chicago. After some success with magazine illustration, he broke with his father and set off on his own.[76] He never got rich but, throughout his long life, found it "lots of fun to be a 'poor artist.'"[77]

Parental objections, as with Anna Lea Merritt, could also be rooted in religious conviction. The austere way of life and teachings of the Church of Scotland around 1880, when David Y. Cameron chose to be an artist, were no more hospitable to the muses than those of devout Philadelphia Quakers. Young Cameron had to contend with the intransigence of a father who was a minister of the church. Intent on steering David to a more practical career, he cajoled him into spending "two rather unhappy years learning something of business with an ironfounder who was a 'stoup' in his father's Church."[78] If David wanted to be an artist, the father made clear, he would have to fend for himself, which is exactly what the son did.

Daughters were especially vulnerable to the parental equation of life in Art and life in Sin or, at the very least, one unsuited for a respectable "lady." To be an artist was for Ilse Bischoff's father synonymous with moodiness and a bad temper. On this understanding she was subjected to a strict regimen of discipline. Whenever she and her brother got into a fight, they were severely punished so that they would never again allow their tempers full play. Having encouraged her artistic leanings as a child, her Prussian-born father had simultaneously tried to control the unbecoming temperament he associated with it. Still, he finally gave his consent, most reluctantly to be sure, for Ilse to study art in France.[79]

One way for daughters to get around opposition was to avoid marriage until they seemed condemned to remain spinsters. Anne Goldthwaite, a Southerner, has left us a charming, tongue-in-cheek, account of a confrontation sidestepped:

> When I was eighteen [1887] I came out with a reception and dance.
> . . . There was nothing to do but get invited to as many parties as
> possible and work hard to attract what beaux we could. . . . I was
> brought up to believe that matrimony was the desired end of a wom-
> an's life and a woman's career. My Aunt Molly's [Goldthwaite's legal
> guardian] favorite quotation (quoted ceaselessly) was, "Gather ye
> rosebuds while ye may," adding, "It is not I, but the dear old bishop
> who says, 'It is better to marry badly than not at all.' " But one sum-
> mer, being home on a vacation from my New York studies, I asked
> Aunt Molly, while she worked among her rosebushes, why she had
> not of late urged me to gather rosebuds. "You are twenty-three years
> old, and a girl doesn't have many chances after that age." As Aunt
> Molly was so wise in the ways of the world, I took to art as a serious
> career and abandoned matrimony.[80]

Like other women barred from seriously studying art until they proved "unmarriageable," she may have lopped a number of years off her age when at last she was able to set off for New York and eventually Paris. Such misrepresentations are common enough and by no means confined to women.

Parents' misgivings, though not totally groundless, were often misplaced. Among the art students in Paris just before World War I, Goldthwaite found no need to "play that I was living in Bohemia" as did many of her friends, including Ethel Mars and Maud Squire, two "nice Middle Western girls in tight, plain gray tailor-made suits, with a certain primness." Eight months later, one would never have recognized them: "Mars had acquired flaming orange hair and both were powdered and rouged with black around the eyes until you could scarcely tell whether you looked at a face or a mask. The ensemble turned out to be very handsome, and their conversation, in public that is, became bloodcurdling." The two enjoyed the legend they laboriously built up but in private—Goldthwaite believed—led exemplary lives.[81]

Even "cultured" parents might not encourage, and perhaps not even allow, a daughter to practice art except to fill the idle hours before marriage. Clare Leighton wrote of her girlhood in an Edwardian world as the "days when Art was highly paid and romantic, and so long as the artists were successful, the doors of Society were flung open wide to receive them." Both her parents were writers; her mother wrote serialized novels for the *Daily Mail* under the name of Marie Connor, while her father, a newspaper man, wrote adventure books for boys. Their world was dominated by a "very special, peculiar class feeling ... [and] a snobbishness that included the celebrated poet or the knighted sculptor." Clare's mother wanted her children to be brought up "most correctly." No hint of anything risqué was allowed to reach their ears, and she certainly would not let them become bohemians. If her daughter had wanted to be a writer, Clare quotes her mother, "it wouldn't have been so bad, but no woman is a lady by reason of being an artist. Only with difficulty can she be a lady in spite of it."[82]

Marie Connor also had definite ideas about education for girls; she took Clare out of school at twelve because she had had far more schooling than necessary: "School takes all the character and charm from a woman." Just the same, Clare was determined to be an artist. In this, she received tacit encouragement from her father, in whom she detected a deep "yearning to be an artist," thwarted by the pressure of having to earn a living by his writing. It was he who bought her the first oil paints as a child. She also had a number of artist relatives as role models. A paternal aunt was an actress; another aunt and an uncle were artists, products of the South Kensington and Royal Academy Schools.[83] Surrounded by artists, she had a conception of life in the studio.

The influence of even one relative could be a significant counterweight to a putdown by unsympathetic parents. The diary of Oliver Hall explicitly acknowledges his good fortune when as "a boy of seventeen, I went to stay frequently with an old uncle who lived in the English Lake District, by name, D. A. Williamson, of Liverpool. He was a landscape painter of a very high order, and full of knowledge as to the receipts and methods of the Old Masters, handed down to him by his father and grandfather, who were painters before him."[84] The more fortunate the circumstances into which an artist was born, the greater the chance of such early contact—through a parent, a relative, a neighbor, a friend of the family, or whatever. There remains the question: How did the etchers from culturally less supportive milieus come to make a decision for Art?

## Starting from Scratch

More than one out of every five among our etchers came from circumstances where incipient talent could easily escape recognition or, even if recognized, be looked upon as a luxury no one could afford to indulge. Not that parents from the lower end of the socioeconomic scale failed to appreciate their children's talent or did not aspire to a better life for them—in fact, a child's ability to draw could be considered a useful skill, a potential means of social ascent, and perhaps even a springboard to fame. McBey, the esteemed Scottish etcher, recalled that during the long years when he worked in a bank to support his grandmother and mother, he "had deep in [his] mind ... secretly nursed the dream that if I could but make a success, no matter how small, of my painting or etching it might prove to be the avenue of escape from the interminable daily grind ... [and] a future not worth facing."[85] He was the illegitimate son of a mother who began to go blind when he was about six. He never knew his father and had been cared for by his maternal grandmother.

Dreams of escape from poverty through art were shared by others, including a disproportionate number of immigrants in both Britain and America. The Klinghoffers had left Poland (then part of the Austro-Hungarian Empire) to seek their fortune in England, where Jews might live without fear of violent anti-Semitism. Clara Klinghoffer's first memories were of their flat off the Whitechapel Road, where the "stairwell ... smelled of mildew. The stone stairs were only lit at night—a feeble open gas flame—and the lavatories on each floor were dirty, and used by lots of people." Things improved somewhat as her father was able to set up a small shop that supplied mill ends to tailors in the business of repairing and refurbishing old clothing—hardly a lucrative kind of business. It was here that the mother first heard that Clara had a talent she ought not to squander. One morning a client had watched the girl sitting in a corner drawing ladies dressed in fantastic clothes of her imagination. "Turning to Clara's mother, he said emphatically, 'You have a very gifted daughter. . . .' [This] fired Mrs. Klinghoffer's imagination: she had a talented child, a *real* artist and that without having had a single lesson! Something must be done about that—but what?" Ill-informed and misadvised, the parents first enrolled Clara at a private institute in Aldgate, where she was happy drawing casts until one morning when the teacher made a pass at her. Shocked, she left the school without explaining why. Fortunately, an advertisement for the reputable Central School of Arts and Crafts came to her father's attention. The principal looked at her drawings and enrolled her immediately.[86]

The father of Raphael Soyer, similarly searching for a better life, left Czarist Russia but headed for the gold-paved streets of America. In the old country, he had been a teacher of Hebrew literature and history, a scholar whose house was a meeting place for young intellectuals and students, a father who spoke to his children of Rembrandt, Raphael, and Michelangelo. Fearful that he and his intellectual friends were spreading seditious ideas among the townsfolk of Borisoglebsk, the authorities forced him to move by refusing to renew his residence permit. In America, the family soon sank into poverty when they lost the money they had brought with them through an unsuccessful lumber venture. But their devotion to the arts never diminished. The sons were encouraged to draw and to make use of all the ready resources of New York City. Even after Raphael (and his twin brother, Moses) had to leave high school to shore up the family finances, they were still able to attend free evening drawing classes at the Cooper Union.[87]

The pride in a son's or daughter's evident skill can move parents of small means to extraordinary efforts. The Welsh parents of Fred Richards set aside a little room in the house where they lived above their small butcher shop for their talented son to use as a studio.[88] Robert Austin's father, a cabinetmaker in Leicester, set his boy "to draw something every day from life, to study nature" and apprenticed him to a lithographic establishment.[89] The mother of German-born Emil Ganso, described by him as a "peasant woman married to a brewery wagon driver," encouraged her son by buying boxes of paints whenever they went to fairs and by showing off his marvelous drawings to the local pastor. But the family was too poor to pay the four-year keep for an apprenticeship with a lithographic firm arranged by this clergyman.[90]

These inequalities in social and economic circumstances could be magnified by the unequal distribution of art training facilities. Those like Klinghoffer and Soyer, who lived in London or New York, had access to rich and varied resources. Others were lucky to be within easy reach of such pacesetting cultural centers as Liverpool and Norwich in England, Glasgow in Scotland, Philadelphia and Boston in the United States. Art institutions in smaller provincial cities—among them Minneapolis, Bristol, and Brighton—were less prestigious but not necessarily inferior to those in the cultural meccas. Mainly, they offered locals a point of entry into the larger art world. But there were many communities with no professional instruction beyond the local artist happy to accept fee-paying students. Some areas, such as the American West in the nineteenth century with its equalitarian tendencies and hostility to aristocratic culture in any form, were virtual art deserts with but a few scattered watering holes. Unless the would-be artist could escape, neither the stimulating influence of a mother nor the "artistic streak" of a family made much difference. No one was likely to take up art, much less painter-etching, without a source of art supplies.

Mahonri Young, the sculptor and etcher, spent his early years in Salt Lake City, where by the 1890s, unlike the rest of the West, there were lots of painters around—"a bunch of fellows who were . . . seriously drawing." Mahonri was allowed to draw alongside them.[91] Not too far away was Brigham Young University, where James T. Harwood taught painting and helped serious young people like Mahonri to get started on their way.

Let us reemphasize, however, that the inequitable concentration of art facilities in a few centers was no great obstacle for the wealthy, able and willing to support their offspring at the "best" art schools, wherever they were located, and to secure for them whatever preliminary instructions they might need to qualify. Nor was sending them off to Europe a problem. But, such support was clearly beyond the reach of parents dependent on the son's (and sometimes the daughter's) earning power. The geographical handicap reinforced any economic handicap, especially in America, with its greater distances and sparser settlement pattern. In this vein, one American printmaker spoke and wrote privately of her personal struggle to overcome both economic hardship and cultural isolation in West Central Illinois, where she was born in 1872. There, she and her father, a wagon maker until factory-made vehicles replaced the old handicrafts, eked out an existence from a small family farm. Helen West Heller, a wood engraver, credited her own love for wood as an artistic material to her father who was constantly whittling, carving duck decoys, and building boats in his spare time. But there was almost no opportunity for her to develop her own artistic interests so long as she remained at home.[92]

## Entry Patterns: Sponsored and Contest

For the culturally and economically disadvantaged, there are in principle only two ways to make it: charting one's own course by seizing whatever opportunity presents itself or relying on some kind of "outside" sponsorship. The careers of our etchers can similarly be divided into those forced to make it "on their own" and those favored either by fortune—with a "sponsor" somehow taking up their cause—or by institutionalized arrangements designed to ferret out young talent and so make a career in art a more viable possibility.

Here we provide no illustrations but only point to a significant national difference in entry patterns: in Britain, the disadvantaged were more likely to have made it into art through what Ralph Turner calls "sponsored mobility," while social ascent for Americans more typically occurred through the self-initiative characteristic of "contest mobility."[93] As Turner describes these mobility systems, where the contest pattern prevails, the winner takes the final prize by participating in an open and drawn-out competition for recognition. Would-be artists are required to battle for training, for a chance to exhibit, and for recognition. Though everyone is free to compete, contestants have constantly to prove themselves in a seemingly endless race. A system of sponsored mobility involves a more ordered but also a more controlled selection process. Those deemed to have the requisite traits for "success" are early singled out for special treatment that facilitates their entry into the world of art until they "arrive" and can do things for themselves.

Just about every etcher, in America no less than in Britain, had some contact with the art-school system or managed to study with one of the recognized masters. The credentials were as important as the training but, as a rule and on the average, the more prestigious the art school the faster the start. Although only a small number of students, even from the elite schools, ever really made it, the schools still exercised important gatekeeper functions. Especially, they were the main channel through which those "on the outside" and with no connections could find their way "in." But the system worked quite differently in the two countries. The extent to which etchers got their training and professional start within or outside the art school system is the subject of the next chapter.

# 6

# Gateways to Art

If the image of the "born artist" is largely a myth, so is that of the "self-taught" artist. One learns to be an artist, usually by going to an art school.[1] The artists we studied were no exception. For all but a very few, the path to recognition originated in the halls of academe though not always, as we shall see, in the Academy.

In the period during which most of our painter-etchers were ready to make a "decision for art," the training of artists, once performed in autonomous work shops with artist apprentices learning their craft from a master, had moved into professional art schools. This "academization" of art instruction, as Pevsner has appropriately called it, began with the founding of the dominant art academies—France's Académie Royale dating back to the seventeenth century, and Britain's Royal Academy to the eighteenth.[2] Those in Philadelphia and New York were established early in the nineteenth. All were intended to advance the interests of visual artists, enhance their status, and make them the equals of poets and philosophers. Attached to each was a school controlled by the academicians.

The teaching in these academies was informed by a theory that stood in sharp contrast to the worship of nature we identify with art criticism in the decades when painter-etching was becoming à la mode. From the perspective of academic pedagogy, true beauty was seen as enshrined in certain arrangements and geometrical shapes that had come closest to full realization in the art of antiquity, with its idealized version of the human figure stripped of all imperfections.[3] This premise gave rise to a well-ordered academic curriculum, with courses in optics, perspective, and anatomy, combined with practical work concentrated on exact reproduction of the minutest details and on the reconstruction of the whole figure from these elements. Students would typically start by copying two-dimensional engravings, then move to the antique casts, and only thereafter be considered ready to draw from the human figure. All too many persevered through long months, and even years, of repetitious exercises sustained only by the prospect of ultimate graduation into the joys of the Life Class.

This tradition carried over into the New World from Europe. So standardized were the acceptable techniques of painting in American schools during the 1880s, according to Joshua Taylor, "that a self-taught painter would have little chance of recognition. His language would not be understood."[4] Even today, when art styles have proliferated and the knowledge of techniques has become so widely denigrated, the art education system continues to play the same gatekeeper role that it did for almost all the artists active during the etching revival.[5]

But the gatekeeping system in the two countries was not identical. The road to recognition in Great Britain, with its publicly subsidized art schools, was clearly marked. Competitive national examinations and state scholarships facilitated the absorption of talent from local schools into the elite institutions, most of them in London. Fierce as the competition for a place may have been, the rules of the game and the steps to be taken were widely known and honored. Once in the system, the young artist could count on support. In America, publicly subsidized (mainly municipal) art schools were scarcer. Young people intent on realizing their artistic ambition, especially anyone from a nonsupportive milieu, had to be considerably resourceful. Acquiring the requisite training was, through most of the nineteenth century, at least partly a matter of luck—stumbling upon knowledge of the right school or the right teacher or finding the means to go to Europe for serious study. Success in this quest also depended to a greater degree than in Britain on how near one lived to one of the better art training facilities.

Both systems had their barriers. We have no way of telling how many poor and/or culturally disadvantaged but talented British children never even made it to the starting gate—that is, to the competition for a place—or whether some of these might have succeeded in America's more open system. What does stand out clearly is the difference in the social origins of painter-etchers in the two countries. A higher proportion of Americans, of the men especially, came from blue-collar backgrounds; among them were a number of immigrants from Eastern Europe. Would-be artists—however humble in origin—found more ways to get on the right track and had a longer time span in which to do so. There were more points of entry and fewer points of no return. But if the gates in America were more open, they were also, as we shall see, harder to find than in Britain.

In this chapter we take a look at the major schools through which our painter-etchers were inducted into art, viewing each institution from the vantage point of the artists who studied there.

## The Schools of Britain

### At the Royal Academy

In the top stream of British art education were a small number of schools that operated outside the state system. The most prestigious, certainly until the turn of the twentieth century, were the Royal Academy Schools at Burlington House in London. By 1889 the Academy could boast that, since its founding, it had given instruction to more than four thousand students.[6] By the time the last of our etchers was ready to enter art, this number would have been far larger.

The Academy was under royal patronage and students paid no fees. Admission was by examination only. Initially a candidate for admission had only to submit the required drawings. But in 1860, to everyone's consternation, Laura Anne Herford, age twenty-nine, had unwittingly been allowed into the Antique School. As she had only put her initials before her name on the drawings she submitted, it had not occurred to the judges that she was a woman. There was no regulation barring women, but none had ever applied and been accepted. After this "mishap," and avowedly for the prevention of fraud, probationers had to repeat their performance within the walls of the Academy. An unofficial quota seems also to have been set on the number of women; at least between 1864 and 1868, no woman was admitted, professedly for lack of room.[7] From 1870 female students were admitted to the number of twelve per year.[8] By then, however, women were turning to other newly established schools with more progressive or, at least, less academic procedures.

A student at Burlington House passed through a prescribed sequence, beginning with the Antique School, where instruction was under the eye of the keeper and his assistant curator, moving on to the Preliminary Painting School, and ending in the Upper Painting School, to be instructed by the Visitors, who were selected in "rotation" from a list of Academicians. In theory, every Academician was required to give a month's tuition to the school, but the most eminent among them did not always take their turn with any regularity.[9] Although a student could at any point be sent back to a lower school, it was possible, according to one report, to pass through all the schools in about eight months.[10] Most stayed longer by far. To cut down on this, studentships were reduced in 1890 from seven to five years and subdivided into periods of three and two years.[11] Students were motivated to work harder by the prospect of scholarships, whose combined total by 1900 came to £12,000. The most coveted of these supported three years of travel and study abroad, a term later reduced to two years.

For the most part, however, the Academy—its rules, curriculum, administration—was impervious to change. It was too inbred an establishment and too steeped in tradition to appeal to many of our would-be painter-etchers. Nor was it easy to meet its exacting standards without lengthy, and sometimes costly, preparation. John Copley went there for five years in the 1890s, only after extensive prior drawing lessons at the Manchester Municipal School of Art. On the advice of a Royal Academician, he supplemented these with private lessons with a well-known portrait painter. At the Academy he came mainly under the influence of William B. Richmond, a portrait and miniature painter, and of George Clausen, who may have taught him to etch.

Another alumnus was Gerald Brockhurst, an authentic prodigy who became a master portrait etcher and a Royal Academician. He was only twelve when he gained admission to the Birmingham School of Art, a state-supported institution with a reputation for instruction in precise draftsmanship. Going on to the Academy schools, he won some of the most sought-after prizes, including the Landseer Scholarship; the Armitage Medal, which in 1910 was worth £30; the Bronze Medal for Design in Monochrome for a Figure Picture; the British Institution Scholarship; and in 1913 a gold medal and Traveling Studentship for his historical painting *The Pool of Bethesda*. Even though etching had no place in the Academy curriculum, Brockhurst more than likely acquired some familiarity with that medium while yet under its tutelage, for he produced two plates the year after he left.

Mabel C. Robinson won admission after attending Lambeth School of Art, the oldest and one of the most highly reputed municipal art schools in London. At the Academy she distinguished herself by winning a silver medal for a drawing and then, while yet a student in 1902, had one of her paintings illustrated in *The Studio*.[12] The small number of women at Burlington House garnered a disproportionate number of the prizes. In 1897, four of twenty-nine awards went to women, including the one to Robinson. Between 1901 and 1910, three Landseer scholarships were won by female students.[13]

The most popular of the feeder schools, however, was not Lambeth but St. John's Wood School of Art. Mr. Bernard Ward, its principal, "had passed more students in the Academy Schools than any other teacher."[14] Its fees, while hardly forbidding, could be further reduced for those attending only on alternate days. Etchers who "prepped" there, like Sylvia Gosse and C. R. W. Nevinson, were more likely to be from materially and culturally privileged families than those who began at one of the many state-supported schools. Gosse had gone to "the Wood," as it was affectionately known, only after attending an English school in Brittany, where she had weekly private lessons from an elderly French painter.[15] And then, despite the five years she spent at Burlington House, she apparently felt, in retrospect, that her period of study with Sickert at Westminster had been the stronger formative influence. Nevinson, on the other hand, bypassed the Academy for the Slade because he found the work of the students there more appealing.

Nevinson has left a vivid account of student life at "the Wood" and its effect on him. There, at the turn of the century, he spent most of his days not in the Life Class but stippling away in "the Antique" with chalk stump and pointed india rubber, only drawing from the model at night. He nevertheless valued what he recalled as a "tremendous grind, demanding a completion of tonal effects and tightness of technique unknown among students today." To begin with, he had been "sloppy" in his technique and so came to believe that, had he gone straight to Paris, an idea suggested but rejected, he would have been "running before he could walk." Moreover, the teaching in the Life Class, which he finally entered, was similar to that at the Académie Julian in Paris: "The draughtsmanship was essentially a painter's method of drawing, and often colour and tone were used rather than the pure lineal draughtsmanship associated with the old masters such as Leonardo and Raphael."[16]

Nevinson nevertheless thrived in this environment. Student life in Edwardian London suited him: these were "grand days" and he could not imagine how he "packed so much work and pleasure into eighteen or twenty hours a day." Studios rented for seven shillings a week. There were "wild dances, student rags as they were called," trips to the opera, and "various excursions with exquisite students, young girls and earnest boys; shouting too much, laughing too often." Academicians served as visitors. Yet, he gradually became aware—

from the people around him, most of them older than he, of "a reaction against what they called the 'pussy' paintings of the Royal Academy." His gnawing doubts about conventions in art grew into certainties when John Singer Sargent, Royal Academician and "the god of St. John's Wood," heralded Slade-trained Augustus John as "the greatest draughtsman since the Renaissance." This convinced Nevinson that "the Slade method of draughtsmanship had a liveliness and intention unknown in the misapplied energy of the old-fashioned dogmas that came to England through the salons of 1870."

The instruction at "the Wood" may not have been that different from that in other places, but it is hard to imagine a social and intellectual atmosphere quite so lively in the art schools of Manchester, Birmingham, or Lambeth. It is equally hard to imagine that Nevinson, had he gone to the Academy Schools, would have found there the same free conviviality. The quality of the instruction in the Upper School was still considered outstanding, but the scuttlebutt, as reported by Nevinson, had it that the reputation of the Academy among prospective students was no longer what it had been. Even so loyal a supporter as C. D. Leslie, a second-generation Royal Academician, was complaining about the fall-off in the number of students of exceptional ability and the admission of a growing proportion of "well-coached dullards."[17] Reforms in the curriculum and admission procedures sought by Academicians, including Leslie, to reestablish the preeminence of the schools had limited success. The post–World War I generation of art students no longer accepted the old ideals, and the administration of the school was pretty much in disarray.[18] By 1927 what remained was "not so much a School, as a rather freely-run life class" with students working when and, to a great extent, as they pleased. Its preeminence as the portal through which passed the respected, rich, and respectable portrait painters of the future was mostly a memory. Meanwhile, several equally viable alternatives had emerged.

## The Slade School of Fine Art

In 1871 Edward Poynter, professor of painting at the Slade School of Fine Art, explained in his opening lecture that this new institution was not meant to compete with the Royal Academy but rather to reform art teaching. While training would still be oriented toward the fine arts, the time spent drawing from the antique with its emphasis on elaborate stippling, rubbing out, and niggling in again would be shortened in a setting more congenial to experimentation. Impressionist influence was evident from its inception, and Alphonse Legros, who in 1876 succeeded Poynter as Professor of Painting, promulgated a realism to reflect life as it is. He subscribed to determined line and brush work, stressing definiteness of stroke.[19] While painting was encouraged through competitions and prizes, Legros put great emphasis on disciplined drawing and, like his predecessor, wanted to keep time spent in the Antique at a minimum. As soon as students evidenced sufficient skill and accuracy in drawing, they were to proceed to the Life Room to draw and paint from the nude. At least once a term Legros gave a demonstration of his own prowess as a draftsman, painting a head accurately and with great speed, completing a portrait in eighty to one hundred minutes. Under Legros and his two successors, Frederick Brown and Henry Tonks, the Slade was to achieve a great reputation for turning out line draftsmen.

One-fourth of our artists, men and women alike, are known to have studied at the Slade—some under Legros, some in the early Brown-Tonks years, and others after the Great War, when Tonks succeeded Brown. Legros, it may be recalled, had been a key figure in the etching revival in France. He continued to train etchers even after his appointment to the Slade, where he set up an etching studio on the top floor of the Gower Street building. Frederick Goulding, the Master Printer, helped him instruct students on Saturday mornings. Among those who trained there were Charles Holroyd and William Strang (who assisted in the etching class while yet a student), as well as Feodora Gleichen, Elinor Hallé, and Dorothy Tennant, all three of whom, though little known as artists today, were early members of the Royal Society of Painter-Etchers (RSPE). Walter Sickert had also studied with Legros at the Slade for several months before going off to join Whistler. But these six names hardly exhaust the long list of Slade students among our painter-etchers.

From its beginning the school appealed to women. Girl students thronged to the school in their "art-embroidered pinafores or overalls."[20] The girls, in fact, may have outnumbered the boys, and their presence in the Life Class could be unnerving to a boy fresh from a public school: "Imagine a large studio, very hot and stuffy, crowded with girls and young men at their easels; and over there, erect on a platform, a curly-haired Italian model, nude except for a loin-cloth. Here was a social revolution. When Ruskin was a boy, society would have been alarmingly shocked by a life-class where young men and women would study together from the nude [without keeping anyone from working]. Nurses in attendance at a hospital could not have been more composed and earnest than the girl students."[21]

Young Will Rothenstein, whose year at the Slade was spent chafing in the Antique Room where Legros thought he might gain a sound basis for drawing, judged the women "austere, as was the atmosphere of the whole school." Hardly any of the older students ever spoke to him and, as he recalled it, men and women rarely met after working hours.[22]

More agitated by the presence of "pretty and original" ladies was a Mr. Slinger, another of Legros's assistants. He kept "devising plans to keep Cupid away," an obsession that came to infect even the more tolerant Legros: "One day a tiny retriever puppy was brought by someone to the school; and I [a woman student], seated on the basement steps, was kissing its tiny forehead and sighing, 'Darling! Darling!' All at once, Legros flashed into view like an angry cat. 'Ha!' he cried indignantly; then changing his tone suddenly: 'Oh! ce n'est pas ce que je craignais!' "[23]

Endeavors to discourage friendships between the sexes obviously fell short of complete success. In the cohort of Augustus John there was certainly much camaraderie between male and female students. Marjorie Lilly of a later generation tells us that in her days at the Slade before the Great War "the girls were curiously apathetic about the men students, taking them for granted as part of the furniture of the place." Deviations were not tolerated. Once when a "pathetic little couple" met in the Antique and wandered about hand in hand, they were hauled into the staff room and reminded that the Slade was not a matrimonial agency: "the poor little girl dissolved in tears."[24]

Notwithstanding occasional amusements, most students worked seriously. Loiterers were the exception. Legros always encouraged the best students, but "even clever girls felt his whip when they didn't work hard enough to improve rapidly."[25] He did not talk much. His English was bad, and what he had to say had to be translated by assistants. Mainly he inspired by example. The Slade, in the words of an early student, was a "happy and diligent oasis, with the immense realities of London lying around it almost unexplored."[26]

It was also socially more respectable than other art schools. The large endowment from the estate of Felix Slade, the lawyer, landowner, and distinguished collector for whom it was named, put the school on a sounder financial footing than other private schools and yet left it free of state regulations and restrictions. Admission was noncompetitive. There were no specific entrance requirements beyond approval of the applicant's drawings by the professor and a short interview. Being part of a university college gave it additional status.[27] Many parents naturally preferred having their children, especially daughters, go to the Slade rather than to South Kensington with its more diverse student body. Tuition in 1900 was 18 guineas a year, the same as at St. John's Wood. There were six scholarships recognizing proficiency in drawing and sculpture, each worth £35 a year for a period not to exceed three years.[28]

In the heyday of the Slade, students were of all ages and nationalities—"aesthetic dandies, foreign immigrants, retired officers, debutantes, blue stockings, intellectuals, Bohemians, and, above all, plenty of beautiful and decorative Slade girls."[29] Nevinson's peer group, just before the Great War, was an odd assortment of people, including

> two outsize Germans, who were dwarfed by a giant Pole with scowling brows, tight check trousers, and whiskers eight inches long. . . . There were Claus and [Rudolph] Ihlee, a retired major or two in white shirt-sleeves and cuffs, and Stanley Spencer with uncombed hair and a cockatoo, looking like a boy of thirteen. Mark Gertler was there, looking, with his curly hair, like a Jewish Botticelli. There were several very old gentlemen; a completely civilized-looking Gilbert Solomon now secretary of the R.B.A. [Royal Society of British Artists]; a long, thin fellow named Helps; Benson, already yellow with cigarette smoking; and I think Paul Nash and Ben Nicholson, very correct and formal. The atmosphere was as solemn as it was uncouth; self-consciousness ruled.[30]

Nash, himself, likened the atmosphere to "a typical English Public School seen in a nightmare, with several irrational characters mingled with conventional specimens."[31]

These unmistakable signs of bohemianism in the accounts by Nevinson and Nash were the heritage of an unusually large group of talented and high-spirited young people who had entered just about the time Legros's tenure had come to an end. Good pupils in any such school, observed D. S. MacColl, a product of the flowering of the Slade under Legros, "come by batches; contagion and emulation spur the leader on and pull others in his train; by general consent [Augustus] John was the center of this second flowering at the Slade."[32] John entered the Slade in 1894, soon after Frederick Brown arrived from his previous position as headmaster of the Westminster School of Art. Brown brought with him Wilson Steer as teacher of painting and, shortly thereafter, Henry Tonks as his assistant professor. Tonks was a surgeon who had impressed Brown with his demonstrations of anatomy in the Westminster evening Life Class. Asked by Brown to join him at the Slade, Tonks left medicine to become the "terrible Tonks" who, together with the more kindly Brown, trained many of those who after the war made names for themselves in British art.

But the school was criticized as too single-minded.[33] It certainly did not fit every temperament. The reticent Brown was a dedicated teacher opposed to any superficial path to success that followed current fashions. His teaching and drawing, like those of Legros, were based on the old Italian masters. One learned to draw with the point and by the character of the contour, rather than by the mass in tone with dark hatching or stippling, which was the practice in the government schools of art. Students had either to accept the basic principle that drawing was the representation and expression of form by the study of contours and nothing more or abandon the course.

Brown formulated these principles, but his assistant professor purveyed them with a sometimes terrifying put-down. Marjorie Lilly remembered Tonks's attack on a new student whose general inefficiency aroused his ire: "Your paper is crooked, your pencil is blunt, your donkey [drawing stool] wobbles, you are sitting in your own light, your drawing is atrocious. And now, 'fixing her with his piercing eye,' you are crying and you haven't got a handkerchief."[34] There may have been method in this madness, inasmuch as he believed that not more than two or three in every thousand students would ever do anything intrinsically worthwhile.[35] Since there was a shortage of space in the Life Room, and Tonks was concerned with maintaining standards, his tactics worked; those without talent—or perseverance—never made it beyond the Antique. John, who had received kindlier treatment, perceived a "natural benevolence under [Tonks's] austere and forbidding mask." Teaching drawing was his passion, and "the Slade was his mistress."[36]

Tonks, with his sharp tongue, nearly put an end to Nevinson's career. On his first morning at the Slade, Brown had looked at the young man's life drawings and told him he could skip the Antique and go straight to the Life Class. In came Tonks to make his inspections. At seventeen, Nevinson was highly vulnerable to the style of verbal whip-lashing so frequently practiced by Tonks, ostensibly for the student's "own good." Without being "unpleasant," the master asked him to define drawing, a thing he did to Tonks's satisfaction by avoiding any mention of either tone or color and using only the word outline. Nevertheless, the intensity of the interrogation shattered the young man's self-confidence. Miserable as this encounter left him, Nevinson managed to get through his first year at the Slade while quickly making his mark in the art world of London: his work was being noticed, he was exhibiting, and he had been encouraged by Walter Sickert and praised by some leading critics. Then came the unexpected: Tonks advised him to abandon art. Nevinson went off to Switzerland where, after much soul-searching, he persuaded himself to ignore the devastating advice.[37]

*Other Private Schools*

In and near London there were other prestigious schools with studio courses. Nevinson took to "dropping in" at Heatherley's, where he learned to paint from the people around him. This school, like St. John's Wood, was geared toward training candidates for the Academy Schools. Founded in the 1840s, Heatherley's could boast that in its first six decades it had graduated no less than twenty-five future Royal Academicians. Two of our women etchers enrolled there: Elyse Lord before the Great War and Cecil Leslie after it ended. Leslie enrolled because students were encouraged to draw from life or the costume model as soon as possible, with no need to spend time in the Antique. When she left Heatherley's, she took with her an old etching press left there by Ernest M. Shepard, who gained fame as illustrator of *Winnie the Pooh*.

Another small private school attended by two of our women etchers was established and run by Louise Jopling (Rowe), the first woman to be elected to the Royal Society of British Artists. Herself married three times, Jopling deplored the common notion that women artists could not combine career and marriage. An excellent teacher, she could give special attention to each student in her small class. The "At Home," held one day every month at the school, "developed occasionally into quite social functions."[38] Winifred Austen, who became a splendid etcher of birds and small animals, and Alice Goyder, a Yorkshire watercolorist who also etched, met in these pleasant studios to remain lifelong friends. They and other Jopling pupils earned more than their share of prizes in art competitions.

The privately run Herkomer School of Fine Arts at Bushey, opened in 1883 in a Hertfordshire village thirteen miles from London, was a somewhat larger enterprise.[39] Sir Hubert Herkomer, its founder, had in mind a "little Art Republic" of students, male and female, working in a cluster of studios. All one hundred—the enrollment limit—lived in the village, which was given over almost entirely to their accommodation. Lodgings were let at a fixed price not to exceed a guinea a week, fairly expensive at that time; tuition was 18 guineas a school year. A corporation owned the buildings and saw to the financing. The professor drew no salary; by 1887, two scholarships worth £30 each were available, one open to a woman, the other to a man.

Herkomer, an etcher as well as a painter, supervised all work. He was reputed to be a harsh taskmaster, impatient with any students who thought they knew more about proper methods of painting than their mentor. He saw no one but himself qualified to judge students' achievements. Those who "failed to reach the highest art" (painting) were to be introduced to other branches of art, such as engraving and etching; there was a thoroughly well organized printing establishment in the professor's own studio, where students might pull their own proofs.

Between classes, students were free to enjoy a game of tennis or chess or to lounge on the grass. In the summer (when hot), men seldom wore coats and the women came out of their studios, their colored pinafores bedaubed with paint. There was a school magazine called *The Palette*, as well as homegrown concerts, theatrical productions, and other diversions after instruction that lasted well into the evening. Herkomer took it for granted that where so many young people were thrown together, friendships between men and women would develop and often be followed by engagement leading to marriage. But he refused, from the start, to enroll married women and, consistent with his belief that wives should devote their lives to the "happiness of [their] husband and children," expelled any woman who married while at the school. Students learned to keep engagements secret lest their professor turn them out.[40]

Mary A. Sloane and Margaret Kemp-Welch were the only two of our etchers to have studied at Bushey. Kemp-Welch, torn between music and art, was persuaded by her older cousin Lucy, the animal painter and then an assistant to Herkomer, that Bushey was the place for her. Still in her teens, she spent several happy years there before going on to the Royal College of Art.[41] Sloane, too, coupled study with a short stint at South Kensington.

## The Royal College of Art

Through the gates of the Royal College of Art passed a great number of our painter-etchers on their way to a career in art. The founding of the school at South Kensington, initially named the Normal School of Design, was part of a general government plan to strengthen the trading position of British goods by upgrading the skills of industrial designers, in whose training Britain lagged far behind France. It evolved to become the National Art Training School and in 1896 received permission to call itself the Royal College of Art (RCA), which we here adopt as the generic term.

To the planners it did not seem feasible to train designers without imparting to them some knowledge of fine art. But given the embryo state of art education, who was to impart the knowledge? So it was that, from the beginning, the RCA was destined to become a center for training teachers for the local and provincial schools of design (and art). For better or worse, the original purpose of the institution became progressively obscured by the "fluctuating motives of students, staff and administration."[42] That local industry failed to come up with sufficient scholarships for tradesmen was but one reason that the school alternated through its long history in its emphasis on one or the other of its several objectives.[43]

Two out of every five men and one of every three women in our sample secured all, most, or some of their training at the RCA. The first of them to arrive, in 1864, the year in which Delâtre, fresh from France, gave demonstrations in printing to the etching class (taught by J. R. Lane, an Academy associate), was John Park from North Shields, Northumberland. The fourteen-year-old boy had won one of the first national scholarships offered to industrial students already engaged in trades that depended on decorative arts; he was graduated in 1871 to become perhaps the youngest art master in the kingdom. Scholarship holders received tuition plus an allowance, which by 1887, amounted to 25 shillings a week for a session of about forty-two weeks. Also admitted free and allotted 10 to 35 shillings a week were students-in-training, a select group who, having taken a first certificate of the third grade from their local schools, would train to become art mistresses and art masters.[44]

These two categories of students were for many years the mainstay of the school. Also qualified to compete for admission and a somewhat smaller weekly allowance were students at the Royal Academy who intended to become teachers after attending either the Life Class or the Upper Division of the Architectural Class for six months. This allowance could, however, be withdrawn if they failed to obtain the Art Class Teacher's certificate and complete the work for the first certificate of the third grade within three terms. Certain students from district and suburban schools of art (such as Westminster at the Royal Architectural Museum and Lambeth) could also be admitted as Free Students for one year. Equally welcome were those who paid fees; there was a separate division for them. Males in these evening classes paid £2 a week, females, £1.

The RCA had been co-ed in principle, but less so in practice, since its founding. First located in Somerset House, it had to move in 1852. The men went to Marlborough House, while the female contingent was sent to Bloomsbury. When suitable space became available at South Kensington a decade later, the women, feeling quite comfortable and happy where they were, refused to rejoin. With the approval of Queen Victoria, they formed themselves into the Royal Female College of Art. But South Kensington had little difficulty in finding its own women students.[45]

Public money spent on art education was primarily meant to help the "male artisan [paid by the hour or week] of the humbler classes," but there was no way to withstand the growing demand for art education among "better-class" females. Those at Bloomsbury were drawn mostly from the middle classes.[46] This class bias carried over to South Kensington and is consistent with one of our findings: the women in our sample who attended the RCA were of higher class origins than the men; several were from definitely privileged backgrounds. Moreover, a teaching philosophy that emphasized draftsmanship as the basis of good design, even for those training as ornamentalists—an unintended tribute to the strength of the Academy tradition—tended to tilt students toward the fine arts. Thus, as early as 1888, more than a quarter of the 426 students attending the RCA were studying to become fine artists.[47]

George Clausen, one of the most distinguished of the early national scholars, was one of these talented apprentices whom study at the RCA lured away from industry. He received his scholarship in 1871, after having attended evening classes for three years while employed as a draftsman. Faculty, he had discovered, did not always treat students with kid gloves. Years later Clausen still recalled these acerbic remarks addressed by Francis Moody, instructor in decorative arts, to a new class of national scholars:

> "Now gentlemen, you come to me here, picked students from all over the kingdom, and I would like to see how much you know. I will ask you to draw now, from memory, some familiar objects." I forget which they were, but I think one was a hansom-cab and another a

dog. . . . Then he [Moody] collected the drawings. Before he put them up, he said, "I have a little daughter at home, ten years old, who has had no instruction in drawing; and last night I asked her to draw the same things I'm asking you to do. Of course yours will be immeasurably better." But unfortunately, when they came to be put up, they were not! Then he said, "Now, Gentlemen, I will tell you what you know. *You know nothing!*" and so he reduced [the students] to a humble and receptive frame of mind.[48]

Nevertheless, Clausen remembered his teachers as "good easy men," who let the students go very much their own way and "muddle through." It was, however, the contact with other students and the London they explored together that he regarded as responsible for his full initiation into the art world.[49]

A full generation later, Sylvia Pankhurst, of suffragette fame, was still experiencing a kind of "scathing criticism" from teachers, which created "abject feelings of incompetence" in her and her fellow students. "On the whole they were a body of very anxious young people. They dreaded the day when their scholarships would come to an end and leave them the task of earning a living in a very precarious profession."[50]

The uncertainties of industrial employment moved many, whatever their original intent, to obtain the Art Master's Certificate that qualified them to teach. As a result, those aiming to be art teachers came to outnumber the prospective industrial designers. One former student contemptuously dismissed those going after certificates as having very little interest in art. These "cakey men," whom no one ever expected to come to any account as artists, he recalled, nevertheless hogged the prizes.[51] Women also took their share but saw themselves passed over for the best teaching posts. In the first decade of the twentieth century, they made up 30 percent of the graduates but only 12 percent of those who became art teachers.[52]

By the time the institution became a Royal College, there was little doubt that it had "more or less forsaken the chief ambition of its founders in favour of the study of fine art and the training of art teachers."[53] The appointment to the directorship of Walter Crane, a socialist who shared the political and aesthetic ideals of William Morris, was intended to infuse new life into the design side of the curriculum. Though he remained head of the college for less than two years, his successor, Augustus Spencer, continued to direct the college toward applied art to an extent that would have astonished the principals of an earlier generation.[54] With a major reorganization in 1901, the curriculum was greatly expanded. Now there were four schools: architecture, painting, sculpture, and design.

What the college never became was a training school for industry. Among students attending during the first decade of the present century, only a third became designers and craftsmen; nearly all the rest had gone into teaching, the majority of them in full-time posts. This put the RCA into strong competition with the Slade, even though only a small minority ended in the "fine arts." In response to this situation, a Royal Commission sitting in 1924 decided that something must be done to get craftsmen scholarship-holders back to the industries upon completion of their RCA course. But the majority of students, either unaware or not greatly concerned that a commission was sitting, did not alter their plans, fully assured that it lacked the power to drive them back if they did not want to go back: "Better a successful artist like Vermeer than a discontented and probably inefficient painter of Delft ware."[55] After the war, when William Rothenstein became principal, the RCA would eclipse the Slade as the leading English school of art.

Each year only about fifty of all the students attending government schools throughout the British Isles were considered advanced enough to be sent on to the RCA. If they did indeed represent the best students in the kingdom, then one could assume that the ability of each would be improved merely by the chance to mix with others equally or more brilliant. That was indeed the underlying principle, and the school environment was certainly hospitable to sympathetic companionship in and out of the classroom, the refurbished quarters "magnificent and palatial" compared with the art schools of Scotland and other parts of the country.[56] There was a lady superintendent whose sphere included the social life of the college and the varied interests of the students outside the curriculum. Men and women participated equally in the limited student governance. The Minute Book of the Students' Common Room is revealing of student concerns before the Great War.[57] These focused on social life—on providing teas and other amenities, as well as such matters as the "behaviour of certain male students in and outside of the Common Room." But then the war raised new issues: there was the matter of Christmas gifts to students serving with the colors, the need for increased government scholarship allowances in view of the "abnormal conditions now obtaining," and a protest against the low salary advertised for an assistant master at the Halifax School of Art. Near the war's bloody end, the officers considered the Sketch Club's proposal for a general meeting to discuss the exclusion from the school of conscientious objectors but unanimously rejected it.

Both the minutes and the RCA student magazine indicate that several artists we studied had been active participants in student life at the college. But for them, as well as for most others, life at the school was remembered most vividly as life in the etching room. Short's early classes had had only five or six students, but under Crane's reorganization, etching had been recognized as one of the advanced technical subjects to be taught in the upper school. No one could be admitted without first demonstrating the requisite proficiency in drawing and approval by the headmaster.[58] So valued did Short's teaching become that his class expanded into a School of Engraving, the most famous of its kind in the world, issuing its own diplomas and with students numbering between sixty and seventy.[59]

More and more it was through the RCA that talented youngsters from all over Britain found their way into art careers. To be sure, some thought the college's routines and regulations too constraining; William Lee-Hankey, for one, in "order to maintain his independence" forfeited his scholarship and took off for Paris. On the other hand, the reputations of the schools of art governed by municipal and county councils of education had come to depend increasingly on the number of RCA medals and scholarships awarded to their students each year. Thus, the Regent Street Polytech (once the West London School of Art) in 1916 boasted by way of an advertisement that it had obtained more medals than any other school in the Kingdom.

And reputation mattered, for in passing the entrance examination for the RCA, the quality of instruction at one's local school could count for as much as native talent. Robert S. G. Dent, an RCA graduate, told us that the Newport Art School, to which he had gone as a teenage boy, had no internal assessment so that, after two years of study, the only thing that counted was how well one did in the external exam. The first time he took it, along with twelve classmates, only one had passed, and he recalled that that person died from a combination of tension and overwork. Bad teaching was clearly at fault. In the better schools, nearly everyone qualified on the first try.[60]

Such obstacles were by no means insurmountable. Fred Richards, also from Newport, but of an earlier generation, had no formal schooling beyond the elementary grades. Private tutoring (by one of his teachers) helped him qualify as an "uncertified teacher" while he took drawing classes at the same local art school later attended by Dent. At age twenty-four, he won the Town Gold Medal for most successful art student of the year. This recognition in a community apparently undistinguished for its love of art spurred his ambition. He saved enough money from his schoolteacher's salary for an August holiday at St. Ives, the artist colony in Cornwall, then spent the next two summers on the Continent at the Bruges School of Painting. In 1907, when he was twenty-eight, he returned from a summer in Tangiers with rough notes to be worked into finished sketches that fall and winter. The Newport Education Authority, impressed by his work, set up a three-year arts and science scholarship to the RCA, naming Richards as its first recipient. There he became a "brilliant student," editor of the student magazine, and a disciple of Frank Short, who redirected his interest away from painting toward etching.[61]

Charles F. Tunnicliffe, a poor boy growing up on a small farm, also found a sponsor in the drawing teacher at his local school. Recognizing that he had something of a prodigy on his hands, the teacher told the boy's parents how their son might make something of his talent if given a chance. The mother was supportive; the father, though skeptical, agreed to let some of Tunnicliffe's drawings be shown to the principal of the nearby Macclesfield School of Art. The upshot was that Tunnicliffe, at age fourteen, received not just a place, but a scholarship to begin his formal training. After six years, the principal considered him promising enough to compete for a place at the RCA. And, once again, he won a scholarship, as well as £80 a year, which made it possible to stay in London for the four years required for a diploma.[62]

Scholarships could not, of course, remove the determined opposition of a parent. The father of Stanley Anderson was so dead set against his son's becoming an artist that he deliberately kept him financially dependent during a seven-year apprenticeship in his own engravers' shop. He was paid no more than the nominal wage, which, by the last year, had risen to 6 shillings a week. Out of this meager income, Anderson paid for one evening's schooling a week at the Bristol School of Art, then once out of his father's clutches, found that the British Institution was awarding a scholarship to the Royal College for an etched portrait. In a few months of day classes, he learned to etch—and well enough—to win. The scholarship provided £1 a week toward fees and keep, which he supplemented by doing some "hack-work for publishing houses."[63] Later he would claim that he had learned mostly from the masters that hung in the museums and by working on his own.

Robert Austin, whose parents sympathized with his artistic ambition, faced a formidable problem of another kind. Apprenticed at age thirteen to a lithographic firm for a mere 4 shillings a week, he attended evening classes at the Leicester School of Art. After several years, while still under contract, he won an RCA scholarship, but the firm to which he was indentured balked at letting him go. A sympathetic foreman, who had long recognized the boy's talent, came to his rescue: somehow he managed not to locate the documents through which the boy had been bound.[64] Free at last, Austin went on to win the coveted Rome Prize for Engraving and eventually succeeded to the professorship of engraving at the RCA.

## The American Schools

Faced in the early years of the Republic with a dearth of art instruction, models, opportunities to display their work, and examples and competition to spur them on, would-be artists were almost required to go to Europe for training. The first formal art school dates back to 1805, when Charles Willson Peale joined with other artists and prominent Philadelphia laymen to incorporate the Pennsylvania Academy of Fine Arts. A similar venture some twenty years later brought into being the National Academy of Design of New York; its Antique School opened in the fall of 1826. While both provided inexpensive education and teaching based on the tradition of their European counterparts, entrance requirements were less than rigorous.[65] In the absence of any well-marked system, this meant that who went where was largely a matter of family support and where one happened to live.

### Philadelphia and the PAFA

In tracing the avenues through which our American artists found their way into art, we begin with the Pennsylvania Academy of Fine Arts (PAFA) in Philadelphia, the first American city to hold an exhibition of original etchings. By the late 1860s, with its student body swelling, the school had instituted some badly needed reforms, including the establishment of admission standards. Between 1871 and 1876, years when a new building at a new site was being constructed to replace the one destroyed by fire, life classes were set up by the Sketch Club, a private society; many of its students turned to the PAFA once classes resumed.[66] In 1876, Thomas Eakins, a product of the Paris atelier of Gérôme, began teaching at the PAFA. The direct approach he took to the drawing of the nude so shocked some members of the conservative Philadelphia community that, ten years later, he was abruptly dismissed.[67] Yet under his tutelage, short as it was, the academy had been transformed into "the most demanding and single-minded art school in America."[68] While Thomas Anshutz, his successor, continued on the course Eakins had set, the PAFA was soon—as we shall see—to face serious competition from New York.

Meanwhile, the PAFA offered its advanced students a unique opportunity to participate in dissections directed by a professor of painting. Every winter, something more than a fourth of the students spent a good part of their time in the dissection room with Eakins, and twice a week all the pupils listened to lectures by Dr. Keen on artistic anatomy. Also, once a year Eakins would take a large class to a suburban bone-boiling establishment, where students could dissect horses in the slaughterhouse. The purpose of this exercise was to demonstrate how beautiful objects were put together. His students might consider this exercise repulsive and certainly less pleasant than copying the frieze of the Parthenon, but if they came with any artistic impulse, Eakins believed, they would not lose it by learning how to exercise it in this hideous way.[69]

The letters of Eliza Haldeman to her classmate and friend, Mary Cassatt, show student life at the PAFA to have been rather rewarding.[70] Both girls came from educated and financially secure families, as did most who entered the academy before the Civil War. They expected to spend up to two years learning to draw before going on to specialize in painting or sculpture. Except for formal lectures on anatomy at the Penn Medical University, most classes were conducted informally without a teacher and with nothing more than on-the-spot criticism by more advanced students or by the curator. Independent study with an established artist outside the academy was the almost indispensable supplement. When the two entered in 1860, women were admitted to instruction in drawing from all but the nude model—eight years later that, too, would be possible, but they were not inclined to wait. They were not, after all, amateur dabblers but determined "to be *professionals*—to master their craft, to exhibit, and ultimately, to sell."[71] They were impatient to go off to Paris once the war ended.

Here is how Haldeman explained to her father what the academy could offer her, in a letter dated 4 February 1860:

> I have commenced taking drawing lessons from Mr. Schuchelle, that is, one of the young ladies at the Academy and myself go to his Studio

once a week, and have him criticise the drawings we made that week, almost all the Pupils at the Academy take lessons in this way. As for painting, I don't think I shall commence it at all this winter. They generally study from the Antique two winters before commencing, and one of the young gentlemen studied two and a half years here, and then went to Paris to finish, when he got there they put him to copying for a year before they allowed him to commence painting, so you see I have plenty of work before I can call myself an artist.[72]

And after nearly two years of drawing instructions from Schuchelle, she reported (on 21 December 1861) that: "We have several new pupils both male and female but Miss Cassatt and I are still at the head [i.e., of the ladies]. Most of the old gentlemen scholars have gone away and commenced to paint. . . . We keep pretty nearly together. She generally getting the shading better and I the form, she the 'ensemble' and I the 'minutia' but I am trying hard to get ahead. I have not taken my Laocoon up yet so I don't know what Schuessele will think of it. The last one he said was better in some respects than hers and worse in others. So it left us equal."[73] Though these efforts left her tired in the evening, there were limited opportunities for fun, some of it at the expense of amateur students who had no intention of becoming artists.

These well-to-do women had an easier time of it than some of their male contemporaries. Stephen Parrish, another Philadelphian, had to give years to establishing a business, which he then sold to support his art habit. Born in 1846, he was past thirty before he could devote himself full-time to the business of becoming an artist while yet supporting a wife and son. About 1882 his studio became the center of a small group of PAFA students, three of them women, who went there once a week to etch. Blanche Dillaye, a native of Syracuse, had been sent to the City of Brotherly Love to study at the Ogontz School, where young women seeking an alternative to the traditional finishing school could acquire a thorough acquaintance with literature, the arts, and science. Following a year of drawing instruction, she had a chance both to teach and begin advanced art studies at the PAFA. Here she took but one lesson in etching. So simple did it seem that she unhesitatingly submitted her name as a contributor to the next PAFA exhibition but then discovered the vicissitudes of the medium. "When the exhibition opened, her labor was represented only by an underbitten plate, an empty frame, the name in the catalogue of a never-finished etching, and the knowledge that etching represents patient labor as well as inspiration."[74] She turned to Parrish for the counsel she needed to become the first serious woman etcher in the United States.[75]

Philadelphia-born Gabrielle Clements, the second of these women, came to the academy in the most roundabout way. She was the daughter of a physician married to a genuine Southern belle; educated in the public schools, Clements was then sent, in 1875, to the highly reputed Philadelphia School of Design for Women.[76] After taking up drawing and lithography there, she went to Cornell University. Only after graduating in 1880 did she return to Philadelphia to study with Eakins at the PAFA and with Parrish.

The third of this trio was Edith Loring Peirce (also known by her married name, Getchell). Coming from Bristol, a Pennsylvania town thirty miles from Philadelphia, she attended the same School of Design for Women as Clements but left for a job in industry. For three years she designed patterns for felt druggets at the Livingston Mills in her hometown. During part of two winters in New York, she studied watercolor painting, moved on to landscape painting in oils, and then, upon her return to Philadelphia, took a studio and enrolled at the PAFA about the same time as Parrish. The two became great friends and, together with two other students, took a four-month trip to Europe. In 1886 she married Dr. Albert C. Getchell, a friend of Eakins.[77]

One of the most successful of the early students at the PAFA was Joseph Pennell, born into a conservative, observant Quaker family. Certain that art was his destiny, he had taken a newly introduced drawing class at the Germantown Friends' School, then sought admission to the PAFA, where tuition was free and the school as good as any in the country. But when he submitted a summer's artwork to the academy, his application was rejected. Nor were relatives willing to help, there being no place for art in the Friends' scheme of salvation. The upshot was "six awful years" as a clerk in a coal company's office. Still hankering for art training and not one to give up, he sent drawings in pen and chalk to the Pennsylvania School of Industrial Art. He was accepted for evening classes but soon expelled for nonattendance. However, his favorite teacher there induced the academy to take a second look, and this time he was accepted. Over objections from the shocked Friends, he gave up his clerk job to make himself into an artist. Still, his troubles were not yet at an end. Enrolled in an evening class in the Antique, Pennell was discouraged by the master, who dispensed criticism with a sneer. He then joined the day class under Eakins and was soon promoted to the Life Class. Although Eakins did not sneer, he could still be brutal, as Pennell learned when he insisted on working in his own way, drawing the model—contrary to instructions—on a large scale and with pen and ink. Pennell was obviously supersensitive. He withdrew to avoid the master's criticisms, thereby depriving himself of the very thing that art school had to offer.[78]

Altogether some seventeen of our painter-etchers came to the PAFA for at least part of their studies. While near half were, like those already mentioned, born before 1870, the academy continued to serve as a gateway to art for others who came of age later in the etching revival, including such well-known printmakers as John Sloan, John Marin, Grace Albee, Peter Hurd, and Benton Spruance.

## New York: The Academy and the League

As a mecca for would-be artists, New York City did not seriously challenge Philadelphia until the latter part of the nineteenth century, when its two leading schools—the National Academy of Design (NAD) and the Art Students League (ASL)—paved the way into art for 51 percent of our American etchers.

The school at the NAD, born in protest against the indifference of American society to the education of young artists, had got off to a bad start. Its entrance requirements were not exactly rigorous and, with students having only to pay their share of the season's fuel and light costs, the school's finances were so shaky that in 1849 it was forced to shut down for three years. To avoid bankruptcy, when it reopened a small entrance fee was imposed.[79] Money was not, however, its only problem. After the Civil War, dissatisfaction with traditional methods of teaching gradually coalesced into a demand for training more "in accord with the training followed by the artists of that time who had studied abroad."[80] In January 1870, the NAD council responded by voting to appoint Lemuel Wilmarth, an experienced teacher trained in Munich and Paris, as the first paid full-time professor. Yet his moves to institute necessary changes were stymied by a council unwilling to charge the fees needed to cover the increased costs.

As the spring term ended in 1875, word spread that the school, so as to save money, planned to close until late December. Given the academy's requirement that students draw from the antique for ten weeks at the beginning of each year, this meant that they could not take life classes until February 1876 and, in effect, would have to repeat a year. They also knew that Wilmarth's appointment had not yet been renewed nor any replacement appointed. Another grievance was the students' lack of access to the school library. All these things prompted Wilmarth and his students to move their drawing classes to another location and, for the purpose of continuing their studies, to form a new association—the Art Students League. While the liberal faction on the NAD council ultimately managed to commit the academy to adequate support and to rehire Wilmarth, their action came too late. The students voted not to return. Before very long, their student-controlled league—where classes were based on the principles of the Paris ateliers—had become a national institution.[81]


*Students of the NAD.* Until after the Civil War, the NAD had a numerically modest enrollment of students from all over the United States plus a small representation from Europe. Most were between eighteen and twenty-four years old. Many had already served some apprenticeship in art—as portrait painters, lithographers, engravers, or sign painters. Though women had been eligible for admission since 1831, they remained a segregated few confined to the Antique. In 1865, after their full integration into the student body, their numbers grew. And as the total number of students rose, the school began, in its diversity, to resemble the population of New York City. By 1901–02, foreign-born students comprised 25 percent of the student body, 33 percent before World War I, and 42 percent (156 out of 367 students) in 1918–19. The largest number of immigrant students came from Russia.[82]

The presence of so many foreign students inevitably became a source of some concern and suspicion. In an atmosphere charged with patriotic fervor and suspicion of subversive activities, the NAD council went on record as "upholding the government of the United States in the present war." Anyone not in sympathy with this action, it declared, would be asked to resign. There was simply "no room for students who are disloyal either in act or talk."[83] Meanwhile the students, too, did their best to prove their loyalty through fund drives and by deed. Among those who interrupted their studies for active service was the future painter-etcher Thomas Handforth, who had entered in 1917 with a university degree but was soon serving with the Army Medical Corps.

Among the many immigrants who found their way to the NAD was William Auerbach-Levy, brought as a child from Brest-Litovsk, Russia, to the Lower East Side of New York. A teacher who recognized his talent arranged for the eleven-year-old to take classes at the academy. His studies there continued through high school and until graduation from the City College of New York. Then, after study in Paris on a scholarship, he returned to teach etching at the NAD. Auerbach-Levy, in turn, taught Paul Cadmus, another of our painter-etchers, who had likewise begun taking art classes at a young age. But for Cadmus, who was American-born, this was no accident; he was sent there by two parents who had met when both were NAD students. Other immigrants at the school included Emil Ganso, whose poverty-stricken background we mentioned in Chapter 5; Mortimer Borne, who as a gymnasium student had won a prize in a national competition while still in Poland and, after coming to New York as a fourteen-year-old, was able to resume art studies interrupted by the onset of war in 1914; and William Meyerowitz, also from Russia, who entered the academy when he was sixteen and, in later years, took special pride in having received all his training in the United States.

Exactly how old Anne Goldthwaite was when she went to New York to study is not clear.[84] Most likely she was thirty-one when her Uncle Henry's offer to pay her expenses rescued her from a dilettantish fate in Alabama. On the way North he cautioned her never to leave the house with her gloves unbuttoned or to carry more than $2 in her purse or "to go out with any man, no matter where or why."[85] When they arrived in Manhattan, Uncle Henry placed his niece in a house for students run by two older girls "sufficiently aged" to serve as chaperones, as would have been normal in the 1890s.[86] She studied hard and progressed splendidly or, at least, "as well as anybody else." At first she heeded her uncle's advice on behavior outside the classroom. If a fellow student asked her company to an exhibition, an everyday occurrence for students, she would meet him inside but not walk with him along the street. But the good Uncle Henry's admonishments were soon forgotten. In her second year she and several of the women students found an apartment; they drew up a "constitution" covering their finances and conduct. They hired a cook no older than themselves, and kept an eye out for small jobs. One such job led her into the etching class taught by C. W. F. (Frank) Mielatz. Her experience there epitomizes the dilemmas facing a "girl student":

> Mr. Mielatz asked four of the students to bring him their portfolios. . . . The New York Water Color Society was to hold an exhibition where for the first time in many years etchings were to be included. . . . There was probably no chance that we could get in, the jury was so severe and we were not good, but he would take our

work down. . . . Before long the three men knew they were in, as they each received an invitation to the stag dinner. But what about me? I couldn't go to the stag dinner. Should there not have been some notice sent me if my prints had been accepted? The stag dinner was on a Friday night, and at seven o'clock Saturday morning (perhaps on his way home from the party), Arronson rang our bell to tell me that my four prints hung with the others! I shall remember him always for that thoughtfulness.[87]

Goldthwaite remained in New York for six years and then, like so many of the Americans, took off for Paris.

The inexpensive training at the NAD provided a golden opportunity for would-be artists from a wide range of backgrounds. But the route by which anyone arrived was not clearly mapped. There was neither a system of feeder schools or of competitive national scholarships through which talent might be groomed by local art teachers to enter the mainstream. The artists we studied mainly got there through their own persistent efforts and/or by what might most appropriately be called the "luck of the draw."

*Students at the League.* The Art Students League, from its inception, was a members' school run by students serious about becoming professional artists. School policies were set by the more advanced students. They made it a place where they could study from the nude or draped model at their own pace with teachers of their own choosing, where classes were scheduled to fit most everyone's needs, and students helped each other whenever the need for practical assistance arose. Fees were to be kept within the means of all who could make their way to the school. The result was a polyglot community with an ambience essentially democratic as well as eminently bohemian: "The impecunious student was there who knows what it is to do his patching and darning and live in an attic room, and the rich swallow-tailed student who can pursue the beautiful without any conflicts with grim necessity, was there. There were feminine students, some rich and some poor, some pretty and some homely, but everybody met on a plane of equality, for art worship was the great leveller." Mainly, however, the real attractiveness of the league resided in the image of excellence it quickly acquired. It became "the place that people went to if they didn't go to the Academy schools."[88]

The pedagogically progressive outlook of the ASL was best exemplified by William Chase, who for two decades was its most popular instructor. Chase believed in careful drawing and taught students to do this with paint and brush. But he rejected the league rule—which echoed that of the NAD—that no student be admitted to draw from life before delivering a satisfactory study of a head or torso from the antique. The disagreement led to a temporary parting of their ways. Joined by Robert Henri, he left the league to direct their own Chase School, known also as the New York School of Art. Students attracted to their evening classes were "men and women who, almost without exception, either worked or earned their living elsewhere, or . . . pursued other studies during the day. Art was to them . . . a matter of fundamental necessity proven, as it were, by the sacrifice of leisure, recreation and, by many, of hard-earned money."[89] League students were similarly motivated and, in other respects, not that different. When Chase, after eleven years, split with Henri, whose teaching philosophy was even more liberal than his own, and returned to the league, he found it sufficiently reformed to provide him with precisely the freedom he had always championed.[90] Formal entrance requirements had been dropped, leaving it to the individual instructors to enforce their own standards of excellence.

What the league offered, in addition to excellent teaching, was a range of choices and a sense of community, which it sought to make available to as many persons as possible. The number and kinds of classes offered increased steadily through the years, as did enrollment. In 1884, there were 468 students; by 1899, almost 1,000. They came, as John Sloan put it, for the "varied menu of nourishment . . . from the conservative to the ultra-modern. A student . . . can choose his studies much as he can choose his food at an Automat."[91] Wanda Gāg, for one, took full advantage of this freedom, staying in any class only long enough to understand the instructor's viewpoint and then, "taking all that was given with a grain of salt," moving on; in this way she resisted the excessive influence of any one teacher. Students were also free to enroll full-time during the day or just take evening classes. Reginald Marsh attended only "sporadically" while free-lancing for newspapers and slicks, after finishing a degree at Yale Art School.[92] A few also studied with Chase or Henri at their New York School or, like Matilde de Cordoba, took concurrent private lessons.

The sense of community, of belonging to an association of like-minded and like-spirited aspirants to a professional career in art, was positively reinforced by an active social life within the league—from daily "penny teas" in the lunch room to annual costume dances enlivened by the antics of a society of students known as the "American

Fakirs." It was equally reinforced, unfortunately, by the hostility of outsiders, fed by sometimes unwelcome publicity. Some of this focused on the annual exhibition of "fakes," first held in 1891 and continued for nearly thirty years. The idea was to burlesque "the paintings of the honored and established few," with parody and pun, sparing no one. Paintings were signed with names so evocative that no one could doubt that a portrait of "Mamzelle DeVeal Rehash" was a caricature of Irving Wiles's portrait of Mlle. Gerville-Reache or that *Mother and Son after Hay* was intended to make horse meat of a horse picture by William J. Hay.[93] The exhibition, for which admission was charged, was a moneymaker; the pictures hung on the walls were auctioned off; proceeds fed a scholarship fund. There were prizes for the best "fakes," as well as $5.03 plus a mince pie for the worst "fake," a prize offered by Zella de Milhau, one of our pioneer women etchers then studying with Chase.

The league also came under attack for championing feminine equality: not only did ladies sit on its Board of Control but they sat in equal number.[94] And it was certainly "radical" to allow women to paint from male models clad only in cloth about the loins. This practice first became a public issue in the early 1880s and, for years, rumor had it that Anthony Comstock, self-anointed suppressor of vice, would lead one of his raids against the life classes. It was not until August 1906 that he struck. With the help of two policemen, he invaded the league office, confiscated the July issue of the student magazine with its drawings of undraped nudes, and arrested the bookkeeper for allowing it to be distributed.[95] The raid outraged many art and literary societies; they saw it as an attack on all artists and on the future of American art. It strengthened student solidarity and rallied the community behind them. Comstock was forced to concede, and as "a Christmas gift," to dismiss all proceedings against the bookkeeper. The Fakirs accepted a fake apology from a fake Comstock at their next auction.

More than a third of our American sample artists attended the ASL. They came from all over the country and stayed, on the average, about two years. Some came as very young people, some after graduation from college, and some as mature adults. Prior art training was not a prerequisite, but the league did make a deliberate effort to reach out for talent; in 1901 it established ten scholarships specifically for out-of-towners, to be awarded in a competition open to students in all art schools and art departments of all colleges in the United States and its possessions.[96] Due largely to these awards, the Minneapolis School of Art became an unofficial feeder school for the league. As two of its students, Adolf Dehn and Wanda Gāg, started for New York on 17 September 1917, Gāg proudly told her diary: "We are two out of twelve [*sic*] of the entire United States and I believe that this is the first time that this honor had been conferred on any member of my school."[97]

New York, however, presented problems even for scholarship holders. For Dehn, there was the military draft; his conscientious scruples brought him a four-month confinement. For Gāg, it was not just a question of money on which to live but also of money to support her orphaned siblings. As before, her Minneapolis sponsors came to the rescue; alumni of her school and friends provided small sums of money toward her "New York struggles," and a loyal supporter, Herschel Jones, paid for her room and board. This did not keep her from going through a "long and agonized period of disillusionment [with] the city of her dreams." It was more than homesickness or the pain of her first serious love affair but anger at the ways of art teachers. The final blow came when half the money she saved from money earned painting lamp shades and other commercial assignments disappeared in a "business smash-up" and made it impossible for her, like many of her fellow students, including Dehn, to take off for Europe.[98]

Isabel Bishop, on the other hand, remembered her experience at the league "as a pretty good period." She entered just at a very high point, when a close-knit bunch of students who later became well-known artists—Arnold Blanch, Peggy Bacon, Alexander Brook, and Yasuo Kuniyoshi—were still around and an influence on students like herself. After an initial stay from 1920 to 1922, she worked in her own studio and then returned in 1925 for another three years to study design and composition. Especially, she liked the feeling of being with a group, not just alone on Fourteenth Street. Later, however, she came to think of her second period at the league as years of "false comfort."[99]

Those students with money, like Helen Loggie from Bellingham, Washington, had an easier time of it. She arrived in 1916, with the effects of the Armory Show everywhere, in a period of excitement, experimentation, and confusion in art. Not in any way financially strapped, she was able to make the most of the city's theaters, ballet, and art galleries. She lived near the school with other art students, learned portraiture from Henri, studied with George Luks, was able to take off for six months in Europe, and upon her return studied privately with Mahonri Young and John Taylor Arms.[100]

## The Ateliers: At Home and Abroad

The formation of the Art Students League had been but part of a nationwide expansion of opportunities for art education in the post–Civil War period, in which established institutions of higher education had taken the lead. Yale University had been the first to establish a Department of Fine Arts, which became a "school" in 1869, and four years later, Syracuse University established a College of Fine Arts. Yet the main impetus had come from the country's remarkable population growth between 1870 and 1890; large stretches of new territory were being settled, while cities doubled and tripled in size. One such boom town was Chicago, where art classes opened in 1866 as part of a newly formed Academy of Design, making Chicago the third city to house such an institution. Although the school was destroyed in the great Chicago fire, another school opened at the Art Institute of Chicago and soon had the largest student body in the nation. By the end of the 1880s, there were art schools at the Boston and Philadelphia museums and in many other large cities, including Cleveland, Kansas City, St. Louis, Minneapolis, Detroit, and Washington, D.C. New York alone had, by 1878, some thirteen schools and associations, including the New York Etching Club, where prospective artists could secure instruction in painting, drawing, modeling, and the various forms of applied art.

But despite the country's increasingly ample facilities, would-be artists were still following the route pioneered by older generations of "imaginative Americans [who had] turned to Europe both for 'inspiration' and for profit."[101] Our painter-etchers were no exception. A majority in each generation spent at least some time abroad, seeking out those places where their teachers had studied, particularly Paris but also Munich, which for a while was its serious rival, especially among young Americans born in Germany or of German heritage. Language posed no problem for Frank Duveneck, a Cincinnati-born artist who went there in 1870. Around him there soon formed a group of young students remembered as "the Duveneck boys." They worked together in the small town of Polling, near Munich, from which they followed their leader on his sketching trips to Venice, Florence, and other Italian cities. One of these was Otto H. Bacher, another German-American from Cleveland, who taught Duveneck to etch. They were two of fourteen Americans who exhibited at the first exhibition of the British painter-etchers in 1881.

*Abroad at Home.* With the return of artists who had distinguished themselves in the European academies, such as Chase, Duveneck, and Twachtman, the quality of instruction in American schools took a giant leap forward. Those students who, for one reason or another, were unable to go abroad, or were still waiting, often managed to study "abroad at home" by entering the studio or summer school run by some eminent artist trained in Europe.

This type of facility seemingly emerged almost spontaneously whenever there was a demand for it. Thus, in Boston, a city which housed some venerable cultural institutions but lagged somewhat behind in professional art training, William Morris Hunt in 1868 responded to a request from a group of women artists by announcing a class in drawing and painting.[102] His notice in the *Boston Transcript* spoke of "an opportunity for *women* to study painting."[103] Ellen Day Hale, one of the few *early* etchers to have studied in Boston, said that Hunt had extended his offer to men but none ever came.[104] Whatever the case, Hunt treated his female students as future professionals. They "were criticized as roughly, made to work as strenuously, praised as frankly, as men."[105] Most were mature women from the elite of Boston society, but there were also some young girls, a few of whom looked forward to a life in art.[106]

As a teacher Hunt was indeed an attractive personality. He was a Proper Bostonian and a product of the atelier of Thomas Couture, whence he had gone to Barbizon to study with Jean-François Millet; he was also one of the city's most distinguished portrait painters. Just before he opened his Boston atelier, he had completed two years of travel in France and Italy and could thus bring to his students a knowledge of French academic practices as well as contemporary French art.[107] For his teaching Hunt drew largely on his own experience. Instead of having students progress in stages from drawing to painting, he emphasized the primacy of the artist's impression or feeling and, presumably in deference to the moral climate of Boston and prevailing practice at the time, did not introduce the nude model.[108] Only when Hale visited a friend at the Pennsylvania Academy, where she attended a few classes in the spring of 1878, did she paint from a nude female model: "I found it hard but nice, she wrote."[109]

Hale was the only daughter and eldest child of Edward Everett Hale, the author of "The Man without a Country." Before coming to Hunt she probably had some drawing lessons from an aunt, who was a writer and a watercolorist as well.[110] Although she also took a class with sculptor William Rimmer at the local school of design, it was her training in Hunt's studio and at the summer school he ran at Magnolia, Massachusetts, that encouraged her to become a professional. Shy and nervous, she was industrious but seemed, to her mentor, overly serious. His advice to her, conveyed through another student, was to do more of the things that other young people did, to have the kind of happiness that belongs to youth, because "he thought it would help [her] painting."[111] Undoubtedly it was his influence that sent her to Europe by 1881. Here, too, it took her some time to screw up her courage to ask Carolus-Duran for admission to his class. She remained apprehensive before every studio visit by a professor but survived these ordeals to become a successful artist.

The first out-of-door summer school in America was started in 1891 at Shinnecock, the Indian name for the land on which it was built.[112] The extension of the Long Island Railroad east from New York City had put the area within easy reach, and the bicycle, perfected in England, made everyone want to explore the countryside. This was just before the automobile was to become popular. In residence each year were about one hundred pupils, the majority of whom were winter students of William Chase, mostly women, from New York. The idea and some of the wherewithal had come from Mrs. William Hoyt, a much-traveled lady who had learned *"plein-air"* painting in Europe. With support from other wealthy residents in nearby Southampton, she set out to woo Chase, then teaching at the Art Students League and freshly returned from a stay in Holland. They gave him land on which to build a house and a studio and sold the land between for people to build cottages on. These, together with the studio, came to be known as the Art Village, a name that still appears on local maps.

Everyone at Shinnecock was encouraged to share their love for the beauty that was in nature as in art by painting together outdoors. Chase's house was three miles from the village, and as he made his way along the connecting road, he would often offer advice to students who set up their easels by the roadside. On Monday mornings, he gave more formal criticisms in the studio building, and these open sessions turned into a diversion for local residents as well. Chase also did demonstration pieces, which he distributed as prizes for special achievements.

Students enjoyed themselves socially. There were cakewalks, charades, and German plays as a reminder of Chase's own student days in Munich. Zella de Milhau, who had supported the Fakirs' fun at the league, was also a moving spirit behind some of the frivolity at

Shinnecock. "Hardly an issue of the *Southampton Press* went by without some reference to this amazing woman. Whether it was for winning the potato growing contest, driving one of the first automobiles in the area, or showing up as a Spanish soldier at a costume party at the Art Village Studio, [she] always managed to steal the show."[113] The Shinnecock adopted her as a daughter of the tribe and named her Chiola, meaning "She Who Laughs," and the house she built in the village was called "Laffalot." That she could also be deadly serious was made clear when she and another woman went to the battlefields of France to drive an ambulance bought with money collected from local residents. A book that recounts her experiences, unfortunately, contains only one etching as frontispiece.[114]

One of Chase's prize students at Shinnecock was Charles W. Hawthorne, who himself became another great art teacher; he founded the Cape Cod School of Art at Provincetown, which for many summers attracted large numbers of students, including some painter-etchers.

*Study Abroad.* Eager as young art students were to study with Chase and Hawthorne or at other art colonies forming throughout the land, they continued to look toward Europe. In the 1860s there had been only about 85 American artists resident in Paris, most of whom arrived after the Civil War. Thereafter their numbers increased rapidly and, according to one conservative estimate, there were at least 150 by the 1870s, and the number kept growing year by year.[115] Some stayed only a few months, others for years, until war or financial catastrophe drove them home.

Cassatt and Haldeman had been part of the immediate post–Civil War exodus. Women were not yet admitted to the Ecole des Beaux-Arts, but there was no dearth of other instruction. Cassatt began with private lessons from Gérôme; Haldeman joined a class for women taught by another prominent Parisian. Neither had any problem in obtaining a permit to copy in the Louvre, where they worked endlessly, except for visits to the countryside, where they could hire local peasants to pose for them. Both ended as students in the atelier of Thomas Couture just outside Paris.

In France, Haldeman assured her parents, they were able to make do nicely with their allowances. "I find it not so very expensive to live here and now that I am out of Paris," she wrote from Ecouen, "I count my 8 hundred [dollars] will last for a year so I suppose this time [a year hence] you will see me home a good painter."[116] Living expenses in Paris were higher than in other European cities. One couple spent the year 1856 in Florence on $600, "which included renting an apartment in a palace and keeping one servant." At the same time the cost of living in Paris was the same as in New York. In the mid-sixties it cost one artist and his wife about $1,000 a year in Paris.[117] This did not prevent the city from being a magnet for throngs of art students of every nationality. Most of our painter-etchers embarked on their pilgrimage to "complete" training they had begun in the States, but there was no obligatory sequence. Those with the means could idle along at a leisurely pace. Traveling scholarships paid the way for Arthur Heintzelman and Lester Hornby, both of whom, before the Great War, left the Rhode Island School of Design to establish themselves in France, which became their home for years. Some others managed only a few months in Paris until they ran out of money.

What could be afforded depended on the needs and pleasures of the individual. A furnished room was cheaper than a studio apartment, even one shared with others. The independent "lady art student" at the turn of the century eschewed the *pension* and lived a solitary existence in her combination bedroom, sitting-room, studio "varied only by the daily visit to the school or *atelier* to which she has attached herself, the incursions of artist friends (if she be emancipated these will be of both sexes); the occasional visit to a place of amusement, when an escort is available; or the equally occasional dinner at a restaurant."[118] The more courageous women could attend mixed classes at Colarossi's, where they would "work shoulder to shoulder with their brother art students, drawing from the costume or the living model in a common spirit of studenthood and *camaraderie*."[119]

Several American painter-etchers got themselves admitted to the elite but tuition-free Ecole des Beaux-Arts. Gérôme was their particular favorite. Anyone not matriculated at the Beaux-Arts, where Gérôme was professor, could still study with him privately or with one or another of its instructors. They could also enroll in one of the numerous private Paris ateliers, of which l'Académie Julian was the most famous. Gustave Boulanger taught there until his death in 1888, as did Jules Joseph Lefebvre, who died in 1911, and Tony Robert-Fleury. Fees ranged from about $3 to $4 a month up to $8. Léon Bonnat, Carolus-Duran, and some other leading artists took private pupils for not much more. Eugene Higgins studied at the Beaux-Arts under Gérôme while at the same time attending Julian's.

The newly arrived—British as well as American—would most commonly find their way either to Julian's or to the Académie Colarossi, its closest rival. At both there were at least three *cours* per day, the morning class, beginning at eight and ending at noon; the *après-midi*, starting an hour later and ending at five; the evening class, running from seven to ten. Competitive exhibitions (*concours*) took place several times a year, with men and women competing for the same awards. We owe to William Rothenstein the following vivid picture of Julian's as it appeared to him when he arrived at the tender age of seventeen, fresh from the Slade, to find "the swarming life there vivid, exhilarating, and pregnant with possibilities." In the early 1890s, it was

> a congeries of studios crowded with students, the walls thick with palette scrapings, hot, airless and extremely noisy. The new students were greeted with cries, with personal comments calculated, had we understood them, to make us blush, but with nothing worse. . . . To find a place among the closely-packed easels and tabourets was not easy. It seemed that wherever one settled one was in somebody's way. . . . Students from all over the world crowded the studios. There were Russians, Turks, Egyptians, Serbs, Roumanians, Finns, Swedes, Germans, Englishmen, and many Americans, besides a great number of Frenchmen. By what means Julian had attracted all these people was a mystery. . . . [He] himself knew nothing of the arts. He had persuaded a number of well-known painters and sculptors to act as visiting professors, and the Académie Julian became, after the Beaux-Arts, the largest and most renowned of the Paris schools . . . there were no rules, and, save for a *massier* in each studio who was expected to prevent flagrant disorder, there was no discipline. I believe the professors were unpaid. You elected to study under one or more of them, working in the studios they visited. . . . So great was the number of students, two models, not always of the same sex, usually sat in each studio. Our easels were closely wedged together, the atmosphere was stifling, the noise at times deafening.[120]

Gradually he became acclimatized to life at Julian's. During his second year he transferred to a new branch at Montmartre, where he found it easier to make friends and involve himself in the artist life of Paris.[121]

Colarossi's may have been less chaotic but hardly less intimidating, as judged by this description of a "mixed class" in 1903:

> One morning there were five girls and half-a-score of men working at time sketches of a Spaniard in matador costume; except that 50 percent of the men were Americans, there was scarcely another instance of two of the workers being of the same nationality. A pretty Polish

girl, in a painting smock so ornamented with the marks of paint brushes that it resembled more than anything else a representation of Joseph's coat of many colours, was working near a Haytian negro [*sic*]; a countrywoman of Marie Bashkirtseff [*Russian*] had her easel alongside that of a merry-faced Japanese. In another corner was an Italian girl of whom great things were expected, and her nearest fellow worker was a sandy-haired Scotsman. All were keen on their work, and even the intrusion of a comparative stranger interfered with them apparently not at all. Had he not been vouched for by one of the students who was an old member of the class, it is not improbable his reception would have been more lively than pleasant.[122]

These foreign students learned to put up with a regular and strenuous routine and some "fagging." Before Kathleen Bruce Scott (later Lady Kennet, the sculptor), who studied there from 1901, reached the school at eight in the morning, she had taken a run, gone for a swim in the river, and had breakfast ("a roll with a cup of chocolate when funds were good"). At noon she lunched in the "usual little restaurant" and was back to work by one. "No tea. Dinner at seven. Occasionally back to the night class, occasionally a club dance or the gallery of the opera, but more usually home to bed." After she won one of the school competitions, she was appointed *massier* and, in exchange for free tuition, was made responsible for posing the model on Monday morning, calling out "C'est l'heure" a quarter before the hour for the model to rest, stoking the fire, and opening the windows at lunchtime. She was one of two women in a class full of men. What a ghastly day it was for her

when, with very knowing looks towards me and a few not too friendly laughs, someone had written up in chalk on the wall, "Tous les nouveaux payent un ponche." . . . All the [newcomers] pay a ponche, but what on earth was a *ponche* anyway. Presently a courteous Norwegian approached me and said, "It is a custom that any new student stands punch to the others" and returned to his place. . . . How on earth was it to be done? Was I to take them to a cafe? Would I have the money? What a well-thought-out torture for a terrified puritan! . . . While I hesitated an ill-bred little Italian started in a half-singing drone, "Tous les nouveaux payent un ponche." One by one they took it up until a great chorus of it filled the room. Suddenly, nearly crying with uncertainty and my heart in my mouth, I too joined in the chorus, "Tous les nouveaux payent un ponche. Je suis nouveau: je paye." A general bravo, and much good-humoured laughter.

Not only did the hot rum punch for sixteen students cost 6 francs—"a shocking blow to [her] careful budgeting," but it was the first time that she had tasted alcohol outside of Communion. Expected to down it to the dregs, she contrived somehow to make it disappear gradually.[123]

Not to be overlooked are those who, like Ernest Haskell, having been repelled by the "stupid academic methods and routine" at Julian's, spurned the ateliers to learn for themselves by copying the Old Masters in the museums and galleries. In spite of frustrations, being an art student in Paris still compared favorably with life as an art student back home, where no one was conscious that such individuals existed, and nobody thought of them as a class but saw each student as a strange person who happened to go astray. In Paris, on the other hand, thought Anne Goldthwaite, "they are in a class whose existence is acknowledged as important and scarcely abnormal."[124] And when could one say that the student in Paris had turned into a certified artist? Did a career begin with a picture hung, with a picture sold? Many American students in Paris were "stimulated to production by premature demands from home for a 'picture.' Their call to art was not always believed in by fathers who had won their money in other ways, and only a grudging consent was given to their trying the experiment at all." Their support was usually contingent on their starting to earn their own living with the brush—or, for that matter, with the etching needle—within one or two years.[125] When Mary Bonner, from San Antonio, Texas, first exhibited three etchings at the Salon d'Automne, the hometown newspaper immediately proclaimed her, whether she was ready or not, a full-fledged artist. Its headline read, SAN ANTONIO GIRL WINS FAME ABROAD.[126]

Americans looked on the lack of foreign experience as a distinct handicap. Many British etchers, especially those from Scotland, also went abroad to study, but the relative ease with which one could skip across the Channel made briefer sojourns of travel and study more typical. Whether one ventured there or not was mostly a matter of choice and rarely a cause for regret. For example, the father of Anna Airy, who became a distinguished painter and etcher, had offered her the finest art education to be had in England or on the Continent. She had chosen the Slade and, thereafter, always felt "too busy working to travel."

In Search of the Self-Trained Artist

What we have written about the availability of art schools is not meant to signal that everyone who wanted a professional art education could obtain it. The odds certainly favored the men over the women, the well-to-do over the poor, the later cohorts over those born earlier, and the residents of a major art center over those living on the periphery. All of our etchers managed, nevertheless, by one route or another, to secure the training that started them on the way to recognition. In dwelling on the institutions that were the gateways to art for most of them, we have omitted or lightly passed over other influential establishments, including those in Scotland and West England as well as some in California and such Midwestern centers as Chicago, Cincinnati, and Detroit. Nor has the part played by university schools of painting or architecture in introducing future etchers to art received its full due.

One basic question: Were there among those we studied any self-taught artists? Strictly speaking, the answer has to be no. The breed, so popular among fiction writers, has eluded our search. Among these near 300, we have come across just 6 with formal training so brief or sporadic to come close to qualifying, but none was without at least some formal training in any precise sense.

Helen West Heller is the only woman among the six. The details of her art education are as obscure as her birth date, which has been placed somewhere between 1872 and 1885. What we know of her personal biography comes mainly from a lengthy document, written shortly before her death, as the first installment of an autobiography, and from a posthumous tribute by a male confidant that repeats much of what Heller herself told him about her own life. Both accounts tend to dramatize and exaggerate her struggles against poverty and real or imagined foes in the art worlds of Chicago and New York. As she would have it remembered, two early attempts to study at an art school in St. Louis failed because the "strong individualism of her artistic temperament could not adapt itself to the conventional training of that time." She subsequently went to Chicago to find work to support her "artistic self-training," but other than a hint that at some point she "briefly" studied art in New York, we lack evidence of any further formal art training.[127]

A second case is that of George Elbert Burr, whose mother gave him art instructions as a boy. At nineteen or twenty he managed to

152 of the building of reputation

spend three months away from the family store to study at the Chicago Academy of Design, enough to bring him some success as an illustrator. *Who's Who* and *Who's Who in American Art* say that he "studied five years in France and Italy," an apparent reference to the chance his travels had given him "to study the diverse prospects and moods of nature and landscape." While Laver, among other art historians, has repeated this information, Burr's cataloguer doubts that he had either the time or the inclination to seek guidance from other artists. That is where the matter rests.[128]

Third, there is George Overbury ("Pop") Hart, who was prone to boast about being self-taught. More accurately, his formal art training amounted to three months at the Art Institute of Chicago and, years later in 1907, another three months at the Académie Julian. To be sure, his impatience with method and convention drove him away from academic circles, but he also learned from his artist friends.

As a fourth candidate we have Ernest Haskell. During a long recuperation from a bad case of typhoid right after high school, he made some sketches—more nearly scratches—while lying in bed. His aptitude was "discovered" when the *New York Mail and Express* took them for publication. Instead of enrolling at Yale, as his parents had hoped he would, he entered art school in Boston for a few weeks of study. Then he took a position as illustrator with the *New York American*, which he left at age twenty-three for a two-year sojourn in Paris, where he studied the old and new masters. The introduction to his catalog, perhaps paraphrasing Haskell, judges that by "working by himself and thinking for himself, he probably learned more than he would have in double the time at either Julian's or the Beaux Arts."[129]

Hart and Haskell may have rejected the formal training to which they were exposed, but Thomas W. Nason, the fifth who might be considered "self-taught," could hardly find the time to spare or even the opportunity for art study. He came from a farm family whose economic circumstances forced him into remunerative employment as soon as he finished high school. He took night courses at business school and in a few years was prospering as the private secretary to a Boston lawyer with extensive mining interests in the West and South America. One year of life classes attended after work, which ended as America entered World War I, was the only formal art education he ever had. After army service and settling down to married life, he began the process of schooling himself in the skills necessary to an engraver in wood and copper.[130]

The last on our list is James McBey. This celebrated Scottish etcher comes closest to being fully self-taught. As a schoolboy in the village where he grew up, near Aberdeen, Scotland, he read and reread a magazine series entitled "A Plain Guide to Oil Painting." At fifteen, while working as a lowly "trotter" at a bank, he read all the 700 to 800 books in the section on fine arts at the local library. With copies from photographic reproductions, he gradually taught himself perspective and chiaroscuro and went on to study the paintings at the Aberdeen Artists Society. At eighteen, he joined a night class at Gray's School of Art, where about thirty pupils were spending months drawing the details of a plaster cast of a rosette about two feet square—"an unattractive subject." His education was cut short when the school closed prematurely. Next he answered an ad offering private lessons from a local artist at 1 guinea a quarter but, after a few evenings, the instructor returned his money with the words, "I can teach you nothing. You will only waste your time by coming here again." Feeling desolate and abandoned, he turned one summer evening to Lalanne's *Treatise on Etching*, which completed his education. He quit his job at the bank to go on a sketching tour to Holland and join the ranks of professional artists.[131]

These vignettes underscore two perhaps obvious points: first, without some kind of formal training, none of these etchers would have been likely to get very far in the art world; second, women who sought a life in art were even more dependent than men on being "allowed in" to the professional art school. Men were at least free to explore a variety of pathways into the art world. In the next chapters, we examine how our artists, having passed the gateways, "got into etching" and "got on" with their careers, achieving recognition and, sometimes, renown.

# 7

## Into Etching: Patterns of Initiation

Once having made a decision for art, how did artists find their way into etching? Most were introduced in the classroom, some in the studio of a friend, still others in a commercial workshop where the fine points of engraving and printmaking techniques might be conveyed with no concern for their fine art potential. A fair number mastered the medium on their own through experimentation after reading a how-to book or copying Old Masters.

Some of the etchers we studied were recruited to the medium early in their art careers, some only after they were well established in a related profession or had built a reputation in another medium. Some sought to learn the medium for instrumental purposes—to be able to reproduce, usually for illustrative purposes, drawings or paintings that might or might not be their own creations; others sought in etching an alternative mode of expression. Yet whatever their motives and whenever they learned, there were but four ways to learn: through formal instruction, either in the workshop or in a professional school; informal instruction in the medium by networking with other artists; or self-instruction, usually with the help of a manual. Yet the way in which any particular artist was initiated into the joys of etching was not so random or chancy as some biographies would have us believe. Not all entry points were equally open to everyone at every point in time. Rather, the pattern of initiation was a function of gender, generation, and nationality.

As to gender, none of the women came to etching via the workshop. Apprenticeships were strictly a male institution, foreclosed by tradition to women. Besides, the class background of most of the women who became etchers would have obviated this route of entry but not art training in school, which, as we have seen, was open to them. Women interested in art flocked to these schools in large numbers and, as a consequence, were more often introduced to the etching

Table 7.1
Mode of Introduction to Etching, by Gender (in percent)[a]

|  | Women | Men |
| --- | --- | --- |
| Apprenticeships | — | 8 |
| Classroom | 66 | 47 |
| Self-taught or informal instruction by other artist | 34 | 45 |

[a] Based on 210 British and American artists.

needle via the classroom than their male counterparts—two-thirds of the women compared to just half of their male colleagues. Men, on the other hand, were more often self-taught and/or had taken up etching in response to the urging and instruction of a fellow artist. Table 7.1 gives the figures based on information available to us.

Getting into etching depended especially on what institutional facilities and advice were available to neophyte artists. Differences between generations had a lot to do with how careers synchronized with the various phases of the etching revival. By the time that most of the men studied had come of working age, the system of indentured apprenticeship whereby men mastered a skill was moribund: fewer than one in ten of those whose entry was ascertainable had come to etching via the workshop, a statistic that probably underestimates the number taking this route, insofar as one can assume that most, if not all, of the British men of the oldest generation on whom we could not obtain this information had also taken the apprentice route. This assumption is based on the overall shift during this period away from training in the workshop toward more formal education in school. The break shows up most clearly between the generation born in the 1870s and the one following, whose members came of age just as the etching classes were beginning to exert their influence. Among the youngest group, born in or after 1900, more than four of every five moved into etching via the classroom (table 7.2). There is another parallel shift not revealed by these figures. The early etchers—i.e., those born before 1870—with no apprenticeship or formal instruction in the techniques of printmaking had more typically picked up the rudiments of their craft either in the studio of a fellow artist or by studying old prints on their own. Those born later more typically learned the techniques of printmaking from texts, by consulting Hamerton, Lalanne, and other manuals that were circulating. It should be added that, because of the underdevelopment

Table 7.2
Mode of Introduction to Etching, by Generation (in percent)[a]

|  | Before 1870 | 1870–79 | 1880–89 | 1890–99 | 1900 and after |
|---|---|---|---|---|---|
| Apprenticeships | 8 | — | 5 | 6 | — |
| Classroom | 40 | 42 | 55 | 62 | 82 |
| Self-taught or informal instruction by other artist | 52 | 58 | 39 | 32 | 18 |

[a] Based on 210 British and American artists.

of its art-school system during the early years, self-instruction with the help of a manual or informal instruction from a fellow artist was more frequent in America.

Finally, the different opportunity structures of Britain and the United States resulted in different patterns of initiation, which reflect, on the one hand, the earlier availability in Britain of more formal instruction in the medium and, on the other, the tradition of self-help and mutuality that characterized the etching movement as it developed in the United States. Thus, a far higher proportion of Americans (27 percent) than of the British (5 percent) were self-taught. And, while in both countries, the most typical route into etching was through the classroom, over half the Americans either learned on their own or informally from another artist.

## Apprenticeship

Some future painter-etchers, especially those who pioneered the movement in France, first became familiar with graphic techniques in an engraving or printing establishment. Charles Jacque, a key figure, had spent some ten years engraving maps. Félix Bracquemond and Auguste Lepère, before they built reputations as artistic printmakers, had worked as reproductive engravers. Whistler, while employed as a draftsman, had taken a two-day course in engraving and etching. Still, by the time the painter-etcher movement got under way, the orientations of craftsmen and fine artists were widely divergent and even antagonistic. Stanley Anderson's father interpreted his son's reluctance to join him in a "steady and dignified" calling as a personal rebuke and rejection. Recounting his struggles to become an artist, Anderson said it had come as "news to him that he was only being forced to

Table 7.3
Mode of Introduction to Etching, by Nationality (in percent)[a]

|  | British | American |
|---|---|---|
| Apprenticeships | 4 | 4 |
| Classroom | 68 | 45 |
| Self-taught or informal instruction by other artist | 28 | 51 |

[a] Based on 210 British and American artists.

follow in the steps of William Hogarth and Thomas Bewick, each of whom—though destined for something higher—had been apprenticed to an engraver and begun his career cutting seals or chasing salvers, tankers and heraldic ornaments."[1] But, then, Hogarth and Bewick had lived and worked in the eighteenth century. It is not surprising that Anderson, born in 1884, should have wanted to escape the kind of apprenticeship that had given a start to so many of the earlier artisan-engravers.

Not only Anderson but every other apprentice in our British sample somehow managed to enter the art-school system, mostly to study printmaking at the Royal College of Art. To be sure, the influence of their earlier training was not easily shaken off. John Park and Charles Bird, both born in the 1850s, though accepted into the Royal Society of Painter-Etchers (RSPE), were never advanced to full fellowship. They failed, it would seem, to become something more than well-trained technicians.

In America, for some sons of craftsmen and some immigrants the workshop remained the entry point even after the art schools had clearly taken over. Often the master—like James Smillie's father, who passed his skills to his son—had himself served an apprenticeship in Europe. Peter Moran had been bound over to a lithography firm but managed to get his "indenture canceled" so that his older brothers might teach him to paint, which he preferred.[2] Others just learned how to etch "on the job." Young Charles W. Dahlgreen, who went to work at twelve, was employed, among other things, as an etcher of swords until he went to art school quite some years later. Rudolph Ruzicka, having arrived in Chicago from his native Bohemia in the 1890s, found a job in a commercial wood engraving house when he was fourteen: "I took my work extremely seriously," he said, "and remember that when the firm which employed me was denounced for employing a minor—(I was found doing a journeyman's job)—I argued very heatedly in Court, claiming that I was not doing factory work, but art work, much to the amusement of everyone in the court room. This happened after about six months in this shop—all that time I received no salary; they then 'raised' me $1.00 a week."[3] Supporting himself with work in process-engraving shops, he attended night drawing classes at the Chicago Art Institute and then took up designing. He moved to New York in 1903, where he was employed for a time as a draftsman in an advertising firm but soon began to devote as much time as he could outside working hours to wood engraving, which by then had become his chosen art.[4]

Likewise, Earl Horter, while still a young boy in Philadelphia, learned to engrave when he went to work as a commercial artist. This was the first phase of what amounted to a lifelong apprenticeship in advertising agencies, during which he continued to hone his talents. Practice and working in his spare time managed to make him into a "fine artist." He sketched and etched during travels at home and abroad, became an avid and distinguished collector of American Indian artifacts, and was an influential teacher who introduced many art students in Philadelphia to modern art.[5]

The youngest of the eleven apprentices in our sample was Russell T. Limbach, born 1904 in Massillon, Ohio. Having spent summers working at local steel mills, he yearned for a white-collar job but never dreamed of going into art. Then, with an assist from his Sunday school teacher, who was a transfer man in a small local lithographic plant, he got a job in the sketch room, where four regular artists took a lot of the company's time to help him. The firm produced art "in the same fashion as Fords are made" and with no idea of the use to which artists might put the lithographic medium. Limbach's eyes were finally opened when he encountered some Whistler prints at an exhibition; in the evening he made some drawings on zinc plates, which he then took to the shop for proofing during the noon hour. Changing jobs, he quickly rose to become head of publicity for the Union Trust Company in Cleveland. By 1928, when he sailed for Europe, he had already won a number of medals, including the silver at the international exhibition of the Print Makers Society of California. Part of that year was spent in Paris taking lessons from a lithographic printer, whose father and grandfather had worked at the same trade. When he returned to Cleveland, it was the depth of the depression and there were no jobs. Somehow he managed. Three years later he went to New York for a visit and found a job as art editor of *New Masses* at a salary enough to live on. He got to know a lot of artists around town and, when the Works Progress Administration started, was asked to help organize the Graphics Division, where he functioned as a supervisor and teacher. Though he had attended the Cleveland School of Art for a brief period, Limbach later claimed not to remember anything he learned there, whereas his "long years of apprenticeship" had brought him "knowledge not obtainable elsewhere."[6]

## The Professional Trainees

Professional etching classes were available earlier and in greater number in Britain than in America. At South Kensington a couple of generations of future painter-etchers spent their Saturdays in the etching class, first with Goulding, then with Frank Short (assisted by Constance Pott), followed in turn by Malcolm Osborne. Many enrolled there explicitly to learn etching and engraving as a field that would help them earn money and assure their careers as artists.

The reorientation of the class under Short goes a long way toward accounting for the high level of technical competence in the British school of etching. Before Sir Frank took over, the students—even under Legros—had spent their time copying exhibits in the Victoria and Albert. Short urged them, instead, to express their own pictorial conceptions.[7] But he also knew how easily the freedom possible in etching could encourage slipshod work.[8] To avoid this, he sought to make his pupils craftsmen first and foremost, and complete masters of their material, so that they would be able to do what they intended with no room for accidents. With his firm manner and strength of will, he challenged students to do their best. He would patiently spend hours advising and helping a student to improve a plate, especially if that student showed aptitude and a passion for the process.[9]

The class quickly became the major incubator for British painter-etchers. If the later generations were not introduced to the fine points of etching by Short himself, it was more than likely that they were taught by someone who had been initiated by him. Constance Pott, his loyal assistant, had first met Short in Goulding's engraving class. As a student at the Royal College of Art (RCA), she had not taken to the ordinary daily round of drawing and design, such as adapting "a lily or rose to wall-paper, tile, or carpet design." The promise of an Art Master's Certificate had likewise failed to stir her ambition. She "drifted into the engraving class . . . discovered her natural métier and felt . . . a spur to serious endeavor," wrote Hardie, who knew her.[10] When Short took over the class in 1891, Pott continued her studies with noteworthy success. With so few enrollees in these early days, there were opportunities for all manner of experimental work, stimulated by Short, who was daring enough to have learned the old technique of mezzotint on his own when there was no one to teach him. Pott, too, was experimental in the technical sense. In 1902 she returned to South Kensington as his assistant teacher of engraving.

Much of the undoubted success of the class under Short was indubitably "due to his skillful, tactful, and energetic second-in-command. Enter the class any Saturday morning, and you will find her by the printing press with up-rolled sleeves, in long blue etcher's blouse, ink-dabber in hand, a copper plate on the heater in front. And while the plate is inked, she will give kind advice as to the botched and bungled plate of the student who stands by. Those who have attended the class bear witness to the energy, enthusiasm, and whole-hearted devotion which have helped many a poor and diffident student, flung into London from some country art school, along the road which has led to a successful career."[11] Her etched self-portrait, *Trial Proof*, exhibited at the Royal Academy in 1900, shows her in "her studio at home," but she was really more at home in South Kensington. Retired in 1924, concurrently with Short, and succeeded by Osborne and Austin, she became a legend—fierce in her loyalty to Sir Frank. Being a Victorian spinster put her under suspicion of having been in love with him. More to the point, she was in love with her work. She never spared herself in giving help when help was needed.

The Saturday classes always seemed too short. Already years before Short and Pott retired, the etching room went into operation two days a week and could be opened, when there was sufficient demand, on additional days. Meanwhile, engraving had become a fifth school at the RCA, with instruction in the processes of etching, aquatint, mezzotint, engraving, wood engraving, and lithography. A student could aspire to a separate certificate for each of these processes and, on obtaining all six, was entitled to a diploma in engraving. The curriculum also included instruction in printing. Students took this in rotation, with everyone printing for a whole day from all the plates in use in the school.[12] The common activity generated a strong sense of fellowship among the etcher trainees, who studied more or less apart from other students, except for the life classes, which they shared with the rest. Their esprit survived into the 1930s when Denise Lebreton Brown, the youngest of our women, was there, first as a student, then as assistant to Osborne. She had decided to enroll at the college after seeing some prints by Robert Austin that were exhibited at the Royal Academy. Both he and Osborne turned out to be all she could possibly have expected from teachers. Like Short, their own mentor, they helped students in every way, even proofing their plates for them. At that time, the class numbered about twenty, of whom about six were women, from whom the same performance was expected as from the men. In her job as assistant, Brown herself instructed many of the students in the technical rudiments with which Osborne preferred not to be bothered.[13]

Through his many students who became teachers, Short's influence extended beyond the RCA. At the London County Council's Central School of Arts and Crafts there was William P. Robins. Robins had been introduced to the art of aquatinting by William Lee-Hankey at Goldsmiths' College. His first plates had been published by Colnaghi's, where Harold Wright, representing that firm, encouraged him to try his hand at etching. Already well on the way to becoming a successful printmaker, Robins hesitated; he had no confidence in his ability to master the technique. Taking the wisest course, he enrolled in the etching class. Once in Short's hands, he quickly developed into a master etcher.[14] After the Great War, in which Robins served, it was his good fortune to receive an appointment as etching master at the Central School. So ecstatic was he about the salary and conditions—£300 for teaching three days a week for forty weeks—that he promised Wright to expect "a rush of fine etchers."[15] Among the "fine etchers" he took under his wing were two women: Elizabeth Fyfe became a finalist in the Prix de Rome in etching after only six months of study, although she may actually have had previous instructions from Frank Emanuel. The other was Rosa Hope, who became an RSPE associate by 1923. Both women combined study with Robins with drawing and painting instruction at the Slade, as did other etchers, including Norman Janes and Anthony Gross.

Around the same time, an especially talented group of young etchers that included Graham Sutherland were joining forces at Goldsmiths' College of the University of London. Then the largest teacher-training college in the kingdom, it also housed a school of art. Etching had become a very popular medium, and most of the faculty had tried a hand at it. Before the Sutherland cohort arrived, a string of Short's students had succeeded William Lee-Hankey as the etching teacher. Frederick Marriott, the headmaster in charge through 1925, thought etching "a good line" for young Sutherland to pursue and probably showed him the basic techniques, but his principal mentors were all first-rank etchers trained by Short.[16] The first was Alfred Bentley; the second, Malcolm Osborne, who replaced his friend when he died of a lingering war injury. And when Osborne left to teach at the RCA, he was replaced, in turn, by Stanley Anderson. Sutherland had both kind and unkind things to say about all three. According to his biographer, he characterized Bentley and Osborne as "very nice men [but] not even technically experimental" and Anderson as a formal and careful crafts-man, precise in technical matters, anxious to help but "almost as hide-bound in his imaginative approach as Bentley and Osborne."[17]

These opinions were not necessarily shared by Sutherland's fellow students. Bouverie-Hoyton remembered the instructors at Goldsmiths' as having put great emphasis on individuality. For them, the right way was "your way"; they were not teaching a method.[18] Robin Tanner, who was then an evening student, put a high value on the very ap-proach Sutherland had criticized as hidebound. Anderson, as he saw it, "shared his knowledge with us as a medieval craftsman might have done with his apprentices. . . . Step by step each one of us followed his directions, and there was no escape. I remember how he kept me grind-ing ink for proving my first plate for a full half-hour. . . . He discov-ered an unground speck or two, which he warned me would scratch the copper. He was not satisfied until I had continued grinding and he had tested the result once more and at last found the shiny black mass 'about right.'"[19]

Whatever the quality of teaching, Sutherland believed he had learned most about etching by working together with his "close little band" of friends at Goldsmiths', which, in addition to Bouverie-Hoy-ton and Paul Drury, included William Larkins. Tanner was not able to participate fully in the group until he stopped going evening only and began to attend full time in 1928. The four, largely left to their own devices, worked together in the well-equipped etching room. One au-tumn day in 1924, Larkins brought in an etching by Samuel Palmer, *The Herdsman's Cottage.* The way he worked amazed Sutherland. "It was unheard of at the school to cover the plate almost completely with work, and quite new to us that the complex variety of the multiplicity of lines could form a tone of such luminosity. . . . As we became famil-iar with Palmer's later etchings, we 'bit' our plates deeper. We had always been warned against 'over-biting.' But we did 'over-bite,' and we burnished our way through innumerable states, quite unrepentant at the way we punished and maltreated the copper."[20] The group was also influenced by F. L. M. Griggs, the most important etcher to follow in the Palmer tradition. Paul Drury's father, an Academy sculptor, had introduced them. However, Sutherland later downplayed the artistic influence that Griggs had on him; only when it came to printing did he acknowledge his debt for having been shown "how thick the ink should be, how to use the hand in wiping it off, how many rags one had to use, and at what kind of stages."[21] He and the others in the group at Goldsmiths' were to develop their own style from other sources of inspiration.

The kind of private instruction Sutherland and the rest had from Griggs was more common among the earlier generations of etchers, but nothing prevented anyone eager to learn from seeking out a master. This was how Hester Frood learned to etch after four or five years of art study plus six months in Paris. The twenty-four-year-old Frood made her way to Kippen-near-Stirling, Scotland, the village where the already famous Cameron lived, in order to make herself known to him. Upon seeing her drawings, she claimed, he said he would make her an etcher. The next year, when she showed up, he invited her to stay with him and his wife.[22] He taught her well and the connection helped. Positive notice came very quickly and made her into a rising star.

None of the teachers of etching in America exerted quite the same pull as the established British masters. More of the training took place through the etching clubs or informally. In Philadelphia, where Sartain had once taught engraving at the Philadelphia Academy of Fine Arts (PAFA), students had to find someone to teach them etching "privately." Even under Daniel Garber, who taught there much later, etching never achieved a dominant role.

The closest counterpart to Short was C. F. W. Mielatz, who succeeded Smillie as chief instructor at the National Academy of Design (NAD) from 1904 until his untimely death in 1919. One of Mielatz's most notable students was William Auerbach-Levy, who was to take his place as etching teacher at the academy. Mielatz also taught Ernest Roth, Anne Goldthwaite, and many others. On the other hand, Raphael Soyer, who attended some of Auerbach-Levy's demonstrations, felt that the class did not offer him much. He had already learned the rudiments of etching from a fellow student at Cooper Union, bought himself a small etching press for $25, and etched at least five plates, four of them portraits. The one of his mother greatly impressed Auerbach-Levy when it was shown to him.[23]

Before the First World War one could also learn to etch at the Art Students League (ASL) from George Bridgman or George Senseney, but courses in etching were not much in demand nor offered with any regularity. The ASL fell in step with the etching revival only in 1921, when it hired Joseph Pennell to teach graphic art (including lithography).[24] He found his teaching handicapped by the poorly equipped classroom: there was only one old copperplate press but, before the second term, he had managed to acquire seven presses. But the caliber of the students and their lack of enthusiasm had disappointed him. Etching appealed to them only, he surmised, because "it was in fashion with dealers and collectors and therefore a sure way to make money." Some could not draw and were appallingly ignorant of art, never having heard of Dürer and with no use for Rembrandt and Whistler, while in the style of New Yorkers they littered the classroom and made no attempt to clean up. By a process of elimination and stern discipline, Pennell soon "collected round him a group of students after his own heart."[25] During the brief period before his death in 1926, he taught Howard Cook, Levon West, Ilse Bischoff, Paul Cadmus, and a number of others. Pennell did indeed carry a tradition of printmaking to the league but did not live long enough to realize fully his ambition to establish an American School of the Graphic Arts.

Various kinds of instruction were to be had in many places—in art schools, at universities, or from individual artists who had somehow mastered the craft. In the early twenties Arthur Millier was doing some teaching in Southern California, "mostly out of [his] own house and largely to architectural draftsmen and young architects. At that time they all wanted to know how to etch and so we had quite a business there."[26] The demand for Millier as a teacher increased as his reputation rose. This brought him some talented students whom he turned into accomplished etchers. Outstanding among them were two women: Loren Barton and Mildred Bryant Brooks. The tribulations experienced by Brooks well illustrate the precarious state of etching instruction in much of America.

Brooks, born in 1903, was lucky to find teachers in high school who recognized her talent. She had expected, upon graduation, to enroll in a College of Fine Arts in Los Angeles. When that closed, she decided on the University of Southern California where, under a special program, she took selected art classes at Chouinard and the Otis Art Institute for college credit. F. Tolles Chamberlin, a former pupil of Bridgman at the Art Students League was her instructor at Otis. He told her that he wanted to make an etcher out of her but apparently lacked the means. His tuition amounted to little more than constructive criticism, hardly enough to make her a real etcher. Before she could even begin to etch seriously, she had married and "for several years found herself so busy with children she didn't have much time for art."[27] Four years later, following an illness and under doctor's orders to find a consuming interest, she resumed her study of art—this time in evening classes at the Stickney Art School in Pasadena. There she came under the tutelage of Millier, who came once a week for a critique of student work. Millier had given her criticism that even he later described as brutal. Under his guidance she had "tackled huge plates packed with detail; when parts were wrong, scraped out hard copper like a he-man, wiped away tears of rage and kept on working."[28] Millier ended by becoming one of her greatest admirers, particularly for her etchings of branching trees. The third person credited by Brooks with teaching her techniques was E. Stetson Crawford, who had studied at the PAFA and in Parisian ateliers and claimed to have been Whistler's first pupil. Brooks printed for him when he was in Pasadena, as she did for a few others.[29]

The search for expert instruction led some Americans farther afield: to the RCA, to Robins at the London Central School, to private study with such recognized masters as William Strang in London or Edouard Léon in Paris. There is ample testimony that Léon, who has not yet been mentioned, "not only knew the technique of etching perfectly, but also how to impart it to others," and would do so for a stipend that seemed even cheap.[30] But there was no fooling around with him. One could learn all the many facets of an etcher's art, including the technique of the color print, which was gaining so much in popularity during the twenties. He had an upbeat style. Instead of pointing out defects, he encouraged his pupils to submit their best prints to the Paris Salon. Such was Léon's influence with the jury that even their first attempts might win a prize or at least an honorable mention. The opinion of his student, Samuel Chamberlain, that "there was no question about his mastery as a teacher" was seconded by others.[31] So many grateful ex-students did Léon acquire that, in later years, he made a special trip to the United States to be wined and dined from New York to Texas. Mary Bonner, from Fort Worth, who had gone to him in 1922, volunteered herself as an official guide and interpreter for his lecture tour on French art.[32] He reciprocated by remaining her faithful sponsor, by helping to launch her on the career prematurely cut short by her sudden and unexpected death in 1935.

## Lateral Entrants

Almost all those artists who were recruited into etching in an institutionalized setting—whether in a workshop, a classroom, or a teaching studio—were near the beginning of their art careers. By contrast those who were essentially self-taught in the medium or who learned the essentials in a more informal setting with the help of friends or colleagues were almost always already well along in their professional careers.

We think of these later learners as lateral entrants. Some may be more aptly described as converts, insofar as they crossed over from a related career field or took up etching after having built a reputation in another artistic medium. The motives behind such crossovers could be either *expressive*—the learning of etching as an end in itself—or *instrumental*—as a means of fulfilling some other purpose, such as supplementing their income. For some lateral entrants, etching proved both pleasurable and profitable.

A number of lateral entrants came from professions that rewarded good draftsmanship but not necessarily under conditions experienced as fulfilling. Their motives were mostly expressive and aesthetic rather than instrumental. For some, like William Ansell, an associate of the RSPE as well as president of the British Institute of Architecture, etching remained very much an avocational sideline. Yet others—including William Walcot and Muirhead Bone in Britain and J. André Smith, Louis Rosenberg, Samuel Chamberlain, and Gerald Geerlings in America—to mention only a few names—actually abandoned architecture, at least for a while. John Taylor Arms, too, was seduced into etching after several years with an architectural firm, his interest aroused by a Lumsden sketch of Benares spotted in a shop window and purchased. With a $12 etching kit that his new bride then gave him for Christmas, he began a long love affair with the medium and became one of its main missionaries. In 1914 he needled his first plate—a copy of a work by Jongkind—with Lalanne's book as a guide. To his great relief, as he later wrote, only one proof survived.[33] Subsequent instruction in etching from a fellow artist, Eugene Higgins, and in printing from Bolton Brown put him on the way to becoming one of the modern American masters of etching.[34] What began as a hobby came, within a few years, to be his life.

Etchers recruited themselves from other professions as well. Frank Short had first trained as an engineering draftsman; Mielatz had had some art training but worked as a surveyor. And that great proselytizer, Haden himself, it may be recalled, was attracted to etching during anatomical studies. At least two other physicians, Dr. Leroy Yale and Dr. B. F. Morrow, participated in the revival as amateur etchers.

Some of our etchers, when already well along in their artistic careers somehow discovered—by mere chance or at the urging of a colleague—that etching was a medium well suited to their temperament. These artist recruits, like other lateral entrants, were enchanted by the ease with which they could run the needle over the blackened surface of the copperplate. Nothing, except perhaps lithography, could better serve the skilled draftsman as a means of direct expression. One great advantage of etching over the stone and even over oil paint was that it did not necessitate the toting about of bulky gear when drawing outdoors.[35]

Some of the most acclaimed etchers took up the medium in a most casual way. John Marin, for instance, had received no encouragement while a student at the PAFA, nor later at the ASL, to pursue his predilection for graphic art. Then, at age thirty-five, just about to sail for Europe, he used the proceeds from his first sale of sketches to purchase a set of Shakespeare illustrated by E. A. Abbey, a copy of Lalanne's *Treatise on Etching*, and several volumes of Rembrandt's etchings. Off he went to France with etching very much on his mind. Fortuitously, he found that his older stepbrother, Charles Bittinger, who had preceded him to Paris, still had an etching press, tools, and surplus copperplates with which he had once experimented. Having found etching not to his liking, he gladly gave his equipment to John but offered no advice. This benign neglect suited Marin. He was a secretive man who preferred to do things his own way. Relying on Lalanne's manual, he took up etching with "predestinate zeal," though probably not without some technical pointers from George C. Aid, an American etcher from St. Louis, who happened to live in the same building. This was all the help that Marin needed to move full speed ahead. In the last quarter of 1905 he produced a dozen etchings, drawing directly on the copper, as had Whistler and Pennell. This do-it-alone approach had its perils: once he dropped a bottle of acid on the carpet of his room, which did not exactly please his landlady, and another time a bottle of iron perchloride broke when a porter dropped his valise and ruined the clothes therein.[36]

Mary Nimmo Moran, by contrast, gladly acknowledged that she had always been the pupil of her more famous husband Thomas Moran, the American landscape painter. Married at age twenty, she took up drawing, watercolor, and oil painting under his guidance. She had never drawn or painted before she met him and, throughout her life, he was supportive and understandably proud of her accomplishments. The family, children and all, would go off on sketching trips, working out of doors during summer months, and soon Mrs. Moran was exhibiting at the National Academy. In 1879, just shortly before he was to accompany an expedition to the then-unexplored Yellowstone Country, Thomas Moran had installed an etching press in his Newark studio. Suggesting that Mary Nimmo might take up etching during his summer's absence, he gave his wife some pointers and left her six waxed plates. Not wanting to chance their ruin, she first experimented on the back of a copper calling plate that she herself had coated, drawing a sketch from memory rather than directly from nature. Once assured that she understood the technique, she took a plate in one hand, her daughter, Ruth, by the other and went outdoors to needle the image of a bridge spanning a river near Easton, Pennsylvania, where she had been summering. She bit both plates, took impressions, and in this way began her involvement with etching.[37]

So naturally talented and enthusiastic was Mary Nimmo that it is hard to countenance a contemporary report that she had been reluctant "to attempt [etching] in the absence of her teacher."[38] However, Moran, on his return, implied that she might have had reason to hesitate. He called her plates "funny-looking things," two of them not worth putting under acid, and the other four "jolly-queer etchings." His wife herself did not think much of them but decided, nevertheless, to send them off to the New York Etching Club. That organization promptly elected her a member, and soon she was considered one of the "best of the women etchers in the country."[39]

Edward Hopper, the painter, is nearly as renowned for his etchings as for his paintings. Asked why he took up etching, he said that he didn't know—"I wanted to etch, that's all."[40] The impetus had come from his acquaintanceship with Martin Lewis, one year older than he and, like Hopper at the time, earning a living in commercial art and illustration. Lewis, one of the future American masters of the medium, had already begun to etch and was able to convey to Hopper its technical intricacies. As it turned out, the Paris and New York street scenes that Hopper etched between 1915 and 1918 were more acceptable to juries than his paintings; by 1920, they were making it into all the prestigious shows, and art journals were giving them favorable reviews. In 1923 two major awards in etching indirectly added to his reputation as a watercolorist and oil painter. Sales of his etchings left him more time to paint and, so Hopper believed, the painstakingly detailed requirements of the medium helped him to hone his skills as a painter.

Yet Hopper cut short his etching career. He made his last plate in 1929, three years before he was elected to the National Academy of Design, an honor he turned down because they had rejected his paintings in years past. Asked if he would print more impressions from his plates, since there would be such a demand for them, he responded: "I don't want to be bothered back in the studio with printing etchings—and I could not stand anyone coming in and printing them in the studio for me. . . . I can't get the proper English ink and I insist on only white umbria paper. Then I pull the ink out of the plate after wiping with a little retroussage of tarleton cloth—I don't think anyone could get the blacks I like—Carl Zigrosser of the Philadelphia Museum once said he thought he could get an etcher to do some printing but I said, NO!"[41] He simply could not bear to turn out work that failed to meet his own exacting standards.

This attitude of Hopper contrasts with that of some other established artists who took up etching more or less as an ancillary activity. They were attracted not so much by the aesthetic potential of the medium as by its duplicative capability, which made it possible to expand the market for their art or to go in for illustration. The motives of these artists were largely, even if not exclusively, of an instrumental character.

Eliza Pratt Greatorex was one such already successful artist to take up the etching needle for instrumental purposes. Greatorex had decided to make art her profession when, at the age of thirty-eight, she was left a widow with three children. Within eleven years, she was elected associate of the NAD, an honor shared at the time with only one other woman. Having made a series of pen-and-ink drawings of Old New York, she was distressed to find all available methods for duplicating them to be unsatisfactory. So that she could be her own interpreter, she decided to learn to etch. Almost sixty-eight years old, she took herself and her two daughters, also artists, to Paris, where in winter 1878–79 she worked in a studio. That summer she etched directly from nature in the French countryside, and within two years she had produced some nineteen or twenty plates. When Koehler published Greatorex's *The Pond* as one of the original etchings in his short-lived *American Art Review*, he described it as "delicate rather than strong, in its inception as well as in its execution."[42]

Some artists made their first acquaintance with the medium early

in their art careers but did not immediately develop any serious interest
in it. "One of the oddest [etching careers] in the annals of the graphic
arts" was that of Frank Benson.[43] It did not get under way until he was
fifty; in actuality, it began in 1882 when, as a twenty-year-old student
at the Boston Museum School, he had, with Lalanne's book close at
hand, etched a small plate of Salem Harbor for the frontispiece of the
student magazine.[44] By the time he produced his second etching thirty
years later, Benson was both critically and financially very successful.
The Corcoran Gallery had just bought his painting *My Daughter* at
the "reduced" price of $5,000. He had turned down a higher offer
from a private purchaser in the hope the work might go to a prestigious institution.[45]

Money was not what triggered so belated a return to etching. The
proofs that Benson had pulled from his early plates were given to
friends or stowed away in portfolios with no plans for their immediate
publication. However, in 1915, whether at his dealer's suggestion or
just to see what would happen, he exhibited a dozen of these prints
along with his paintings at the Guild of Boston Artists.[46] His sports-
man-artist depictions of wild fowl, huntsmen, and fishermen proved
enormously popular. Sales were so encouraging that after a week the
Guild asked Benson for more impressions. As demand grew, some of
them rapidly became collectors' items. A print published at $40 could
advance in an incredibly short time to a figure five times greater.[47]
Such unanticipated success could only spur Benson's enthusiasm for
etching birds in flight or at rest—"ducks on the wing, pintails passing,
grouse alighting, geese resting." Over the last thirty years of his life, he
turned out 355 etchings and drypoints, with all editions printed by
Benson himself.[48] Having early in life become one of the best-known
American painters, he found it easy late in life to repeat that success as
an etcher.

The interest in Augustus John as an etcher was and to some extent
remains largely an offshoot of his reputation as a painter. Already
famous, though not rich, he took up etching rather casually, at the
suggestion of Benjamin Evans, a classmate at his school in Bristol as
well as later at the Slade. His first plate was a portrait of Evans.[49] It
was etched in 1901, when John was teaching at Liverpool Art School
to support his family. Other portrait etchings soon followed. Most
were done for practice, printed "with varying degrees of skill," and
with "little idea of making any profit by the exhibition or publication
of proofs."[50] Given John's reputation, they nonetheless soon found
their way to the market. When Campbell Dodgson, who had been

acquiring prints and drawings by living artists for the British Museum print room, inquired whether John might let him have a selection, the artist was more than agreeable; he was provoked into a period of great productivity for a one-man show at the newly opened Chenil Gallery. Its preparation involved something of a salvage operation. John's previous plates had to be searched out, then cleaned and scraped as they were found. They were given numbers rather haphazardly and with "no relation to the order of production or any other principle of arrangement."[51]

Of the 82 etchings shown at Chenil, the 15 dated 1906 were likely prepared "somewhat hurriedly" to meet the exhibition deadline. These Dodgson judged to be "without genuine inspiration." In his opinion, the "greater . . . and also, with few exceptions, the best part [of John's work] had been produced before 1906."[52] Although this first show was followed by several others, John's output soon slowed. Over the remaining fifty-five years of his life, he produced no more than fifty more plates—the last in 1920. He never tried to cash in on the etching frenzy, as he surely could have. He was probably too busy as a draftsman and painter to devote the sustained attention demanded by a medium which "did not suit his temperament; it was too slow and too small."[53] Certainly, John never regarded his etchings as a major part of his artistic oeuvre; he never exhibited with the RSPE nor did he include even one etching in the major retrospective of his work organized by the Arts Council in 1948. Yet some critics—Frank Rutter, for one—believed that, like Whistler, John might ultimately be recognized as a greater etcher than painter.[54] Be this as it may, the notoriety he had earned as a painter helped him build a reputation in this secondary medium.

John Copley, a contemporary of John, had learned to etch as a student but readied no plates for publication until he was past fifty and one of Britain's leading lithographers. Throughout the years of the etching craze, he continued to make lithographs, undeterred by the temptation to cash in on the vogue. Yet Copley took up etching just as the medium in its pursuit of novelty and technical wizardry seemed to be nearing creative exhaustion.[55] This was in 1925, when he was too ill to handle the heavy lithographic press and the doctor advised moving to a warm climate. The Copleys selected Alassio in Italy where they both spent time etching.[56] His prints (as well as those by his wife, Ethel Gabain) enjoyed a "kind reception," and he "found it interesting and exciting using a new medium," but as he confided to Frank Weitenkampf, he still liked lithography best.[57] His oeuvre nevertheless includes about 155 etchings, most produced in the last twenty years of his life, after the medium had gone out of fashion. Editions were usually small. Still, since he was doing so much etching in addition to painting, it began to strike him as a "little absurd" not to belong to the RSPE. Yet he wondered, "how on earth [he] could fit into that galère," given his more painterly technique. His hesitation was unfounded; his admission, under a special rule by which the society could "elect artists of repute without an election" was unanimous.[58] Neither the lure of profit or fame had much to do with Copley's return to etching.

Similarly, Dame Laura Knight came to etching with her reputation already assured. Then forty-six and generally recognized as "England's foremost woman painter," she had not previously tried her hand at printmaking. Was the booming market for etchings an incentive to give it a try? One explanation she offered makes her decision sound completely fortuitous. It seems she had broken her wrist and could not paint when she happened to pick up a manual at a bookstall in the Charing Cross Road that made etching seem deceptively simple and easy.[59] A friend let her have an old press that had been stored away in a damp cellar—"an amateur affair not made for real use, which you could lift with one hand."[60] Fortunately, she had another friend who knew a bit, but not much more, about printmaking than she did. Knight and this friend, John Everett, a nephew of John Everett Millais, learned together. Lacking money for proper equipment, they used tools made from odds and ends Everett picked up at market-stalls and warehouses in strange parts of London.

On their first attempt, they thought it "a miracle to get any impression from that little warped press, on which Everett had to sit and turn the handle at the same time." They tried aquatinting, using a loan copy of Goya's *Caprichos* as their guide. The broader method appealed to Knight more than pure line etching.[61] Next Knight bought George Clausen's old press, found a printer in David Strang, and was soon showing both etchings and aquatints at the Academy and elsewhere. Lumsden, explaining that Dame Laura had not been producing them for "very long," featured two of her aquatints in his highly popular manual, praising her Goya-like figure-subjects as "technically faultless." One depicted a male Spanish dancer, the other two flirtatious young women on a bank holiday—subjects that Lumsden thought were "not likely to appeal to the average collector."[62] And, at first, that seemed to be the case. Bond Street was anything but receptive. The first "laconically minded" dealer to see her prints told her she still had " 'a long way to go!' He shuffled my bundle of prints like a pack of playing cards: they were not his stuff. . . . I packed up . . . and bolted to Harold [her husband], waiting for me outside. He took my portfolio. I was worn out having trekked to other dealers that morning all equally sour countenanced." She was ready to burst into tears.[63] But she only had to be patient—years before the market went bust, her prints were selling well. This does not mean that her original motive had been mainly commercial. In fact, she soon tired of the "printing, signing and packing up parcels to meet the orders for all the various prints" and other chores that went with success.[64]

Ill health, broken bones, love, even death can affect a career in most unanticipated ways. The story of Anna Lea Merritt, whom the reader already has encountered as a young girl seeking art education in her native Philadelphia, represented, for Koehler, "one of the few rare instances in which true conjugal love can be traced as a motive power in art."[65] Merritt, by then a well-established painter, wished to memorialize her deceased husband, an art restorer and art critic, with a collection of his writings that included a very personal recollection of his life.[66] Mr. (Charles) Kegan Paul, her compassionate publisher, suggested an engraver who might do a portrait for the frontispiece. Not liking the portrait shown her, she decided to etch one herself, though she had never etched before.

Kegan Paul agreed to wait while she mastered the medium, but he did not have to wait very long.[67] With Hamerton's book as her guide, Merritt took a close look at the etchings by Van Dyck and Rembrandt at the British Museum, secured the necessary tools, and set to work: "The portrait ... which was very soon etched, quite amazed Mr. Kegan Paul. He asked me to do others for other memoirs—also he wished I could produce at least twenty-two more etchings to illustrate our book. This I succeeded in doing—half of the etchings are careful copies of little pen-sketches which had finished Mr. Merritt's letters to me during my winters in America—most of them exquisite compositions. The rest were my own designs to illustrate *Robert Dalby and the Professor* [her husband's novel]." She had help from Mrs. Edwin Edwards, wife of a member of the Old Etching Club, in learning how to print, and this saved her a long journey to a printing establishment. Charles W. Cope, another member of the Old Etching Club, showed her how to put a white paper screen between the copperplate and the light to help her see the shining copper lines in the "black varnish." Usually working by gaslight with a water globe, she found that "nearsighted eyes had a great advantage." By removing her specs, she could see "the minutest lines, for which most people would need a magnifying glass."[68]

Having learned to etch for a very special purpose, Merritt produced fifty-three or more plates during her lifetime but never felt as fully at home etching portraits as in painting them. She agonized over Koehler's request that she contribute an etched portrait to a series on American celebrities. Portrait etching was fraught with perils not found in landscape etching: "A slight divergence from the line intended is of little consequence in a tree but of great [consequence] in a nose and owing to the glimmering on the copper and the frequent necessity of *reversing* I find *exactness* difficult in this branch of art."[69] She nevertheless thought it worth the try. Her portrait of Louis Agassiz, when completed, seemed surprisingly good to her[70] but did not please Koehler, who preferred to substitute a reproductive etching she had made of a drawing by George Richmond of Gilbert Scott. "In a fit of vexation, after hearing [Richmond's] criticism, [Merritt] put in a few *touches* in imitation of his and bit them accidentally too deep.... There was no curing it."[71] Koehler continued to prefer this plate even though, in her judgment, it was fit only to be destroyed.

## Self-starters

We have seen how the techniques taught in the commercial workshops and introduced into the curriculum of art schools were a stimulus to future etchers and how the medium spread informally through the artists' own networks. Some were lured by the aesthetic of the etched line or by the richer tones of drypoint and aquatint, brought to their attention in the ordinary course of their work or while browsing through museums and galleries. Their numbers were bound to swell as etching grew more popular and the number of exhibitions expanded. Other motives, some of them highly practical, reinforced this aesthetic appeal.

The remaining question is how artists with no prior knowledge about or experience with the medium learned about etching and how to etch. For instance, the Western artist George Burr needled and printed two etchings when he was no more than twelve years old. It seems implausible that this Missouri youth could have reinvented the process for himself, but we have no idea where he might have turned for instruction. It is highly unlikely that his mother, Burr's only drawing coach, could have had any experience with etching a full six years before the formation of the New York Club and eight years before Koehler's campaign to popularize original etching in America. Did he somehow come across in that small town one of the few manuals then available? Where he secured a plate is easier to imagine: in 1871 his father had added a tin shop to his hardware business, and it was there that Burr did his printing.[72]

John Sloan, famous chronicler of life on the sidewalks and in the tenements of New York City, ventured into etching as a youth, while holding a job as assistant cashier in the retail department of Porter and Coates, a leading Philadelphia bookstore. The store also sold fine prints. With permission from the head of the print department, Sloan soon busied himself making pen and ink copies of original works by such as Dürer, Rembrandt, Hogarth, Cruikshank, Leech, and others, copies that he sold for $5 apiece. Working in the bookstore gave him easy access to the standard works on printmaking. His first etchings, mostly reproductive, date from about 1888, when he was seventeen. They include an original portrait of his sister Marianna. *Schuylkill River*, another early print, was much in the style of Whistler and one of the few that "looke[d] like an etching from the connoisseur's point of view." It occurred to Sloan that "had I pursued the direction here suggested my etchings might have become quite popular."[73] Instead it took years for Sloan to be critically regarded as a "fine artist" and to reap the financial rewards from his art. Today, of course, his etchings command high prices.[74]

The artist might start with drypoint, scratching directly on the plate with a sharp object, and thus skipping the more demanding procedure of grounding and biting. Marguerite Kirmse, who became a highly successful animal portraitist, made her first intaglio print with a Victrola needle on a piece of old copper to give to a friend as a birthday present. She had come to New York from her native England seeking a musical career, but by 1930 she was selling more etchings (mostly of dogs) than any other living artist.[75]

Bertha Jaques, too, found her own way into etching. She had been a student at the Art Institute of Chicago and, at age thirty, was comfortably married to a dentist. On a visit to the World's Columbian Exposition, she saw for the first time prints by the leading etchers of the day—Bracquemond, Buhot, Whistler, Haden, Tissot, Zorn, Cameron, Short, and more. These she could savor at her leisure, day after day, thanks to a seasonal pass she received for the daily arrangement of flowers at one of the exhibits.[76] After this she turned to the treatises by Hamerton and Lalanne and to the Art Institute to look over their Rembrandt and Meryon prints for clues about the technical aspects of etching.[77] Then, she recalled, "I took it up alone in my own home, that is, without any help except that of my husband who made my tools."[78] Her first print was made on a thin sheet of copper that came from a hardware store and was meant for the bottom of kettles. She grounded it according to Hamerton's instructions, using wax, asphaltum, and pitch. For tools she had a paperhanger's wooden roller covered with leather and a discarded dentist's drill. She drew a sail boat and shore line, then immersed the plate in the acid bath: "Immediately things began to happen. The acid attacked the little copper lines shining through the black wax ground and a row of opalescent green bubbles arose with fascinating regularity. I was so busy watching it that the acid was half way through the plate and the boat nearly wrecked before I could make up my mind to interfere. When I did, and the thin ground was removed with turpentine, the lines proved to be too deep."[79]

Not everyone who tried to learn by experiment succeeded. Anne Goldthwaite's interest in the technique was roused when she applied for work at a business called the Cheltenham Press and was told by the proprietor that, were she an etcher, he could readily find work for her. Being enterprising, he decided, then and there, to make an etcher of her. Goldthwaite remembered that "he had a large flat book on etching by Lalanne. This he would read to me while I, with etching ground, roller and needle, would try to follow Lalanne's instructions. The book was an English translation, and I might have read it myself to better advantage, but for some mysterious reason this did not seem permissible ... he supplied the plates and the services of his printer [who engraved plates, visiting cards, invitations, etc.]."[80] It did not take her long to decide that she would do better at Kimmel and Voight's, who were "real printers of etchings." In this she proved mistaken. During the long time she spent there she was kept in the office and never allowed into the printing room: the firm's young printer was afraid of women. Her own "good behavior" was, however, duly rewarded with presents, one at a time, of trial proofs by such notables as Swain Gifford, Anders Zorn from Sweden, and Whistler. Still eager to learn, she heard that "there existed such things as etching classes" and made her way to Mielatz's class at the NAD, where we have already encountered her as its sole female enrollee.

Twenty years later Peggy Bacon, studying at the ASL, still found no printmaking instruction there. In 1917 a fellow student gave her the idea of using a heavy steel needle to cut a drawing into a zinc plate. The plate, when inked, made duplicates. She and her friend found an old printing press that had been left in the corner of the life class room. So attractive did she find drypoint that it quickly came to supersede painting as her primary medium. Two years later she took an evening etching class taught by Mahonri Young, mostly because it gave her access to a press and the few critiques that he offered.[81]

Self-instruction, though more frequent in America, was by no means unheard of in Britain—especially among the Scots. Lumsden, to whose book so many would later turn, had himself learned from a manual.[82] Muirhead Bone's interest was sparked by a volume of Meryon reproductions he came across in Glasgow's Mitchell Library. Apprenticed to an architect, he was soon making his "painstaking pen-drawings" of Glasgow "look as like etchings as I could—even to dipping them in tea to improve their tone!"[83] Later, while in art school, a fellow student showed him how to smooth the unused backs of small zinc visiting card plates. These Bone used, employing a sewing needle fixed with sealing wax in a bit of wood, to make his first drypoints. Not until the next winter did he consult Hamerton's treatise and so get into etching: "I busied myself with drawings of streets, shipyards, and harbour scenes for my first set of Glasgow etchings" and, by a "great stroke of luck," was able to purchase "for a very modest sum" the printing press that D. Y. Cameron left behind when he moved to Edinburgh.[84]

Most striking is McBey's account of his self-introduction to the medium. Etchings had been mentioned in books he read at the local library but, until he came across Lalanne's *Treatise*, he had no idea how they were made. After studying the requirements, he "felt it within [his] power to make one etching by using substitutes." He readied a plate and, with a small mirror and two darning needles in his pocket, picked himself a deserted part of the harbor front. "The ease with which the needle, as it touched the black wax surface, made the copper-coloured line was almost uncanny." He finished, went home, and "straightaway immersed [the plate] in a bath of half nitric acid and half water. Everything happened according to Lalanne, whose treatise I had handy, open at the page."[85] His next problem was finding a copperplate press like the one described in the manual.

It was just possible that the copying press in the bank [where he worked] would do the job: "Surreptitiously I took the plate and the few accessories necessary and tried it. Nothing happened. The pressure obviously was too dissipated. It was mortifying to be defeated so near to my goal." A week later it occurred to McBey that the mangle in the basement might do the job if the top rollers were screwed down tightly enough: "I cut a piece of linoleum for a traveling plank and ran it a little way through the rollers. On it I placed my copper plate, inked and wiped; then the dampened paper; then three pieces of blanket. I screwed down the pressure all it would take and slowly turned the handles till the blankets were clear at the other side of the rollers." He managed surprisingly well and ended with "a perfect print." This was his start. With a steel piston rod discarded in a junk yard and the assistance of an uncle who was a blacksmith, he transformed the mangle into a powerful machine that functioned perfectly as long as the plates were not too large.[86]

## The Diffusion of Etching

As a number of our examples have suggested, the more seasoned etchers were always ready to share their knowledge with neophytes. Smillie had come across Charles Platt and given the young man some pointers. Cameron had taken up etching in 1887 after a chance discovery of his drawing by George Stevenson, a painter-etcher, who then taught him; Mielatz, too, was taught by J. J. Callahan, an amateur etcher, who had seen him sketch.

Searching biographies, one detects ripples by which the medium spread not only through the schools but also informally from person to person. In Philadelphia, Peter Moran taught Stephen Parrish, who in turn taught Gabrielle Clements, Blanche Dillaye, and Edith Peirce Getchell. When Ellen Day Hale was in Paris, she learned etching from Clements. They became great friends and later, as winter residents in Charleston, South Carolina, they—or, at any rate, one of them—taught Alice R. H. Smith, a well-known painter and watercolorist, who then taught Elizabeth O'Neill Verner, in whose national recognition the locals still take considerable pride. Hale and Clements, by then "old ladies in their sixties," became prime movers behind the formation of the Charleston Etchers Club and of an etching class as well as of the acquisition of a printing press by the local museum.[87]

Networking was also important in New York. Here Martin Lewis had shown his good friend, Hopper, what he had largely learned for himself, and then, with the zest of a new convert, Hopper had carried the message to Walter Tittle, his neighbor in a Washington Square studio. Tittle had watched his neighbor

busy messing about with bottles of acid, porcelain trays, balls of ground, etc. with an eagerness born of new interest. Occasionally he would show me his experiments, and use me as a model for his plates. He urged me to try this medium, pursuing his propaganda in this direction with remarkable persistence. He adopted a cookoo-clock [*sic*]

technique, popping his head through our connecting door with mo-
notonously repeated advice: 'Make an etching, make an etching,' and
so on indefinitely. The door would slam to escape a missile or bar a
rush, then open again: 'Buy a copper plate, buy a plate, buy a plate!'
As drops of water wear away stone, he forced me into an activity that
I had really craved for a long time.[88]

Such informal recruitment was more common in the years before
the teaching of etching became institutionalized into regular classes. It
survived longer in America, where for many years the etching societies
did what the schools had left largely undone. Much of the thrust came
from a small number of genuine enthusiasts, as untiring as Haden but
also more self-effacing in their campaign on behalf of the medium. As
should by now be obvious, two names stand out: John Taylor Arms
and Bertha Jaques. Their enthusiasm for sharing the fruits of a discovery that both had made essentially on their own was truly contagious.

Arms's proselytizing efforts were legendary. They began even before he moved into the presidency of the Society of American Etchers
in 1931. Diaries he kept reveal a busy schedule of activities to promote
etching among various official and unofficial bodies. Hundreds of artists were no doubt prompted to needle their first plate after watching
one of his many public demonstrations. Even after the market collapsed, his efforts did not flag. Thus, there is still in circulation a
"demonstration plate" of the Grolier Club Library, dated 9 March
1941, etched and printed on those premises and duly editioned for
distribution to members of the club.

Less well known but equally active as a proselytizer was the durable Bertha Jaques, secretary-treasurer of the Chicago Society of Etchers, whose key role in popularizing etching in America we have discussed. Always on the lookout for new talent, she encouraged many
neophytes and personally taught some of them to print or even printed
for them. Hers, she alleged in 1900, was the "only printing press west
of New York." It may have only seemed so to her. Printmakers from all
over the world were forever stopping by just to print their plates on her
press or, more often, to have her print them. She was always helpful
and, like Arms, in great demand as a lecturer: from 1894 to 1933 she
gave 140 talks and demonstrations around the country.[89]

More than that, printmakers constantly solicited her detailed advice: "There may be others," she responded to one inquirer, "who can
tell you more about presses than I can, but I doubt if any secretary gets
more letters concerning them, who is not in the business. Not daily,

but almost weekly am I importuned to direct aspiring etchers to a small and inexpensive press, which, in its box weighs 200 pounds, but the average press such as should be used for large plates runs from 800 to more. I am forced to give the discouraging information that there aint no such critter." She had purchased her own "baby press" weighing 200 pounds around the turn of the century for fifteen dollars from a man who didn't know what it was worth and wanted to get rid of it. Jaques, not eager to discourage her correspondent, tried to hold out some hope—there might be a man who would sell his press, there was a very small wooden press that could print plates not over five by seven—but she finally declared herself helpless. If a small, affordable press could be found, she promised, "I shall be glad to send information concerning blankets, ink, paper and all the necessities."[90]

Having now considered in this and the last chapter how the artists studied made their decisions for art and then for etching, we now turn to consider the personal and social factors that enabled them to build more or less successful reputations in the field.

# 8 🐉

# On the Road to Recognition: The Personal Context

The reputation of an etcher was built on a three-fold foundation: recognition of talent by insiders, proof of that talent through creative printmaking, and access to a network for getting one's prints into circulation. To achieve each of these, most artists had to struggle, sometimes against highly unfavorable odds. Only those whose reputations as painters were already well established had an easier time of it; they did not have to strive for the visibility that others still sought through their etchings.

In building their reputations as artists, etchers were somewhat disadvantaged vis-à-vis painters, whose work had always been more valued. We have already recounted how grudgingly the art establishment, dominated by painters, accorded status to engravers as creators of original work. The discrimination against them persisted. All too often the etchers found their work, even when accepted for exhibition, poorly positioned and hung so that it was difficult for visitors to appreciate its full charm. And no matter how popular etchings became, the art market, no less than the academy, continued to accord them only secondary status.

Some of this disadvantage had to do with qualities intrinsic to the medium. Typically, etchings are small and delicate and therefore not as well suited for display in an exhibition that attracts crowds. Before the rise of galleries, an enterprising artist might send a single previously publicized painting on a traveling exhibition and count on the collection of entry fees to generate income and publicity for the sale of engraved renderings of a highly touted work. Museums, too, had a strong predilection for large canvases. Walter Sickert knew all too well that his bid for glory suffered from his penchant for painting sketches instead of more finished pictures. "I am clear-sighted enough," he confided to a fellow artist, "to realize that the backward position I am in . . . is partly my own fault. I have done too many slight sketches, and too few considered elaborate works . . . not more than half-a-dozen museum pieces . . . in twenty-seven years! And that is *too few*."¹ Nor had Sickert's penchant for small etched sketches of "low-class life" done much to shore up his reputation. Even those which had been acquired by curators or had found their way into public collections by some other route were unlikely to be touted as major acquisitions and would be brought out only for specialized exhibitions. And while these etchings and drawings might be included in a heavily advertised retrospective, the paintings usually attracted the attention and drew the largest crowds.

Etchers are aware that their creations tend to get lost in exhibitions. They do not catch the eye and cannot be viewed from a distance, while seeing them under glass (for their protection) hides their full charm. For this reason, William Strang had declined an invitation to send two etchings to a forthcoming Paris exhibition. "Owing to the extremely limited space," he explained to the organizer, "the showing of [only] two etchings would give so small an idea of an etcher's work that it would be of no use sending."² But etchers also have a certain advantage. Whereas a painter commands attention only if the "right people"—and enough of them—can be induced to come to a showing, the etcher has the capability of producing multiple images—all originals—from a single plate. These impressions are easily transportable and can be sent to whoever might be interested, demonstrating what Walter Benjamin calls the displacement of cult value by exhibition values as a result of mechanical reproduction.³ Etchers are in a position to increase their visibility with editions of their prints, provided of course that they maintain quality.

James D. Smillie had already earned himself some laurels. He was president of the American Watercolor Society, a founding member of the New York Etching Club, and on the way to becoming a member of the National Academy. Yet his incessant concern over where he stood "in the race"⁴ repeatedly crops up in the many letters he wrote. As he confided to Koehler in 1879, "there is probably no better channel or quicker way for me to reach the public and make a reputation, if I am going to have one, than through [Koehler's] *American Art Review*—consequently it will be to my interest to avail myself of that publication to send out some of my most important work." He singled out his not yet completed etching of *Cedars by Moonlight*, of which he had already sold a few impressions to fellow artists. Would Koehler give Smillie $100 for the plate, let him keep fifteen proofs, and publish the print, which would obviously (given the large edition) have to be steel-faced, as soon as he conveniently could? Smillie "had intended at first to keep my more important plates but not believe[d] that it will be policy [politic?] for me to wait before I can invest in that way until I am more widely known by the public"[5] A few months later, still at work on the plate, he was imploring Koehler to delay its release "until the October or November number [of the *Review*]. The people whose attention I strive to get are widely scattered during the summer time, and are then not so easily interested in art matters. Consequently, I feel it a right time as well as in the right place."[6] Smillie expressed the same concern when he questioned the edition size of *Poets and Etchers*: "To print but a thousand [copies] would make the enterprise practically a failure" for artists looking to the volume to publicize their art and themselves.[7]

Like other artists, Smillie knew that he could not build a reputation simply on quantity. He bemoaned the flood of inferior etchings that kept good work from catching the right eye. Opportunities for publicity had to be seized before the bubble burst, even though no one could ever fully control his own fortunes.

In this and the next chapter, we look at how our etchers built reputations. The presentation is organized around the contextual influences on the process—the personal and the social. The personal context refers to the immediate circumstances that facilitate or inhibit an artist's ability to be productive and to get his or her work into circulation, in particular the financial situation, place of residence, and personal connections. While we take up the matter of "mutuality"—partnerships in art—we mostly leave the matter of marriage and gender effects for special treatment in later chapters. The influences discussed in this chapter are "personal" in the sense that they are idiosyncratic rather than general to etchers or to etchers during a particular period. We designate as "social" the changes in the opportunity and reward structures traceable to economic conditions and the state of the art market, changes that simultaneously affect all members of the art community.

## Does Money Matter?

Most professional artists are not bohemians eking out a marginal existence—not the French Impressionists, like Manet, Monet, and Degas in the nineteenth century, nor even all of the European avant-garde painters active during the first quarter of this century.[8] Nor, by any stretch of the imagination, did it hold for the artists we studied. Though they complained—often for good reason—about low earnings, most managed to maintain a comfortable middle-class life-style. Nevertheless, only a small minority of the most successful were able to meet their financial obligations solely from sales to collectors, museums, and the like.

How then did they manage? Hard data on individual income are difficult to come by. To arrive at an informed judgment on sources of livelihood and how these changed over the years, we had to rely on information on jobs held and other income-producing activities, on how an artist's prints and other artworks were marketed, and on family background. While these data rarely allow us to state with any confidence what part of any artist's income in any given time period came from commissions, from illustration, from commercial work, from teaching, and so forth, they do tell us how important the sale of prints was to his or her economic well-being.

For about 70 percent of the British and 78 percent of the Americans, etchings and/or other prints were—during some phase in their lives—a *supplementary* or *significant* source of income (table 8.1). What varied across generations, reflecting changes of the taste cycle, was the proportion for whom this income was a significant means of support, that is, who largely depended on sales of prints for their livelihood. Etchers born between 1880 and 1889 were best positioned to have benefited from the etching vogue—for half of them the sale of prints was significant. But among the generation born 1890 and after, etching continued to be a major source of income but more for Americans than for British.

We also find national differences in the *main* sources of income (table 8.2). Somewhat over one-fourth of the British but more of the Americans—over one-third—lived primarily off sales of their artwork, including paintings, sculpture, prints, and commissioned portraits. Most others in both countries depended mainly on income from teaching, illustration, or commercial work. For about one-fourth in each country teaching and, in some cases, curatorial jobs were the economic mainstay; 15 percent in Britain and 12 percent in the United States depended on illustrating. For all others, commercial employment, architecture, photography, or writing was the main source of income. Though the proportions who derived their livelihood from such "other" sources are just about the same, fewer of the British worked in commercial enterprises, while three Americans spent some part of their working life in jobs not at all related to art. Not one of the British had done so.

Table 8.1
Sale of Etchings as a "Significant" or "At Least Supplementary" Source of Income, by Generation (percentage of each generation)

| | British (N = 121) | | American (N = 172) | |
|---|---|---|---|---|
| *Birth Cohorts* | Significant | At Least Supplementary | Significant | At Least Supplementary |
| Before 1870 | 24 | 65 | 31 | 69 |
| 1870–79 | 21 | 66 | 29 | 93 |
| 1880–89 | 50 | 79 | 50 | 81 |
| After 1889 | 32 | 76 | 49 | 74 |
| All Artists | 31 | 71 | 42 | 78 |

Table 8.2
Main Source of Income for Etchers (in percent)[a]

| Main Source of Income | British (N = 114) | American (N = 151) |
|---|---|---|
| Art | (15) | (12) |
| Prints | (11) | (23) |
| Illustration | 15 | 12 |
| Portrait/mural commissions | 3 | 3 |
| Commercial and miscellaneous other | 4 | 11 |
| Teaching/curatorial | 28 | 26 |
| Private (inheritance or spouse) | 26 | 14 |

[a]Estimated from biographical data and sales records.

More significant is the difference in the proportion with a main income from private sources. Though by the nineteenth century private patronage of artists had greatly diminished, 14 percent of the Americans but almost twice as many of the British could count on family support—on allowances from parents, generous inheritances, or a spouse with a comfortable income. While this kind of cushion seldom removed all pressure to earn income, it would certainly have reduced it. By far the most frequent recipients of such bounties in both countries were women.

This preliminary accounting suggests four related, yet distinct, questions about the influence of money, or the lack of it, on artistic output:

1. Did artists whose financial well-being was assured thereby lack the necessary drive to produce?
2. Did dependence on print sales affect the *quantity* of an artist's output?
3. Did the need to sell affect the *quality* of the product?
4. Was it counterproductive to have to work at a job not directly related to one's primary artistic activity?

## Was Financial Security a Disincentive?

Surely, it is better to be too rich than too poor. Yet economic theory postulates that it is the need to make a living that encourages the self-employed to work harder. Thus, it was said that since Edouard Manet "had an independent income, there was not the same pressure [on him] . . . to produce and sell as on, say, Pissarro," who, with a large family, and six children to support, was in a far more difficult position.[9] And, indeed, while Manet painted only 286 canvases between 1855 and 1883, Pissarro produced 710 between 1851 and 1890, and by 1910 this total had risen to 1,267.

Other things being equal, family wealth seems an obvious asset. It frees the artist from the pressure to turn out salable work in quantity and provides the leisure that is believed to foster creativity. Few of our painter-etchers were born to wealth, but near a fifth had some private means of support. Without the financial incentive to produce and sell, were they relatively less productive than others less favored by fate? With regard to painters, this kind of question is difficult enough to answer; for etchers it is even more complicated. For the painter, the number of canvases is a reasonable, if flawed, measure of productivity, but the output of printmakers can be measured either by the number of finished plates or by the total number of impressions pulled from those plates.

We found the lack of a financial incentive to have had a more discernible effect on the size of editions and number of impressions printed than on the number of plates. While self-approval and the approval of peers sufficed to keep the well-to-do etcher etching, why bother to print more than a handful of impressions of a plate if sales did not matter? The American, Cadwallader Washburn, for instance, born into a family with very considerable mineral holdings in Minnesota, could travel endlessly in search of inspiration and, unencumbered by the need for sales, put outrageously high prices on his prints. Though his productivity, judged by number of plates, was high, it was far lower when measured by the number of impressions. Likewise, Reginald Marsh, with a munificent inheritance from his grandfather, never bothered to print a full edition of most of his plates.

There are exceptions to the pattern. Helen Loggie, the daughter of a wealthy businessman in Bellingham, Washington, had the resources to pursue "a lifelong love affair with art and literature." Sent to Smith College and then to the Art Students League in New York City, she also could travel in Europe. Before she was thirty, she had etched and exhibited between seventy-five and ninety plates, but then, returning to the Northwest, she began a long-lasting, long-distance collaboration with John Taylor Arms, the master etcher. For twenty-five years, until his death in 1953, she sent him her plates along with a few proofs pulled on her old Sturges press. Arms would then see how her plate performed on various expensive papers. When the best combinations of inking and paper had been decided, the plates were sent for editioning to David Strang, the most sought-after printer in England.[10] Loggie was in a position to pay for the shipping, the printing, and for the finest Italian, French, or English rag papers.[11] Considering these expenses, there was little, if any, profit for her in printing full editions of her works, but she did so nevertheless. Had she not loved to draw, she told friends in 1965, she would never have etched, but this was the only way to get her drawings, mostly of Northwest landscapes and, especially its trees, distributed. By continuing to show her etchings at competitive and invitational print and drawing exhibitions long after the vogue had passed, she acquired an audience and, by selling at a loss—something artists with no private means could not afford to do—she also found buyers. In this way, she worked to build a reputation. Her last plate, made in 1960 when she had long suffered from arthritis, remained uneditioned.

The weight of biographical evidence suggests that an assured income from any source, even if it did not guarantee financial independence, was more of an opportunity than a hindrance, especially in getting started. Young Alden Weir made it to Paris with an allowance from the wealthy widow of one of his baptismal sponsors; William Merritt Chase got there with help from a syndicate of wealthy St. Louis businessmen who underwrote his expenses. For others a Prix de Rome or a traveling scholarship brought the freedom to develop and a head start in building a reputation. Lacking such patronage, some young printmakers found dealers willing to invest in them: thus, when

Anthony Gross, who had learned to etch at the London Central School while yet a teenager, was without funds to continue his studies abroad, a dealer offered to sponsor him at £6 a month—a guarantee sufficient, as the artist saw it, to make him independent and "free to earn it anywhere."[12] For the five years of their contractual relationship, he was free to travel to Spain, Morocco, Algeria, Italy, and Sicily, producing a considerable body of work that he could be sure would sooner or later be shown.

## Did Dependence on Sales Increase Print Productivity?

Searching for an answer, we looked at income in still another way: How dependent was the artist on the income from prints? The ones who looked upon their prints as their main source of livelihood for at least some part of their career were judged to be *print-dependent*; those with several sources of income, one of which was prints, were judged to be *partly print-dependent*. A third group of *print-independents* includes those with private means, for whom the income from etchings mattered little, if at all.

When we then cross-tabulated the degree of print-dependency with print-productivity—using as measures both the number of extant plates and actual impressions printed—the unambiguously dependent proved to be, on the average, the most productive. Yet only in Britain is there a consistent increase in plate production as dependence on print income increases (table 8.3). In America, the relationship is less clear: while those most dependent on print income turned out more plates, the print-independent were more productive than those whose income was only partly dependent on the sale of prints. It seems that among the thirty-four Americans whose well-being was not at all dependent on such sales, there were at least three unusually high producers—Benton Spruance, Grace Albee, and Cadwallader Washburn—who account for the high average output of this group.

Our analysis supports to this extent the common belief that need is a spur to effort: the economic incentive stimulates productivity, which in turn stimulates the growth of reputation. The unambiguously print-dependent in Britain needled three and one-half times as many plates and pulled about four times as many impressions as those not dependent on sales. And while the association is not so dramatic in America, the productivity of the print-dependent there was about twice that of all others (table 8.3).

Still, a "yes" answer to our question is not unqualified: first, our

Table 8.3
Productivity, Measured by Average Number of Plates Produced, According to
Artists' Dependence on Income from Etching

| Income from Prints | British ($N = 121$) | American ($N = 151$) |
|---|---|---|
| Significant | 212 | 190 |
| Supplementary | 99 | 93 |
| Not important | 59 | 133[a] |

[a] This figure is brought up by a few high producers of independent means who pulled small editions.

data are not unflawed. It must be acknowledged that information on any artist's oeuvre, even that based on a catalogue raisonné, is subject to some error. Unless a fully annotated collection has been set aside, the cataloguer has to rely in good part on the memory of the artist (or a surrogate), and this can prove faulty. Accuracy depends also on the cataloguer's own fund of knowledge and on the care taken with the cataloguing. Some were satisfied to list only those plates that were in fact "published," while others were inclined to list every plate, no matter how experimental, including those for which no impression had survived or could be found. Productivity figures vary accordingly. Furthermore, some catalogs compiled while an artist was still alive and productive unavoidably lack information on prints that were yet to come. And far more problematic are the productivity estimates for the many artists whose work still remains uncatalogued; we based these on whatever documents we could find—exhibition lists, museum holdings, advertisements, publication notices, personal correspondence, memorabilia—and, in a few cases, they are no more than educated guesses.

Second, the selective survival of records favors artists with established reputations. The better known the artist, the more likely it is that his or her oeuvre will be fully documented; conversely, the oeuvre of the less well known artist, however industrious, is likely to be undercounted. In this way differences in productivity levels are likely to be exaggerated. This is not, as in the case of Old Masters, a function of overattribution but of the thoroughness, even zeal, with which the documentation has been pursued. To locate an unknown print by a major artist is more rewarding than to catalog the oeuvre of a lesser figure. Aware that the gap in productivity might thus be exaggerated, we recalculated our figures, comparing only those in the British sample whose output could be documented with a high degree of certainty. And, as anticipated, the gap narrowed, but the observed relationship, however attenuated, between productivity and print-dependency persists. Here again, as with the Americans, the closing of the gap between the print-independent and those only partially print-dependent is almost totally accounted for by two deviant cases. Neither Arthur Briscoe nor Martin Hardie had any financial need to etch, yet both were high producers, each having published 189 plates. The average output of the eight other print-independents was only 78.

## Does the Need to Sell Affect the Quality of the Product?

Artists worry that in the quest for security they may subvert their more lofty ambitions. Thus, Umberto Boccioni, a member of the Futurist movement who died in World War I, confided to his diary: "I am not discouraged over my own powers but over my financial means, which don't ever seem to increase without the most ignoble self-prostitution."[13] Although few of our painter-etchers seem to have agonized in their letters and diaries—at least in such extreme language—about debasing their art for money, such charges are not unheard of. One finds throughout the etching revival criticism of some artists, beginning with Charles Jacque, for catering to demand and turning out pastiches of indifferent quality. Is there any telling evidence that making etchings for income is associated with a deterioration of quality?

Essentially, artists made prints for three reasons: to please themselves, to make money, and/or to reach a wider public and thus make a name for themselves. An artist might be motivated by pleasure, money, and ambition all at the same time, and the primary motivation could change over the course of a career. During the earliest phases of the revival, artists did not expect to reap much financial benefit from their etchings. Alden Weir, the American Impressionist painter, avowed that he drew on copper "for the sole reason that it had the mystery of a new path." He found it easy to carry around in his pockets a half-dozen plates with which to fill up odd moments. Gradually, and under the influence of his friend and fellow artist, Henry Twachtman, he "got so interested in a certain charm that etching only possesses" that he acquired his own press and would often pull prints in the early hours of the morning.[14]

Money to be made from prints was particularly tempting to the young artist whose reputation was not yet secured. Thus Peter Hurd, born early in the century, turned to lithography as a way of achieving solvency during the depression. Though he had been gaining attention as a painter, he found it impossible to support himself with commissions and the small number of paintings he had been able to sell. Originally inspired by George Bellows, he tried his hand at lithography but took it up seriously only when he came to believe that "there would be a demand for [his] lithographs at prices ranging from ten to twenty dollars per print."[15] The hunch proved correct. Sales of lithographs "played a significant part in keeping bills paid." Still, producing to order had its frustrations. After finishing a print to be sold as a Christmas card, he confided to his diary that, "[If] it had been four times as large it would have been much better—more textures more careful—subtle handling." He was similarly concerned that its Western subject matter, consisting of five shepherds singing around a campfire before a starlit tepee, might strike the people of Pennsylvania, where he had been working, as "too bizarre to allow for popularity around here." What kept him working were the sales a friend in New Mexico was making for him, plus assurances from his printers that he could expect more buyers.[16] But as he developed a reputation as a painter, the financial incentive weakened and he no longer pursued his printmaking with the same energy.

Incentives were to change even more dramatically for Arthur Millier. After his discharge from the Canadian Army in 1919, this California artist resumed his art studies in San Francisco, supporting himself with odd jobs until he returned to Los Angeles. In 1921 he won a scholarship to the Art Students League but was warned that, with the country in the midst of an economic depression, he should not venture to New York without some assured means of subsistence. Having studied etching in San Francisco, Millier now took up the medium and had little trouble selling his etchings "around town." For several years, these sales supported a growing family. He also taught etching, mostly in his own house: "At that time they all wanted to know how to etch so we had quite a business there. And it was the architects and their draftsmen, the doctors and the lawyers who bought prints, and they were very helpful because they would send me to another ... whenever the going began to get rough and I didn't know how I was going to pay the gas bill why I'd stick a bunch of prints in a portfolio and go out in an afternoon or morning. This worked for a number of years until they could see me coming."[17]

Millier abandoned etching when it ceased to provide the income he needed, though he continued to seek recognition as an artist. After a series of jobs, including sales work for a local gallery and writing reviews for newspapers, he discovered he had more talent as a critic than as a salesman of prints. When the art critic of the *Los Angeles Times* resigned, he took over.[18] A few years later, he gave up his artistic ambitions, reasoning that he could hardly be impartial were he reviewing shows to which he might send. Only when he retired from the *Times* did he once again take up the etching needle—but for a quite different, intensely personal, reason. Earlier, needing to sell prints, he had been depicting urban scenes; now he wanted to record, for posterity, the vanishing rural landscape of California—a "useless [and] a silly obsession," he confided to his wife. "I, the great unappreciated Millier, will show them in a few lines on paper what California is really like." He feared that his etched impressions would have little meaning for anyone else, so that his last attempt "for a morsel of eternity" might only be "a kind of conceit."[19] Concerned for his reputation, he etched, above all, for the fulfillment it gave him. These prints were issued in rather small editions.

Were Millier's later etchings, produced from purer motives, better than the ones he did in the earlier period? One critic commented on the greater looseness of his late style, almost as if he were sketching. But this change might have come anyway with greater maturity. Besides, Millier had never created with an eye solely focused on what would sell.

No one doubts that artistic integrity is apt to suffer when financial considerations override all others. Some painters are judged to have frittered away their talent in accepting fashionable portrait commissions. Similarly, the reputation of an etcher who catered to the apparently insatiable demand for picturesque townscapes, quaint architectural views, idyllic landscapes, sentimental kitsch, and other subjects then fashionable could not be sustained for very long. There was, for example, William Lee-Hankey: having once forfeited his scholarship to the Royal College of Art (RCA) in order to maintain his artistic independence, he was later criticized for adopting "the well-worn theme of motherhood and [playing] upon its seeming banality in exquisite variations." His popularity began to peak while the demand for etching was still on the rise in the 1920s. Even his admirers wished that he might enlarge the range of his subject matter and introduce variety into his technique, including one critic who nonetheless insisted that the artist was "no manufacturer clinging to a formula" and that each plate was the result of "an esthetic emotion."[20]

Of course, the motivation of an etcher who repeats a formula found to please a public need not be crassly commercial. Thus, there is the example of Hedley Fitton, whose elaborately detailed and over-sized etchings were catalogued and highly praised in the first two decades of this century. Many were published in editions of 250 and sold at a premium to a small band of admirers, who acquired them as personal possessions and not, as so many collectors, for resale at substantial profits. An acquaintance remembered him as a man who, though "interested" in the prices his etchings fetched, was "never deflected [by them] from pursuing his high standard for dealing with the public at large. No artist had less of the commercial spirit, none detested more deeply modern methods of self-advertisement."[21] Nevertheless, when he died in 1929, it was thought that "his claim to remembrance will be little," and Guichard, a half-century later, panned his etchings. They "competed with Dendy Sadler reproductions for destruction during etching purges. . . . Some that were perhaps too heavy to leave their abodes have managed to survive."[22]

Demand affects quantity more directly than subject matter. On this score artists are prone to misjudgments. Hurd, whom we just discussed, had made a lithographed self-portrait. Thinking that "it would have only very limited interest or market value, [he] had the printer make only a few impressions before polishing the stone" but then found, to his surprise, that certain collectors specialized in artists' self-portraits. When a curator inquired about his, Hurd had but one unsold print from the small edition.[23] Sometimes the influence of demand can be charted by the number pulled from each plate. Frank W. Benson took up etching in 1912. That year he published twelve plates, another twelve in 1913, and eleven in 1914. But the total yield from these early plates rose dramatically—from 112 the first year to 189 the next and 384 in 1914—as they attracted attention.[24] Benson, who was still doing his own printing, had limited the edition size to 35 for drypoints and 50 for etchings. But as demand kept rising, he began printing as many impressions as a plate might yield. By 1917, some editions were running to 150, which became the norm for his published plates during the 1920s.

In so stepping up his output, Benson did not, however, abandon his concern for quality. He was never accused of prostituting his art for money. But he could hardly have been averse to the profits it brought. Few etchers, save perhaps McBey, enjoyed this popular painter's almost instantaneous financial success as an etcher. The publication price of his new plates was rarely under $60, and for some it went as high as $125—a tidy sum equal to about one-fourth of the price of a new car! Benson once confided to A. J. Philpott, a critic, that his "personal profit from the sale of etchings had averaged about $80,000 a year" during the boom years.[25] What kept him going is hard to say. He did not etch so he could eat. He had been doing well financially long before his etchings began to sell. Indeed, he owned four houses in Salem, Massachusetts, one of which, occupied by a recently married daughter, had burned down in the 1914 fire.

Printing is tedious and costs money. No artist has any incentive to print (or have printed) beyond what the market can absorb—plus the few extras for self and friends. To this extent, then, an artist's admirers create the supply. One etcher might wish to limit quantity in order to realize high prices from a more select clientele. Another might set a limit out of considerations that are purely aesthetic. Cameron, for one, wanted the size of his editions to be determined only by the durability of the copper. He ceased printing as soon as a plate showed the slightest sign of wear. On the same ground, he resisted steel-facing a plate to make large printings possible, holding to the view that the thin film of the harder metal, however impossible to measure, impaired the quality of the lines and the resonance of the masses.[26] On this point, he disagreed with many other authorities, among them Frank Short, who had found two prints from the same plate, one taken before and one after steel-facing, to be indistinguishable.

Could it have been that Cameron, in playing the perfectionist, was appealing to the "discriminating" collector, who only wanted the best and the most expensive? This is unlikely; many other etchers shared his view and accepted whatever financial loss it might cause them. Harry Wickey had been encouraged by William Ivins, the curator of prints at the New York Metropolitan Museum of Art, to show his drypoints to some of the best dealers around the city. Carl Zigrosser at Weyhe was the only one to accept any on consignment. But then, after the Met bought three and other artists, among them George Bellows and "Pop" Hart, had commented favorably on Wickey's work, he found the dealers more receptive. His editions, however, had been small; some were never completed because the plates showed signs of wear, and Wickey considered it "entirely unethical to retouch them once this had occurred. A number had been given to artist friends, and when I finally had a market there were very few on hand to sell. I was not greatly concerned by this fact, for the work had served to establish my reputation as a sincere artist, and that was compensation for the time being."[27] Wickey, who was then in dire financial straits, valued his reputation more than the potential proceeds that enlarged editions could have brought him.

One woman who achieved her economic goals without sacrificing her artistic standards was Helen Hyde, a color etcher from San Francisco whose early successes as a painter in Paris would have completely satisfied a less ambitious or less talented woman. Even if her paintings and watercolors "did not set the Seine afire," they were mentioned respectfully. She was only twenty-two when she won a first honorable mention in the Salon.[28] After she returned to San Francisco, possibly because of the "ruthless rejection" of one of her pictures by the Salon,[29] she gained wide admiration for her color prints—etchings, drypoints, and aquatints, as well as woodblocks of children—Chinese, Japanese, Mexicans, and Southern blacks. *Totty*, the first of her children, as she liked to think of them, was a "wee chubby child sitting on a doorstep absorbed in her own interests." The public ignored *Totty*, whom Hyde called "my unappreciated first." It was a simple etching in black and white, a failure until she "smudged some paint on her and, lo the missing something was supplied. Totty was complete and established her right henceforth to appear in colored clothes."[30] Successful experiments in color printing followed, and once a local dealer agreed to handle "her children," there were requests for them from all over the country. The leading galleries in New York, Boston, Kansas, Denver, and Chicago carried them.

Her success in marketing these color prints was not entirely fortuitous. Financial acumen, united to executive ability of a high order, was another of Hyde's talents.[31] She had, she wrote as her career began virtually anew, always wanted to support herself by her work. Yet she had consistently refused to "abase" her art purely for money-making or to "do clap-trap work to catch the public eye and fancy. I believe in artists living up to the best there is in them and going on in their own way. In time people will say, 'See that person going so steadily along, turning neither to the right nor the left; he must be going somewhere.' Then they begin to tag along and soon there will be plenty of followers."[32] To read her correspondence is to understand how the quality of her work combined with persistence, pluck, charm, and good business sense helped her develop the requisite market channels. In San Francisco, she "had the press behind her." Mrs. William Randolph Hearst had bought six or seven of her prints, and Hearst himself had gone to the gallery to photograph them for his papers. Her entry point to New York was the Macbeth Gallery, which handled contemporary paintings. Along with a painting, she sent some of her color etchings to the owner "just in case he wanted to do something with them." She was aware that Macbeth did not handle prints but "I would like my little heathen to be in your hands." As customers, seeing the etchings, requested copies, she found herself "chained to her printing press," with Macbeth functioning as a print dealer without ever having meant to. The relationship was formalized. She asked him about prices: "Some or *most* of the dealers think they are low but I don't want to raise them until I am sure of my ground."[33]

Her distributional network in place, Hyde went to Japan in 1899 to study color woodblock techniques. During her fifteen years in Tokyo and Nikko, while she experimented with the process, she took care to maintain, even expand, the outlets in the United States for her prints. When Macbeth moved, she turned to Klackner's as her New York outlet. As she explained, there might have been more "artistic places," but she felt that her children were far better off with Klackner's, who wanted them, "than with more artistic and snooty people who might take them on tolerance." In Japan, after giving up trying to print all her own work, she could easily have issued larger editions with the printers she had trained and now supervised. In fact, they were disappointed at not being able to print by the thousands as was their custom. Financially her success was "as complete and permanent as the assurance of her place in the art world," wrote Bertha Jaques.[34]

For the printmakers who had found a safe niche in the expanded market, there was always the temptation to repeat a success and thus play it safe. Yet to be sought out by dealers also put the artist in a strong position to resist the pressure, if not always the temptation, to sacrifice artistic integrity by catering to the market. Thus, financial incentives apparently affected reputations in contradictory ways. The prospective income from prints was for many a spur to productivity but enhanced a reputation only to the extent that the enlarged output did not damage the etcher's standing with other artists.

## Is a Job Counterproductive?

In their reminiscences, some etchers recalled, with expressions of dismay, how the market crash forced them into teaching or illustration or what some considered the ultimate debasement—commercial work. But was working at any of these jobs necessarily counterproductive?

To begin with, we note that even before the market crash most of our etchers, unable to support themselves solely or mainly by the sale of their artwork, had to look to other sources of income. Especially in America, with its more individualized, competitive contest to prove oneself, artists had to fend for themselves, making the most of whatever opportunities came their way—teaching a course here and there and from time to time or free-lancing at illustration, poster design, or whatever. The British, with opportunities more contingent on sponsorship, were more likely to have found one relatively secure position and stayed with it. The differences in national opportunity patterns are reflected in the kinds of jobs held. Although slightly more British than Americans obtained their main income from teaching, more Americans than British had taught at some time or other—many of them in a temporary job without a salary high enough to live on. When supplementary sources of income are taken into consideration, 42 percent of the British and 52 percent of the Americans derived at least part of their livelihood from teaching. For Americans, illustration was likewise more important as a source of supplementary income, rather than as main income, which it had been for a significant number of the British. The reverse was the case when it came to commercial work. Although it held little attraction for most artists on both sides of the Atlantic, more Americans were attracted to this sector by its evident earning potential. The difference between the etchers in the two countries remains even when supplementary income is taken into account. The breakdowns for *main* income are shown in table 8.2.

Some jobs held by those in impecunious circumstances could not have advanced their artistic careers. Two of our Americans—Ernest Roth and Emil Ganso—worked in bakeshops while seeking to break into art. Roth's classmates at the NAD had nicknamed him "the baker"; he worked nights—on the one to eight A.M. shift—at his father's bakery so as to leave afternoons and evenings open for art classes. However, staying awake in class required some effort. Despite instructors who worried about his health, he only gave up this job when, rewarded by modest sales, he was able to rent a little house in an out-of-the-way area of Staten Island, New York. He turned this into a practical studio, where he expected "to be able to devote all his time to his art."[35]

Ganso turned to baking out of far greater need. Arriving in the United States with hardly a penny to his name, he found casual employment in bakeries on shifts that lasted from twelve to fourteen hours—even sixteen on Saturday night. He took to "visiting" the classes at the NAD but found it hard to stay alert: "Just imagine me falling asleep with a nice nude model right in front of me," recalled the artist, whose most acclaimed prints (and paintings) would be of nudes.[36] Ganso's account of his early years evokes images of *la vie de bohème*. About 1915–16 he teamed up with Jan Matulka, another artist, sharing a bare room in an empty house on Fourteenth Street, where no one collected the rent and they lived cheaply with the help of the bread, cakes, and rolls Ganso received at bakeries where he unsuccessfully sought employment.

Later the two were able to continue their makeshift existence in a rented apartment, painting as often as circumstances allowed. One day's work for Ganso meant a week's food; if there was a second day's work, this was set aside for the upcoming rent. When there were enough jobs to stretch money beyond rent and food, they would hire a model for Sunday painting. The pressure on Ganso relaxed during World War I, when the bakers won an eight-hour day and he landed a job as foreman in one of New York's largest baking plants. All this time he was not just painting but etching, having found a press abandoned by another artist in their apartment building. Some nine years after his arrival in America, Ganso managed to crash the no-jury exhibition of the Society of Independent Artists with three nudes he had painted on a double bed sheet rather than on canvas, which was expensive. Only in 1925, when he was well hooked into the art world, did he feel he could "wipe the flour and sweat from his face and [leave] the full-time oven for the full-time easel." At the opening of his first print exhibition, the Weyhe Gallery "served the cake he had baked as a farewell gesture to his old profession."[37]

Like these two bakers, others of our etchers at one time or another took on odd jobs as watchmen, hotel clerks, and dishwashers; they picked fruit, worked on ferry boats, shipped out to sea, surveyed land, sailed as hands on fishing boats, and did things that in no way drew on their artistic skills. Others painted signs, decorated homes and churches, and, before the advent of press photography, found employment as newspaper illustrators. Yasuo Kuniyoshi managed to free summers for painting by photographing the art of his fellow painters.

*Teaching and productivity.* The conventional alternative to such freelancing was a secure teaching post. For some this was not just a means to an end. Rather they viewed it as less diverting than more highly paid commercial work, where the demands of the client more nearly determined output. On balance, teaching has to be considered more of an asset than a liability: "Not the least of the benefits from teaching," wrote Harry Wickey, "was the fact that I was allowed to develop in my own way without worry of whether I was producing work that would sell. I, too, was growing, and my contact with students helped considerably, for on more than one occasion their freshness of vision helped to clear up a troublesome problem for me." One of his bright students observed that, "Harry keeps the class going so he can etch and he etches so he can keep the class going."[38] Nor did William Robins's teaching responsibilities at the London Central School make him less productive. At least one critic thought that "the additional experience . . . gained . . . by the practice of teaching . . . had carried his technique to greater perfection."[39]

Whether a teaching job was for a career more an asset than a liability depended on a number of factors: the prestige of the institution where the artist was employed, where it was located, and how large a commitment of time and energy was required in the fulfillment of one's duties. Well-positioned teachers of etching with access to equipment, to assistants, and to students could devote themselves to their art. Frank Short, Malcolm Osborne, and Robert Austin not only gained visibility as professors of engraving at the RCA, they also produced, during their tenure there, some of their best-known plates. While their selection was a capstone to prior accomplishments, this did not hold for Susan Crawford, who at twenty-six was appointed assistant in the Department of Etching at the Glasgow School of Art, where she taught for twenty-four years, until her death in 1918. Initially trained at the school, she had then studied abroad, a practice she continued during working holidays and between terms. As the only Scottish woman then a fellow of the Royal Society of Painter-Etchers (RSPE),[40] she was a reliable contributor to its annual exhibitions as well as to exhibitions abroad. During her relatively short lifespan, she etched over one hundred plates, mostly topographical. Reviewers thought them "charming," "clever," and even "creative when not concerned with representation."[41] It would seem that her teaching did not deter her from maintaining her contacts with the larger art world; it also made her a central figure in Glasgow's art community and "a favorite among her fellow-artists."[42] She was thus spared the fate of some nationally recognized women artists whose accomplishments went unacknowledged in their hometowns. Quite to the contrary, her prints were among the central attractions in the school's annual exhibitions, and she was welcomed into Glasgow's leading women's clubs— the Glasgow Literary and the Society of Lady Artists, which combined "the social with artistic elements in its pleasant club house."[43]

Teaching could, however, cut into time for creative work. A heavy schedule or administrative load could take its toll on productivity, especially if the employing institution was removed from the mainstream of art. Dorothy Burt Martin, for example, spent most of her working life as an art mistress in the sequestered environment of a residential school. Born in 1882, she had first trained in the Midlands (Wolverhampton), gone on to the Royal College of Art, held several short-term teaching appointments, and ended by spending thirty years as the head of the Art Department at the prestigious Roedean School (for girls) in Brighton. Fortunately, the headmistress thought it to the advantage of the school to give Martin one day a week to go to London, "whether she used it to make paintings of special flowers for the Royal Horticultural Society or to follow a course in the History of Art at the Courtauld Institute, to go to Exhibitions, or generally to keep in touch with her artist friends, and . . . to give up one evening in the week to train students in etching at the Brighton School of Art." Etching was her first and continuing love; a former student enrolled at the RCA had been "amazed" to find Martin in Sir Frank Short's "[Saturday] class . . . [working away] with all the enthusiasm . . . of the twenty-year old students." Martin never gave up "learning." Having mastered one craft—be it embroidery, pottery, or modeling—she was always ready to master the next: "At each of her annual exhibitions of etchings and paintings one was surprised afresh at the amount of work she had achieved during the year, in addition to her teaching."[44]

Martin nevertheless failed to build a great reputation even though she exhibited regularly at the Brighton Art Club and at the Society of Women Artists. She never, as far as we have been able to tell, had a gallery or dealer to represent her, printed a full edition of any of her plates, listed herself in the directory of the *Fine Prints of the Year*, or sought election to the RSPE. Was it that her profound loyalty to the school and to her students ("ready at all hours of day or night to do things for others") made her less productive or personally ambitious? Nevertheless, her landscape etchings, hardly well known, did find their way to the print room of the Victoria and Albert, where Guichard, who inspected them, classified her as a "major" etcher. How many other talented etchers teaching in residential schools under similar circumstances were simply never heard from? We know only those who were sufficiently successful to be included in our study. One of these, Gertrude Hayes, who for many years taught art at the famous Rugby School, was also one of the most productive among our British women.

Roi Partridge was one who looked back upon his many years of teaching—at Mills College in Oakland, California, where he had also directed the art gallery and chaired the art department—as the "peak period of his productivity as an artist." He got the job in 1920, when he badly needed it. At thirty-two, he had already achieved a good deal of recognition, winning some of the most coveted prizes for etching. But, with a wife and three children to support, he "found it hard going to live exclusively as an artist."[45] Bertha Jaques, in recommending Partridge to the manager of a print-dealing firm in Boston, described him when they first met as

> an enthusiastic student of the martyr type, prepared to carry his banner to the heights or die. A friend told me he was sleeping on the floor, had one suit of clothes and couldn't turn his back unless he had his coat on. He cooked his own food and lived mostly on cereals from principle. He wrote me, without boasting, of having acquired enough money to buy a cape, much needed, but on the way to the store, he saw a beautiful Japanese print in a window and bought it instead. It was always his idea that the food for the spirit was worth more than clothing or food for the body. It was his devotion to principles that made me feel whatever he started after he would get. About that time I heard of him and began to sell his prints which surprised him greatly. The confidence it brought, and the patronage, was quite a lift. He came home [from Paris] about the time the war broke out, proposed to a girl he had been corresponding with, but had never seen, and went to see her as soon as he landed in Seattle. . . . With no money or anything to support a wife, they were married and had a desperate struggle for a time, especially as three boys came in two years, the last in a pair. He said he would die before he would do commercial work, but thought better of it, took a position to do designing, got strongly on his feet and was offered a position as teacher of art in the Mills College, one of the largest schools for girls in the country. . . . This took only part of his time and has enabled him to go on with his etching.[46]

After five years of teaching, Partridge had not, he wrote, lost "interest in etching. I have nearly three months in summer and some days each week to spend in the field and in my workshop."[47] The artist, who became best known for his linear depictions of California's wooded and mountainous terrains, was able to make a virtue of necessity. It was a dearth of funds that had first turned him toward landscapes for subject matter rather than to costly studio work.[48] Now, with money from teaching, he could see to some creature comforts while immersing himself in the outdoors. He bought a little piece of land with a small house on it, then bought the adjoining piece with a shack, remodeled it himself, and rented it out. Going to the woods for trees and shrubs, he made the place beautiful. When he was able to buy a secondhand car and a dress suit, he joked that "his downward career was complete." When he finally did give up teaching, he told us two years before his death at 96, it was to devote the full time of his remaining years to etching.

Those who taught in the secondary school system found it harder to keep up with their own artwork, and a disproportionate number of these were women. Two who persevered were Blanche Dillaye, an American, and Marion Rhodes, from Yorkshire in North England. Dillaye, an early art educator, taught for many years at the Ogontz School in Philadelphia, which she herself had attended. The school had been founded by her aunt, a pioneer in the struggle for reform in "girls education" by acquainting them with literature, art, and science, as an alternative to the old curriculum of "samplers and accomplishments."[49] This exacting educational experience turned Dillaye into an exponent of the gospel of ambition and hard work. She signed many of her drawings with a tiny sketch of a snail as a play on her French name, pronounced "delay," and took as her motto Shakespeare's tribute to the snail: "He goes but slowly, but he carries his house on his head." A handsome woman, she was also "nervous energy personified." She excelled not only as a teacher but also as an organizer and played a vital role in activating the Philadelphia art community. As an artist, she drove herself all her life—during the years she taught and after she was able to give it up. Her early work was praised for its accurate drawing, good handling of light and shade, and a fine discernment in choice of subject matter; her later work was praised for its mastery of technique. Teaching seems not to have held her back. Before she was fifty—and she lived to be eighty—a newspaper declared that "few women of America have risen to as high a place in the art world as that held by Blanche Dillaye."[50]

Marion Rhodes, born in this century, was enrolled at the Leeds College of Art when her father was killed in an accident. With no intention of abandoning art, she nevertheless found it prudent to fulfill the requirements for a teaching certificate, which by that time included a course on etching. After some years of teaching in the provinces, she found an art teacher's job in London that she was able to combine with part-time evening studies under William Robins at the Central School. Economic necessity kept her in teaching, but a career in etching had become her primary goal. Determined not to let teaching interfere, she resisted all temptation to advance in the pedagogical hierarchy: "You can't be a head mistress and go on with your work." For fourteen years she taught only part-time because she wanted "the middle part of [her] life to be productive." At West Ham High School, she could finish at 3:30 and then go, twice a week, to the Central School. At the Enfield Country School, where she taught subsequently, she found a "good atmosphere" that allowed her to keep up with her art.

Though still a neophyte when etching went out of fashion, Rhodes never ceased producing plates. Between 1928 and 1940, with hardly a market and no financial incentive, she had produced about 150 etchings, aquatints, and softgrounds. Nor did she slow up during the disruptive period when her school was bombed to the ground during the Second World War. She even secured a special permit to needle an etching of St. Paul's during the German blitz. In 1941, aged thirty-four, she was elected an Associate Royal Etcher; in 1953, she became an R.E. Until at least the end of the 1970s, she continued to work in the older style of the 1920s and 1930s and never missed a chance to exhibit in the annual exhibition. Some of her plates were fully editioned, but she never tried for a "one-man" show or sought an agent, a road that, as she saw it, was "all right if you want to make a living at it." She enjoyed creating and, believing etching was "for ordinary people to have an original at a reasonable price," wanted to share this enjoyment with others.

Comfortable with her own modest life-style, she chose to put low prices on her prints. Retired from teaching in 1960, she had not, when we spoke to her twenty years later, "retired from the etching press." In fact, she had bought a small one to be able to work at home.[51]

*Illustration and Reputation.* Fewer etchers earned their main livelihood from illustration than from teaching. But two of every three Britons and two of every five Americans derived significant supplementary income by illustrating books or magazines. Yet most were loath to be labeled as "illustrators." The term, as Howard Simon points out in a history of the subject, "has often been used as a kind of epithet to hurl at the modern artist who dares to embody an idea in the medium of print." He intended his book, among other things, to serve as a reminder that the greatest of artists, including Dürer, Raphael, Mantegna, Rembrandt, Hogarth, Goya, Cruikshank, and Toulouse-Lautrec, did not neglect illustration.[52]

Most of our etcher-illustrators would have defined themselves as fine art, rather than commercial, illustrators, a working distinction based on the degree of control the artist exercises over the conception of the image and its printing. Given the association of their metier with reproductive engraving, which they had long tried to escape, etchers were especially sensitive to implications that their work was in any sense less genuinely creative, or artistic, than that of painters or sculptors. To earn one's way by illustrating was to court such criticism: "The only thing" blocking Ruth Gannett's election to the National Academy was "that she has done a great deal of illustration," so Dorothy Lathrop, herself an associate of the academy, wrote in thanking Grace Albee for endorsing Gannett's nomination. Being a woman and illustrator, Lathrop felt she knew how "real" artists felt about illustration, and this did not give her "much confidence about going to Academy meetings."[53]

Notwithstanding such discrimination, there were certain advantages in being an illustrator. Pennell, who had supported himself by such work while attending the Pennsylvania Academy, pointed these out in his own blunt fashion: "Illustrating, despised by the Professor, held in contempt by painters, looked down upon by the students, was not [in 1881] the favorite path along which the incompetent could struggle or promenade. . . . But when I began to get going, I found that the painters were willing enough to come to me, to whom they had scarce spoken before, for tips about work. I believed, as I do now, that illustration is a most serious, a most important form of art. . . . Really, though, all art is illustration and always has been from the beginning of time."[54] Pennell and an artist friend had heard that Peter Moran and the Smillies (James as well as George) were making etchings and drawings of pictures and getting paid a dollar an hour for it. Proudly he recalled his and his friend's disrespect for tradition and professional etiquette and their "wild desire to get some of the dollars. . . . What we were asked to do was to make pen-and-ink sketches from photographs of well-known pictures by European artists. This we did, and so well that we were given lots more—or I was—and as we virtually could select our artists, we tried to do our best."[55]

The recognition Pennell so quickly gained as an illustrator, mainly for *The Century*, brought him his first major etching commission. In 1882 he was asked to go to Italy and illustrate, with twelve etchings, a series of W. D. Howell's articles on Tuscany. The magazine offered him $50 for a print from each plate, his passage back and forth, and a railroad ticket to Florence from London. Pennell immediately knew that his "name would be made and jumped at the chance of six months' work for six hundred dollars," learning only later that Charles A. Platt had refused a similar offer. With these etchings he made his name in the European art world: "An illustrator receives more publicity from a magazine which publishes illustrations than any other artist, for though large numbers of people may see in one city an art exhibition, an illustrated magazine is an art gallery for the world—or was in those days."[56]

Pennell illustrated not just for the money but because he loved it. Others turned to it as their best option. When Otto Bacher first came to New York in 1889, "very few things were open to an artist for a livelihood. I had to choose from three things,—either paint portraits, teach or illustrate. I chose the latter . . . to make a beginning and earn a living" but, he added, "*not* as life work."[57] Likewise, Mahonri Young, an etcher who would become better-known as a sculptor, first worked as an artist for a Salt Lake City newspaper and then again in New York while studying at the Art Students League. "Illustrations," he recalled, "were really the only place" to earn a living. Teaching jobs and commissions for portraits went to those who were already well recognized[58] but, in these days before photography was in wide use, most newspapers employed artists. They used them more or less as reporters, much as television today deploys camera crews.

Illustrators' reputations as artists were more closely linked to their illustrations than teachers' reputations as artists were linked to their teaching. Not surprisingly, artists who tried illustrating often found publishers' demands inconsistent with their own ideals of artistic excellence. Upon his return from overseas service with the American Expeditionary Force, Harry Wickey found a "welcome home" from the *Saturday Evening Post* with a request that he illustrate a story. It was like "exposing myself to smallpox again," he later wrote. Three pictures he sent were used, and paid for, but there also came a letter stating that they were not quite up to the usual *Post* standard. The incident confirmed his conviction that illustration was not for him.[59] He left this lucrative field for such odd jobs as stretching canvases and working as a general handyman.

Illustration could consume an inordinate amount of an artist's time and psychic energy. For F. L. M. Griggs, who was not always in the best of health, it could be downright physically exhausting. Yet he persisted because, until his debut as a renowned etcher, his drawings for the *Highways and Byways* series in Britain were his main source of support. "Three week's [*sic*] or a month's cycling on end traversing the hilly South Wales countryside," he complained to F. O. Macmillan of the publishing house, "would, I'm afraid, sap a good deal of one's enthusiasm . . . [and] produce fatigue fatal to artistic effort." A motor bike, Griggs suggested, might save a good deal of time and strength, and be of use for subsequent volumes. Could Macmillan give him an advance? The quality of his illustrations would gain, indirectly. But Macmillan saw things from a business perspective. He was irritated by repeated delays whenever Griggs felt inspired to include places that interested him but had not been specified in the author's itinerary.

Griggs's long relationship with the firm was marked by many disputes over payment for unsolicited drawings. In such cases Griggs, often in need of cash, had to depend on the publisher's goodwill, but when the dispute was over the quality of the reproductions, he was more intransigent. Though financially strapped, he would offer to send the right paper—it had to be "quite smooth"—and to pay for proofs by his friend, the printer Emery Walker, whom he considered far superior to the man Macmillan was using. He was particularly distressed by the illustrations in the Nottinghamshire book: "I know the drawings were among my best—they will appear as by far the worst I have done for you."[60]

That an image as published did not do justice to the artistry of its creator was a common complaint. William Strang, anxious that his etched portrait of Rudyard Kipling be properly printed by Macmillan's, offered to take it to Goulding himself to superintend its printing.[61] Rothenstein protested the publisher's use of his Gitanjali drawing to advertise books by the Indian poet, Rabindranath Tagore, as a violation of his copyright agreement. Again, the issue for Rothenstein was less that of money than principle. He was appalled by the poor printing that had failed to do justice to the drawing and, thereby, could blemish his reputation.[62]

On the whole, the early decades of the etching revival were especially hospitable to talented illustrators. Visibility through quality could hardly hurt. New processes of reproduction were not only cheaper than reproductive engraving but, in the hands of a skillful printer, could yield copies closer to the original than hitherto possible. Lester Hornby's reputation was enhanced when the art historian, William Howe Downes, praised his illustrations in *An Artist's Sketchbook of Old Marblehead*. Publishers, especially of magazines, competed for the best artists to illustrate their texts. Editors even built articles around the drawings or etchings of an artist whose work they admired, a practice that survived into the 1930s and 1940s, when *Life* magazine, notwithstanding its reliance on photographs, also commissioned illustrations from artists. Earlier the rise of the *beau livre* signaled that books themselves could be conceived and treated as art objects: some deluxe editions actually used original etchings for illustrations.[63]

Wood engravers found it easier than intaglio printmakers to reconcile their artistic ambitions with their illustrating. The medium had been extensively used by reproductive engravers for precisely this purpose. Then, early in the twentieth century, there came into being—in Britain more than in America—a new school of wood engravers with "a common philosophical vision and a dominant aesthetic language." Its adherents were determined not to be mere *reproducers* of illustrations but to communicate their messages by illustrating fine books.[64] Several of the painter-etchers we studied were part of the movement, Clare Leighton being the most prolific as well as financially most successful. Her career dates from 1925 when, fresh out of the Slade, she set herself up in one room, where she painted and gave private drawing lessons. She had had an offer of an excellent teaching job and an inspectorship right in London. That would have guaranteed her a permanent income, but she refused, believing "you can't do both" and that "to deny the other force . . . is the unforgiveable sin." Instead, Leighton gave lessons during the day, which left her free to paint and make decorative woodcuts of farm things, animals, and people at night and on holidays. Soon the pictures and etchings she sent to art papers and publishers found takers, and people began to know her name.[65]

As an illustrator, employing mostly wood engravings, Leighton really had two professional lives—the first in Britain, the second in the United States. During an active career of over fifty years, she produced over 700 prints; she illustrated forty-nine books, some of which she authored, and won a number of print prizes. Interestingly, the catalog of her retrospective at the Boston Public Library was titled "The Artist and Her Work," not "The Work of an Illustrator." This underscores the way Leighton thought about and presented herself—as a "fine artist" or at least as a "fine art illustrator." Almost all the engravings she made for books were separately editioned for exhibition and sale in leading print shows. Near 35,000 impressions of her works were printed, so that her name became familiar to print collectors as well as to book aficionados.

By contrast, wood engraver Dorothy Lathrop, who won major awards both as an illustrator and printmaker, was far better known in the book world for, unlike Leighton, she published but few of her prints separately.[66] What she sent to exhibitions, which she did but rarely, was "just for fun in what time was left over from illustrating." Not counting on sales, she set her prices for individual impressions so low that even when she sold a print, she found herself "in quite a sizeable hole." There were dues to be paid, exhibition fees and shipping costs, not to mention agents' fees. For an out-of-towner living in

Albany, New York, exhibiting was "an expensive business."[67] Preferring not to expend the time and money, it was far more difficult for her, as a fine art illustrator, to build a reputation as a fine artist.

The mother of five sons, Grace Albee was the only woman in our sample with a large family, but she and her artist husband had private means and so were not dependent on her artistic work for income, or, for that matter, on his. She preferred rural themes, often depicting summer scenes near the family summer home in Bucks County, Pennsylvania. Her wood engravings, like those of Leighton and Lathrop, earned her election to the National Academy and countless other honors and awards. When she illustrated, which she did occasionally, the subjects were entirely of her own choosing, but she made no determined effort to market her work as fine prints, never had a dealer, and did not even acquire a social security card until she was seventy-two. Albee's personal records, as meticulously detailed as her wood engravings, indicate that between 1922 and 1940, she engraved eighty-five blocks, including a few bookplates. If full editions were sold at prices listed in her record books, they would have yielded an annual income of about $4,500 a year—a tidy sum for those years. Could she have earned more had she turned her talents to illustrating? Did she not do so because she had no inclination for it or was it simply that she did not badly need the money and thus could devote herself to building a reputation as an artist-engraver? Apparently, she did not feel impelled in this direction. A 1962 entry in her diary indicates that an admirer, William Connor, with whom she corresponded, felt she was too modest, insufficiently aware of the importance of her work. He urged her to prepare a catalogue raisonné to further enhance her reputation. The thought of doing this, it seems, had never occurred to her.[68]

The point is that those artists without some assured income faced hard choices—whether to teach, illustrate, seek portrait commissions, or accept commercial work. None of these jobs was necessarily counterproductive, yet insofar as they were but means to an end, each had its advantages and disadvantages.

## The Importance of Place and Time

What greatly mattered in reputation building was being in the right place at the right time. The right place for almost everyone was in, or close to, a center of artistic activity. In France this meant quite obviously Paris, where the major schools, museums, and galleries were concentrated. The center for English artists was in and around London, but Glasgow, Liverpool, and Bristol were also good places to be. Before New York emerged as the authentic capital of the American art world, it had been almost mandatory for American artists to launch their careers in Europe. J. Alden Weir, while a young man in Paris, was advised in a letter from his older artist brother "to make [his] reputation over there, for it's [a] hard and *vague* thing over here—if made over there it's more enduring and profitable."[69] Of those American etchers who went abroad for study, some remained for the better part of their productive lives. Long-term residents of Paris included George Aid, D. Shaw MacLaughlin, Caroline and Frank Armington, Lester Hornby, and Arthur Heintzelman. All were younger than Weir by a generation or more.

While the "right place" was mainly a matter of geography, the "right time" was a matter of personal biography. If there was a right time to work abroad, there was a right time to return. Thus, expatriates who stayed too long risked losing their rightful place in their own country. Furthermore, what counted for etchers, as much as for painters, was access to a distribution system that could make their oeuvre widely available. For the successful etcher, however, the market was truly international. Not only Keppel in New York but Goodspeed's in Boston and Roullier in Chicago were only too eager to represent American etchers working abroad, while the more successful British would actually designate (and number) a specific part of their editions for the American market.

Geographical barriers were less of an obstacle in Britain than in America: not only were distances smaller, but close cultural and social connections between London and various subsidiary centers served as points of entry into the national art world. In the United States lack of access to a major distribution system meant that some etchers well recognized in the West were little known in the East. Nevertheless, even in the United States, long before the etching cycle reached a climax, the modern age of rapid transportation and the quick dissemination of news from the major art markets was reducing the pockets of isolation.

Travel to faraway places off the beaten pathways, sometimes at considerable risk and great discomfort, could be converted into a reputational asset. Etchings of exotic scenery and eccentric customs had a special appeal in an age when most people still relied on artistic renditions to acquaint themselves with places they could never expect to see for themselves. To cite some examples: until Mortimer Menpes exhibited etchings produced during a trip to Japan in the 1880s, he had been known mostly as one of Whistler's pupils. In the decades before World War I, Ernest Lumsden achieved his first real visibility with etchings of India, as did Charles Cain with views of Mesopotamia, and Thomas Handforth with Burma and Thailand. Wanderlust could even enhance the reputation of an already established artist. In 1927, as he was approaching fifty and sensing a need of a "refresher," Fred Richards cut loose from his teaching duties and set off for Alexandria, Egypt, which he made his headquarters. Then, sending for his printing press, he went on an artistic exploration of the Near East.[70] First going up the Nile to Khartoum and Omdurman, he next headed east to Port Sudan and then, after kicking up thousands of miles of desert dust, ended with a short stay in Jidda. After trips to Jerusalem, Haifa, Beirut, and Damascus—not then sights familiar to modern-day video viewers—he disappeared for the better part of a year into Persia. His book, *A Persian Journey*, provided an "etcher's impression of the Middle East . . . unique in the abundant literature of Persian travel. . . . His drawings convey . . . the elusive, almost unearthly beauty of light and shade and of line which more than compensates for the lack of colour in Persian architecture."[71]

Women, though more constrained in their ability to travel, could be equally adventuresome. Far-off places had fascinated Lucille Douglass ever since an uncle presented the little girl with a worn set of Hezekiah Butterworth's travel books. After the First World War, when this American Southerner was an accomplished painter in midcareer, she took up residence in the Orient and set out on the sketching expeditions that brought her special attention in the art world.[72] In China a houseboat became her studio; for a while she was on the staff of the *Shanghai Times* and would journey into out-of-the-way districts, where communication was difficult and travel often hazardous. In the 1920s during the revolution, when fighting was at its fiercest in the Yang-Tze Valley, she went, heedless of consular advice, into the mountains to sketch a lovely temple she had been told about. When she arrived with her two coolies, it was swarming with rebel soldiers. She sent the coolies ahead, alighted from her chair, set up an easel, and calmly began to paint. Soon the entire company of soldiers crowded around to watch her work. When finished with her sketch, she gathered up her belongings, received the officer's salute, and left unmolested.[73]

Returning to the United States only to lecture on the Far East or exhibit her art, she soon had collectors all over the world. After she painted the Temple of Angkor, the French Colonial Government commissioned a series of etchings of this magnificent ruined Khmer city for display at the 1927 French Colonial Exhibition in Paris. These etchings, together with some two dozen pastels of similar subjects, were the basis for a Washington exhibition under the patronage of the French ambassador and were, in 1934, used for illustrating *New Journeys in Asia* by Helen Churchill Candee, who had accompanied Douglass to Angkor. The prints from the set, published in editions of ten, were sold at the then-staggering publication price of $100 per impression!

Their wanderlust certainly took Richards and Douglass to the right places at the right time—just as the popularity of etchings reached its peak. But what of those who stuck to home that was neither New York nor London? Not being near enough to the center was to risk obscurity, a fate that both Anna Airy in Ipswich, England, and Blanche McVeigh in Fort Worth, Texas, each in her way had to make a special effort to escape.

Anna Airy was a successful painter in oil and watercolor as well as an etcher but never so nationally renowned or as much in the limelight as Dame Laura Knight, her senior by five years. Their careers do, however, to some extent run parallel. In 1917, the two were the only women to be commissioned to do canvases for the Canadian War Records Office. They worked in the same camp, where their presence caused some stir.[74] Airy—but not Knight—worked in still another "man's world" when the War Memorials Committee commissioned her to paint four large canvases of munitions factories, an assignment that she considered a great feather in her cap. The conditions under which she worked were strenuous, and she found herself "fast qualifying for the pit. . . . They roll out the red hot shell cases in batches within 4 feet of me to cool off! . . . [B]ut the general swelter and steam and the dust and the swearing are going to make a ripping picture I think!"[75] Yet Airy, who painted the same kind of large canvases so admired by the Academy as Knight, never was elected to membership. Wherein lies the difference?

Both artists were forceful personalities, but Knight had fewer qualms about seeking help in storming that male bastion and was able to overcome opposition to women with the help of A. J. Munnings, a powerful friend, who kept putting her name forward again and again until he succeeded.[76] Airy, according to those who knew her well, would never have lowered herself to ask anyone to put her up. Set in her ways, she was intent on doing everything for herself without help. Equally important was Airy's decision, in the mid-1930s, to abandon

London for a permanent base in Playford, near Ipswich, where her family had maintained a home for many years. There, distanced from major distribution channels, she remained, aware that the cultivation of reputation required that one be visible. She always alerted her students to the large wastage in every artist's output, advising them that "if the work can be got out, by sale, or auction, and start on its lucky or unlucky chance in the world, *something* will come through in the course of time, and find the resting-place it deserves . . . sooner or later someone who does know will spot that work, and then the fun begins: the work is recognized and the connoisseur begins to take notice."[77]

Airy herself worked away in an unheated, unelectrified studio, insisting she was too busy to travel—even to Paris. Though she did not abandon her London contacts, much of her energy was devoted to the Ipswich Art Club. A member since 1903, forty years later she became the first woman to serve as its president. On taking office, she instituted a stricter policy of selection that resulted in smaller exhibitions and higher standards. President until her death in 1964, the club memorialized her with an award to honor her interest in young artists.[78] In this capacity, she had a hand in putting their community on the cultural map as a place for artists to work without risking invisibility.

Blanche McVeigh, an etcher from Texas, worked against even greater odds in Fort Worth, a community that, in the 1920s was certainly not the "right place" for a young woman with serious artistic ambitions and no assured income. She had taken art courses in St. Louis, Philadelphia, New York, and Chicago, and had traveled abroad for six months. Daniel Garber, her teacher at the Philadelphia Academy of Fine Arts, had found her "born to the etching press." But as an etcher in Fort Worth she was an isolate. It was a backwater that did not take its artists seriously and even less so if they were women. At a time when McVeigh's etchings were being shown at the Women's Club, the *Fort Worth Press* carried her picture, in its "Society and Clubs" section, together with those of three other professional artists with the caption: "Art is the Hobby of these Girls."[79] Later, supporting herself by managing an art supply store, she took it on herself to transform Fort Worth into a community more caring and knowledgeable about fine art. Together with two of the other "girls" pictured in the *Press*, she opened the Texas (later Fort Worth) School of Fine Arts. She kept in touch, through correspondence and participation in the exhibitions of etching societies, with the centers of the artistic world. As president of the Fort Worth Art Association, she was the first to bring to town examples of the work of Derain, Matisse, Picasso, and other moderns.

A retrospective of her work in 1953 was coupled with the claim that "she had been as well-known nationally as any Texas artist."

Still, being in the hinterland had made it hard to build a reputation. She knew few people who could advise her how to go about this. When, during the war, she wrote John Taylor Arms, then president of the Society of American Etchers, for an "invitation" to submit work for membership, he had to explain that this was against the rules. Most diplomatically, he expressed his hope that she would *feel* like submitting her work for this purpose. Arms, whom she had never met, thought highly of her work. When she thanked him for including her name in the yearbook of the *Encyclopaedia Britannia*, he assured her that it would appear on anyone's list of contemporary American etchers.[80] McVeigh did win many prizes and praise but, being in the "wrong place," she had always to depend on long-distance advice about marketing. Disappointed at not having heard from Kennedy and Company in New York about prints she had sent, she had to be gently advised by another art dealer that Weyhe's might have been more receptive. The same dealer offered to ask Kennedy's "to show me your work. Maybe they don't have this Angel aquatint, and I can tell them what they're missing."[81] It must be said that her range of subject matter was limited. Her "Negro genre," depicting little black angels looking like "grown folks," would have scant appeal to collectors today. Fort Worth seems to have done little to extend her horizons and encourage her to try new things. And she herself did not want to appear "arty."[82]

## In the Face of Adversity

To experience hardships from time to time and in various forms is the human lot. The saga of the hero tells of a person who, beset by a run of misfortune, overcomes it and endures. In the aggregate, our artists were not unduly afflicted. They did not live tragic lives, but a fair number had to cope with illness, their own or that of people close to them, and with a multitude of problems that disrupted, or threatened to disrupt, their careers. Five ended their lives by suicide, three in response to illness and all of them at a fairly advanced age. A remarkable degree of resiliency in the face of adversity accounts for the success of some of the rest.

Illness, indirectly, had paved the path to art for Theodore Roussel and Ernest Lumsden. Both families had slated their sons for the military. Lumsden's health broke down after only a short time aboard the

HMS *Worcester*, thus allowing the young man who had always shown an aptitude for art to go to Reading to study under Morley Fletcher.[83] Roussel had already passed his examination for the Ecole Spéciale Militaire when a "grave illness" intervened. He went to Rome to recuperate but, owing to a fever he caught there, stayed longer than planned and worked on his art. By the time he returned to France, the 1870 war with Germany was imminent and he was called to active service. With the war over, and luckily having received only a slight wound, he left the army to pursue an artistic career that took him to England.[84]

An American whose chronic disability brought him into art was Paul Landacre.[85] While he was studying horticulture at Ohio State, a crippling infection left him with a stiff and twisted right leg and little strength in his arms, which he was never again able to raise above his head. Back in his native California, he began, during long therapeutic walks, to sketch the animals, birds, flowers, and trees he saw about him. Realizing that, if he persevered, his drawing talent might furnish an independent living and restore his self-esteem, he enrolled in art classes and started to work in advertising agencies. Meanwhile, anxious to move away from purely commercial art, he experimented with etching, drypoint, mezzotint, and lithography until he found his forte in wood engraving. His first great success as an illustrator, *California Hills and Other Wood-engravings from the Original Blocks*, was published in a signed numbered edition of 500 and chosen one of the "Fifty Books of the Year."[86]

In order to assure quality, Landacre insisted on printing all his own work on a press found in an abandoned mining camp; it had taken two months of incredibly messy labor, disassembling and cleaning every one of its rusted and grimy parts, to get it back in working order. Given his handicap, he could not have managed without assistance from his wife, who not only took care of the household and the finances but helped push the lever of the press when he had to print a large block.[87] So totally was he dependent on her that he committed suicide shortly after she died.

George Elbert Burr experienced the debilitating effects of poor health and near exhaustion all his life. From childhood he had been afflicted with bouts of hay fever, which he escaped for a month every summer by leaving Missouri for Chicago and the lakes region. His state of health had nothing to do with his decision for art but was the main consideration behind his move to Denver, with its sunny climate and great opportunities for sketching out-of-doors. Quickly, Burr became one of the ablest pictorial interpreters of Western mountains and desert scenes.[88] Mostly he worked on what pleased him, but his thirty-five-plate *Desert Set*, completed in 1921 and judged his "immortal contribution to the etcher's art," can, in a circuitous way, be traced to his ill health.[89] The set was to be published in an edition of forty, with plates numbered according to the sequence in which they had been finished. The plan was to sell thirty sets intact for $750, but even when the price was raised to $1,200, most sold within a few years. A relative suggests that Burr "might never have taken on the task had he not sought (possibly on the doctor's advice) to escape the rigors of the Colorado winters" by making for Palm Springs, the Mohaje Desert, and the Coachella Valley.[90]

All this took meticulously demanding studio work, followed by printing, matting, and distribution of the finished prints to dealers, all of which Burr did himself. When these exertions began to take their toll, he was forced to take "a complete rest, after a very active winter's work, and especially as he has a disabled arm, which has probably been overtaxed"[91] by his use of an old hand press that lacked gears and required considerable strength to operate. Thereafter, he spent his winters in Tucson and in 1924 sold his Denver home to resettle in Phoenix, where he continued to work as much as his health permitted, seeking to satisfy the seemingly never-ending demand for his work. "Have had a very busy winter with the bisness [*sic*] end of my work," he wrote to Frank Weitenkampf of the New York Public Library in 1927, ". . . and I am not husky as of the days before the flu, and soon tire," but he added that some of his new etchings were "I think, my best work."[92] Now sixty-eight, he was nevertheless inclined to limit himself "while still having 'a lot of fun' with my work when I am able to be up and around. Have finished quite a lot of new plates in the past three years, and water colors as well. . . . Most of the twenty-five new plates I've printed in very limited editions, of from four to ten prints, and have destroyed the plates, in that way, I have the joy of creation without the real work of printing . . . So long as I can work a little for the joy of it."[93] Burr, having suffered poor health all his life, carried on in this spirit until his death in 1939 at the age of eighty.

We have already met the Copleys and told of his return to etching. The couple's surviving son, thirty-five years after his parents' death, remembered his father as a "semi-invalid" cared for by his mother, with whom he shared an artistic partnership for nearly four decades.[94] There are constant references in the Copley correspondence to her husband's illnesses: Ethel would explain that "bad attacks" had forced him to give up all thoughts of work, or that he was forbidden to talk on the telephone. In one letter, Copley regretted that his attacks were making "hopeless holes" in the work of his wife. A few years later, he said he was too ill to even draw.[95] Yet, according to the son, it was his father who, in the last twelve years of his parents' lives, became a healthy old man, grown stronger by the need to physically care for his wife in her own periods of incapacity. Indeed, it was in these years, during and after World War II, that he did so many etchings, some of his best.[96]

From 1938, it had indeed become Ethel's turn to struggle against personal tragedy and her own illness. First came the death of the younger son who had been studying for a medical degree followed by the removal of one kidney and a second rare operation on the remaining kidney. During the war, she obtained an official assignment to record women's work in factories, farms, and camps in remote areas. The "physical effort as her health declined was considerable. . . . When with age and illness she grew very thin she worried about her appearance and turned to eccentric hats, blue rinses, some sinister black stuff which she brushed on her hair with a tooth brush, white face powder and dark red lipstick. Then she set out to wherever she had to go."[97] Their son marveled at "the energy and guts of both of them." Harold Wright, their faithful dealer, acknowledged their courage "in working on, steadily and conscientiously, despite all the lack of warm and steady encouragement to do so" when there was no longer a market for their black-and-white work nor even a dealer prepared to exhibit it.[98] John refused to shed "tears over what might have been." Changing fashions meant only that "an artist, who works over some 50 years, has a long pull at the start, then perhaps ten years of ease and glory, and a long old age of comparative neglect. . . . Often enough his work at the unrecognized beginning is brilliant and at the forgotten end is the finest of his life." None of this, he believed, should make much difference to a good artist's work.[99]

Illness was just as likely to strike in midcareer, sometimes with detrimental effects, as in the case of Charles Holroyd who, as a Slade student, had been judged capable of memorable achievement. A superior draftsman and a meticulous worker, he was early elected to the Royal Society of Painter-Etchers. But while Holroyd went on to play a crucial role in the British art world, as an artist—and, certainly, as an etcher—he never fulfilled the high hopes of his friends and admirers.[100] Henry Newbolt remembered him as a vital presence in the art world—a "commanding figure, big in stature" with a calm assurance and a wonderful knowledge of the world of pictures.[101] His appointment as keeper at the National Gallery of British Art (Tate Gallery) had been expected to provide him with the financial security needed to pursue his own work. At first, "his official duties . . . [did] not occupy too much of his time."[102] But after he advanced to the directorship, administrative frictions and job-related anxieties of the gravest kind brought on ill health that kept him from fresh work and even from printing full editions from earlier plates. He died prematurely in 1917, having used himself up in worrying about protecting the museum collections from both German zeppelins and suffragette violence.[103] The cruelest blow came when Mary Richardson (alias "Polly Dick") on 10 March 1914 managed to evade the watchful eyes of gallery detectives and take an axe to Velasquez's *Venus* and "destroy the picture of the most beautiful woman in mythological history."[104] Without meaning to, she also put an end to Holroyd's career as an artist.

Artists, and especially etchers, depend on their eyes. One cannot etch without very acute sight. We learn that "just at the zenith of his career as an etcher, . . . [J. Alden] Weir's eyes began to fail and he was obliged to relinquish the close work on plates, especially as he often did so at night."[105] More tragic were the consequences for Matilda de Cordoba, an American portrait etcher, who went nearly blind from the arduous strain of etching. When years later, after an eye operation, she returned to art with the same insistence and vitality, she never was able to recapture the worldly success she had hitherto enjoyed.[106] On the other hand, Herman A. Webster, an American whose eyes had suffered gas damage in World War I, recovered sufficiently after eight years to resume etching with renewed vigor. His *Soir de Fête, Italy* won the 1930 Henry F. Noyes Prize, awarded by the Brooklyn Society of Etchers (figure 35).

Finally, there are those who fought gallantly, not always successfully, to continue as artists against the ravages of old age. Our admiration goes to Nora Fry Lavrin, whom we interviewed in 1978 when she was 81; her husband, Janco (John) Lavrin, Emeritus Professor of Slavonic Languages at the University of Nottingham, was then in his nineties. She had been heralded just before the collapse of the print market in England "as an etcher who promises to count." We had come across some of her work in the Ashmolean Print Room. A sketchbook of their honeymoon trip to Yugoslavia shows the newly-weds, as they prepare to leave, hastily printing a plate for Colnaghi's and hanging the impressions on a clothes line to dry. Now, near half a century later, there was Nora Lavrin, in their modest apartment in

West London, crippled by arthritis and with two artificial elbows, still working away (at illustrating) in her little study and more intent on talking about current events and her current projects than about the past.

Francis Dodd put an end to his own life because he feared, his widow said, that neuritis in his right shoulder might affect his work; he was then almost seventy-five years old.[107] Likewise, Edward Julius Detmold shot himself through the chest. He had not spoken of suicide but was reported to have been depressed on account of his failing eyesight;[108] the twin brother, with whom he had once collaborated, had been a suicide fifty years earlier. Only two of the suicides come near close to fitting the persistent but erroneous stereotype of the suicide-prone artist misunderstood in his own time.[109] William Walcot, "anxious, frustrated, and in despair with a time that was out of joint, ended his own life" during World War II when he was near seventy and facing financial disaster.[110] But there was more uncertainty about what had moved William Strang to suicide in 1921, just after his election as a full member of the Royal Academy—but as an engraver, not as a painter. Since he had been exhibiting paintings continuously for twenty years, the election is said to have infuriated him. But did the disappointment plunge him into suicidal despair? We shall never know.[111]

## Mutuality

Many of our artists climbed the ladder to recognition in tandem. About a fourth—of both the British and the Americans—were married to or lived for many years with another artist. The proportion of shared careers may actually have been higher, inasmuch as some, no doubt, shielded their liaisons, past marriages, and divorces from public view. In other cases, personal information is scanty. Nevertheless, the data we have hardly reinforce the many accounts, some of them pure fiction, about the disruptive effects of bohemian life-styles and unrequited love on artistic careers. To the contrary, they suggest that mutual support and inspiration enabled many of the etchers we studied to remain creative by contributing to their psychological well-being.

The Armingtons, no less than the Copleys, whom we have chronicled, shared with each other most of their lives and their careers. "Life," fifty-year-old Caroline Armington observed in 1925, when both Frank and she were doing well with their etchings, "is such a happy rush."[112] Theirs has been called "the greatest art and love story in Canadian history" and seemed to be "nourished further by the passionate regard each had for art. . . . Instead of being envious, each took a great pride in the achievements and success of his mate."[113] Caroline Wilkinson and Frank Armington first met in 1891 at Saturday lessons in the studio of an Ontario artist. Frank was fifteen and she one year older. Both were determined to be artists and, by 1900, had made their way, though separately, to Paris where, by chance or prior arrangement, they met again and were shortly thereafter married. But Frank's health played havoc with their plans. Weakened by a childhood bout with spinal meningitis, he was warned to give up art for some "less strenuous, less demanding means of making a livelihood." Back in Canada, he tried journalism, business, and heading an art department in a boarding school. Four years of this were enough. They decided to return to Paris, this time as their permanent home.

Both enrolled at the Académie Julian, with Caroline attending the classes reserved for women. And both got their start by painting portraits. Affected by the Impressionist movement, they changed to doing landscapes. Frank was the first to take up etching. In 1908, when his wife was winning critical acclaim for her oil paintings of French and Belgian peasant women, he won honorable mention for his prints at the Société des Artistes Français. Two years later he had become an associate of the RSPE, an honor Caroline either never aspired to or never achieved, even though she, too, had meanwhile discovered her own affinity for the needle and copperplate. In a kind of *pas de deux*, they reversed roles. Frank gave up his membership in the RSPE; by the late twenties he was not etching at all, while Caroline gradually abandoned watercolor and oil painting to work exclusively at etching. Over a lifetime, she produced 557 etchings and drypoints.

The Armingtons exhibited jointly in Europe and the United States throughout their lives. Honors, awards, and sales multiplied, though less so for Caroline because, as a male admirer explained: "Caroline had the disadvantage of being of the wrong sex for her time. Early in her career, an agent advised her to conceal her femaleness under unisexual initials." She would have none of this. Also, it was Caroline's job to hold the household together. Seizing the business reins, she sold the prints and paintings for which Frank could never bring himself to ask money. She kept the books, the records, and the accounts, and even saw to it that he signed his lithographs and etchings and performed other mundane tasks he was prone to neglect. When they finally deserted Paris in 1939, they were reported to have had $200,000 in savings, a fortune in those days. What not even their friends knew was the poor state of Caroline's health. Believing the German Luftwaffe to be an even bigger potential threat, the couple reluctantly sailed for New York City. When Caroline died in a hotel three days after their arrival, her lifelong companion was "inconsolable." Yet to the astonishment of all who knew him, he quickly remarried, radically changed his will, cutting out a relative and the American Church in Paris as beneficiaries. Upon his death just two years after Caroline's, the posthumous management of their shared reputation was left in the hands of a second wife, who had had neither a part in its development nor any great interest in its survival.[114]

Marriages between artists were inevitably endangered by unwelcome comparisons of their work. Thus, Grace Albee may have been a better etcher than her husband but turned to wood engraving as her medium to avoid such "unseemly" competition. And as she accumulated awards and gained recognition for her work, she sought to minimize the disparity. Following her election to the National Academy of Design, she immediately mobilized her contacts to work for his election to that same body.[115] She had met Percy at art school and was married to him in 1913, upon completion of her course. His junior by seven years, she devoted a good part of the next fifteen years to rearing their five sons, the last born in 1927, without altogether forsaking her art. During the war, she made a poster, displayed in the center of the Providence Bank, encouraging people to buy Liberty Bonds for children. In 1921 the Albees held a joint black-and-white exhibition at the Providence Art Club, which was also a center of their social life.

Her career really took off when the Albees, encouraged by enthusiastic letters from Arthur Heintzelman, her brilliant schoolmate at the Rhode Island School of Design, moved to Paris, where they spent the five years from 1928 to 1933. She took six one-hour lessons in wood engraving from Paul Barnet, the director and founder of the Institut d'Esthétique Contemporaine. Within one year, she was exhibiting in the Paris spring Salon as well as the Art Institute of Chicago; the year following, her work was reproduced in *The Studio*, with commentary by Malcolm Salaman. In 1932, she had a one-woman exhibition at the American Library in Paris, a rare honor for an American artist.

How had she managed? They had put the children in L'Ecole Alsacienne and used their apartment at 7 rue Campagne Première as a studio, each choosing a small corner with a north light. Her north light had not, however, served much of a purpose, as the only time she found free to work was after nine o'clock at night until the "wee small hours" of the next morning. All the while, she was also taking a class in French, so she had to keep up her "pep." Still, she might not have managed a career and such a large family at home and in Paris without some support from her husband's well-to-do family, founders of the Keith-Albee Vaudeville Circuit.[116] Once launched on their way, both were quite successful, holding numerous two-person shows between 1928 and 1949 in which Percy, principally a mural painter, showed drypoints along with Grace's wood engravings. Grace accumulated awards, with *Junked* (figure 57) a big hit at the Artists for Victory Exhibition. Late in the 1940s, with the war over, she wrote on the fly cover of her diary: "What I do with my time, besides the usual house-hold duties involving three meals a day and the cleaning up after, reading the paper, brushing up and dusting, watering plants, feeding the animals and etc. etc." In fact, what she was doing, besides keeping a diary, was making engravings, which she gave up only after her husband died in 1959. After a major operation, which she barely sur-vived, she once more took up the graver, but "with limited output." She was cataloguing the graphics by Percy, which she had given to museums in his memory; in response to a request, she had also begun to catalog her own.

A third lifetime partnership was that of the Zorachs—William, who made his mark as a sculptor, and Marguerite, the printmaker, painter, and embroiderer of tapestries. "It is rare in the history of art," observed Tarbell about their early years,

> for two artists as talented as Marguerite and William Zorach not only to marry, but to share such close artistic interests. The painter whose style was closest to that of Marguerite Zorach from 1913 through 1920 was William Zorach. Both artists had undergone similar experi-ences in Paris during their formative periods, and after their marriage in December 1912, the factors that shaped their respective styles were nearly identical. They had the same friends, attended and showed in the same exhibitions, and painted in the same places. Their media, their interests, and their styles diverge after 1920, but during the first years of their marriage, certain similarities can be found in the works of each.[117]

William Zorach affirms in his autobiography that art had never been a source of conflict; nor was there any rivalry between them. They had done what each could do best. Harmony rested, in large part, on accommodation, on negotiating the differences between two persons reared in completely different worlds. He had been brought as a four-year-old to Cleveland, Ohio, from a little village in Lithuania by parents whom he described as Old World people and religious Jews. Poverty had compelled him to quit school and learn a trade. He supported himself as a lithographer before making his way to New York and, from there, to Paris, where the two met.[118]

Marguerite, born Thompson, came from a family with social credentials. Her father was a prominent lawyer and her mother could trace her ancestry to early settlers in Massachusetts. She herself had been a brilliant student at her high school in Fresno, California, and was destined for Stanford. Her parents had neither encouraged nor supported her study in Paris and were no more reconciled to her ambitions upon her return home from four years abroad. They hoped that she would forget about being an artist and settle into local society. This was not to be. After a new spurt of creative activity that followed a sojourn in the Sierra mountains and a successful exhibition in Fresno, she turned her back on California and went East to marry Bill, but not before she had "framed a few of her more traditional paintings for her parents, set aside a few works for herself, and then hauled all her other early paintings, prints, and drawings to the Fresno town dump."[119] Very few of her very early etchings survived this dumping. After their marriage, both she and her husband continued to experiment with the prints that are now being recognized as "an unusually fine but neglected aspect of their artistic development."[120] But after the birth of her second child in 1917, Marguerite no longer found the hours of uninterrupted concentration necessary to "work out her personal visions on canvas." She took to designing wool embroidered tapestries that "rightfully belong to the realm of fine art."[121]

Artistically and in their social outlook, the Zorachs were more "radical" or "modern" than the Copleys, the Armingtons, or the Albees. Their life-style more nearly fits the popular image of the artist as a bohemian. But they coped in similar ways. Marguerite handled the money matters, so that "Bill never had to bother about such things."[122] He did, however, share the housework and the rearing of their children. In his posthumously published autobiography, he refers to the

> tendency among men to transform the loved one into a mother image. . . . I had that tendency, but Marguerite . . . was not going to be any man's mother. To her, marriage was a partnership. . . . If one partner possessed a particular quality or ability, he should use it for the common good. Work, ideas, accomplishments were to be shared. She was happy to do the cooking, to make her clothes and the chil-

dren's, and in the very early days she made my shirts out of pongee silk. But she felt that the care of the house and children was the responsibility of both of us. I evidently had sewed on buttons and darned my own socks when I was a boy at home. These jobs she never took over nor did she ever look after my personal belongings [as his mother had].[123]

He admitted to "plenty of arguments." She liked order and beautiful surroundings, while he did not care about possessions. And, though he was a "one-woman man," he said that Marguerite expressed occasional annoyance "at the women who 'understood' me and told me what a great artist I would be if I could only shake off her influence— for theirs."[124] The partnership lasted for over fifty years to their mutual benefit.

Where such partnerships dissolved, it was often for reasons that had nothing to do with art and cannot, in any event, be explored with the kind of data we have at hand. Differential success does, however, create problems, particularly when the career of one advances at the expense of the other or when comparisons unfavorable to one are constantly made. Wanda Gág thought that "two artists would get along just horribly [as marriage partners]. . . . Why, we would be forever criticizing each other's work, and (who knows) perhaps be jealous of each other and each other's models. . . . I want a man who appreciates art, and who is willing to let me draw when I'm in a drawing mood. He can be lots smarter than I in other things (in fact I'd *rather* have him be) but in art I want him to be just a little below me. Sounds selfish, I know, but that's the only way we would harmonize."[125]

Otherwise, exogenous marriages can offer the economic stability conducive to productivity, which two artists struggling together often find hard to attain. Thus, before Mabel Dwight left Eugene Higgins, to whom she was married, they were "desperately poor" and living (around 1913) in a tumbledown house on East Sixty-first Street in New York City. Zigrosser tried, albeit with "scant success," to sell Higgins's "rather melancholy etchings" at Keppel's.[126] A bout with tuberculosis that required hospitalization had gotten Higgins into a big financial hole, leaving his wife to "bear the trials" of their economic misfortune.[127] Success came to Dwight, a painter, only when, in her fifties and no longer with Higgins, she took up lithography and became known "as a master of the *comedie humaine* for caricatures depicting the streets and cafes of Paris, the subways and studios of Manhattan, Coney Island and Harlem."[128]

Artist-couples who shared a mutually fulfilling life were not necessarily married or of different gender. We know little about some of these mutualities. In the time most of our artists lived, it was the custom to refer to two women artists as long-time companions. Male artists who cohabited were typically referred to as close friends. Whatever the "real" nature of their mutuality, it is evident that some, like Ellen Day Hale and Gabrielle de Vaux Clements, pooled their talents and put their stamp on each other's work, including their etchings.[129] In another collaboration between two inseparable friends, Malcolm Osborne saw to the posthumous printing and distribution of the last etching by his studio mate, Alfred Bentley. More publicized was the relationship between Clara Mairs and Clement Haupers, her much younger housemate. They defied gossip and came to be fully accepted in their community. Maud Squire and Ethel Mars escaped to Paris, where they found the environment more tolerant of their bohemian life-style.

Do women artists, like their male colleagues, need a wife? There is no question that most of the men etchers in our sample had helpmates who strove to ensure them domestic tranquillity and freedom from day-to-day household responsibilities. Some women received similar support from a spouse. There was some of this sharing between Marguerite Kirmse, who mainly etched dogs, and her husband, with whom she ran a kennel. Better yet to be married, as was Gene Kloss, to a poet who understood her aesthetic needs and could adapt his life to fit hers. Both she and Phillips found their inspiration in the surroundings of Taos, New Mexico, where they anchored Gene's 1,200-pound etching press. When family responsibilities mandated that they live part of each year in Berkeley with their widowed mothers, they bought another secondhand press. The economic struggle was difficult but not inhibiting. While neither wanted to teach, he took on "various supportive jobs" to free Gene to make the etchings that "sold fairly well at minimal prices." And while she, as a septuagenarian, was yet working at her press, Phillips prepared, wrote, and saw to the publication of a catalog to bolster interest in her work. In this sense he was the "wife" that so many women needed.[130]

As long as a wife was expected to sustain the domestic and emotional well-being of the entire family, the burden of economic support fell more heavily on the husband. He was expected to provide the income, and most married men etchers did. However, when divorce, widowhood, or just hard times put this burden on the women, it could, even if unwelcomed, be the making of a career. Until her husband's unexpected death, art had been for Elizabeth O'Neill Verner more of an avocation than an activity to generate income. Now she suddenly found herself with two adolescent children, a mortgage on their family residence, and no apparent means of support. When her former art teacher suggested that she could make a living as a professional artist, she converted the shed behind the house into a studio and then into a showroom for her etchings, mostly of local scenes. The plates that she needled in a passage next to her bedroom were printed with a press at the local museum. Everything had to be planned around the children's activities. Once she obtained her own press by the sale of some stocks, her son and daughter took to helping after school—David pulling the copper press, Betty showing the studio, explaining the process, and exhibiting the finished etchings to the visitors who came by every day.[131]

Mildred Bryant Brooks had not been widowed but became the breadwinner when her husband lost his job during the Great Depression. For the next eight years, it was her printmaking, teaching, lecturing, and printing for other artists that kept her "little family well and happy." Most of this work had to be done at night when other duties could be suspended for a few hours. Within a few years her etchings were being exhibited at the Smithsonian and acquired by some of the major museums. In 1934, she won the John Taylor Arms prize of the Society of American Etchers for the "best piece of technical execution in pure etching." All this was accomplished at a price. While she loved her "busy almost frantic life . . . and would not have had it otherwise," she needed "some leisure for creative work, and respite from the harass of financial embarrassment. I want to be able to etch for a full year—everything that I have within myself . . . must somehow come out. . . . Surely after a year of uninterrupted joyous work and serious study, I will be better prepared to give my . . . family some of the advantages that I feel they deserve and must have!"[132] In writing this, she was dreaming of a Guggenheim Fellowship, but we do not know if she ever went so far as to apply. Meanwhile, etching was going out of fashion and, as the Second World War began, she encountered difficulty in obtaining foreign inks, German paper, and copperplates for her prints. Gradually, especially as her vision deteriorated, she turned to freelance work as an interior decorator and painting murals in private homes and offices. Her major contribution came during the years of hardship in the 1930s.[133]

A Closing Note

Gender has been a constant theme mediating the effects of these personal contingencies on the productivity and visibility of our etchers. Not yet directly examined is whether and how much women felt at a disadvantage vis-à-vis men, how they coped with such disadvantage, and the implications of their response on their reputations. Some women exhibited regularly in exhibitions arranged by the many societies of women artists, whereas others sought to avoid such company as well as the label, wishing to be recognized only as artists, regardless of gender identification. We have postponed a more detailed discussion of gender effects until we turn to the question of the "disappearing lady-etchers" in Chapter 10. The effect of gender on the building of reputation is closely linked to explanations of its survival or nonsurvival and it seemed best to treat the two together. But, before this, in Chapter 9, we complete our inquiry into reputation building by examining the social and historical contexts in which it takes place.

Figure 1. Allart van Everdingen (Dutch), [Three Goats by the River], etching, seventeenth century

Figure 2. Charles Jacque (French), Retour des champs, etching, ca. 1866

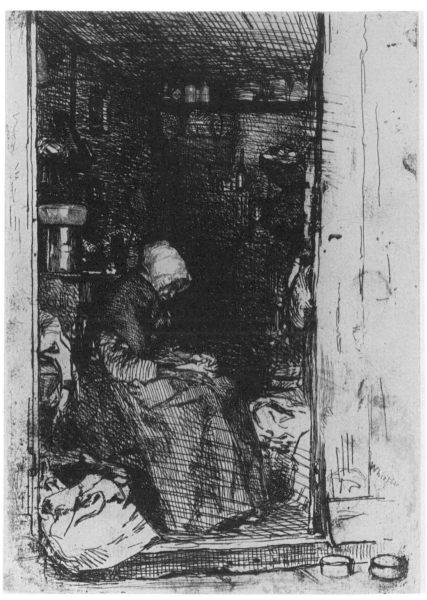

Figure 3. J. A. McN. Whistler (American), La Vieille aux loques, etching, 1858

Figure 4. Charles Meryon (French), L'Arche de pont de Notre-Dame, Paris, etching, 1853

Figure 5. Francis Seymour Haden (British), Horsley's Cottages, etching, 1853

Figure 6. Armin Landeck (American), Studio Interior, Number 1, etching, 1935

Figure 7. Mary Nimmo Moran (American), 'Twixt the Gloamin' and the Mink
When the Rye Came Home, etching, 1883

Figure 8. Frank Short (British), Wintry Blast on the Stourbridge Canal, drypoint, 1889

Figure 9. Catherine M. Nichols (British), At Oulton Broad, Suffolk, drypoint, ca. 1892

Figure 10. David Y. Cameron (British), The Rialto, etching, 1900

Figure 11. D. Shaw MacLaughlan (Canadian), Sketch of Notre Dame, etching, 1900

Figure 12. Constance M. Pott (British), Morning Post, The Strand, etching, 1905

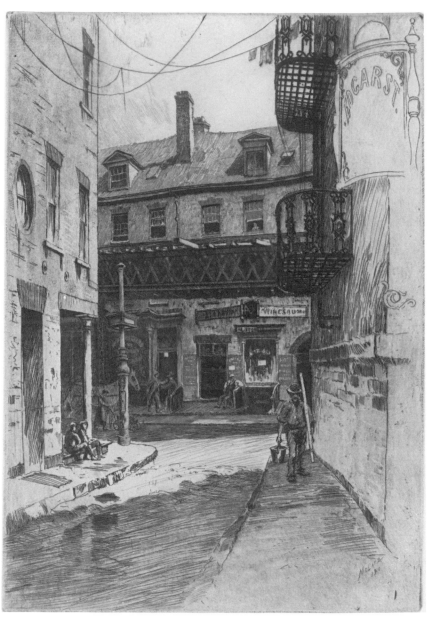

Figure 13. C. F. W. Mielatz (American), Edgar Street, etching, 1910

Figure 14. William P. Robins (British), The Old Willow, drypoint, 1913

Figure 15. Minna Bolingbroke (British), Norfolk Marshes, etching, 1916

Figure 16. Roi Partridge (American), Dancing Waters, etching, 1911

Figure 17. George Elbert Burr (American), Mount Chapin, Estes Park, aquatint, ca. 1915

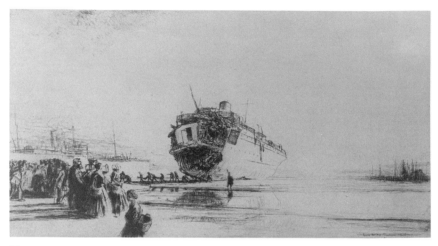

Figure 18. James McBey (British), The Torpedoed Sussex, etching with drypoint, 1916

Figure 19. C. R. W. Nevinson (British), That Cursed Wood, drypoint, 1918

Figure 20. Percy Smith (British), Death Awed, etching, 1919

Figure 21. Kerr Eby (American), Dawn, the 75's Follow Up, drypoint, 1919

Figure 22. Percy F. Gethin (British), The Traveling Circus, Sligo, etching, 1913

Figure 23. John Sloan (American), The Movey Troupe, etching, 1920

Figure 24. Laura Knight (British), At the Folies Bergères, etching and aquatint, ca. 1925

Figure 25. Nora Lavrin (British), The Showman (The Italian Marionettes), etching and drypoint, ca. 1930

Figure 26. Franklin T. Wood (American), Dr. Faust, etching, 1933

Figure 27. Molly Campbell (British), Burlington House, etching, 1915

Figure 28. Peggy Bacon (American), Aesthetic Pleasure, lithograph, 1932

Figure 29. Edmund Blampied (British), Driving Home in the Rain, etching, 1915–16

Figure 30. Walter Richard Sickert (British), Maple Street, etching, ca. 1920

Figure 31. Sylvia Gosse (British), Homeward Bound, soft ground etching, 1920s

Figure 32. Anne Goldthwaite (American), Cotton Wagon, etching, ca. 1920

Figure 33. Orovida Pissarro (British), Man and Beast, aquatint, 1924

Figure 34. Winifred Austen (British), Chickens and Snail, etching, probably done in the 1920s

Figure 35. Herman A. Webster (American), Soir de fête en Italie, etching, 1928

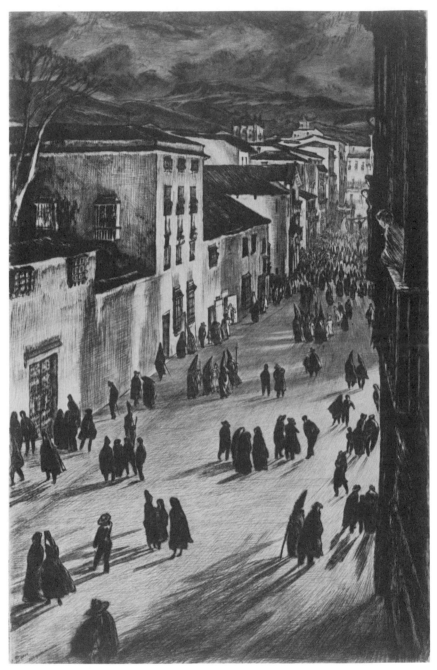

Figure 36. Muirhead Bone (British), Spanish Good Friday, Ronda,
drypoint, 1925

Figure 37. Robin Tanner (British), Christmas, etching, 1929

Figure 38. Augustus John (British), The Serving Maid, etching, ca. 1905

Figure 39. Arthur W. Heintzelman (American), Three Score and Ten, etching, 1919

Figure 40. Malcolm Osborne (British), Mrs. Herberden, etching, 1923

Figure 41. Ethel Gabain (British), Hebe, drypoint, 1926–28

Figure 42. Paul Drury (British), Head of a Negro, etching, 1925

Figure 43. Elizabeth O. Verner (American), Cyrus, etching, late 1920s/early 1930s

Figure 44. Greta Delleany (British), The Towpath, etching, ca. 1922

Figure 45. Hester Frood (British), Normandy Farm, etching, 1925

Figure 46. Eveleen Buckton (British), [Sunset], aquatint, ca. 1924–29

Figure 47. Mildred Bryant Brooks (American), Spring, etching, 1932

Figure 48. Gerald K. Geerlings (American), Black Magic, New York 1928, etching with aquatint, 1929

Figure 49. John Taylor Arms (American), Study in Stone, Cathedral of Orense, etching, 1933

Figure 50. Martin Lewis (American), Glow of the City, drypoint, 1929

Figure 51. Ernest Roth (American), Greenwich Village from 38 Grove Street, etching, 1937

Figure 52. Marion Rhodes (British), St. Mary-le-Bow, Cheapside, etching, ca. 1943

Figure 53. Stanley Anderson (British), The Reading Room, line engraving, 1930

Figure 54. Aileen M. Elliott (British), Boat Builders, Cairo, etching, ca. 1928

Figure 55. Denise L. Brown (British), Breton Market, etching, 1934

Figure 56. Robert S. G. Dent (British), The Hospital Ward, etching, 1934

Figure 57. Grace Albee (American), Junked, wood engraving, 1939

Figure 58. Irwin D. Hoffman (American), Job 16:18 "O earth cover not my blood / Nor let my cry have resting place," etching, ca. 1941

# 9

# Social and Historical Contexts

The shift from client-oriented production, to please a patron, to market-oriented production, in anticipation of an indeterminate demand, has created new forms of competition.[1] Artists trade on reputations assumedly based on the uniquely individual character of their work; yet the sheer number of competitors makes it hard to stand out against the crowd. In fact, reputations are equally dependent on social factors—on the strategic relationships an artist forms with other members of the art world and with persons who can function as mediators to the outside. Some etchers made names for themselves as participants in the collective effort to elevate etching to the status of a fine art, while others who found the medium suitable to their artistic temperaments were able to ride the crest of a wave they did not themselves create. Individual artists were further affected by developments outside the art world, some of which—like war and economic depression—were totally beyond their control.

In this chapter we look at reputation building as a collective process influenced by two sets of factors: the placement of the artist within networks and the opportunity structure as changed by external events. Dissident artists have often banded together against an art establishment reluctant to recognize them as peers, hang their work, and admit them as members. In this respect, the etchers did not differ greatly from the Impressionists and other avant-garde groupings.[2] Acceptance into the collaborative network of the etching societies was for many the first step toward the building of a reputation. It brought them the recognition they needed as a springboard. The extension of that recognition into renown required more praise from influential critics, attention from the art public, representation by a major gallery, and, of course, sales to wealthy collectors or, better yet, to museums. The artist had somehow to link up with strategically placed mediators of reputation.

Nor are reputations, individual as well as collective, built in a historical vacuum. Here we focus on the disruptive effects of two wars on artistic careers in order to illustrate the potential stimulus of such dislocations toward institutional innovation and of the actual war experience toward the release of creative energies. This does not mean, of course, that the arts always flower during war or that the stress caused by war was not also a hindrance.

## The Technological Imperative

Making an etching is, technologically, a rather complex undertaking, with the outcome directly dependent on a thorough mastery of the process. An etching—the print—evolves through three distinct steps: (1) the drawing of an image on a properly grounded metal plate; (2) the "biting" of this plate by repeated immersions in acid and "stopping out" to make corrections; and (3) the printing of the image from the plate. None of this is simple, and many plates go through literally dozens of corrections before the artist is fully satisfied with the result. Only the first of these steps—the drawing of the image—parallels what other visual artists do; for the second and third there is no equivalent. An etcher needs to know what strength of acid to use, at what temperature, and how long to submerge the plate in the acid to realize a line of a given strength or to achieve certain tonal values. Different acids attack the metal in different ways; some bite right down into the plate to deepen the grooves, others tend to spread. And when it comes to printing, effects depend on the paper and ink used, the wetness of the paper, how the ink is applied, the wiping of the plate, and the pressure applied in running the plate through the press. All this may look easy to a novice who merely watches. Yet, so many are the variables that no one, no matter how experienced, can ever be certain how a plate will print before seeing the resultant proof. Technically and artistically satisfying results come partly through trial and error.

To master these technical difficulties, printmakers have usually been ready to share their knowledge of techniques and materials not only with friends or fellow artists in adjoining studios but also, not infrequently, with inquiring strangers. For example, a veteran etcher like Bertha Jaques, who after twenty-five years of printing described herself as "still learning"[3] and "always interested in etching experiments, remembering my own difficulties [and] . . . eager to be of every help possible,"[4] took time to send the following detailed instructions to a pen pal, a watercolorist, whom she had been encouraging to etch:

. . . to answer your questions . . . as they come. . . . The drying of prints is many and various; all depending on the kind of paper and the heaviness of the lines. For instance: etchings that have heavy lines where the ink stands up, should not be put under pressure until the ink is dry, which may take several days. . . . With rather heavy paper that keeps its shape, and not too heavy lines, I lay my print, just off the press, on a blotter, and put another over it. . . . After a week perhaps the whole pack can be put under pressure. . . . Another way with vellum or heavy paper, is to lay wet print on board, have plenty of pins or sharp tacks and hammer; drive pins in about an inch apart all around the print at the edges and set it up to dry. . . . You see, it is merely a question of your paper and the printing, and the way you like to do the work. Soft Japan paper does not stretch with pins and tacks as does vellum or heavy paper.[5]

Collaboration came most naturally in workshops, where printmakers working side by side could experiment together with unfamiliar techniques. Among the more famous was Atelier 17, organized by William Hayter in Paris during the 1920s and later moved to New York. It was expressly set up for the exploration of new ways of gravure. The workshops of the Works Progress Administration Federal Art Project, founded in the 1930s to give work to the unemployed, similarly encouraged artists to try their hand at a whole range of printmaking techniques, including etching. Jacob Kainen, who joined the project in its first month, recalled the "enthusiasm" with which participating artists greeted the opportunity to both survive economically and "work in a spirit of camaraderie with other artists and skilled craftsmen. . . . It was in the shop that the printmakers felt most truly at home. There they could proof their blocks, plates, and stones in company of outstanding professionals. . . . There was no 'star' system—we were all in the same boat. We were stimulated by each other's presence."[6]

That the production of etchings calls for quite different skills at different stages is a second impetus toward collaboration. The reader may recall the "first born" of the New York Etching Club (see Chapter 4), which was jointly created by three artists, each demonstrating a different step in the process. Such collaboration was not quite as idiosyncratic as it may seem. Whistler, himself a highly skilled printer, could always get free help and was never shy about asking. Frank Short recalled how Whistler was in the habit of dropping by to talk over technical matters, sometimes bringing a batch of plates to have re-biting grounds laid for him, on occasion asking Short to take out or lighten lines on a plate. The last time they printed together was in July 1900, when Whistler came to Brook Green with nine or ten plates and they printed a few proofs each. Whistler, "as usual, worked a little in dry-point between each proof." It was Short's impression that "he liked some one to print with him—some one that he could leave the ink and the press to, and be only concerned himself with the wiping. I was always a little surprised that he left the ink mixing to me—'Make it your own way,' he would say, 'a dark *nutty* brown.'"[7]

Printing a full edition, especially a large one, could be tedious. Muirhead Bone, in the habit of doing his own printing, lamented that the job had become "an awful burden." He had just bought a bigger press and was looking for some assistance. He "like[d] 'proving' a plate and doing a few proofs"—to see if the image he strived for had actually been achieved or if the plate needed further correction—"but whole issues make a most tremendous grind. I don't wonder Haden had Goulding to do the grind for him."[8] The problem was to find a printer able to complete the job according to the artist's specifications as Goulding had done. Could one entrust one's plate—and thereby one's reputation—to a printer who, as some complained, "had the inflexibility of a crude machine without the machinery's susceptibility of adjustment . . . [whose] absurdly limited knowledge and vocabulary made it useless to appeal to him in terms outside the every-day patter of his trade"?[9] These formidable middlemen could stand between etchers and their public.

One response to this problem was to make a virtue out of necessity. Roi Partridge, for one, took the position that the American etchers, particularly in the Western part of the country, were fortunate in having to do their own printing, as there were no professional etching printers. This kind of etcher "is not, as is often the case in Europe, only half an etcher, one unable to produce his own art children."[10] There is some question whether one could be a competent etcher and not know how to ink a plate properly, wipe it, and get a satisfactory impression on paper. Some never mastered the process, so that their plates fared better in the hands of a seasoned professional on the ground that "what really counts is what is said on the plate."[11] Even Haden, champion of self-sufficiency, paid tribute to Auguste Delâtre for his unequaled skill in knowing how to impart to Haden's prints the "richness in coloring, the true impression of art as opposed to the mechanical." He acknowledged, perhaps a bit too grudgingly, that his etchings owed the Frenchman "a great deal." But he left himself a way out, insisting that there were times when one required "a finer and less robust treatment" that only the artist can understand and which "Delâtre would be the first to appreciate."[12]

At least two-thirds of all the etchings exhibited at the annual shows of the Royal Society of Painter-Etchers (RSPE) between 1890 and 1910 are said to have been printed either by Goulding or one of his shop assistants.[13] A small number he inscribed "F. Goulding imp" to certify that he took special satisfaction in the result; his "full right to such a monogram" was never contested.[14] Certainly, his reputation rests more on the many he printed, not only for Whistler, but also for Haden, Legros, William Strang, Pennell, and Auguste Rodin, than it does on his own etchings.

Delâtre and Goulding were only the most famous of a line of highly reputed copperplate printers, which included Henry E. Carling, David Strang, and Frank Welch in England and Frederick Reynolds, Peter Platt, and Charles S. White in America. All three Americans had, at one time or another, printed for John Taylor Arms. An expert printer himself, Arms relied on them to print the editions of most of his plates and later on David Strang, who, during a year in America, printed supplements to many of Arms's earlier editions. After Strang returned to England, Arms continued to send him plates to print and then patiently—or impatiently—waited for the return of impressions by surface mail.[15] When it came to meeting deadlines, Arms could also count on assistance from Ernest Roth and from Kerr Eby in pulling trial proofs; both lived nearby in Connecticut. On at least one occasion the three worked together on a plate: the buildings in *Medieval Pageantry* were needled by Arms; Eby did the figures and trees and, assisted by Roth, printed the edition.[16] The less experienced, mindful that it was "much easier to make an etching than to print it well," might approach the selfless Bertha Jaques, who found herself so swamped with requests for help that her husband urged—only half-jokingly—that she "hang out a shingle . . . , saying 'Professional Printing Done Here,' " which is what some others did in order to supplement their incomes.[17]

A third impetus toward collaboration had to do with the cost of equipment. Without a good press, the quality of prints was bound to suffer. At the time, those capable of printing larger plates cost at least $800, a sum many artists, especially the younger ones, would have found hard to accumulate. Along came Lee Sturges, a well-to-do member of the Brooklyn and Chicago etching societies. Unable to find the right kind of press, he designed one and had it built to his specifications. When he offered to build additional models and sell them at cost, which he estimated at $100, advances in the costs of labor and materials raised this to $280, putting it out of reach of most individuals.[18] The alternative was finding a press to share. The facilities at the Royal College of Art (RCA) in London, at the National Academy of Design (NAD) in New York, or at the Philadelphia Print Club became meeting places where etchers could print and at the same time enjoy the advice and companionship of other printmakers. Even in out-of-the-way Provincetown, Massachusetts, some 200 artists pooled resources to form an association and purchase, as one of its first projects, an etching press available to all members.[19]

Fourth, and last, printmakers are better positioned than painters to band together in collective marketing ventures. Most etchings are inexpensive enough to tempt the inexperienced buyer. In promoting their medium with offers of free prints to the associate members of their societies, etchers did not face the same problem as the art unions, limited as they were to a few original pictures distributed by lottery every year; all but the few lucky winners had to make do with engraved facsimiles. Paintings are expensive, and painters, dependent on the patronage of only a small number of collectors, were understandably less concerned over general publicity for their art than over the price of their own paintings, a subject of endless bickering between the officers of these organizations and artists. The etching societies, on the other hand, could stir interest by presenting original prints to members at no great cost to themselves. Some prints were literally given away for publicity purposes—in one case as a bonus to new subscribers to *The New Republic*.[20]

For the same reason, individual etchers could show their most salable prints in several societies or place them with dealers in several cities more or less concurrently. Thus, Arms could report with some satisfaction that in December 1924, after a year of almost uninterrupted work in Europe, his *Rue Sauton*, etched the previous April and on the market in France and England for some months, had just been published in America.[21] It was even more common for British etchers to reserve a specified number of impressions for the American market, where the etching societies, hardly idle themselves, managed in many instances to put together duplicate traveling exhibitions in a circuit where original prints were rarely seen. And if an etching turned out to be in special demand in one place, a supply could usually be made available at the stated price, at least until the edition gave out. Etchings could even be ordered individually through the mail or on a subscription basis, mainly from publishers and their agents, with collectors signing up for impressions of as yet unpublished plates. There was little economic incentive for an etcher to withhold a print. Many found it useful to participate in a variety of collaborative enterprises.

## Support Networks: Insiders and Mediators

Reputations are built through networks that carry word of an artist's achievement. It takes more than sending to annual exhibitions to attract attention. Juries have their preconceptions, even blatant biases, about what is good and what is mediocre. Besides, they cannot give all submissions their full attention, and the entry of an unknown may be passed over. Even an entry that passes muster may still be badly hung or simply get lost among the hundreds competing for attention. The channels whereby artists move into the mainstream are so clogged that rarely is there a chance for a work to "speak for itself." Without some publicity many a promising artist falls by the wayside.

The relevant networks are of two kinds: *insider* networks that develop around the production of art and *mediator* networks that link artists to the art public. Each is central to one component of reputation. The insider networks through which individuals gain recognition and acceptance by other artists also lead to the development of a collective identity and sense of shared fate. But especially as etching gained popularity and the field of worthies became crowded, the influence of insiders—of the etching societies and similar circles—declined relative to that of the mediators who wrote about, exhibited, marketed, or otherwise took a strong interest in their work. It is through the mediator networks that etchers, individually and collectively, became renowned.

### Hierarchical Networks

Insider networks, to which we turn first, involve both hierarchical relationships between artists of manifestly unequal standing and lateral relationships among art students or artists joined together in a common purpose. Young artists need guidance. Not surprisingly, it was generally some respected member of the artistic community who served as counselor and sponsor for many a fledgling etcher. The first important contacts of a neophyte often came through teachers respected by other artists and known to dealers, critics, and curators. They served as conduits to other important individuals who, as gatekeepers, could open many doors. Frank Short would often have responsibility for the print section of major exhibitions, or to cite a specific example, Smillie alone was delegated to select the artists for the important etching exhibit at the 1904 Louisiana Purchase Exhibition in St. Louis. Also, unpaid officers of the etching societies assisted many neophytes through introductions to strategic persons that led to jobs, commissions, dealer contracts, invitations to exhibit, and nomination to artistic societies with limited membership. Some went out of their way, quite unofficially, to scout for unrecognized talent. Thus Bertha Jaques exhibited justified pride in having discovered her "first Simon-pure genius" when he was lighting the street lamps of San Francisco. No one out there had recognized John Winkler's "worth" until he was "introduced" through her Chicago society. After that, the "world was waiting at his door."²²

Anyone with a recommendation from a prestigious school like the Royal College of Art had a head start, but hierarchical networks also worked for those on the "periphery." Constance Copeman from Liverpool, a favorite of John Finnie, the distinguished painter who taught there, had taken up etching under his personal tutelage. Two years after Finnie became a fellow of the RSPE, Copeman was elected an associate, but with the death of Finnie in 1907, she lost her sponsor. Not living in London, she had no opportunity to make herself visible by working on committees, which might have bettered her chance of being put up for election as a full fellow. Out of sight, out of mind? At any rate, she remained an associate during the three decades of her membership.

In America, also, it helped those with an eye on honorific election to have a friend in court. As a member of the council of the National Academy, John Taylor Arms was strategically placed to propose printmakers for consideration or to become the key sponsor for an aspirant. The influence he wielded as a council member from 1938—and as vice-president after 1941—was considerable. One year he sponsored Grace Albee and got her elected associate by a large majority; the next year, Doel Reed, Victoria Huntley, and Adolf Dehn also made it with his support and a fourth printmaker he seconded lost by only three votes. Subsequently, he also proposed Stow Wengenroth and Armin Landeck and got them elected. But his influence was not unlimited. Helen Loggie, whom he also sponsored, had to wait until 1949 to become an associate.

In sponsoring others, mentors also consolidated their own reputations by seeing to the advancement of disciples who would carry on in the same style. Thus, hierarchical networks tended to be the channel favored by those prepared to conform, whereas it was the lateral networks on which mavericks were more inclined to rely.

*Lateral Networks*

Elders do wield authority, and each cohort of newcomers has to compete for visibility against those already entrenched in the hierarchy. The process finds expression in the succession of generations.[23] There being only limited room at the top, neophytes temperamentally disinclined to take the path laid out for them by their mentors risked outright rejection. If nevertheless determined to go their own way, they had to depend on the help of like-minded peers. When Nevinson was advised by Henry Tonks, his teacher at the Slade, to forget about an art career—a story we have already told in Chapter 6—he reacted as any strong-willed twenty-one-year-old would: "Had [Mark] Gertler [a fellow student] told me seriously that I was wasting my time I should have been heart-broken, but as things were I managed to bear up." After some months of floating, he went back to London, where his old "gang" from the Slade, now calling themselves Neo-Primitives, had more or less formed up again. When later he went to Paris, it was with another friend from St. John's Wood, his earlier art school, in whose company he "quickly forgot the Tonks nonsense about abandoning art."[24]

Many support networks did indeed date back to art school, where students had come under the spell of a genuine spirit of camaraderie. Augustus John, William Orpen, and Albert Rutherston, known as the "Three Musketeers," met at the Slade during the mid-nineties. They were always together and, not content with working in trio all day, would meet in some studio at night where they could draw. They also included within their circle Ambrose McEvoy, the painter and etcher Edna Waugh (later Lady Clarke Hall), and several other talented women.[25] While the ways of Orpen and John were to diverge, and several of the women, in John's words, "came to nought under the burden of domesticity,"[26] the word of their alleged precocity got their reputations off to a fast start. A decade after the John generation of students had left the Slade, a patron intent on encouraging young artists published a volume on drawing at the Slade in which four members of the group, including John and Orpen, were still featured together.[27] And these student-day linkages were still being recalled in the obituaries of these artists more than half a century later.

Groups of young artists often coalesce around a single dominant figure—a fellow student of apparent talent, as in the above case, or a

young artist only a few years their senior. American students dissatis-
fied with the teaching at the Munich Academy first flocked to the
nearby studio of twenty-nine-year-old Frank Duveneck; they followed
him to Florence and Venice, where they became known as the "Duveneck boys." Otto Bacher, the only one to have had prior experience with
etching, brought along an etching press and introduced the "boys,"
including Duveneck, to the medium. His methods were a mighty rev-
elation "to those who, after reading Hamerton's treatise, had become
discouraged with the long processes" recommended by him.[28] Their
work on the copperplate, Bacher's included, also benefited from contacts with Whistler, who happened to be in Venice at the same time.
The affinity was noted when Bacher, Duveneck, George Edward Hopkins, and Theodore M. Wendel sent work to the first exhibition of the
RSPE: "Those familiar with Mr. Whistler's method of etching," wrote
*The Times*'s reviewer, "will at once recognize that in Mr. Bacher he has
found a most formidable rival."[29] This was high praise indeed. Haden
and Legros actually mistook the three etchings of Venice by Duveneck,
whom no one in London knew, for Whistler's. Rumor had it that the
Duveneck name was made up to circumvent a stipulation in Whistler's
contract with the Fine Art Society that his twelve etchings of Venice be
shown at no other gallery.[30] Etchings by members of the Duveneck
circle also traveled to the Boston Museum of Fine Art; some were
subsequently published by Koehler. Despite this promising start, all
members of this group abandoned etching within a few years.

Lateral networks developed quite spontaneously among art students and among artists working in nearby studios; many spent additional time together on sketching trips or summered in the same art
colony. These links were often as much a product of happenstance—of
where the artist lived or where the studio was located—as of design.
Both in the United States and Britain, there were many residential
clusters of etchers. In Britain they were grouped together in residences
or studios in Brook Green, in the Hammersmith section of London, or
on Fitzroy Street in Camden Town. In New York, before the turn of the
century, artists were housed together in the upper stories of the YMCA
building at Fourth Avenue and Twenty-third Street, in the Studio Building at 51 West Tenth Street, and in the Holbein Studios on West Fifty-
fifth.[31] Greenwich Village and Union Square were centers. Propinquity
fostered the networks through which reputations were collectively
built. It is in fact remarkable how often and how early the paths of
some of our best-recognized etchers crossed—in Paris, in New York, in
their summer residences.

There were, moreover, no clear lines of demarcation between the support networks of painters and etchers but rather much overlapping.[32] In fact, for many etchers the connection to painters was critical. John Sloan, for example, credited Robert Henri, the painter, with inspiring him and William Glackens, Everett Shinn, James Preston, and George Luks through his "magic ability as a teacher."[33] All had at one time or other illustrated for the *Philadelphia Press*. What had attracted these young men to Henri was his championing of a new kind of American art, different from the largely derivative works that dominated the National Academy of Design. As one by one they moved from Philadelphia to New York, they remained in contact and were once again drawn to Henri, who had likewise relocated there. It was to his old friend Glackens that Sloan owed his commission as coillustrator—with Glackens, Luks, and Shinn—for the translated edition of the novels of Paul de Kock.[34] The illustrations, begun while Sloan was still in Philadelphia, would be his first important etchings.

The group stuck together. Although by 1906 Henri had become a full academician and Glackens an associate, juries were still rejecting some of their work. Sloan was having even greater difficulties. His New York diary, begun in 1906, indicates how cool a reception he was encountering. Pisinger Modern Gallery, where Henri, Luks, and Glackens were also exhibiting, had managed to sell exactly one set of his New York etchings to Henry W. Ranger, the landscape painter, who had requested that Sloan sign them as a personal favor. Sloan hoped that this sale would be "very good advertising as Ranger is very well known." Only a few days later, he learned that the gallery was removing his paintings for more "salable stuff." Other frustrations followed in short order: his etchings were rejected by Keppel, by the Cooperative Society, by Klackner Art Publishers, and finally by Wunderlich, the art dealer who specialized in engraving, where the "clerks were interested . . . [until] the manager . . . threw cold water on said hopes." Sloan also had an introduction to Russell Sturgis, the art writer, who told him that his etchings lacked charm and their message "could be best expressed in words." The set he had left as a gift was returned as "too costly," but Sturgis kept the one print he liked, thereby breaking the set.[35]

The most painful slap in the face was the return to Sloan of four etchings that had been invited by Mielatz, of the committee on etchings at the Water Color Society Exhibition. The explanation by Mielatz was that other members had thought them "too vulgar" for a public exhibition. Sloan then requested that his six others prints also be taken down but this was refused as "contrary to the rules." All the while, his paintings were faring no better at the National Academy. Of two he submitted to the 1907 exhibition, one was "fired"; the other received no more than a rating of second quality and was badly hung. In this misery he was in good company. Henri's paintings had received the same indifferent rating from a jury of which he himself was a member; he decided to withdraw all of them. Feeling unappreciated and ill-treated, the members of the Henri circle, within days of these rejections, developed a plan for an "exhibition of the 'crowd's' work next year." Sloan was to take charge of the moneys and Henri of the correspondence.[36] They were joined by Arthur B. Davies and Ernest Lawson, two artists who had just been defeated for academy membership, and later by Maurice Prendergast, whom Davies apparently brought in, to form the cooperative project for which they are remembered as "The Eight." Yet Sloan continued to feel that he had "never done anything anybody wanted."[37] It took another five years to sell his first painting. Not content simply to wait, he set out on a vigorous campaign to sell his etchings and paintings by sending an illustrated brochure to a list of 1,600 prospective buyers selected from *Who's Who*. A set of his thirteen city etchings, now in high demand, was offered for $35, a low price. Sloan could afford to do this only because "I am my own publisher and all distributors' profits are eliminated. I hope you will be interested and send me an order." The offer resulted in exactly two sales, one to the Newark Museum. Only after the Metropolitan Museum of Art, after long delay, purchased his *Dust Storm* were his sales sufficient to devote himself to painting full time.[38]

Lateral support groups were as important to young etchers searching for their own distinctive style as to young painters. Especially in the 1920s, when the achievement of distinction in modern etching was delayed by keen competition among "such a host of candidates," groups of etchers could more readily build reputations collectively than individually. We have already written of the young English etchers at Goldsmith's College who turned to F. L. M. Griggs, an older etcher, rather than to their own teachers for advice. Having too much individuality to be regarded as "mere continuators" irrevocably committed to any definite artistic tradition, they joined together, as friends, to develop an expressive style of their own.[39] In America, such lateral support groups were likely to be both more encompassing and more organized. To read the histories of American printmaking is to be aware of the importance of collective enterprise in stylistic development. Lithography flourished in the togetherness of artists in Woodstock, New York; innovations in color printing came with the influx of artists to Provincetown just before World War I; the silkscreen process, or serigraphy, took off in the 1930s when nurtured by the Federal Arts Project and proselytized by a group that included Elizabeth Olds, Harry Gottlieb, and Louis Lozowick. As the depression deepened, the more "socially conscious" American printmakers joined the American Artists' Congress to undertake a project intended to publicize a "deep-going change that has been taking place among artists . . . a change that [was taking] them . . . into the street, into the mills, farms, mines and factories. More and more . . . are filling their pictures with their reactions to humanity about them, rather than with apples or flowers." Even the abstract artists, Ralph Pearson pointed out in an introduction to their 1936 exhibition of one hundred prints, "note their concern with social issues and subjects, at least as a source of inspiration, as indicated by their titles."[40]

## Mediator Networks

As artists free themselves from dependence on their mentors, linkages with the outside world become more important. While lateral networks may provide the platform from which to launch a rising star, the achievement of renown beyond the world of teachers and peers requires the assistance of influential intermediaries. For some artists, mediators were readily at hand; the artist had to do no more than cash in on family connections. Most others, in establishing such ties, had to exercise considerable initiative and to persevere.

### Making Connections

Muirhead Bone was one artist who started with very little beyond his very evident talent. His interest in art, like that of so many others, had been roused by a drawing master. Archibald Kay, a member of the Royal Scottish Academy, took Bone and Francis Dodd, his other favorite pupil, into his evening class, where the two boys became close friends. Together they next attended Kay's larger evening class at the Glasgow School of Art. Dodd was awarded a scholarship that allowed him to go to Paris, but for Bone, given his family situation, there was no choice. He went to work as he finished school at fourteen. Turned down as an apprentice designer for a calico mill and as a book illustrator for a local firm, he spent the next three years in an architect's office. Each day he would finish his work as quickly as possible and escape to the streets and docks where he could draw. At eighteen, he had done with architecture. He took a job in a home crafts shop that closed over the summer so that he was free to join Dodd, now back from Paris, for three months of "serious" painting on a part of the coast frequented by Glasgow artists. Determined to make himself a real artist and with enough jobs to keep him going, he set up in a small studio, was elected to the Glasgow Art Club, and even had pictures in its annual exhibition. His network had begun to expand.

Early in 1898, Bone, now twenty-two, made his first drypoints with the help of a fellow student. He studied Hamerton and busied himself with drawings of streets, shipyards, and harbor scenes for his first set of Glasgow etchings and then, with introductions from Dodd in hand, sought visibility in London. Drypoints sent at the invitation of Bernard Sickert, whom Bone had met through Dodd, had already been hung at the New English Art Club. He also had from Dodd an introduction to D. S. MacColl, a well-connected and influential Glasgow painter, writer, and art critic. When Bone called on him, he met Tonks, who happened to be at the house; through MacColl, he also met William Strang and Dunthorne, the dealer, who bought one of Bone's prints but otherwise showed no great interest. Lord Carlisle, a relative of one of his Glasgow patrons, introduced him to Legros and J. P. Heseltine. But even though Bone had been able to use his Glasgow network and connections to enlarge the circles in which he was known, he did not yet have an active gallery connection.

Bone's next trip was to Manchester, where Dodd, to whose sister he was soon to become engaged, was living. As there were not enough local patrons in Manchester to bring Bone the regular income he needed to marry, he went to Ayr (Scotland) for a year, trying to establish himself as an art master but without being able to secure a single pupil. Then, in 1901, his etchings were hung at the big International Exhibition at Glasgow and, happily for Bone, noticed by Campbell Dodgson as well as Charles Aitken, the director of the Whitechapel Art Gallery (and later of the Tate Gallery), "whose friendships (made in person the year following) were to influence [Bone's] life deeply." But even after the Glasgow exhibition, Bone still felt "rather gloomy" about his prospects: his career "did not . . . advance at all."[41] He was particularly downcast because not one of his etchings would be used to illustrate a book by MacColl. The publisher did not think they reproduced well. As Bone told MacColl, it would not have mattered if Legros, Zorn, Meryon, Haden, or Charles Keene's works were not represented—all were more or less classics. But he had been "a *local* black-and-white man" and was counting on this book, which was not to be a "local product."⁴² Ultimately, *A Rhenish Evangeliarium*, the most successful of Bone's Glasgow Exhibition etchings, was illustrated in MacColl's *Nineteenth Century Art*.

Bone was ready by now to settle in London. MacColl, forever supportive, helped him secure the use of a house in Chelsea, where he made the acquaintance of other members of the New English Art Club and soon became a member himself. He devoted much of his time to pencil drawings. So eager was he to have his architectural drawings appear in the *Architectural Review*, of which MacColl was the editor, that he would let MacColl "settle a fee as small as you like and be quite glad."⁴³ He was further indebted to MacColl for asking Robert B. Ross at the Carfax Gallery about an exhibition for Bone. It was here that Dodgson bought a picture for the Contemporary Art Society to present to the Tate. MacColl and Dodgson, Bone gratefully recalled, were "the first helping hands I had in London."⁴⁴ Bone's real break came when he met Gustav Mayer, of the Obach publishing firm, who offered to publish his *Southampton from Eling* as part of a portfolio if the artist would deliver ten plates of equal quality along with the required number of proofs.⁴⁵ This portfolio, published in 1904, contained some of Bone's most highly praised plates.⁴⁶ Thereafter, it was through the Society of Twelve, which Bone helped found—along with such other rising stars as William Strang, Cameron, George Clausen, Rothenstein, Shannon, and Conder—that his etchings came to the attention of a larger public and brought his first renown.

*Publicity and Publicists*

Just to have an outlet that helped make ends meet did not suffice for a national reputation. Neither was an illustrating commission much of a reputational plus unless it led somewhere. Like Bone, those who specialized in architectural drawing—Griggs, Mielatz, Charles Henry White, and others—had to place their drawings and etchings where they would be seen by the right people. A print on consignment at a gallery easily gets lost, but a well-advertised exhibition, especially one backed by an illustrated sales catalog with a biographical sketch of the artist, enhances visibility.

A gallery director as savvy as Harold Wright of Colnaghi's, knowing the value of the right publicity, would actively collaborate with exhibiting artists to produce articles and brochures on their life and work. With "constant and kindly persistence [he] unraveled the shrouds of mystery of past prints and events" about the Copleys for his article in *The Print Collector's Quarterly*, timed to coincide with a forthcoming exhibition.[47] Copley, filled with gratitude, acknowledged that Ethel Gabain and he really could no longer complain about want of recognition. "I believe," he wrote Wright, "it was your little book, more than anything else, that set it all going."[48] In like manner, Frederick Keppel in New York, Roullier in Chicago, and Louis Holman of Goodspeed's in Boston had promoted the etchings of artists they represented with a booklet, sometimes with a fully annotated and up-to-date list in the appendix. The ultimate credential was, of course, the publication, during an artist's lifetime, of a catalogue raisonné.

It must be noted that the fine print trade, like the art business in general, attracted a fair number of dealers who conducted their business with an eye to more than the bottom line. Carl Zigrosser, of Weyhe's in New York City, took special satisfaction in having "encouraged, perhaps with more enthusiasm than discretion, a great number of American printmakers."[49] He too had offered gallery space and, in some cases, booklets to rouse interest. Encouragement could also mean financial support in the form of loans or retainers. Not only Zigrosser but other dealers, S. P. Avery for example, assisted young artists, sometimes surreptitiously, to hold body and soul together. The ubiquitous Harold Wright likewise took a personal interest in those in whom he believed. Ethel Gabain expressed her gratitude when, in the hospital about to undergo a risky kidney operation, she confided: "You have been our friend for so many years, and such a real friendship it has been between us through so many years of struggle and difficulty and you have done so much for us—that we wanted to tell you ourselves. . . . If the time came when my prints had to be dealt with I know I am leaving them in good hands, that you would do the best you could for the family as you will." Mrs. Wright, she recalled, had even given her wise advice about the Copley children, now grown, when they were still babies.[50] Outside counsel could take many forms: years later Mielatz still recalled "with an air of warm thankfulness" how Wunderlich, founder of the house later known as Kennedy and Company, had warned him that it would be a mistake to turn out plates simply because they would sell.[51]

The economic component, inextricably present in even the friend-liest dealer-artist relationship, was usually irrelevant to the critic's championship of etchers. At least this held for Malcolm Salaman, who regularly wrote on prints for *The Studio*, the *Bookman's Journal and Print Collector*, and other publications from a conviction reminiscent of Hamerton and Koehler. His strong pro-Whistler opinions, expressed in the *Manchester Courier* when a young man, had put him at odds with his editors. Asked to modify his comments, Salaman had refused, as he proudly informed Whistler, with "a letter after your own heart."[52] Decades later as editor of the richly illustrated *Fine Prints of the Year*, he introduced, along with the work of established printmakers, that of many who were yet unknown. When he died in 1940, it was justly said of him that "many an etcher today can look back and acknowledge his start on a career to the encouragement of Malcolm Salaman."[53]

Indeed, he had taken special joy, and some credit, for his part in launching McBey on his meteoric rise to stardom. In a little back room at Goupil's, where Salaman had gone late in 1911 to look over some modern color prints, he had chanced on a group of etchings by a man whose name he did not recognize. Nor could the gallery manager provide any information on the artist. Salaman recalled that he left "in a state of eagerness to make everybody else acclaim the young etcher," whose show, when it opened, had attracted few visitors.[54] Attendance quickly picked up, as did sales, in response to enthusiastic press notices by Salaman and by James Greig, critic of the *Morning Post*. Greig exhorted his readers to buy even if, like Sir James Murray, a Trustee of the National Gallery of Scotland, they had never before bought a single etching.[55] Within three and a half months, Goupil's had sold a phenomenal 220 prints plus another 138 at Davidson's in Glasgow, where McBey opened two months later.[56] When Richard Gutekunst, the print dealer, to whom Greig had introduced the artist, offered to act as his publisher (conjointly with Davidson), he received so many applications for McBey's etchings that he feared being overwhelmed with orders. Not eager to risk "people pestering me for things I could not give them," he decided to hold back on another exhibition; he had "a horror of creating another movement similar to what ha[d] been done in [the case of] Cameron and Muirhead Bone."[57]

On his part, McBey also felt overwhelmed by his unexpected celebrity status. People looked upon him, he confided to Greig, "as a sort of mild Messiah": the other day, Hardie had brought to his studio "an artistic lady—Miss Katherine Kimball A.R.E.—who, had she not been forcibly restrained, would have broken a box of ointment of spikenard [a fragrant and very costly ointment of ancient times]—very precious—over my head." Gutekunst, he went on, "looks on me as an angel of light, and enquires delicately after my state of health, and when I am likely to consider seriously thinking about a new etching. Davidson's of Glasgow keep on ordering, and wish to buy up my next six plates. They, too, distress themselves lest I work too hard, fearing lest they kill the gander that lays the golden eggs." He also mentioned Hutcheon, of the *Morning Post*, who appreciated his etchings and had framed them, and the "*Nottingham Guardian*, which sighed in vain for McBeys at the Painter-Etcher show," where he had been rejected for associate membership. Others were showing him added deference now that there had been thrown on him a "martyr's cloak."[58] A friend reported that at a high tea with Short and his pupils it had been mentioned that McBey had been to a portraitist; this was met with "a sort of gasp and silence, which said more plainly than words 'the bloody upstart.' "[59] All this was the direct consequence of massive critical attention.

Some well-to-do collectors sought out artists for the prestige, some for the pure pleasure they derived from such associations. To cater to these desires, it was common for artists to hold open house in their studios. While such personal relations are still cultivated, the setting for them has changed. One collector described his first meeting with the by-now famous McBey as a professionally managed luncheon with a would-be patron. He became determined to meet the artist, whom he greatly admired, under more "human circumstances" and, when he succeeded, took obvious delight in the fact that their "acquaintance ripened into friendship," that it became his "privilege to enjoy both a master's work and a master's mind."[60] The collector, a journalist who became a highly successful advertising executive, listed himself in *Who's Who* as an author of "books on print collecting." The book, in which his friendship with McBey is described, was privately printed and issued by the family with Season's Greeting for Christmas 1948.

It is easy to forget that the relationship between artist and patron was far closer before the dealers came to interpose themselves. Such friendships did, and still do, flourish. A particularly close relationship developed between Griggs and the Fleet Street journalist Russell Alexander. The two met during Alexander's visits to the Cotswolds and kept up "a close and intimate correspondence [in which] Griggs poured out, in long letters, the difficulties and the triumphs and the joys he encountered in his etchings."[61] It was to Alexander that Griggs entrusted the cataloguing of his etched work.[62] A planned biography never materialized. Thomas Simpson, another British collector, had the audacity to act as a special champion for the few contemporary etchers he particularly admired. Since he knew of no critic who had done so, he decided to "boldly come out into the open for the purpose of sifting the wheat from tares."[63] Acknowledging the perils of prophecy, he offered would-be collectors his predictions of the "probable final importance" of certain modern and contemporary etchers, which he sorted into five classes.[64] Leading Class I was Meryon, followed by Whistler. The recommended list of thirteen included the Scottish trio of Cameron, McBey, and Bone and three Englishmen—Haden, Short, and William P. Robins. None was American, but Clarence Gagnon, a Canadian, also made the list. This splendidly illustrated, limited edition book, published just as the postwar boom was getting under way, must have had some influence on the market.

*Getting Into the Archives*

Two activities can enhance living artists' reputations while giving them a better chance of being remembered in days to come. Both involve strategies that may ultimately enshrine artists in the archives and so perpetuate their name and fame. Writing, or being written about, and better still, being collected by public institutions can achieve this end.

Every artist needs spokespersons, but those working in a minor art need them even more. The literati are the acknowledged purveyors of fame.[65] Or, put another way, writers create a literary context that gives the work and its creator their special distinction. The world of art and the literary world do indeed intersect at many points, most directly when artists are writers or double as professional critics—Sickert, for example, whose comments on the art scene appeared in some of the leading journals of opinion, or Arthur Millier, whose occasional pieces led to his full-time position as art critic for the *Los Angeles Times*.

These two were hardly the only gifted writers among our etchers. William Strang, A. Hugh Fisher, Edna Clarke Hall, and Peggy Bacon had published poetry. Many more wrote books for children or on subjects suitable for illustration, and a few scored some literary success with autobiographical accounts—of their career, their childhood, travels, memorable associations, and experiences. They also wrote about art—Holroyd about Italian art and Philip Kappel about all kinds of antiquarian subjects on which each had become an expert. Margery Ryerson, editor of Robert Henri's *The Art Spirit*, was a frequent contributor to art journals as well as general interest publications.

Whether or not one wrote mattered less than one's connections to the literary scene. Sickert, Rothenstein, and John frequented the Café Royale and became influential players in the London world of arts. Joseph Pennell, an alien to London, managed his own entrance when, on his way to Europe on an illustrating commission for *The Century*, he called on Edmund Gosse, a leading literary figure and the magazine's European representative. The two became friends, and when in the winter of 1885–86 the Pennells came to live in London, Gosse introduced them to famous literary figures, such as Thomas Hardy, Walter Pater, Andrew Lang, Rider Haggard, and Henry James, who were regular guests at his house.[66] It was also at Gosse's that Pennell met George Bernard Shaw, who secured him a post writing art criticism for *The Star*, a London evening paper. Pennell admitted that he had "wanted ... to become famous ... [and] succeeded in getting rather well known and in and out of endless scrapes" as a critic, the first of his many ventures into writing.[67]

The ultimate validation of a reputation, the visible emblem of the artist's importance, came through museum purchases. Aware of this, both etchers and their dealers normally provided information on such acquisitions in even the shortest biography. Yet etchers faced an extra difficulty, inasmuch as before the Great War most museum directors and curators had their sights set on the art of the past and were disinclined to invest in modern etchings, oblivious to the fact that the "price of a single masterpiece of painting would establish and maintain handsomely a Print Department."[68] The few with confidence in the lasting artistic merits of the modern print had to show the way by example and by their writing. To cement the merging relationship with museums, several of the print societies sought to hold their exhibitions in public galleries. The Chicago Society of Etchers went farther, using the proceeds from sales to purchase some modern etchings for donation to the Art Institute of Chicago. The Cleveland Print Club did much the same for that city's Museum of Art.[69]

Even sympathetic curators had to be selective, not only in what they bought but also in what they accepted as gifts, to prevent their museums from becoming "dumping grounds" and their facilities for restoration and cataloguing from being overtaxed. Despite his long-standing friendship with Hans Singer, keeper of prints at the Dresden Museum, Pennell approached him gingerly in telling him of the extraordinary success he had had with his London set. He was keeping about ten proofs each, he wrote, proposing to offer them to a few museums and galleries. "But before doing so—I write to ask you, if you think they are wanted? And secondly what course—if they are wanted should be pursued. I would also like to let Dr. Lehrs have a set in Berlin." At the same time, in order to protect his reputation, Pennell did not want it said that he "gave" the etchings, though "I am extremely glad to do so, for I *never gave* a gallery, even the Philadelphia

Academy, my old school, which is always wanting things—or any public institution anything before."[70]Meanwhile, aware of the genuine admiration Singer had for his work, Pennell was looking forward to an article the keeper was preparing for *The Studio*. Singer had publicly judged Pennell's work "unsurpassed" when it came to "artistic sensitivity and ingeniously free treatment in his field."[71] Pennell was not one to mind this kind of overstatement.

In sum, successful etchers were highly enterprising. They did not allow opportunity to go begging, and they worked hard to overcome whatever obstacles lay in their way. But they did not build their reputations all by themselves. Recognition came largely from the network of peers with whom many collaborated, partly in response to the technological imperative of the medium. Movement beyond this world of insiders usually required mentors and other mediators. The reputation of an etcher, like that of all artists, was promoted through the efforts of the dealer, critic, and museum network. Writers, especially, create a literary context that takes the place of what Walter Benjamin called the "aura."[72] Over the long run, writers can legitimate artistic worth and help an artist's works to find a place in those archives where cultural treasures judged to merit preservation are housed.

The Historical Context

Reputations, individual and collective, are not built in a historical vacuum. To begin with, the success or failure of any artist's efforts to build a reputation is inextricably linked to the changing status of the medium, style, or genre in which he or she works. Such changes in status are themselves closely linked to changing life conditions. Thus, the growth in the popularity of painter-etching coincided with a very significant increase in public demand for art, a direct beneficiary of the rise in discretionary income made possible by economic growth during the latter part of the nineteenth century. Some of this money flowed into prints. Meanwhile, advances in the methods of pictorial reproduction through various photographic processes were changing the nature of print collecting. Engravings had long been valued primarily as records of flora, of fauna, of distant lands, and of anything of which there were no other images. Now, tutored by critics, the new collectors began to seek prints primarily for their artistry.

Artists are always affected by economic conditions and by fashions that impinge directly on the art market. To supplement our discussion (Chapter 4) on the effect of the Great Depression and the rise of abstract art, we now focus on the far more disruptive effects of war. War plays havoc with routines. When a nation feels threatened, patriotism becomes the order of the day. Restrictions are imposed and resources diverted to areas of higher priority to the war effort. Of the two world wars, the 1914–18 conflict had the more serious effects by far. It shattered the unfettered optimism in the inevitability of human progress and for the first time brought into play the full power of a new machinery of destruction. Fighting men were the inevitable victims. Their loss was deeply felt in France and Britain, their armies suffering a shocking number of casualties in the battles of the Somme and around Verdun without achieving any significant military advance. Yet, perverse as it may seem, what looms as an obvious obstacle also creates new opportunities for those poised to take advantage of them. Some, but only some, of our etchers owe much of their considerable reputations to their active participation as military combatants or noncombatants, especially in the Great War.

### Obstacles and Interruptions

With the outbreak of war in 1914, French authorities immediately imposed travel restrictions that inconvenienced artists. No longer could they freely roam the countryside for picturesque subjects. In searching biographies, one encounters tales of artists, even some on official assignment, who were detained on suspicion of spying when found sketching in forbidden territory.[73] Some of these tales may themselves be suspect, but the restrictions were nevertheless real. Some expatriate Americans, who had used Paris as a base for sketching trips all over Europe, simply returned home to wait out the war. Others in the art world had to cope with more personal restrictions on their ability to do business as usual: the highly respected Gutekunst was forced to close his London establishment because of his German origin. Some had only to change, or distract attention from, their heritage: thus, the etcher Amelia Bauerlé became Amelia Bowerley.[74] More generally, artistic activity slowed as energies and resources were absorbed by the war. There were fewer exhibitions, fewer exhibitors, and fewer sales. One of the casualties of America's entry was *The Print Collector's Quarterly*, which suspended publication for the duration with its last 1917 issue.

The most direct effect was on young men of military age. The statistics tell their own story. Of those men in our sample who were of draft age either in World War I or II, nearly two out of three (63 percent) of the British saw active service, as did one of every three (33 percent) of the Americans.[75] Many of the British volunteered for the

Artists' Rifles. Mobilized the day after war was declared, it was one of the first Territorial battalions to be sent to France. Upon its arrival there in October 1914, the unit was immediately sent to the front, but later the unit was converted into a reserve for the regular British Expeditionary Force, supplying officers to every branch. Some of our etchers were assigned to camouflage units, others put to work in making maps, visual training aids, or given assignments that called on their skills as draftsmen; it is remarkable nevertheless how many served in the ranks as ordinary soldiers and in assignments that made no use of their professional skill.

Even the ones ineligible for active combat sought to enter the fray. Nevinson, then under the influence of the Futurists who looked upon war as a great cleansing force, knew he would fail a physical because of a limp but responded to the "urge to do something, to be 'in' the War." He went to Dunkerque to join the Red Cross ambulance corps. A few months were all that he could take; he was sent home to London where he found "life still unshaken" but was sadder for having seen war.[76] Thereafter, responding to an appeal from the Chelsea Arts Club, Nevinson enlisted as a private in the Royal Army Medical Corps assigned to a London hospital. Then, just as the unit was to ship out, he was discharged after an attack of rheumatic fever. On the other hand, it has been said that Gerald Brockhurst, on account of his intense commitment to pacifism, refused military service. Records do show, however, that he was discharged from service in May 1916 for "reasons of health."[77]

Neither Nevinson nor Brockhurst was the most serious war casualty in our sample. Percy Gethin fell in the Battle of the Somme; Alfred Bentley died a premature death as the consequence of having been gassed. Herman A. Webster, an American then living in France and a volunteer for the ambulance corps, did not recuperate from war injuries affecting his eyesight until years after the war.

Nor, for that matter, were women's careers totally exempt from the disruptions of war. Constance Copeman made dolls for children in order to contribute something.[78] Bertha Gorst, from nearby North Wales, asked an American bookplate collector to let her put off his request "for the present. I can think of nothing but egg collecting (for the wounded) and sandbag-making and drilling girls. . . . 'Woodland deer, and horses hares' are very remote from my imaginative mind at present."[79] Orovida Pissarro was among the many women who moved from London to the country to help with agriculture.[80] Zella de Milhau, an American, drove an ambulance. She was awarded several medals, including the Croix de Guerre, for bravery under fire and courageous service.[81] Amelia Bowerley and Mabel Louisa Robins, both British, paid the ultimate price; they were victims of the influenza epidemic that swept Europe in 1918. Margaret Kemp-Welch lost most of her plates in one of the sporadic attacks by zeppelins on the city of London.

In World War II, Eric Ravilious, a promising British printmaker, died in the Battle of the Atlantic, but mostly it was work rather than lives that was at risk. The home and studio of A. Hugh Fisher fell victim to German bombs during the Blitz. His cabinets and tools were destroyed; his coppers, books, and prints were buried in the debris.[82] At age seventy-four, Fisher had already made his reputation, but for younger artists the consequences of such losses early in a career must have been serious.[83] Several American etchers, though immune to the Blitz, were persuaded to donate plates to meet the copper shortage brought on by the war.[84]

## Opportunities for War Artists

Belligerents have always found artists useful. But the Great War marked the first time that governments directly employed artists to provide psychological armaments in the form of posters, cartoons, and propaganda and in developing an effective camouflage in the field. Moreover, some far-sighted officials in Britain saw a need for official war artists to create a pictorial record of the war that could be permanently preserved in a war museum.

*Great Britain.* The idea that artists might succeed in conveying the experience of war better than any official record was slow to take shape. The first to have artists produce pictures of the home and war fronts were the Germans, and by 1915 reproductions of these had appeared in American publications.[85] On the French side, it had been almost impossible for artists of war, even the most famous, to get into the area then called "the front." Frederick Villiers, who finally obtained permission, produced some very accurate drawings, many done on the spot and in a frontline trench, which appeared in *Illustrated London News.* Officially sanctioned, these were the only drawings to become widely available during the first two years of conflict.[86]

The impetus for the appointment of British war artists came from two directions: from artists themselves and from officials eager for a better documentation of the achievements of the country's fighting men. A spokesman for the art community was William Rothenstein. The idea had come to him during a visit to the Belgian front, where he had been taken up in a "sausage" balloon for a full vista of the lines stretched along the Yser. It was consistent with his beliefs, expressed earlier, that the state and municipalities should employ artists so as to compensate for the gradual diminution of private patronage. His proposal, made to the War Office through a friend, was received sympathetically by Lord Northcliffe, who wanted to copy the Germans by sending "distinguished artists to the front" but did not think the British authorities were yet ready to do so.[87]

On this last count his lordship was wrong. Exactly such an enterprise was about to be sanctioned by the propaganda arm of the government, where Charles F. G. Masterman, the Liberal politician, who from 1914 on headed what was then called the Special Department, had decided to recruit artists to make up for the paucity of good photographs. The presence in this department of several eminent representatives of the British art world—among them Campbell Dodgson—had influenced that decision.[88] Within a month of Northcliffe's pessimistic assessment, Britain had its first official war artist in the person of Muirhead Bone.

The selection of Bone is testimony to the importance of networks. In the spring of 1916, he had just turned forty but was facing call-up and preferred to be used as a war artist. He first asked his brother, a journalist, to intercede with Lord Newton, who was then at the Foreign Office in charge of foreign propaganda.[89] Convinced that the King would not "want his records to be simply bound volumes of the *Daily Mirror*," he once again turned to his old sponsor for advice on how to get the monarch (or Queen Mary) to accept that "I'm the best man and that it ought to be done." He would be willing, he wrote MacColl, to devote all his drawings and etchings for the next two years to such a project. Surely, he implored him, it would be a wiser and more economical use of himself than guarding some gas work threatened by the Germans.[90] Bone also had supporters on Masterman's staff: there was Dodgson, who may have argued that Bone's etchings of London demolition scenes made him a natural to record battle field devastation, and A. P. Watt, a literary agent, who had bought at auction a canvas that Bone had donated to the Red Cross.[91]

By July he had a six-month contract; by August he had donned a uniform and was in France. He returned to England in December to render home-front activity and record life at the Grand Fleet, an assignment interrupted by another much shorter stay in France. All his drawings were to go to the government, which had free rights of reproduction and could select whatever it wanted of the originals for its archives. Meanwhile, they were being regularly reproduced in the *War Pictorial*, an official magazine with a large circulation. Campbell Dodgson selected 200 to be reproduced in *The Western Front*, consisting of ten monthly issues, starting January 1917, each with twenty drawings by Bone.[92] Close to 400,000 copies were printed, 35 percent for the American market. The publisher also promised a large-sized deluxe edition that would give full effect to the artist's work. It was printed in one, two, or three colors according to the character of the original. So flooded was the market that, except for the special over-size reproduction of his highly publicized drawing of tanks rolling into attack, which sold well all over the world, many issues had to be given away.[93] The public was nonetheless interested in war art, and the response to Bone's drawings, when shown in London, was generally favorable. One reviewer observed that before the war Bone had been repeating a few successes until they "nearly became monotonous, and one felt that the artist needed a new stimulus, some fresh subject or inspiration." As a war artist, he had discovered new subjects and expanded his scope.[94]

Bone's good fortune in finding a position that exactly fitted him contrasted with that of McBey, who when posted to France lacked the liberty to draw where he pleased. After several rejections for military service because of bad eyesight, he had been commissioned a second lieutenant in 1916 and given a secret but most uninteresting assignment. Sketching was against regulations and had to be done surreptitiously. For many subjects, McBey had to depend on thumbnail notes and sketches made on small cards held in the palm of his hand or even inside his pocket. When his attention was drawn to a torpedoed passenger ship that lay beached near Boulogne, he went out night after night to sketch it. From endless local notes and composition studies there finally evolved, when he was on leave, an etching of the *Sussex*, hailed as "a landmark in the progress of [his] art" and later described, by his cataloguer, as "one of the noblest, most spiritual of his plates."[95] (See figure 18.) An exhibition of his war drawings, including some of the Somme, at Colnaghi and Obach drew much favorable comment.

With the reorganization, in 1917, of what had been a separate propaganda arm into first a department, then a ministry, of information under Lord Beaverbrook, more appointments of official war artists soon followed. Beaverbrook had already played a significant role in the Canadian government's development of a war artists' scheme. By offering attractive commissions, he had recruited artists of stature, including such painter-etchers as Anna Airy, David Cameron, Augustus John, and Laura Knight. In the spring of 1917, McBey found himself, likewise upon recommendation of Dodgson, assigned as an official war artist with the British Expeditionary Force in Egypt. His brief was "to make drawings of appropriate war scenes in Egypt and Palestine for the purposes both of propaganda at the present time and of historical record in the future" along the model of Bone's *The Western Front*.[96] Though left to himself, his work was made difficult by the intense heat and lack of transport. For months he carried on as best he could, moving around on foot or hitching rides, yet missing some of the finest material around him. He arrived too late to witness the fall of Gaza but managed to get to Jerusalem on the day of the official entry of the Allied forces just before Christmas. These obstacles notwithstanding, he made nearly as many drawings (299) as Bone,[97] yet circumstances were such that they never received the publicity intended by the propaganda department. Delayed by censors and photographers at GHQ Cairo, they arrived in London only after the German spring offensive of 1918 had overshadowed the militarily less significant victories in the Near East. Although some drawings were carried by *War Pictorial* and other periodicals and eleven were included in *The Desert Campaigns* published by Constable, the planned booklets along the lines of *The Western Front* never materialized.

Once home in February 1919, McBey proceeded, as Bone never did, to turn his sketches and notes into etchings. Among them was *Dawn: The Camel Patrol Setting Out*, which set auction records during the twenties. It depicts the Australian Camel Patrol, which McBey, while waiting for the campaign to start, had accompanied on a five-day reconnaissance into the Sinai Desert. Through these etchings McBey emerged from the war with his reputation as much enhanced as Bone's.

Not every war artist benefited. The Western Front landscapes which the Canadians commissioned from Cameron, the third of the Scottish "big three," added nothing to his reputation. To the contrary, at least one art writer judged that the artist had relied too much in the paintings he did on conventions successfully used in his depictions of Scottish Highlands. While neither the fighting nor its effect on the landscape was ignored, his rendering of war scenes managed somehow "to avoid the unpleasant aspects of the front and make a featureless landscape into an interesting, if not a beautiful, picture."[98] None were ever translated into etchings.

*Unofficial War Artists*. No one will ever know how much unofficial art, such as that produced by McBey in his spare time, was created (and then lost) by the men who saw action. Some of our artists who were under thirty when the war broke out earned their credentials with works derived from their frontline experience. Several later received appointments as official war artists. The first of them was Nevinson. In the enforced leisure that followed his medical discharge from the army, he had put his experience to account. His paintings, which combined elements of the Cubist and Futurist styles, when shown in group exhibitions were praised by such critics as Frank Rutter, Lewis Hind, and Paul Konody; the last was art adviser to Lord Beaverbrook. Konody's especially warm response led to a one-man show at Leicester Galleries. Despite a slow start, attributable to wartime conditions, the show sold out.[99] After Konody followed up with a complimentary monograph, the way had been cleared.[100] Nevinson went to France as an official war artist; seventeen of his pictures were reproduced in the February 1918 issue of *British War Artists at the Front*. When he repeated some of his wartime compositions in drypoints and lithographs (figure 19), they were hailed by Dodgson as a pioneer example of a "new movement in English graphic art."[101] Nevinson was elevated to the status of a minor celebrity.

A good deal less meteoric was the rise of Paul Nash, who had volunteered through the Artists' Rifles, was commissioned in 1916 upon completion of a course as map instructor but not sent to the front until February 1917, when things were quiet. Letters he wrote during this hiatus speak of the sunshine that "made everything look full of colour and alive," of "larks singing," of the "curious beauty" connected with graves and burials. Just having posted six drawings to his wife for mounting, framing, and exhibition at Goupil's, he was trying to convey his vision in words:

> Here in the back garden of the trenches it is amazingly beautiful—the mud is dried to a pinky colour and upon the parapet, and through sandbags even, the green grass pushes up and waves in the breeze, while clots of bright dandelions, clover, thistles and twenty other plants flourish luxuriantly, brilliant growths of bright green against the pink earth. Nearly all the better trees have come out, and the birds sing all day in spite of shells and shrapnel. I have made three more drawings all of these wonderful ruinous forms which excite me so much here. . . . It sounds absurd, but life has a greater meaning here and a new zest, and beauty is more poignant. I never feel dull or

careless, always alive to the significance of nature who, under these conditions is full of surprises for me."[102]

He promised another batch of drawings in a month or less. After a week in which he found himself too busy, literally, even to write, he still referred to these "wonderful trenches at night, at dawn, at sundown." His mind would never lose the picture of "a wide landscape flat and scantily wooded and what trees remain blasted and torn, naked and scarred and riddled."[103] Two months later, he was sent home to recover from a painfully dislocated rib, suffered in a fall into a trench during a moonless night just before the big battle.

Nash was able to convert his mishap into a golden opportunity by working up his sketches for an exhibition of twenty war drawings at Goupil's and then, through his connections, returning to France as a war artist instead of a regimental officer. Though he had missed the battle of Passchendaele, he was able to make twelve drawings of that infamous battlefield, viewing it from a new perspective. Where he had perceived beauty, he now saw the "most frightful nightmare of a country more conceived by Dante and Poe than by nature, unspeakable, utterly indescribable." His drawings could only give "some vague idea of its horror, . . . [of] the normal setting of the battles taking place day and night, month after month. . . . Sunset and sunrise are blasphemy, they are mockeries to man." Instead of an "artist interested and curious," he came to define himself as a "messenger who will bring back word from the men who are fighting to those who want the war to go on forever. . . . Feeble, inarticulate may be my message, but it will have a bitter truth, and it may burn in their lousy souls."[104] Masterman greeted these drawings, when shown to him, with surprising enthusiasm. He commanded that they be exhibited. With help from Nevinson, a Slade classmate, he started to make lithographs of his war subjects. He also painted oils and soon found himself commissioned to do a huge panel for the Imperial War Museum that kept him busy in London until the end of the war. Among his most powerful works are his woodcuts of no man's land.

Many unofficial artists of the war were never officially, or only belatedly, recognized. Percy Smith, an early volunteer, was assigned as a gunner to a fifteen-inch howitzer crew. Before leaving for France, he had produced but twelve etchings, of which two were actually issued in an edition. Serving with the Royal Marine Artillery, he managed on occasion to steal time away from his duties to sketch what he observed of war. A few scenes were scratched directly onto plates smuggled out to him between the pages of magazines; other sketches were only later transferred to copper. All this was accomplished at some risk—twice he was arrested as a spy. Twenty-two plates were "done unofficially during 1916, 1917, and 1918. A few impressions were taken by the etcher as opportunity offered when on leave from the Front."[105] His most memorable, *Dance of Death*, a set of seven allegorical etchings of the Great War (figure 20), was executed during a period of rest and recuperation that he had the good fortune to spend away from Flanders in a British Channel town, where he had access to a press. The set, not finished until 1919, was put away on a shelf until seen by Campbell Dodgson, who wrote about it for *The Print Collector's Quarterly*,[106] and by Martin Hardie, who purchased a set for the Victoria and Albert. Considered one of Smith's major works, the *Dance of Death*, published in an edition of one hundred, lives on while his drypoints of the battlefield are all but a memory. Apart from twelve sets published by Colnaghi's in 1925, proofs are practically nonexistent. Smith himself destroyed some early impressions because they did not meet his exacting standards.

Their scarcity and bad timing account for the failure of Ian Strang's wartime etchings to enhance his reputation. He enlisted as a private in 1914. Prior to this he had produced forty-four etchings, all of them depicting architecture or architectural landscapes. Now in the Imperial War Museum in London there can be seen twenty of his etchings based on studies made in the trenches but needled after the war's end. Konody, who saw them when they were first exhibited, ranked them with "the most convincing and most accomplished etched records of the war zone."[107] But since Strang printed only about a dozen impressions of each before canceling the plates, they never became widely known. An article on Strang's etchings, published in *The Architect's Journal* on 21 March 1928, on "the tenth anniversary of the beginning of the most critical battle in the Great War," did not even mention his war etchings; nor did an article in *The Studio* in September that same year. And very few of them were ever illustrated in the war books that flooded the market just after the war ended.[108] His etching, *Knocked Out Tanks*, though derived from his personal impression of "the first appearance of tanks on any battlefield," was greeted as no more than an attempt to duplicate the success Bone had had with the same theme.

*United States.* The United States entered the First World War late and, unlike Britain and Canada, failed to look for its best artists to send to the front. To be sure, a Division of Pictures was formed under the Committee on Public Information, headed by George Creel, mostly to supply the various parts of the government with posters and other publicity material. In January 1918, authority was obtained to commission eight men to serve as official war artists in France. The War Department sent illustrators, rather than painters, to produce work "suitable for reproduction in the press." Even as drawings intended for illustration, the pictures were hardly a success. Of the 196 offered to magazines, only 51 were accepted for publication.[109]

The first war artist to arrive in France was J. André Smith. Trained as an architect, he described himself as a self-taught etcher who took up the needle only for relaxation. For the Committee on Public Information, he completed 105 drawings and produced a good many more on his own. In December 1919, Arthur H. Hahlo, the print dealer, published a limited edition book in which one hundred of these were illustrated together with a signed original proof etching of troops marching past a ruined church. Neither the etching nor the drawings were especially evocative. Smith himself described them as an "unsensational record of things actually seen," the majority having been made for the War Department's official records.[110]

The pictorial record left by Smith and other War Department artists compares unfavorably with the etched work of two unofficial war artists. The first is Lester G. Hornby, who had gone to France to study and made himself part of the Parisian scene. Already recognized by invitations to exhibit in prestigious salons and international exhibitions, by articles in *The Studio*, and by the illustrating commissions that came his way, the war moved him to return home. Within two years he was back, first operating on his own and then with passes as a sketch correspondent. He accompanied the American troops in their push at Château-Thierry and Belleau Woods, donning his helmet, readying his gas mask, and creeping along between the American guns and the high fagot camouflage on the German side of the road, learning what it meant to have shelling come "nearer and nearer."[111] Out of such authentic experience came thirty-seven etchings of the Great War; his drawings, too, were widely illustrated in newspapers and magazines.[112]

The June 1919 issue of *Harper's* carried an eight-page insert of drawings, entitled "From a Soldier's Sketchbook," by another unofficial war artist (figure 21). Sergeant Kerr Eby, born in 1889, the same year as Nevinson and Nash, had published ten etchings by 1915. When he resumed printmaking after a four-year gap, it was with war subjects—in drypoint, pure etching, mezzotint, and lithograph—which stand as "the expression of one who lived the experience day by day, month by month ... [and] were etched when the horror and nobleness, ruin and tragic beauty of it all were fresh and vivid things in Mr. Eby's mind."[113] While most of his war etchings were issued in 1919, he kept returning to the theme years later. His etching, *September 13, 1918—St. Mihiel Drive*, based on a drawing of the Twenty-sixth Division coming out of action in Château-Thierry and considered one of the great American war prints, first appeared in 1935 in an exhibition of his prints and drawings entitled "The Tragedy of War."[114] Like most of the great war prints, it was a pacifist statement. Eby himself was pleased to be labeled a pacifist if this meant believing "that there can be and are other ways of settling differences between Christian nations than murdering youngsters—and that lawful, not to say, sanctified, wholesale slaughter is simply slobbering imbecility."[115]

Neither Hornby nor Eby gained the kind of fame as war artists that the British artists—especially Bone, Nevinson, and Nash—did. Not only had America been touched less directly by the slaughter, but also the novelty had worn off by the time their work appeared. Examples of British art had preceded them across the Atlantic and, with the war over, most people wanted to get back to "normalcy." Interest in their depictions of the war as experienced by soldiers revived as the pacifist movement gained ground in the 1930s.

*World War II.* We begin by pointing out that by September 1939, when Hitler's armies attacked Poland, even the youngest of the male artists studied had turned thirty, which put them past the age of military utility in any but a noncombatant specialty. Understandably, only two of the British and three of the Americans performed regular military service. In fact, many were near the end of their careers, soon to be bypassed by the movement toward abstraction, which came to dominate the postwar era. We have also to point out some basic differences between the two wars. In 1914 troops had received their marching orders with an exuberance that could not possibly have survived the unequal encounter with the machinery of modern war. The World War II generation was more realistic, its idealism moderated. During the second war the artist's attention was not focused on one riveting theme—on no man's land, that strip of ravaged earth and chopped off vegetation between trenches, stretching for hundreds of miles, as the single dominant image. Both the Blitz and the unfamiliar surroundings in which troops fought provided a variety of new subject matter for art. Although the Kaiser's artillery had sent some shells toward Paris and some zeppelins had flown over London, these incursions had not stirred consciousness in the way that the deliberate attacks on civilians did during World War II. There was also more to cover as the troops of both nations fought major campaigns in theaters clear across the world.

For established artists who had been trying to make a go of it in the depressed economies of the thirties, the war provided welcome and well-paying employment opportunities. The British War Artists' Advisory Committee, headed by Kenneth Clark, did not differ greatly from its predecessor. Artists were sent out to cover the war both on the home front and in the more distant war theaters.[116] Not surprisingly, the names of Bone, Nevinson, Knight, and others associated with the Great War reappeared on the British lists, but there were other official war artists with lesser credentials. Two of these were younger painter-etchers: Graham Sutherland and Anthony Gross. Sutherland's first major assignment was to make pictures of the debris and damage caused by the air raids on London. Next he was sent to document the contribution of mine workers to the war effort; Edward Sackville-West, the critic, considered the pictures he produced a "new point of departure" for the artist.[117] This is of scant relevance to his reputation in etching, a medium he had forsaken years before, but his reputation as a painter, which the war enhanced, enhanced the survival power of his reputation as an etcher.

In contrast, Anthony Gross's service as a war artist brought a five-year halt to his progress as an etcher: a plate etched in 1940 remained unpublished until 1948. When war was declared, Gross had been in Paris collaborating on a cartoon film but immediately returned to London to offer himself as a war artist—to "paint in and behind the lines" in France, where he knew the language and had contacts. Soon he was making drawings for the War Office. By December 1940, Gross had a captain's commission and found himself aboard a troopship en route to Egypt, Syria, India, and Burma. Returned to England, he landed with the troops at Arromanches on D-Day; in 1945 he was in Torgau to sketch the formal rendezvous between the Russians and Americans. His many war drawings, of which a good number were deposited in the Imperial War Museum, say nothing very profound about war and the suffering that goes with it. Only two of his etched works treat actual war subjects—the 11 o'clock parade at the guards depot in Caterham and the shelling of Dover. Artistically he benefited from having to confront a subject and "work out how to do it, starting from scratch. It is fascinating, especially when I can remember periods where I seem to have gone on sleeping for years doing more or less the same thing."[118] He kept moving ahead with a steady output of drawings, etchings, and paintings, ultimately to become a full member of the Royal Academy.

Once again, the American effort was less coordinated than that of the British. It took the War Department about a year after Pearl Harbor to set up an Art Advisory Committee, chaired by artist George Biddle, brother of the attorney general, to oversee the dispatching of artists to active theaters.[119] Six months after the program went into operation, Congress refused funds. *Life* magazine, which already had its own war artist correspondents, agreed to offer contracts to the civilians who had already been sent overseas by the military. The original understanding had been that all work produced by the government-recruited artists would be given to the government for a national war art collection. After the war, when *Life* exhibited some of their works along with those of its own reporters, the catalog indicated that all belonged to the magazine. At least one artist took exception: Howard Cook wrote that he had never worked for *Life* and hoped that his work would finally be installed in "official government quarters" as had originally been intended.[120]

While America lacked a stable of prominent former war artists on which it could draw, it did have John Taylor Arms, who ranked close to Bone as an etcher of architectural subjects. Arms, who had been a naval officer in the First World War, now offered to make drawings of navy yards, industrial plants, and the like, at his own expense and without even the prospect of a commission, just as soon as Naval Intelligence was able to establish his "respectability."[121] His prints and drawings would become the property of the Navy Department. He further proved his usefulness by needling four etchings of ships, which were printed in large editions, with 500 of each put on sale in naval PXs at $5 each. He also helped organize Artists for Victory, a group of civilian artists, whose members were eager to use their skills in the service of the war. Irwin D. Hoffman, another painter-etcher, became its director.

Several of the American artists we studied, now middle-aged, still managed to get quite close to the fighting. Among them was Kerr Eby, no stranger to war. He landed with the American marines at Tarawa, the Pacific island that saw some of the bitterest fighting, where, against orders, he slipped in with the third assault wave. He continued with them to the jungle warfare in Bougainville, sleeping on the hard coral, slogging through the jungle mud, sharing the minor pleasures and the major discomforts of the marines at war, and making some starkly realistic drawings. Exhibited around the country, these were hailed by the *New York Times* as "one of the finest things to have come directly out of the war."[122] Unfortunately, the strains from the hardships of war were to take their toll. He died in 1946, at age 57, after a brief illness, with no time to make etchings from his drawings.[123]

The leader of the War Art Unit was Howard N. Cook, forty-two years old at the time. This printmaker and illustrator had taken up fresco painting on a Guggenheim Fellowship in Mexico and thereafter executed several important murals. Directly commissioned as a war correspondent with the rank of colonel, he shipped out on a troop transport to picture the emotional impact of the war on the various types of combatants. Neither he nor other artists in his unit had been adequately prepared for life in the war zone and the exacting demands upon them. Once there and able to make the seriousness of their purpose understood, they "were given practically unlimited opportunity for observation, for travel, and finally for participation in combat."[124] The unit's biggest adventure was going ashore with the task force at Rendova Island, New Georgia. They had to dig their own foxholes. Cook himself went through a species of shock, losing count of time and dates, writing to everybody and mixing up addresses, but he managed to work by concentrating on vivid mental impressions and sketching them while they were still white hot, as soon as he was back at the base.[125] These provided the material for paintings done over a two-year period on his return home. He also etched a portrait of himself in a foxhole.

Cook meant his work

> to reflect the horror, the struggle and the life in the jungle. It is not a pleasant picture but to my mind it is as true as the mud that hangs from the men's boots. . . . The color is conceived to express and heighten the mood of the paintings. They are not pretentious in size or execution but I believe that, as a set, they carry considerable punch and I like to think also as an anti-war crusade, for there are no heroics in them at all and I believe they represent quite a personal approach to what a sensitive individual felt. It is a result in psychological terms and not merely surface pictorial, incident making and farthest of all from photographic representation.[126]

These pictures were evidently too raw for *Collier's Magazine*, which abruptly terminated a contract with him. This dashed his hopes of wider exposure through a national publication. However, in its eagerness to have the artist off their hands, the magazine left him free to approach galleries for an exhibition.

Cook was as convinced as some of the Great War artists that the emotional shock of the war experience had proved a "release from my former painting, that it helped to establish a warm contact with our fellow men in their suffering and work and also, seeking release from tension, to find stirring beauty in nature which itself reflects the impulsive drama of human life."[127] After prior showings at Kennedy Galleries (New York) and in Minneapolis, he opened with an exhibition of large watercolors and war paintings at the Frank Rehn Gallery in New York that met with much praise. Sales were another matter. His hope that the war drawings might be kept together and go as a unit into some collection remained unrealized.[128] At least, he hoped, the Whitney Museum, which owned only one or two of his drawings and some prints, would acquire a painting, or that one or two collectors might decide to do the same. In fact, there were no sales at the exhibition![129] His only consolation was that his *Exodus*, an aquatint of a group of Free-French soldiers toiling up the path along a jungle canyon in New Caledonia, of which he also made a gouache, was awarded the Henry F. Noyes Prize of the American Society of Etchers. But by this time Cook's most productive period as a printmaker lay well behind him. His reputation was coming to rest more on the paintings he was turning out than on the handful of new prints he made.

## Other Influences

To separate the effect of war on reputations from other concurrent influences is difficult. The movement toward modernism and abstraction and long-term changes in the market for art went hand in hand with developments directly related to war. The First World War came right upon the heels of the breakthroughs of modernism. Roger Fry had stirred up a mild storm with his espousal of Post-Impressionist painting then being exhibited in London, while America was trying to assimilate the art from the famous Armory Show. As the Second World War began, few artists had yet fully recovered from the effects of the Great Depression and the market for etchings had all but disappeared.

Of the official war artists in World War I, Nevinson and Nash had been the most successful in melding their new subject matter with the new style. Their work was in close accord with the spirit of modernism, just as it was gaining ground. But after the war, Nevinson seems to have reverted to a more conventional approach. None of the others—with the possible exception of Nash, who is not in our sample[130]—ever allied themselves with any of these movements.

By World War II, more artists had absorbed this modernist spirit into work that retained an essentially realistic, representational, figurative flavor. This was certainly true of Sutherland and goes a long way in accounting for his rise into prominence. In a quite different way it holds also for Gross, whose prewar etchings already showed signs of French influence. Among Americans, there were Cook, Ganso, Dehn, and other progressive printmakers favored by Zigrosser at Weyhe. The point is that many of the painter-etchers, even some who considered themselves "modernists," came to feel bypassed after the war. The cleavage was sharpest in America, where abstract expressionism and its derivatives came into full dominance. Feeling themselves unappreciated and pushed aside, a number abandoned printmaking or, if they continued, did so on a much smaller scale and/or in a vastly different style.

Enterprises based on the principle of public support for the arts, enunciated by William Morris and used by Rothenstein to press for the war artist scheme, did not carry over into the postwar world. The Federal Arts Project of the Works Progress Administration (WPA), which had given employment to so many printmakers, was seen mostly as a temporary make-work expedient. Britain, too, by the late thirties had a "Recording Scheme," modestly financed by The Pilgrim Trust. Artists employed under this scheme were to record buildings at risk, somewhat along the lines of the guide books commissioned by the WPA but not so encompassing. To give work to "starving artists" was a secondary objective.[131] When war broke out and the War Artists' Advisory Committee took over, it effected just such a rescue of Graham Sutherland, whose main support for his painting had come from the money he earned teaching at the Chelsea School of Art. With the school about to be evacuated and facing the loss of his job, Sutherland thought of leaving London for the countryside, perhaps to live with his mother. The connection he had to Kenneth Clark, of the War Artists' Advisory Committee, led to his first assignments and subsequently to the contract that made him the first fully employed war artist under the new scheme.[132]

The collapse of the etching market had forced Stanley Badmin, early recognized as a master etcher, to take on more and more commercial work. Even though he also taught and kept sending, quite regularly, to the Royal Watercolour Society, his prospects came to rest more and more on commercial illustration, for which he became known. Early in the war the Ministry of Information had him organize exhibitions and make posters to promote the war effort but, junior by three years to Sutherland, he was called up in 1942 and joined the Royal Air Force. Badmin had put in for camouflage but was turned down. Why? The artist wondered whether it was because he had "recognized fascism too early" or whether they wanted public school lads, sort of officer types.[133] The military set him to work on an operational model of proposed landing sites based on aerial photographs. Though this assignment left him much free time to paint and sketch, even to take on the odd job that came from the Ministry of Information, it was not the kind with which a creative artist furthers a reputation. After the war, it was hard for him to get back on the right track. While his commercial work flourished, it was not until the mid-1950s that he once more began participating in major watercolor exhibitions and, though etching was his favorite medium, he never produced another. His reputation as an etcher rests solely on the prewar work.

Gerald K. Geerlings's military service earned him the Legion of Merit with an oak leaf cluster but did little for his standing within the artistic community. Like Badmin, he had dropped out during the depression and gone back to being an architectural draftsman and consultant. After volunteering for active duty, he was commissioned a captain in the army and pioneered the development of aerial perspective drawings that were later used in target maps to guide the aerial bombing. Not until he retired after nearly forty-two years of architectural practice did he resume his printmaking activity in the seventies.[134] R. Stephens Wright, on the other hand, did not give up etching or painting until the war intervened. As an employee of Douglas Aircraft, he worked at production illustration, making perspective drawings for persons who did not know how to read blueprints and could not work from them. "This," as he put it, "was no art work." First, he had to punch a time clock like others; then he became head of production-illustration, did a handbook for the company, was made a vicepresident, and even got himself involved in sales promotion, which caused him to stay on at Douglas for four months after the war. Then, drawing on this experience, he started three different schools to teach perspective to engineers. Other enterprises, like the etched stationery called Rome Productions he developed with an associate, could hardly help him regain his prewar reputation as "one of the most remarkable engravers of the younger American school" and a winner of a gold medal at the 1937 International Exhibition in Paris.[135] Because the "conservative" style in which he worked had gone out of fashion, there was little point in going back to this old medium. But he continued to paint portraits and hold exhibitions in West Coast galleries right into the eighties.

## A Summing Up

In this chapter we have drawn attention to the social and historical elements that go into the building of a reputation. Because reputations do not exist in a historical vacuum, it is difficult to generalize. Historical influences do not alter one basic fact: that reputations are produced collectively in several meanings of the term. To feel secure in their identity as artists, etchers needed recognition from "insiders." All had friends among fellow artists; most worked alongside others and could turn to colleagues and teachers for help; even the loners benefited from what their predecessors had done and their contemporaries were still doing to elevate the status of etching as one of the fine arts. But to be recognized by peers, mentors, and other insiders is the first step, in most cases even the indispensable prerequisite, toward the achievement of renown. It gives the artist a certain momentum but not enough to guarantee the kind of acceptance we have called renown. Further ascent requires the publicity that only mediators have the capability to provide.

To be sure, the reputations of etchers were also affected by larger historical forces—among them the movement of artistic taste that coincided with the etching cycle, rising standards of living followed by the depression, national policy toward the arts, and the dislocations of lives and markets by war. In this chapter we have focused on war to illustrate a second and equally basic fact; namely, that perverse as it may seem, even a cataclysm of the magnitude of the Great War has positive effects. Institutions are forced by necessity to look more favorably on innovations that might otherwise have never been given a thought, while new experiences sometimes release creative energies in individuals. Not every artist was positioned to take advantage of these opportunities. The careers of some came to a tragic end; others gained a new lease on life. Nothing remained the same—neither the individuals nor the art world in which they had been accustomed to function.

Having now completed, with this chapter, our general inquiry into the building of reputation—following our artists from their parental homes to their schools, through their initiation into etching and their struggles for recognition—we now take up in Part III the question of the survival or nonsurvival of reputation. Fittingly, we begin by searching for an answer to the specific question that first stimulated our interest in this matter: Why had so many of the once well recognized British lady-etchers been so forgotten?

# Part III

The Survival of Reputation

# 10

# The Case of the Disappearing Lady-Etchers

The case of the disappearing "lady-etchers" is a veritable mystery that begs for solution. A year-by-year examination of *Year's Art* we undertook in 1977 first called their fate to our attention. It turned up an impressive list of British women etchers who, from the outset of the etching revival until its virtual demise, had been regularly represented in major exhibitions, elected to honorific societies, and applauded by art critics and writers. Yet, with few exceptions, neither their names nor their works seemed to have survived. What, we wondered, had happened to them?

Women artists had been an integral part of the revival. As early as 1893 a noted French etcher, in reviewing the annual exhibition of the Royal Society of Painter-Etchers (RSPE) referred to the "real talent" of its "Ladies"—both fellows and associates.[1] Frederick Wedmore's *Etching in England*, published in 1895, singled out women for special attention, as did the Victoria and Albert's Martin Hardie in 1906.[2] To cite just one more authority—Hans Singer in *Die moderne Graphik* (1912) devoted an entire section to the British "lady-etchers," noting the esteem in which they were deservedly held.[3]

These lady-etchers, so called by art writers at the time, were more recognized by their peers than were women painters or sculptors or, even, watercolorists. In the 1880s, when the Royal Society of Painter-Etchers was organized, no woman painter had yet been elected to the Royal Academy as an artist solely and purely on the basis of her artistic achievement.[4] They were equally ineligible to be fellows of the Royal Institute of Painters in Water Colours or members of the newly formed (1886) antiestablishment New English Art Club. Many of these groups remained closed to women until after the Great War. Lady Feodora Gleichen, the first woman to become a fellow of the Royal Society of British Sculptors, received this honor only posthumously in 1922. She also etched and had been a Royal Etcher since 1884. In fact, 15 percent

269

of all fellows and associates in the RSPE between 1880 and 1930 were women, a share that increased as the revival gained momentum. While the early dominance of men and a slow rate of attrition contributed to their underrepresentation among the fellows, whose number was not to exceed fifty, they fared better here than in any other society save the Society of Miniature Artists.

In spite of their prominence, their presence was frequently overlooked. To take one example: the book by Sir Francis Newbolt, an associate of the RSPE, prepared in celebration of their fifty-year jubilee and illustrated with members' etchings to exemplify their "good work."[5] Of the 85 artists whose work was reproduced, 10 (or 12 percent) were women. The illustrations appear in alphabetical order by artist's name. As the result of this artifact, three of the first five plates are by Anna Airy, Elizabeth Armstrong, and Winifred Austen. Yet, such was the male myopia that the reviewer for the *Times Literary Supplement* (22 January 1931) did not include among the many names mentioned that of a single woman etcher. The writer found that "there is enough work of the younger *men* [italics ours], to entitle any society to respect and favour."

The mystery of the disappearing lady-etcher is Janus-headed; it looks both to the past and to the future and raises two questions: why should women in etching have been so successful, compared to women in painting, watercolor, and sculpture, in gaining recognition? Why were they so much less successful in converting this recognition into more lasting renown? In raising this second question we recognize, of course, that the end of the etching boom wiped out many artists—men as well as women. Our point here is that some were more forgotten than others and that these, especially among the British, were more likely to be the women.

This forgetfulness has a material side that can be documented. Today one encounters disproportionately fewer examples of these women's work among the stock of print galleries, on display in museum print rooms, or in sales catalogs than those of their male contemporaries. And we are not talking of a minuscule output easily lost. Thirty-nine women working in England and Scotland, all with some national recognition, listed 706 plates in *Fine Prints of the Year* (1923–38); the total number of impressions amounted to over 40,000. Or consider another statistic: fifty-four of the British women in our sample together pulled some 200,000 impressions over their lifetime. Professional women etchers may have produced somewhere between

750,000 and 1,000,000 impressions over the revival years.[6] Were men and women etchers equally forgotten (or remembered, if you will), one would expect to come across one print by a woman for every eight or so prints by a man.[7] Our own count, made in 1976–77, of prints in leading print galleries in both the United States and Britain yielded a figure closer to one in twenty for sales catalogs and near one in fifty in gallery stock.

Since then two things have happened: first, interest in women artists and their history has grown as part of the explosive growth of interest in women's history during the 1970s. The feminist movement in particular has inspired an active search for forgotten women. An exhibition entitled "Women Painters: 1550–1950," with 150 works chronicling 400 years of work, drew throngs when it opened in December 1976 at the Los Angeles Museum of Art and later at the Brooklyn Museum.[8] Second, there has been a resurgence of interest in English etchings of the revival period after their "long slide into obscurity."[9] As a new generation of print lovers began collecting them, prices began to rise and impressions began to emerge from out-of-the-way storage places. This rescued a few individuals from oblivion without, however, eliminating the female disadvantage. If some of the lost women have been rediscovered, so have most of the men.

## Is Etching for Women?

To turn first to the puzzle of the past. Why did women fare as well as they did in the etching world? At first glance etching, which involves sharp instruments, acids, and ink-stained fingers, appears to be the kind of dirty work that fastidious women would rather avoid. As the satirical poet Thomas Hood, himself trained as an engraver, suggested: "It scarce seems a lady-like work that begins / In a scratching and ends in a biting!"[10] Singer, too, despite his extravagant praise of some women, expected female participation to be limited by a technique he found "unfortunately not entirely appetizing. Whoever has seen the hands of a professional etcher will understand what I mean."[11] But there is a flip side to this argument, one advanced by a commentator in the *Gazette des beaux-arts* writing about the same time as Hood: "To women falls the practice of the graphic arts, those painstaking arts which correspond so well to the role of abnegation and devotion which the honest woman happily fills here on earth, and which is her religion." Referring to their willingness to attend to detail, he continued, "Who else but women would have the careful patience to hand-color botanical plates, pious images, and prints of all kinds?"[12] A more empathetic Martin Hardie observed:

> Of all the varied branches of art, few could appeal to feminine sympathy with stronger claim. It is an art that requires lithe, supple, pliant fingers, a firm yet sensitive touch—the "light hand" that figures in another sphere of woman's work. It is an elusive, baffling, subtle art. The copperplate seems to become a sentient thing—of whims and fancies; it is uncertain, coy, and hard to please as woman herself; it calls for humoring and light caresses. It is an art that requires patience and self-control, a close attendance upon petty trifles, during the slow biting of the acid, the re-grounding and re-working, the elimination of this detail, the addition of that, the burnishing of a stubborn line. Lastly, an etching is essentially dainty and delicate in the final form it takes. *It is an art in which woman is destined to excel.*[13]

The first woman etcher of whom there is any record was Anna Maria Schurmann (or van Schurman), a child prodigy of Dutch parentage, who died in 1678.[14] Angelica Kauffmann, born in 1741, was the one British woman etcher who attained before the nineteenth century the kind of recognition accorded to men. Many other women who etched, especially during the latter half of the eighteenth century, could be disregarded as amateurs, and some were, literally, Ladies.[15] But women were also to be found among the most accomplished professional engravers and reproductive etchers. In other words, as the art of painter-etching revived, women were not so much attracted to a medium because it became popular as already attracted to a medium that came into vogue. And, however dirty the job, most did their own printing or, like the men, entrusted the job to professional printers only when the task of printing large editions became too onerous. Some taught neophyte etchers to print, and others were prevailed upon to help out on jobs for which their busy male peers did not have time.

Etching is a medium that often necessitates helpers, especially during the printing phase. Assistance in wetting paper, drying, preparing inks, smoothing blankets and, of course, turning the handles of the press is always welcome. Down through the ages, women have been initiated into the etching process because husbands, brothers, and fathers pressed them into service.

## Factors Facilitating Success

The medium that welcomed women out of the parlor (though not out of the kitchen) into the workroom helps account for the large number of women who etched, acid and dirty hands notwithstanding, but does not explain their success as artists. The relative ease with which women could enter the field did act as a predisposing factor. Older, more established professions may bar qualified entrants on the basis of race, ethnicity, class origin, and, of course, gender; however, the perceived necessity for these ascriptive criteria of eligibility is diminished in newer and more socially marginal areas of artistic activity. This helps explain why the RSPE was open to women from the start: good etchers were needed if the status of the painter-etcher was to approximate that of the painter and sculptor. Painter-etching was not as yet the preserve of a group with vested interests. With no privileges to protect, they could concentrate on the quality of the works sent to their first Allcomers Exhibition, not on the gender of the senders. A number of senders were women, and their work was good enough to merit an invitation to membership. Other etching societies practiced a similar openness. Fifteen percent of the inaugural members of the Society for Graphic Art, the closest British competitor of the RSPE, were women.[16]

There nevertheless persists an apocryphal story about Mary Nimmo Moran; she is alleged to have been invited to fellowship because— with her entry signed "MNMoran"—the organizers did not know she was a woman. That story, like some similar ones about women artists breaking down barriers, is a wishful myth, repeated by those who have no qualms about making the male establishment appear even more narrow-minded than it was. The letter of invitation, archived in the Easthampton Free Library, is clearly addressed to "Mrs. Moran." This is not to deny that other more subtle prejudices, enough to intimidate women, persisted. In her application to the RSPE in 1894, while yet a student, Constance Pott signed herself simply "C. M. Pott, Esq," which is also how her election was announced in *The Times*; she had "never dared to acknowledge her inferiority of sex in submitting her work."[17]

From here on, what helped women to establish themselves were those characteristics of the medium that virtually mandated cooperation, out of which grew opportunities for informal and easy contacts based on a mutuality of goals, such as have always linked favored students to their teachers or led some like-minded artists to group themselves around a dominant personality. For women brought up in

Victorian or Edwardian England with an ingrained fear of seeming "too forward" or too self-seeking, such collaborative relationships eased their integration into the art world and, where these extended to marketing, made this necessary activity less distastefully competitive for them. While the distribution of etchings was, to some extent, taken over by publishers and print sellers acting as artists' agents, the proliferation of societies for exhibiting and marketing prints, as well as the clubs made up of what were essentially subscribers, made contact with a potential clientele easier.

One needs to understand that during the period in which many of the lady-etchers came of age, the middle-class milieu in England discouraged self-assertiveness as unladylike, all too often resulting in an ingrained incapacity to act in what were then defined as masculine roles. In plain words, the woman etchers could not allow themselves to appear unseemly aggressive or boastful. In providing clear channels for achieving recognition, their integration into professional networks reduced, but did not eliminate, conflict between the feminine role as traditionally defined and these women's desire for success.

We see then that the relative success of women etchers during the revival was encouraged by (1) the greater openness of this still somewhat marginal "fine art," (2) certain characteristics of the medium, and (3) the well-defined network of professional organizations and marketing channels. We mean to emphasize that the formalization and routinization of institutional arrangements not only facilitated entry into the field but made advancement less dependent on self-promotion than it still was in some other artistic and humanistic endeavors. These factors, which generally facilitated the building of reputation, were especially important in helping women to cross the first threshold toward success. The monetary and honorific rewards sustained their motivation to follow what came to be a well-marked path from the etching class into the professional etching world. The woman etcher following this path became a professional without undue, or what might appear to her unseemly, forwardness. These arrangements also functioned to screen out, by self-selection, anyone with a weak commitment to an artistic career.

Given their positive effects for women, it seems ironic that Anna Lea Merritt, an Anglo-American portrait etcher, should have deplored them in an open letter specifically addressed to women artists. The tendency toward overorganization in art training, she wrote in 1900, was stifling originality, creativity, and innovation.[18] What she failed to recognize was that formalization might work to the woman artist's advantage, putting her under less pressure to cultivate personal connections with patrons and dealers. Nor did the women etchers suffer as much as women painters and sculptors in being excluded from the casual conviviality of what had been (and remained) a man's world of clubs, with its close connections to the establishment. Their own organizations served their immediate needs.

## Two "Obvious" Explanations

Why should these lady-etchers have been far more forgotten than their male peers? When we first posed the question to persons familiar with the British art scene, we typically received one or both of two answers: The women must not have been very good and/or they probably got married, had children, and dropped out.

### "They Weren't Very Good, Were They?"

This contention is the harder to refute. After all, the quality one perceives in a work of art has to do with how one looks at it. Yet this ready-made explanation was advanced by respondents who could not have seen much, if anything, of these women's oeuvres. Indeed, its inaccessibility was for them sufficient proof that they could not have been very good. On one occasion, when we showed a dealer Pott's masterly *Morning Post, The Strand* (figure 12), she did not hesitate to acknowledge its superb quality but was equally quick to point out that it had little commercial value. That last observation is inarguable. Certainly none of the British lady-etchers was so renowned and widely collected as a number of the men.

Whoever looks at the prints by these women will find them of variable quality: some are superb; a number at the other extreme lack refinement and originality. There is, however, a tendency among art writers and critics to judge a woman by comparing her work to that of better-known men. The converse almost never happens; rarely is a man's work judged against that of a woman.

Here are some comments from a contemporary work on the etchers of the period: "Winifred Austen is probably the best etcher of birds to appear so far this century, greatly surpassing the better-known American, F. W. Benson in accuracy. She also portrayed small mammals with equal charm." Laura Knight, the etcher, is "a virile exponent of mixed method, using aquatint, soft-ground and line engraving as well as pure etching and drypoint. . . . In at least one plate, *Sleeping Dancer*, human sympathy lends a touch of greatness to the realism, and that rare element contributes to a masterpiece. . . . In some of her works, such as *Acrobats*, Laura Knight resembles Nevinson, and all her etchings are tinged with the same modern feeling." The listing on Sylvia Gosse begins: "The best of Sickert's pupils in etching. . . . Sometimes there seems little to choose between pupil and master." And finally, speaking of Clara Klinghoffer, "In the British Museum there are four etchings, a good one, *Girl Combing Her Hair* could easily be mistaken for a [Julius] Komjati."[19]

Were these women less worthy than the men? Perhaps they could not match the very best, but they seem, according to these citations, as good as most of them and certainly not clearly outclassed. As for the rest, we judge them only as seen through the eyes of their contemporary peers, as evidenced by election to artistic societies, acceptance of their work in juried exhibitions, prizes won, and critical acclaim. Our method of selecting etchers for this study assured that every one of the women in the sample had the same minimal recognition for her achievements in etching as her male counterparts.

An equally relevant question is whether the women, more often than the men, dealt with once-popular subjects now out of favor. The appeal of allegorical subjects and romanticized family and peasant themes, frequently encountered in the nineteenth century, has certainly diminished. While some subjects may never lose their appeal, depictions of historical events, of demolished buildings, and other matters of record cater to more idiosyncratic tastes. This holds especially for portraits of persons once prominent and admired but of little interest to new generations.

Some etchings by both men and women have struck us as archaic, overly sentimental, and no longer "stylish." Nowadays few connoisseurs are likely to appreciate Amelia Bowerley's decorative mermaids or Eileen Soper's "active little creatures [who] have never sinned and bear no resemblance to the modern child."[20] But the same holds, no doubt, for William Lee-Hankey's numerous sentimental studies of women and children and for the dourness of many of William Strang's etchings, with their pseudo-classical atmosphere. Strang also etched 160 original portraits, including one well-known likeness of Rudyard Kipling. Generally, men would have had an easier time in obtaining commissions for portraits of famous men, but both women and men etched portraits of people they knew or who interested them. The only etchers in our British sample whose reputations rest *primarily* on such portraits are Gerald Brockhurst and Augustus John. Women etched theatrical and circus personalities but favored topographical scenes, for which there was an important market, but so did many of the men. All in all, we discovered no consistent differences in subject matter that could account for the differential survival of the reputations of men and women.

## *"They Got Married and Dropped Out"*

The second explanation for the disappearance of the women etchers derives from a widely held stereotype that remains hard to shake: women who marry abandon their careers to devote themselves to family and children. Even the feminist, Germaine Greer, cites "love" as a major obstacle on the road to success for women artists and illustrates it with the sad story of Edna Waugh Clarke Hall, "one of the brilliant Slade girls . . . [who] virtually abandoned painting at nineteen." In a note, hidden in the back pages, Greer acknowledges that Clarke Hall continued with her artwork after her marriage but points to her slow progress, to the more than ten years she took to complete her etched illustrations for *Wuthering Heights*, now in the Tate.[21] Clarke Hall may have taken her time with this series of twenty-four plates—her favorite medium being watercolor—but she was no dropout. This is attested by the Bond Street exhibition of her work in 1979, just before her one hundredth birthday.

Only half the women ever married, and only one out of five had children (table 10.1). These demographics reflect the hard choice women had to make between family and career, especially the earlier generations. The ones born before 1870 were least likely to have ever married but, if married, were just as likely as the rest to have had children. Their families were small, with no more than one or two children, and the women in every generation tended to marry late. Just three of the women, one being Hall, married before age twenty-five. The other two were Wendela Boreel, who took a wounded war hero as husband, and Elyse Lord, who claimed to have married at eighteen but whose marriage certificate gives her age as twenty-three.[22] Here again there is a generational difference: the average age at first marriage of those born before 1870 was thirty-five; for those younger, it was thirty-one. Two women were remarried after being widowed, both to fellow artists.[23]

But whether married or not, most of these women had long careers. We have of course no way of estimating how many talented women did drop out after an early marriage *before* ever achieving any kind of reputation. Our case against the "dropout" hypothesis rests on its failure to explain the disappearance of the recognized British lady-

Table 10.1
Percentage of Artists Married and with Children, by Generation[a]

| Generation | Percent Married | | Percent with Children | |
|---|---|---|---|---|
| | Women | Men | Women | Men |
| Victorians | 31 | 94 | 14 | 59 |
| Late Victorians | 64 | 79 | 23 | 64 |
| Edwardians | 58 | 92 | 17 | 50 |
| World War I | 58 | 88 | 40[b] | 63 |
| All generations | 52 | 88 | 24 | 59 |

[a] Based on 121 British artists for whom marital status and number of children were ascertained.
[b] Includes one never-married artist with an adopted or illegitimate child.

etchers. It can be bolstered by some vignettes of the effect of marriage on women of different generations.

*The Victorians.* Born before 1870, the pioneers of the revival were in every sense Victorians. Fewer of them ever married and none, so far as we could ascertain, before reaching thirty. Minna Bolingbroke, from Norwich, had been a founding member of the Norwich Art Circle and a productive artist when at age thirty-seven she married the Norwich etcher Charles Watson, with whom she had once studied etching. She moved to London to join her husband but kept her own name. Asked about this, she explained that she had not intended a feminist gesture but felt that there were already enough Watsons in art.[24]

After her marriage, she continued to participate in major exhibitions for at least another thirty-two years. Her work is frequently judged in relation to that of her husband, with whom she shared many sketching trips abroad, often drawing and then etching the same Gothic facades in a similar style, one somewhat reminiscent of Whistler's Venice set. Present-day critics tend to dismiss Bolingbroke's etchings as purely derivative. Guichard, with characteristic neglectfulness, includes only Watson but not his wife in the mainstream of British etching. She is relegated to the status of a "minor etcher," despite the repute in which she was held by contemporaries. Singer, for one, found it to her credit that she did *not* take over Watson's manner in its pure form and singled out for special praise her unusual talent for doing birds.[25] Wedmore went so far as to suggest that with her "drypoints of plump birds, and live stock of the farmyard . . . Miss Bolingbroke may follow in the track of a great Frenchman, and may meet with a success akin to some extent to that of Bracquemond's masterpiece, 'Le Haut d'un battant de Porte.' " This was indeed high praise.[26]

Elizabeth Adela Armstrong was thirty, already a fellow of the RSPE, and regularly showing oil and watercolor paintings in leading London galleries when she married Stanhope Forbes. He was working in Cornwall, which is where they made their home. She continued to work and remained an active member of the Newlyn School, even after the birth of their son, until her sudden death in 1912 at age fifty-three. Hers is, nevertheless, one of the few documented cases of how marriage, even if only circuitously, ended an etching career. Etching, she explained, "was a branch of art of which I was intensely fond, and one of the few modes of expression which I could pursue more easily in London than elsewhere. Afterwards, when I had settled in Cornwall, the difficulty of having the trial proofs pulled while actually at work, proved too discouraging, and gradually, to my regret, I found myself compelled to lay aside my etching tools, and I ceased to contribute work to the society to which I had felt it such an honour to belong."[27] Her problems may have been aggravated by her preference for drypoint, which she found more difficult to visualize without pulling a proof. She is another of the women described by Greer in *The Obstacle Race* as having sacrificed art for "Love": Armstrong, she writes, "worked in the fragile medium of water-colour, leaving grander genre and history compositions to her better-known husband."[28] A kinder male critic simply notes that work by both husband and wife was frequently reproduced in *The Studio* and that Elizabeth Armstrong's often appeared "a more domestic variant of his very rugged images."[29]

*Late Victorians.* The fourteen British women born between 1870 and 1879 embarked on their careers in the late years of Queen Victoria's reign. Their working years coincide closely with the decades when etching was à la mode. Some of the long-lived among them were still exhibiting their etchings during and after the Second World War. The nine among them who married were hardly less productive artistically than those who remained single. In fact, two were among the most productive women etchers—Winifred Austen, who did not marry until forty and became a widow within five years, and Gertrude Hayes, art mistress at the Rugby School, who after being married to one member of that faculty, when widowed, married yet another. Both of Hayes's husbands etched, but neither was as well recognized or commercially successful as she.

The marrieds of this generation also include the three women artists best known to the public. Laura Knight, the first woman R.A., and her husband, Harold, whom she met at an art class in Nottingham, built their careers together. Hilda Cowham, too, had met her husband at art school and married him at twenty-eight. She became the first woman to illustrate for *Punch*. More precisely, she is the first whose gender was evident to readers. The *Dictionary of British Book Illustrators and Caricaturists* indicates that Helen Hoppner Coode (1859–82) preceded her but signed her drawings with a monogram. Katherine Cameron, a younger sister of David Y. Cameron, had been associated with Charles Rennie Mackintosh and the Art Nouveau movement around Glasgow. Through her popular illustrations of children's books, she extended her reputation beyond Scotland.[30] She was fifty-four when she married Arthur Kay, an important art collector. Given his close ties to a wide circle of people important in art, the marriage could not in any sense have been a hindrance to her career.

Of the three Late Victorians with children, neither Cowham, who had a son, nor Edna Clarke Hall, who had two sons, dropped out. The third mother was Bertha Gorst. For some time we thought she might be one of our deviant cases, a woman who had abandoned a career for marriage. She was one of seven women and seven men selected for study, all of them born before 1880, who had exhibited every year for at least ten years without being elected fellows of the RSPE. We wanted to understand what might have impeded their progress. From standard biographical dictionaries and the RSPE roster we learned that Gorst had been born in 1873 near Birkenhead, North Wales, had studied at the Birkenhead and Liverpool Schools of Art, and was an associate from 1902 through 1929, but any clues as to her "fate" kept eluding us. It seemed unlikely that she had retired at age fifty-six, so we began to imagine that, having struggled long enough against family demands, she might finally have given up on art. That she was married we knew, since she was listed as "Mrs. Aiken." Beyond that we had no luck in locating a death certificate, a marriage certificate, a will, or any bit of evidence that might help track her down. Nor did the trail grow any hotter on discovering that in 1912 Alfred Fowler, of Kansas City, had published a set of bookplates by Bertha Gorst, "also known as Mrs. John G. Aitken."[31] The new spelling proved only another dead end. Quite by accident, we next picked up the scent among the papers of the bookplate collector, Herman Theodore Radin, in the New York Public Library. There were three letters from a Bertha Aikin in Llangollen, North Wales; we now know the correct spelling. In that picturesque

Welsh town, by one of those incredible strokes of luck that sometimes reward the historian as detective, the trail ended. There a series of coincidences led us to the unofficial town archivist, Miss Sarah Pugh-Jones, then in her nineties, who, it turned out, had been a friend of Bertha Gorst. The two had worked together on a number of social welfare projects both during and after the Great War. Both had actively campaigned for women's suffrage. Framed on her wall were two Gorst etchings, an appealing landscape (*The Linden Tree*) and a rendering of *The Cloister Cathedral, Chester*.

Marriage, we discovered, had interfered with Mrs. Aikin's career but in a most roundabout way. Before marrying at thirty-eight, she had lived with her father and three sisters, helping to support the family by etching the historic sites of nearby Chester, with its Roman walls and picturesque streets. These she marketed through a Chester print dealer. After her marriage, Aikin built for his wife and son—born a year later—a handsome stone mansion with a freestanding studio in the walled garden. There she had her own etching press and, with her husband's encouragement, continued to etch and work in watercolor almost until her death in 1938. But she no longer had any financial need as an incentive to market her prints nationally. A few were sold locally; some were awarded as valued prizes to supporters of Welfare House, a new type of care center for children built and supported by the Aikins, which did become the all-absorbing project of her later years. But a dropout she certainly was not.[32]

Marriage is, of course, only one of many possible distractions. It certainly cannot account for Gertrude Hayes's failure to advance to full fellowship in the RSPE. She may have produced and put into circulation as many as 15,000 impressions of her plates, many of them much admired at the turn of the century. She became an A.R.E. at twenty-five, while still single, a full four years before her first husband was elected. Why, despite this apparent precocity, she never advanced to R.E. is not clear nor why the promise of a brilliant future was never realized. In all likelihood, she became deeply involved in the life of the school where she was a major figure, a diversion to which men are equally susceptible. Had she been a man, she might have had more alternatives. But her marriage never kept her from a financially rewarding but, in the long run, unexceptional career.

*Edwardians and the Great War Generation.* The Edwardians, born in the eighties, began training for their careers just as the age of Victoria gave way to the short reign of Edward VII, an era often described as a lull between two storms: the Boer War from 1900 to 1902, which resulted in nearly 10,000 casualties, most of them British; and the Great War, which wiped out a generation of Britain's young male elite. We had assumed that this carnage would have had its greatest effect on the marriage rate of those born in 1890 or after, whom we thought of as the Great War generation. But the proportion ever married was not different from that of the Late Victorians or Edwardians. What we did find, looking at our data from another perspective, was a suggestive, if not compelling, difference between the proportions of the *never* married among those twenty-one or younger when the war began (47 percent) and the rest of the Edwardians (35 percent).

Other differences between these two generations reflect certain liberalizing influences and the wider social circles in which the more emancipated women of the Great War generation were able to move. For one thing, though divorce was almost unheard of among those born before 1890—there was one case—it had become more common without reaching epidemic proportions among those born later.[33] For another, those of the Great War generation who married were less likely than their predecessors to marry a fellow artist. Of nine who ever married, Freda Marston was the only one to marry a painter. Many of the rest had husbands who were journalists and writers, a few of them foreign-born. And it is only among the Great War generation that we find permanent emigrants who left England to settle in another country. We have not yet determined the later whereabouts of two artists: Lillian Whitehead's trail disappears after 1939, when she was forty-five, and that of Doris Boulton after 1946, when she was fifty-two. They may have been among the emigrants; neither the British nor the Scottish registry has their death certificates.

Among these more modern women, as among the earlier generations, we could not find a case where marriage—or "Love," as Germaine Greer puts it—ended an artistic career. She does write, as have so many others, of the "Sickert women" who sacrificed their hope of becoming great artists at the altar of this "archetypal teacher-lover." All three happen to be in our sample, and we shall return to the question of whether their reputations gained or lost from this association. As regards Thérèse Lessore, who became Sickert's third wife, Greer acknowledges that opinion on her was divided. She quotes a critic who believed that Lessore, "like so many others who came beneath the Sickert spell[,] . . . began to turn out echoes of him rather than her strange little interiors." Then, without naming names, she notes that "other critics can be found who insist that she [Lessore] kept her individuality to the last."[34] Guichard, too, judges Lessore, the etcher, to be a "faithful imitator of her husband."[35] This judgment is hard to fault. But are there not etchings by Whistler that closely resemble those of Jacques and Rembrandt just as there are etchings by Pennell, Menpes, and Sickert that lean heavily on Whistler? More to the point, Lessore came to etching late, with a considerable reputation as a painter. It was Sickert who led her to take up etching in order to exploit her drawing talents. "Love," in Greer's terminology, simply steered Lessore in a new direction. In this instance, in contrast to the mutuality of other artistic couples, the inspiration may have been predominantly one way.

## The Nonsurvival of Reputation

Obviously, the disappearance of the lady-etchers is not adequately explained either by their lack of commitment to their profession or their lack of talent. Nevertheless, one expects to find some relationship, however loose, between a lifetime reputation and its survival over time. To reiterate, all our etchers, women and men alike, had been well recognized in artistic circles for accomplishments in printmaking, but only a minority had achieved the level of renown that would have made their names familiar to their contemporaries and attracted the interest of historians, critics, wealthy collectors, and museum goers eager to become cognoscenti.

To pin this down, we judged the reputation of each artist while alive using previously discussed measures about acceptance in exhibitions, prizes, and critical acclaim. Each of us did this separately. When done, we discussed and reconciled our differences until the two of us were satisfied. The result was a four-category ranking. To be in the top category, an artist had to have earned some degree of renown for his or her artistic achievements and/or as an important personality on the art scene. As for the rest, we differentiated among high, medium, and moderate success as an artist. Renown was scored as 4; artists less than renowned or with very limited renown were rated from 1 to 3 according to how well they had been recognized in their lifetime. In applying the classification scheme, we made every effort not to be influenced by our own preferences or by the name recognition these artist enjoy among collectors today or the prices their prints commanded on the art market of the early 1980s.

The women studied had, in the aggregate, been less recognized in their lifetime than the men. Only four British and four American women, compared with sixteen British and twenty America men, met our criteria for lifetime renown. The same gender disparity shows up when the reputation scores for men and women are averaged (table 10.2). Once again the men are a good notch ahead of the women. But should this gender disparity be taken as evidence that the achievements of the lady-etchers were inferior to those of the men? We think not. While no one can deny that the quality and characteristics of the artist's work form the base on which a reputation is built, other things have to be factored in. For one thing, the appreciation of an artistic work and the price it commands hinge to a large extent on what is known about the persona of its creator. This is what gives a reputation its staying power. If women were less successful at making themselves visible than were the men, this goes a long way to explain the gender disparity in lifetime reputation.

We cannot complete our description of this state of affairs without mentioning that most men in our sample were neither so much more renowned nor so much better recognized in their lifetimes than the women as to clear up to our full satisfaction the mystery of the lady-etchers' disappearance. To demonstrate that the female disadvantage is in fact cumulative, we similarly assigned values between 0 and 4 as an index of the posthumous reputations of all artists deceased before the end of 1985. Etchers given the value 0 are the ones who have pretty much fallen into oblivion: they no longer have a reputation to speak of. The remaining four values gauge the degree of surviving interest in an etcher's prints: 1 was given for limited interest confined to a small circle of knowledgeable specialists; 2 to artists for whose prints there is a recognized market; 3 to artists for whom the demand is great enough to have driven up the prices for their prints to a significant degree; and 4 to "important artists" whose prints continue to be coveted by dealers and collectors.

There is no doubt that the descent into oblivion was indeed greatest for the British women—twenty-three out of fifty-seven (or 40 percent) of those known no longer to be alive, compared with only three out of sixty (or 5 percent) of the British men placed in the 0 category. The second part of table 10.2 gives the gender disparity in posthumous reputations for all the etchers we studied in the two countries. The increase in gender disparity points to the presence of other influences that compound the original handicap under which women labored in achieving recognition for artistic achievement in their lifetime. If such recognition were the single determinant of posthumous reputation, would the women have proved to be even more disadvantaged in death than they were in life?

Table 10.2
Lifetime Reputation and Posthumous Reputation, by Gender

| | Lifetime Reputation | | |
| | Women | Men | Gender Disparity |
| --- | --- | --- | --- |
| Britain | 1.9 | 2.3 | .4 |
| United States | 2.0 | 2.8 | .8 |
| | Posthumous Reputation | | |
| | Women | Men | Gender Disparity |
| Britain | .9 | 1.9 | 1.0 |
| United States | 1.2 | 2.4 | 1.2 |

Let it also be said that we do not conclude that male prejudice and deliberate discrimination, both real enough, can provide a full explanation for the "disappearance" of the lady-etchers. One key to the puzzle, as we shall show, lies in whether there are survivors able and willing to act as mediators to posterity. The lack of such mediators worked to the disadvantage of women but had similarly adverse effects on the posthumous reputations of some of the men.

The contrast in the fates of men and women etchers serves as a strategic vantage point from which to extend our examination, in the last chapter, of the social determinants of reputation and its survival. In the rest of this chapter we focus specifically on three kinds of factors that help to explain the mysterious fate of the lady-etchers:

1. External circumstances at the intersection of history and biography that are beyond the artist's ability to control.
2. The consequences of personal decisions that are within the control of the individual artist.
3. Relationships negotiated by artists using their inherited or acquired social and cultural capital, some of which are theirs to control, some not.

## A Time to Be Born and a Time to Die

Not only were many of the women born at the wrong time, they also lived too long and were more likely to have died at the wrong time—when both etching and their personal reputations had long gone into eclipse. Such matters of life and death—certainly not of the etcher's own doing—help us understand why the British women were less remembered than their male counterparts.

Being "born at the wrong time" means that the Victorian women grew up and came of age in a society that did not prepare them to advance their reputations in the competitive world of art. They were never schooled in the art of self-promotion; their whole upbringing worked against it. To women reared in a solidly middle-class Victorian home, as most were, such self-serving behavior would have been defined as unseemingly aggressive and not at all "lady-like." Men, by contrast, were under pressure to succeed and hence less inhibited when it came to competing for attention and touting their talents. They also controlled the directorships of museums, the curatorial jobs, and the editorships, positions in which incumbents could always extend a helping hand to a budding young artist.

Dying at the "wrong time" had a more direct influence on the survival of reputation. Both the men and the women of the British revival exceeded the average life expectancy, but the women exceeded it more than the men. On the average, they lived seventy-eight years; the men, seventy-two. But averages tell only part of the story. Proportionately twice as many women survived into their eighties and nearly every fifth woman had a ninetieth birthday. The difference is even more pronounced in the two generations whose working lives synchronized most closely with the etching cycle. The late Victorians, born in the 1870s, outlived their male contemporaries by an average of fourteen years; the Edwardians, in their forties at the height of the boom, lived eight years longer on the average. Thus, their reputations were, paradoxically, casualties of their remarkable longevity. It meant not only that they outlived their colleagues and friends but also, if married, that they typically outlived their husbands and sometimes even their children. A disproportionate number died decades after the peak of the etching cycle, at a time when the medium and their personal reputations were in eclipse. Their deaths no longer had much news value. Consequently, fewer women than men were memorialized in newspaper or journal obituaries, a major source of biographical data for reference works on artists. *The Times* of London carried obituaries on 80 percent of the men but only 33 percent of the women, a difference far larger than the gender disparity in lifetime reputations. The explanations for some omissions are of course idiosyncratic and have nothing to do with longevity. The death of one-hundred-year-old Edna Clarke Hall should have been worthy of notice, but it came when *The Times* was on strike.[36]

Even when it was printed, a woman's death notice could easily be overlooked; the standard British practice seems to have been to list

Table 10.3
Survivors of Artists, by Gender (in percent)

|  | Women (N = 46) | Men (N = 56) |
|---|---|---|
| Spouse | 20 | 64[a] |
| Adult children | 7 | 16 |
| Sibling | 3 | 9 |
| Mother | — | 2 |
| Fellow artist or close friend | 13 | 2 |
| Other relatives | 52 | 4 |
| Essentially none | 4 | 2 |

[a] Includes one artist survived by a woman companion.

married women, even those with established professional identities, under their married name. Mindful of the potential consequences, Anna Airy, known in her private life as Mrs. Pocock, included a specific request in her will that her tombstone and "any obituary notice for publication should appear in the name 'Anna Airy' as my married name 'Anna Pocock' will be entirely useless and defeat the purpose of this publicity."[37]

The effects of longevity were compounded by the high proportion of women who, by choice or circumstance, remained single. This cut down the survivorship rate. There was no loving husband or children to do all the things that had to be done to preserve the artist's work and keep alive her memory. Far fewer women than men had a spouse or children to mourn them (table 10.3). Those who lived longest had no one left with enough knowledge and energy to send a memorial notice to *The Times*, write a tribute to the deceased or, at least, to see to it that the all but moribund etching societies did so.

### Three Forgotten Victorians

Among the most forgotten of the British lady-etchers were three truly distinguished Victorians, whose individual biographies we now search for clues as to their fates.

Catherine Maude Nichols, who had a claim to distinction, was born too early and died at the wrong time. Affectionately known by her friends as Kate, she listed herself in *Who's Who* as the "First Lady Fellow of the Royal Painter-Etchers." This was not literally true. She had been preceded by Mary Nimmo Moran, an American, and by Lady Tennant, who resigned within the year. Yet Nichols was certainly the first authentic British lady fellow and one of the most productive. She needled upward of 200 plates, most of them drypoints, examples of which are to be found at the Victoria and Albert, the British Museum, the Norwich Art Gallery, and in the Norwich Central Library, some of them donated by Seymour Haden. The print room of the Ashmolean in Oxford also houses some small and exquisite drawings by Nichols, part of a collection of the work of nineteenth-century draftsmen, including Charles Keene and Charles Jacque, bequeathed by Charles Emanuel, a connoisseur of drawings and prints.

In her lifetime Nichols received much praise. Singer called her energetic, which she certainly was, and said her works could hold their own in any company. It was her fate, nevertheless, to be consistently judged as a woman in a man's world. According to *The Studio*, "Her etchings are among the best that the lady artists of our time have produced."[38] *The Times* considered her success "one of the many proofs that in some branches of art women are becoming serious rivals of men."[39] An article in the *Women's Penny Paper*, a popular magazine, in an obvious hyperbole, went so far as to dub her the "Meryon of Norwich."[40] Nichols herself felt that she was better known abroad and in the United States than in her hometown. In this she may have been right. An article in *The Bookman*, an influential journal, chided Norwich for neglecting her work even after she had reached maturity as an artist.[41]

Guichard, in 1977, nevertheless relegated her to the status of a "minor etcher," and her work is hardly in high demand. Some of her prints can be, or may already have been, flushed out from the old houses of Norwich where they once hung on walls. The persistent collector might even be able to uncover an occasional drypoint by Nichols among the batches of battered prints displayed in some shop or print stall. One plausible explanation for the current neglect is that her work did not wear well. Administrators at the Castle Museum in Norwich, in rejecting suggestions that they give her a retrospective exhibition, pointed out that her work, though "very good of *its period*," had become dated.[42] Whether they meant that painter-etching generally, as practiced during the revival, or just Nichols's etchings, were dated is not clear. By 1960, the museum was certainly helping to relegate her to the dustbins, responding to an inquiry that she was "not a very outstanding artist" and that what might appeal to many as a charming pastel landscape "would not have a very high market."

Before the decade ended, a would-be donor was told the etchings and engraving he offered were only of local interest and at present had "no value" as works of art, an evaluation then amended to read "very little" value.[43]

There is no reason to consider the etchings and drypoints by Nichols any more dated than those of her contemporaries—male or female. Most are of city streets, architecturally interesting buildings, and rural landscapes. She did many sketches (water scenes) along the Norfolk Broads (figure 9). It seems that the Castle Museum staff was judging the value of her etchings in terms of her standing as a painter. Of the several paintings by her that had been purchased by subscription and presented to the museum, none was hanging in the gallery at the time we visited it; nor was the portrait of Nichols commissioned by friends and formally donated to the museum after her death on view at the time. Although Nichols had "nourished ambitions in regard to the media of oil and water" and her "hunger for attainment" had remained with her to the last, even a friend acknowledged that her color usually was "too low in tone," probably because she lacked the necessary foreign study. "She became aware as the years wore on that her lasting claim to distinction lay in her skill as a dry-point etcher."[44]

Alas for Kate Nichols! She was born too early to press this claim to the fullest. The institutionalized training facilities through which woman were initiated into the world of painter-etchers were not yet in place when she prepared to become an artist. And, with the ties that bound an unmarried women of her class background to Norwich, she did not find it easy to develop the informal contacts that expedited the careers of later generations. On the other hand, despite her upbringing as a proper Victorian lady, she did not develop that ingrained incapacity to promote herself, which held back so many of her female contemporaries. Had she not seen to her own interests, she might not have become the "first" Lady Fellow of the RSPE.

What clues we have into her character suggest that she was anything but a shrinking violet. Nor was she unmindful that it would take publicity to extend her reputation beyond the confines of her hometown, where people knew her. She was aware that she had to toot her own horn, as no one would toot it for her, and so acted as her own press agent at every opportunity. There is, for instance, her biographical entry in Clement's *Women in the Fine Arts*. Consisting of readily available information that the compiler supplemented with a questionnaire sent to individuals, it was for years the only available biographical reference on women artists.[45] Some of our women did not respond or, if they did, modestly supplied only routine biographical data. The entry on Nichols amounts to a self-advertisement stocked with information that only she could have supplied, such as the official letter of thanks she had received for sending to exhibitions in Munich and the fact that she had worked "in the open at Barbizon, in Normandy, in Cornwall," and other places. In the same spirit, she did what she could to create her own legend when she was interviewed. In one such interview, she went out of her way to mention that she "had been told" she was the first *English* woman to have stayed in Barbizon. That her name was scarcely as well known as it should be, she attributed to her "individuality," her "lack of attraction toward the sort of subjects that take with the general public," and her like for "queer old places with character in them." She had plenty of appreciation from artists, she told the interviewer, and as she was not starving, need not worry herself about popularity.[46]

The artistic and fiercely independent "presence" she cultivated may have been too strong for Norwich taste but would not have attracted more than passing attention in London circles. Friends described her as a distinctive, interesting, and delightful personality and as an intellectual of great charm. From time to time she wrote for magazines and newspapers; she also published a novel and an account of her midlife conversion to Catholicism. In her Norwich garden, she gave delightful parties. Everybody liked her for her "rare gift of appearing to give her whole and undivided attention to anybody to whom she talked." The sympathy she exhibited toward people extended so far into the animal world as to seem "absurd and exaggerated." She had a tame rat and rabbits that hopped around her studio. Its ceiling was never dusted because she saw the beauty in cobwebs and dust and, probably, could not bring herself to kill spiders.[47]

The bravado she displayed in Norwich belies the pathos revealed in her hesitant, almost obsequious, approach to the men whose judgments could make or break an etcher's career. In the RSPE she did not always carry herself with the easy self-assurance one expects of a fellow who is part of the club; as a lady fellow, she felt constantly on guard for her right to be there. The need she experienced to cloak what might otherwise be seen as "forwardness" in a feminine guise comes out in letters she wrote when sixty years old. The first is to Frank Short as he was selecting prints for an upcoming summer exhibition at the Royal Academy. "I am sending a strong *little* thing to the R.A. (drypoint). Do help me if you can to get it in—you might tell the hanger to turn a *kindly* eye! It is a *strong* one: won't disgrace us." In the same letter she gingerly asked him to intervene for her in the Franco-British Exhibition in 1908, also handled by Short. "I should like to send another strong little etching to the Franco-Shepherd's Bush as well as the one you kindly selected (Old Houses, Lakenham) but I suppose space is very limited." Was she supposed to wait for the "Franco-people" to ask for it?[48] Short did not reply but sent her inquiry on to Sir Isidore Spielmann, the British organizer for the entire exhibition, who likewise failed to reply. Three weeks later Nichols herself wrote Spielmann to ask him directly if he would kindly tell her when she was to forward her "exhibit." In pencil, she added "for which I have a form of invitation"; she enclosed a stamp and envelope to assure a reply. In still another letter to Spielmann about a season ticket to the exhibition, she complimented him on how "lovely the whole thing is." Only as an afterthought did she get to her main reason for writing, which was to draw his "attention to a little omission in my case: they have omitted my letters R.E. after *my name in the catalogue*, and as they have put them after the names of the other Fellows I know it *is* a mistake. Perhaps you would kindly rectify it in a new edition."[49]

Was she a feminist? Her ambivalence about this is revealed in an interview in 1889. On the one hand, she harbored an obvious resentment against such bias as she and others had encountered. Men, she said, had all the power and would make laws in their own favor. On the other hand, she subscribed to the view that "men and women have different parts to play in the world." She found it downright "ridiculous" to be waited on by a broad-shouldered young man in a shop selling nothing but veils and lace-edgings and ribbons. As for etching, she could not see that it mattered whether you were a man or a woman "if you have the gift."[50]

Nichols, who passed away in 1923 after a long bout with cancer, may also have died too early to reap the benefits of the developing craze for etchings. Especially, she missed out on *Fine Prints of the Year*, with its regular illustrations of contemporary artists. But, unlike some others, her death did not go unnoticed. An obituary in *The Times* was captioned "A Woman Etcher."[51] However, the local press paid more attention to her social pedigree and to the fact that, as the oldest daughter of the mayor, she had once presented a bouquet of roses to Queen Alexandra, then Princess of Wales. Present at her funeral "was a fairly numerous congregation, well representative of the city in general, but more especially of the deceased lady's artistic connexions."[52] A little more than a month after her death, most of her personal estate, left to a brother, was put up for sale at auction in a sale billed as an "opportunity for collectors." A practically complete catalog of plates, prepared by a Mr. Arthur Batchelor, not listed as being among the mourners, appears to have been for sale on this occasion, but we have been unable to locate a copy.

Prospective bidders had been told that all plates of her engraved work had been destroyed. The prints from them left in the studio were sold in lots of about a dozen, each containing one or two first-rate impressions. A number of city and county people had engaged in "particularly keen competition for many of the etchings." But it would be a long time before *Cow Hill, Norwich*, one of her best-known prints, would again fetch the £8.8.0 it went for in 1923.

Minna Bolingbroke was another early fellow of the RSPE. She had exhibited paintings, etchings, and at least one lithograph at major shows for fifty years until she was near seventy, then continued her active interest and participation in the art world for at least another eight years. Surely her passing would not have gone unremarked? In fact, when she died on 4 May 1939, aged eighty-two, in Kensington, London, where she had lived most of her adult life, there was no mention of her passing in any London paper—at least nothing we could locate. She was buried in Norwich, the city in which she had been born and reared, a member of a well-established mercantile family. Yet not even the papers in her hometown gave her a full obituary. A routine notice of the funeral appeared in the *Eastern Daily Press* under her married name and with no references to mourners or eulogies. There is little information on her life save that contained in standard biographical dictionaries. While some etchers' works regained some popularity in the 1970s, the life and oeuvre of Bolingbroke lay buried too deeply to be exhumed. The odd print might turn up in Norwich or even in London, where a copy of her one lithograph, pulled by Frederick Goulding and from his private collection, sold for £3 ($5.50) in 1976. Guichard only lists her name—misspelled as well—among the hundreds of minor etchers.

Her husband, Charles J. Watson, had died during the heyday of the etching boom, when the death of a well-known etcher was still news. On that occasion, Frank Short, who was a close friend, had written a commemorative letter to *The Times*. The archives of the Norwich Art Museum contain clippings of other obituaries, one with an inscription in Minna's hand that reads "My dear husband died November 1, 1927," followed by a refrain from an old Coster song, "When we part as part we must, I pray to God I'll be the fust." Watson had been at work cataloguing his many etchings, a project left unfinished. Bolingbroke devoted years to its completion and to arranging for its publication. The enterprise absorbed much of her remaining energy and may be what kept her from ever exhibiting again in a major show after Watson's death. Though she wrote the text for this catalog, she did not in any way let the reader know that she herself had been a recognized etcher nor was there a hint of her close professional collaboration with her husband. Correspondence with the Bodleian Library in Oxford, to which she wished to donate a copy, identifies her only as "Minna R. Watson (Mrs. C. J. Watson)."[53] As the catalog was privately printed, it would not have been automatically deposited in this and other British copyright libraries.

Bolingbroke's own works can be found in several museums. Every one of those in the Victoria and Albert had been acquired prior to 1920. The British Museum, which has a larger collection of her etchings, accessioned its last one in 1970; it is a very early work, perhaps her first, and in poor condition. We can only wonder if it was accepted to fill a gap finally recognized as interest in British painter-etching was about to pick up. Clearly she did not time her death well. With no loving husband or children, she had no one to do for her what she had so willingly done for her husband. Her brother and sister were both dead; their children were her closest survivors. Most of the close circle of painter-etchers of which she and her husband had once been a vital part were gone, and Short, who had seen to a proper obituary for Watson, now a very old man, failed to do the same for Bolingbroke, or perhaps *The Times* just failed to print it. Given the political and economic troubles facing Britain in 1939, the death of an accomplished but not renowned painter-etcher was hardly a priority news item. The only catalog to identify her prints is a small notebook, handwritten in pencil, of seventy-three plates she produced between 1885 and 1918. Her nieces and nephews presented it to the library of the Castle Museum, where surely it does not see daylight very often.

Constance Pott, the third of our forgotten Victorians, was another who lived too long, dying at ninety-five in 1957, when etching was moribund and her mentor, Sir Frank Short, long deceased. When the two retired simultaneously from the Royal College of Art in 1924, each had been presented with an identical leather-bound volume with the names and addresses of their former students embossed on its vellum pages. That list, which we have not seen, undoubtedly includes a goodly number of subsequently successful painter-etchers. A photograph in the Ashmolean Museum, sent by way of thanks to each of the students, shows Short seated at a table examining a print, with Pott looking over his shoulder.[54] When she began her twenty-three-year stint as assistant to Short, she was one of only two women to have ever been employed to teach at the RCA.[55] Nevertheless, this once-legendary figure has virtually disappeared from memory, along with most of her work. Frank Hardie, in editing the running record of his father's etched work, identified one oft-mentioned sketching companion as the "now largely forgotten Constance Pott."[56] He remembered meeting her during his childhood but had no idea what had happened to her.

To begin with, we, too, knew nothing about Pott beyond those basic facts by which she was selected into our sample: she had become an A.R.E in 1894, four years later a full fellow, and her prints had been singled out for special mention by influential critics of the day. Hardie referred to her "conspicuous success" and judged her etching "of sufficiently fine quality to claim entry into the most select collections."[57] In a second article, he extolled her as both an experimental etcher and a teacher.[58] Singer, too, paid her what was intended as the highest of compliments: he saw an affinity between her London scenes and those of Whistler but found Pott's "more feminine, dainty and soft." "Extraordinary" was how Frederick Wedmore described her command of techniques.[59]

Her etchings add up to some 125 plates, which makes her one of the most productive of the Victorian women etchers and, beyond a shadow of doubt, the most versatile. She used aquatint, softground, sugar aquatint, drypoint, line engraving, mezzotint, and had even made a few lithographs.[60] Examples of these can be found in major British museums, especially the Victoria and Albert. The print room of the New York Public Library also has clippings that identify her as a "contemporary etcher whose work is greatly in demand."

This evidence of full recognition moved us to learn more about her and her etchings. Our search for the "missing" Pott testifies to the perils of dying at the wrong time. When we searched for an obituary, none could be found. Nor could any of the London print dealers we queried provide any clues. At Colnaghi's, which had handled her work, the head of its modern print department did not recognize the name. It was obvious that few of her prints had ever come on the market. To be sure, Guichard ranked her among the "major etchers," emphasizing her association with Short and describing her prints as "agreeable pieces with period charm." There was evidence that, after her retirement, she had continued to take an active interest in etching and other etchers. Thus, in 1938, she had attended the funeral of Job Nixon, whose etching career was cut short when he was killed in a car crash.

Her will, drawn up in June 1952, set up a trust fund leaving most of her money (near £17,000) for Johannes Matthias Daum, one of her last pupils at the RCA, to use as income for the duration of his life. About him we know only that he had some success as an etcher during the boom years, that two of his etchings were reproduced in *Fine Prints of the Year*. Why was he named her chief beneficiary? And, more to the point, did he feel honor-bound to preserve her memory?

The puzzle is that Constance Pott, with all her talent and connections, should be so little remembered and remarked. Her reputational "problem" has at least something to do with her longevity: she outlasted nearly all her contemporaries and many of her pupils. Those who still survived in 1957 had abandoned etching for other artistic pursuits in which she was no longer a central figure. Given these circumstances, it would have been difficult to persuade a gallery or museum to organize a special retrospective as a memorial. All her prints and books were left to two sisters but, so far as we can tell, these never found their way into a public collection. The Pott etchings at the Victoria and Albert and the British Museums were all early accessions. Those at the Ashmolean came from the collection of Charles Holroyd, who died in 1917.

Could Pott herself have done more to assure the survival of her artistic reputation? We do not know if she kept a running record of her work, but even if she did not, she could have remedied this during the many years that followed her retirement from active teaching. No such catalog has surfaced. Nor have we even come across a catalog of a large solo exhibition. Probably she was content to exhibit a large number of prints in annual group shows and never had one. To understand this reluctance for self-promotion, we have to consider her background and the milieu in which she lived and worked.

She grew up in West London as the oldest daughter in a large household that was solidly upper middle class. Sheppers, Pelly, Price and Pott, the family firm, was listed on the stock exchange. She lived and died in her father's home in South Kensington, close by the Royal College, but she kept a studio in Knightsbridge. Henry Pott, her father, left an estate of over £148,000 and an ironclad will that was thirteen pages long, providing trusts for his wife and nine children, six of them daughters of whom only one was married. To his wife he left the carriages and horses plus a library of books, pictures, and prints, which on her death were to pass to her oldest daughter Constance. But the daughter's inheritance was by no means unencumbered. Also included in the will was an elaborate scheme by which each of the children, in turn, was to choose a remembrance from among the things that had been in her mother's boudoir. Each daughter, in addition to money in trust, received £2,000 outright, a less generous share than the sons, who were also the executors of the estate.

Mrs. Henry Pott was both an author and an amateur artist who occasionally illustrated her own books. Though not an etcher, she was part of the circle that revolved around Frederick Goulding and Frank Short. One of her books, *Philomir or Self's the Man*, has illustrations by Raymond Ray-Jones, R.E., and A. Hugh Fisher, A.R.E., "after the author's original drawings"; a cover designed by Eli Wilson, A.R.E.; as well as a foreword by Frank Short.[61] A second book by Mrs. Pott, entitled *Quite the Gentleman*, provides a look into the Victorian world in which Constance Mary was enmeshed. Originally written when Constance was sixteen for the "amusement and benefit" of all the Potts' children "with no idea of publication," it was reissued in 1913. In a new preface, Mrs. Pott expressed her hope that the old-fashioned notions she had espoused would be as "true and helpful" to the children of her children as the latter had declared them to be. In "fictitious" letters to a boy away from home, his parents advise him that the object of the school is to make him into an English gentleman— "large hearted, large minded, unselfish, upright, honourable"—and that "goodness and intellect will always hold their own against either 'blood' or 'money.' " While the parents insist that their son cultivate his mind, his sisters back home are taught by a governess and assume responsibility for keeping him "well posted in the family news."[62]

One etcher, too young to have been Pott's student, remembered her—perhaps only by reputation—as an "old maid; very, very Victorian, very much respectable."[63] She engaged very much in "good works." Her students at the RCA seem to have been quite appreciative, even fond, of this self-effacing woman, whose old-fashioned sensibilities they sometimes offended with their spoofs as, for example, when the honorary degree of "the Schools Associateship" was conferred on her. Through the "happy inspiration" of one etching student, a subscription was got up to make her a "presentation of clothes" on this occasion—all duly reported in the student magazine. In the next issue, there was an apology together with a correction: She had received the "full Associateship degree," an academic rank, and the "clothes" presented consisted of "a cap and gown."[64]

Meanwhile, she remained "Miss Pott" to everyone, even in the inscriptions on impressions of their etchings given her by friends. Yet she emerges as flesh-and-blood in the little notes on the prints she gave to others and still more so when, in the few bits of correspondence we have come across, she writes of "family worries and sickness [that made it] impossible to concentrate and work" or of the "war and the trouble of those years . . . [which] have lowered the nerves and made people more susceptible to anything that comes their way." Her pride in her workmanship comes through in her refusal to sign proofs of a bookplate commissioned by a collector because she felt them to be "very poorly printed and not a credit to the plate," and she followed this up with instructions to the collector's printer.[65] One conjures up a picture of Constance Mary Pott in her long later life, assuming the responsibilities of her matriarchal mother, whose namesake she was, at the expense of her own career and doing nothing to conserve her own reputation.

Her prints, being of "little value," because they were by an "unknown," had not often come into circulation until quite recently. Hoping to purchase for illustrative purposes some good examples of the work of the forgotten lady-etchers, we kept asking about Pott but to no avail. Then, in 1979, one came to us through an American *amateur d'estampes* with a keen eye but very limited funds; he had purchased *Morning Post, the Strand* (figure 12) as part of an auction lot for a few shillings and, learning of our interest, was happy to trade it for another etching. Meanwhile, our consistent inquiries about Pott and her "fate" seem to have helped resuscitate her reputation. Within four years, eight other Potts made their way to us from several sources. It was hard to resist but we finally did when the asking prices began to reach $200.

## A Contrary Case

Is there ever a right time to die? Even to raise the question sounds ghoulish. Still, we point to the case of an etcher who died young *before* she had the chance to realize her full promise but, as a result, gained a limited "immortality." Elizabeth Fyfe, known to all her friends as "Bessie," died in Switzerland in 1933, just after her thirty-fourth birthday, following a long bout with tuberculosis. The first indication that she would have to go to the hospital came in a letter written nine years before. By then, she had been a Prix de Rome finalist. Hailed as "one of the most original and accomplished young etchers" in the 1920s, she had won attention from art critics and connoisseurs in Great Britain, America, Italy, and elsewhere. Her complete etching oeuvre amounted to just over 1,600 impressions from fifty-two plates.[66] Yet she somehow survives, at least as a minor figure, while others once far better known do not. Guichard, for one, lists her with the "majors." A good representation of her better prints is in the British Museum and in the Victoria and Albert. One or two turn up on the market from time to time.

While Fyfe's best-known etchings convey rather lofty religious themes that suggest a somber side, she was definitely a modern woman—a classical dancer who enjoyed reading, rowing, and, like many young people in those postwar days, motoring. That she has not simply disappeared has something to do with the tragedy of her dying so young. While she was in the hospital, her teachers, dealers, friends, collectors, and fellow etchers rallied round to organize an exhibition of her work, complete with a catalog, and then used the proceeds from sales to help pay for the care she needed.[67] Harold Wright of Colnaghi's, who had been her dealer, kept sending her cheerful notes and remitted the proceeds from sales without subtracting the usual commission; he also arranged to have her etchings printed by David Strang, the leading printer of the day, when she herself was no longer physically able to do this.[68] With so many of Fyfe's friends well positioned in the art world, her passing could hardly escape notice. Hers was in fact one of the very few obituaries to appear in the influential *Print Collector's Quarterly*. As to the preservation of her work, Wright gave a complete set of Fyfe's prints to a sister in Manchester while also making certain that no others still awaited discovery. Thus, the many persons mobilized by the tragedy of her premature death helped keep alive the memory of the persona and contributed to the preservation of her work.

### Omissions

Thus far, our inquiry into the puzzling fate of the lady-etchers has focused primarily on matters over which they had no control—when they were born, when they died, and whether they had caring survivors. But it should also have become clear that some of their plight was of their own making. More women than men failed to take certain steps that would have helped to project their reputations beyond their lifetime.

There is, first, the size of the artistic output they left behind. Women, on the average, produced fewer plates than the men and pulled fewer impressions from those they made (table 10.4). These averages, if anything, underplay the differences due to the presence among the women of a few superproducers. In terms of plates and especially in terms of the number of prints, the output of Clare Leighton (quite well known) exceeds that of all other British men and

Table 10.4
Productivity, by Gender

|  | Women (N = 59) | Men (N = 63) |
|---|---|---|
| Average number of plates | 84 | 153 |
| Average number of impressions | 3,619 | 5,033 |

women. The number of impressions by women is also swelled by several with a few prints published in large editions through members of the Printsellers Association. When we look at the *median*, instead of the average, number of impressions for all artists, which was somewhere around 3,000 for a lifetime, twice as many men as women exceeded that number. Let us hasten to add, however, that many of our figures on individual productivity are no more than informed estimates based on catalogs and museum holdings. Nevertheless, the contrast, no matter how we choose to measure productivity, is clear.

In aggregate the women were clearly under less *economic* pressure to make available for sale all the impressions their plates could yield. Some, if single, could get by quite adequately, though not live in luxury, on income derived from an inheritance or on an allowance from their families. More of them came, if not from affluent homes, then at least from comfortably middle-class backgrounds that provided some kind of cushion. This was not true of everyone; a few had lost their fathers and had to struggle but they were, in this respect, better off than the men. Only 5 percent came from modest or poor family backgrounds, compared to 25 percent of the men. Similarly, the economic well-being of married women, with some notable exceptions, did not depend to the same degree on what they earned from their art. Our data on "main source" of income bear this out. Though there were far fewer married women than married men in our sample, more women lived mainly off the income of a spouse, and more had some kind of inheritance on which they could draw (table 10.5). It stands to reason, therefore, that fewer of them had the same compelling motive to establish a long-term relationship with a dealer-agent who would have pressured them to produce a supply of prints large enough for profitable promotion.

Second, the women were less inclined to keep the kind of records that greatly facilitate the identification of the artist's work. Far fewer women than men kept good records that included information on

Table 10.5
Main Source of Income, by Gender (in percent)

|  | Women (N = 58) | Men (N = 59) |
|---|---|---|
| Art and prints | 12 | 37 |
| Illustration | 16 | 14 |
| Portrait/mural/commercial, etc. | 2 | 12 |
| Teaching/curatorial | 21 | 36 |
| Private (inheritance or spouse) | 50 | 2 |

when and where plates were etched, the number of states and their differences, size of editions, and other information that is indispensable when it comes to the subsequent preparation of a complete catalogue raisonné. Such omissions impede the future identification of surviving work and, as a consequence, result in an underestimation of productivity. Few students of art history are moved to expend much time and energy in documenting the oeuvre of a minor artist whose tracks are hard to follow. And why did fewer women than men keep good records? Some, like some of the men, had disdain for what is after all a clerical task; some claimed to be unmindful of posterity but, mostly, they rarely had anyone—like a wife or daughter—who would assume almost complete responsibility for keeping such records. For these and for other reasons the list of lady-etchers whose work has been fully and adequately catalogued is very small indeed.

Third, fewer women took steps to ensure proper custodianship for their work. At least this is what we glean from their wills. Hardly any of those we located contain explicit instructions on what was to be the disposition of prints and plates still in the artist's possession at the time of death. Especially, they were less likely than their male colleagues to have bequeathed their works to a museum or to someone who they could be sure would provide for their preservation, keep them together, or dispose of them in a way that would best protect the artist's hard-earned reputation.

What difference did it make if women failed to take such steps—to be big producers, to print full editions of their plates, and to keep good records? Such omissions, it can be shown, have been cumulative in their detrimental effect. Reputations have suffered accordingly, though not always to the point of total oblivion. We turn to four case histories: the first two failed to take such steps, the second two acted out of greater self-interest.

## A Distaste for Self-Promotion

We look first at the careers of two quite productive and talented women, both of them single, whose work is scarcely known today, in part because they scoffed at self-promotion, failed to keep good records, and were rather casual about providing for the posthumous conservation of their work.

Margaret Kemp-Welch, who died in 1968, had been an eager and happy participant in the late-Victorian world. She had grown up in a cultured family with a love for pictures and good music; two cousins were also professional artists. Margaret developed a liking for travel, which her parents provided ample opportunity to satisfy. They also allowed her to maintain a studio in the garden of the family house, where she sometimes taught. A younger cousin, who went to her for drawing lessons while on holiday from boarding school, recalled her as "a delightful teacher, inspiring, thorough and great fun [who] earned her bread and butter as Head of the Art Department at Clapham High School for Girls, in London," where she was "much loved and respected."[69] She was equally popular with her nieces, with some of whom she shared an interest in music and amateur theatricals.[70]

Her quite considerable etched output was well received by the influential critics of the day. Singer praised her for "not playing up to the sentimental."[71] When shown at group exhibitions, her prints were often singled out for praise. Wedmore, in a backhanded compliment to women, found her *In the Marsh* and some other etchings "so good that they should almost suffice to enable their authors to survive the deplorable disadvantage of being only women. Quite hopefully," he added, "one may look on the artistic future of these ladies—on the public recognition of it."[72] Also, an entry in the widely used Thieme-Becker biographical dictionary praises "the skill with which Kemp-Welch masters the difficult technique of aquatinting . . . [which] makes her topological and scenic prints desirable objects for collectors."[73]

From all indications, Kemp-Welch had no great inner compulsion to immortalize herself through her work, which, according to our best estimate, amounted to about 120 plates, from which as many as 4,000 prints may have been pulled. The surviving work cannot be anywhere near as large. She lost most of her early plates and the impressions from them in 1918, when a bomb from a zeppelin destroyed her studio. Yet this mishap hardly accounts for the thoroughness with which she has been forgotten. A contributing factor was her obvious distaste for record keeping. She never had a dealer to prod or assist her in this task, for which her busy academic and professional schedule left her little time. Often she did not even sign, title, or number her prints. When we asked the niece who had custody of what remained of her art about this, her response was, "She wasn't the kind who would. . . . She wasn't boastful."[74] A request to send biographical materials for Clement's compendium on women artists likewise remained unanswered. Her will included instructions on how her paintings, watercolors, and prints might be distributed to relatives and friends but absolutely nothing about offers to museums or sale through galleries. As a result, though both the Victoria and Albert and British Museums had long owned examples of her etchings and aquatints, these do not reveal the full scope of her talent. Still, sufficient of her work is conserved, some in public trust and more of it in private hands, so that the case of her disappearance is by no means closed even though the artist herself failed to take some small steps toward the perpetuation of her reputation. Whether anyone will ever come along with the energy and incentive to take the giant steps now required to restore it remains questionable. She was another of the once well received women whom Guichard in 1977 relegated to a "minor" status.[75]

Greta (Margaret Annie Mary Adelaide) Delleany, one of our Edwardians, was thought a "marvelous artist" by those who knew her work, but few knew the full scope of her achievements, not only in etching but also in pastel.[76] The reason: she was pathologically shy. She had to be pushed into submitting her etchings to the Royal Academy show and would not allow any article to be written about them. Frank Short, her instructor, probably had to submit on her behalf the print which made her an A.R.E. She never became a fellow, likely because she would never think of advancing her own candidacy. *Towpath*, reproduced in the first volume of *Fine Prints of the Year*, was submitted for consideration by Colnaghi's, which had published it (figure 44).

Born in Stoke Newington (North London), she had, after the early death of her mother, been sheltered by her father, a bank clerk, to whom she was overattached. When he died, she was "lost." He had, however, left a modest inheritance, on which, given her Spartan habits, she was able to make do by living cheaply off-season in guest houses in Kent and Sussex. This is how she had found her way to Cheltenham. There she attached herself to the school of art, whose principal, the painter-etcher Robert S. G. Dent, let her use the equipment, and she let him criticize her work. She would sit etching while he taught classes, leaning over to rap his knuckles whenever he said anything of which she did not approve.

She was too shy and frightened to do anything like teaching. Thus, other than what modest income she may have had from etchings and drypoints sold mainly through British and American etching societies, she probably never earned a penny in her life. She must have produced about forty of these, which, printed in editions of fifty to one hundred, sold for 1 or 2 guineas apiece. For her own pleasure, she also made a large number of clichés-verres, which she gave to her many friends. When she died in 1968, she willed what she most treasured to Dent, requesting that he select examples of her best work to give to her friends and to art galleries at his "unfettered discretion." Carrying out the request proved a grim job. Delleany had been a hoarder who threw nothing away. Dent took near everything to his college, sent cards to friends, and had a kind of "jumble sale." Whatever remained unsold, he brought back to his house. Years later, when a provincial gallery owner specializing in watercolors came to look at Dent's work, he was also shown some of Delleany's. Her beautiful pastels, this dealer estimated, were worth hundreds and hundreds of pounds; he took fourteen of her pastels and some of her prints, framed them, and easily sold the whole lot.

So it was that Greta Delleany, who never sold very much in her life, became a "big name" in a small part of the world. Since she had signed only what she exhibited, Dent found himself issuing certificates to assure anxious collectors that these were indeed authentic Delleanys. Within months of hearing this account, we came across signed copies of her etchings in three galleries—two in Boston, the other in Washington, D.C. None of these dealers knew anything about their creator—not even that she was British—but they had found the work appealing.

### A Few Exceptions

Eveleen Buckton, a Late Victorian who died aged ninety in 1962, is today remembered better than she might otherwise be because she took some steps to perpetuate her reputation. She was the fifth daughter of a distinguished scientist, and niece of another.[77] Though born into a large family, she outlived her siblings and had for many years resided alone in Hampstead, London. Though she left her very considerable estate to a nephew, she specifically requested that her trustees select out some of her "drawings, etchings, watercolors, and sculpture" for the British Museum and public galleries in the United Kingdom and abroad. Just what these trustees selected is impossible to say, but her work is well represented in the British Museum, most of it

acquired before her death. Her prints are also in the Ashmolean, the
Victoria and Albert, and the Bradford Gallery.

Buckton, a product of the Slade, had begun as a watercolorist and
sculptor and did not come to etching until she was about fifty. She was
one of those "mature practitioners" whom Short was happy to admit
to his class because they could draw. She produced a number of plates
in the 1920s but, as an etcher, only came into her own after the decline
of the market. In 1937, the year she was made an A.R.E., a Buckton
print appeared in *Fine Prints of the Year*; a second was in the 1938
volume. Ignoring fashion, she etched the last of her over sixty plates in
1959 when she was eighty-seven years old and did most of her own
printing as well. Given the limited demand for etchings in these lean
years, the total number of impressions issued from her plates may be
less than 2,000. Yet a remarkably large number have surfaced in the
years since her death. Though hardly renowned in her lifetime, her
memory has not, like that of other contemporaries, been totally obliterated.

An independent soul, she had evidently not been trained to "lady-
like" passivity, or perhaps she deliberately refused to play that role.
According to a nephew, she had traveled extensively to many remote
places to work directly on the spot, had walked immense distances,
climbed with skilled mountaineers in search of subjects that "composed"—a favorite term of hers. The outbreak of World War I had
caught her sketching in Austria. For such suspicious doings, the military had arrested her several times, causing her to lose much of her
work and equipment. And in Italy during World War II, she had once
more fallen under suspicion. An etcher thirty years her junior recalled
her as a very tall woman who wore a big hat and stockings that she
rolled down. When asked, as a kind of joke, if she would like to go to a
football game with the young men in her class, she surprised them by
saying yes, and she also joined them at the races.[78] She was also given
to expressing her opinions quite fearlessly. Her nephew thought her
fully dedicated to her art as well as to her friends and relations "whom
she stood by in any crisis or emergency." One of these, probably her
nephew, must have cared enough to conserve what was left of her
work, though at the time of her death it could have had little monetary
value.

Next, we turn to Dame Laura Knight, the painter and Royal Academician, who took most of the steps she should have, but not all. The
most renowned of the lady-etchers, she was also the most well publicized. Though she came to etching late in her career, she was the only

woman to be included in the *Modern Masters of Etching* series.[79] Over a decade, beginning in 1923, she produced some fifty plates, printing twenty to fifty impressions of her aquatints, fifty to seventy-five of her etchings, and one hundred copies of her one line engraving. But with the crash, so she recalls in her second autobiography, "the hope of selling any etching became forlorn: on a bottom shelf in my studio lie four big boxes filled with prints, unsought untouched for many years." Yet while "most of the artists who solely employed this pictorial form of art suffered a knock-out blow," her own suffering "was small by comparison."[80] She did not entirely abandon printmaking. In 1934, in 1943, and again in 1956, when nearing eighty, she made plates for presentation to members of the Print Collectors Club, and she was still exhibiting prints when she was near ninety.[81] Her total oeuvre probably comes to near 4,000 impressions.

It bothered Laura Knight not one bit that her assertiveness might be considered unladylike. Having had to make her own way, she had no qualms about promoting her reputation and did whatever she could to see to it that she would be remembered the way she wished to be remembered. Thus, she wrote not just one but two autobiographies—the first in 1936, the second in 1965. The year before her death, she superintended the selection of works, including some of her etchings, for an exhibition that was expected to be a final celebration of her long career. She managed to star even in this, her memorial, which her presence turned into a media event. On video, she appeared with "a scotch in one hand and cigarette in the other. . . . Dressed in a magenta-coloured gown, her white hair 'modelled by Miss Worth, you know,' and bound by a black velvet ribbon, she sat in a blue satin chair on Private View Day and received her friends: artists—famous and not yet established—politicians, society figures, dancers, personalities from most walks of life. She was in her element."[82] Two more exhibitions followed. In each of these, Dame Laura had her say; in Nottingham, where both she and her husband had gone to art school, she intervened to insist that one of her paintings *not* be included.[83]

Widowed in 1961 and childless, she had no close survivors; so she left it to her solicitors, as executors of her will, to dispose of her drawings, etchings, manuscripts, and other effects in accordance with instructions she had drawn up. Some money was to go to the Royal Academy and its schools, but she requested—giving no reason—that there be no scholarship prize or award in her name, that her ashes be scattered, and that there be no mourning for her. But from everything else she did it was clear that she had no intention of being forgotten.

Dame Laura had every reason to believe she would remain a "star." Nevertheless, today her prints are not as coveted by collectors as one might have anticipated, given both the publicity and the high praise that had been showered on her work. Ernest Lumsden wrote that her figure subjects "based on the Goya tradition showed tremendous power in design and draughtsmanship, and [were] technically faultless."[84] Several critics referred to one or more of her prints as masterpieces. Yet, at least not until recently, Knight's prints have commanded nowhere near the attention or price of an Augustus John. In 1977, to cite an example, John's small etched portrait, *The Serving Maid* (figure 38), sold for $260 while Knight's aquatint, *At the Folies Bergères* (figure 24), once equally acclaimed, was selling for $75.[85] So great a difference in the posthumous standing of these two renowned artists could hardly have been anticipated. They had been born just months apart and been friends for many years. Both were R.A.s, though John was elected before Knight, and both were the kind of flamboyant personalities who make good press copy. Each left two published memoirs. And both had attained an early success as painters before they ever thought of taking up etching. John's foray into etching had preceded Knight's; he had etched more plates, most of them between 1901 and 1910, many of which were slight, offhand sketches dashed off with little respect for the medium. Critics divide on their artistic merit. Some would agree that John's reputation as a painter has exaggerated the worth of his minor activities. Others consider some of his small portraits "among the most perfect etchings of the time."[86] Whatever their true merit, John's etchings are better known and have been more sought after than those of Knight.

Why then did Dame Laura's reputation not stand the test of time as well as she and her admirers had every reason to expect? For one thing, she did not live quite long enough to be able to exploit the renewed interest, beginning late in the 1970s, in the work from the revival period. But most puzzling, and perhaps most significant, is the lack of anything approaching a definitive catalogue raisonné of her printmaking. None appeared in her lifetime and none has appeared as of this writing: the *Modern Masters* volume beautifully reproduced some of her best prints but otherwise offered only meager information. The one biography of her life was clearly not intended as a contribution to art history and fails to mention her etching career.[87] By contrast, the first catalog of John's etchings was issued in 1920 and updated by 1931.[88]

The explanation for this "oversight" may be sought in Dame Laura's long-lasting but complicated relationship with her husband Harold Knight, also a painter. Three years older than she, he had inspired her when they first met in art school as teenagers.[89] Though she continued to acknowledge his superior aesthetic wisdom and always treated him as the greater artist, it was her huge canvases, with their daring colors and depictions of ballet dancers and circus performances, that drew the crowds when the two exhibited together, as they often did. And she managed to get herself elected an associate of the Royal Academy a year before that honor was bestowed on him—reportedly with her help.[90] In tempering Harold's natural resentment, Laura often walked a tightrope, though neither of her autobiographies is candid about this. In promoting her reputation as a painter, she was reluctant to pursue her self-interest too obviously. The marriage was especially strained in the years of the Great War, made even more difficult when their many friends in the Cornwall art colony ostracized Harold for registering as a conscientious objector. Also, he had fallen hopelessly, but deeply, in love with another woman.[91] In the trying years after the war, when Laura took to printmaking, she may have been loath to make too much of a success he could not share, since the medium held no attraction for him. Both her autobiographies dwell on her and Harold's many trials and triumphs in painting; that neither book had much to say about her triumphs as a printmaker is revealing.

Meanwhile, both John's and Knight's reputations as painters have had their ups and downs, but since her death, it is fair to say, hers has been more often down than up. Contemporary critics no longer consider Knight a "major" painter. Had she held her place as a renowned painter, her etchings would surely be valued more. But if Germaine Greer is right in predicting that Knight's "drawings and aquatints are much finer and more suggestive than her finished oil paintings, and upon them her enduring reputation will eventually rest,"[92] someone will first have to prepare the catalog that Knight herself failed to make ready.

Let us add here that the etchings of Orovida Pissarro, the one British woman whose work is fully catalogued, today command good prices. In fact, her reputation has actually been enhanced since her death in 1968. "Orovida," as she signed her prints, was a prodigious producer. She etched 107 plates, from which she pulled about 8,000 impressions in different states, all of them systematically documented in a 150-page album, which she herself bequeathed to the Ashmolean Museum. In this album at least one state of nearly every one of her prints is hinged, pasted, or laid in opposite an appropriate handwritten entry. It forms the basis for the definitive catalog of her etchings and aquatints published in 1969.[93] Orovida's record-keeping activity is equally evident in a similar album with pasted photographs of her paintings, identified by handwritten titles and notes on size and sales, also in the Ashmolean. To assure the survival of her work, she donated these records to that museum, along with impressions from almost all her plates.

## Moving in Circles

A third set of factors informs our inquiry into the disappearance of the lady-etchers. While most of the women and their work have been forgotten, some have been less forgotten because they are linked in memory to other artists—almost always men—who are remembered. Social ties to the famous can promote the posthumous survival of a reputation and, indirectly, of the artistic output on which that reputation is based. In this respect, the British women had an advantage but also a unique handicap.

The advantage was not an advantage of gender but a consequence of their social origins. More of the women than the men were born into the "right" circles, where from childhood on they glimpsed the important intellectual, literary, artistic, and political personalities of the day. The ability to enter this world was, to this extent, inherited rather than cultivated in the course of an artistic career. The particular handicap for the women etchers was their exclusion from many male preserves—not only from artistic societies and elite positions in the art establishment, but also from the easy conviviality of clubs where so much "business" is conducted. Even when allowed in, it was usually not as artists in their own right but only as "adjuncts" to important men. This kind of discrimination lives on beyond the grave. A number of women etchers survive in the collective memory mostly because they moved within the orbit of artists (or other important figures) who continue to command attention.

The close affiliation of three women—Thérèse Lessore, Wendela Boreel, and Sylvia Gosse—has contributed to their continued visibility as etchers. Gosse, by far the most distinguished etcher of the three, might well have made it "on her own," but it is unlikely that the etchings of Wendela Boreel and, especially, those by Thérèse Lessore would command quite the attention that they do today had these women not been part of the Sickert circle. Still, Lessore already had a reputation as a painter before she became his third wife in 1926. It is said that he fell in love with her paintings long before he fell in love with her, having written about her work and contributed a preface for the catalog of her first solo show. Though never in any formal sense his student, a *Times* obituary nevertheless identified her mainly as "Sickert's pupil . . . his feminine counterpart."[94] In 1974 her work, along with that of Gosse and Boreel (and two other women), was featured in a London exhibition with the catchy (though, to feminists, offensive) title, "The Sickert Women and the Sickert Girls." The catalog says that little is known about Lessore and she "is usually discussed only in relation to Sickert, yet a closer investigation reveals an artist in her own right with an extremely interesting and forceful personality."[95] Included in the show were fourteen of her oils and watercolors, but no etchings.

To be sure, Lessore probably pulled no more than 400 impressions from her plates; few, if any, still circulate. Despite its scarcity, her etched work is better represented in public collections, mostly through the Sickert Trust, than that of others who moved in less-celebrated circles. She was married to Sickert for less than half her professional life but is remembered as "Mrs. Walter Sickert," and that is also how her few surviving letters in manuscript collections are catalogued.[96] Having devoted most of her last years to caring for the invalid Sickert and having identified her interests so completely with his, she might not mind. The point is that had she not become Mrs. Sickert, she might hardly be remembered and least of all as an etcher.

Boreel, though a favorite pupil of Sickert's, played a less central role than the other two in Sickert's life. Her "rediscovery" in the 1980s is a fortuitous sequitur to the increasing interest in the Sickert story. Beginning in the 1960s, he became the subject of a number of biographies, including one by Marjorie Lilly, herself a "Sickert girl."[97] Boreel, born in 1895 and then still living in France, provided an authentic link to the Sickert past.

As is true of Lessore, critics hardly ever look at Boreel's etched work without comparing it to Sickert's, although some have judged it superior to or at least as good as his. Malcolm Salaman called her "an instinctive etcher" whose "daintily vivacious" conception was her own.[98] Frank Rutter referred to one of her etchings as "like an early Whistler in its precision of drawing," while a *Times* reviewer found her handling of the medium freer, looser, and slicker than her master's.[99] Boreel saw herself as less imitative of Sickert than either Gosse or Lessore: "Sickert taught me a lot but I think I developed as myself, unlike Sylvia Gosse who I think followed him too slavishly . . . as did Thérèse Lessore."[100] Still, however much she may have wished to

downplay the stylistic linkage with Sickert, the story of her first encounter with him has found its way into near every gossipy account of
Sickert's life and contributed to his reputation as a male chauvinist.
This came about while Boreel was attending his evening class at Westminster Technical Institute; when he asked her to stop in at his office
afterward, she was frightened, expecting to be expelled for incompetence. To her surprise, he said, " 'Your drawing is far too good for here.
I'll install you in a studio in Mornington Crescent where you will paint
each morning and then come to me in the afternoons.' So I became
Sickert's 'petit nègre,' to do all, and to be at his beck and call. . . . I
used to mix his paints and square his canvasses. . . . Then there were
Sickert's famous breakfasts during which [two other women students]
and myself would rush around clearing up, dashing down Charlotte
Street to get rolls, marmalade, butter and coffee."[101]

This story serves feminists as a horrific example of the exploitation of the female by the male artist: "It does not require either a vivid
imagination, or an excessively soured one, to picture the master encouraging slight emotional attachments, affairs and adoration in place
of the deeper ones he had no time for, and using his only too willing
worshipers as drudges. . . . One of the 'Sickert girls' [Boreel] has told
us in her own words how this might come about."[102]

Accounts of Boreel's association with Sickert abound. For our
purposes, it really matters little what the truth was—whether Gosse
and Lessore were jealous or whether Sickert meant to marry Boreel or
only to bed her down (one version she has given). There is some evidence to support the Boreel-Gosse rivalry hypothesis: around 1917,
Marjorie Lilly tells us, Sickert had "a craze for gouache painting,"
stimulated by the brilliant studies produced by "his pupil and friend,
Wendela Boreel," and that Sylvia Gosse, not to be outdone, began to
work in gouache, in no time at all contributing "some first-class examples in this difficult medium."[103]

Mainly, the Boreel case demonstrates how much the survival and
revival of reputation has to do with the circles in which an artist
moves; she is linked in history with more than one famous circle. Now
that Boreel's work has been rediscovered, she could easily become
more than just a footnote in the Sickert story, for she was not only a
serious artist but a colorful personality, who was born into and lived in
a series of privileged circles. Her mother was American, her father, first
secretary of the Dutch Embassy in London. Her sister, also a Slade
student and a Sickert favorite, married the Argentine ambassador to
Britain.[104] Through her parents who lived in Tite Street opposite

Whistler's White House and John Singer Sargent's studio, she met Frank Schuster and his sister, Adela, the wealthy friends and benefactors of Oscar Wilde who had also lived on the street. At their home, which was the focus of artistic life on the street, she met and mingled with other members of Britain's literary and artistic elite, including its foremost composer, Edward Elgar, and poets such as William B. Yeats, Siegfried Sassoon (whose portrait she etched), and Thomas Hardy. Through Sickert she met important art critics like Paul Konody, Frank Rutter, and Roger Fry.

Then, after the Great War ended, she moved on to a faster track. She married a young New Zealander, Leslie Wylde, who had lost a leg during the war, and the couple became part of the "gay twenties" with an abandonment reminiscent of the F. Scott Fitzgeralds. Frank Schuster had brought "Anzy," as her husband was nicknamed, to Boreel's first solo exhibition. Schuster, who had paid off Oscar Wilde's debts after his death, had been struck by a coincidence when he first met Anzy convalescing in hospital: his name was Wylde and, like Wilde, he had a hooded eye. Schuster all but adopted Wylde and later left him all his money.[105] Well-heeled and well-connected, the young couple lived in style; they moved on the fringes of the fashionable and ultraconservative, appeasement-oriented, Cliveden set that surrounded Lady Nancy Astor in the pre–World War II years.

Boreel's etchings reflect the changing circles in which she moved. There are the impressions of theaters and boxing matches in the prewar years spent with Sickert. In the 1920s, there are her old nurse, portraits of Leslie Wylde and their son, the Hyde Park nannies, and the Royal Enclosure at Epsom Downs. Then, in the 1930s, there are the unemployed and a frankly anti-Semitic print dated 1932 titled *The Jew at the Café Royal (A Sight of Things to Come)*.[106] The café, near Piccadilly, was at that time a favorite meeting place for the literary and artistic elite. Later, in the 1940s, when Boreel, caught in France during World War II, managed to make her way to the United States, she etched people skating in Central Park.

Boreel was one of the etchers who lived long enough to see interest revive in her etched work, but more than just its evident quality, what brought it on to the marketplace were the circles in which she had moved and the linkages to famous people that made her a persona and guaranteed her some place, however minor, in the collective memory.

Sylvia Gosse also lived almost all her life surrounded by literary and artistic circles of which she was an integral part, yet she never exploited these close contacts in the furtherance of her own career. She chose to watch from the sidelines rather than occupy center stage. She assisted Sickert not only with his painting and teaching but devoted a good deal of time and energy to handling his finances and helping out, often "in such an unobtrusive way that half the time he did not even know that the help had been given."[107] This does not mean that she was a doormat to be trampled or a lovesick calf, as Boreel implied.[108] It was just that, as she wrote her dealer who was anxious that she find her "particular place" among contemporary painters, " 'Ne vous faites pas de la bile' as they say here [in Everneu]. . . . I'm afraid I was not blessed—or otherwise—with the gift of ambition by any fairy god-mother at my christening."[109]

Nevertheless, she was not above caring whether or not her reputation endured. In correspondence late in life about an exhibition being planned by the Ashmolean, she wrote: "What fun to have a finger in one's own (possible?) memorial Exhibition."[110] Also, she expressed her pleasure at finding that her works were selling well at auction: "That Gosse has now come into her own [as a critic had written] seems to be true," she wrote.[111] She lived to see her paintings fetch increasingly high prices and took pleasure in this even when her name was misspelled—as "Goss"—in an exhibition.[112]

It was in her father's house that Sickert, who often came to Edmund Gosse's Sunday evening gatherings, first suggested that Sylvia ought to take up etching. As to exactly when and under what circumstances Sickert made the suggestion, the evidence is contradictory. There are at least three versions of the story.[113] Whatever the case, once Sickert took notice of her, she moved into his orbit and thereafter never sought to extricate herself. While yet in her twenties, she became his assistant and coprincipal at Rowlandson House, the school Sickert had opened at 140 Hampstead Road. Her job was to show students how to do the craft part—laying ground, grinding ink, printing, and so on. Meanwhile, she got on with her own etching. Sickert himself was bored and impatient with students who had no ability, so the risk was that the school might soon have no pupils. It fell on patient Sylvia to take on the teaching of the untalented, leaving the better ones to Sickert. The idea of the school (officially known as the Sickert and Gosse School of Drawing and Painting) had been to make some money, and it also fell to Gosse to put their finances in some kind of order.[114]

Once Sylvia took on the job of rescuing Sickert from financial disaster, it appears to have become a habit. It was she who made it possible for him to marry his second wife, Christine, by solving his money problems, when through a stroke of good luck an "anonymous" purchaser was found for a large picture that had not sold! When Christine lay dying a few years later, it was Sylvia who nursed her and supplied the necessary support that got him back to working once more. Years later, during World War II, when Sickert was ill and Thérèse Lessore, his third wife, needed help to care for him, it was Sylvia who came to the rescue. She persisted in her self-appointed mission even after Sickert's death. (Thérèse had survived him by only three years.) Among other things, to help perpetuate interest in Sickert's printed work, Sylvia donated her collection of his etchings to the Victoria and Albert.

The obvious question is: To what extent does the survival of her reputation rest on her own achievements? Are we dealing with more than a satellite effect? Gosse's etched work consists of some 150 plates, printed in small editions, so that the total impressions probably number under 4,000. Examples pulled from many of these plates have found their way—mainly as gifts from the artist or others—to most of the major print repositories in England. At last count the Victoria and Albert had 15; the Ashmolean, 36 (as well as some lithographs); and the British Museum, 76. Gosse's portrait of Sickert, presented by the poet, Siegfried Sassoon, hangs in the Tate Gallery. What is lacking is a fully annotated catalogue raisonné. It is hard not to believe that with the growing interest in women artists in the Camden Town group and in modern etchings that one may be in the making.

Whatever the merits of Gosse's work, there is hardly a printed reference to it that does not invoke the association with Sickert and the Camden Town group. Yet, like the other "Sickert women," she was never officially a member of that group—in large part because Sickert joined the others in opposing membership for women. To admit them, however worthy, he apparently believed, was to open the doors wide for the entry of the artists' wives and lady-friends. Only later, when the Camden Town group merged with the London group and needed more members to support a larger gallery, was the exclusionary rule reversed. Then, both Gosse and Lessore were among those admitted.

A very brief biography of Sylvia Gosse begins, "It is virtually impossible to portray as complex a personality as Sylvia Gosse's seems to have been in a few short sentences. Even intimate friends describe her as a 'living contradiction.' "[115] The most informative but not very well known biography of the artist was written by a friend of many years, who had "long felt that Gosse's work deserved to be known to a wider public" and hoped her book would serve this purpose. Kathleen Fisher, its author, explained that her friend, Sylvia, had shunned any form of publicity, finding it most distasteful and, presumably, would not have welcomed this posthumous effort.[116]

In this rather appealing book, Fisher, who was also Sylvia's pupil, nowhere indicates or even hints that Sylvia had been in love with Sickert or longed to marry him but lost out twice to women who were her good friends. Rather, so she surmises, Sylvia felt strongly that a woman painter should never marry, even though her own mother, Nellie Epps, a painter encouraged by her husband, had continued to exhibit (and also to write) long after her children were born. Gosse herself was not a crusading New Woman, not even a suffragette. In fact, she was shocked when her sister, Tessa, chaperoned by her aunt, Lady Laura Alma-Tadema, a well-known portrait painter, insisted on marching to Downing Street for Votes for Women. Sylvia thought the vote was bound to come sometime and could not understand how marching would help.

Whether Gosse did or did not disavow marriage, the theme of Gosse the spinster, with her unfulfilled dream of being Mrs. Sickert, constantly surfaces; it is part of the legendary lore spread within the art world. Gosse herself would no doubt have deplored this; she hated gossip and backbiting. Still, the tale of unrequited love undoubtedly contributes to the Gosse persona and thus may prove the telling factor that will help sustain interest in her art and perpetuate her reputation.[117]

## The Mystery of the Disappearing Lady-Etchers: Case Closed?

Why did the British women more often than the men fail to convert their success and recognition into lasting fame? Why were they more forgotten than their male contemporaries? These are the two questions we have tried to answer.

We have found no merit in two explanations: one that is based on alleged flaws in their work, the other that implies a certain lack of seriousness.

We have to acknowledge that women were less likely to have achieved, in their lifetimes, that level of renown which most nearly assures the posthumous survival of artistic reputation. Here the women were less adept than the men. While their work was accepted for exhibitions, won them awards, gained them commissions and other forms of recognition from fellow artists, they were less successful at marketing their art. Some who had independent means, through inheritance or marriage, were not pressed to make editions of their prints for distribution. They were also less willing to seek, or adept at securing, the kind of publicity that leads toward celebrity status. Yet such publicity is the essential element not only in the survival of a reputation but in its "rediscovery," should it be temporarily lost.

Among the nonaesthetic factors that contributed to their "disappearance," some were of the women's own making and some were beyond their control. Some were born too early in a Victorian Age that made room for them as artists but not as active competitors for public attention. Their upbringing left them more socially inhibited and less skillful at self-promotion than their male counterparts. Longevity, mortality patterns, and the hard choices that professional women had to make in deciding whether or not to marry or to have children all combined to put their posthumous reputations at risk. Fewer women did marry and, if married, few had children. Living so long, many "died at the wrong time," when painter-etching was no longer in fashion, and/or they left behind no survivors with a sentimental or vested interest in seeing that their reputations survived.

Also, many women failed to keep the records that could facilitate the future identification of their work or took care that their work was preserved and kept in the public domain. Some had no stomach for such a self-serving task; others were too occupied to take the time and, besides, had no "wives" to take over this task. Whatever the reason for such omissions, these suggest that they were less concerned than the men about winning lasting glory as artists.

An additional handicap was the women's restricted access to springboards for promotion. Certain professional positions and other public roles through which a man might make a name for himself were unavailable to women. Some came within the orbit of a famous man but thus risked merging their own images with that of their mentor.

Have we solved the "mystery"? Perhaps not entirely. But we invite our readers to look at the illustrations in this book and judge for themselves whether all of the "forgotten" women deserve their neglect. In the next chapter we shall try to show that some of the same factors that serve to explain the "fate" of these women also help to explain the "fate" of some of the men.

# I I

# Reputation and the Collective Memory: A Summing Up

The past lives on within the present and nowhere more vividly than in the arts that appeal to the eye. Throughout the world, architectural monuments dot the landscape. Everywhere, it seems, there are museums and archives to house the meticulously identified and carefully labeled relics of years long gone. Sanctified by age, they remind onlookers of a rich cultural heritage. The objects are there to be looked at, studied, catalogued, admired. Some can be bought by those with a passion to possess. That the things on display also command a price can be seen whenever a "museum-quality" item comes up for sale at auction or finds its way into one of the galleries that cater to curators and collectors alike.

In this chapter we take a more general look at the selective survival of reputation within the collective memory, an elusive concept not be confused with what historians know or have been able to unearth about the past. What Halbwachs, who introduced the term into the sociological vocabulary, meant by *la mémoire collective* was something less erudite and less oriented toward factual detail, a living image of the past that was, in a very real sense, a collective property; in short, a form of folk knowledge more or less.[1] The image shared by people in some social universe is made up not only of what people actually recall and then pass on but also of things that have somehow been recovered, embellished, or even invented to serve some contemporary cause.[2] One can, in fact, draw boundaries between groups based on the past that people share. The world of critics, curators, connoisseurs, collectors, and dealers in etching is similarly bounded by shared name recognition.

Although we have been dealing specifically with etching as one of the arts, our inquiry has been less concerned with the objects themselves than with things less material, namely the ideas attached to these works and, more particularly, the association of these works with their creators. There is a view, espoused by Thomas Carlyle and still common among men of letters, that the greatness of poets, preachers, kings, and others, which presumably includes artists, rests on accomplishments that transcend the historical climate in which they flourished. We do not dispute the influence of the deed on what people will remember about the doer. Glory leaves an afterglow and will give those who, for whatever reason, have achieved fame in their lifetime a hold on the attention of future generations. But, as William Goode has pointed out, small differences among a few top performers, none unequivocally superior to the rest, often result in large disparities of acclaim.[3] Just as there are other factors that account for these disparities, so supposedly extraneous influences cause differences in how well a reputation projects to posterity.

Survival in the collective memory is closely tied to the survival of tangible objects that recall the deceased. Legends are built on accounts of a person's feats and achievements, sometimes on nothing more than a document testifying to his or her existence. A picture of the person, whether in stone, on a coin or stamp, or in a drawing or photograph, is a further help; so is having one's name connected with a particular concept, place, gadget, or style. The posthumous reputations of visual artists are more specifically linked to surviving examples of their creations; neither documents testifying to their achievements nor authenticated copies suffice. Nothing can substitute for the originals, for objects wrought by the artist's own hand. Consequently, so runs our argument, what artists do in their lifetime to facilitate the preservation and future identification of their oeuvre has a significant effect on whether, and how well, their names will be known to posterity.

Of course, the survival of these tangible objects is not all-determining. Artists build reputations by working in an accepted genre or style.[4] But tastes change and so do aesthetic standards. Painter-etching was not the only art to fall out of fashion, particularly in a period when innovation in art was being accepted more readily than ever before.[5] Parallel cases can be found in the downgrading of the painters working in the nineteenth-century French academy style or, as previously mentioned, of the "rebellious" Pre-Raphaelites in Britain. In the 1880s, the popularity of pictures by Dante Gabriel Rossetti, Holman Hunt, and John Millais had reached unprecedented heights but then dropped precipitously.[6] Yet the names of some of these artists remain household words. No matter how much their work may fluctuate in value, they survive the passage of time. Today there is renewed interest even in Bouguereau and some of his influential Academy contemporaries. Still others experience the kind of posthumous "rediscovery" so vividly chronicled by Haskell[7] for Botticelli, El Greco, Vermeer, and others brought back to "life" after a long period in which they had been all but forgotten, and even despised, to be thereafter elevated and enshrined as Old Masters. Such rediscovery is greatly facilitated when the conditions for remembering are present.

What accounts for the durability of reputation? Searching for generalizability, we expand our discussion of the British lady-etchers to include both men and women in Britain and America, then go on to consider the conditions for remembering in other fields of endeavor.

We begin by reminding the reader once more of the distinction between two aspects of reputation. Recognition, as we have defined it, resides in the esteem with which peers and other significant "insiders" hold the work of an artist. But achievement of recognition alone does not make an artist famous. There have always been so-called etcher's etchers, much admired by peers, who nevertheless remained "undiscovered." The road to renown, the more cosmopolitan form of recognition, depends on the kind of publicity that only critic and dealer promotion can provide. Only eleven of our etchers ever achieved the kind of celebrity status that should have guaranteed the survival of their works and assured them a place in the pantheon of the truly renowned. All were better known for their painting than their etching: they were Augustus John, Walter Sickert, Laura Knight, and Graham Sutherland among the British, and J. Alden Weir, Mary Cassatt, Arthur B. Davies, John Marin, John Sloan, Raphael Soyer, and Paul Cadmus among the Americans.[8] While all others whose lives we studied had been well recognized as etchers, just one in six had achieved some degree of renown, that is, their names had become established currency outside the more intimate world of fellow artists and a handful of admiring clients.

Where lifetime renown is insufficient to assure the survival of tangible reminders of achievement, on what does the durability of reputation depend? Four things can make a difference:

1. the artist's own efforts, in his or her lifetime, to protect or project his/her own reputation
2. the availability of others who, after the artist's death, have a stake in preserving or giving a boost to that reputation
3. linkages to artistic, literary, or political networks that facilitate entry into the cultural archives

4. symbolic associations with emerging cultural or political identities.

In what follows, we occasionally draw on the very rich biographical source material on the most renowned etchers in order to explicate, or underline, how the posthumous reputations of less well recognized artists are affected. Some factors that sustain the reputations of the renowned may well make the difference between survival and oblivion in the cases of those who—like the forgotten lady-etchers—are less well known.

## Lifetime Initiatives

Artists are mortal and not everyone thirsts for immortality. The chance that artistic success (recognition) will keep a name alive for future generations is enhanced by initiatives taken by the artist during his or her lifetime. Artists can influence their posthumous reputation by making it easier for others to keep them visible when they themselves are no longer in a position to do this for themselves.

Anything that an etcher did to assure the preservation of a cache of works both *sufficient in number* to catch the eye of dealers, collectors, curators, and art historians and *easy enough to locate and identify* contributed to the survival of a reputation. This meant that the artist had to have produced a critical mass of work, kept adequate records to guarantee its proper attribution, and made arrangements for its proper custodianship.

### Artistic Output

With regard to artistic output, one cannot, over the long haul, have too much of a good thing. Before its displacement by photography, printmaking was an effective means for enlarging the easel painter's public. Thus, in his lifetime, Rembrandt's etched work was widely known. Guercino, his Italian contemporary, having seen various of these etchings, assumed "that [Rembrandt's] work in colour is likewise of complete exquisiteness and perfection."[9] Another case in point: the year after Whistler's death, he was—and probably still is—remembered more as an etcher than as a painter. His pictures had seldom been bought nor often been seen in galleries, while his etchings were "scattered in hundreds of homes and exhibitions . . . [and had] gained him the universal admiration and recognition of the world."[10]

What can be fatal is rarity, but rarity is not the same as scarcity in relation to demand. Only the work of a select group recognized as masters—like Jan Vermeer van Delft or Giorgione—appreciates from being almost impossible to obtain. But "there must be many painters comparable to [these two] . . . whose work is rarer still . . . but is not worth anywhere near as much."[11] The few surviving early impressions of Rembrandt etchings seldom come on the market but, if they do, fetch a pretty penny. Yet, according to one study of the art market, it is still "much easier to buy an etching by Rembrandt than by his less distinguished forerunner, Hercules Seghers, and there are far more engravings by Claude than by his fellow Lorrainer, Jacques Bellange."[12] By the same token, when the limited number of plates and small editions by the renowned American painter Edward Hopper are up for sale, they command a high price. A small oeuvre had the opposite effect on Franklin T. Wood, Hopper's less well known contemporary. Though an etcher's etcher, his prints were neither sufficiently publicized nor widely enough distributed to sustain any demand once the etching vogue had passed.

The oeuvre of etchers, like that of other artists, is complete within their lifetime. Therefore, the death of a renowned artist tends to drive up the price of whatever is still available. Sometimes the productive period can be extended, as in the case of Goya, whose plates came into the possession of the Spanish government. Many posthumous editions ("restrikes") have been printed and put on sale, several being of rather indifferent quality. This runs counter to the practice of most modern etchers, who destroy or "cancel" their plates by defacement once an edition is complete and refuse to sign any impression where the printing falls short of their own standards. Plates deteriorate and cannot yield more than a limited number of the brilliant and "authentic" images for which an artist strives. Cancellation prevents possible damage to the artist's reputation through the unauthorized release of inferior impressions. There is, however, no demand for restrikes by any but the most renowned artists. Significant posthumous editions exist for only two etchers in our sample, Weir and Reginald Marsh, neither of whom looked to his prints for income. Both left a significant number of uncanceled plates still capable of yielding impressions. Weir's daughter, a skilled printer, pulled small editions from several dozen plates remaining in his studio.[13] After Marsh's death a collection of thirty plates was donated to the Whitney Museum by his Yale classmate and friend, William Benton, a United States senator. Published in editions of one hundred, these constitute about three-fourths of all impressions ever pulled from Marsh's many plates.[14]

Artists dependent on prints for a livelihood have a strong incentive to provide publishers and dealers with a steady supply. Some may compromise their integrity by turning out pastiches, sentimental kitsch, or whatever the market will take. Yet, as we have pointed out earlier (Chapter 8), the danger to artistic reputation resident in the economic pressure to produce is often exaggerated and its positive side overlooked. Other things being equal, there is much to be gained from developing a clientele and producing an oeuvre for later promotion, acquisition by museums, and preservation by those who treasure it. Contrariwise, the absence of an economic incentive can be counterproductive and sometimes was. Marsh was hardly the only etcher with no need to sell, who rarely printed more than a few impressions for friends, colleagues, and the occasional patron. Nor did those in this "fortunate" position go out of their way to build the kind of relationships that could have worked to their mutual benefit. Enterprise in marketing one's prints not only helped to build a reputation but to sustain it over the years.

## The Existence of Records

The chances for survival are increased when the artist keeps a record that facilitates future identification of his or her work. A specialist on the print world may invest years in searching out all extant prints, in all their states, by a renowned artist but would not spend the energy and time it would take to trace the steps of a "minor" figure who has made it hard to trace them. Etchers generally feel impelled to document their work, making notes on technical details concerning each plate: when and where it was needled, on what kind of ground, the length of time it was in the acid-bath, the strength of the solution and its temperature, the changes and corrections made at each stage, the size of the edition and, if applicable, the number of prints pulled in each state and whether and when the plate was canceled. These notes, when saved, provide a record that is almost a sine qua non when it comes to preparing a catalogue raisonné that signals that the artist deserves to be taken seriously. Arms went even farther: he gave an impression from every one of his 448 plates (in their various states) to his wife in case anything happened to him; collections only somewhat less complete were assembled for each of his two sons and for an artist friend.[15]

Yet for every Arms there was at least one other with evident disdain or no stomach for these clerical tasks—some because they felt too busy, others because they thought their reputations should rest exclusively on the merits of their art. "Account-keeping," as they saw it, was only for would-be profit makers. Some who could not or would not take on this job for themselves were fortunate enough to find others to do it for them. According to the daughter of Thomas Moran, her father's "dislike for writing ... extended also to his correspondence and record-keeping; indeed, he avoided anything that distracted him from his all-consuming passion, the making of pictures."[16] This daughter was his inseparable companion for twenty-seven years after her mother's death, managing all her father's affairs. Other daughters and wives have done no less. "I'm glad that I managed to salvage the etchings themselves," wrote the former wife of B. J. O. Nordfeldt to his widow. "As I told you, Nord was not in the least interested—in fact rather impatient with me for trying to date, catalog and keep them in order—kept saying: 'Why bother?' He used to send off a bunch of prints to dealers without even making a list either for the dealer or himself! After that I always enclosed a list either for the dealer to sign and return, and in at least one case that turned out to be a most fortunate thing."[17] Sometimes a friend or admirer felt called on to take over, as did Russell George Alexander, a journalist and staunch admirer of the etched work of the Cotswold artist, F. L. Griggs.[18] Augustus John, who was most careless about all such matters, turned to Arthur Clifton. Being the manager of the Chenil Gallery, where John first showed his etchings, Clifton naturally had a stake in assuring the success of the exhibition.[19]

Where such records were kept by neither the artist nor by a surrogate, whether son, daughter, or an admirer, the posthumous reputation was at risk. Though Sickert has been judged by at least one curator as one of the most seminal printmakers of the twentieth century, the prints of this otherwise renowned artist are today less well known than they might otherwise be because of his casual attitude toward sales and prices.[20] For him etching was mainly a means for making his images widely available. He insisted on low prices, kept no records, and even balked at embellishing an etching with a signature. He was fortunate insofar as he had an admirer in Harold Wright, who began cataloguing his prints after the artist's death. This effort, though never finished, stirred interest in this neglected aspect of Sickert's work, and he was in any event a sufficiently important (renowned) painter, so-called minor master, and art-politician that he was never in any real danger of being forgotten. Since his death in 1942, there have been two biographies and three books on his career as a painter. The writings on Sickert the painter have sustained interest in his etchings even while they are hard to find. For artists whose reputation rested chiefly on their etchings, a Sickert's selling habits and inattentiveness to record keeping would have been fatal unless, of course, there was someone to keep track.

## Conservation and Distribution

Artists can help preserve their reputations by providing for proper custodianship of their work. Most commonly, etchers present impressions to print rooms in libraries and museums, which improves the likelihood that these will physically survive. But to be archived in a solander box hardly guarantees the visibility of a print. Museums usually favor paintings over etchings (and drawings) in assigning their limited permanent exhibition space, and their etchings are not often displayed. Except when part of a special exhibition, they remain tucked away in print cabinets, available only to the scholar or to the dealer/collector in search of authentication. Still, even when hidden from public view, these etchings remain as reminders of their creator's existence. The reputation of the artist still gets a boost, however slight, when the acquisition is listed in the museum bulletin and perhaps even accompanied by a brief biographical note. Just being in the museum allows the work to endure and the artist to be "discovered" by some future scholar.

Also, the thirty to one hundred fine impressions that the copperplate typically yield makes it relatively easy for the etcher to be generous. Some prints given away to friends and other artists end up in prestigious collections. Moreover, curators who would be fearful of asking a painter to donate a painting are not so hesitant about approaching printmakers. Artists not yet established feel honored by such requests, pleased to know that they were not only acceptable but desired. For others these requests can give rise to a dilemma: Should it get around that they had given away, rather than sold, their prints to a public collection, would this damage their standing? This can be resolved by the subterfuge of attaching as a condition that the donation be recorded as an "anonymous gift." One etcher responded to a curator's request for his prints by directing him to a wealthy patron who owned a large collection of his work and could perhaps be persuaded to donate some to the print room.[21]

The artist's reputation stands to benefit most when the body of work is kept together, thus assuring future identification. Unless the artist is already famous, the dispersal of an estate (or the contents of a studio) by way of the auction block or by consignment for sale deprives prospective researchers of the cache of prints they need to make their effort seem worthwhile. Nor is it likely that anyone will ever again be able to acquire an inventory large enough to guarantee profit to a dealer ready to promote the "forgotten" artist as a unique rediscovery by organizing an exhibition followed by a sale or just holding on to the work and waiting for its time to come.

The etchers we studied varied in the effort they made to get their work into museums and to have it registered as part of the artistic heritage. The octogenarian Frank W. Benson felt that "after years of work devoted to etching and drypoint I find myself with a mess of prints that constitute a record of those years. It consists of singe prints of each plate as it was proved by trials and printed by myself. . . . My intention was to leave a record as a thing of common interest to my children, who were young when the plan was formed. By consultation with them I found that all wished to have the collection preserved in some institution provided with facilities for its preservation and exhibition." With this assurance, Benson put his collection into the archives.[22] Sylvia Gosse, who did so much to keep the name of Sickert alive by acquiring and donating examples of his work to museums, was less careful about conserving her own. Responding in her late years to the inquiry of a curator anxious to build up his Camden Town holdings, she wrote that she had become a "steady reducer of property in her old age" and no longer had any catalogs of her exhibitions and "but a few etchings." After some searching, she uncovered a "rather appalling number" returned to her by Colnaghi's after the death of Harold Wright, head of their print department, but she could remember neither their titles nor dates. She had, she explained, long given up on keeping full records. Asked about one of the etchings, she could do no more than identify it as having been done "about 1917" and ended with the suggestion that the curator "give it any name" he wished.[23]

This attitude was certainly not shared by all women. Katherine Kimball, once a well-recognized but by no means renowned etcher, took the initiative in getting herself into at least one prestigious print collection. Born in 1866, she was nearly seventy when, as an expatriate living in England, she wrote to the curator of graphic arts at the Smithsonian, introducing herself as "an American citizen . . . no longer young . . . at one time a member of several well known art societies [with] work in the permanent collections of several high grade museums." She had "on hand" twelve or fifteen proofs, made when her "eyes were at their best," that might be of interest. Could she send them "on approval" at anywhere from $6 to $15?[24] In response, she was apprised that such purchase would be against the policy of the Smithsonian; she should direct her inquiry to the Library of Congress.

This is how, we believe, some of her architectural and scenic views of French cities which the library acquired by purchase found their way into its print collection. Considering that the etching vogue was all but over, the initial inquiry must have taken a certain amount of self-assurance. Her work can also be found in such public collections as the New York Public Library, the Boston Museum of Fine Art, the British Museum, the Victoria and Albert, and even the Bibliothèque d'Art et d'Archéologie in Paris.

Wills filed by the etchers give clues to just how concerned (or unconcerned) they were to have a hand in their future reputations. Some contain precise instructions for the custodianship of their work.[25] Anna Airy, who died childless, used her will to maintain full control over the distribution of all articles pertaining to her professional career by designating the public galleries where she wanted them to go. The very practical advantages to be gained under some estate laws may have made it easier for tax lawyers and enterprising museum officials to persuade artists to include such provisions in their wills. Considerations of this sort probably carried even more weight with the heirs. Whatever the motive, it made it more likely that a representative collection of prints by the deceased (and sometimes even of their papers and notes) would be archived.

Mainly, etchers in Britain—and, so far as we can determine, in the United States,[26]—left the contents of their studio along with the rest of their property to relatives or friends. Whether these found their way into public archives or were widely dispersed by way of gift giving or sales was entirely up to the heirs. A few artists were quite ready to leave such decisions to persons with a strong financial interest in such residue. Elyse Lord, a reclusive and rich widow when she died in Abingdon near Oxford, was content to leave all her prints and, to this extent, entrust her "fate" to her publisher. Contrast this with the express wish of Joseph Webb. Born in 1908, he came to etching rather late and executed but twenty-four plates (plus five lithographs, seven bookplates, and two Christmas cards) before World War II.[27] Their "imaginative qualities [gave] him high rank in a limited but distinguished class" of connoisseurs.[28] In a will drawn up in 1962, eight months before his death, he stipulated that the sum of £6,000 "be used for exhibiting my graphic work and if possible to exhibit such assembled exhibition in various counties. I desire the reproduction of the most important 'imaginative mystical' painting to be reproduced in full colour and published[,] any sales &/or royalties from these sources to be devoted to the financing of this work." The £6,000 was a significant part of his estate, more than he left to any close relative or friend.

Inheritors in need of (or greedy for) money were tempted to sell quickly and to the highest bidder. As a result, control over the estate often fell into the hands of dealers, who had their own priorities. But even those mindful of their responsibility to perpetuate the memory of the artist often found it difficult to formulate a clear plan for distributing or archiving the etched work. Cecil Leslie, who died in 1980, left everything in her studio to Pauline H. Clarke, her close friend, several of whose books she had illustrated. When a year later, we visited the writer, she had already given a few of Leslie's aquatints to the British Museum. The remainder had been lovingly stored with the rest of Leslie's papers and pictures in Clarke's own studio, in the hope that she might yet be able to arrange a memorial exhibition, perhaps in Cambridge, where she lived, before putting the work up for sale. Financial gain was not a consideration for her. We also found two daughters, justifiably proud of the prints, drawings, and paintings their mothers had produced, similarly at a loss as to how best to make use of them. Each had carefully stored and preserved them in pristine condition for decades. Thus the prints of both Roselle Osk, who lived in Manhattan and later in Long Island, and of Aileen Mary Elliott, who had lived in Southampton and Wokingham in England, had survived but done little to perpetuate the artist's reputation.

Given the survival of a critical mass of fine work, the failure to keep a full record and to arrange for its custodianship does not in itself ordain the eclipse of an artistic reputation, yet these oversights tend to be cumulative in their effect. An artist whose work is scattered and difficult to identify suffers from double neglect. There is no effective demand for etchings by artists whose names are known by only a handful of specialists, about whom there is no biographical information, no catalog, nor even a checklist to serve as a reference to holdings in museums and print rooms. Even when the odd print turns up, it is unlikely to resonate any memories. Since one can hardly tout as a special "rarity" a print by an unknown, it neither commands the price nor stirs the interest it would if by a "known artist."

## Survivors

Once an artist dies, his or her reputation comes to rest irrevocably in other hands. Only a small minority will have achieved the renown and gained a following sufficient to carry them through the ages. The remembrance of most, including artists once well recognized within an esoteric circle of admirers, is highly dependent on survivors with an emotional and/or financial stake in the perpetuation of their reputation. Especially those who made no effort to control their own fates need a helping hand.

Marital and familial status affect the probability that artists will leave behind survivors dedicated to preserving or promoting their reputations. Financially strapped widows with young children will go to some lengths to assemble, possibly at a dealer's urging, what remains of the artist's work and records. When George Bellows died quite unexpectedly at the age of forty-two, just as he was rising to stardom, he left behind a wife and two daughters. The entire capital his widow, Emma, possessed consisted of 600 paintings plus thousands of unsold drawings and lithographs. These she managed carefully. One show, arranged by Bellows himself, had already been due to open. Emma soon saw to it that a major show of the whole series of Bellows's lithographs would be held at Keppel's, which had been the principal outlet for his prints. "Disinclined to let the public become too familiar with [his late work] too soon," she was eminently successful in managing his estate over the years so as to maximize her income from it.[29] Bellows had portrayed his wife as "a beautiful, self-possessed, and slightly imperious woman—attributes which Emma used to good advantage in protecting her husband's artistic interests during the nearly thirty-five years she was to survive him."[30]

Important as the economic incentive may have been, it was not the sole criterion that guided her sales. Bellows's biographer assures us that

> she never sold a picture or a drawing unless she was certain the bearer understood it and would appreciate it. She became a holy terror to museum directors if they hung a Bellows too low or in the wrong light. . . . [She] was determined to publish a photographic record of George's work for all the world to see. In 1927 she had Alfred Knopf and Company reproduce all of George's lithographs, 195 in all, in a handsome, cloth-bound volume. This she followed two years later with a numbered 2000 copy edition of 143 photographs of his paintings. . . . She personally looked to the condition of the canvases and saw to their framing. . . . In 1940, . . . H. V. Allison, who had been Keppel's specialist in the Bellows field . . . set up a gallery of his own; and his son Gordon approached [her] for the privilege of handling the Bellows prints. She graciously consented. . . . Once the gallery was established she made it the display case for the Bellows oils as well. From that time on, H. V. Allison and Co. has

been the sole outlet for the estate of George Bellows, holding a small exhibition almost every year, presenting always a little unfamiliar material and some that is better known.[31]

Her enterprise had much to do with the steady growth in demand and in price for the work of Bellows, who never suffered the eclipse some other famous artists experienced after their deaths.

Being a painter and with his printmaking confined to lithography, Bellows is only marginally associated with the painter-etcher movement. But there are numerous other examples—though few so well documented—of a loving wife, husband, son, daughter, or close companion seeking to create some "monument" by which to honor the memory of an artist who was primarily an etcher. Even if they could not arrange the kind of definitive retrospective mandated for a star like Bellows, they could, as a tribute, collect the prints (and other works), perhaps to offer them to a museum where they would, hopefully, be preserved and made available for study.

After H. J. Stuart Brown, an amateur etcher with high recognition, died in 1941, his daughter took "the first opportunity" to write Harold Wright what she hoped was

> an intelligent letter on the subject of Daddy's etchings etc. . . . Prints and plates of my father's are, of course, being stored together as you suggest. His 'Private Collection,' I shall certainly keep intact in the meantime and, as you suggest, in the end, I should like to give it, in the memory of him to some Museum, where his work would be appreciated. It will never be broken up I can assure you—and I will arrange, if anything untoward should happen to me, that you are got in touch with at once—to see (if you wouldn't mind) that all this is carried out.[32]

Since Brown, though eligible for inclusion, was not chosen into our sample, we have not searched down the final destination of his collection. Guichard believes that a Brown etching deserves a place "in every collection of British etchings," but this is precluded by their scarcity.[33] Despite an article and catalog in the *Print Collector's Quarterly*, he is among those less remembered today.

Several survivors did what they could to expedite the cataloguing of their husbands' etched oeuvre. Some went to even greater lengths. In a beautiful volume, Theresa Bernstein, then ninety and herself a painter (and etcher) of some note, attempted a "summing up" of the life and work of her husband, William Meyerowitz, who had died a few years before at age ninety-four.[34] Survivors like Bernstein, who are themselves artists, are best positioned to help the reputation of the deceased. Clement Haupers, the lifelong intimate friend and artistic companion of Clara Mairs, helped prepare the catalog for the memorial exhibition her friends and collectors sponsored at the Minnesota Museum of Art. During the forty-two years they lived together, he had worked closely with her, assisting in the production and printing of much of her output.[35] And during the two decades in which he survived her, he continued to help; he culled and arranged for the archiving of their papers now readily available in four microfilm reels from the Minnesota Historical Society.[36]

Where there is no immediate close family, more distant relatives or a circle of friends and admirers may take on the commemorative task. Such was the case for two popular American bachelors born in the 1860s, "Pop" Hart and Alexander Shilling. They traveled widely— Hart to the South Seas and Mexico, Shilling mostly to the Low Countries and Europe. They were successful enough with their art to support a modest life-style, selling their work when in need of money for whatever it fetched. Shilling paid with etchings for dental services, and it would not have been out of character for Hart to have done the same. We can be sure that neither gave a hoot about keeping a record. But both were personally popular, and their numerous friends went out of their way to memorialize them.

When Shilling died, members of the Salmagundi Club in New York, where he had been a popular figure, arranged for a privately printed memorial volume. *The Book of Alexander Shilling* contained essays of appreciation and personal reminiscences together with illustrations of a representative selection of his paintings and etched work.[37] The only other listing, equally incomplete, is of thirty-nine etchings in *American Prints in the Library of Congress*.[38] Likewise, Hart's numerous admirers helped arrange for memorial exhibitions and for significant purchases of his prints by the Library of Congress. But it was the "strong devotion" of a niece who befriended the aging Hart that "preserved his art for posterity" when, decades later, she presented some of his watercolors, along with papers she found scattered around his cottage, to the Library of Congress and then willed to the Zimmerli Art Museum in New Brunswick, New Jersey, some 5,000 watercolors, drawings, prints, and paintings that served as the basis for a book to bring Hart "back to life."[39]

The likelihood that there will be survivors with a financial or emotional stake in the perpetuation of a deceased artist's reputation is further affected by longevity. While those who, like so many of the British lady-etchers, enjoy a long life may have more time for achievement, others struck down on the verge of a promising career—in a tragic accident, as a suicide, as the result of incurable disease, as a wartime casualty—may be better remembered than they might have been had they lived out their full lives. They are more apt to leave behind bereaved mothers and needy spouses with dependent children; they also leave people in their art world who, aware that life can be unfair, feel the need for some kind of memorial to mark the artist's departure, even if the oeuvre is not, by the usual measures, that extraordinary. It is unlikely, for example, that anyone would still take note of the British etcher, Percy Gethin, had he not died, just a few days before his forty-second birthday, in the Battle of the Somme. *The Times* printed both an obituary and a personal tribute to this artist "of great promise," even though his work, of which there was only a modest amount, had not been widely exhibited. Gethin's widowed mother, determined to keep alive the memory of her son, secured the assistance of his friends. Nine years after his death, there appeared a book on Burgundy and Morvan, written by a collector and illustrated with Gethin's etchings.[40] Another year later there followed a well-promoted printing of forty impressions from four of Gethin's surviving plates, of which, like most of his work, there existed only a few impressions. The project was publicized through an article in the *Print Collector's Quarterly*.[41] The result was something less than a boom for Gethin etchings, and the prints by him that have turned up recently still bring only modest prices. There simply are not enough of them. No one will ever know what Gethin might have produced had he lived, but at least there is documentation of the work he did produce, with several examples having found their way into major print rooms. Guichard devotes twenty lines to Gethin, while the names of the once better known, such as the long-lived Bolingbroke, are simply listed along with those of some 1,000 other etchers.[42]

Longevity does not inevitably work to the detriment of a reputation. A few of the younger etchers lived long enough to be given a "second chance" by the recent (late 1970s) renewal of interest in prints from the revival period. This was true of Robin Tanner, born in 1904, who, after the market collapse, abandoned etching for a more secure teaching career. Having issued only eight plates by 1930, he finished just six more over the next sixteen years, then stopped etching until 1970. A careful worker, he never canceled or destroyed a plate, preferring to use it as long as it would "yield perfect impressions."[43] Then, encouraged and promoted by Robin Garton, a London dealer in prints, he began issuing impressions from new plates as well as from some earlier ones that were still in prime condition and followed this with a catalogue raisonné. Even though Tanner's etchings had been well received in the twenties, it is doubtful that his early output would have been sufficient in quantity to sustain his reputation without this stimulus. Thus, the new flurry of interest in this genre has flushed out not only surviving prints but also a few surviving etchers.[44]

## Linkages in Memory

To advance our argument: the durability of reputation is linked to the artist's leaving behind both a sizable, accessible, and identifiable oeuvre and persons with a stake in its preservation and promotion. What momentum these provide will be reinforced by the artist's proximity to an institutional system for archiving. This can be seen most clearly in the case of established painters advantageously positioned by reason of their association with some school or period or region. Both curators and collectors will seek to acquire not only their oils but their drawings and prints as well. More generally, any linkage to important artistic and literary circles or to a political and cultural elite adds to the artist's posthumous visibility. Such links can go some way toward making up for a dearth of more tangible reminders of lifetime accomplishments.

### The Satellite Effect

"Major" artists typically serve as symbolic markers for art historians, curators, and cataloguers. Some of the glow from the luminaries then falls on the lesser figures within their orbit. To be identified as someone's student or someone's follower can be an obstacle in *building* a reputation but in the long run converts into a plus. Directly, the association adds to the artist's credentials;[45] to the master's it adds even more, since influence is demonstrated through one's artistic progeny. Indirectly, some unknown or less well known followers gain visibility from the association. Printmakers, too, are often lumped into groups according to style or because they worked in the same place at the same time; for example, "The Stamp of Whistler" was an exhibition organized to document his influence as a graphic artist.[46] Included in it—along with prints by such leading figures as Manet and Pissarro, Legros and Wilson Steer, Hassam and Twachtman—were some all but forgotten etchers.

One of these "forgottens" was George C. Aid, born in 1872 in Quincy, Illinois, who had studied at the School of Fine Arts in nearby St. Louis and then, after working as a staff artist for two local newspapers, had gone off to Paris for study at the Académie Julien, as had so many aspiring American artists of his day. In Paris, he had some considerable success both as a painter and etcher, being one of only twenty-five Americans whose work was illustrated in the special 1902 issue of *The Studio* on modern etching and engraving. He also earned an honorable mention in the Salon des artistes français and a silver medal at the Louisiana Purchase exhibition in St. Louis. In 1906, he was given a special showing in Paris, along with two other Americans, and while yet a resident of that city linked up with Albert Roullier of Chicago, who became his American agent. Just before the Great War, Charles DeKay described him as an "artist of note who made a sensation a few years ago with etchings conceived and carried out on a magnificent scale."[47] To some extent, his reputation was a casualty of the war. Due to its disruptions, only a few of the paintings through which he had established his reputation in Europe ever made their way to America, so that in the long run the reputation he had acquired as a painter did little to enhance interest in his etchings once the fashion had passed. More than sixty years after the war, Aid's skillfully executed depictions of quaint buildings, streets, bridges, and harbors were reintroduced to the public as a "more detailed and careful variant of Whistler's vignetted scenes." Even then, the carefully documented "Stamp of Whistler" catalog only revealed the neglect into which Aid's work had fallen. His one etching in the show is identified as having "been completed by 1910 when [it] was given to the Toledo Museum"; yet this etching *Rotterdam*, so listed in a 1914 catalog of an Aid exhibition, is the same as the one in *The Studio*, which pinpoints the date as 1901 or 1902. Without this tie-in to Whistler, it is to be doubted that Aid's work would ever again have seen even this much light of day.

Another whose memory received a mild boost through her associations with Whistler is Elizabeth Adela Armstrong, better known as Mrs. Stanhope Forbes, who "made no irresistible bid for fame, nor sought with any perspicacity a market for herself, being content with a proof or two from her exquisite plates."[48] A painter and watercolorist, she is mostly remembered in connection with her husband, a Royal Academician and founder of the Newlyn School of Artists, which she helped him to put on the map late in the nineteenth century. A personal friend of the couple published a joint biography, still not impossible to get a hold of.[49] It includes a long letter in which the artist recounts her life before she settled in Cornwall. Then, a decade after Elizabeth's premature death in 1912, her husband presented a collection of her drypoints to the Victoria and Albert as a lasting and suitable memorial to the artist. This presentation became the occasion for a write-up in the *Print Collector's Quarterly* and, together with the biography, made her a likely candidate for rediscovery. She was included in the Whistler exhibition although she may never have met the master—or, if she did, it was only after she had given up etching. The link came through Mortimer Menpes, a Whistler pupil who printed for Forbes. Her first experimental plate, a study of heads, made use of a figure from Whistler's *Speke Hall*, which she could only have copied while working with Menpes.[50] In 1981, the Friends of the Newlyn Art Galleries gave her (and her husband) a major retrospective. In order to raise money for the local museum, they used the occasion to sell a recently discovered cache of her rare etchings, turned over to them by a great-niece who had treasured them enough to assure their survival. The question: without the Newlyn School or the Whistler connection, would there still have been interest in her prints near a century later? And would the purchasers have been willing to pay the £30 to £90 they were being charged?

The future reputation of Katherine Cameron likewise rests to a large degree in the hands of the "Glasgow Boys," that avant-garde circle of painters which formed around Charles Rennie Mackintosh in the 1890s. Her standing as an artist is bound to rise or fall as the reputation of his circle—now on a swift ascent—is adjusted. When she died at ninety-four, the obituary in *The Times* remembered her as "one of the last survivors of the first generation of Glasgow artists to study under Francis H. Newbery [at the School of Art] . . . and put Glasgow with its own cool elegant brand of art nouveau on the map of the art world around 1900."[51]

*Elite Connections*

Proximity to some elite, whether through family or the artist's own achievement, provides the cultural capital and connections that clear the road to lasting renown.[52] First of all, it helps to have a close relative who is a famous artist. One cannot easily separate the enduring visibility of Orovida Pissarro, a creative and truly experimental etcher, from that of her father, Lucien, and her eminent grandfather, Camille. Signing herself "Orovida" did not keep critics from reminding the public that she was indeed a Pissarro. In 1943 she participated in an exhibition of "Three Generations of the Pissarro Family"; after her death, Leicester Gallery held another by the same title. Her original, craftsmanlike, modern decorative prints would have earned her a fine reputation regardless of such connections but would not likely have drawn as much attention. In 1921, when she was just twenty-eight and had been etching for only seven years, four of her prints were sold in a New York auction of master etchers, though not, of course, at the same price as the Whistlers, Meryons, and Zorns.[53] That same year Weyhe also gave her a joint exhibition with Marie Laurencin, the celebrated French artist, while Campbell Dodgson, who had become a consistent patron, saw to it that impressions of her prints went to the British Museum.

The names of some artists will be remembered nearly always in association with that of a better-known family member. To avoid being overshadowed by the more illustrious artists with whom they were associated, some changed their names. Orovida simply dropped hers. But the survival power of a reputation will nonetheless be enhanced rather than diminished by the association the name suggests.

Beyond the artistic connection, anyone closely related to persons of eminence is apt to leave traces in the papers of their famous relatives. Some clues to the personal history of the reticent Stephen Parrish, the Philadelphia etcher and father of the renowned illustrator Maxfield Parrish, turn up in the history of this distinguished Quaker family and in reminiscences of his son. Sylvia Gosse turns up in books by and about her family. So does Gwen Raverat, granddaughter of Charles Darwin; she is also the author of a delightful book about her childhood that was a bestseller on both sides of the Atlantic.[54] In addition, in the years before the Great War Raverat became part of a circle that centered around Rupert Brooke, the poet who became a national cult figure when he died as a soldier in a "corner in a foreign land" far from England. Bonded together by their rebellion against Victorian stuffiness, the group included Eric Gill, the writer and illustrator; Virginia Woolf and others of the Bloomsbury Group; both the Keynes brothers—John Maynard and Geoffrey; along with Jacques Raverat, the young Frenchman whom Gwen Darwin eventually married. There are glimpses of her in the voluminous correspondence of this group, much of it archived, much of it the material used by biographers.[55]

The greatest posthumous advantage comes from a tie-in to a literary circle like the Bloomsbury Group, where artists and writers cross paths. Writers have always functioned as articulate spokespersons for other arts. Etching and the unrecognized genius of Charles Meryon, it will be remembered, were first publicized by Baudelaire, the poet-critic. The artistic-literary connection is best exemplified by Marcellin Desboutins, who also wrote plays and was a major figure on the cultural landscape of nineteenth-century France. Across the Channel, Sir William Rothenstein conducted a thirty-year correspondence with Rabindranath Tagore, published in 1972, whose work he had sought to publicize before this Indian poet won the Nobel prize.[56] Also, William Butler Yeats, Thomas Hardy, Ezra Pound, John Jay Chapman, and numerous other literary figures were among Rothenstein's friends, all of whom appear in the fascinating three volumes of his reminiscences.[57] Sickert, a gifted writer himself, was on close terms with Osbert Sitwell. A volume of his art criticism, edited by Sitwell together with a long introduction, appeared five years after Sickert died.[58] Evidence of the long friendship of Bone with Hugh Walpole, the novelist and collector, is preserved mostly in their correspondence, which documents how much Walpole did to spread the word about Bone.[59]

Men, it should be clear, had an advantage but not a monopoly with regard to elite connections. Clare Leighton, in both her lives—one in England, one in America—was tied into literary circles through friendship. She herself was a minor literary figure, much as were Sickert and Rothenstein. Her writings reveal some of the turning points in her life subsequent to the events she recounted in her childhood reminiscences. We have been told that, in her old age, she was writing an autobiography. More to the point is that her literary acquaintances have included her in their own reminiscences. In the early 1920s, Leighton fell in with two Oxford graduates, both feminists and pacifist activists, who introduced her into the intellectual and literary circles of London. One was Vera Brittain, author of *Testament of Youth*, an autobiography that amounted to a powerful condemnation of war. Much of it revolves around Clare's brother, an aspiring poet and Brittain's fiancé, who was killed in France half an hour before he was due to begin his Christmas leave and marry Vera, but Clare also appears in it. First published in 1933, the book had a second life during the Vietnam conflict, first as a series on British television, then on PBS *Masterpiece Theater*, followed by a new paperback edition. Leighton is also featured in the edited letters of Winifred Holtby, the novelist who was the other member of the literary pair.[60] Holtby played an important part in launching Leighton's career by having her illustrate what became Holtby's two best-known novels as well as stories she wrote for the *New Leader*.[61] Leighton's literary circle also included Henry Noel Brailsford, a political journalist, to whom she was once married. Still, the endurance of her reputation, in Britain and then in America after her emigration, is largely due to her own efforts—her prodigious output of high quality wood engravings, the fourteen books she wrote and the forty-nine she illustrated, as well as her formidable skill in publicizing herself and her work. Beyond this, and as long as her two literary friends remain cult figures, her persona will live, albeit as only a minor figure, in the feminist movement.

In the United States artistic-literary networks were more loosely knit. One finds them in New York, of course; yet, on the whole, printmakers tended to move within their own circles and colonies. Conspicuous among these was the short-lived association between writers and artists in Provincetown during the First World War. The colony included the playwright Eugene O'Neill, Mabel Dodge Luhan, and John Reed along with several artists in our sample associated for a time with the Provincetown Printers, namely B. J. O. Nordfeldt, Marguerite Zorach, Margaret Patterson, and Maud Squire.[62] They joined in the production of plays, with the artists contributing the scenery. Some artists developed more lasting relationships with literary notables. Philip Kappel's friendship with John P. Marquand, which endured for twenty-five years, began with the artist showing the novelist some plates he had made. Kappel illustrated two of Marquand's *Timothy Dexter* books, and Marquand, by then a best-selling novelist, contributed an introduction to Kappel's own *Jamaica Gallery*. Kyra Markham as a young art student, torn between becoming an actress or going into art, had first lived with Floyd Dell, a Chicago writer, and then for several years with Theodore Dreiser. She "appears" as Sidonie in the novel *This Madness* but stars as herself in Dreiser's diaries during the years they spent together.[63]

One of the more intriguing cases is that of Marion Greenwood, a lithographer and a muralist of some distinction, about whom biographical facts, beyond the standard listings, were hard to come by. But then, quite unexpectedly, she showed up as a central figure in the biography of Josephine Herbst by Elinor Langer.[64] Herbst, a young radical in the 1930s, had once been regarded as one of the most important "women writers" in America but had since been largely forgotten. In seeking to unravel the mystery of Herbst's disappearance, the biography also introduces us to the persona of Greenwood. Both the linkage and information improve her chances for rediscovery.

## Figures in a Landscape

Any symbolic association that makes an artist stand out from the crowd boosts a posthumous reputation. The connection may be no more than fortuitous and a function, so to speak, of proximity. Or it may be that a part of the art public perceives a congruence between some relevant aspect of its own identity and the characteristics it ascribes to the artist. Such ideological congruence also fosters "rediscovery" as long as other conditions for remembering are met.

### Highlighting

Geographical location or historical coincidence can draw attention to artists living and dead. Sometimes, as in the case of portraitists, both function together insofar as a portrait that preserves for posterity the image of a famous person also adds to the visibility of the portraitist, all the more so when the portrait exists in multiples. In this sense, there exists a symbiotic relationship between artist and sitter similar to that between illustrator and author. Assumedly, there will be a continuing demand for some portraits by Walter Tittle, who burst on the scene with a portfolio of prints of the major players in the 1922 Disarmament Conference and later etched such literary giants as Joseph Conrad, Rudyard Kipling, and George Bernard Shaw. Portrait prints of famous persons usually attract more attention and command higher prices than others of equal quality by the same artist.

It matters little whether the sitter is satisfied. In fact, the rejection of a portrait by a distinguished subject can augment a reputation even if not exactly in ways the artist may wish. This happened to the painted portraits of two of our etchers. Graham Sutherland had to stand by while Lady Churchill destroyed his commemorative portrait of Sir Winston, commissioned by the House of Commons. When *The Times* front-paged the story, Sutherland, at least for a few days, achieved the celebrity status that three decades of artistic production had never yielded. Peter Hurd's name became a household word during a dispute over his commissioned portrait of Lyndon Johnson. The sitter, displeased, called it "the ugliest thing I ever saw."[65] Such controversies serve the press as pegs on which to hang references to the artist's name.

Similarly, when the carousing sailors painted by thirty-year-old Paul Cadmus for the Public Works Art Project roused the wrath of Navy officials, the controversy brought notoriety and overnight fame to the struggling young artist. Cadmus had previously made some drypoints and etchings. Informed by journalists that the Navy planned to scuttle *The Fleet's In*, he declared that "they can tear up my canvas, but they'll have a sweet time eating copper."[66] So incensed was the artist by this move to eradicate his picture that he was determined to preserve the image in an an etched plate and made it the first of an ambitious series of etchings, each after an already completed painting. While the controversial mural, though never deliberately destroyed, was long hidden, there was so great a demand for the etching based on it, printed in an edition of fifty, that Cadmus himself no longer owned an impression, and a copy of it hardly ever appears on the market. Today the etching is never exhibited without some reference to the controversy. The notoriety from this incident certainly helped draw attention to other very considerable achievements by this artist. His reputation rests more directly on his paintings and is further supported by links to the New York cultural establishment. Both parents were artists, his brother-in-law director of the New York ballet, and he counted among his friends W. H. Auden and E. M. Forster. His life and work have been recorded in a book and a Ph.D. dissertation.[67] He has had exhibitions in several museums. Still alive in 1986, he was able to appear in a television documentary.

Symbolic associations can also be based on origin. For example, an artist who lacks national renown can still be designated a region's most conspicuous contributor to the national scene or celebrated as the representative of a particular ethos or culture. Small museums, partly by necessity, will self-consciously capitalize on their locale as a source of artistic inspiration. What better way than to "rediscover" the role a local artist played in a prominent art movement? Artists bypassed by Paris, London, or New York museums and galleries in their competition for blockbuster exhibitions can be elevated to stardom in smaller places. In this way Tacoma-born Thomas Handforth, an illustrator of children's books with some recognition but limited renown as an etcher, is featured as the greatest artist of the West Coast port he left as a young man; its public library has a Handforth Room and a collection of his prints, some of them on permanent display. Similarly, special exhibitions of prints by Elizabeth O'Neill Verner, a local etcher who died in 1979, can still be seen regularly in Charleston, South Carolina. Her studio, carefully restored by her daughter, is a stop on a historical walking tour.

Recorders of the past, like the portraitists of the famous, are favored when it comes to name recognition. They become associated with the nostalgia they depict. Seldom have etchers been commissioned to record historical moments, yet Maxime Lalanne in France and Muirhead Bone in England are remembered partly for their etchings of urban demolition; the New York scenes that C. F. W. Mielatz and Charles H. White etched early in this century are now being treasured as a record of a bygone era and, in the process, attention is drawn to their names. The Great War has served a similar function for others. In the 1930s, as memories of it gained a new salience, relevant prints of both Percy Smith and Kerr Eby were included in books that articulated the growing revulsion against the earlier slaughter.[68] The peace movement may yet bring them and other war etchers a third life.

*Ideological Congruence*

The fluctuating importance of feminism and antiwar sentiment touches on the phenomenon of ideological congruence: those whose art can be made to serve a broader cause, such as defining an emerging identity or dramatizing new aspirations, are more likely to be granted a prominent place in the collective memory.[69] This hinges to some extent on their ability to depict broad themes, like injustice and suffering, or to encapsulate human foibles in ways that catch people's fancy, as did Honoré Daumier and Théophile Steinlen, two French printmakers, who are remembered today more because of the wide exposure given their political statements—Daumier's satirical depictions of the bourgeoisie, Steinlen's sympathetic portrayals of the poor—than for their extraordinary artistic achievements. They really had no confreres among the nineteenth-century British. Although William Strang was a socialist, his art was less openly political. He and other British etchers were more inclined to express their social concerns by embracing the aestheticism of a William Morris, which retains a certain appeal but has not been appropriated by any current political movement.

Many American printmakers saw their art related to the cause of the dispossessed. John Sloan, Glenn Coleman, William Gropper, Adolf Dehn, Louis Lozowick, and others are remembered in part, though by no means solely, for their contributions to the magazine, *Masses*, and its successor, *New Masses*.[70] Furthermore, their printmaking activity, more often than that of the British, extended into the depression. A good number of them, including some women, became involved in the social and political struggles of the 1930s. Mabel Dwight, Minna Citron, and Elizabeth Olds abandoned the usual pretty scenes in favor of bread lines, industrial strikes, and other symptoms of economic malaise; Irwin Hoffman, Reginald Marsh, and Raphael Soyer graphically portrayed the homeless in soup kitchens and missions, warming their hands over sidewalk grates. Examples of this "socially conscious" art were assembled by the American Artists' Congress in a nationwide exhibition of duplicate exhibits of one hundred prints. In line with its stated purpose of bringing "art to the people," these prints were sold cheaply. Many of the exhibitors were little known at the time; few ever made much of a reputation for themselves. But as personal memories of these times recede, interest in these prints, with their stirring images of a troubled past, is reviving. The volume of reproductions from that exhibition has been reprinted, and some of the almost forgotten artists are to that extent being "resurrected."[71]

A still more telling illustration of how artists long dead may be captured to serve as symbols of an emerging cultural identity is the resolute effort to identify and catalog women artists. Ideological motivations that fasten on gender have given some nearly forgotten women etchers a "new life." Feminism has been the force behind the growing effort to document their rightful place in history. Exhibits of forgotten women have become popular. Yet it is the conditions for remembering, as set forth in this chapter, that will determine who among the women artists becomes a candidate for resurrection.

## The Survival of Reputation

Entry into the collective memory is subject to the selectivity necessitated by the limits of space. Some artists stand out from among the rest despite small differences in actual or imputed achievements. The many "runners-up" can be dismissed as simply not important enough to merit our attention.[72] In a statement that echoes Burckhardt, Herbert Read holds that "the qualities in [a work of art] that survive the ideas and aspirations of a particular age to appeal to the aesthetic faculties of succeeding ages ... are to be regarded as primarily the creation of individuals endowed with exceptional skill or sensibility."[73] But undiscovered talent abounds in examples of misplaced temperaments. There may simply be more geniuses than we can possibly recognize.[74] And, once overlooked, posterity will never know—except in the rarest of circumstances—to whom to attribute their works should these be later unearthed. This has been the fate of many folk artists, whose names were never attached to works that, at the time, were not considered to have artistic value.[75] Some painter-etchers have fared no better. Without contesting the validity of aesthetic criteria for judging art and its creators, we have chosen to focus on the social processes that mediate between the qualities said to inhere in the object and the response of the art public.

We note in passing that the very conception of "genius" as the possession of extraordinary gifts is itself a historical product and amenable to sociological analysis.[76] There is an extensive literature, psychological and anthropological, that suggests what in one setting is defined as charismatic can from another perspective be analyzed as pathological. This applies even to unique renderings of reality, long praised as signs of artistic genius, that are now attributed to physiological impairment. The peculiar distortions in El Greco's paintings suggest astigmatism; the style of Cézanne's paintings is shown to be consistent with his near-sightedness. And the mystery that we read into the late styles of Rembrandt and of Turner suggests ophthalmic deficiencies associated with age: the fuzziness and breadth in Rembrandt's late portraits may be due to the reduced refractive power of aging eyes; the increased blurring and dominance of red and orange in Turner, to the progress of a cataract. These existential influences are of little interest to admirers.[77]

Works of art, even those that survive, do not speak for themselves; someone has to speak for them—if not the artists themselves, then at least some effective surrogate. In addition, as our investigation of etchers suggests, the posthumous reputations of artists are significantly affected by what is known about their personae. Are reputations in other sectors of culture production subject to similar influences? The question is worth pondering.

Name recognition certainly means a great deal in literature, where new authors have more difficulty getting their work recognized than those whose names are already known to the publishing world. Coser, Kadushin, and Powell note that no more than about 1 percent of all first novels in the United States get published;[78] novels submitted by authors with one or more successful books in print fare far better. When Doris Lessing, a contemporary author with a large following, used a pseudonym in publishing two modest but very well written naturalistic novels, no one paid them much attention. There were few reviews and they quickly disappeared from bookstores. Reissued not long after as *The Diaries of Jane Sommers* by Lessing, they immediately made news.[79]

The pattern exemplified by the current literary celebrity system is certainly not new. As an "experiment," Anthony Trollope wrote two stories in which he tried to disguise his style. Although he heard them favorably mentioned by readers, as a "new" author he "had no real success. . . . Another ten years of unpaid unflagging labour might have built up a second reputation," he concluded. "But this at any rate did seem clear to me, that with all the increased advantages which practice in my art must have given me, I could not induce English readers to read what I gave them, unless I gave it with my name."[80]

Once a creative artist has gained renown, the name attached to his or her work functions much like a brand label. The imprimatur of the creator, living or dead, validates the quality, value, and—where relevant—the price of the work. Even with old wine, stored until its taste has begun to deteriorate, one can still relish the label. So, too, the celebrity status of authors long gone directs attention to work that otherwise would be of little interest. Writing some decades after the death of Samuel Johnson, who had once dominated the London intellectual scene, Macauley observed that while "the memory of other authors is kept alive by their works, it is the memory of Samuel Johnson that keeps many of his works alive."[81]

The advantages of an author's favorable entry into the memory process tend to be cumulative. Johnson had his Boswell. More generally, literary pacesetters whose names once were household words continue to provide a frame for judging work even after they are long gone and the style in which they wrote has been superseded. Not only is the hierarchy, once established, maintained over time with only some modification; it more or less replicates the hierarchy one finds among academics and literary historians.[82] Anyone not in the mainstream will be left out, a condition that has deleted many women from the ranks of great writers.[83]

Today's listeners are no less captives of musical history. The music critic of the *New York Times* opined a few years ago that we had reached a stage in Western culture "where it would not be possible for music by an unknown composer to be accepted as great art."[84] Among the musical pieces that disappeared from concerts and are no longer recorded, for no other reason than the emerging consensus among scholars that they had been falsely attributed, are the *Jena* Symphony supposedly by Beethoven, the *Toy* Symphony by Haydn, and the *Wiegenlied* by Mozart. The art market, too, operates on the assumption that there can be "no such thing as a masterpiece by a painter who is not currently dubbed as a great master."[85] Surely this edict, attributed to a Paris-based dealer in nineteenth-century French art, puts a severe restriction on the number of works deserving of our admiration. Competition for those so designated is keen. As for the rest, they are consigned to the margins until the seemingly insatiable demand stimulates the kind of discovery—or rediscovery—that enhances their value. Similar to the notion of master is the notion of *auteur*, namely a director accepted as a creative artist. The label lifts his films out of the commercial cinema and makes him a natural candidate for retrospectives.[86]

It is the writers who function as the articulate spokespersons for other arts. As Charles Horton Cooley observed, "other and non-literary sorts of fame are certain and enduring very much in proportion as they interest the literary class. The latter, being artists or critics of art, have a natural predilection for other arts as well as their own, and cherish the fame of painters, sculptors, actors, and musicians."[87] A tie-in to any such circle is a tremendous advantage. Just think for a moment of the part Leo and Gertrude Stein played in promoting the fame of artists who aroused their enthusiasm. Their virtually open house was frequented, among others, by such influential English critics as Roger Fry, Clive Bell, C. Lewis Hind, and Frank Rutter. "Hardly any American artist or writer who went to Paris, which was becoming increasingly popular among the American avant-garde, failed to visit them."[88] The influence of their collection on other collectors snowballed. The names of Cézanne, Matisse, Picasso, and other of their favorites got around. The rapid ascendancy of Jackson Pollock during a later period has likewise been attributed to the activities of a small and especially influential social network who "committed themselves to bringing about [his] artistic success *before* he had even begun to paint the pictures which brought him fame; and that the activities of Pollock's influential promoters forced other uncommitted actors to 'take his work seriously' . . . [until it] became part of taken-for-granted art knowledge."[89] The case, while perhaps extreme, indicates the extent to which renown is based more on what Liah Greenfeld would describe as charismatic qualities than on the creator's rational adaptation to public demand.[90]

Posthumous reputations are closely linked to the preservation of tangible reminders of artists' lives and their achievements. Not everything is preserved. The chances of survival are improved where a large number of copies exist in a durable medium and are valued by contemporaries. When it comes to quantity, printmakers have a certain advantage over other artists. The survival prospects of work by productive etchers with access to market channels are good, even though an image on paper is more vulnerable than one chiseled in stone or painted on a wall or canvas. But number and distribution do not assure the preservation (and identification) of the requisite oeuvre unless some value attaches to it. Thus, of the hundreds of copies of the *New England Primer* printed in the colonies before 1727, not one has ever been located because, unlike family Bibles from the same period, they were not treasured as heirlooms.[91] Although the initial impetus to preservation may come from a bereaved widow or loving daughter moved by her loss to assemble the creations, papers, and other ephemera of a deceased, this is no more than a first step. There must be others who share this interest. What obviously matters most in the long run is the proximity of the deceased to institutions with organized arrangements for the archiving and restoration of the historical evidence. This is also the conclusion of Gilbert Shapiro and his collaborators from their study of which of the parish *cahiers* of 1789 survived.[92] Particularly those who enjoyed power and esteem in their lifetime are also more likely to have had friends with influence and connections to archives.

Not long ago at the Frick Collection in New York there was an exhibition of works by a once "celebrated unknown." François-Marius Granet was a painter of oils, a watercolorist, the foremost art official in Paris, and the author of a small autobiography. Many of his larger paintings were destroyed in the 1848 uprisings in Paris; the abolition of his office put an end to his fame. He died in 1849, leaving boxes with hundreds of watercolors. Two things that kept his name alive were a fine portrait of Granet by Ingres and a museum in Aix-en-Provence that bears his name. Not until 1947 did any scholar dig into the residues of his life and career. The recent exhibition, his first in America and slated to travel, consisted of sixty watercolors, all in excellent condition after 150 years in the protective darkness of their boxes.[93] Without them, Granet could hardly have survived as an artist even to the limited extent that he did.

As to what it is that has to survive, there is in the visual arts no substitute for the original—as there may be in the literary and performing arts. Pictures are valued not just for what they portray but for the authentic touch of the artist, believed to be irretrievably lost in any copy, no matter how difficult it is for the naked eye to detect the difference; it is equally lacking in a fake, even one so expertly done that it has required a new technology to cast doubt on its genuineness. Pictures are what Nelson Goodman calls "autographic." The aesthetic properties of a picture, he holds, "include not only those found by looking at it but also those that determine how it is to be looked at."[94] This does not hold for other "allographic" arts, the record of which is preserved in notations that must first be translated into words or sound before their meaning can be assimilated. In these cases, the original manuscript is of no interest, except perhaps as a source document. Certainly, no one would claim that the appeal and "value" of a literary work was diminished when printed in a large edition on poor paper and weakly bound—even if the edition is pirated. Or, as Goodman puts it, "Haydn's manuscript [of the *London Symphony*] is no more genuine an instance of the score than is a printed copy off the press this morning. . . . Copies of the score may vary in accuracy, but all accurate copies, even if forgeries of Haydn's manuscript, are equally genuine instances of the score."[95] In principle, a single legible copy available for duplication suffices to sustain the reputation of a writer or musician; a theatrical script or a musical still needs, of course, to be realized in the interpretations of performers.

In music, especially, much original material has been lost simply because certain commercial productions were considered ephemeral. For many years, no scores or parts for George Gershwin's *Of Thee I Sing*, the first musical to win a Pulitzer prize, were known to exist. Then a project was launched by the National Institute for Music Theater to recover for the archives what might yet be salvaged of performance materials from old Broadway musicals, and the score turned up. In England, it took the tireless efforts of a son, himself a theatrical agent, to revive the frolicsome musical, *Me and My Girl*, by Noel Gay, one of the great names in his heyday. In the 1930s this London show had had a record run of 1,646 performances.[96]

Given that the work, or at least an acceptable notational statement, has been preserved, the collective memory is further influenced by the means available for dissemination. In the past, the more enterprising painters relied on engravers to copy their work and make it known to a larger public. But these engravings were not duplications of the original work, the way any copy of a literary text is, but generalized, abstract reports about iconography and composition in another medium.[97] The autographic character of the original is lost because the engraver cannot render accurately the surface, the brushstrokes, and the nuances of shading and color through which the personality of the artist is revealed. Moreover, each reproductive medium has its own bias. As the color print (or slide) takes over as the preferred reminder of images in paintings, the visibility of artists who paint in flat tones that lend themselves to reproduction in greater verisimilitude will increase.[98]

Similar factors affect reputations in the performing arts. The availability of theaters with suitable stages and seating helped determine which renaissance plays were ever revived and when, while the musical instrumentation and specialization of orchestras has much to do with which composers fill the standard contemporary musical repertoires.[99] Such selections by producers and musical directors, in turn, influence the reputations of those who created these works. Modern technology has further changed the survival process. Film, sound tracks, and videotape have made it possible to record and permanently store what once could only be experienced "live." Conductors, musicians, dancers, and actors can bid for the same immortality that had hitherto been reserved for the creators of the scores and scripts kept alive by their performances. The authenticity of the "original" performance is best preserved in sound reproduction. Blaukopf suggests that the advent of the technically perfected stereo record promoted the music of Gustav Mahler by making it possible to realize fully the "considered spatial pattern of sound" contained in the technical directives of the composer's musical notations for his Eighth Symphony, where the sound of a church organ is combined with the voices of singers and the strains of the orchestra.[100]

Another determinant of lasting fame has to do with uniqueness and its measurement. Especially in modern sport, an increasingly precise technology for scoring and preserving achievement has fostered a new concept of record that invites comparison in nearly every kind of athletic competition.[101] Even exceptional feats tend to be overlooked unless written into an official record book that then becomes the basis for bestowing recognition through awards and commemorative devices.[102] Though records are continuously being surpassed, some record holders stand a better chance of surviving in memory, having passed some kind of a "natural" marker, like the four-minute mile; Roger Bannister, the first to cross this barrier, made front-page news, and is still better remembered than several runners who have since been clocked at even faster times.

Clear and presumably "objective" criteria for the verification of achievement also exist in science. Competition among investigators in the same area centers on priority, which in the present system can usually be ascertained with some accuracy. To measure importance and "greatness" by counting the number of times a work is cited is more questionable, particularly in the more humanistic disciplines where the new cannot easily be distinguished from the old. There are names that scholars feel compelled to cite, if only to demonstrate that they have not been omitted out of ignorance. On the other hand, they need not identify the source of their ideas if it is not also known to others. This gives senior professors, if so inclined, the freedom to appropriate the ideas of students without acknowledgment. Students are under the opposite constraint. As a consequence, academics in departments with large numbers of graduate students accumulate more citations than are due them. References to a mentor's work becomes mandatory, even though other scholars may have been first to formulate the same ideas.

## Time and Obliteration

The cultural contributions of "modernist" artists and scientists are similar in many respects. Both seek an "original" vision, a way of looking at the world as no one has done before. Yet what each means by originality is quite different. The difference hinges on obsolescence. Whereas every new scientific discovery supersedes or improves on earlier formulations, the arts and humanities continue to look to the past for inspiration. Originality in art rests on the uniqueness of the irreproducible achievement. "If Raphael had died in his cradle," Burckhardt points out, "the *Transfiguration* would assuredly have never been painted."[103] The world would have been poorer for it. This "timelessness" of the artistic contribution contrasts sharply with the orientation in science, where original discoveries will not be accepted unless and until they have been replicated. Originality resides in being the *first* to identify a phenomenon, to give it the formulation that is accepted and utilized by others, and perhaps even to have one's name attached to it.[104] Surely others would have arrived at the same results later. For scientists time marches rapidly, though some, long gone, are still feted today.

The influence of extraneous factors is illustrated by the rather exceptional case of Gregor Mendel, who must, by any objective standard, rate with the far better known Charles Darwin as having made a path-breaking contribution to our understanding of evolution. Darwin's idea ran contrary to theological doctrine and brought him almost instant fame; the first printing of *The Origin of Species* quickly sold out. Mendel, on the other hand, received recognition only belatedly and after his observations had been independently verified. The centennial of Darwin's work was widely celebrated, while the hundredth anniversary of Mendel's paper in 1965 was much noticed only in Czechoslovakia and the 1984 centennial of his death "went completely unnoticed by the institutions of science."[105] The name of Darwin remains a household word associated with the idea of evolution, which he did not even invent but made popular by contributing an explication of the mechanism of natural selection. Here also Alfred Wallace and Edward Blythe, two contemporaries, had come close to understanding the same process. What is more, Darwin had actually observed Mendelian ratios in snapdragons but failed to draw the appropriate conclusions.

Why should Darwin's be a household name while that of Mendel is scarcely known beyond the scientific community? The answer is almost too simple: there is a far larger residue of information about Darwin than about Mendel to provide grist for the academic mill. Darwin left an autobiography, scientific sketches, and hundreds of letters on just about every subject. There is no comparable source material to remind us of Mendel, nearly all of whose notes were burned at his death. A curriculum vitae, submitted with an application to secondary school, and ten letters he wrote to the botanist Karl Naegeli plus another handful to his family are all that remain to tempt the scholar. Geography also worked against Mendel. Moravia, where he spent most of his life as a monk, was hardly a center of science, and no one would look there, rather than to the proceedings of the Linnean Society of London, for startling breakthroughs. Because of this isolation, Mendel's work never became the basis for a Mendelian school.

In the assessment of presidential reputations, and those of others in public life, the "impossibility of agreeing on yardsticks" is an even greater stumbling block. The powers and responsibilities of the executive office have changed, and its occupants have had to cope with vastly different contingencies, but ultimately the reputation of each chief executive will rest on the truckloads of records that every administration generates through the normal institutional processes. Writing in 1966, Bailey noted that the collections left by Washington, Jefferson, Lincoln, Franklin Roosevelt, and Wilson were huge, while those of McKinley and Coolidge were "as thin as their reputations."[106] His "bibliographical law"—the bigger the collection of presidential papers, the bigger the president—may no longer apply today, when every presidency generates records filling warehouses. Presidential reputations, like those of artists, are equally affected by the accidents of life and death. Some live long enough to produce memoirs giving their own version of events or to see to the establishment of a library that will not just house their papers but serve as a permanent monument. Theodore Roosevelt went so far as to write "posterity letters" just for the record. The abundance of other information makes the success of such personal initiatives questionable, all the more so since the selection of public figures for commemoration depends less on the record of the past than on whether or not it can be made to appear relevant to the aspirations of people today.[107]

The same can be said of the timeless art of the past. The works that have survived are hardly the locus of a single value known as "beauty"; they are, in the word of George Boas, "multivalent.... Certain of their values are experienced by some people, others by others." There is no a priori method, other than by fiat, for determining which of the many values are properly "aesthetic." Even the Mona Lisa, a universally recognized masterpiece, has undergone change. It was first praised by Vasari, who called it unfinished, for its "fidelity to nature"; by mid-seventeenth century, the excellence of the painting was said to reside in the "finish" given it by Leonardo. Two hundred years later, at the height of the Romantic era, Théophile Gautier discovered her "enigmatic" smile. What counted from then on was not the faithful rendition of the sitter but how the artist had managed to evoke the eternal feminine, the *femme fatale*.[108]

In an equally fascinating account, Jane Tompkins shows how Nathaniel Hawthorne established his claim to lasting fame. His fiction, she points out, "did not distinguish itself at all clearly from that of the sentimental novelists [of his day]—whose work we now see as occupying an entirely different category." What Hawthorne did have were good connections to the institutional networks through which reputations were made. It was the critics in certain literary journals whose high praise elevated his status above that of some others whose work was more popular. A later generation of critics continued to praise Hawthorne's stories but singled out works that had not been widely read in his time. So it came about that the stories most admired today are not those that had made him a great writer in the eyes of his contemporaries, and even those works still considered "great" are now judged important for quite different reasons.[109] Tompkins's analysis calls attention to the importance of the "reader," not only in the reception of literary texts but in the decoding of popular visual fare, as in television.

In stressing the role of the reader, we must not overlook the role of the mediator who signals the right interpretation. What Becker calls "posthumous editing" is most directly built into all of the performing arts, where each director or conductor puts his own stamp on the work.[110] In this respect musicians, as Gustav Mahler was moved to observe in 1905, are in the "worst" position. Everyone can read (and supposedly everyone can make out what there is in a picture), but "a musical score is a sealed book. Even the conductors who can decipher it present it to the public imbued with their varying conceptions. The important thing is to create a tradition."[111] This is exactly what Mahler set out to do, using his position with the Vienna Court Opera to give performances of his own work all over Europe. Conductors and players can be as crucial as reviewers. Because of the cost of rehearsal time, orchestras are inclined to stick to the "classics" that their members already know how to play, which is another reason why composers, once bypassed, have difficulty in regaining their place in the musical repertoires.[112] Mahler's posthumous success has been achieved with the help of convincing champions such as Leonard Bernstein, Bruno Walter, and Otto Klemperer. By the the 1980s, his symphonies had been almost as amply recorded as those of Beethoven.[113]

Disparities between posthumous reputations are further aggravated by the tendency to resolve any ambiguities of authorship in favor of the more renowned, a phenomenon which Merton has christened the Matthew effect—"for unto every one that hath shall be given."[114] When two researchers collaborate and publish their results jointly, the greater credit usually goes to the more renowned. Perhaps it is only realistic to assume that innovative ideas come only from seasoned scientists with known track records, but this cannot be universally true. Once a name becomes attached to a discovery, those who paved the way hold interest only for historians. This results in a certain "misallocation of credit," corrected only insofar as some researchers, once having built their own reputations, are in a position to obtain retroactive recognition for their part in earlier collaborative work.

There is a parallel in art to this "misallocation of credit"; it rests on the manifestly false assumption that any masterpiece must be the work of some renowned master. Scholars seeking to identify an unquestionably solid corpus of Rembrandt paintings are discovering that some of his "authenticated" works were, in fact, painted by others. Earlier scholars and curators, reflecting the attitude of Romanticism, had been inclined to believe otherwise: Only a true genius, like Rembrandt, would have been able to portray humanity with the same subtle tones, and "any painting that looked at all Rembrandtesque had to be by him."[115] Endeavors to correct this bias have resulted in reattributions, and his oeuvre has shrunk by nearly one-half. Reduced in size, what remains becomes even more valuable. On the other hand, the Dutch virtuoso had about one hundred pupils, all of whom strove to produce paintings like his, yet their names, having been lost, are doomed to be lost forever. Identifications like "follower of" or "in the school of" Rembrandt continue to evoke the great painter's name and to attest to his influence.

In science, too, posterity has some leeway when it comes to what Kuhn has identified as the "unusually troublesome class" of accidental discoveries by researchers who, so to speak, stumble on a previously unknown phenomenon that they do not yet fully understand.[116] The class includes such breakthroughs as the discovery of oxygen and the principle of the preservation of energy, where the full import of laboratory observations by several scientists emerged only gradually as the full range of contemporary ideas was brought to bear on them.[117] Each such case left several claimants for the posthumous honors. Just who will become the "discoverer" according to the schoolbooks read by future generations will depend on the kind of selective processes operant among our printmakers.

Most decisive technological breakthroughs have come through the work of several experimenters. The telegraph is a good example. From 1822 on, P. Schilling von Canstadt in Germany had devised a code, similar to the one later developed by Samuel F. B. Morse, and tried it out on electromagnetic devices. Two Englishmen carried these experiments further, took out a patent, and in 1838 saw the first telegraphic connection installed between Paddington and West Drayton. That Morse is now remembered as *the* inventor has much to do with the code that is still in use. Another example: Thomas Edison and Joseph Swan contributed equally to the development of the incandescent lamp but "Edison, as with all his inventions, took full advantage of the patent laws." Swan was blocked until the two joined in the Edison and Swan United Electric Light Company Limited.[118]

To return to etching. Here, as in other areas of activity, small and nonmeasurable differences in lifetime recognition can result in significant disparities of posthumous acclaim. The etcher's achievement is refracted through initiatives taken in the artist's lifetime, through survivors acting as links to posterity, through networks that bring their work into the museums and archives, and through their availability as a symbolic focus for a variety of sentiments that may have nothing to do directly with art. Peculiar to etching as a form of printmaking is that the much-admired images, unlike those of painters, exist in multiples that are neither copies nor fakes. Each impression is a unique original, different in at least some minor way from all other prints yielded by the same plate. For the *amateur d'estampes*, on whom the marketability of etchings and the reputations of their creators ultimately depend, the mystique of the print lies in the opportunity to hold in one's hand a true original that gives a sense of communication with the artist across time. In this precise sense, the persona of the artist as well as the work itself comes to be etched in memory.

# Appendixes

# Printmaking Techniques

There are four major methods of "artistic" printmaking: *intaglio* prints, which include both etching and engraving, are produced by forcing ink into the hollowed grooves of a metal plate, which is then run through a press under considerable pressure; *relief* prints, mostly from woodblocks or linoleum, where the whites are cut away and the ink rolled on the "high points" to be printed on the surface; *planographic* prints, usually made from specially prepared stones but sometimes from zinc plates, where the transfer of the image drawn is based on the immiscibility of oil and water, and, finally, *serigraphic* techniques, where the artist's drawing produces something like a stencil through which inks are then forced.

The serigraph was developed only in the 1930s and did not really come into its own until after the Second World War. But many painter-etchers also tried their hand at lithography and the woodblock and were equally at home with these media. A few actually found them more suitable for their artistic purposes. In emphasizing the distinction between original and reproductive work, we have sometimes glossed over other distinctions and written as if etching, drypoint, aquatint, and so forth were interchangeable, when in fact they are not. Some people refer to the entire genre of intaglio prints as "engravings." What follows is a brief listing of major terms.

**Engraving.** Use of the burin to cut grooves into a hard plate (usually steel) to produce the lines and cross-hatchings characteristic of older prints.

**Pure etching.** Covering a plate (usually copper) with wax ground, drawing the image with a needle, repeated insertion of the plate into acid until it is ready for printing (also called "proofing").

**Drypoint.** Dispenses with grounding and acid bath in favor of directly "scratching" the image on the copper (or zinc) plate with a sharp and hard point; often used in conjunction with etching because it gives rich darks not easily achievable with etched lines.

**Aquatint.** Similar to etching except that, instead of relying on lines, the artist uses a resin powder (or some other means) to give the plate a finely grained surface, which (after immersions of different length of time) produces an image built up of tones more than lines.

**Line engraving.** Involves drawing with the burin but in a freer fashion and without the detailed cross-hatching that characterized reproductive engraving as previously practiced.

**Soft-ground etching.** Another variant in which the etching ground is deliberately kept soft so that it will stick to the drawing the artist makes on a paper placed over it and thus create the exposed lines for the acid to bite into.

**Mezzotint.** An older technique somewhat in disuse, where the plate is roughened with a roulette to allow it to hold ink and the artist builds the image by scraping in order to "smooth out" the places intended as highlights.

# Artists in the Statistical Sample

These two lists, arranged chronologically, contain the names of artists on whom specific biographical information was sought. Quantitative statements (but not illustrative material) are based on this sample only. The less than perfect match in age between the men and women is due in large part to our corrections of information initially taken from listings in authoritative directories, some of which turned out to be inaccurate. Sometimes the year of birth was difficult to ascertain. Where there was conflicting information, we relied on the best source documents available; where there was no information, we placed artists chronologically according to what we knew about their careers.

Similar problems were encountered with death dates. For artists assumed to be deceased but with no corroboration, dates are given as ?; where we knew the artists had survived into the 1980s but had no further information, dates are shown as †.

Some artists—mostly the women—exhibited under more than one name. The one less used is shown in parentheses.

Included in the British sample is a subsample of eight women and eight men who remained associates in the Royal Society of Painter Etchers for long years—even until honorable retirement—without ever advancing to the rank of fellow. They were included because we wanted to know whether (or how) their careers were blocked. These men and women, identified by an asterisk after their names, were also matched, as far as possible, in the same way as the rest of the sample.

*British Etchers*

| Women | Men |
|---|---|
| Nichols, Catherine M. (1847–1923) | Baskett, Charles E. (1845–1929)* |
| Hallé, Elinor (1856–1926) | Roussel, Théodore (1847–1926) |

Bolingbroke, Minna R. (1857–1939)

Illingworth, Adeline (1858–1942)

Berkeley, Edith (Savill) (1859–1909)

Forbes, Elizabeth (Armstrong) (1859–1912)

Piper, Elizabeth (1860–1956)*

Gleichen, Lady Feodora (1861–1922)

Pott, Constance M. (1862–1957)

Martyn, Ethel King (1863–1946)

Copeman, Constance G. (1864–1953)*

Harrison (Godman), Jessie (1864–post 1936)*

Fell, Eleanor Mitchell (1866–1946)*

Stewart, Ethel I. Waldron (?–ca.1924//27)

Crawford, Susan F. (1868–1918)

Sloane, Mary A. (1868–1961)

Heriot, C. I. Robertine (1869–?)

Clutterbuck, Julia E. (1871–1932)*

Buckton, Eveleen (1872–1962)

Hayes, Gertrude E. (1872–1956)*

Gorst, Bertha (1873–1938)*

Cowham, Hilda (1873–1964)

Simpson, Janet S. C. (1873–ca. 1972)

Park, John (1851–1919)*

Menpes, Mortimer (1855–1938)

Bird, Charles (1856–1916)*

Short, Sir Frank (1857–1945)

Fitton, Hedley (1857–1929)

Strang, William (1859–1921)

Dawson, Nelson (1859–1941)

Sickert, Walter R. (1860–1942)

Holroyd, Sir Charles (1861–1917)

Duff, John R. K. (1862–1938)

Cameron, Sir David Y. (1865–1945)

Fisher, A. Hugh (1867–1945)*

Gaskell, G. Percival (1868–1934)

Manning, W. Westley (1868–1954)*

Lee-Hankey, William (1869–1952)

Hall, Oliver (1869–1957)

Rothenstein, Sir William (1872–1945)

Ansell, William (1872–1959)*

Briscoe, Arthur E. (1873–1943)

Walcot, William (1874–1943)

Gethin, Percy F. (1874–1916)*

Bauerlé (Bowerley), Amelia (1874–1916)

Cameron, Katherine (1874–1965)

Kemp-Welch, Margaret (1874–1968)

Robinson, Mabel C. (1875–1953)

Goyder, Alice Kirkby (1875–1964)

Austen, Winifred (1876–1964)

Knight, Dame Laura (1877–1970)

Clarke Hall, Lady Edna (Waugh) (1879–1979)

Gosse, Sylvia (1881–1968)

Frood, Hester (1882–1971)

Airy, Anna (1882–1964)

Martin, Dorothy Burt (1882–1946)

Gabain, Ethel (1883–1950)

Delleany, Greta (1883–1968)

Kershaw, Mary E. (1884–1968)

Lessore, Thérèse (1884–1945)

Lord, Elyse (1885–1971)

Raverat, Gwen (1885–1957)

Jefferies (Hartnell), Katherine (1886–1970)

Campbell, N. Molly (1888–1971)

Dobson, Margaret S. (1888–ca.1952//53)*

Fish, Anne Harriet (1890–1964)

Boulton, Doris (1892–?)

Dodd, Francis (1874–1949)

Copley, John (1875–1950)

Hardie, Martin (1875–1952)

Bone, Sir D. Muirhead (1876–1953)

Griggs, Frederick L. (1876–1938)

Smart, Douglas I. (1877–1970)

John, Augustus (1878–1961)

Richards, Fred C. (1878–1932)

Bentley, Alfred (1879–1923)

Simpson, Joseph (1879–1939)

Osborne, Malcolm (1880–1963)

Smith, Percy (1882–1948)

Robins, William P. (1882–1959)

Detmold, Edward J. (1883–1957)

Lumsden, Ernest (1883–1948)

McBey, James (1883–1959)

Anderson, Stanley (1884–1966)

Warlow, H. Gordon (1885–1942)*

Blampied, Edmund (1886–1966)

Strang, Ian (1886–1952)

Litten, Sidney M. (1887–1949)

Nevinson, C. R. W. (1889–1946)

Rushbury, Sir Henry (1889–1968)

Woollard, Dorothy (1893–†)

Pissarro, Orovida (1893–1968)

Whitehead, Lillian (1894–?)

Boreel, Wendela (1895–†)

Marston, Freda (1895–1949)

Elliott, Aileen Mary (1896–1966)

Lavrin, Nora Fry (1897–1985)

Sherlock, Marjorie (1897–1973)

Fyfe, Elizabeth (1899–1933)

Leslie, Cecil Mary (1900–1980)

Leighton, Clare (1900–†)

Klinghoffer, Clara (1900–1970)

Hope, Rosa S. (1902–72)

Gibbs, Evelyn (Lady Willatt) (1905–†)

Soper, Eileen (1905–†)

Rhodes, Marion (1907–†)

Brown, Denise L. (1911–†)

Brockhurst, Gerald (1890–1978)

Nixon, Job (1891–1938)

Todd, A. R. Middleton (1891–1966)

Janes, Norman (1892–1980)

Cain, Charles W. (1893–1962)

Squirrell, Leonard (1893–1979)

Webb, Clifford (1895–1972)

Austin Robert S. (1895–1973)

Wedgwood, Geoffrey (1900–1977)

Bouverie-Hoyton, Edward (1900–†)

Tunnicliffe, Charles F. (1901–79)

Sutherland, Graham (1903–80)

Drury, Paul (1903–87)

Gross, Anthony (1905–84)

Badmin, Stanley (1906–†)

Webb, Joseph (1908–62)

Dent, Robert S. G. (1909–†)

## American Etchers

In America, there was no official recognition similar to becoming a fellow of the Royal Society of Painter-Etchers. Election to the National Academy of Design might serve as a rough equivalent but few etchers (and even fewer women etchers) made it into this body. Lacking a roster of nationally recognized etchers from which to build and expand our sample, we compiled a list of women etchers from the following sources: the exhibitions of etchings by women at the Boston Museum of Fine Art (1887) and at the Union League Club in New York (1888); the membership rosters of the Philadelphia and New York Etching Clubs in the 1880s and 1890s; those favorably mentioned in surveys of American etching and engraving, such as the Special Numbers of *The Studio* (1902 and 1913); the listings of etchers in the compendium of American artists and etchers by Michigan State University (1913), in the *American Yearbook of Etching* (1914), in the volumes of *Fine Prints of the Year* (1923–38), and in the volumes of *Fifty Prints* (1926–38); those with a favorable showing in the popularity survey taken by the magazine *Print* (1936); and inclusion in *American Prize Prints* by Albert Reese (1947). As in Britain, each woman was paired by birthdate with a male contemporary.

There is one difference, however. American printmakers were less likely to insist on the sharp distinction made by the RSPE between painter-etchers and engravers on the one hand and artists who favored the lithograph or woodcut on the other. All were pretty much part of the same network. Our selection procedure thus brought into the American sample 35 artists whose reputations as printmakers are more closely tied to their lithographs or woodcuts (as indicated by an "L" or "W" after a name) than to their etched or engraved work. B. J. O. Nordfeldt, Margaret Patterson, Emil Ganso, Reginald Marsh, and Howard Cook are only a few among those equally accomplished in several of the print media.

*American Etchers*

| Women | Men |
|---|---|
| Greatorex, Eliza (1819//20–97) | Smillie, James David (1833–1909) |
| Moran, Mary Nimmo (1842–99) | Gifford, R. Swain (1840–1905) |
| Cassatt, Mary (1844–1926) | Moran, Peter (1841–1914) |
| Merritt, Anna Lea (1844–1930) | Parrish, Stephen A. (1846–1938) |
| Dillaye, Blanche (1851–1931) | Weir, J. Alden (1852–1919) |
| Hale, Ellen Day (1855–1940) | Bacher, Otto H. (1856–1909) |
| Getchell, Edith L. (Peirce) (1855–1940) | Burr, George Elbert (1859–1939) |
| Clements, Gabrielle de Veaux (1858–1948) | Shilling (Schilling), Alexander (1859–1937) |
| Oakford, Ellen (?–?) | Platt, Charles Adams (1861–1933) |
| Jaques, Bertha (1863–1941) | Davies, Arthur B. (1862–1928) |

Congdon, Ada Irene Vose
(1865–?)

Kimball, Katherine B.
(1866–1949)

Patterson, Margaret (1867–1950)

Coover, Nell (?–?)

Hyde, Helen (1868–1919)

Goldthwaite, Anne (1869–1944)

de Milhau, Zella (1870–1954)

Gearhart, May (1871–1951)

Heller, Helen West
(1872–1955) W

Squire, Maud Hunt (1873–1955)

DeCordoba, Matilde (1875–1942)

Armington, Caroline (1875–1939)

Thorne, Diana (1875–?)

Dwight, Mabel (1876–1955) L

Merrill, Katherine (1876–1962)

Mairs, Clara (1878–1963)

Stevens, Helen B. (1878–1954)

Newton, Edith (1878–?) L

Oberteuffer, Henrietta Amiard
(1878–1962)

Lum, Bertha (1879–1954) W

Colwell, Elizabeth (1881–?)

Verner, Elizabeth O. (1883–1979)

Osk, Roselle H. (1884–1954)

Mielatz, Charles F. W.
(1864–1919)

Dahlgreen, Charles W.
(1864–1955)

Washburn, Cadwallader
(1866–1965)

Myers, Jerome (1867–1940)

Hart, George Overbury ("Pop")
(1868–1933)

Gallagher, Sears, (1869–1956)

Marin, John (1870–1953)

Sloan, John (1871–1951)

Kinney, Troy (1871–1938)

Aid, George C. (1872–1938)

Higgins, Eugene (1874–1958)

Haskell, Ernest (1876–1925)

Armington, Frank W.
(1876–1941)

MacLaughlan, D. Shaw
(1876–1938)

Hutty, Alfred (1877–1954)

Wood, Franklin T. (1877–1945)

Webster, Herman A.
(1878–1970)

White, Charles Henry
(1878–1918)

Nordfeldt, Bror J. O.
(1878–1955)

Roth, Ernest (1879–1964)

Lewis, Martin (1881–1962)

Horter, Earl (1882–1940)

Hornby, Lester G. (1882–1956)

Coulter, Mary J. (1885–1965)

Kirmse, Marguerite (1885–1954)

Ryerson, Margery (1886–1989)

Bonner, Mary (1887–1935)

Crosman, Rose (1887–?)

Zorach, Marguerite (1887–1968) W

Norton, Elizabeth (1887–1985) W

Miller, Helen P. (1888–1967)

Douglass, Lucille (1889–1935)

Albee, Grace (1890–1985)

Boyer, Alice Rive-King (1890–?)

Ford, Lauren (1891–?)

Lathrop, Dorothy (1891–1980)

Markham, Kyra (1891–1967) L

Buell, Alice Standish (1892–1960)

Levy, Beatrice S. (1892–1972)

Gág, Wanda (1893–1946)

Barton, Loren (1893–1975)

Bacon, Peggy (1895–1987)

Rosenthal, Doris (1895–1971) L

Good, Minetta (1895–1946) L

McVeigh, Blanche (1895–1970)

Loggie, Helen (1895–1976)

Blanch, Lucile (1895–1981) L

Bernstein, Theresa (1896 [1890?]–†)

Pearson, Ralph M. (1883–1958)

Ruzicka, Rudolph (1883–1978)

Hansen, Armin C. (1886–1957)

Arms, John Taylor (1887–1953)

Meyerowitz, William (1887–1981)

Woiceske, Ronau (1887–1953)

Partridge, Roi (1888–1984)

Nason, Thomas (1889–1971)

Auerbach-Levy, William (1889–1964)

Kuniyoshi, Yasuo (1889–1953) L

Eby, Kerr, (1889–1946)

Ostrowsky, Abbo (1889–1975)

Rosenberg, Louis C. (1890–1983)

Heintzelman, Arthur W. (1890–1965)

Wickey, Harry (1892–1968)

Lozowick, Louis (1892–1973) L

Landacre, Paul (1893–1963) W

Millier, Arthur (1893–1975)

Allen, James E. (1894–1964)

Winkler, John W. (1894–1979)

Ganso, Emil (1895–1941)

Reed, Doel (1895–1985)

Chamberlain, Samuel (1895–1975)

Dehn, Adolf (1895–1968) L

Riggs, Robert, (1896–1970) L

Andrus, Vera (1896–1979) L

Durieux, Caroline (1896–1989) L

Coughlin, Mildred (1896–?)

Murphy, Alice H.-(1896–1966)

Citron, Minna (1896–†)

Tait, Agnes (1897–?) L

Olds, Elizabeth (1897–†) L

Hill, Polly Knipp (1900–†)

Huntley, Victoria H. (1900–1971) L

Burrage, Barbara (1900–?) L

Murphy, Minnie Lois (1901–62) L

Brooks, Mildred (1901–88?)

Bishop, Isabel (1902–88)

Kumm, Marguerite (1902–†)

Kloss, Gene (1903–†)

Bischoff, Ilse (1903–76)

Mason, Alice T. (1904–71)

Lee, Doris (1905–83) L

Lowengrund, Margaret (1905–57) L

Bianco, Pamela (1906–†) L

Blumenschein, Helen (1909–†) L

Greenwood, Marion (1909–70) L

Blanch, Arnold (1896–1968) L

Geerlings, Gerald K. (1897–†)

Handforth, Thomas (1897–1948)

Marsh, Reginald (1898–1954)

Locke, Charles W. (1899–1983) L

Soyer, Raphael (1899–1987)

West, Levon (1900–1968)

Lucioni, Luigi (1900–1988)

Kappel, Philip (1901–81)

Hoffman, Irwin D. (1901–89)

Cook, Howard N. (1902–80)

Borne, Mortimer (1902–†)

Wright, R. Stephens (1903–†)

Hurd, Peter (1904–84) L

Spruance, Benton (1904–67) L

Sternberg, Harry (1904–†)

Limbach, Russell T. (1904–71) L

Cadmus, Paul (1904–†)

Landeck, Armin (1905–84)

Wengenroth, Stow (1906–78) L

Taylor, Prentiss (1907–†) L

Hirsch, Joseph (1910–81) L

# Notes

## Abbreviations Used in the Notes

| | |
|---|---|
| AAA | Archives of American Art, Washington, D.C. |
| AMPR | Ashmolean Museum Print Room, Oxford, England |
| ASL | Art Students League |
| BL | British Library, Manuscript Division, London, England |
| BPL | Boston Public Library, Boston, Mass. |
| EI | Essex Institute, Salem, Mass. |
| GU | Glasgow University |
| LAMA | Los Angeles Museum of Art, Los Angeles, Calif. |
| LC | Library of Congress, Division of Manuscripts, Washington, D.C. |
| NMAA | National Museum of American Art, Washington, D.C. |
| NYPL | New York Public Library, New York, N.Y. |
| RCA | Royal College of Art, London, England |
| RHC | Harry Ransom Humanities Research Center, Austin, Tex. |
| RSPE | Royal Society of Painter-Etchers |
| SCHS | South Carolina Historical Society, Columbia, S.C. |
| SYRU | George Arents Research Library for Special Collections, Syracuse University, Syracuse, N.Y. |
| V&A | Victoria and Albert Museum Library, London, England |

## Chapter 1

1. Walpole, "The Etching," pp. 18–21.

2. According to *Print Prices Current*, 1933–34, an impression of "The Balcony" was sold for £199 at auction.

3. Walpole, "The Etching," pp. 18–21. The etcher is Allart van Everdingen (1621–75), Dutch. Neither the etching in this book (figure 1) nor any other in the oeuvre of Everdingen matches the description in the story.

4. The other major printmaking techniques are planographic (printing from a flat surface where the transfer of the image hinges on the immiscibility of oil-based ink and water) and relief prints (printing from blocks to which the ink is applied with a roller so that only raised portions of a block are covered). The silk screen print and related techniques were not developed until the 1930s.

5. The so-called Veblen effect, after Veblen in *Theory of the Leisure Class*.

6. The number varies from just a few to the literally hundreds of copies possible after the soft copperplate is electrolytically faced with steel.

7. Marron, Foreword to *Marron Collection of American Prints*, p. 12.

8. Locke, *Essay Concerning Human Understanding*, pp. 476–79.

9. Holroyd, *Augustus John*, p. 71.

10. Baudelaire, *Painter of Modern Life*, p. 1.

11. E. B. White, "How to Tell," p. 74.
12. Kristeller, "Modern System of the Arts," p. 508.
13. Zilsel, *Entstehung des Geniebegriffs.*
14. Vasari, *Lives of the Painters.*
15. Ruskin, *Political Economy of Art*, p. 29.
16. Ibid., p. 56.
17. Ibid., pp. 126–27.
18. See Boime, *Academy and French Painting*, chap. 11.
19. For a brief description of the major methods, see Appendix A: Print-making Techniques.
20. Fry, "Art-History," pp. 4 and 7.
21. Reitlinger, *Economics of Taste*, chap. 6.
22. Fry, "Art-History," p. 9.
23. The sources were Hind, *History of Engraving and Etching*; Laver, *History of British and American Etching*; Emanuel, *Etching and Etchings*; the sixteen volumes of *Fine Prints of the Year*; and the periodical *The Bookman's Journal and Print Collector.*
24. Membership (or associate membership) in the National Academy of Design could not serve us because few etchers (and even fewer women etchers) were ever selected and because its practices changed significantly over the years.
25. Besides Hind, *History of Engraving and Etching*, Laver, *History of British and American Etching*, and *Fine Prints of the Year*, our sources included catalogs of two early exhibitions of women-etchers—one at the Boston Museum of Fine Art in 1887 (see Koehler, "Introduction"), the second at the Union League Club of New York in 1888 (see Rensselaer, "Introduction")—and the membership rosters of the Philadelphia and New York Etching Clubs in the 1880s and 1890s, along with other lists and exhibition material.

## Chapter 2

1. C. Vosmaer, cited in the Preface to Hamerton, *Etching and Etchers*, 4th ed.
2. Hood, *Complete Poetical Works*, p. 384.
3. S. H. Monk, University of Minnesota, cited in E. Partridge, *Dictionary of Catch Phrases*, p. 37.
4. Charlot, Foreword to *American Printmaking*, pp. 7–8.
5. Monk cited in E. Partridge, *Dictionary of Catch Phrases*, p. 37n.
6. Lecture by Frederick Goulding to the Art Workers' Guild, cited in M. Hardie, *Frederick Goulding*, pp. 70–71.
7. Emanuel, *Etching and Etchings*, p. xii.
8. Hind, *History of Engraving and Etching*, p. 106.
9. Ibid., p. 105.
10. For a good selection of illustrations, see Freedberg, *Dutch Landscape Prints.*
11. Hind, *History of Engraving and Etching*, p. 170; Hamerton, *Etching and Etchers*, 1st ed., p. 73.
12. Hind, *History of Engraving and Etching*, p. 170.
13. Slive, *Rembrandt and His Critics*, p. 29n.
14. Haden, *Etched Work of Rembrandt*, passim.
15. Hind, *History of Engraving and Etching*, p. 173.
16. Fuchs, *Rembrandt in Amsterdam*, p. 54–57.
17. Laver, *History of British and American Etching*, p. 2.

18. For useful summaries of the "Rembrandt story," see White and Konody, "Rembrandt van Rijn," and J. Rosenberg, *Rembrandt.*

19. Slive, *Rembrandt and His Critics*, p. 29.

20. Fuchs, *Rembrandt in Amsterdam*, p. 66.

21. See Hind, *History of Engraving and Etching*, p. 172; also Fuchs, *Rembrandt in Amsterdam*, p. 65, and J. Rosenberg, *Rembrandt*, p. 330.

22. Samuel van Hoogstraten, cited in Slive, *Rembrandt and His Critics*, p. 97.

23. See Fuchs, *Rembrandt in Amsterdam*, p. 66.

24. Ibid.

25. Ibid., p. 62.

26. Bartsch, *L'Oeuvre de Rembrandt.*

27. For the definitive account of this "madness" and its effect on British taste, see D'Oench, " 'A Madness to Have His Prints,' " pp. 63–81.

28. Hamerton, *Etching and Etchers*, 4th ed., p. 81.

29. Reed and Wallace, *Italian Etchers.*

30. Carlson, "The Painter-Etcher," pp. 25–27.

31. Grant, *Dictionary of British Etchers*, p. 13.

32. Rosenthal, *La Gravure*, p. 237.

33. Wortley, "Amateur Etchers," pp. 189, 191.

34. Oppé, "Earl of Aylesford," passim.

35. B. W., "Imitations of Rembrandt by B. W." This author bases himself on Edward Edwards, *Anecdotes of Painting*, published in London by Leigh and Sotheby in 1808. Sparrow, *British Etching*, pp. 84–85, also contains a detailed account and gives as its source a typescript copy of Benjamin Wilson's autobiography, which was later published.

36. See Grant, *Dictionary of British Etchers*; also Hind, *History of Engraving and Etching*, p. 240.

37. D'Oench, " 'A Madness to Have His Prints,' " p. 63.

38. Hitchcock, *Etching in America*, p. 50.

39. Among the best known of these accounts are Laver, *History of British and American Etching*; Singer, *Moderne Graphik*; Watrous, *Century of American Printmaking*; Wedmore, *Etching in England*; and Weitenkampf, *American Graphic Art.*

40. Three hundred of his etchings and drypoints had been completed by 1848.

41. There really are only thirteen; the fourteenth is a reworked state of his first etching.

42. Leipnik, *History of French Etching*, p. 87.

43. Rensselaer, "American Etchings," p. 9. Keppel, *Golden Age of Engraving*, does not attribute this to Dupré alone but refers to it as "a saying among the French artists."

44. Wickenden, "Charles Jacque," p. 83.

45. Leipnik, *History of French Etching*, pp. 77–78.

46. For a detailed account, see Bradley, "Some French Etchers and Sonneteers," pp. 183–212.

47. Leipnik, *History of French Etching*, pp. 84–85.

48. Ibid. Also Keppel, *Golden Age of Engraving*, p. 123.

49. "Silhouettes d'artistes contemporains," pp. 348–55. She learned from Meryon "à vernir sa planche."

50. Schneiderman, *Prints of Haden*, p. 22.

51. Leipnik, *History of French Etching*, p. 92.

52. Abbott, "Lady of the Portrait," p. 323.
53. *Gazette des beaux-arts*, 1st ser., no. 14 (1863): 190.
54. Cited in Keppel, *Golden Age of Engraving*, p. 87.
55. Bailly-Herzberg, *L'Eau-forte de peintre*, 2:20–21.
56. Charles Baudelaire published a short article entitled "L'Eau-forte est à la mode" in *La Revue anecdotique* (2 April 1862), which later appeared in *Le Boulevard* (14 September 1862) under the title of "Peintres et aqua-fortistes" and was then reprinted in Lemaître, *Baudelaire*, pp. 411–15.
57. Baudelaire, *Art in Paris*, p. 221.
58. This formulation is adapted from that of Martin Hardie, curator for prints and drawings at the Victoria and Albert; see his *Frederick Goulding*.
59. Bailly-Herzberg, *L'Eau-forte de peintre*, p. 38.
60. Ibid., p. 47.
61. See Keppel, *Golden Age of Engraving*, pp. 3–5.
62. Hamerton, *Etching and Etchers*, 4th ed., p. 152.
63. Cited in Weisberg, *Etching Renaissance in France*, p. 28n.
64. M. Hardie, *Frederick Goulding*, p. 145.
65. Bailly-Herzberg, *L'Eau-forte de peintre*, pp. 45–46. Her source for the statistic is unclear.
66. Hamerton, *Etching and Etchers*, 4th ed., p. 148.
67. Hind, *History of Engraving and Etching*, p. 321.
68. M. Hardie, *Frederick Goulding*, p. 145.
69. Leipnik, *History of French Etching*, p. 99.
70. For information on Delâtre's life and role, see M. Hardie, *Frederick Goulding*, pp. 146–47.
71. Bradley, "Some French Etchers and Sonneteers," p. 190; see also his "Meryon and Baudelaire," pp. 587–609.
72. Rosenthal, *La Gravure*, p. 370.
73. Baudelaire, *Art in Paris*, p. 219.
74. Hitchcock, *Etching in America*, p. 27.
75. See Mourey, "France," and Cate and Hitchings, *Color Revolution*.
76. Salaman, "Great Britain," p. 3.

Chapter 3

1. M. Hardie, *Frederick Goulding*, p. 144.
2. Sparrow, *British Etching*, p. 155.
3. Schneiderman, "Genesis of English Landscape Etching," pp. 193–95.
4. Sickert, "Old Ladies of Etching-Needle Street," p. 304.
5. Laver, *History of British and American Etching*, p. 45.
6. M. Hardie, *Frederick Goulding*, p. 25, refers to the case as "Prince Consort v. Strange"; *The Times* gives the name on the docket as "Prince Albert v. Strange." Spielmann in "Art Forgeries" touches on the case.
7. Based on Minutes of the Etching Club deposited in the Library of the Victoria and Albert Museum. The account in Laver, *History of English and American Etching*, chap. 5, is also based on these minutes. We have also made use of Laver, "Seymour Haden," and Sparrow, *British Etching*, chap. 5.
8. Laver, *History of British and American Etching*, p. 47.
9. "Rules of the Etching Club," promulgated at its first regular meeting on 2 July 1838 and amended on 7 November 1839.
10. Farr, *English Art*, p. 355. See also Jacomb-Hood, *With Brush and Pencil*.

11. Quoted in Laver, *History of British and American Etching*, p. 51. See also Palmer, *Life and Letters*, pp. 315, 377.

12. M. Hardie, *Frederick Goulding*.

13. At least there are no minutes between 27 February 1872 and 25 April 1876.

14. Laver, "Seymour Haden," p. 91.

15. M. Hardie, *Frederick Goulding*, p. 149.

16. Laver, *History of British and American Etching*, p. 55.

17. Minute book, 2 May 1860.

18. Letter by George du Maurier cited in Weintraub, *Whistler*, p. 75.

19. Hamerton, *Autobiography*, p. 319.

20. Hamerton, *Etching and Etchers*, 4th ed., p. 239.

21. Ibid., p. 129.

22. Ibid., pp. 241–42.

23. Hamerton, *Etching and Etchers*, 1st ed., pp. 70–71. The story is retold in another context in Huish, "Etching in England," p. 148.

24. Hamerton, *Etching and Etchers*, 4th ed., p. 219. Many original etchings were published in *Portfolio* during the years of its existence from 1879 to 1893.

25. *The Etcher*, December 1880, p. 24.

26. From a manuscript written while Haden was president of the RSPE; reproduced in Keppel, *Golden Age of Engraving*, opposite p. 133.

27. Wedmore, *Etchings*, p. 138.

28. Sparrow, *British Etching*, p. 204; see also Hamerton, "Mr. Seymour Haden's Etchings," p. 595.

29. Sparrow, *British Etching*, pp. 204–5; Schneiderman, "Genesis of British Landscape Etching."

30. J. Pennell, *Etchers and Etching*, p. 183.

31. Schneiderman, *Prints of Haden*.

32. Dodgson cited in Sparrow, *British Etching*, p. 40.

33. J. Pennell, *Etchers and Etching*, p. 183.

34. M. Hardie, *Frederick Goulding*, p. 24.

35. Laver, *History of British and American Etching*, p. 74.

36. F. Newbolt, *Royal Society of Painter-Etchers*, is based on the minutes of the society. Inquiries at the current RSPE office suggest that these either are in deep storage or no longer exist.

37. Herkomer, *Etching and Mezzotint*, cited in Laver, *History of British and American Etching*, p. 75.

38. Huish, "Etching in England," p. 148

39. F. Newbolt, *Royal Society of Painter-Etchers*, p. 25.

40. For details, see Weintraub, *Whistler*, pp. 259–62. There are several versions of the story. For Whistler's account, see Fine Art Society, *Correspondence by J. A. McN. Whistler, respecting to etching of Frank Duveneck attributed to Mr. Whistler by F. S. Haden* (London, 1881).

41. Haden's annual report to RSPE for 1889; see F. Newbolt, *Royal Society of Painter-Etchers*.

42. M. Hardie, *Frederick Goulding*, pp. 113ff.

43. An estimate, based on *Year's Art*, of the average edition size for plates published by members of the Printsellers Association at the time was over 300.

44. F. Newbolt, *Royal Society of Painter-Etchers*, p. 31.

45. *Year's Art*, volumes for 1888–92.

46. F. Newbolt, *Royal Society of Painter-Etchers*, pp. 31–32.

47. Wedmore, "Royal Society of Painter-Etchers," pp. 22–23.

48. Slater, *Engravings and Their Value*, p. 88.

49. Salaman, "Print Collectors' Club," p. 210.

## Chapter 4

1. Four of the eight daughters of English-born John Sartain became engravers. Sartain taught etching to Thomas Moran and S. J. Ferris. See Wray, *Etching in the United States*, p. 53.

2. Rensselaer, "American Etchers," p. 487.

3. Five of the founding members of the National Academy of Design were classified as engravers. See E. Clark, *National Academy of Design*, p. 195. Other well-known painters who began their artistic careers in this way include Asher B. Durand, John Kensett, John W. Casilear, and Winslow Homer.

4. Dunlap, *Rise and Progress of the Arts*, 3:184.

5. Koehler, *American Etchings*, p. 7.

6. Dunlap, *Rise and Progress of the Arts*, 3:144.

7. Isham, *History of American Painting*, p. 290, compares their "neat execution" with the later work of men such as Lalanne.

8. Chapman, *American Drawing Book*.

9. Letter by Gifford to Koehler, 1 August 1879, Koehler Correspondence, AAA.

10. Wray, *Etching in the United States*, p. 53.

11. Castagnary cited in Bailly-Herzberg, *L'Eau-forte de peintre*, 1:212.

12. Wray, *Etching in the United States*, p. 54.

13. Hitchcock, *Etching in America*, p. 60.

14. Letter to Koehler cited in his *American Etchings*, p. 23.

15. Letter by Farrer to Koehler, 5 October 1879, Koehler Correspondence, AAA.

16. Hitchcock, *Etching in America*, p. 31. At least one New York firm (F. B. Patterson) secured the requisite plates and etching tools as a means of interesting such fine art illustrators as E. A. Abbey and C. S. Reinhart. In 1872, the firm published a portfolio of etched views of old New York by Farrer as a supplement to portfolios of French etchings it had begun to carry.

17. Wray, *Etching in the United States*, p. 60.

18. Ibid., pp. 62–63.

19. Letter by Smillie to Koehler, 23 July 1883, Koehler Correspondence, AAA.

20. New York Etching Club, *Exhibition Catalog* (1882), pp. 5–6.

21. Hitchcock, *Etching in America*, pp. 5–6.

22. Hartmann, *History of American Art*, p. 137.

23. Koehler, *New York Etching Club*, cited by Tyler, *American Etchings*, p. xi. See also Wray, *Etching in the United States*, p. iii; Weitenkampf, *American Graphic Art*, pp. 12–13; and Watrous, *Century of American Printmaking*, p. 7.

24. E. R. Pennell, *Joseph Pennell*, 1:45.

25. Cheney, "Notable Western Etchers."

26. Tyler, *American Etchings*, p. x.

27. Wray, *Etching in the United States*, p. 54,

28. J. Pennell, *Adventures of an Illustrator*, p. 74.

29. E. R. Pennell, *Joseph Pennell*, 1:75.

30. Lalanne, *Treatise on Etching*.

31. Norton, *Prints at the Essex Institute*, p. 55. *Marblehead Neck*, the demonstration etching, is in the collection of the Boston Museum of Fine Arts.

32. For estimates of print runs based on Koehler Correspondence, see Bruhn, *American Etching*, p. 16.

33. Letter by Henry Farrer, 15 October 1879, Koehler Correspondence, AAA.

34. Letter by Falconer (n.d.), Koehler Correspondence, AAA.

35. Cited in *New York Times*, 24 December 1882.

36. Letters by Smillie to Koehler, 3 December 1882 and 17 June 1885, Koehler Correspondence, AAA.

37. Watrous, *Century of American Printmaking*, p. 16.

38. C. Clark, "Five American Print Curators," p. 85.

39. Cited in Schneider, "Birth of American Painter-Etching," p. 188.

40. Koehler, "Introduction," p. 12.

41. Hitchcock, *Etching in America*, pp. 59ff.

42. Wray, *Etching in the United States*, p. 60.

43. Hitchcock, *Etching in America*, refers to a memorandum prepared by Keppel that shows the share of modern etchings as follows: 1875, 2 percent; 1876, 2 percent; 1877, 9.5 percent; 1878, 21 percent; 1879, 9 percent; 1880, 15 percent; 1881, 26 percent; 1882, 33 percent; 1883, 73 percent; 1884, 60 percent; and 1885, 62 percent.

44. Smillie, Introduction to *Catalog of Etching Proofs*, p. xi.

45. Rensselaer, Introduction to *Women Etchers of America*, pp. 5–6.

46. Weitenkampf, *American Graphic Art*, p. 35.

47. Watrous, *Century of American Printmaking*, p. 18.

48. Koehler, "Vereinigte Staaten," p. 196.

49. Letter from James D. Smillie to Koehler, n.d. [1902], Koehler Correspondence, AAA.

50. William Chase, Frank Duveneck, Henry Twachtman, Stephen Parrish, R. S. Gifford, Henry Farrer, and Thomas and Peter Moran had abandoned etching for painting. The first two were also teaching, as was J. Alden Weir, whose printmaking activity after the early nineties was confined to a few experimental lithographs. Robert Blum and Otto Bacher had turned to illustration, mostly pen-and-ink, as their main source of livelihood and painted rather than etched in pursuit of artistic goals. Charles A. Platt was on the way to becoming a successful architect.

51. Undated letter from Smillie, replying to Jenkins's letter of 16 March 1902, Smillie Papers, AAA.

52. Watrous, *Century of American Printmaking*, p. 31.

53. C. Clark, "Five American Curators," p. 85.

54. Weitenkampf, *Manhattan Kaleidoscope*, p. 116.

55. Goldman, Introduction to *One Hundred Prints*, p. 16.

56. Watrous, *Century of American Printmaking*, p. 31.

57. The Print Collector's Bulletins of painter-etchings for sale by Keppel, covering twenty-six artists, were published between 1904 and 1909. The pamphlets in Roullier's series are undated but were published before 1912.

58. F. Watson, "American Etchers," p. 382.

59. *Print Collector's Quarterly* 1 (February 1911): 7.

60. Unsigned note, *Prints* 6 (February 1936): 157; and Cheney, "Notable Western Etchers," p. 738.

61. Stevens, "Exhibition of Contemporary American Etchings," p. 949.

62. As reported in volumes of the *American Art Annual*.

63. Cheney, "Notable Western Etchers," pp. 738–39.

64. *American Art Annual*, vols. 12–17.

65. Gearhart, "The Brothers Brown," pp. 288–89.

66. *Print Letter* 1 (3) (December 1922), LAMA.

67. Ibid., 1 (5) (August 1922).

68. Ibid., 2 (1) (October 1923); emphasis in original.

69. Ibid., 5 (2) (November 1926).

70. See *Yearbook of American Etching*.

71. Constitution, New York Society of Etchers, NYPL; our emphasis.

72. Though it is sometimes traced to a meeting at the Salmagundi Club in 1915, the Society's report of 1917 gives the founding date as April 1916 "at a meeting called by Mr. Paul Roche" (NYPL).

73. Ibid.

74. Article IX, Constitution, *Painter-Gravers of America*, in the Print Room, NYPL.

75. Grafly, *Philadelphia Print Club*, p. 1.

76. Print Club of Cleveland, *Fifty Years in Review*, p. 11.

77. Letter by Pennell, 11 November 1920, cited in E. R. Pennell, *Joseph Pennell*, 2:229.

78. See J. Pennell, *Graphic Arts*, p. 6.

79. Letter from Earl H. Reed to Pennell, 19 October 1911, Pennell-Whistler Collection, LC.

80. We counted only etchings, drypoints, aquatints, and modern line engravings, but not mezzotints and stipple engravings reminiscent of an older tradition.

81. Campbell Dodgson in *Fine Prints of the Year* (1936), p. 21.

82. The estimate appears in *Print Letter* (of the Honolulu Print Makers) 4 (1) (1938), in Print Room, NYPL.There was also an American College Society of Print Collectors, organized in 1930, to stimulate understanding of the graphic arts among undergraduates. Membership was open to institutions ready to commit themselves to establishing permanent collections available to the student body. An advisory committee selected two prints each year published in a limited edition for distribution to members. See listing in *American Art Annual*, in volumes 29 and after.

83. Comment by Dodgson, *Fine Prints of the Year* (1936), p. 21.

84. Sparrow, *Memories of Life and Art*, p. 90.

85. *Year's Art* (1948).

86. Sabin, "Colour Prints," p. 19.

87. Simpson, *Modern Etchings*, p. 15.

88. *Bookman's Journal and Print Collector* 6 (July 1920).

89. Simpson, *Modern Etchings*, p. 62.

90. DeKay, "Popularity of Etchings," pp. 249–51.

91. J. H. Slater gives sales from 1918 to 1920 in *Bookman's Journal and Print Collector* 6 (1920): 96.

92. McBey, "Etchings," p. 97.

93. Rinder, *D. Y. Cameron*, p. 217.

94. *The Rose Window, Notre-Dame de Paris* by Hedley Fitton, a contemporary of Cameron, scored a similar success—though at a lower level—at a Paris sale, where it was knocked down for 3,000 francs, about three times the amount normally commanded by other Fitton etchings.

95. Dutcher sale. See Delteil, *Manual de l'amateur d'estampes*, 2:467.

96. Slater, *Engravings and Their Value*, p. 26.

97. Wyckoff, *Wall Street and the Stock Markets*, p. 179.

98. McKinzie, *New Deal for Artists*, p. 5.

99. Menzies, "Art in the Showroom," p. 70.

100. Interview with Marion Rhodes, R.E., 1980.

101. Rowland, "Decline of Etching," pp. 24, 22.

102. Quoted in Berthoud, *Graham Sutherland*, p. 57.

103. Hutchinson in *Fine Prints of the Year* (1934), p. 13.

104. *San Francisco Chronicle*, 11 September 1929, cited in Schutz, *My Share of Wine*, p. 94.

105. Schutz, *My Share of Wine*, pp. 97ff. In 1939 Bard Brothers reproduced twenty-four of his etchings for a book entitled *New York in Etching*. Processed by intaglio gravure from copperplates, they looked nearly like original etchings; Schutz, *My Share of Wine*, p. 109.

106. Geerlings, "Interview," p. 54.

107. Hutchinson in *Fine Prints of the Year* (1934), p. 13.

108. Cf. Buckland-Wright, *Etching and Engraving*.

109. American Institute of Graphic Arts, *Fifty Prints of the Year* (1926).

110. Letter from John Taylor Arms to Philip Kappel, 16 May 1949, Philip Kappel Papers, AAA.

111. Letter from Ralph M. Pearson to George Biddle, 25 November 1956, Biddle Papers, LC.

112. Ralph M. Pearson to George Biddle, 24 April 1958, in ibid.

113. See Mellerio, *La lithographie originale*.

114. See Flint, *Provincetown Printers*.

115. Dows, "New Deal's Treasury Art Program," p. 43.

116. Kainen, "Graphic Arts Division," p. 175.

## Chapter 5

1. Sparrow, *Memories of Life and Art*, p. 80.

2. Ruskin, *Political Economy of Art*, p. 31.

3. Kris and Kurz, *Legend, Myth and Magic*.

4. Merritt, *Love Locked Out*, p. 9.

5. Goodrich, *Raphael Soyer*, p. 27.

6. Tunnicliffe, *My Country Book*, cited in Niall, *Portrait of a Country Artist*, pp. 19–20.

7. Marin, *Selected Writings*, pp. viii, 77.

8. Roberts, "Mortimer Menpes," p. 106. The story is repeated in *Who Was Who*.

9. Interview with Isabel Bishop, Oral History Collection, Columbia University.

10. Gardner, "Child as Artist," pp. 146–56.

11. Getzels and Csikszentmihalyi, *Creative Vision*, pp. 30ff.

12. McBey, *Early Life*, p. 10.

13. Browse, *Sickert*, p. 14.

14. Salaman, "Miss Eileen Soper's Etchings," p. 262.

15. Clipping, Roll N-79, NYPL in AAA.

16. Dodgson, "Maurice and Edward Detmold," pp. 374–75.

17. Rinder, *D. Y. Cameron*, pp. xxi–xxii.

18. Rutter, *Theodore Roussel*, pp. 2–3.

19. Raverat, *Period Piece*, p. 64.

20. Gág, *Growing Pains*, passim.

21. Wickey, *Thus Far*, pp. 23–24.

22. McBey, *Early Life*, p. 10; and Rothenstein, *Men and Memories*, 1:16–17.

23. Nonetheless, Getzels and Csikszentmihalyi, *Creative Vision*, p. 50, indicate that "fine art" students were high on aesthetic and low on economic values.

24. Swanwick, *I Have Been Young*, p. 60.

25. A. H. Fisher, *Through India and Burma*.

26. These include, among others, James David Smillie, James McBey, John Taylor Arms, Helen West Heller, Wanda Gág, Clare Leighton, and (probably) Mabel Dwight.

27. Gray, *Predicaments*, chap. 3.

28. Pelles, *Art, Artists and Society*, p. 65.

29. Jacob also overshadows his uncle Salomon van Ruisdael.

30. Greer, *Obstacle Race*, p. 12. See also Harris and Nochlin, *Women Artists*, passim.

31. Gág, "These Modern Women," p. 691.

32. Gág, *Growing Pains*, p. xix.

33. Personal interview with Denise Lebreton Brown (Mrs. Frank Waters), 11 March 1978.

34. Dunbar, *Laura Knight*, pp. 13–14.

35. Knight, *Oil Paint and Grease Paint*, p. 1. Much of the same material is repeated in her second autobiography, *Magic of a Line*.

36. Letter by Ernest Blumenschein, 9 March 1940, Blumenschein Papers, AAA.

37. Blumenschein Papers, AAA.

38. U. Johnson, Introduction to *Paul Cadmus*.

39. Burke, *J. Alden Weir*, pp. 23–55.

40. See Dunlap, *Rise and Progress of the Arts*, 3:184.

41. Letter by James David Smillie to S. R. Koehler, 19 August 1889, Koehler Correspondence (AAA).

42. This is how Weitenkampf remembers him; see *American Graphic Art*, p. 19.

43. Letters from Smillie to Koehler, 21 June and 20 April 1881, Koehler Correspondence, AAA.

44. Cited in Ashmolean Museum, Introduction to *Etchings and Aquatints by Orovida*, p. 10.

45. Meadmore, *Lucien Pissarro*, p. 90.

46. For example, Furst, "Orovida's Exhibition," p. 44.

47. Ashmolean Museum, Introduction to *Etchings and Aquatints by Orovida*, p. 10. Letters by Orovida in the archives of the Ashmolean contain many references to family finances.

48. Pissarro, *Letters to His Son*, p. 265. Camille, who died when Orovida was not yet ten, had produced more prints—127 etchings and 67 lithographs—than any other Impressionist.

49. *The Times*, 13 August 1968.

50. Meadmore, *Lucien Pissarro*, p. 71. See also B. S. Shapiro, *Impressionist Printmaker*.

51. Jacomb-Hood, *With Brush and Pencil*, p. 16.

52. Guichard, *British Etchers*, p. 61.

53. Macdonald, *History and Philosophy*, p. 124.

54. Merritt, *Love Locked Out*, p. 13.

55. Ibid., pp. 14–15. People told Merritt that she must be mistaken, that William Holman Hunt (1827–1910) had never made a watercolor of his famous painting. Years later Hunt himself assured her that he had indeed made a small watercolor replica, and it later turned up at an auction.

56. See Parker and Pollock, *Old Mistresses*, chap. 1.

57. Hale, *Mary Cassatt*, p. 31. Also Mathews, *Cassatt and Her Circle*, pp. 16–18, 22–36.

58. Johnson and Greutzner, *Dictionary of British Artists*, p. 207.

59. K. Fisher, *Conversations with Sylvia*, p. 23.

60. Raverat, *Period Piece*, p. 60.

61. Ibid., p. 64.

62. Ibid.

63. Nevinson, *Paint and Prejudice*, pp. 5–12.

64. Griff, "Recruitment and Socialization of Artists," pp. 149–50.

65. Rothenstein, *Men and Memories*, 1:17–21.

66. John, *Chiaroscuro*, p. 30.

67. Ibid., p. 31.

68. *Evening Standard*, 19 January 1929, cited in Michael Holroyd, *Augustus John*, p. 36.

69. Marin, *Selected Writings*, p. viii.

70. Helm, *John Marin*, pp. 6–8.

71. The information on Evergood, an etcher not included in our sample, comes from Baur, *Philip Evergood*; Lippard, *Graphic Work of Philip Evergood*; and from the Philip Evergood Papers, AAA (Roll 429).

72. Swanwick, *I Have Been Young*, p. 62.

73. Goodrich, Introduction to *Prints of Reginald Marsh*, p. 8.

74. Tarbell, *Peggy Bacon*, p. 4.

75. Muncaster, *Wind and the Oak*, p. 11.

76. T. M. Fisher, "George Elbert Burr," pp. 124–25.

77. Seeber, *George Elbert Burr*, p. 2.

78. Caw, *Sir D. Y. Cameron*, p. 2.

79. Bischoff, *Six Dogs—Drive Slowly*, p. 52.

80. Breeskin, *Anne Goldthwaite*, p. 19. There is good reason to believe that Goldthwaite was some years older when her aunt concluded she would never marry.

81. Ibid., p. 25. Maud Squire and Ethel Mars, who became friends of Gertrude Stein in Paris, were depicted in her story, "The Making of Americans," as "Miss Furr and Miss Skeen." See Toklas, *What Is Remembered*, p. 47.

82. Leighton, *Tempestuous Petticoat*, pp. 31–33.

83. Best known among them was John Leighton, a figure and landscape painter (1822–1912).

84. Cited in Muncaster, *Wind and the Oak*, p. 11.

85. McBey, *Early Life*, p. 46.

86. Stoppelman, Introduction to *Clara Klinghoffer*, p. 5.

87. Gettings, *Raphael Soyer*, p. 8.

88. Collins, *Artist-Venturer*, p. 17.

89. Mories, "Robert S. Austin," p. 181.

90. Salpeter, "Emil Ganso," p. 59.

91. Interview with Mahonri Young, Oral History Collection, Columbia University.

92. Heller's at times paranoiac account of her life can be found among the papers of Fay Gold [Fanny Helfand], AAA. Written when she was eighty-three, it was intended as the beginning of an autobiography. A somewhat similar account of her life is given by Harms, "From Dark to Light," pp. 30–34, 67–68.

93. Turner, "Sponsored and Contest Mobility."

Chapter 6

1. Of 468 Chicago artists listed in the 1938–39 volume of *Who's Who in American Art*, only two claimed to be "self-taught." Likewise, only 4 percent of British artists exhibiting in the late 1970s were found to have "evaded the art-school system entirely." Clive Ashwin, of *The Studio*, cited in Cresson, *Arts and the Academies*, pp. 17–18.
2. Pevsner, *Academies of Art*.
3. See Quentin Bell, *Schools of Design*, chap. 1, for a good summary of the "academic ideal."
4. J. C. Taylor, *Fine Arts in America*, p. 125.
5. See, for example, Moulin et al., *Les Artistes*, passim.
6. M. H. S., "Schools of the Royal Academy," p. 473.
7. Ibid. See also Hutchison, *History of the Royal Academy*, p. 118, for citations of relevant Royal Academy Council Minutes.
8. Morgan, "Lost Opportunity of the Royal Academy," p. 415.
9. M. H. S., "Schools of the Royal Academy," pp. 473–76.
10. Davson, "Art Students and Some Art Schools," p. 646.
11. Leslie, *Inner Life of the Royal Academy*, p. 4.
12. *The Studio* 25 (1902), p. 38.
13. "Royal Academy Schools List of Prizes and Prize Winners," RA ms. SP/4//2, Spielmann Correspondence, V&A.
14. Davson, "Art Students and Some Art Schools," p. 646.
15. Mories, "Sylvia Gosse," p. 11. See also the letter from Gosse to Ian Lowe, 10 March 1968, Curatorial Files, AMPR.
16. Nevinson, *Paint and Prejudice*, pp. 21–32, as are the quotes and summaries in the next paragraph.
17. Leslie, *Inner Life of the Royal Academy*, p. 64.
18. R.A. Annual Report, 1927, pp. 30–41, cited in Hutchison, *History of the Royal Academy*, p. 166.
19. Fothergill, *The Slade*, p. 8.
20. Jacomb-Hood, *With Brush and Pencil*, p. 13.
21. Sparrow, *Memories of Life and Art*, pp. 108–9.
22. Rothenstein, *Men and Memories*, 1:22–24.
23. Sparrow, *Memories of Life and Art*, p. 96.
24. Lilly, *Sickert*, p. 125.
25. Sparrow, *Memories of Life and Art*, p. 98.
26. Ibid., p. 108.
27. Macdonald, *History and Philosophy*, p. 269.
28. Davson, "Art Students and Some Art Schools," p. 647.
29. Ibid.
30. Nevinson, *Paint and Prejudice*, p. 34.
31. Nash, *Outline*, p. 90.
32. D. S. MacColl, "Augustus John," in Fothergill, *The Slade*, p. 7.
33. Letter by Gosse to Wright, 27 November 1921, Wright Papers, GU.
34. Lilly, *Sickert*, p. 118.
35. Everett, *Bricks and Flowers*, p. 73.
36. John, *Chiaroscuro*, pp. 42–43.
37. Nevinson, *Paint and Prejudice*, chap. 3 passim.
38. Cooke, "Girl Students," p. 579. See also Jopling, *Twenty Years of My Life*.
39. Herkomer, *My School and My Gospel*.

40. Ibid., pp 62ff.

41. Personal interview with Frances Hazeldine, goddaughter of Kemp-Welch, 21 June 1978.

42. Board of Education, *Report on Advanced Art Education.*

43. Frayling, *Royal College of Art*, passim.

44. Prospectus of the Royal College of Art, 1887.

45. Cooke, "Girl Students," pp. 573–74.

46. Class backgrounds of students in the Government Schools of Design are difficult to analyze. See Macdonald, *History and Philosophy*, especially pp. 143ff.

47. Ibid., p. 161.

48. Clausen, "Recollections of the Old School," pp. 155–61.

49. Ibid.

50. Pankhurst, *Suffragette Movement*, pp. 172–73.

51. Speed, "Reminiscences of S. K.," p. 36.

52. Board of Education, *Report.*

53. Board of Education, *Report on Advanced Art Education.*

54. Whitley, "London Schools," p. 19.

55. Article by John Adams, "The Art Student and Industrial Design," *R.C.A. Students' Magazine* (1924), RCA.

56. Address by Cameron to RCA students, 3 December 1912, as reported in "Common Room News," *R.C.A. Students' Magazine*, RCA.

57. This book is located in the library of the RCA.

58. Prospectus of the RCA, 1901, RCA.

59. Diploma statistics are from *The Studio*, cited by Frayling, *Royal College of Art*, p. 69.

60. Interview with R. S. G. Dent, 19 July 1980.

61. Collins, *Artist-Venturer.*

62. Niall, *Portrait of a Country Artist.*

63. M. Hardie, "Etchings of Stanley Anderson."

64. Robins, *Seventeenth President*, p. 9.

65. Keppel, *Golden Age of Engraving*, p. 36.

66. Brownell, "Art Schools of Philadelphia," p. 739.

67. This widely accepted explanation was recently challenged by Kathleen Foster, Curator of the Pennsylvania Academy, who announced that she would show that Eakins was fired because high educational standards were driving away students with more modest goals. See *New York Times*, 18 June 1986, p. 22.

68. J. C. Taylor, *Fine Arts in America*, p. 124.

69. Brownell, "Art Schools of Philadelphia," pp. 742, 745.

70. Mathews, *Cassatt and Her Circle*, chap. 1. The original letters are in the collection of the Pennsylvania Academy of Art.

71. Ibid., p. 17.

72. Ibid., p. 24.

73. Ibid., p. 26.

74. Willard and Levermore, "Blanche Dillaye," pp. 244–45.

75. See Clement, *Women in the Fine Arts*, and Dillaye, *Memorial Exhibition.*

76. Kershaw, "Philadelphia School of Design," p. 187.

77. Sources give conflicting information on the sequence of Getchell's art study. For the most conscientious effort to put together a chronology, see Davidson, *Eleanor Norcross, Amy Cross, and Edith Loring Getchell.*

78. E. Pennell, *Joseph Pennell*, 1:34–35.

79. E. Clark, *National Academy of Design*, p. 69.

80. Ibid., p. 90.

81. Fink, "National Academy of Design," pp. 9–10, and Landgren, *Years of Art*, pp. 18-19.

82. Fink, "National Academy of Design," pp. 5–14; for changes in the students' provenance, see p. 11.

83. From the Minutes of the Academy, cited in E. Clark, *National Academy of Design*, p. 159.

84. Breeskin, *Anne Goldthwaite*, pp. 21–23. See also Goldthwaite's Introduction to the Museum's exhibition catalog *Anne Goldthwaite*, which is taken from her unpublished autobiography.

85. Goldthwaite, Introduction to *Anne Goldthwaite*, p. 13.

86. Breeskin, *Anne Goldthwaite*, p. 21.

87. Ibid., p. 22.

88. Landgren, *Years of Art*, pp. 49, 57.

89. Kent, *It's Me Oh Lord*, p. 76.

90. See Henri, *Art Spirit*.

91. Speech by John Sloan accepting the president's chair of the ASL, 1931, cited in Landgren, *Years of Art*, p. 90.

92. Goodrich, Introduction to *Prints of Reginald Marsh*, p. 8.

93. Landgren, *Years of Art*, p. 74.

94. Ibid., p. 24.

95. Ibid., p. 52. Comstock was an inspector for the United States Post Office conducting his crusade for an association that called itself the New York Society for the Suppression of Vice.

96. Ibid., p. 78.

97. Gág, *Growing Pains*, p. 468. She, Dehn, and Lucile Lundquist (later Blanch) arrived together in 1917. Others from Minneapolis soon followed, including Arnold Blanch and Elizabeth Olds. Marguerite Kumm, younger than these four, bypassed the League for the Corcoran School of Art in Washington, D.C. Clara Mairs, still another etcher from Minnesota, did not, so far as we know, attend the Minneapolis School of Art but studied with Daniel Garber at the PAFA.

98. Gág, "These Modern Women"; see also A. O. Scott, *Wanda Gág*.

99. Interview with Isabel Bishop, Oral History Collection, Columbia University, N.Y.

100. Unpublished manuscript by Dorothy Koert, cited in Whatcom Museum, *Beyond the Veil*, [no pagination].

101. Josephson, *Portrait of the Artist as American*, p. 45.

102. Sharf and Wright, *William Morris Hunt*, p. 17. See DiMaggio, "Cultural Entrepreneurship," and Baltzell, *Puritan Boston and Quaker Philadelphia*, on cultural institutions in nineteenth-century America.

103. Cited in Richard T. York Gallery, Introduction to *Ellen Day Hale*.

104. Ellen Day Hale Papers, AAA. See also Hoppin, "Women Artists in Boston," pp. 17–46.

105. Hoppin, "Women Artists in Boston," p. 19.

106. Almira B. Fenno-Gendrot, *Artists I Have Known* (Boston: The Warren Press, 1923), cited in Sharf and Wright, *William Morris Hunt*, p. 17.

107. Sharf and Wright, *William Morris Hunt*, p. 18.

108. Ibid., pp. 20–21.

109. Letter by Hale, 19 March 1878, cited in Hoppin, "Women Artists in Boston," p. 37.

110. Atkinson, *Letters of Susan Hale*.

111. Hoppin, "Women Artists in Boston," p. 39.

112. Pisano, *Students of William Merritt Chase*.

113. Ibid., p. 6.

114. Erskine, *Thank God for Laughter*.

115. Fink, "American Artists in France," p. 34n.

116. Letter by Haldeman, 8 March 1867, cited in Mathews, *Cassatt and Her Circle*, p. 43.

117. Fink, "American Artists in France," p. 34.

118. Holland, "Lady Art Students in Paris," p. 226. This description of British students would also have fit many American students at the time.

119. Ibid., p. 228.

120. Rothenstein, *Men and Memories*, 1:36–43.

121. Ibid., p. 58.

122. Holland, "Lady Art Students in Paris," p. 228.

123. K. B. Scott, *Self-Portrait*, pp. 30–32.

124. Breeskin, *Anne Goldthwaite*, p. 26.

125. Whiteing, "The American Student," p. 266.

126. *San Antonio Express*, 25 January 1925, p. 12, cited in George, *Mary Bonner*, p. 32.

127. Letter from Helen West Heller, 18 October 1955, Fay Gold Papers, AAA; Harms, "From Dark to Light," pp. 30ff.

128. Seeber, *George Elbert Burr*, p. 197.

129. Pousette-Dart, *Ernest Haskell*, p. 13.

130. Whitehill, "Evolution of a Printmaker," pp. 15–23.

131. McBey, *Early Life*, pp. 18, 34, 41, 40.

## Chapter 7

1. M. Hardie, "Etchings of Stanley Anderson," pp. 227–28.

2. "Peter Moran," p. 135.

3. Cited in Whitehill, Introduction to *Rudolph Ruzicka*, p. 6. Whitehill was director of the Boston Athenaeum, 1946–73.

4. Ibid.; also Ivins, *Wood-Engravings of Rudolph Ruzicka*, p. 1.

5. Flier for the exhibition of Horter's drawings, paintings, and prints at the Hahn Gallery, Chestnut Hill, Pennsylvania, May 1980, and several obituary notices.

6. *Cleveland Sunday News* [no date], Russell Limbach Scrapbook, and letter by Limbach to Sam Golden, 22 May 1945, Limbach Papers, Wesleyan University Library, Middletown, Conn.

7. Many etchings by these former students were put in the RCA Library and then given to the V&A Print Room, where they are available for examination.

8. *The Times*, 25 April 1945.

9. Salaman, "Sir Frank Short, R.A., P.R.E., Master Engraver."

10. M. Hardie, "Women Etchers of Today," pp. 438–39.

11. Ibid.

12. Prospectus of the RCA, 1921–22.

13. Interview with Denise Lebreton Brown (Mrs. Frank Waters), 11 March 1978.

14. Salaman, "Etchings and Drypoints of W. P. Robins," p. 117.

15. Letters by W. P. Robins to Harold Wright, undated (one postmarked 29 July 1920), Wright Correspondence, GU.

16. Berthoud, *Graham Sutherland*, p. 47.

17. Ibid., p. 47.

18. Interview with Edward Bouverie-Hoyton, 14 June 1981.

19. Tanner, *Etching Craft*, pp. 12–13.

20. Berthoud, *Graham Sutherland*, pp. 51–52, citing Sutherland's foreword to *The English Vision*, catalog of an exhibition at the William Weston Gallery, London, October 1973.

21. Berthoud, *Graham Sutherland*, p. 54, based on an interview with Sutherland, November 1979.

22. Unpublished biography of Hester Frood, prepared 6 February 1966, in response to a request from the Ashmolean, in possession of Alan C. Campbell (nephew), Woodmancote, Surrey.

23. Gettings, *Raphael Soyer*, pp. 3, 9.

24. Landgren, *Years of Art*, which is a semiofficial history of the ASL. E. R. Pennell, *Joseph Pennell*, 2:271, gives October 1922 as the date of her husband's first class.

25. E. R. Pennell, *Joseph Pennell*, 2:272.

26. Interview with Brooks by Betty C. Hoag, 4 May 1975, Tape 48, Interviews with Artists, AAA.

27. Interview with Brooks, cited in Laguna Beach Museum of Art, *Southern California Artists*, p. 38.

28. Ibid.

29. Ibid., p. 39.

30. Chamberlain, *Etched in Sunlight*, p. 26.

31. Ibid., p. 28; also telephone interview with R. Stephens Wright, 1985.

32. George, *Mary Bonner*, pp. 48–49.

33. Arms, "A Self Estimate."

34. Fletcher, *John Taylor Arms*. The account of his self-initation appears in other sources. See Pelletier, "John Taylor Arms," p. 911, and Bassham, *John Taylor Arms*.

35. McBey, *Early Life*, p. 42.

36. Helm, *John Marin*, pp. 13–14; Zigrosser, Introduction to *Complete Etchings of John Marin*, pp. 7–8.

37. Based on her own straightforward account in an incomplete autobiographical sketch in her own handwriting, Pennypacker Long Island Collection; also F. M. Benson, "Moran Family," pp. 66–84. For a more recent account incorporating other material from the above collection, see Friese, "Mary Nimmo Moran," pp. 4–7.

38. Benson, "Moran Family," p. 78.

39. Friese, "Mary Nimmo Moran," p. 7.

40. O'Doherty, *American Masters*, p. 17.

41. Reminiscences of Hopper, Lahey Papers, AAA.

42. *American Art Review*, May 1881.

43. Dodd, *Generation of Illustrators*, p. 152.

44. Printed by J. A. Daniels, a well-known Boston printer, after steel-facing. Benson says that he personally printed all later proofs. See letter from Benson to Arthur Heintzelman, 2 July 1947, Essex Institute, Salem, Mass.

45. Letters from Frank Benson to Mr. McGuire, 12 December and 20 December 1912, in Director's Correspondence, Corcoran Gallery, Washington, D.C.

46. Dodd, *Generation of Illustrators*, p. 153.

47. Ibid.

48. F. Benson, *Etchings and Drypoints.*

49. John, *Chiaroscuro*, p. 43.

50. Dodgson, *Catalog of Etchings by John*, p. vi.

51. Ibid., p. viii.

52. Ibid.

53. Holroyd, *Augustus John*, p. 264.

54. Rutter, *Art in My Time*, p. 91.

55. Copley, Introduction to *John Copley and Ethel Gabain*, p. 2.

56. Salaman, "Gossip about Prints."

57. Letter from John Copley to Frank Weitenkampf, 8 January 1928, Weitenkampf Correspondence, AAA.

58. Letter from John Copley to Harold Wright, 3 August 1947, Wright Correspondence from Artists, GU.

59. Knight, *Magic of a Line*, p. 333. The accident is not mentioned in her earlier autobiography, which is a much fuller account.

60. Knight, *Oil Paint and Grease Paint*, p. 272.

61. Ibid.

62. Lumsden, *Art of Etching*, p. 323.

63. Knight, *Magic of a Line*, p. 333.

64. Ibid.

65. Koehler, "Works of American Etchers—Anna Lea Merritt," p. 230.

66. H. Merritt, *Art Criticism and Literature.*

67. A. L. Merritt, *Love Locked Out*, p. 119.

68. Ibid., pp. 119–20.

69. Letter from Anna Lea Merritt to Koehler, 18 July 1879, Koehler Correspondence, AAA.

70. Ibid., 23 September 1879.

71. Ibid., 27 October 1879.

72. Seeber, *George Elbert Burr.*

73. P. Morse, *John Sloan's Prints*, p. 62.

74. Kraft, *John Sloan*, pp. 7–8.

75. *Art World*, 6 May 1930. Clipping in Vertical Files, NMAA.

76. Letter from Bertha Jaques to Tolman, director of the Graphic Arts Division, Smithsonian, 3 November 1940, Vertical Files, NMAA.

77. Lovely and Pierce, Introduction to *Bertha E. Jaques.*

78. Letter from Bertha Jaques to Leila Mechlin, 25 October 1930, Mechlin Papers, AAA.

79. Letter by Jaques, no date given, cited in Lovely and Pierce, *Bertha E. Jaques*, p. ii.

80. Breeskin, *Anne Goldthwaite*, p. 21.

81. Tarbell, *Peggy Bacon*, pp. 9–10.

82. Salaman, "Etchings of Lumsden," p. 92.

83. Bone, "From Glasgow to London," p. 151.

84. Ibid., p. 152.

85. McBey, *Early Life*, p. 43.

86. Ibid.

87. Myers, "Re: Printing," p. 9.

88. Unpublished diary by Walter Tittle, AAA.

89. Lovely and Pierce, Introduction to *Bertha E. Jaques*, p. iv.

90. Letter from Jaques to Alice R. H. Smith, 5 January 1920, Smith Letters, SCHS.

Chapter 8

1. Letter from Sickert to Anna Hope Hudson (about 1907), cited in Baron, *Sickert*, p. 102 (emphasis in original).

2. Letter from William Strang to Isidore Spielmann, 22 December 1899, Spielmann Letters, V&A.

3. Benjamin, "Work of Art," pp. 224–25.

4. Several letters from Smillie to Koehler, 1879–80, Koehler Correspondence, AAA.

5. Ibid., 27 November 1879.

6. Ibid., 16 March 1880.

7. Letter from James D. Smillie to Benjamin Holt Ticknor, 10 June 1881, Ticknor Papers, LC.

8. H. C. White and C. A. White, *Canvasses and Careers*, esp. pp. 129–40; T. Shapiro, *Patrons and Politics*, pp. 72–76.

9. H. C. White and C. A. White, *Canvasses and Careers*, pp. 133–34.

10. See Whatcom Museum, *Beyond the Veil*.

11. Entry for 5 March 1945, Arms Diaries, AAA, indicates that Arms took Loggie out for dinner in New York City at the Swiss Pavillion, remarking that it was "delicious and expensive." The entry does not indicate who paid the bill.

12. Reynolds, Introduction to *Etchings of Anthony Gross*, p. 6.

13. T. Shapiro, *Patrons and Politics*, p. 76.

14. Pach, "Peintres et graveurs contemporains," pp. 214–15.

15. Meigs, *Lithographs of Peter Hurd*, p. 15.

16. Journal entry, 2 November 1934, cited in Hurd, *My Land Is the Southwest*, p. 133.

17. Interview with Arthur Millier by Betty Ochrie Hoag, 4 May 1965, Interviews with Artists, AAA.

18. Millier also wrote anonymous reviews for the *Christian Science Monitor*, *Time*, and the *Art Digest*.

19. Letter by Millier to his wife, dated "Christmas 1965," Millier Papers, AAA.

20. Laver, "Art of William Lee-Hankey," pp. 14–20.

21. Letter signed F. R. L., *The Times*, 23 July 1929.

22. Guichard, *British Etchers*, p. 37.

23. Letter from Peter Hurd to Frank Weitenkampf, 12 November 1939, Letters to Weitenkampf, AAA.

24. F. Benson, *Etchings and Drypoints*.

25. Cited in Ordeman, *Frank W. Benson*, p. 17.

26. Rinder, *D. Y. Cameron*, p. xxx.

27. Wickey, *Thus Far*, p. 66.

28. Norman Springer in the *San Francisco Bulletin*, 26 May 1919.

29. Emerson, "Helen Hyde," p. 430. On the advice of Macbeth, the New York art dealer, she had submitted the painting for "one of the prizes," only to find that it was not even accepted for exhibition. But she also felt that, "however things have been going my way so much lately for my own good perhaps, it is just as well to have a drawback now and then." See letter from Helen Hyde to Macbeth, 16 April 1899, Macbeth Gallery Records, AAA.

30. Jaques, *Helen Hyde*, p. 10.

31. Ibid., p. 27.

32. Ibid., pp. 24–25.

33. Letter from Helen Hyde to Macbeth, 11 May 1899, Macbeth Gallery Records, AAA.

34. Jaques, *Helen Hyde*, p. 25. Other quotes in this paragraph come from letters to Macbeth Gallery between 1896 and 1919, the year of Hyde's death. Letters, diaries, and accounts of work sold, which are in the manuscript collection of the California Historical Society (San Francisco), were not examined.

35. Laurence, "American Etchings at St. Louis," p. 279.

36. Salpeter, "Emil Ganso," p. 100. Our sketch is largely based on this article.

37. Zigrosser, *World of Art and Museums*, p. 42.

38. Wickey, *Thus Far*, pp. 77, 76.

39. Dodgson, "English Landscapes of Robins," p. 93.

40. Katherine Cameron, the other well-known Scottish "lady-etcher," did not become an R.E. until late in her life. Crawford was one of the few nationally recognized etchers, male or female, resident in Glasgow.

41. Singer, *Moderne Graphik*, p. 328.

42. *Scottish Life*, 28 April 1900, p. 1065, has a photograph showing Crawford wearing pince-nez spectacles. For another posthumous appreciation, see the obituary in the *Glasgow Herald*, 26 April 1918.

43. Caw, *Scottish Painting*, p. 212.

44. From a memoriam by Dame Emmeline Turner for *Magazine of the Roedean School*, 1949.

45. From 1915 to 1934, Partridge was married to Imogen Cunningham, a member of the famous f/64 group of photographers, which included Ansel Adams, Maynard Dixon, and Dorothea Lange. The name of Cunningham is undoubtedly more familiar than that of Partridge. Much of the following material is based on an interview with the artist in 1982.

46. Letter from Roi Partridge, 12 March 1924, Holman Files, BPL.

47. Letter from Roi Partridge to Frank Weitenkampf, 11 February 1926, Letters to Weitenkampf, AAA.

48. Steinberg, "Roi Partridge at Ninety-One."

49. The school, founded as the Chestnut Street Female Seminary, is today part of the community college system.

50. Information on Dillaye comes from George U. Stevens, "Autobiography of Modern Artists," Stevens Collection, AAA, which includes clippings from many newspapers; from Clement, *Women in the Fine Arts*, p. 110; from Weitenkampf Correspondence, Roll 86, AAA; from clippings in Holman Files, BPL; from Macbeth Gallery Papers, AAA; and from the Philadelphia Art Alliance, *Memorial Exhibition*.

51. Interview with and personal letter from Rhodes to authors, 1980.

52. Simon, *500 Years of Art in Illustration*, p. xiii.

53. Letter from Dorothy Lathrop to Grace Albee, 12 January 1969, Albee Papers, AAA.

54. J. Pennell, *Adventures of an Illustrator*, p. 57.

55. Ibid., p. 77.

56. Ibid., p. 101.

57. Notman, "Some More of the Book Illustrators."

58. Interview with Mahonri Young, Oral History Project, Columbia University, N.Y.

59. Wickey, *Thus Far*, p. 63.

60. Letters from F. L. M. Griggs, 4 May 1902 and following, Macmillan Correspondence, BL.

61. Letter from William Strang, 1 June 1897, in ibid.

62. Letters from William Rothenstein in ibid.

63. As an example, see John Sloan's illustrations for the two-volume edition of

W. Somerset Maugham's *Of Human Bondage*, published for the Limited Editions Club.

64. Woodruff, Foreword to *History of British Wood Engraving*, p. 17.

65. Letter from Winifred Holtby, 15 April 1925, cited in Holtby, *Letters to a Friend*, p. 319ff.

66. In 1929 Lathrop won the Newberry Medal, then the Caldecott Medal for illustrating, and the Eyre Medal for wood engraving. In 1946, she received a purchase prize from the Library of Congress for her print, "Goldfish."

67. Letter from Dorothy Lathrop to Grace Albee, n.d. [May or June 1967], Albee Papers, AAA.

68. Albee notebook, in ibid.

69. Letter from John F. Weir to J. Alden Weir, 25 February 1875, cited in Young, *Life and Letters*, pp. 63–64.

70. Letter from Fred Richards, 1925, cited in Collins, *Artist-Venturer*, p. 131.

71. Letter from Fred Richards, cited in ibid., p. 160.

72. Obituary in *New York Sun*, 27 September 1935.

73. Interview with Lucille Douglass, *Washington Post*, 15 April 1928.

74. Knight, *Oil Paint and Grease Paint*, p. 24. Airy's canvas *Cook-house at Withy Camp* is reproduced in Konody, *Art and War*.

75. Letter by Anna Airy, 8 June 1918, cited in M. Ross, *Robert Ross*, pp. 329–30. This and other wartime paintings by Airy are in the Imperial War Museum in London.

76. Dunbar, *Laura Knight*, p. 82. For other evidence of Munnings's friendship with the Knights, see his autobiography, *Artist's Life*, passim.

77. Letter from Anna Airy to Dr. John Dickson, 1 February 1962, concerning the watercolors of his wife, Evangeline Dickson, which is in the Dicksons' possession.

78. Airy also served as president of the Ipswich Museums. Webber, Introduction to *Centenary Exhibition*.

79. Clipping, 17 July 1931, Blanche McVeigh Papers, AAA.

80. Letters by John Taylor Arms to Blanche McVeigh, 1 May 1943 and 13 August 1946, McVeigh Papers, AAA.

81. Letter by Maynard Walker to Blanche McVeigh, May 1951, in ibid.

82. First of a series of articles by Janice Conley, n.d., in ibid..

83. *The Times*, 2 October 1948; *Who Was Who*; and Lumsden, *Catalogue of Exhibition*.

84. Rutter, *Theodore Roussel*, pp. 4–5.

85. Lehman, *Paul Landacre*.

86. See Landacre, *California Hills*.

87. Lehman, *Paul Landacre*, pp. 70–71.

88. Seeber, *George Elbert Burr*. Also Cheney, "Notable Western Etchers," and T. M. Fisher, "George Elbert Burr," pp. 324–29.

89. R. Morse, "George Elbert Burr," p. 74.

90. Seeber, *George Elbert Burr*, p. 42.

91. *Rocky Mountain News*, 24 June 1923, cited ibid., p. 44.

92. Letter from George Burr to Frank Weitenkampf, 22 May 1927, Letters to Weitenkampf, AAA.

93. Letter from George Burr to Leila Mechlin, n.d. (about 1929), Mechlin Correspondence, AAA.

94. Copley, Introduction to *John Copley & Ethel Gabain*.

95. Letter from John Copley to Weitenkampf, Letters to Weitenkampf, AAA.

Other relevant letters by Copley in Wright Correspondence from Artists, AMPR.

96. Copley, Introduction to *John Copley and Ethel Gabain.*

97. Ibid. Other information concerning Gabain's illnesses in her letters to Harold Wright, Wright Correspondence from Artists, AMPR.

98. Letter from Wright to the Copleys, in ibid., dated 24 May 1949. It is possible that this letter, among the Wright papers, was never mailed.

99. Letter from John Copley to Wright, 8 July 1949, in ibid.

100. Baldry, "Paintings and Etchings of Holroyd," p. 292.

101. Newbolt, *My World,* p. 214.

102. Baldry, "Paintings and Etchings of Holroyd," p. 292.

103. Obituary, *The Times,* 19 November 1917.

104. Mackenzie, *Shoulder to Shoulder,* p. 261.

105. Zimmerman, "Julian Alden Weir," pp. 306–7; see also Young, *Life and Letters,* p. 184.

106. De Cordoba, *Etchings, Drawings, Lithographs.* See also the obituary in the *New York Times* written by her niece (Mercedes Matter). Erroneously, an obituary had appeared in the *American Art Annual,* 10:76, as early as 1913 when she would have been 38. Johnson and Greutzner, *Dictionary of British Artists,* published in 1976, gives her death as 1912, which may be the year in which she became legally blind.

107. *The Times,* 12 March 1949.

108. *Montgomeryshire Express and Times,* 6 July 1957.

109. Wittkower and Wittkower, *Born under Saturn,* chap. 6, found a remarkably small number of self-inflicted deaths among artists.

110. *Dictionary of National Biography,* s.v. Walcot.

111. Athill, Introduction to *William Strang.*

112. Letter by Caroline Armington to Frank Weitenkampf, n.d. (February 1925), Weitenkampf Correspondence, AAA.

113. Brockman, *Caroline and Frank Armington.* Based on interviewing persons who had known them.

114. Frank Armington's obituary (*New York Times,* 23 September 1941) indicates that he had married Jessie F. Clark. We have no information on why the will was changed or whether it contained any special provision about what to do with their joint work.

115. For instance, see letter from Arthur W. Heintzelman to Albee, 6 January 1943, Albee Papers, AAA; this collection, however, was not catalogued and in boxes at the time we consulted it.

116. Edward Albee, author of *Who's Afraid of Virginia Woolf?,* is a nephew, not a son, as sometimes erroneously assumed.

117. Tarbell, *Marguerite Zorach,* p. 41.

118. Zorach, *Art Is My Life.*

119. See letters by Marguerite Zorach to her husband, written before their marriage, William Zorach Papers, LC. The citation is from Tarbell, *Marguerite Zorach,* p. 35.

120. Ibid., p. 49.

121. Ibid., p. 50.

122. Letter by Marguerite Zorach to Samuel C. Cooper, 27 December 1961, after her husband's death, Zorach Papers, LC.

123. Zorach, *Art Is My Life,* p. 189.

124. Ibid., p. 183.

125. Scott, *Wanda Gág,* p. 104; letter to the author (née Schmidt).

126. Zigrosser, *My Own Shall Come to Me*, p. 125.

127. Letters by Higgins, n.d. (1910) and 27 February 1910, in Macbeth Gallery Records, AAA.

128. Zigrosser, *Artist in America*, pp. 145–46.

129. Hale, *Life in the Studio*, p. 108. See also correspondence between Hale and Clements, Hale Papers, AAA.

130. Kloss, *Gene Kloss Etchings*, pp. 9–11.

131. Bassman, *Born Charlestonian*.

132. Letter by Mildred Bryant Brooks to R. P. Tolman, Smithsonian Institution, 1 November 1937, in Vertical Files, NMAA. Brooks was then thirty-six.

133. Laguna Beach Museum of Art, *Southern California Artists*, p. 36, based on an interview with the artist held at the museum.

## Chapter 9

1. Wackernagel, *Florentine Renaissance Artist*, p. 285.

2. Rogers, "Batignolles Group," pp. 194–220.

3. Letter from Bertha Jaques to Alice R. H. Smith, 6 September 1923, Smith Letters, SCHS.

4. Ibid., 5 January 1921.

5. Ibid., 6 September 1923.

6. Kainen, "Graphic Arts Division," p. 166.

7. Cited in E. R. Pennell and J. Pennell, *Life of Whistler*, 1:283.

8. Letter from Bone to Hugh Walpole, dated 28 August (about 1924), Walpole Papers, RHC.

9. Reminiscences of A. H. Palmer, cited in M. Hardie, *Frederick Goulding*, p. 123.

10. Partridge, "Gentle Prayer on Etching," in *Print Letter*, LAMA.

11. Thorne, "Portable Press," in ibid.

12. Burty, "L'oeuvre de Haden," p. 273.

13. M. Hardie, *Frederick Goulding*, p. 39.

14. Letter from Haden to Goulding, 4 April 1896, cited in ibid., p. 36.

15. David Strang, a son of William Strang, was author of a widely used text, *Printing of Etchings and Engravings*.

16. Fletcher, *John Taylor Arms*, p. 177.

17. Letter from Jaques to Alice R. H. Smith, 15 October 1925, Smith Letters, SCHS.

18. Ibid., 5 January 1921.

19. *American Art Annual*, 13:243.

20. These six prints (by Sloan, etc.) issued in editions of between 500 and 1,000 are today in high demand. The other artists were Peggy Bacon, John Marin, Ernest Haskell, Edward Hopper, and Kenneth Hayes Miller—of whom all but the last two are in our sample.

21. Letter from John Taylor Arms to Frank Weitenkampf, 22 December 1924, Letters to Weitenkampf, AAA.

22. Letter from Bertha Jaques to Alice R. H. Smith, 17 September 1921, Smith Letters, SCHS.

23. Pinder, *Problem der Generationen*.

24. Nevinson, *Paint and Prejudice*, pp. 42–43, 46, 48.

25. These were, according to Rothenstein, *Men and Memories*, 1:334, John's sister Gwen, Mary Edwards (who married McEvoy), Grace Westry, Ida Nettleship

(who became John's first wife), Louise Salaman, Ursula Tyrwhitt, and Gwen Salmond (later Lady Matthew Smith), all of whom attended the Slade at the same time.

26. *The Times*, 1 February 1958, in an obituary note on Lady Matthew Smith.

27. Fothergill, *The Slade*.

28. Letter from H. M. Rosenberg to Margery Ryerson, 17 August [1923 or 1928], Ryerson Papers, AAA. See also Duveneck, *Frank Duveneck*, p. 89, and Bacher, *With Whistler in Venice*, p. 9.

29. Cited in Anderson Gallery Auction Catalog of the estate of Otto Bacher, 1910, NYPL.

30. E. R. Pennell and J. Pennell, *Life of Whistler*, 1:295–96. See also Bacher, *With Whistler in Venice*, p. 138. Whistler may have spread this rumor himself to spoil the opening of the exhibition for Haden, with whom he was feuding.

31. Weitenkampf, *Manhattan Kaleidoscope*, p. 122.

32. The first exhibition of the Impressionist painters was held under the name of the Society of Artists, Painters, Sculptors, and Etchers. The original nucleus, whose members had met as students, were later joined by others, including Bracquemond, the peintre-graveur, who was a friend of Degas, but who played only a minor role in this group. See Rewald, *History of Impressionism*.

33. John Sloan notes on deposit in the Delaware Art Center, Wilmington, Delaware, cited in Kraft, *John Sloan*, p. 19.

34. Brooks, *John Sloan*, p. 46.

35. Sloan, *John Sloan's New York*, pp. 30–31, 28, 31, 32.

36. Ibid., pp. 33, 108, 120, 109, 112, 118.

37. Cited in Brooks, *John Sloan*, p. 172.

38. J. D. Morse, "John Sloan," pp. 57–58.

39. Ogg, "Etchings of Sutherland and Drury," pp. 77, 79, 92. Sutherland and Drury were the youngest artists ever to become subjects of a full-length article in this journal. The article could have been extended to include Bouverie-Hoyton and Larkins, the other two members of the group with Robin Tanner, the evening student a fifth.

40. American Artists Congress, *Graphic Works*, p. 5. For a recent general review of the history of graphics in the United States, see U. E. Johnson, *American Prints and Printmakers*, and Watrous, *Century of American Printmaking*.

41. Bone, "From Glasgow to London," p. 156.

42. Letter from Bone to MacColl, 1 October 1901, MacColl Papers, BL; our emphasis.

43. Ibid., 24 October 1901.

44. Ibid., 20 March 1937.

45. Ibid.

46. Dodgson, "Muirhead Bone," pp. 63–64.

47. Letter from John Copley to Wright, 11 May 1923, Wright Papers, GU.

48. Ibid., 23 December 1924.

49. Zigrosser, *World of Art and Museums*, p. 44.

50. Letter from Ethel Gabain, 14 October 1938, Wright Papers, GU.

51. Weitenkampf, *Manhattan Kaleidoscope*, p. 147.

52. Letter by Malcolm Salaman to Whistler, 2 January 1889, Whistler Collection, GU.

53. Obituary notice in *The Studio* 119 (February 1940): 102.

54. Salaman, "James McBey," p. 18.

55. Letter from Murray to Greig, 4 December 1911, Greig Papers, BM.

56. Letter from McBey to Greig, 10 March 1912, in ibid.
57. Letter from Gutekunst to Greig, 13 May 1913, in ibid.
58. Letter from McBey to Greig, 10 March 1912, in ibid.
59. Letter from McBey to Greig, 22 May 1914, in ibid.
60. Kynett, *Treasure Trove*, p. 10.
61. Comstock, *A Gothic Vision*, p. 12.
62. Alexander, *Engraved Work of F. L. Griggs*.
63. Simpson, *Modern Etchings*, p. 12.
64. Ibid., p. 30. The listing was as follows: I. Meryon, Whistler; II. Zorn, Haden, Bone; III. Legros, Forain; IV. McBey, Cameron; V. (Marius) Bauer, Gagnon, Lalanne, Lepère, Robins, Short.
65. Cooley, "Fame," p. 117.
66. E. R. Pennell, *Joseph Pennell*, 1:155–56.
67. Ibid., p. 160.
68. Carrington, "Note by the Editor," p. 181.
69. E. R. Pennell, *Joseph Pennell*, 2:100.
70. Ibid., pp. 33–34; emphasis in original.
71. Singer, *Moderne Graphik*, p. 359.
72. Benjamin, "Work of Art."
73. Rothenstein, *Men and Memories*, 2:305–6.
74. Bauerlé's father was a well-known artist and art teacher, Karl-Wilhelm-Friedrich Bauerlé, who came to England in 1869. His daughter changed her name "around 1909" because of "tensions" that led her to deny her "ethnicity." See Singer, *Moderne Graphik*. Elyse Lord also of German origin, took even greater pains to hide her German parentage by being absolutely uncommunicative about her early years and private life.
75. The precise numbers: 20 of 32 British artists, 13 of 40 Americans.
76. Nevinson, *Paint and Prejudice*, p. 95ff.
77. Fletcher, *Complex Simplicity*, p. 13.
78. See obituary of Mary Cox Palethorpe, Copeman's partner, in the Liverpool *Courier*, 4 June 1988; also, bibliographic entry on Copeman in *Merseyside Painters*.
79. Letter from Gorst to Herman Theodore Radin, 5 September 1916, Letters to Radin, NYPL.
80. Ashmolean Museum, *Etchings and Aquatints by Orovida*, p. 11. She spent a year with the Women's Emergency Corps.
81. See "Zella de Milhau," and Erskine, *Thank God for Laughter*, for accounts of her war experience.
82. Whitmore, "A. Hugh Fisher," p. 381.
83. Among others suffering a loss were Stanley Anderson, Edward Bouverie-Hoyton, Paul Drury, and Marion Rhodes.
84. "List of Etchings in order done," by Walter Tittle, Tittle Papers, Wittenberg University; also Schutz, *My Share of Wine*, p. 110. Neither artist was in the statistical sample.
85. Tippett, *Art in the Service of War*, p. 23.
86. Gallatin, *Art and the Great War*, p. 138.
87. Rothenstein, *Men and Memories*, 2:134, 206.
88. Harries and Harries, *War Artists*, p. 7.
89. Letter from Bone to MacColl, 3 May 1916, MacColl Papers, BM.
90. Ibid., 14 May 1916.
91. Harries and Harries, *War Artists*, p. 9

92. Bone, *The Western Front*.

93. Harries and Harries, *War Artists*, p. 78.

94. Gibson, "British Artists in the War Zone," p. 178.

95. Ibid., p. 185; also M. Hardie, *Etchings and Drypoints by James McBey*, p. xv.

96. Letter from Willson to McBey, 28 April 1917, cited in Harries and Harries, *War Artists*, p. 24.

97. Based on McBey, *Early Life*, pp. 117–19, and Harries and Harries, *War Artists*, pp. 24–26.

98. Tippett, *Art in the Service of War*, p. 59.

99. Nevinson, *Paint and Prejudice*, p. 115.

100. Tippett, *Art in the Service of War*, p. 59.

101. Quote from introduction to Dodgson and Montague, *C. W. R. Nevinson*.

102. Letter by Nash, 7 March 1917, cited in Nash, *Outline*, pp. 188–91.

103. Ibid., 6 April 1917, p. 194

104. Ibid., 13 November 1917, pp. 218–19.

105. Notes by William Rothenstein accompanying the publication in 1925 of *Twelve Drypoints of the War 1914–1918* by Colnaghi's, which published the series.

106. Dodgson, "Mr. Percy Smith's 'Dance of Death.'"

107. Chenil Gallery, Introduction to *75 Etchings of the Battlefield*.

108. Walker, "Etchings of Ian Strang," p. 139.

109. Gallatin, *Art and the Great War*, p. 24.

110. J. A. Smith, *In France with the A. E. F.*

111. Letter by Hornby, 29 July 1918, cited in Holman, *Hornby's Etchings*, p. 10ff.

112. For example, Melleterre, "How the War Was Won."

113. Arms, *Kerr Eby, A.N.A.*

114. Eby, "War," p. 80.

115. Eby, *War*.

116. A. Ross, *Colours of War*, p. 23.

117. Cited in Harries and Harries, *War Artists*, p. 199.

118. Cited in A. Ross, *Colours of War*, pp. 149–50.

119. Biddle, *Artist at War*, p. 1.

120. Varga, "Life's Art Program," p. 121. See also letter from Cook to Captain Herman W. Williams, Jr., of the Corps of Engineers, 10 August 1945, Cook Papers, SYRU.

121. Arms, "Diaries," 11 April 1942, AAA.

122. Edward Alden Jewell in the *New York Times*, 6 May 1945.

123. Dodd, *Generation of Illustrators*, pp. 164–65.

124. Letter from Howard N. Cook to Capt. Loren Fisher (U.S. Army), 30 August 1946, Cook Papers, SYRU.

125. Howard N. Cook, interviewed by Mr. Darragh Aldrich on Radio Station WCCO (Minneapolis-St. Paul), 7 March 1945.

126. Letter from Cook to Frank Rehn, 29 October 1944, Cook Papers, SYRU.

127. Ibid., 12 September 1945.

128. Ibid.

129. Ibid., 8 January 1946.

130. Material from printmakers *not* in our sample, because there were no women to match them with, is occasionally used for illustration but not for quantitative generalization.

131. Beetles, *S. R. Badmin*, p. 23.
132. Berthoud, *Graham Sutherland*, chap. 5.
133. Beetles, *S. R. Badmin*, p. 23.
134. Czestochowski, *Gerald K. Geerlings*, pp. 18, 30.
135. Life history based on telephone interview, 1985. The quote is from Camille Mauclair, "Redmond Stephens Wright," p. 3.

## Chapter 10

1. Buhot, "Onzième Exposition," p. 198. Mentioned by name were Crawford, Harrison, Bolingbroke, Piper, and Nichols.
2. Wedmore, *Etching in England*; M. Hardie, "Women Etchers of Today."
3. Singer, *Moderne Graphik*, pp. 324–29.
4. Angelica Kauffmann was elected in 1768, shortly after the Academy was founded. According to the entry for Kauffmann in the Thieme-Becker, her success was based in large part on "extra-artistic" factors, such as her precocity and "femininity," as well as a personality that earned her the goodwill of many important people.
5. Newbolt, *Royal Society of Painter–Etchers*.
6. Estimate is based on the number of women etchers listed in Guichard, *British Etchers*.
7. Derived on the assumption that listings in *Fine Prints of the Year* for men and women are equally representative of their total output.
8. Harris and Nochlin, *Women Artists*.
9. Guichard, *British Etchers*, p. 11.
10. "Etching Moralized" (1844); see Hood, *Poetical Works*, p. 384.
11. Singer, *Moderne Graphik*, p. 235 (author's translation).
12. *Gazette des beaux-arts*, 1 October 1860, cited in Harris and Nochlin, *Women Artists*, p. 56.
13. M. Hardie, "Women Etchers of Today," p. 380.
14. The first spelling is as in Koehler, Introduction to *Exhibition of Women Etchers*. The "van Schurman" appears in the introduction by Weitenkampf to *Engravings, Etchings and Lithographs by Women*, held at the Grolier Club fourteen years later. Neither the name Schurman nor van Schurman appears in Hind, *History of Engraving and Etching*.
15. Wortley, "Amateur Etchers," pp. 189–211.
16. Society of Graphic Arts, *Catalogue of Inaugural Exhibition*.
17. M. Hardie, "Women Etchers of Today," pp. 438–39. Pott herself was Hardie's probable source. But since Frank Short, an influential member of the RSPE, was thoroughly familiar with her work, it is unlikely that the selection committee did not know that they were admitting a woman.
18. A. L. Merritt, "Letter to Artists."
19. Guichard, *British Etchers*, pp. 24, 45, 39, and 44.
20. Ibid., p. 60. Soper's illustrative drawings actually resemble those of E. H. Shepard's for *Winnie the Pooh*, A. A. Milne's classic.
21. Greer, *Obstacle Race*, pp. 36–67; regarding Clarke Hall, see p. 53.
22. She was born Elise Müller, and the claim may have been part of the fiction by which she sought to conceal her German origin during the First World War.
23. Somewhat over a fourth of all women in mid-Victorian England never married, but among the educated classes to which most of our British lady etchers belonged, the proportion of never-marrieds would have been considerably higher. See Best, *Mid-Victorian Britain (1851–70)*, p. 120.

24. Singer, *Moderne Graphik*, p. 328.
25. Ibid.
26. Wedmore, *Etching in England*, pp. 159–60.
27. Birch, *Stanhope and Elizabeth Forbes*, p. 67.
28. Greer, *Obstacle Race*, p. 113; in fact, a number of her oils were shown at the Royal Academy.
29. Getscher, *Stamp of Whistler*, p. 196.
30. Caw, *Scottish Painting*, pp. 414–15.
31. Addendum to chap. 21 of Levis, *Descriptive Bibliography*.
32. Personal interview with Sarah Pugh-Jones, 1 July 1983. She also showed us some memorabilia and several etchings by Gorst. Other traces of the artist's work survive in prints presented to Welfare House (Langollen) years after her death, and in a biographical sketch Pugh-Jones wrote for the *Journal of the Society of Bookplate Collectors*. We have been unable to locate the latter.
33. Thérèse Lessore, whose second marriage was to Sickert, is the one divorcee in the earlier generations.
34. Greer, *Obstacle Race*, pp. 48–49. She seems to base this on the biography by Majorie Lilly, *Sickert*, p. 114, which she does not actually cite.
35. Guichard, *British Etchers*, p. 47.
36. To keep the record complete, the *Times Index* includes the obituaries that appeared in the *Daily Telegraph* during this period, including those of Clarke Hall and Charles F. Tunnicliffe.
37. The British Registry at Somerset House, London, houses her will and that of many other etchers.
38. Issue dated April 1903.
39. Issue dated 26 February 1906.
40. Interview with Nichols, 7 October 1889, *Women's Penny Paper*, n.d., Colman and Rye Collections, Central Library, Norwich, England.
41. Article, dated 1931, in ibid.
42. Response to a letter of inquiry regarding Nichols, 21 November 1945, Correspondence File in the library, Castle Museum, Norwich, England.
43. Responses to letters of inquiry regarding Nichols, 1 December 1960 and 29 January 1968, in ibid.
44. "Death of Miss C. M. Nichols," *Eastern Daily Press*, 31 January 1923.
45. Clement, *Women in the Fine Arts*, pp 250–52.
46. Interview with Nichols, 7 October 1889, clipping from *Women's Penny Paper*, Colman and Rye Collections, Central Library, Norwich, England.
47. H. S. S., "A Norwich Artist," *Eastern Daily Press*, 22 February 1943.
48. Letter from Nichols to Frank Short, 28 March 1908, Spielmann Letters, V&A.
49. Letters from Nichols to I. Spielmann, 15 April and 28 July 1908, in ibid.
50. Clipping in *Woman's Penny Paper*, n.d., Colman and Rye Collections, Central Library, Norwich, England.
51. *The Times*, 2 February 1923.
52. *Eastern Daily Press*, 3 February 1923.
53. Correspondence is attached to the copy of the catalog of Charles F. Watson in the Bodleian Library, Oxford.
54. A copy of the accompanying citation is in AMPR.
55. Frayling, *Royal College of Art*, p. 77.
56. F. Hardie, *Prints of Martin Hardie*.
57. Hardie, "Women Etchers of Today," 1 September 1906.
58. Ibid., 8 September 1906.

59. Singer, *Moderne Graphik*, p. 328; also Wedmore, "Prints and Drawings," p. 102.

60. Preparing a plate for mezzotint requires considerable strength, and not many have been able to master the technique, yet both Pott and Mary Sloane, her friend and contemporary, performed this task successfully.

61. C. M. Pott, *Philomir*. The copy in the British Library is dated 1915.

62. Mrs. Henry Pott, *Quite a Gentleman*.

63. Personal interview with Edward Bouverie-Hoyton, 14 June 1981.

64. *R.C.A. Student Magazine* 2 (January 1913): 45, and (February 1913): 60.

65. Concerning her troubles, see letters of 8 June and 3 November 1920, 4 April 1921, and 5 June and 10 September 1922. For pride in workmanship, see letter dated 8 May 1923. All in Letters to Radin, NYPL.

66. Furst, in *Apollo Magazine*, January 1930, p. 69; also *Cimento, Rivista Illustrata di Belle Arti*, Naples, 1929. The fifty-two plates include two woodcuts and twenty wood engravings that were commissioned for illustration.

67. Catalog and letters from Catherine E. Marshall, with a list of purchases and purchasers; see Wright Papers, GU.

68. Letters from Fyfe are both in Wright Papers, GU, and Wright Correspondence from Artists, AMPR.

69. Personal letter from Reverend Noel Kemp-Welch to authors, 10 June 1978.

70. Personal interview with Frances Hazeldine, niece and god-daughter of Kemp-Welch, 21 June 1978.

71. Singer, *Moderne Graphik*, p. 329.

72. Wedmore, *Fine Prints*, p. 247.

73. Thieme and Becker, *Allgemeines Lexikon*, s.v. "Margaret Kemp-Welch."

74. Personal interview with Frances Hazeldine, 21 June 1978.

75. Sometimes the work of Margaret Kemp-Welch is mistakenly attributed to her cousin, Lucy Kemp-Welch, well known as a watercolor painter. In the Bradford Museum of Art we found one of her prints so identified. See also Clement, *Women in the Fine Arts*, p. 191, who quotes Wedmore praising "Lucy" for work Margaret showed at the RSPE exhibition.

76. Quotation from a personal interview with R. S. G. Dent, R.E., 19 July 1980, who had been a friend of Delleany and graciously answered our many questions about her and others.

77. George Buckton, her father, was a fellow of both the Royal Society and of the Linnaean Society; her mother's brother, William Odling, was a professor and distinguished chemist.

78. Interview with R. S. G. Dent, 19 July 1980.

79. Salaman, *Laura Johnson Knight*. Elyse Lord was later included in a series on the modern masters of *color* etching.

80. Knight, *Magic of a Line*, p. 333.

81. She had an exhibition in Syracuse, New York, for example. See her letter to James Swann of the Chicago Society of Etchers, cited in Dunbar, *Laura Knight*, p. 224.

82. Dunbar, *Laura Knight*, pp. 226–27.

83. David Phillips (Director, The Castle Museum and Art Gallery, Nottingham), cited in Dunbar, *Laura Knight*, p. 228.

84. Lumsden, *Art of Etching*, pp. 322–23.

85. Prices listed by Bond Street printsellers.

86. For praise, see Hind, *History of Engraving and Etching*, p. 330–31; for criticism, see Guichard, *British Etchers*, p. 44.

87. Dunbar, *Laura Knight.*
88. Dodgson, *Catalog of Etchings by Augustus John*; and Dodgson, "Additions to the Catalogue," pp. 271–87.
89. Knight, *Magic of a Line*, p. 74.
90. Knight, *Oil Paint and Grease Paint*, p. 312.
91. Dunbar, *Laura Knight*, pp. 90–91.
92. Greer, *Obstacle Race*, p. 113.
93. Ashmolean Museum, *Etchings and Aquatints by Orovida.*
94. *The Times*, 11 December 1945.
95. Haenlein, *Sickert Women.*
96. As, for example, in the MacColl Papers, BL.
97. Lilly, *Sickert.* Others are by Baron, Browse, and Sutton.
98. Salaman in *Fine Prints of the Year*, 1925. Her keen eye for character, he noted, could be seen in portraits of her husband, of the poet Siegfried Sassoon, and best of all, of her devoted old nurse.
99. Cited in Haenlein, *Sickert Women.*
100. Ibid. From an autobiographical sketch explicitly written for this catalog.
101. As told to Michael Parkin. See also Parkin Gallery, *Etchings of Wendela Boreel.*
102. Greer, *Obstacle Race*, p. 47.
103. Lilly, *Sickert*, pp. 67–68.
104. Privately tutored, Boreel was hardly uneducated; she was versed in, among other things, Greek philosophy—or, at least, her diary shows, according to Parkin, that she had read Plato and Aristotle.
105. Schuster assumedly was a homosexual. According to Boreel, Sickert had once said with a wink in Schuster's direction that "a pansy in my time was a flower." The Wyldes also inherited a considerable sum of money from Elgar.
106. In the catalog of her 1980 exhibition at Parkin Gallery. Some of Boreel's "best friends" may have been Jewish, as were certainly her two main benefactors, Adela and Frank Schuster.
107. Lilly, *Sickert*, p. 148.
108. Thwaite, *Edmund Gosse*, p. 369, asserts that Sickert was the love of Sylvia's life, "though she was not his," without citing any evidence for this statement.
109. Letter from Sylvia Gosse to Harold Wright, 6 January 1922, Wright Correspondence from Artists, AMPR; quoted with permission.
110. Letter from Sylvia Gosse to Ian Robertson, Keeper of Western Art, 22 May 1966, Curatorial Files, AMPR; quoted with permission.
111. Ibid., n.d. [about May 1965].
112. "Tiresome of them," she wrote, "to have botched my Gosse—will try and forget it but my French hieratic name means a very great deal to me." This same error showed up in a Christie's auction catalog and marred her pleasure, even though her works fetched prices she had never dreamed of in "the good old working days." K. Fisher, *Conversations with Sylvia*, pp. 32–33.
113. One account has Edmund Gosse consulting Sickert about his daughter's career. After studying the paintings her father showed him, Sickert pronounced his judgment: "One thing I am certain of: she should become an etcher. I shall teach her etching. She can come to me and we shall do etching together." K. Fisher, *Conversations with Sylvia*, p. 33. Haenlein, *Sickert Women*, puts Sir Edmund in a less favorable light. Sickert had taken an immediate interest in her work. It was his encouragement that had given her the impetus to branch out for herself over the

objections of a father who did not want to see his unmarried daughter set up as an independent painter. She gives no source for this. A third version is in a letter by Sylvia, written not too long before she died. She indicated that she had been working on her own for several years when she "met Sickert," who told her to come over to his studio, looked at her drawings, and told her to come back the next day and learn to put them on the copper. Letter to Ian Lowe, 10 March 1968, Curatorial Files, AMPR; quoted with permission.

114. K. Fisher, *Conversations with Sylvia*, pp. 33–34. The school was in operation until the beginning of World War I.

115. Haenlein, *Sickert Women*.

116. K. Fisher, Foreword to *Conversations with Sylvia*.

117. Ibid., pp. 50–51. See also Browse, *Sickert*, p. 40: "so great was the bond between the three of them [Sickert, Gosse, and Lessore] that it was a matter of speculation to their mutual friends as to which of them he would finally marry."

## Chapter 11

1. Halbwachs, *Collective Memory*.

2. Lewis, *History*.

3. Goode, *Celebration of Heroes*, p. 67.

4. This is discussed in greater detail in Kubler, *Shape of Time*; Becker, *Art Worlds*.

5. For example, Rosenberg, *Tradition of the New*; Crane, *Transformation of the Avant-garde*.

6. Reitlinger, *Economics of Taste*.

7. Haskell, *Rediscoveries in Art*.

8. Of these, Cadmus, born in 1904, is the only one still alive as of this writing.

9. Cited in Keen, *Sale of Works of Art*, p. 142. This has become a deliberate strategy. To increase their visibility, the German expressionist group "Die Brücke" issued yearly portfolios of original prints to "associate" members on a subscription basis, as the etching societies had done.

10. Menpes, *Whistler As I Knew Him*, p. 87.

11. Taylor and Brooke, *Art Dealers*, p. 8.

12. Keen, *Sale of Works of Art*, p. 142.

13. Ely, Introduction to *Etchings by J. Alden Weir*.

14. Associated American Artists, *Prints of Reginald Marsh*.

15. Letter by John Taylor Arms to Leila Mechlin, 7 November 1941, Carl Zigrosser Collection (AAA). The collection also comes up repeatedly in the Arms Diaries (AAA).

16. Fryxell, Introduction to *Home-Thoughts from Afar*, p. 15.

17. Letter from Margaret Nordfeldt to Emily Nordfeldt, 12 February 1963, Nordfeldt Papers, AAA (Roll D-166).

18. Alexander, *Engraved Work of F. L. Griggs*.

19. Dodgson, *Etchings by Augustus John* (1920).

20. On Sickert's influence on the art, see Wilton, Foreword to *Walter Sickert*, p. iii.

21. Letter by Arthur W. Heintzelman to Frank Weitenkampf, Letters to Weitenkampf, AAA.

22. Letter from Frank W. Benson to Arthur W. Heintzelman, 2 July 1947, Benson Letters, EI.

23. Letters from Sylvia Gosse to Ian Robertson, Keeper of Western Art, dated 22

February, 29 March, and 20 May 1965, Curatorial Files, AMPR; quoted with permission.

24. Letter from Katherine Kimball to R. P. Tolman, 1 August 1937, Vertical Files, NMAA.

25. British wills are catalogued and are (with only some exceptions) available for inspection at central registries in London and Edinburgh. For information on the posthumous disposition of the American artist's oeuvre, we have relied almost exclusively on secondary sources.

26. Based on anecdotal and often sketchy information, mostly from secondary sources.

27. Harold Wright's notes on the work of Webb, Wright Papers, GU.

28. Fell, "Some Topics of the Moment," p. 268.

29. C. H. Morgan, *George Bellows*, p. 295.

30. Sadik, Introduction to *Portraits by George Bellows*, p. 10.

31. C. H. Morgan, *George Bellows*, pp. 296–97.

32. Letter from Brown to Wright, 21 May 1941, Wright Papers, GU.

33. Guichard, *British Etchers*, pp. 30–31.

34. Meyerowitz, *William Meyerowitz*.

35. Minnesota Museum of Art, *Etchings by Clara Mairs*. Haupers, twenty years younger than Mairs and a former regional director of the WPA Federal Art Project, had also helped to mount an exhibition of her works two years before she died.

36. Microfilm MN 456, Minnesota Historical Society, St. Paul, Minn.

37. Cortissoz, *Book of Alexander Shilling*.

38. Beall, *American Prints*.

39. Gilbert, *George Overbury "Pop" Hart*.

40. Crowdry, *Burgundy and Morvan*.

41. Wright, "Etchings and Lithographs of Gethin," pp. 69–91.

42. Guichard, *British Etchers*.

43. Tanner, *Etcher's Craft*, p. 34.

44. For example, a set of three etchings of nudes, each in editions of one hundred, the first etchings by the octogenarian Paul Cadmus in thirty years, were available from the Sylvan Cole Gallery in New York City.

45. Moulin, *Marché de la peinture*.

46. Getscher and Staley, *Stamp of Whistler*.

47. DeKay, "George C. Aid, Etcher," pp. 446–49.

48. Sabin, "Dry-Points of Elizabeth Armstrong Forbes," p. 76.

49. Birch, *Stanhope and Elizabeth Forbes*.

50. Getscher and Staley, *Stamp of Whistler*, p. 196.

51. Obituary of Katherine C. Kay, *The Times*, 24 August 1965.

52. On "cultural capital," see Bourdieu, *Distinction*.

53. Anderson Galleries, New York City, 28–29 March 1921; see also note in *The Bookman's Journal and Print Collector*, 6 May 1921, p. 33.

54. Raverat, *Period Piece*.

55. The most recent biography of Brooke paints an unflattering, even disturbing, portrait of this circle of young aesthetes, who called themselves the Neo-Pagans, Brooke and the Raverats being the most outspokenly anti-Semitic among them. See Delany, *Neo-Pagans*, p. 187.

56. Lago, *Imperfect Encounter*.

57. Rothenstein, *Men and Memories* and *Since Fifty*.

58. Sickert, *A Free House!*

59. For the many favors he did, see his correspondence, Walpole Papers, RHC.

60. Holtby, *Letters to a Friend.*

61. Holtby's novels are *Anderby Wold* (1921) and *The Crowded Street* (1924).

62. For a discussion of this group, see Flint, *Provincetown Printers.*

63. Riggio, *Theodore Dreiser*, passim.

64. Langer, *Josephine Herbst.*

65. On Sutherland, see Berthoud, *Graham Sutherland*, pp. 187–200, 299–302; on Peter Hurd's portrait of Johnson, see *New York Times*, 6 January 1967.

66. U. E. Johnson, Introduction to *Paul Cadmus*, p. 9.

67. Kirstein, *Paul Cadmus*; Eliasoph, "Paul Cadmus."

68. P. Smith, *Sixteen Drypoints*; Eby, *War.*

69. Barry Schwartz has looked at this phenomenon from the opposite perspective, namely at how monuments in the national capital selectively preserve the memory of names and events. See Schwartz, "Social Context of Commemoration," and *George Washington.*

70. Zurier, *Art for the Masses.*

71. American Artists' Congress, *Graphic Works.*

72. Goode, *Celebration of Heroes*, chap. 4.

73. Read, *Art and Society*, p. 133.

74. Cooley, "Fame," p. 122; see also Kubler, *Shape of Time.*

75. Becker, *Art Worlds*, p. 256.

76. Zilsel, *Entstehung des Geniebegriffs*; also G. Becker, *Mad Genius Controversy.*

77. Trevor-Roper, *World through Blunted Sight.*

78. *Books*, p. 60. We assume that this is a statistic based on manuscripts submitted to publishers, many of which make the rounds and are rejected several times.

79. Lurie, "Bad Housekeeping."

80. Anthony Trollope, *Autobiography*, cited in Becker, *Art Worlds*, p. 24.

81. Macaulay, *Life of Samuel Johnson*, pp. 48–49.

82. Rosengren, "Time and Literary Fame" and "Literary Criticism."

83. Tuchman and Fortin, "Women Writers"; Tompkins, "Masterpiece Theatre"; and Tuchman, *Edging Women Out.*

84. Henrahan, "Listeners Are Captives."

85. Weschler, "Strange Destiny," p. 83.

86. Kapsis, "Reputation Building," pp. 15–35.

87. Cooley, "Fame," p. 119.

88. Rewald, *Cézanne, the Steins, and Their Circle*, pp. 16, 18.

89. Mulkay and Chaplin, "Aesthetics and the Artistic Career," pp. 133–34 [our emphasis].

90. Greenfeld, *Different Worlds*, pp. 4–5.

91. Murphey, *Our Knowledge of the Historical Past*, p. 145.

92. Shapiro, Markoff, and Duncan, "Selective Transmission of Historical Documents."

93. Russell, "Frick Brings Back a Celebrated Unknown."

94. Goodman, *Languages of Art*, p. 112.

95. Ibid, pp. 112–13.

96. *New York Times*, 10 August 1986.

97. Ivins, *Prints and Visual Communication*, p. 143.

98. Wind, *Art and Anarchy*, p. 77.

99. On the theater, see Griswold, *Renaissance Revivals*; on symphony repertoires, see Mueller, *American Symphony Orchestra.*

100. Blaukopf, *Gustav Mahler*, p. 143.

101. Guttmann, *From Ritual to Record*, p. 51.

102. Schmitt and Leonard, "Immortalizing the Self."

103. Burckhardt, "Great Men of History," p. 176.

104. Merton, "Priorities in Scientific Discoveries," pp. 286–324.

105. Lewontin, "Darwin, Mendel and the Mind," pp. 8–10, which forms the basis of the account that follows.

106. Bailey, *Presidential Greatness*, p. 54.

107. Schwartz, *George Washington*.

108. Boas, "Mona Lisa in the History of Taste," pp. 207–34.

109. Tompkins, "Masterpiece Theatre," pp. 633 and 640.

110. Becker, *Art Worlds*, pp. 210–17.

111. Cited in Blaukopf, *Gustav Mahler*, p. 174.

112. Mueller, *American Symphony Orchestra*.

113. *New York Times*, 13 April 1986, Sect. ii, p. 27.

114. Merton, *Sociology of Science*, p. 445.

115. Egbert Haverkamp-Begemann, cited in the *New York Times*, 25 November 1985.

116. Kuhn, "Energy Conservation," pp. 321–56.

117. Twelve men, each on his own, had grasped the essential concept usually credited to Helmholtz.

118. Derry and Williams, *Short History of Technology*, pp. 624f, 732–33. One of the authors "learned" as a boy in Germany that electric light had been invented by Werner von Siemens.

# Select Bibliography

## Archives

Austin, Tex.
  Harry Ransom Humanities Research Center, University of Texas
    Hugh Walpole Papers
Boston, Mass.
  Public Library (Fine Arts Library)
    Louis Holman Files
Charleston, S.C.
  South Carolina Historical Society
    Alice R. H. Smith Letters
East Hampton, N.Y.
  Free Library
    Pennypacker Long Island Collection
Glasgow, Scotland
  Glasgow School of Art, Library
    Clipping File
  Glasgow University Library
    Harold J. L. Wright Papers
    Whistler Collection
Liverpool, England
  Brown Library
    Vertical Files
London, England
  British Library, Manuscripts Collection
    Frances Cornford Letters (re Raverat)
    James Greig Papers (Ms 9809)
    D. S. MacColl Papers
    Macmillan Correspondence
  Royal College of Art Library
    Minute Book
    *R.C.A. Students' Magazine*
  Victoria and Albert National Art Library, Manuscript Collection
    Isidore Spielmann Letters
    Minutes of the Old Etching Club (Ledger Book)
Los Angeles, Calif.
  Museum of Art
    *Print Letter*. Published by Print Makers Society of California
Middletown, Conn.
  Library, Wesleyan University
    Russell T. Limbach Papers

*399*

New York, N.Y.
  Columbia University
    Oral History Collection
  New York Public Library
    Letters to Herman T. Radin, 1911–1944
    Print Room
Norwich, Norfolk, England
  Central Library
    Colman and Rye Collections of Local History
Norwich Museums Service (Norwich Castle Museum)
    Curatorial Files
Oxford, England
  Ashmolean Museum Department of Western Art, Print Room
    Curatorial Files
    Orovida Pissarro Letters
    Harold J. L. Wright Correspondence from Artists
Philadelphia, Pa.
  Philadelphia Museum of Art Archives, Archives of American Art/Carl
    Zigrosser Collection
Salem, Mass.
  Essex Institute, James Duncan Phillips Library
    Curatorial Files
St. Paul, Minn.
  Minnesota Historical Society
    Clement B. Haupers and Clara G. Mairs Papers (MN456)
Springfield, Ohio
  Wittenberg University
    Walter Tittle Papers
Syracuse, N.Y.
  George Arents Research Library for Special Collection, Syracuse University
    Howard Cook Papers
Washington, D.C.
  Archives of American Art, Smithsonian Institution
    Grace Albee Papers
    John Taylor Arms Diaries
    Ernest L. Blumenschein Papers
    Faye Gold [Fanny Helfand] Papers
    Ellen Day Hale Papers
    Philip Kappel Papers
    S. R. Koehler Correspondence
    Lahey Papers
    Macbeth Gallery Records
    Blanche McVeigh Papers
    Arthur Millier Papers
    B. J. O. Nordfeldt Papers
    Oral History Collection
    Margery Ryerson Papers
    Smillie Papers
    George U. Stevens Collection
    Walter Tittle Diaries
    Letters to Frank Weitenkampf

Corcoran Gallery
Director's Correspondence
Library of Congress, Manuscripts Division
Clara Barton Papers
George Biddle Papers
Pennell-Whistler Collection
Benjamin Holt Ticknor Papers
William Zorach Papers
National Museum of American Art, Library
Vertical Files

## Published Sources

Abbott, Katherine E. "The Lady of the Portrait: Letters of Whistler's Mother." *Atlantic Monthly* 136 (1925): 319–28.

Alexander, Russell. *The Engraved Work of F. L. Griggs, A.R.A., R.E.: A Catalogue.* Stratford-upon-Avon: Shakespeare Head Press, 1928.

*American Art Annual.* Vols. 1–37. Washington, D.C., 1989–1945/48. Continued as *American Art Directory.* Vols. 38–. New York: R. R. Bowker, 1949—.

American Artists' Congress. *Graphic Works of the American 30's.* 1936. Reprint. New York: Da Capo Press, 1977.

American Institute of Graphic Arts. *Fifty Prints of the Year.* New York: 1926–38.

Arms, Dorothy Noyes. *Kerr Eby, A.N.A.* Vol. 8. *American Etchers.* New York: Crafton Collection, 1930.

Arms, John Taylor. "A Self Estimate." Introduction to *John Taylor Arms, A Man for All Time: The Artist and His Work.* Edited and compiled by William Dolan Fletcher. New Haven, Conn.: Sign of the Arrow, 1982.

Ashmolean Museum. Department of Western Art. Introduction to *A Catalogue of Etchings and Aquatints by Orovida.* Oxford, 1969.

Associated American Artists. *The Prints of Reginald Marsh.* Catalog of the exhibition 13 September to 2 October 1976. New York, 1976.

Athill, Philip. Introduction to *William Strang, R.A., 1859–1921.* Catalog of the exhibition at Graves Art Gallery, Sheffield, England, 6 December 1980 to 18 January 1981.

Atkinson, Caroline P., ed. *Letters of Susan Hale.* Boston: Marshall Jones, 1918.

B. W. "Imitations of Rembrandt by B. W." *Connoisseur* 7 (1903): 124–25.

Bacher, Otto H. *With Whistler in Venice.* New York: The Century, 1909.

Bailey, Thomas A. *Presidential Greatness: The Image and the Man from George Washington to the Present.* New York: Appleton-Century-Crofts, 1966.

Bailly-Herzberg, Janine. *L'Eau-forte de peintre au dix-neuvième siècle: La Société des Aquafortistes (1862–1867).* 2 vols. Paris: Laget, 1972.

Baldry, A. L. "The Paintings and Etchings of Sir Charles Holroyd." *The Studio* 30 (1904): 283–92.

Baltzell, E. Digby. *Puritan Boston and Quaker Philadelphia: Two Protestant Ethics and the Spirit of Class Authority and Leadership.* Boston: Beacon, 1982.

Baron, Wendy. *Sickert.* London: Phaidon, 1973.

Bartsch, Adam. *Catalogue raisonné de toutes les estampes qui forment l'oeuvre de Rembrandt.* 2 vols. Vienna, 1797.

Bassham, B. L. *John Taylor Arms: American Etcher.* Catalog of the exhibition at Elvehjem Art Center, Madison, Wis., 21 February to 6 April 1975.

Bassman, Marlo Pease. *Born Charlestonian: The Story of Elizabeth O'Neill Verner*. Columbia, S.C.: State Printing Company, 1969.

Baudelaire, Charles. *Art in Paris: Salons and Other Exhibitions*. London: Phaidon, 1965.

————. *The Painter of Modern Life*. Translated by Jonathan Mayne. London: Phaidon, 1964.

Baur, John I. H. *Philip Evergood*. New York: Praeger, 1960.

Beall, Karen F., ed. *American Prints in the Library of Congress: A Catalogue of the Collection*. Baltimore, Md.: John Hopkins University Press, 1970.

Becker, George. *The Mad Genius Controversy*. Beverly Hills, Calif.: Sage, 1978.

Becker, Howard S. *Art Worlds*. Berkeley, Los Angeles, and London: University of California Press, 1982.

Beetles, Chris, ed. *S. R. Badmin and the English Landscape*. London: Collins, 1985.

Bell, Quentin. *Schools of Design*. London: Routledge and Kegan Paul, 1963.

Benjamin, Walter. "The Work of Art in the Age of Mechanical Reproduction." In *Illuminations*, pp. 217–51. New York: Schocken, 1969.

Benson, Frances M. "The Moran Family." *The Quarterly Illustrator* 1 (April–June 1893): 66–84.

Benson, Frank W. *Etchings and Drypoints by Frank W. Benson, an Illustrated and Descriptive Catalogue*. Vols. 1–4 compiled and arranged by Adam E. M. Paff. Vol. 5 compiled and arranged by Arthur W. Heintzelman. Boston and New York: Houghton Mifflin, 1917–59.

Berthoud, Roger. *Graham Sutherland: A Biography*. London: Faber and Faber, 1982.

Best, Geoffrey. *Mid-Victorian Britain (1851–70)*. New York: Schocken, 1972.

Biddle, George. *Artist at War*. New York: Viking, 1944.

Birch, Mrs. Lionel. *Stanhope A. Forbes, A.R.A. and Elizabeth Armstrong Forbes, A.W.R.S.* London, New York, and Melbourne: Cassell, 1906.

Bischoff, Ilse. *Six Dogs—Drive Slowly*. New York: Viking, 1953.

Blaukopf, Kurt. *Gustav Mahler*. Translated by Inge Goodwin. London: Allen Lane, 1973.

Board of Education. Introduction to *Report of the Committee on Advanced Art Education in London*. London: H.M. Stationery Office, 1936.

————. *Report of the Departmental Committee on the Royal College*. London: H.M. Stationery Office, 1912.

Boas, George. "The Mona Lisa in the History of Taste." *Journal of the History of Ideas* 1 (1940): 207–34.

Boime, Albert. *The Academy and French Painting in the Nineteenth Century*. New York: Phaidon, 1971.

Bone, Muirhead. "From Glasgow to London." *Artwork* 5 (Autumn 1929): 145–60.

————. *The Western Front: Drawings by Muirhead Bone*. Garden City, N.Y.: Doubleday, 1917.

Bourdieu, Pierre. *Distinction: A Social Critique of the Judgment of Taste*. Cambridge, Mass.: Harvard University Press, 1985.

Bradley, William Aspenwall. "Meryon and Baudelaire." *Print Collector's Quarterly* 1 (1911): 587–609.

————. "Some French Etchers and Sonneteers." *Print Collector's Quarterly* 4 (1914): 183–212.

Braudy, Leo. *The Frenzy of Renown*. New York: Oxford University Press, 1986.

Breeskin, Adelyne Dohme. *Anne Goldthwaite: A Catalogue Raisonné of the Graphic Work.* Montgomery, Ala.: Museum of Fine Arts, 1982.

Brockman, A. McKenzie. *Caroline and Frank Armington.* Two Mountains, Quebec: Montreal Print Collectors Society, 1985.

Brooks, Van Wyck. *John Sloan: A Painter's Life.* New York: E. P. Dutton, 1955.

Brownell, W. C. "The Art Schools of Philadelphia." *Scribner's Monthly* 18 (September 1879): 737–50.

Browse, Lillian. *Sickert.* London: Rupert Hart-Davis, 1960.

Bruhn, Thomas P. *American Etching: The 1880s.* Storrs, Conn.: William Benton Museum of Art, 1985.

Buckland-Wright, John. *Etching and Engraving: Techniques and the Modern Trend.* London: The Studio, 1953.

Buhot, Félix. "Onzième Exposition annuelle de la Royal Society of Painter-Etchers." *L'Art* (1893):197–98.

Burckhardt, Jacob. "The Great Men of History." In *Reflections on History*, pp. 172–203. London: Allen and Unwin, 1943.

Burke, Doreen Bolger. *J. Alden Weir: An American Impressionist.* Newark: University of Delaware Press, 1983.

Burty, Philippe. "L'oeuvre de M. Francis Seymour-Haden." *Gazette des Beaux-Arts*, ser. 1, 17 (October–November 1864): 271–87, 356–66.

Carlson, Victor. "The Painter-Etcher: The Role of the Original Printmaker." In *Regency to Empire: French Printmaking 1715–1814*, pp. 25–27. Catalog. Minneapolis, Minn.: Minneapolis Institute of Arts, 1984.

Carrington, Fitzroy. "A note by the Editor." *Print Collector's Quarterly* 2 (April 1912): 180–83.

Cate, Phillip Dennis, and Sinclair Hamilton Hitchings. *The Color Revolution: Color Lithography in France, 1890–1900.* Santa Barbara, Calif., and Salt Lake City, Utah: Peregrine Smith, 1978.

Caw, James L. *Scottish Painting: Past and Present (1620–1908).* Edinburgh: T. C. and E. C. Jack, 1908.

———. *Sir D. Y. Cameron, R.A., R.S.A., R.W.S., L.L.D.* Old Water-Colour Society's Club, no. 7. London: Old Water-Colour Society's Club, 1949.

Chamberlain, Samuel. *Etched in Sunlight.* Boston, Mass.: Public Library, 1968.

Chapman, John B. *The American Drawing Book.* New York: Redfield, 1858.

Charlot, Jean. Foreword to *American Printmaking 1913–1947: A Retrospective Exhibition*, by the American Society of Graphic Artists. Catalog. Brooklyn, N.Y.: Brooklyn Museum, 1947.

Cheney, Sheldon. "Notable Western Etchers." *Sunset Magazine* 21 (December 1908): 737–44.

Chenil Gallery. Introduction to *75 Etchings of the Battlefield and Other Scenes by Ian Strang.* London: Chenil Gallery, 1920.

Clark, Cynthia. "Five American Print Curators." *Print Collector's Newsletter* 11 (July–August 1980): 85–87.

Clark, Eliot. *History of the National Academy of Design.* New York: Columbia University Press, 1954.

Clausen, George. "Recollections of the Old School." *The RCA Students' Magazine* [about 1913]: 155–61. (Volume and date on copy available were illegible.)

Clement, Clara Erskine. *Women in the Fine Arts.* Boston and New York: Houghton Mifflin, 1905.

Collins, William J. T. *Artist-Venturer: The Life and Letters of Fred Richards, Etcher and Author.* Newport, Wales: R. H. Johns, [1948].

Comstock, Francis Adams. *A Gothic Vision: F. L. Griggs and His Work.* Boston: Boston Public Library, 1966.

Cooke, Grace. "Girl Students in the London Art Schools." *Girl's Realm* 1 (April 1899): 572–79.

Cooley, Charles Horton. "Fame." In *Social Process*, pp. 112–24. New York: Scribner's, 1927.

Copley, Peter. Introduction to *John Copley and Ethel Gabain.* Catalogue of the exhibition at Garton and Cooke, London, 13 November to 6 December, 1985.

Cortissoz, Royal, Horatio Walker, and Howard Giles. *The Book of Alexander Shilling.* New York: The Paisley Press, 1937.

Coser, Lewis M., Charles Kadushin, and Walter W. Powell. *Books: The Culture and Commerce of Publishing.* New York: Basic Books, 1982.

Crane, Diana. *The Transformation of the Avant-garde: The New York Art World, 1940–1985.* Chicago: University of Chicago Press, 1987.

Cresson, Hugh. *The Arts and the Academies: The Romanes Lecture for 1979–80.* Oxford: Clarendon Press, 1980.

Crowdry, William H. *Burgundy and Morvan.* London: Christopher, 1925.

Czestochowski, Joseph S. *Gerald K. Geerlings, from the Permanent Collection of the Cedar Rapids Art Association.* Catalog. Cedar Rapids, Iowa, 1986.

Davidson, Sandra. *Eleanor Norcross, Amy Cross, and Edith Loring Getchell.* Catalog of the exhibition, 11 November to 11 December 1980, Watson Gallery, Wheaton College. Norton, Mass., 1980.

Davis, Fred. *The Yearning for Yesterday: A Sociology of Nostalgia.* New York: Free Press, 1979.

Davson, Florence Sophie. "Art Students and Some Art Schools." *The Girl's Own Paper* 21 (1900): 646–47.

De Cordoba, Matilde. *Etchings, Drawings, Lithographs.* Catalog of the Memorial Exhibition, 27 January to 10 February 1951. New York: Pen and Brush Club, 1951.

DeKay, Charles. "George C. Aid, Etcher: A Leading American in this Branch of the Graphic Arts." *Arts and Decoration* 4 (1914): 446–49.

—————. "The Popularity of Etchings." *Art and Decoration* 10 (1919): 249–51.

Delany, Paul. *The Neo-Pagans: Rupert Brooke and the Ordeal of Youth.* New York: Free Press, 1987.

Delteil, Loys. *Manuel de l'amateur d'estampes des XIXe et XXe siècles.* Paris: Dorbon-Aîné, 1925.

Derry, T. K., and Trevor I. Williams. *A Short History of Technology from the Earliest Times to* A.D. *1900.* New York and Oxford: Oxford University Press, 1961.

*Dictionary of National Biography.* 21 vols. Edited by Sir Leslie Stephen and Sir Sidney Lee. London: Oxford University Press, 1914–. Supplements edited by L. G. Wickham Legg and E. T. Williams.

Dillaye, Blanche. *Memorial Exhibition of Watercolors and Etchings.* Catalog. The Philadelphia Art Alliance, May 1932.

DiMaggio, Paul. "Cultural Entrepreneurship in Nineteenth Century Boston." *Media, Culture and Society* 4 (1982): 33–50, 303–22.

Dodd, Loring Holmes. *A Generation of Illustrators and Etchers.* Boston: Chapman and Grimes, 1960.

Dodgson, Campbell. "Additions to the Catalogue of the Etchings by Augustus

John, R.A." *Print Collector's Quarterly* 18 (1932): 271–87.

———. *A Catalogue of Etchings by Augustus John, 1901–1914.* London: Chenil Gallery, 1920.

———. "The English Landscapes of W. P. Robins, R.E." *Bookman's Journal and Print Collector* 12 (1925): 93–96.

———. *The Etchings of James McNeill Whistler.* London: The Studio, 1922.

———. Introduction to *British War Artists.* London, February 1918.

———. "Maurice and Edward Detmold." *Print Collector's Quarterly* 9 (1922): 373–405.

———. "Mr. John's Etchings." *Country Life,* November 1, 1919, pp. 545–47.

———. "Mr. Percy Smith's 'Dance of Death.'" *The Print Collector's Quarterly* 8 (October 1921): 323–26.

———. "Muirhead Bone." *Die graphischen Künste* (Vienna) 29 (1906): 53–65.

Dodgson, Campbell, and C. E. Montague, eds. *C. R. W. Nevinson.* British Artists at the Front, pt. 1. London: 1918.

D'Oench, Ellen G. "'A Madness to Have His Prints': Rembrandt amd Georgian Taste, 1720–1800." In *Rembrandt in Eighteenth Century England,* pp. 63–81. New Haven, Conn.: Yale Center for British Art, 1983.

Dows, Olin. "The New Deal's Treasury Art Program: A Memoir." In *The New Deal Art Projects: An Anthology of Memoirs,* edited by Francis V. O'Connor, pp. 10–49. Washington, D.C.: Smithsonian Institution Press, 1972.

Dunbar, Janet. *Laura Knight.* London: Collins, 1975.

Dunlap, William. *History of the Rise and Progress of the Arts of Design in the United States.* 3 vols. 1836. Reprint. New York: Benjamin Blom, 1985.

Duveneck, Josephine. *Frank Duveneck: Painter-Teacher.* San Francisco, Calif.: John Howell, 1970.

Earle, Helen J., ed. *Biographical Sketches of American Artists.* Lansing: Michigan State University Library, 1913.

Eby, Kerr. *War.* New Haven, Conn.: Yale University Press, 1936.

———. "War." *Prints* 6 (December 1936): 80.

Eliasoph, Philip. "Paul Cadmus: Life and Work." Ph.D. diss., State University of New York at Binghampton, 1979.

Ely, Caroline W. Introduction to *Catalogue of an Exhibition of Etchings by J. Alden Weir.* New York: Frederick Keppel, 1927.

Emanuel, Frank. *Etching and Etchings: A Guide to Technique and Print Collecting.* New York and Chicago: Pittman, 1930.

Emerson, Gertrude. "Helen Hyde and Her Japanese Children." *American Magazine of Art* 7 (1916): 429–35.

Erskine, Mel [Mary Emily Lawton]. *Thank God for Laughter.* New York: C. Kendall, 1936.

*The Etcher: Examples of the Original Etched Work of Modern Artists.* Vols. 1–5. [London], 1879–83.

Everett, Katherine. *Bricks and Flowers: Memoirs.* London: Reprint Society, 1951.

Farr, D. L. A. *English Art, 1870–1940.* Oxford: The Clarendon Press, 1978.

Fell, H. Granville. "Some Topics of the Moment." *The Connoisseur* 101 (1938): 265–68, 274.

Fine Art Society. *Correspondence by J. A. McN. Whistler, respecting Etching of F. Duveneck, attributed to Mr. Whistler by F. S. Haden.* London: Fine Art Society, 18 March 1881.

*Fine Prints of the Year: An Annual Review of Contemporary Etchings, Engravings, and Lithography.* 16 vols. London: Halton and Truscott Smith, 1923–38.

Fink, Lois Marie. "American Artists in France, 1850–1870." *American Art Journal* 5 (November 1973): 32–49.

———. "The National Academy of Design." In *Academy: The Academic Tradition*, edited by Lois Marie Fink and Joshua Taylor, pp. 5–14. Washington, D.C.: National Collection of Fine Arts, Smithsonian Institution, 1975.

Fisher, A. Hugh. *Through India and Burma with Pencil and Brush.* London: T. Werner Laurie, 1911.

Fisher, Kathleen. *Conversations with Sylvia: Sylvia Gosse—Painter 1881–1968.* London and Edinburgh: Charles Skilton, 1975.

Fisher, Theo Merrill. "George Elbert Burr." *American Magazine of Art* 10 (February 1919): 124–29.

———. "Katherine Cameron's Etchings of Flowers." *American Magazine of Art* 10 (July 1919): 323–25.

Fletcher, William Dolan. *Complex Simplicity: Gerald Leslie Brockhurst and His Graphic Work.* New Haven, Conn.: Eastern Press, 1984.

———. *John Taylor Arms, A Man for All Time: The Artist and His Work.* New Haven, Conn.: Sign of the Arrow, 1982.

Flint, Janet Altic. *Provincetown Printers: A Woodcut Tradition.* Washington, D.C.: Smithsonian Institution Press, 1983.

Fothergill, John, ed. *The Slade: A Collection of Drawings and Some Pictures by Past and Present Students of the London Slade School of Art.* London: R. Clay and Sons, 1909.

Frayling, Christopher. *The Royal College of Art: One Hundred & Fifty Years of Art & Design.* London: Barrie and Jenkins, 1987.

Freedberg, David. *Dutch Landscape Prints of the Seventeenth Century.* London: British Museum Publications, 1980.

Friese, Nancy. "Mary Nimmo Moran: A Biography." In *Prints of Nature: Poetic Etchings of Mary Nimmo Moran.* Catalog of an Exhibition at the Thomas Gilcrease Institute of American History and Art, University of Tulsa, Okla., 7 September to 2 December 1984.

Fry, Roger. "Art-History as an Academic Study." In *Last Lectures.* New York: Macmillan, 1939.

Fryxell, Fritiof. Introduction to *Home-Thoughts from Afar: Letters of Thomas Moran to Mary Nimmo Moran.* Edited by Amy O. Bassford. Easthampton, N.Y.: Free Library, 1967.

Fuchs, R. H. *Rembrandt in Amsterdam.* Greenwich, Conn.: New York Graphic Society, 1971.

Furst, Herbert. "Orovida's Exhibition at the Redfern Gallery." *Apollo* 4 (July 1926): 44–46.

Gág, Wanda. *Growing Pains: Diaries and Drawings, 1908–1917.* New York: Coward-McCann, 1940.

———. "These Modern Women: A Hotbed of Feminists." Published anonymously. *The Nation,* June 22, 1927, pp. 691–93.

Gallatin, Albert E. *Art and the Great War.* New York: Dutton, 1919.

Gardner, Howard. "The Child as Artist." *Journal of Communication* 29 (Autumn 1979): 146–56.

Gearhart, Edna. "The Brothers Brown—California Painters and Etchers." *American Magazine of Art* 20 (May 1929): 283–91.

Geerlings, Gerald K. "Interview." *Print Review,* no. 16 (1982): 48–59.

George, Mary Carolyn Hollers. *Mary Bonner: Impressions of a Printmaker.* San Antonio, Tex.: Trinity University Press, 1982.

Getscher, Robert H. *The Stamp of Whistler.* Catalog of the exhibition, Oberlin College, Allen Memorial Art Museum, 2 October to 6 November 1977. Oberlin, Ohio, 1977.

Gettings, Frank. *Raphael Soyer: Sixty-five Years of Printmaking.* Washington, D.C.: Smithsonian Institution for the Hirshhorn Museum, 1982.

Getzels, Jacob W., and Mihaly Csikszentmihalyi. *The Creative Vision: A Longitudinal Study of Problem Finding in Art.* New York: Wiley, 1976.

Gibson, Frank. "British Artists in the War Zone—Muirhead Bone and James McBey." *The Studio* 69 (January 1917): 178–85.

Gilbert, Gregory. *George Overbury "Pop" Hart; His Life and Art.* New Brunswick and London: Rutgers University Press, 1986.

Goldman, Judith. Introduction to *One Hundred Prints by 100 Artists of the Art Students League of New York, 1875–1975.* New York: Art Students League, 1975.

Goldthwaite, Anne. Introduction to *Anne Goldthwaite, 1869–1944.* Catalog of the exhibition held at the Museum of Fine Art, 22 March to 1 May 1977. Montgomery, Ala., 1977.

Goode, William J. *The Celebration of Heroes: Prestige as a Social Control System.* Berkeley and Los Angeles: University of California Press, 1978.

Goodman, Nelson. *Languages of Art.* 1976. Reprint. Indianapolis, Ind.: Hackett, 1988.

Goodrich, Lloyd. Introduction to *The Prints of Reginald Marsh.* Catalogued by Norman Sasowsky. New York: Clarkson Potter, 1976.

⸺. *Raphael Soyer.* New York: Praeger, 1967.

Grafly, Dorothy. *A History of the Philadelphia Print Club.* Philadelphia: Print Club, 1929.

Grant, M. H. *A Dictionary of British Etchers.* London: Rockcliffe, 1942.

Gray, Basil. *The English Print.* London: Adam and Charles Black, 1934.

Gray, Cecil. *Predicaments: On Music and the Future.* London: Oxford University Press, 1936.

Greenfeld, Liah. *Different Worlds: A Sociological Study of Taste, Choice and Success in Art.* Cambridge: Cambridge University Press, 1989.

Greer, Germaine. *The Obstacle Race.* New York: Farrar Straus Giroux, 1979.

Griff, Mason. "Recruitment and Socialization of Artists." In *The Sociology of Art and Literature: A Reader,* edited by Milton Albrecht, James Barnett, and Mason Griff, pp. 145–59. New York: Praeger, 1970.

Griswold, Wendy. *Renaissance Revivals: City Comedy and Revenge Tragedy in the London Theater, 1576–1980.* Chicago: University of Chicago Press, 1986.

Guichard, Kenneth. *British Etchers, 1850–1940.* London: Robin Garton, 1978.

Guttmann, Allen. *From Ritual to Record: The Nature of Modern Sport.* New York: Columbia University Press, 1978.

Haden, Francis Seymour. *The Etched Work of Rembrandt.* London, 1877.

Haenlein, Charlotte. *The Sickert Women and the Sickert Girls.* Catalogue of the exhibition at the Parkin Gallery (London) in collaboration with the Maltzahn Gallery (London), 18 April to 18 May 1974.

Halbwachs, Maurice. *The Collective Memory.* Translated from the French. 1950. Reprint. New York: Harper Colophon, 1980.

Hale, Nancy. *The Life in the Studio.* Boston: Little, Brown, 1969.

———. *Mary Cassatt.* Garden City, N.Y.: Doubleday, 1975.

Hamerton, Philip G. *An Autobiography, 1834–58, and a Memoir by His Wife, C. E. Hamerton, 1858–1894.* London: Seeley, 1897.

———. *Etching and Etchers.* 1st ed. London: Macmillan, 1868. 4th ed. Boston: Little, Brown, 1912.

———. "Mr. Seymour Haden's Etchings," *Scribner's Magazine* 29 (August 1880): 586–600.

Hardie, Frank. *The Prints of Martin Hardie.* Oxford: Ashmolean Museum, 1975.

Hardie, Martin. *Etchings and Drypoints from 1902 to 1924 by James McBey.* London: P. D. Colnaghi, 1925.

———. "The Etchings and Engravings of Stanley Anderson." *Print Collectors' Quarterly* 20 (July 1923): 221–46.

———. *Frederick Goulding: Master Printer of Copper Plates.* Stirling, Scotland: Eneas Mackay, 1910.

———. "Women Etchers of Today." *The Queen,* 1 September 1906, pp. 380–81, and 8 September 1906, pp. 438–39.

Harms, Ernst. "From Dark to Light: An Appreciation of the Life Work of Helen West Heller, 1872–1955." *American Artist* 21 (November 1957): 30–34, 67–68.

Harries, Meirion, and Susie Harries. *The War Artists: British Official War Art of the Twentieth Century.* London: Michael Joseph, in association with the Imperial War Museum and the Tate Gallery, 1983.

Harris, Ann Sutherland, and Linda Nochlin. *Women Artists 1550–1950.* Los Angeles, Calif.: County Museum of Art, 1976.

Hartmann, Sadakichi. *A History of American Art.* Boston: L. C. Page, 1902.

Haskell, Francis. *Rediscoveries in Art: Some Aspects of Taste, Fashion, and Collecting in England and France.* 2d ed. Oxford: Phaidon, 1980.

Hayden, Arthur. *Chats on Old Prints.* London: T. Fisher Unwin, 1909.

Helm, MacKinley. *John Marin.* New York: Pellegrini and Cudahy, 1948.

Henrahan, Donal. "Listeners Are Captives of Musical History." *New York Times,* April 13, 1986, sec. 2, p. 25.

Henri, Robert. *The Art Spirit.* Compiled by Margery Ryerson. Philadelphia and London: Lippincott, 1930.

Herkomer, Hubert. *Etching and Mezzotint Engraving: Lectures Delivered at Oxford.* London: Macmillan, 1892.

———. *My School and My Gospel.* London: Constable, 1908.

Hind, Arthur M. *A History of Engraving and Etching from the 15th Century to the Year 1914.* 3d ed. 1923. Reprint. Boston: Dover, 1963.

Hitchcock, J. R. W. *Etching in America.* New York: Whitestokes and Allen, 1886.

Holland, Clive. "Lady Art Students in Paris." *The Studio* 21 (1904): 225–31.

Holman, Louis A. *Hornby's Etchings of the Great War.* Boston: Charles E. Goodspeed, 1921.

Holme, C. Geoffrey, ed. *Etchings of Today.* London: The Studio, 1929.

Holme, Charles, ed. *Modern Etchings, Mezzotints and Drypoints.* London: The Studio, 1913.

Holroyd, Michael. *Augustus John.* Harmondsworth, Middlesex: Penguin, 1976.

Holtby, Winifred. *Letters to a Friend.* Edited by Alice Holtby and Jean McWilliams. London: Collins, 1937.

Hood, Thomas. *The Complete Poetical Works of Thomas Hood.* Edited by Walter Jerrold. London and New York: Oxford University Press, 1920.

Hoppin, Martha J. "Women Artists in Boston, 1870–1900: The Pupils of William Morris Hunt." *American Art Journal* 13 (Winter 1981): 17–46.

Houfe, Simon. *Dictionary of British Book Illustrators and Caricaturists, 1800–1914*. Woodbridge, Suffolk, England: Antique Collector's Club, 1978.

Hubbard, E. Hesketh. *On Making and Collecting Etchings*. Breamore, Hamptonshire: Print Society, 1920.

Huish, M. B. "Etching in England." *Magazine of Art* 1 (1878): 146–48, 217–20.

Hurd, Peter. *My Land Is the Southwest*. College Station: Texas A & M University Press, 1983.

Hutchison, Sidney C. *The History of the Royal Academy, 1768–1968*. London: Chapman and Hall, 1968.

Isham, Samuel. *The History of American Painting*. New edition with supplemental chapters by Royal Cortissoz. New York: Macmillan, 1936.

Ivins, William I. *Prints and Visual Communication*. Cambridge, Mass.: Harvard University Press, 1953.

———. *Wood-Engravings by Rudolph Ruzicka*. Booklet printed in connection with an exhibition at the Newark Public Library, 5 March–31 March 1917. Newark, N.J.: Newark Museum Association, 1917.

Jacomb-Hood, G. P. *With Brush and Pencil*. London: John Murray, 1925.

Jaques, Bertha. *Helen Hyde and Her Work*. Chicago: Libby Company Printers, 1922.

John, Augustus. *Chiaroscuro: Fragments of an Autobiography*. London: Jonathan Cape, 1954.

———. *Finishing Touches*. Edited with an introduction by Daniel George. London: Jonathan Cape, 1964.

Johnson, J., and A. Greutzner. *The Dictionary of British Artists 1880–1940*. Woodbridge, Suffolk, England: Antique Collector's Club, 1976.

Johnson, Una E. *American Prints and Printmakers*. Garden City, N.Y.: Doubleday, 1980.

———. Introduction to *Paul Cadmus/Prints and Drawings*. American Graphic Artists of the Twentieth Century, monograph 6. Brooklyn, N.Y.: Brooklyn Museum, 1968.

Jopling, Louise. *Twenty Years of My Life, 1867 to 1887*. London: John Lane, 1925.

Josephson, Matthew. *Portrait of the Artist as American*. New York: Harcourt, Brace, 1930.

Kainen, Jacob. "The Graphic Arts Division of the WPA Federal Art Project." In *The New Deal Art Projects: An Anthology of Memoirs*, edited by Francis V. O'Connor, pp. 155–75. Washington, D.C.: Smithsonian Institution Press, 1972.

Kappel, Philip. *Jamaica Gallery*. London: Macmillan, 1961.

Kapsis, Robert E. "Reputation Building and the Film Art World: The Case of Alfred Hitchcock." *Sociological Quarterly* 30 (Winter 1989): 15–35.

Keen, Geraldine. *The Sale of Works of Art: A Study Based on 'The Times-Sotheby Index of Fine Arts.'* London: Thomas Nelson, 1971.

Kent, Rockwell. *It's Me Oh Lord*. 1955. Reprint. New York: Da Capo Press, 1977.

Keppel, Frederick. *The Golden Age of Engraving*. New York: Baker and Taylor, 1910.

Kepplinger, Hans-Matthias. *Realkultur and Medienkultur: Literarische Karrieren in der Bundesrepublik*. Alber Broschüre Kommunikation, bd. 1. Freiburg and Munich: Alber, 1975.

Kershaw, J. D. "Philadelphia School of Design for Women." *The Sketch Book* 4 (April 1905): 187–91.

Kirstein, Lincoln. *Paul Cadmus*. New York: Imago Books, 1984.

Kloss, Phillips. *Gene Kloss Etchings*. Santa Fe, N.M.: Sunstone Press, 1981.

Knight, Laura. *The Magic of a Line*. London: William Kimber, 1965.

————. *Oil Paint and Grease Paint*. New York: Macmillan, 1936.

Koehler, S. R. *American Etchings: A Collection of Twenty Original Etchings*. Boston: Estes and Lauriat, 1886.

————. Introduction to *Exhibition of American Etchings*. Catalog. Boston Museum of Fine Arts, 1881.

————. Introduction to *Exhibition of the Women Etchers of America*. Catalog. Boston: Museum of Fine Arts, 1887.

————. *New York Etching Club: Twenty Original Etchings*. New York, 1885.

————. "Vereinigte Staaten von Nordamerika." In *Die Radierung*. Vol. 3 of *Die vervielfaeltigende Kunst der Gegenwart*, edited by Richard Grau, pp. 193–220. Vienna: Gesellschaft der verfielfältigende Kunst, 1892.

————. "The Works of the American Etchers VIII.—Anna Lea Merritt." *American Art Review* 1 (1880): 230.

Konody, Paul G. "On War Memorials." In *Art and War: A Selection of the Works Executed for the Canadian War Memorials Fund*. London: Canadian War Records Office, 1919.

Kraft, James. *John Sloan, a Printmaker*. Washington, D.C., International Exhibitions Foundation, 1984.

Kris, Ernst, and Otto Kurz. *Legend, Myth and Magic in the Image of the Artist: A Historical Experiment*. Translated from the German by Alastair Laing and revised by Lotte M. Newman. New Haven and London: Yale University Press, 1979.

Kristeller, Paul O. "The Modern System of the Arts." *Journal of the History of Ideas* 12 (1951): 496–527.

Kubler, George. *The Shape of Time*. New Haven and London: Yale University Press, 1962.

Kuhn, Thomas S. "Energy Conservation as an Example of Simultaneous Discovery." In *Critical Problems in the History of Science*, edited by Marshall Claggett, pp. 321–56. Madison: University of Wisconsin Press, 1959.

Kynett, H. H. *Treasure Trove: Rambles with the Sketches of James McBey*. Privately printed by author, 1948.

Lago, Mary M., ed. *Imperfect Encounter: Letters of William Rothenstein and Rabindranath Tagore, 1911–1941*. Cambridge, Mass.: Harvard University Press, 1972.

Laguna Beach Museum of Art. *Southern California Artists 1890–1940*. Laguna Beach, Calif.: Museum of Art, 1979.

Lalanne, Maxime. *A Treatise on Etching*. Translated by S. R. Koehler. London: W. and G. Foyle, 1880; Boston: Estes and Lauriat, 1880.

Landacre, Paul. *California Hills and Other Wood-engravings from the Original Blocks*. Los Angeles: Bruce McCallister, 1931.

Landgren, Marchal. *Years of Art: The Story of the Art Students League of New York*. New York: Robert M. McBride, 1940.

Langer, Elinor. *Josephine Herbst: The Story She Could Never Tell*. Boston: Little, Brown, 1984.

Laurence, Alfred E. "American Etchings at the St. Louis Exposition." *Brush and Pencil* 12 (May 1903): 269–80.

Laver, James. "The Art of William Lee-Hankey." *Bookman's Journal and Print Collector* 10 (1924): 14–20.

————. *A History of British and American Etching*. London: Benn, 1929.

———. *Museum Piece*. London: Andre Deutsch, 1963.

———. "Seymour Haden and the Old Etching Club." *Bookman's Journal and Print Collector* 10 (June 1924): 87–91.

Lehman, Anthony L. *Paul Landacre: A Life and a Legacy*. Los Angeles: Dawson's Book Shop, 1983.

Lehman, Harvey G. "The Creative Years: 'Best Books.'" *The Scientific Monthly* 45 (1937): 65–75.

Leighton, Clare. *Tempestuous Petticoat: The Story of an Invincible Edwardian*. New York: Rinehart, 1947.

Leipnik, F. L. *A History of French Etching from the Sixteenth Century to the Present Day*. London: John Lane, 1924.

Lemaître, Henri, ed. *Baudelaire: Curiosités esthetiques; L'Art romantique; et autres oeuvres critiques*. Paris: Garnier Frères, 1962.

Leslie, G. D. *Inner Life of the Royal Academy*. London: John Murray, 1914.

Levis, Howard C. *Descriptive Bibliography of Books in English Relating to Engraving*. 1912. Reprint. London: William Dawson, 1974.

Lewis, Bernard. *History: Remembered, Recaptured, Invented*. Princeton, N.J.: Princeton University Press, 1975.

Lewontin, R. C. "Darwin, Mendel and the Mind." *New York Review of Books*, October 10, 1985, pp. 8–10.

Lilly, Marjorie. *Sickert: The Painter and His Circle*. London: Elek, 1971.

Lippard, Lucy. *Graphic Work of Philip Evergood*. New York: Crown, 1966.

Locke, John. *An Essay Concerning Human Understanding*. Edited by Alexander Campbell Fraser. Oxford: Clarendon Press, 1894.

Lovely, Deborah, and James O. Pierce. Introduction to *Bertha E. Jaques*. Exhibition at the Lovely Fine Arts Gallery. Oakbrook Terrace, Ill.: Lovely Fine Arts, 1985.

Lowenthal, David. *The Past Is a Foreign Country*. New York: Cambridge University Press, 1985.

Lumsden, E. S. *The Art of Etching*. London: Seeley, Service, 1925.

———. *Catalogue of Exhibition*. Edinburgh: Daniel Shackleton, n.d.

Lurie, Allison. "Bad Housekeeping." *New York Review of Books*, 19 December 1985, pp. 8–10.

M. H. S. "Schools of the Royal Academy." *The Graphic*, 4 May 1889, pp. 473–76.

Macaulay, Thomas Babington. *Life of Samuel Johnson*, edited by Charles Lane Johnson. 1830. Reprint. Boston: Ginn, 1928.

McBey, James. *The Early Life of James McBey: An Autobiography 1883–1911*. Edited by Nicolas Barker. Oxford: The University Press, 1977.

———. "Etchings: the Quick and the Dead." *The Bookman's Journal and Print Collector* 9 (1923): 92–100.

MacColl, D. S. *Nineteenth Century Art*. Glasgow: Maclehose, 1902.

Macdonald, Stuart. *The History and Philosophy of Art Education*. New York: American Elsevier, 1970.

Mackenzie, Midge. *Shoulder to Shoulder*. New York: Knopf, 1975.

McKinzie, Richard D. *The New Deal for Artists*. Princeton, N.J.: Princeton University Press, 1973.

Marin, John. *The Selected Writings of John Marin*. Edited by Dorothy Norman. New York: Pellegrini and Cudahy, 1949.

Marron, Donald B. Foreword to *The Gloria and Donald B. Marron Collection of American Prints*. Catalog of the permanent collection. Santa Barbara, Calif.: Santa Barbara Museum of Art, 1981.

Massey, William Thomas. *The Desert Campaigns*. London: Constable, 1918; New York: G. P. Putnam's, 1918.

Mathews, Nancy Mowil, ed. *Cassatt and Her Circle: Selected Letters*. New York: Abbeville Press, 1984.

Mauclair, Camille. "Redmond Stephens Wright, Etcher." *Pencil Points* 15 (January 1934): 3–8.

Maugham, W. Somerset. *Of Human Bondage*. Illustrated by John Sloan. New Haven, Conn.: Yale University Press, for the Limited Editions Club, 1938.

Meadmore, William Sutton. *Lucien Pissarro: un coeur simple*. 2d rev. ed. New York: Knopf, 1963.

Meigs, John, ed. *Lithographs of Peter Hurd*. With an introduction by Andrew Wyeth. Lubbock, Tex.: Baker Gallery Press, 1968.

Mellerio, André. *La Lithographie originale*. Paris: L'Estampe et l'affiche, 1898.

Melleterre, General. "How the War Was Won." Translated by Herbert Adams Gibbons. *Harper's Monthly* 138 (March 1919): 433–45; (April 1919): 598–612.

Menpes, Mortimer. *Whistler as I Knew Him*. London: Adam and Charles Black, 1904.

Menzies, W. G. "Art in the Showroom." *Apollo* 11 (1930): 70–72.

Merritt, Anna Lea. "Letter to Artists, Especially Women Artists." *Lippincott's Monthly Magazine* 65 (1900): 463–69.

———. *Love Locked Out: The Memoirs of Anna Lea Merritt*. Edited by Galina Gorokhoff. Boston: Museum of Fine Arts, 1982.

Merritt, Henry. *Art Criticism and Literature*. London: Kegan Paul, 1879.

*Merseyside Painters*. Exhibition Catalog. Liverpool: Walker Art Gallery, 1978.

Merton, Robert K. "Priorities in Scientific Discoveries." *American Sociological Review* 22 (1957): 286–324.

———. *The Sociology of Science*. Edited by Norman Storer. Chicago: University of Chicago Press, 1973.

Meyerowitz, Theresa Bernstein. *William Meyerowitz: The Artist Speaks*. Philadelphia: The Art Alliance Press, 1986.

Minnesota Museum of Art. *Etchings by Clara Mairs (from the Abby Weed Grey Collection)*. Catalog of the permanent collection. Minneapolis: Minnesota Museum of Art, 1976.

Morgan, Charles H. *George Bellows: Painter of America*. New York: Reynal, 1965.

Morgan, H. C. "The Lost Opportunity of the Royal Academy: An Assessment of Its Position in the Nineteenth Century." *Journal of the Warburg and Courtauld Institute* 32 (1967): 410–20.

Mories, F. G. "Robert S. Austin, A.R.A., R.W.S., R.E." *The Artist* 17 (August 1939): 781–84.

———. "Sylvia Gosse." *The Artist* 35 (March 1948): 10–12.

Morse, John D. "John Sloan, 1871–1951." *American Artist* 16 (January 1952): 24–28, 57–59.

Morse, Peter. *John Sloan's Prints: A Catalogue Raisonné of the Etchings, Lithographs and Posters*. New Haven, Conn.: Yale University Press, 1969.

Morse, Reynolds. "George Elbert Burr and the Western Landscape." *Art in America* 34 (2 April 1946): 73–90.

Moulin, Raymonde. *Le Marché de la peinture en France*. Paris: Les Editions du Minuit, 1967. Translated by Arthur Goldhammer and abridged as *The French Art Market*. New Brunswick, N.J.: Rutgers University Press, 1988.

Moulin, Raymonde, Jean-Claude Passeron, Dominique Pasquier, and Fernando Porto-Vazquez. *Les Artistes: Essai de morphologie sociale.* Paris: La Documentation Française, 1985.

Mourey, Gabriel. "France." In *Modern Etchings and Engraving: European and American,* edited by Charles Holme. London: The Studio, 1902.

Mueller, John H. *The American Symphony Orchestra: A Social History of Musical Taste.* Bloomington: Indiana University Press, 1951.

Mulkay, Michael, and Elizabeth Chaplin. "Aesthetics and the Artistic Career: A Study of Anomie in Fine-Art Painting. *Sociological Quarterly* 23 (Winter 1982): 117–38.

Muncaster, Martin. *The Wind and the Oak: The Life, Work, and Philosophy of the Marine and Landscape Painter, Claude Muncaster.* London: Robin Garton, 1977.

Munnings, A. J. *An Artist's Life.* 3 vols. London: Museum Press, 1952.

Murphey, Murray G. *Our Knowledge of the Historical Past.* Indianapolis and New York: Bobbs-Merrill, 1973.

Myers, Lynn Robertson. "Doing and Creating: Biographical Sketch." In *Mirror of Time: Elizabeth O'Neill Verner's Charleston,* pp. 7–15. Catalog of the exhibition held at the McKissick Museum, 19 August to 30 September 1983. Charleston, S.C., 1983.

Nash, Paul. *Outline: An Autobiography and Other Writings.* London: Faber and Faber, 1949.

Nevinson, C. R. W. *Paint and Prejudice.* New York: Harcourt Brace, 1938.

New York Etching Club. *Exhibition Catalog.* Printed annually. New York, 1882–93.

Newbolt, Francis. *The History of the Royal Society of Painter-Etchers and Engravers, 1880–1930.* London: Print Collectors' Club, 1930.

Newbolt, Sir Henry. *My World as in My Time.* London: Faber and Faber, 1932.

Niall, Ian. *Portrait of a Country Artist: Charles F. T. Tunnicliffe, R.A.* London: Gollancz, 1980.

Norton, Bettina A. *Prints at the Essex Institute.* Museum Booklet Series. Salem, Mass.: Essex Institute, 1978.

Notman, Otis. "Some More of the Book Illustrators: Otto Bacher." *Saturday Review, New York Times,* February 16, 1907, p. 94.

O'Doherty, Brian. *American Masters: The Voice and the Myth.* New York: Random House, 1973.

Ogg, David. "The Etchings of Graham Sutherland and Paul Drury." *Print Collector's Quarterly* 16 (1929): 77–100.

Oppé, A. P. "Fourth Earl of Aylesford." *The Print Collector's Quarterly* 11 (1924): 262–92.

Ordeman, J. T. *Frank W. Benson: Master of the Sporting Print.* Brooklandville, Md.: J. T. Ordeman, 1983.

Pach, Walter. "Peintres-Graveurs Contemporaines: M. J. Alden Weir." *Gazette des Beaux-Arts,* Ser. 4 6 (September 1911): 214–15.

Painter-Gravers of America. *First Annual Yearbook.* New York, 1917–18.

Palmer, Samuel. *Life and Letters of Samuel Palmer, Painter and Etcher.* Written and edited by A. H. Palmer. London: Seeley, 1892.

Pankhurst, E. Sylvia. *The Suffragette Movement: An Intimate Account of Persons and Ideals.* London, New York, and Toronto: Longman's, Green, 1931.

Parker, Rozsika, and Griselda Pollock. *The Old Mistresses: Women, Art and Ideology.* New York: Pantheon, 1981.

Parkin Gallery. *The Etchings of Wendela Boreel.* Catalogue of the exhibition at the Parkin Gallery (London), 1 to 18 October 1980.

Partridge, Eric. *A Dictionary of Catch Phrases: British and American, from the Sixteenth Century to the Present Day.* London and Henley: Routledge and Kegan Paul, 1977.

Partridge, Roi. "Gentle Prayer on Etching." *Print Letter* (mimeo) 8 (December 1929).

Pelles, Geraldine. *Art, Artists and Society.* Englewood Cliffs, N.J.: Prentice Hall, 1965.

Pelletier, S. William. "John Taylor Arms: An American Mediaevalist." *Georgia Review* 30 (Winter 1976): 907–38.

Pennell, Elizabeth Robins. *The Life and Letters of Joseph Pennell.* 2 vols. Boston: Little Brown, 1929.

Pennell, Elizabeth Robins, and Joseph Pennell. *The Life of James McNeill Whistler.* 2 vols. Philadelphia: Lippincott, 1909.

Pennell, Joseph. *The Adventures of an Illustrator, Mostly in Following His Authors in America and Europe.* Boston: Little, Brown, 1925.

––––––. *Etchers and Etching.* 4th ed. New York: Macmillan, 1936.

––––––. *The Graphic Arts.* Chicago: University of Chicago Press, 1921.

"Peter Moran." *Art Journal* 4 (1878): 133–37.

Pevsner, Nicolas. *Academies of Art.* Cambridge: Cambridge University Press, 1940.

Philadelphia Art Alliance. *Memorial Exhibition of Watercolors and Etchings by Blanche Dillaye.* Catalog. Philadelphia, May 1932.

Pinder, Wilhelm. *Das Problem der Generationen in der Kunstgeschichte Europas.* Berlin: Frankfurter Verlags-Anstalt, 1926.

Pisano, Ronald G. Introduction to *The Students of William Merritt Chase,* pp. 4–8. Exhibition at the Parrish Art Museum (Southampton, N.Y.) and Hecksher Museum (Huntington, N.Y.), 28 September–11 November 1973.

Pissarro, Camille. *Camille Pissarro: Letters to His Son Lucien.* Edited with the assistance of Lucien Pissarro by John Rewald. New York: Pantheon, 1943.

Pott, Constance M. *Philomir, or Self's the Man.* London: R. Banks, 1915.

Pott, Mrs. Henry. *Quite a Gentleman.* London: Banks and Son, 1913.

Pousette-Dart, Nathaniel. *Ernest Haskell: His Life and Work,* New York: T. Spencer Hutson, 1931.

Print Club of Cleveland. *The Print Club of Cleveland: Fifty Years in Review.* Cleveland, Ohio: Print Club of Cleveland, 1970.

*Print Letter.* Mimeographed newsletter of the Printmakers Society of California. Copies available in the library of the Los Angeles Museum of Art.

*Print Prices Current.* 21 vols. Compiled by E. H. Courville and E. L. Wilder. London, 1919–40.

*Print,* vols. 1–8, 1930–38.

Raverat, Gwen. *Period Piece.* New York: Norton, 1952.

Read, Herbert. *Art and Society.* New York: Macmillan, 1937.

Reed, Sue Welsh, and Richard Wallace. *Italian Etchers of the Renaissance and Baroque.* Catalog. Boston: Boston Museum of Fine Art, 1989.

Reitlinger, Gerald. *The Economics of Taste: The Rise and Fall of the Picture Market 1760 to 1960.* New York: Holt, Rinehart and Winston, 1961.

Rensselaer, Marion Schuyler van. "American Etchers." *Century Magazine* 24 (February 1883): 483–99. Reprinted by Keppel and Co., 1884.

––––––. Introduction to *Exhibition Catalogue of the Work of Women Etchers of*

*America.* New York: The Union League Club, 1888.

Rewald, John. *Cézanne, the Steins, and Their Circle.* London: Thames and Hudson, 1986.

———. *The History of Impressionism.* Rev. ed. New York: Museum of Modern Art, 1961.

Reynolds, Graham. Introduction to *The Etchings of Anthony Gross.* Catalog. London: Victoria and Albert Museum, 1968.

Richard T. York Gallery. Introduction to *Ellen Day Hale.* Catalog of the exhibition at the York Gallery, 17 October to 14 November 1981. Boston, 1981.

Riggio, Thomas P., ed. *Theodore Dreiser; American Diaries 1902–1926.* Philadelphia: University of Pennsylvania Press, 1983.

Rinder, Frank. *D. Y. Cameron: An Illustrated Catalogue of His Etched Work with Introductory Essay and Descriptive Notes on Each Plate.* Glasgow: Maclehose and Sons, 1912.

Roberts, Chalmers. "Mortimer Menpes: The Man and His Methods." *Harper's Monthly Magazine* 101 (October 1900): 703–11.

Robins, W. P. *Seventeenth President of the Royal Society of Painters in Water-Colour.* Old Water-Colour Society's Club, no. 33. London: Old Water-Colour Society's Club, 1958.

Rodden, John. *The Politics of Literary Reputation: The Making and Claiming of George Orwell.* New York: Oxford University Press, 1989.

Rogers, Maria. "The Batignolles Group: Creators of Impressionism." In *The Sociology of Art and Literature: A Reader*, edited by Milton C. Albrecht, James H. Barnett, and Mason Griff, pp. 194–220. New York: Praeger, 1970.

Rosenberg, Harold. *The De-Definition of Art.* New York: Horizon, 1972.

———. *The Tradition of the New.* New York: Horizon, 1959.

Rosenberg, Jakob. *Rembrandt: Life and Work.* London and New York: Phaidon, 1968.

Rosengren, Karl Erik. "Literary Criticism: Future Invented." *Poetics* 16 (1987): 295–325.

———. "Time and Literary Fame." *Poetics* 14 (1985): 157–72.

Rosenthal, Léon. *La Gravure.* Paris: Librairie Renouard, 1909.

Ross, Alan. *Colours of War.* London: Jonathan Cape, 1984.

Ross, Margery, ed. *Robert Ross: Friend of Friends.* Oxford: Jonathan Cape, 1952.

Rothenstein, William. *Men and Memories.* 2 vols. London: Faber and Faber, 1931–32.

———. *Since Fifty.* London: Faber and Faber, 1939.

Rowland, Stanley. "The Decline of Etching." *Apollo*, July 1940, pp. 22–24.

Ruskin, John. *The Political Economy of Art.* London: Smith Elder, 1868.

Russell, John. "The Frick Brings Back a Celebrated Unknown." *New York Times*, December 2, 1988.

Rutter, Frank. *Art in My Time.* London: Rich and Cowan, 1933.

———. *Theodore Roussel.* London: The Connoisseur, 1926.

Sabin, Arthur K. "Colour Prints in Stipple and Mezzotints." *Connoisseur* 1 (September–December 1901): 19–27.

———. "The Dry-Points of Elizabeth Armstrong Forbes, formerly E. A. Armstrong (1859–1912)." *Print Collectors' Quarterly* 9 (1922): 75–100.

Sadik, Martin. Introduction to *Portraits by George Bellows.* Catalog of the exhibition at the National Portrait Gallery, 4 November 1981 to 3 January 1982. Washington, D.C., 1981.

Salaman, Malcolm C. "The Etchings and Dry-points of W. P. Robins." *Bookman's*

*Journal and Print Collector* 5 (1922): 112–19.

————. "The Etchings of E. S. Lumsden, R.E." *Print Collectors' Quarterly* 8 (1921): 91–119.

————. "A Gossip about Prints." *Apollo* 6 (1927): 180–82.

————. "Great Britain." In *Modern Etchings, Mezzotints and Drypoints*, edited by Charles Holme, pp. 3–104. London: The Studio, 1913.

————. *The Great Painter-Etchers from Rembrandt to Whistler*. London: The Studio, 1914.

————. "James McBey—A Master Etcher." *Bookman's Journal and Print Collector* 5 (October–November 1922): 17–22, 50–55.

————. *Laura Johnson Knight*. Modern Masters of Etching, no. 29. London: The Studio, 1932.

————. "Miss Eileen Soper's Etchings of Childhood." *Studio* 85 (1923): 262–66.

————. "The Print Collectors' Club." *The Bookman's Journal and Print Collector* 4 (July 1921): 208–10.

————. "Sir Frank Short, R.A., P.R.E., Master Engraver." *Bookman's Journal and Print Collector* 5 (1922): 186–94.

Salpeter, Harry. "Emil Ganso: Handy Artist." *Esquire*, July 1938, pp. 59, 99–102.

Schmitt, Raymond L. and Wilbert M. Leonard II. "Immortalizing the Self through Sport." *American Journal of Sociology* 91 (1986): 1088–1111.

Schneider, Rona. "The American Etching Revival: Its French Sources and Early Years." *American Art Journal* 14 (1982): 40–65.

————. "The Birth of American Painter-Etching, 1866-1882." M.A. thesis. Graduate Division, Queens College, City College of New York, 1978.

Schneiderman, Richard S. *A Catalogue Raisonné of the Prints of Sir Francis Seymour Haden*. London: Robin Garton, 1983.

————. "The Genesis of English Landscape Etching." Ph.D. diss., State University of New York at Binghampton, 1977.

Schutz, Anton, *My Share of Wine*. Greenwich, Conn.: New York Graphic Society, 1972.

Schwartz, Barry. *George Washington: The Making of an American Symbol*. New York: Free Press, 1987.

————. "The Social Context of Commemoration: A Study in Collective Memory." *Social Forces* 61 (1982): 374–402.

Scott, Alma Olivia. *Wanda Gåg: The Story of an Artist*. Minneapolis: University of Minnesota Press, 1949.

Scott, Kathleen Bruce [Lady Kennet]. *Self-Portrait of an Artist*. London: John Murray, 1949.

Seeber, Louise Combes. *George Elbert Burr*. Flagstone, Ariz.: Northland Press, 1971.

Shapiro, Barbara S. *The Impressionist Printmaker*. Boston: Museum of Fine Arts, 1973.

Shapiro, Gilbert, John Markoff, and Silvio R. Duncan. "The Selective Transmission of Historical Documents: The Case of the Parish *Cahiers* of 1789." Unpublished paper, Department of Sociology, University of Pittsburgh, 31 March 1987.

Shapiro, Theda. *Patrons and Politics: The European Avant-Garde and Society, 1900–1925*. New York: Elsevier, 1976.

Sharf, Frederick A., and John H. Wright. *William Morris Hunt and the Summer Art Colony at Magnolia, Massachusetts, 1876–1879*. Salem, Mass.: Essex Institute, 1981.

Sickert, Walter R. *A Free House! or, the Artist as Craftsman. Being the Writings of Walter Richard Sickert,* edited by Osbert Sitwell. London: Macmillan, 1947.
———. "The Old Ladies of Etching-needle Street." *English Review* 10 (January 1912): 301–12.
"Silhouettes d'artistes contemporains: Mlle. Gabrielle Niel." *L'Art* (2d ser.) 1 (1894): 348–55.
Simon, Howard. *500 Years of Art in Illustration: From Albrecht Dürer to Rockwell Kent.* Garden City, N.Y.: Garden City Publishing Company, 1945.
Simpson, Thomas. *Modern Etchings and Their Collectors.* London: John Lane, 1919.
Singer, Hans W. *Die moderne Graphik.* 1st ed. Leipzig: E. A. Seemann, 1912.
Slater, John H. *Engravings and Their Value: A Guide for the Print Collector.* 4th ed. London: L. Upcott Gill, 1912.
———. *Engravings and Their Value: A Guide for the Print Collector.* 6th ed. London: Bazaar Exchange and Mart, 1929.
Slive, Seymour. *Rembrandt and His Critics, 1630–1730.* The Hague: Nijhoff, 1953.
Sloan, John. *John Sloan's New York Scene: From the Diaries, Notes and Correspondence, 1906–1913.* Edited by Bruce St. John with an introduction by Helen Farr Sloan. New York: Harper and Row, 1965.
Smillie, James D. Introduction to *Catalogue of Etching Proofs Exhibited at the National Academy of Design.* New York: New York Etching Club, 1891.
Smith, J. André. *In France with the A.E.F.* New York: Arthur H. Hahlo, [1919].
Smith, Percy. *Sixteen Drypoints and Etchings of the Great War.* London: Soncino Press, 1930.
Society of Graphic Arts. *Catalogue of Inaugural Exhibition.* London: Suffolk Street Galleries, S.W.1, 1921.
Sparrow, W. Shaw. *British Etching from Francis Barlow to Seymour Francis Haden.* London: John Lane, The Bodley Head, 1926.
———. *Memories of Life and Art through Sixty Years.* London: John Lane, 1925.
———. *Women Painters of the World: From the Time of Caterina Vigri (1413–1463) to Rosa Bonheur and the Present Day.* London: Hodder and Stoughton, 1905.
Speed, Harold. "Reminiscences of S. K." *The R.C.A. Students Magazine* 2 (December 1912): 35–38.
Spielmann, M. H. "Art Forgeries and Counterfeits." *Magazine of Art* 27 (September 1903): 549–53.
Steinberg, Steve. "Roi Partridge at Ninety-One." *San Francisco Sunday Examiner & Observer* (Arts Section), October 12, 1980.
Stevens, Thomas Wood. "An Exhibition of Contemporary American Etchings." *Art and Progress* 4 (May 1913): 949–53.
Stoppelmann, J. W. F. Introduction to *Clara Klinghoffer, 1900–1970.* Catalog of the exhibition at the Belgrave Gallery (London), 4 to 16 November 1976, and 26 March to 28 May 1977.
Strang, David. *The Printing of Etchings and Engravings.* London: Ernest Benn, 1930.
Sutton, Denys. *Walter Sickert: A Biography.* London: Michael Joseph, 1976.
Swanwick, H. M. *I Have Been Young.* London: Gollancz, 1935.
Tanner, Robin. *The Etcher's Craft.* Bristol: Friends of the Bristol Art Gallery, 1980.
Tarbell, Roberta K. *Marguerite Zorach: The Early Years, 1908–1920.* Catalog published in connection with an exhibition held at the Smithsonian Institu-

tion, National Collection of Fine Arts, 7 December 1973 to 3 February 1974. Washington, D.C., 1973.

————. *Peggy Bacon: Personalities and Places.* Washington, D.C.: Smithsonian Institution Press, 1975.

Taylor, Gary. *Reinventing Shakespeare: A Cultural History from Restoration to the Present.* London: Weidenfeld, 1989.

Taylor, John Russell, and Brian Brooke. *The Art Dealers.* New York: Scribner's, 1969.

Taylor, Joshua C. *The Fine Arts in America.* Chicago: University of Chicago Press, 1979.

Thieme, Ulrich, and Felix Becker. *Allgemeines Lexikon der bildenden Künstler.* Leipzig: William Engelmann, 1907–. Supplements by Hans Vollmer. Leipzig: E. A. Seemann, 1961–.

Thorne, Diana. "The Portable Press." *Print Letter* 8 (March 1930). Mimeographed newsletter.

Thwaite, Ann. *Edmund Gosse: A Literary Landscape, 1849–1928.* Chicago: University of Chicago Press, 1984.

Tippett, Maria. *Art in the Service of War.* Toronto, Buffalo, and London: University of Toronto Press, 1984.

Toklas, Alice B. *What Is Remembered.* New York: Holt, Rinehart and Winston, 1963.

Tompkins, Jane. "Masterpiece Theatre: The Politics of Hawthorne's Literary Reputation." *American Quarterly* 36 (1984): 617–42.

Trevor-Roper, Patrick. *The World through Blunted Sight: An Inquiry into the Influence of Defective Vision on Art and Character.* Indianapolis and New York: Bobbs-Merrill, 1970.

Tuchman, Gaye. *Edging Women Out.* New Haven, Conn.: Yale University Press, 1988.

Tuchman, Gaye, and Nina E. Fortin. "Women Writers and Literary Tradition." *American Journal of Sociology* 90 (1984): 72–96.

Tunnicliffe, Charles F. *My Country Book.* London and New York: The Studio, 1942.

Turner, Ralph H. "Sponsored and Contest Mobility and the School System." *American Sociological Review* 25 (1960): 855–67.

Tyler, Francine. *American Etchings of the Nineteenth Century.* New York: Dover, 1984.

Varga, Margit. "Life's Art Program." In *Work for Artists,* edited by Elizabeth McCausland, pp. 118–22. New York: American Artists Group, 1947.

Vasari, Giorgio. *Lives of the Painters, Sculptors and Architects.* 4 vols. Translated by A. B. Hinds and revised and edited with an introduction by William Gaunt. New York: Dutton, 1963.

Veblen, Thorstein. *The Theory of the Leisure Class.* 1899. Reprint. New York: Modern Library, 1934.

Wackernagel, Martin. *The World of the Florentine Renaissance Artist: Projects and Patrons, Workshop and Art Market.* Translated by Alison Luchs. Princeton, N.J.: Princeton University Press, 1981.

Walker, R. A. "The Etchings of Ian Strang." *The Print Collector's Quarterly* 18 (1931): 129–49.

Walpole, Hugh. "The Etching." *Good Housekeeping,* April 1924, pp. 18–21.

Warner, W. Lloyd. *The Living and the Dead.* Yankee City Series, vol. 5. New Haven, Conn.: Yale University Press, 1959.

Watrous, James. *A Century of American Printmaking (1880–1980)*. Madison: University of Wisconsin Press, 1984.

Watson, Charles J. *Catalogue of the Etched and Engraved Work of Charles J. Watson*. With a biographical note by Mrs C, J. Watson. London: Emery Walker, 1931 [for private circulation].

Watson, Forbes. "American Etchers of the Present Day." *Arts and Decoration* 4 (August 1914): 381–84.

Webber, Michael. Introduction to *Centenary Exhibition of the Ipswich Art Club, 1874–1974*, 23 September to 11 October 1975. Ipswich, Suffolk: Ipswich Art Club, 1975.

Wedmore, Frederick. *Etching in England*. London: George Bell and Sons, 1895.

———. *Etchings*. London: Methuen, 1911.

———. *Fine Prints*. 2d ed. Edinburgh: John Grant, 1910.

———. "Prints and Drawings at the Victoria and Albert." *Connoisseur* 17 (1910): 99–103.

———. "The Royal Society of Painter-Etchers." *Studio* (1895): 22–26.

Weintraub, Stanley. *Whistler: A Biography*. New York: Weybright and Talley, 1974.

Weisberg, Gabriel. *The Etching Renaissance in France, 1850–1880*. Catalog of the exhibition at the Utah Museum of Fine Arts, 13 February to 14 March 1971. Salt Lake City, 1971.

Weitenkampf, Frank W. *American Graphic Art*. New York: Henry Holt, 1912.

———. Introduction to *Catalogue of a Collection of Engravings, Etchings and Lithographs by Women*, 12 to 27 April 1901. New York: Grolier Club, 1901.

———. *Manhattan Kaleidoscope*. New York: Scribner's, 1947.

Weschler, Laurence. "A Reporter at Large: A Strange Destiny." *The New Yorker*, 16 December 1985, pp. 47–86.

Whatcom Museum. *Beyond the Veil: The Etchings of Helen Loggie*. Text by Thomas Alix Johnston and Dorothy Koert. Bellingham, Wash.: Whatcom Museum of History and Art, 1979.

White, E. B. "How to Tell a Major Poet from a Minor Poet." In *Quo Vadimos*, pp. 68–74. New York: Harpers, 1939.

White, Harrison C., and Cynthia A. *Canvasses and Careers: Institutional Change in the French Painting World*. New York: Wiley, 1965.

White, John Forbes, and Paul Konody. "Rembrandt van Rijn." In *Encyclopaedia Britannica*. 11th ed. 22:80.

Whitehill, Walter Muir. "The Evolution of a Printmaker." In *The Work of Thomas W. Nason, N.A.*, edited by Francis A. Comstock and W. F. Fletcher, pp. 15–23. Boston: Boston Public Library, 1977.

———. Introduction to *Rudolph Ruzicka*. Exhibition Catalog. New York: Grolier Club, 1948.

Whiteing, Richard. "The American Student at the Beaux Arts." *Century Magazine*, December 1881, pp. 259–72.

Whitley, W. T. "London Schools." In *Arts and Crafts*, edited by Charles Holme, pp. 3–24. London: The Studio, 1916.

Whitmore, Elizabeth. "A. Hugh Fisher, A.R.E." *The Print Collector's Quarterly* 28 (October 1941): 381.

Wickenden, Robert J. "Charles Jacque." *The Print Collector's Quarterly* 2 (1912): 74–101.

Wickey, Harry. *Thus Far: The Growth of an American Artist*. New York: American Artists Group, 1941.

Willard, Frances E., and Mary A. Levermore, eds. "Blanche Dillaye." In *A Woman of the Century*, pp. 244–45. 1893. Reprint. New York: Gale Research, 1967.
Wilton, Andrew. Foreword to *Walter Sickert as Printmaker*. Catalog by Aimée Troyen. New Haven, Conn.: Yale Center for British Art, 1979.
Wind, Edgar. *Art and Anarchy*. New York: Knopf, 1965.
Wittkower, Rudolf, and Margot Wittkower. *Born under Saturn: The Character and Conduct of Artists. A Documented History from Antiquity to the French Revolution*. New York: Random House, 1963.
Woodruff, Alan W. Foreword to *A History of British Wood Engraving*. Edited by Albert Garrett. Tunbridge Wells, Kent: Midas Books, 1978.
Wortley, Clare Stuart. "Amateur Etchers." *The Print Collector's Quarterly* 19 (1932): 189–211.
Wray, Henry Russell. *A Review of Etching in the United States*. Philadelphia: R. C. Penfield, 1893.
Wright, Harold J. L. "The Etchings and Lithographs of Percy Francis Gethin." *Print Collector's Quarterly* 14 (1927): 69–91.
Wyckoff, Peter. *Wall Street and the Stock Markets: A Chronology, 1644–1971*. Philadelphia: Chilton, 1972.
*Yearbook of American Etching*. Introduction by Forbes Watson. London: John Lane, The Bodley Head, 1914.
*The Year's Art*. Compiled by M. B. Huish (and A. C. R. Carter). London, 1880–1948.
Young, Dorothy Weir. *The Life and Letters of J. Alden Weir*. New Haven, Conn.: Yale University Press, 1960.
"Zella de Milhau, Etcher." *American Magazine of Art* 14 (May 1923): 249–53.
Zigrosser, Carl. *The Artist in America*. New York: Alfred A. Knopf, 1942.
———. Introduction to *The Complete Etchings of John Marin: A Catalogue Raisonné*. Philadelphia: Philadelphia Museum of Art, 1969.
———. *My Own Shall Come to Me*. Casa Laura, 1971 [privately published].
———. *Prints and Their Creators: A World History*. New York: Crown, 1974.
———. *A World of Art and Museums*. Philadelphia: The Art Alliance Press, 1975.
Zilsel, Edgar. *Die Entstehung des Geniebegriffs: Ein Beitrag zur Geschichte der Antike und des Frühkapitalismus*. Tübingen: J. B. C. Mohr, 1926.
Zimmerman, Agnes Saumarez. "Julian Alden Weir—His Etchings." *Print Collector's Quarterly* 10 (October 1923): 288–308.
Zorach, William. *Art Is My Life*. Cleveland, Ohio: World Publishing Co., 1967.
Zurier, Rebecca. *Art for the Masses, (1911–1917): A Radical Magazine and Its Graphics*. With contributions by Earl Davis and Elise K. Kenney. New Haven, Conn.: Yale University Art Gallery, 1985.

## Interviews and Correspondence with and about Artists in the Sample

Mortimer Borne, letter received 28 March 1984
Edward Bouverie-Hoyton, 14 June 1981
Denise Lebreton Brown (Mrs. Frank Waters), 11 March and 18 June 1978
Pauline Clarke (Mrs. Hunter Blair), regarding Cecil Leslie, 17 August 1981
Robert S. G. Dent, 19 July 1980, also regarding Greta Delleany
Evangeline Dickson, Dr. John Dickson, and Jack Haste, regarding Anna Airy, Winifred Austen, Alice Goyder, and Leonard Squirrel, 19 August 1981
Alan Campbell Frood and Patricia Ann Frood, regarding Hester Frood, 29 August 1981

Dr. John F. Goyder, regarding Alice Kirkby Goyder, letter received 10 May 1978
Kenneth Guichard, 2 March 1978
Frances Hazeldine, regarding Margaret Kemp-Welch, 21 June 1978
Irwin D. Hoffman, 24 September 1981
Jacob Kainen, 15 March 1980, regarding WPA artists
Reverend Noel Kemp-Welch, regarding Margaret Kemp-Welch, letter received 10
    June 1978
Barbara Latham, regarding Howard Cook, telephone interview, 19 April 1984
Nora Fry Lavrin and Janko Lavrin, 16 May 1978
Roi Partridge, 8 September 1982
Jane Piper, regarding Earl Horter, telephone interview, 9 April 1985
Virginia Poli and Kenneth Poli, regarding Roselle Osk, 28 February 1983
Sarah Pugh-Jones, regarding Bertha Gorst, 1 July 1983
Marion Rhodes, 21 August 1980
Hyman Segal, regarding Anne Harriet Fish, 14 July 1981
Jane Thistlethwaite (Mrs. Frank Thistlethwaite), regarding Norwich and Minne-
    sota artists, 22 August 1978
Elizabeth Elliott Whiteley and Abranel Saxby, regarding Aileen Mary Elliott, 10
    August 1982
Redmond Stephens Wright, telephone interview, 22 March 1985

# Acknowledgments: Institutional Resources

Listed here are the many institutions where we worked during our search for the lives of our artists. While some, such as the Bodleian in Oxford and the Library of Congress, were more used than others, we list all alphabetically. Where possible, we note the individuals who offered special assistance.

Archives of American Art, Washington, D.C., Boston, and New York (Garnett McCoy and Judy Throm)

Ashmolean Museum, Library of Western Art and Print Room, Oxford

Associated American Artists, New York (Hilda Castellon; Sylvan Cole, Jr.; Stephen Long; Estelle Yanko)

Atelier d'Art, Deux Montaignes, Quebec (A. McKenzie Brockman)

Atkinson Art Gallery, Southport, Merseyside, England (Diana de Bussy, Keeper of Fine Art)

Bethesda Gallery, Md. (Betty Duffy and John Duffy)

Bodleian Library, Oxford

Boston Public Library (Sinclair Hitchings, Keeper of Prints, and Theresa Cederholm, Curator, Fine Arts Department)

Bradford Public Library and Art Museum, Bradford, England

Bradford University, Department of Sociology, Bradford, England (Helen Roberts)

Brighton Public Library, Brighton, England

Bristol Art Gallery, Bristol, England

British Library, London

British Museum, Print Room, London

Colingdale Newspaper Library, London

Corcoran Gallery of Art Archives, Washington, D.C.

Davidson Gallery, Seattle, Wash. (Sam Davidson)

Duke University Library, Durham, N.C.

East Hampton Free Library, Long Island Collection, N.Y.

Edinburgh Public Library

Essex Institute, Salem, Mass.

Fitzwilliams Library, Cambridge University

Frank Melville Library, State University of New York at Stony Brook
Gallaudet University for the Deaf, Library, Washington, D.C. (with assistance from Prof. Deborah Sonnenstrahl)
George Washington University, Library, Washington, D.C.
Glasgow School of Art, Library
Harbor Gallery, Cold Spring Harbor, Long Island and New York City (Dorothy Schneiderman)
Harvard University Art Library, Boston
Historical Society of Philadelphia, Archives
Ingeborg Gallery, Port Washington, N.Y. (Gert Wirth)
Ipswich Art Museum, Ipswich, England
Laguna Art Museum, Laguna, Calif.
Library of Congress, Department of Prints and Drawings (Bernard Reilly) and Manuscripts Division, Washington, D.C.
London Gallery, Washington, D.C. (Sally Cremin)
Martin Summers Gallery, New York
Massachusetts Institute of Technology, Art Library, Cambridge, Mass.
Mitchell Library, Glasgow
National Gallery of Art, Library, Washington, D.C.
National Humanities Center, Library, Research Triangle Park, N.C. (Alan Tuttle, Rebecca Sutton)
National Portrait Gallery, Washington, D.C. (Mark Pachter, Historian)
Newlyn Museum and Art Gallery, England
New York Public Library and Print Room
Norwich Public Library, Norwich, England
Palace of the Legion of Honor, Library, San Francisco, Calif.
Penzance Public Library, Penzance, England
Records Office, William Brown Library, Liverpool
Records Offices, London and Edinburgh
Robin Garton and Gordon Cooke Fine Prints, London
Royal College of Art, Library, London
Royal Society of Painter-Etchers, London (Malcolm Fry, Michael Blaker)
Ruthven Library and Records Office, North Wales
Ryerson Library, Art Institute of Chicago
St. Antony's College, Oxford
Seattle Public Library, Wash.
Society of American Graphic Artists, Archives, New York (Steven Yamin, Secretary)
Studio One, Oxford, England (Betty Clark)
Tacoma Public Library, Wash. (Gary Reese, Manuscript Librarian)
Truro Library and Records Office, South Wales
University of North Carolina Library, Chapel Hill

University of Oregon Library, Eugene (Hillary Cummings, Curator of
    Manuscripts and Special Collections)
University of Pennsylvania, Library
University of Washington, Libraries, Seattle
Victoria and Albert Museum, Library and Print Room, London
Walker Art Gallery, Liverpool
Wesleyan University Library and Art Center, Middletown, Conn.
Whatcom Museum, Bellingham, Wash.
William Morris Gallery, London (Peter Cormack, Librarian)
Worcester Art Museum, Mass. (Timothy Riggs, Curator)
Worcester Historical Museum, Mass.
Worcester Historical Society, Mass. (Mrs. Goss, Librarian)
Zeitlin and Ver Brugge, Los Angeles (Carolyn Bullard, Gallery Director)

# Index